2017

To N.

My attempt to comp
involvement of educated and
professional classes in the genocide,
of which members of my family
were victims.
Many thanks for your invaluable
advice in writing this book.

Tom

Thomas Lehner

The Clash: Weimar Classicism and Buchenwald Barbarism

Austin Macauley
Publishers Ltd.

A CIP catalogue record for this title is available from the British Library.

ISBN 9781786299741 (Paperback)
ISBN 9781786299758 (Hardback)
ISBN 9781786299765 (eBook)

www.austinmacauley.com

First Published (2016)
Austin Macauley Publishers Ltd.
25 Canada Square
Canary Wharf
London
E14 5LQ

Dedication

This book is dedicated to the memory of my father Josef Lehner, brother Paul Lehner and grandparents who perished during the Second World War and to my loving mother.

About the Author

Thomas Lehner CBE, MD, FMedSci is professor of Basic and Applied Immunology at King's College, London. He published over 300 articles on immune responses to infections and to stress. He struggled over many years with the critical question: 'how was it possible for a highly cultured German people to carry out mass murder?'.

Acknowledgments

I owe a great debt of gratitude to Professor George Steiner whose consistent writing of the paradoxical link between culture and barbarism during the Nazi period in Germany, as well as his advice has influenced my choice of the subject matter of the book. My good friend, the late Professor Ludwik Finkelstein OBE has been most helpful in numerous discussions about the early Judeo-Christian relationship and the development of the Holocaust. He enabled me to think through the complexities involved and in his gentle way correct my misconceptions. Dr. Edward Kessler MBE, director of the Woolf Institute in Cambridge, has advised me on my writing and drew attention to alternative views. He also made me aware that whilst I may well be recognised in the field of medicine I am unknown in the humanities, which may cause difficulties. I am grateful to Lord Jonathan Sacks for his valuable advice and encouragement in formulating my thoughts. I have been greatly supported by my good friends, Professors Michael Denman, Norman Joels, Ivan Roitt, Jeremy Turk and Neville Woolf. Collectively they read most of my writing, suggested important revisions and corrected many errors, for which I am truly grateful.

I wish to thank Dr. Michael Stolleis, professor of Public Law at the Goethe University in Frankfurt am Main who confirmed the record about Hitler gaining German nationality after several rejections by a 'trick'. I learned a great deal from my discussions with Dr. Robert Jay Lifton, professor of Psychiatry and Psychology at the City University of New York and Mount Sinai School of Medicine, who interviewed directly several German concentration camp doctors and published the findings in this book. I greatly appreciate the effort exerted by several librarians at the Heidelberg University in letting me read the original doctoral thesis of Josef Goebbels and when I was unable to find the acknowledgement to his Jewish supervisor they inspected the thesis with great care to see if it was tampered. I gained insight in one of the sons of a leading Nazi, Nicolas Frank, who cannot forgive his father, Hans Frank, responsible for the murder of millions of Poles and Jews when he was Governor General in occupied Poland. I owe a great debt of gratitude to many German historians and librarians who encouraged me by asking similar questions to mine, when I visited the universities of Jena, Heidelberg, Hamburg, Berlin as well as the Kaiser Wilhelm Institute and the Weimar libraries.

I learned a great deal in discussions with the late professor Charles Dent at University College, London, Dame Janet Vaughan at the University of Oxford and Dr. Keith Mant, professor of Forensic Pathology at Guy's

Hospital Medical School who were appointed to advise on the nutritional intake, especially in Belsen Bergen concentration camp. I gained a great deal of insight and understanding of German history and anti-Semitism through the numerous lecturers I was privileged to attend at the Wiener Library, The German Historical Institute, London and Pears Institute of the Birkbeck College, London.

My sincere thanks to Mrs. Kathy Doyle for her forthright and able assistance in organising the book and most of the figures over many years and Jonah Lehner for his help with the computer, formatting and the Index. I should like to extend my thanks to Mr. Connor Browne and the Production Team of Austin Macauley Publishers Ltd. for their helpful advice and meticulous editing of the book.

Finally, I cannot adequately thank Greta, my wife, for her support and putting up for many years with my moods, seclusion and irritability when immersed in dealing with the greatest tragedy played out in our time.

Foreword

This book tackles one of the great puzzles of my life and tries to answer the great unanswered question of my youth. I have known for some time that it was in production and I am excited that it is finally here.

As a young boy, Germany was all around me. I was brought up in Hendon Central, around the corner from the site that would later house Brent Cross shopping centre; I have never lived in another country; I speak only English; and neither of my parents were raised in Germany. So why do I say that as a young boy Germany was all around me?

I am the son of two refugees. My father had been born in Lwów, then in Poland, and had been deported as a young boy to the border of Siberia. And my mother grew up in Holland and is a survivor of Belsen concentration camp.

My mother's father was a man called Alfred Wiener, a cultured German and Arabist who devoted his life to studying the rise of Nazism, documenting its rise and recording its crimes. My favourite picture of him is in his study in his famous library, at his desk, surrounded by his books. It captures not just him but the family atmosphere in my own home.

For my father was deeply influenced by his father in law. He was given hundreds of Alfred's books as an engagement present and added thousands to them. I recall him in a similarly studious posture, his nose in a large volume. While he was a Pole by birth it was the culture and German background of Alfred Wiener that suffused our home. Only as a young adult did I appreciate that the continental food, the décor in the homes of the old family friends we visited, the accents we heard, were not typical.

And as this became clearer to me something else became less clear. Germany had been intellectually dazzling, culturally brilliant. Yet Germany had also stolen our property, made an exile of my grandfather, imprisoned my mother, and killed my grandmother. Living in my childhood environment meant living every day with people who had personally been victims of German violence. Every person we knew, it seemed, had their own story of the miracle which alone allowed them to escape.

How could these two things co-exist? How could one of the world's greatest cultures produce its greatest act of degradation?

It is puzzling over this that has led Thomas Lehner to produce this extraordinary study – a tour de force of learning and inquiry. It doubles as a review of intellectual life in one part of Germany at one time, and a review of the Holocaust in that same area.

By bringing together, say, the history of Buchenwald with the history of Weimar culture and the Universities of Jena and Heidelberg the reader is permitted to grope toward greater understanding. To see the way that intellectual life came under the sway of politics and how great academics made themselves servants of a debased ideology is to appreciate a little better how an entire country gave itself over to murder and racist atrocity.

One is left with the disturbing thought that the sheer power of German cultural life made Hitler's rise easier. It perhaps contributed to a reverence for authority and to a desire that the purity of social life should reach the same standards as the purity of art and science. As many great liberal thinkers, such as Karl Popper, have argued, this is a very dangerous desire.

What gives this book its drive and urgency is that what Dr. Lehner discovers is not really something he wants to know or live with. That such crimes should come from the great culture which he so respects and, in particular his fellow medics, for whom he naturally has fellow feeling, pains him deeply.

What makes this book special is that he faces this fact unflinchingly as page by page he gradually reveals it. In doing so he demonstrates the qualities that were missing in some of the cultured people he writes about. Without courage and independence, where are we?

Lord Daniel Finkelstein
Associate Editor, The Times
15th August 2016

CONTENTS

INTRODUCTION

'If you want the present to be different from the past, study the past'

Baruch Spinoza, 1632-1677

'What experience and history teach is this – that nations and governments have never learned anything from history or acted upon any lessons they might have drawn from it'

G.W.F Hegel 1770-1831

'The lack of resistance to the Jewish persecution does not necessarily indicate acceptance, but rather 'lethal indifference'

Ian Kershaw, 2008

'The only ultimately valuable thing in the universe is the individual human being and the ultimate sin is to degrade or humiliate another human being. The doctrine according to which I must respect other human beings'

Immanuel Kant, 1724-1807

'Pathetic that the German people submit to any mad scoundrel who appeals to their lowest instincts, who confirms them in their vices and teaches them to conceive nationalism as isolation and brutality'

Thomas Mann's interpretation of Goethe's thinking, 1939

'Stood on the great plain
in the falling snow,
Ten thousand soldiers marched
to and fro
Looking for you and me,
my dear,
Looking for you and me'

W.H. Auden;
Refugee Blues, 2003

'Libraries, museums, theatres, universities, research centres can prosper next to the concentration camps' George Steiner, 1971	'You will remember not in vengeance -in a determination that these things shall not occur again' Sir Hartley Shawcross' summing up the Nüremberg Trial, 1946

As a child of the Second World War, reflecting on the atrocities perpetrated by the National Socialist regime in Germany, its collaborators in Austria and elsewhere in Europe, I embarked on the quest for an answer some fifty years ago. The decision to study the horrendous and painful history of Genocide was difficult, especially when I read what German and Austrian medical 'colleagues' were capable of perpetrating face-to-face with children and adults. An innate compulsion, however, was difficult to resist, propelled by what appeared to be passive acceptance of Nazi atrocities by the Western culture; 'let bygones be bygones and look forward to the future'. I was also reminded as a medical student at University College Hospital Medical School, when I was on Professor Charles Dent's clinical unit. He witnessed the ultimate evil and human suffering inflicted on the inmates of the concentration camp in Bergen – Belsen, as he was a member of the British delegation of medical scientists investigating the effect of diet on people recuperating from near death caused by starvation. Indeed, large number of prisoners were dying, despite, or as it turned out, because of the sudden excessive calorie intake. My second encounter, about five years later, was at Guy's Hospital Medical School, when I needed to learn a new research technique and arrangements were made for me to spend a week in Dame Janet Vaughan's Department at the Churchill Hospital. She was also the Principal of Somerville College, Oxford. In 1945, she was a member of the medical delegation attempting to offer the most appropriate diet for the starved inmates in Belsen concentration camp. Some years later at Guy's Hospital, I had the good fortune of having many discussions with Keith Mant, professor of Forensic Pathology who headed the Special Medical Section of the British Army's War Crimes Group in Germany. He interviewed a large number of perpetrators and victims involved in medical atrocities committed at the Ravensbruck women's concentration camp.

The critical significance of the Jewish genocide has emerged gradually after the war, when the atrocities carried out by German cultured people have come to light. Sir Max Hastings has expressed this most succinctly in 2014. "The war aims of the Germans in the First World War were little different to those of Hitler 35 years later, except for the Jewish genocide." The moral justification of the 'Good War' emerged only with the liberation of the concentration camps and discovery that two millennia of Christianity and two centuries of the Enlightenment has made little difference to man's inhumanity to man, except employing more efficient and sophisticated means of mass murder. Hastings conclusion is in line with the Nüremberg trial of the Nazi leaders, as among a number of indictments, the only one which proved to carry the convincing force of law was that of 'crimes against humanity', in which the practices of civilised nations were violated.

The astonishing revelation faced humanity that in the latter half of the twentieth century, the unimaginable, unspeakable, anti-human, anti-Christian, and anti-Enlightenment deed was committed in the heart of Europe by a highly educated, cultured, science-endowed, enlightened, and disciplined people. They set upon a minority of identifiable people by their religion, which academics of renowned universities converted into a racial identity, responsible for all the ills and calamities that affected the good people of the German 'Volk'. Some Christian scholars established a seat of learning linked with the university to free the Bible of Jewish contamination. The universities were busy establishing chairs in eugenics, re-named 'racial hygiene', and eminent lawyer's enacted laws to deprive the dastardly minority of all freedom, liberty, and protection under the law. Doctors of medicine educated by some of the most celebrated medical schools, taught in the art of healing, became the arbiters of life and death and perpetrators of some of the most inhumane medical experiments.

The politicians showed them the way, the people joined in by brutal force, let loose on the undefended minority, and the country's resources were mobilised to eradicate the source contaminating the peace-loving 'Volk'. The anointed 'Führer' emerged, of Austrian provenance, naturalised to German citizenship by subterfuge. He led the good people, university professors, bishops, lawyers, doctors, and artists under the all-embracing umbrella of the 'Führer Principle', interpreted as the Word, religion, law, science and medicine of the new order. And the silent majority, the innocent bystanders, remained silent.

Six million children, women, and men were sacrificed at the altar of Nationalism, Racism, Religion, Enlightenment, and Eugenics. Can it happen again, and remember, any minority can be targeted and all people in some countries can be a minority – 'the other' This is what the 'Thousand Year Reich' achieved in twelve years, a documented template of genocide, which another anointed, charismatic leader can readily follow with the 'will to power' and the silent majority to maintain its 'innocent bystander' status.

The prime objective of this book is an attempt to examine and forestall another disaster, that is nearer than people are prepared to envisage. To convert the 'Thousand Year Reich to Thousand Year Memory', to analyse, deploy, and mobilise all means of the humanities, the ethically endowed scientific establishment, and the depth of human psyche, the stirrings of the selfish gene, the retrograde signals of atavism, the very essence of existence required to prevent the suffering, pain and depravity of genocide. This is the categorical imperative of the twenty-first century, a legacy of the German-led genocide, to investigate 'the signatures of the template of genocide'.

I resolved to attempt to answer the question, 'Why' and to learn about the people of the country where it all happened. After many years of hesitation about the subject matter, I abandoned my initial intention to re-analyse the atrocities perpetrated by some German and Austrian doctors during the Nazi period. A great deal had been published already and not many people would wish to read, indeed can endure reading about doctors selecting for life and death innocent children, women, and men, or about the horrendous experiments perpetrated on human beings. Moreover, I had great regard for the healing profession, which I had joined, traditionally considered to be the most humane and worthy vocation. There have been many decent and caring German men of medicine who made fundamental contributions to the healing profession. I admired especially the scientific contribution to the biology and pathology of cells and liberal mind displayed by Rudolf Virchow of the Charité Hospital in Berlin.

To my surprise, after meeting and getting on well with German medical scientists at numerous international conferences, I decided to seek an answer to this crucial question from German historians. I asked, "how was it possible for a most cultured people in the centre of Europe in the twentieth century to perpetrate the ultimate evil? Deprive a peaceful religious minority of freedom, livelihood, shelter, leading to deportation to concentration camps designed for mass murder?" I asked this question of historians from the Max Planck Institute in Berlin, the Free University of Berlin, and those of the Universities of Jena, Heidelberg, Hamburg, Nüremberg, and Munich. To my astonishment, a frequent answer was "we are asking the very same question ourselves". This was both healing to my personal deep wound and validating my question, so far unanswered.

I decided to focus on Western Culture and Civilization, knowing fairly well that the meanings of these two critical words-concepts are hopelessly mixed up. However, since I took a firm decision to write about the 'German Question' and Germans demonstrably differentiated 'Kultur' (Culture) from Civilization (both defined below), I adopted this line of argument. The outstanding literature of Goethe and Schiller drew my attention to the eighteenth century Weimar classicism and the ancient seat of learning in the adjacent University of Jena. Within a short distance to the west is Eisenach, where Johan Sebastian Bach was born and where Martin Luther attended school and later hid in the local Wartburg castle to escape imprisonment by the Pope and where he translated the New Testament into German. Thus, the epicentre of great literature and poetry in Weimar, music and religion in Eisenach, and the humanities (Fichte and Hegel) and sciences (Haeckel) in Jena, served all my requirements of culture and by all accounts civilization. The fatal proximity of Buchenwald concentration camp, within about five miles north of Weimar, and the unprecedented barbarity perpetrated there, presented the reverse side of civilization. The triangular constellation of Weimar – Jena – Eisenach, and its proximity to Buchenwald, all in the state of Thuringia, served as a focus to reflect on Culture versus Barbarity during the Third Reich (Fig 1).

The working definition of civilization used in this book is based on the principle of natural justice, by reasoning humanity, abiding by individual freedom, and gaining material welfare, which does not harm others – it is the opposite to barbarism. Culture refers to human appreciation, expression and development of education, reason, ideas, and all branches of the arts that elevate the sense of well-being, happiness, and spiritual fulfilment.

From the very start, I became aware that even restricting my enquiries to a microcosm of Culture and Civilization in this small part of Germany, lands me in the vast territory of German history, religion, literature, philosophy, law, medicine, and natural and social sciences. Furthermore, to make the narrative comprehensible in terms of the prevalent voices of the perpetrators and victims, I was obliged to broaden my account beyond Thuringia. Buchenwald concentration camp was built early in Thuringia because it was the first National Socialist state in Germany and the first priority of the party was to eliminate any opposition real or imagined by building the camp. Why choose the site next to Weimar of all places is a mystery of the 'Übermensch' (superman) mentality of the National Socialist; a pride in the spiritual heights of German 'Kultur', linked by a quirk of reason to preservation of that Kultur and eliminating any real, alleged or elected enemy.

The Thüringen state governing body under Wilhelm Frick and Fritz Sauckel demonstrated very early all the subsequent features of the fascist

'Third Reich', by its extreme nationalism, racism, and anti-Semitism. The latter thrived in Thuringia, as indeed in the rest of Germany, as the longest hatred and animosity related to the origin of Christianity and its split from Judaism. To appreciate the potential source of conflict, I found it essential to struggle with the history of early Christianity, trying especially to come to terms with the historical Jewish Jesus, a focal point of the narrative, despite the lack of any direct written word by Jesus himself. I am aware that this book is littered with a vast number of controversies, and I hope not too many inaccuracies. It is inevitable that some of my interpretations will be contested, as there is hardly an issue that is not mired in controversy. I must have blasphemed against both the Jewish and Christian religious beliefs and my only defence is that most of these offences are not entirely of my own making.

As a medical scientist, devoted to experimental work with a substantial number of publications in the scientific literature, I am painfully aware that I am not offering primary data. My approach is eclectic, relying almost entirely on the meticulous research of specialists in the fields of history, theology, philosophy, literature, law, medicine, and sociology. However, I am offering an overall, albeit brief account of a critical period of Judeo-Christian Civilization in Western Europe, that in many ways illustrates the uncontrolled movements of the tectonic plates of Civilization and its tenuous relationship to Culture as defined above. The antagonism between Christianity and Judaism has regrettably led to a native fratricide; the brotherly love each preaches has turned into mutual polemics, with Christianity gaining ascendancy after Constantine's conversion in the fourth century and exercising its might thereafter. The high moral and ethical values that monotheism has engendered have failed to prevent disasters throughout the ages of Christian civilization. The vitriol of Martin Luther was initially turned on to Catholics, whilst "the Jews are the best blood on earth". However, very soon all the venom was diverted against the Jews when they rejected Luther's bidding to convert to his reformed Christianity. He published an extremely damaging narrative, 'On the Jews and their lies', which had serious repercussions right up to the National Socialist period.

The great hopes of the enlightenment had liberated the Jewish people from their oppressive existence and deprived freedom and the prevailing rights of citizenship. The enlightenment has made it possible for rational debate and science to develop, unhindered by religious restrictions and ancient dogmas. Mankind had been liberated to exercise fully its power of reasoning, leading to immense scientific advances, and great improvements in our lives. Regrettably, despite all the lofty ideals and declarations of human freedom, the aphrodisiac of power, devoid of morality, empathy, and altruism has not abated. Evil, if anything, has been enhanced by modern advances in communication, organisation, science, and efficiency of weaponry. George Steiner has steadfastly argued of the juxtaposition of art with barbarity; "libraries, museums theatres, research centres…can prosper next to concentration camps".

The critical question that calls for an answer, though eighty years delayed, is how could a stateless Austrian, with uncertain provenance, a school dropout, failed artist, army corporal with a criminal record, imprisonment, and sham naturalised German citizenship become the 'Führer' of the most cultured, scientifically endowed country in Europe? The short answer is that the German people were waiting for the Messiah, the one who will put right all the wrongs, real or imaginary, Germans have suffered, materially and spiritually. The Führer emerged with an impressive charisma and leadership, underpinned by nationalism, promising greatness of the German Volk. He identified in their midst the scapegoat, the perfidious Jew, who was responsible for all the past, present, and future ills. And the 'Volk' listened, the churches knew it for two thousand years, and their well inscribed memories were entrenched by Martin Luther's doctrine. The Academia saw the brilliance of a Gundolf and Heine in literature, Mendelssohn and Marx in philosophy, another Mendelssohn in music, Einstein and Haber in Science, and Ehrlich in medicine, to mention only some of the outstanding men of enlightened Germany. 'The Jews were everywhere, they took over the country and were responsible for all the calamities; the solution is clear and calls for righteous action'.

An attempt to answer the burning question, 'how was it possible' is the subject of this book. This question was asked among others by Friedrich Meinecke, the renowned German historian in his book 'German Catastrophe'. "Must we not always be shocked at the precipitous fall from the heights of the Goethe era to the swamp of the Hitler period? We Germans ask ourselves how was this possible". My aim was an attempt to correlate and as far as possible interpret the multiple complex interacting factors, which may identify the root causes, the factors responsible for the persistence of the prejudice and hatred. To analyse human necessity for a scapegoat that harks back to the time of animal sacrifice and differentiate the villain from the innocent bystanders. The outcome of this conundrum is that the 'Thousand Year Reich' has converted 'The Jewish Question' into 'The German Question'.

Ultimately, the analysis of the German problem boils down to the two diverse cultures that of Goethe versus Goebbels – Culture versus Barbarity. Goethe the liberal, freedom-loving man of culture who owed nothing to the Church or Universities, unlike Goebbels, Doctor of Philosophy from the famous university of Heidelberg with strong early ties to the Church, turned into the harbinger of hatred, venom, and propagating evil. Goethe wrote profound poetry, plays, and literature, establishing the cultural status of the German language. He was a man of innate wisdom, not expressed in learned treatises, but in literary narratives and poetry that reached deep in the innermost sanctum of the soul. He established a culture and civilisation that Germans and Europeans have tried to emulate. 'Back to Goethe' was the cry after almost every disaster in Germany. Goebbels was the frustrated writer who found his 'nirvana' in Hitler's hate and prejudice, pinning his life's ambition to an evil ideology of supremacy, racism, and denigrating all but the 'Volk' and the 'Führer'. He was responsible in his own words for 'the big lie', using the spoken word, radio, and films to depersonalise a people who nourished him in his intellectual and emotional development.

An attempt to analyse and interpret the genocide in terms of the complexities of theology, art, ethics, morality, law, medicine, and the sciences is a daunting task. Yet there has been a constant inner need over the last half a century to reflect, interpret, express, and perhaps burst the bubble of incomprehension of reason as opposed to mindless prejudice. My early objective was to attempt 'meta-analysis', that is correlating the multiple factors, which create the complexities of civilization that can turn into barbarity. The basic studies of this multifactorial problem have been kept within the impermeable walls of theology and academia, largely out of reach of the informed reader. Historical treatises are usually written for historians, scientific works for scientists, medical studies for doctors, and religious tracts for theologians. The non-specialised general, informed reader has seldom the opportunity to read an overall account of this critical period in Western Christian Civilization. My hope is that this account might get through to the informed readership and receive the critical assessment of the thinking man and woman. The difficulties encountered were too great for the aimed 'meta-analysis' and preliminary enquiries into other methods of analyses of multifactorial problems, such as 'systems biology', 'game theory', algorithms – would have required some mathematical formulation and collaboration with experts in these fields that was as yet difficult to accomplish.

I have avoided discussing Islam, primarily because it has not been directly involved in Western Judeo-Christian Civilization and the

Holocaust, though otherwise, it is of immense importance and calls for a different treatise. I have also deliberately abstained from discussing the birth of Israel, which had been argued as possibly the only positive outcome of the 'Shoa' (Holocaust). The issue is enormously complex, as Zionism harks back long before the emergence of National Socialism and the subject has been frequently dealt with elsewhere. My aim has been to discuss, however inadequately, the co-existence of culture with barbarism and I have my doubts, if the all-important subject of modern Israel would necessarily help to clarify this objective. It would also raise new issues, both of Islam and the prevalent anti-Israeli sentiments, in Europe, as well as the Middle East. I have abstained from discussing other genocides, especially the tragedies of the Armenian genocide, which began in 1915 in Turkey and claimed over a million Armenians. Nearer the present time, I have also avoided the genocides in Cambodia and Rwanda, all of which are tragic, but they have not taken place in the heart of European Christian culture and the Enlightenment, as has been my primary objective.

Having decided to focus initially on the State of Thuringia, I selected the Friedrich Schiller University of Jena, in preference to Erfurt, as Jena was linked to Weimar from its foundation in 1558 by the elector John Frederick the Magnanimous, when Jena was regarded as a centre of the Reformation. Later in the 18th century, Jena's reputation was boosted by the classical culture of Weimar, with Goethe and Schiller among other literary giants. The university demonstrates the transition from a classical seat of learning, having renowned teachers and students in literature, philosophy, science, and medicine for over four centuries, into a model fascist establishment. The Humboldtian principles of upholding the freedom of ideas, humanities, research and teaching were converted to the 'Führer Principle', of Hitler's National Socialist ideas of the supremacy of the German 'Volk', at the expense of the rest of humanity. In order to ascertain if Jena was a special case, divorced from the fate of the other universities in Germany, I extended my enquiries to the University of Heidelberg, on the basis that it was the oldest (1386) and arguably the most famous university in Germany. This proved particularly rewarding, as it demonstrated a liberal attitude without religious bias that prevailed as far back as the 17th century, when the 'dangerous atheist' Baruch du Spinoza was invited to the chair in Philosophy. Yet, like Jena, the university was transformed by academics imbued by nationalism and racism, into a Nazi university, governed by the 'Führer Principle'.

Long before the advent of Nazism, individual academics relentlessly voiced their anti-Semitism under the cloak of 'free speech' of Universities, which has often developed into 'free abuse'. Johann Gottlieb Fichte at the University of Jena referred to Jews in 1793, "a mighty, hostile state, which is permanently at war with every other". Heinrich von Treitschke, one of the most influential historians of his time, member of the Reichstag and professor at the Universities of Berlin, Heidelberg, Kiel and Freiburg, made his oft repeated statement about 1880 that "Jews are Germany's misfortune". From the early 1930, Jewish professors and lecturers were ostracised and attacked by others, such as Professor Philipp Lenard at the University of Heidelberg and the student body was encouraged in anti-Semitic heckling and abuse of some teachers.

In accord with Nazi ideology, lawyers shamelessly went ahead to promulgate restrictive laws, reversing the progress of liberty and freedom earned by previous generations. They must have realised that euthanasia, based on dubious medical criteria, is morally flawed and that mass killing cannot be tolerated in a civilised world. The extra-judicial status acquired by Himmler and Heydrich's SS, and Müller's Gestapo hordes, exercised 'No Limits in the 'Extra-Territorial' concentration camps.

My greatest surprise, disappointment, pity, and shame was to discover that medicine, my own chosen vocation, which has been traditionally held in such high esteem by all religions and humanity, deserves the severest opprobrium for its disgraceful behaviour. 'Healers turned Killers' as succinctly expressed by Robert Jay Lifton, with doctors of medicine selecting men, women, and children for murder. The lucky individuals passing the triage of life or death at the very entrance of the 'Vernichtungslager' (Extermination Camp) were worked and starved ultimately to death. A number were selected for the most infamous medical experiments perpetrated on human beings, by doctors qualified at some of the best German and Austrian Medical Schools. All the barbarities were in full swing, whilst Beethoven and Mozart were played, Goethe and Schiller were read and recited, and 'Kultur' with its ennobling, spiritual élan, thrived side by side of murder at large, as consistently argued by George Steiner.

For twelve years, Germany pursued war on three fronts: the Eastern front first against Czechoslovakia, Poland, and after an interval, against Russia, the Western front initially against France and Britain and later Britain and the United States. The third front was the unilateral formally undeclared racial extermination war against the defenceless Jewish people. The war against Jews, referred to as the 'Holocaust', is derived from the biblical sacrifice of an animal offering consumed by fire. However, the Hebrew word 'Shoah' for catastrophe, is nearer to the unique event, for which new laws had to be enacted – 'crime against humanity' and

'Genocide'. I also use the terminology 'Swastika versus Star of David' to emphasise the direct conflict between two grossly unequal forces in the undeclared war of annihilation of a religious minority. Hitler and his acolytes succeeded in the only historical heritage of the Thousand Year Reich, 'the memory of the killing fields of the Holocaust'. Indeed, the 'Jewish Question' mutated into the 'German Question', surprisingly declared by Hans Frank at the Nuremberg Trial, "A thousand years will pass and the guilt of Germany will not be erased".

I dealt briefly with the Catholic, Protestant, and Jewish responses to the Holocaust, trying to analyse and comprehend volumes of writings, despite a palpable void of meaningful interpretation. George Steiner argued with his powerful intellect, "We will not be capable of thinking of the Shoah, albeit inadequately, if we divorce its genesis and its radical enormity from theological origins". There was little or no opposition from the Catholic and Lutheran Churches to Hitler's Germany with the notable exception of four Protestant theologians, Karl Barth who had to leave Germany, Dietrich Bonhoeffer who was imprisoned in Buchenwald concentration camp and murdered, Martin Niemöller and Heinrich Grüber, both of whom were incarcerated in Sachsenhausen and Dachau, but fortunately survived.

There was little, if any, formal resistance from the academic establishment or from the German population at large, with some honourable individual exceptions offering support for their Jewish colleagues, friends, and neighbours. The shining exceptions were the brave students of the 'White Rose' opposition, who lost their lives but salvaged Goethe's, Schiller's, and Humboldtian humanitarian ideals of Germany. They were led by Professor Kurt Huber, arguably the only academic actively opposing the Nazi regime, in stark contrast to Martin Heidegger the brilliant philosopher but flawed human being.

An intriguing notion of German-Jewish affinities by no lesser individuals than Goethe and Thomas Mann might apply to a love-hate relationship shown in the extreme by Goebbels. His mentor and supervisor of the PhD thesis in Heidelberg was the Jewish professor Max von Waldberg, and his girlfriend to whom he was strongly attached was also Jewish. In science, Philipp Lenard, a Nobel Prize winner in physics, mentored by the half-Jewish professor Heinrich Hertz, helped by Albert Einstein to interpret the results, both of whom he acknowledged and greatly revered, turned perversely into a mindless hatred and a movement against 'Jewish Physics'. The philosopher Martin Heidegger also had a Jewish mentor professor, Edmund Husserl, who was instrumental in appointing him to the chair in Philosophy at the University of Freiburg, and another

Jewish professor, Emil Lask, whose ideas Heidegger failed to acknowledge in his major concept of 'Being and Time' (Da Sein). He had an intimate relationship with his Jewish PhD student Hannah Arendt, yet he joined the Nazi party, became Rector of the University of Freiburg, and endorsed the 'Führer Principle' guiding the University. He watched his mentor Husserl being humiliated and dismissed from the University and never uttered a word of remorse for his despicable behaviour.

The final chapter deals with the post-war 'collective amnesia', followed almost a generation later by a breach of the taboo subject by the Church and the beginning of realisation of Germany's moral abyss, with expression of culpability, responsibility, and apology for the tragedy. The universities, centres of learning, and the legal profession, so far have failed to do the right thing and admit their responsibility for some of the harm, when they dismissed a large number of political and Jewish academics and lawyers, with little or no opposition from their colleagues. The exception has been the Kaiser Wilhelm Society – renamed the Max Planck Society. Under the presidency of Hubert Markl, investigating its war-time history, the Society admitted "the deepest regret, compassion, and shame at the fact that crimes of this sort were committed, promoted, and not prevented within the ranks of German scientists." The medical profession after constant denials, despite mountains of evidence, fully admitted its culpability in the Holocaust in 2012, about sixty-seven years after the tragic period.

A short account is presented on some hopeful signs, of which the declaration of Vatican II is the most significant, as well as important Christian and Jewish theological treatises, outlining ways of revising traditional teaching and engaging in serious studies of ecumenism between the Abrahamic religions. There is as yet little evidence that the split between 'Culture and Civilization', has been adequately studied. The complicity of academia in universities, the learned professions, especially law and medicine, linked with an institutional anti-Jewish polemic maintained by the churches, are the basic issues raised in this account. 'Holocaust denial' will not be discussed as the historical veneer attempted by David Irving and other anti-Semites have been demolished in the 'Lipstadt Trial' and brilliantly documented by professor Richard J. Evans in his book 'Lying about Hitler: History, the Holocaust, and the David Irving Trial' (2000).

However, the emergence of revisionist historians, concerned about the posthumous historical image of Germany, riddled with guilt, poor self-esteem, indeed shame of the released barbarity of the 'Kultur Volk', will be briefly discussed. The vexed question of the 'innocent bystander' referring to the vast majority of the German civilian population is open to debate, and can be phrased in Churchillian terms. “We did not know, we were not told – and you did not ask!”. The memory of the killing fields of the Holocaust, in the midst of an advanced Western Christian Civilization imbued with the ideology of the Enlightenment must not be put to rest, until the multifactorial causes have been adequately researched, identified, and acted upon. The coexistence of Culture and Barbarism should be of critical concern to the entire Western Civilization, if another human catastrophe is to be averted. The words of the German writer W. G. Sebald are appropriate. “No serious person can think about anything else than the Holocaust”.

Finally, the chapters and some sections are introduced by a ‘montage of Aphorisms’, to offer the essential message in succinct, well-thought-out phrases by distinguished individuals with a depth of understanding of the culture, civilization, and the human condition, and adding a few of my own humble contributions. As the book covers a broad area aimed at the general readership, to quote all the references would be difficult, inappropriate, and dissuade the very readership it is hoped to reach. However, I give the major sources of my information in the select bibliography at the end of the book.

'WELTSCHMERZ' – COSMIC PAIN

I read Goethe, the German soul of culture – wisdom – judgment and ask – why.

I read Schiller, the Nation's poet, "The Ode to Joy – we are all brothers" and ask – why.

I listen to Bach's lofty sonatas and partitas, the 'Ur-musik' and ask – why.

I am moved by Beethoven's quartets that reach the very essence of one's being and ask – why.

I am struck by Dürer's prescience of "Four horsemen of the Apocalypse" and ask – why.

I meditate at the ephemeral nature of the great and the good and ask – why.

And wonder – has 'Weltschmerz' turned into 'German Question', why murder millions of innocent souls, 'Warum'!

CHAPTER 1: THE FEDERAL STATE OF THURINGIA; THE PROTOTYPE OF A NAZI STATE

I. **Introduction**
II. **Early History of Thuringia**
III. **Weimar Classicism**
IV. **Goethe in Weimar (1775-1832)**
V. **Friedrich Schiller (1759-1805)**
VI. **Johann Gottfried Herder (1744-1803)**
VII. **Weimar Republic**
VIII. **Thuringia – a prototype of a Nazi state**
IX. **Anti-Semitism in Thuringia**
X. **Claims of National Socialism on Goethe, Schiller and Herder**

THE FEDERAL STATE OF THURINGIA AND THE WEIMAR REPUBLIC

The centre of literature, poetry, music, theology, and scholarship, in fatal proximity with the ultimate evil of a centre of brutality, should be of concern to all who value Western civilization, culture and religion.

(Author)

I. INTRODUCTION

After years of reflections on Western Culture and Civilization, I arrived at a representative microcosm about 30km apart, between Jena, Weimar, and Eisenach, within the state of Thuringia in Germany. This epicentre of high culture, advanced academic attainments of University scholarship was in fatal proximity with the ultimate evil perpetrated in the concentration camp of Buchenwald. The coexistence of Goethe and Schiller in Weimar, Bach and Luther in Eisenach and the humanities, theology and sciences at the University of Jena, with unprecedented barbarity in Buchenwald is a reality that should be the concern of all who value Western Civilization and Culture. The following account will focus on The Federal State of Thuringia, a microcosm of culture in Weimar – Jena – Eisenach versus Barbarity in Buchenwald (Fig. 1). Each of these is described in a separate chapter, except Eisenach, which is presented in separate sections of Martin Luther and the 'Institute' in Eisenach.

Fig.1 The Federal State of Thuringia, with Weimar – Jena – Eisenach and Buchenwald

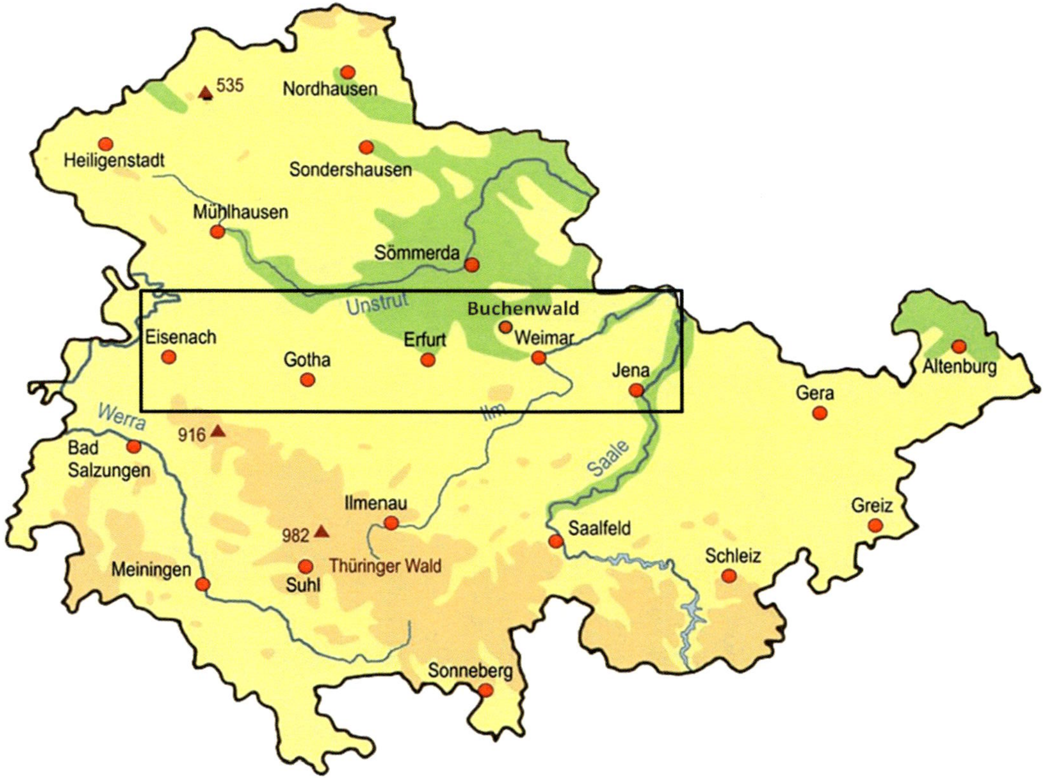

A working definition is presented here to appreciate the two concepts, which are conventionally related or mixed, and on which the ideas presented here are based. Civilization refers to the principle of natural justice, by reasoning humanity, abiding by individual freedom, and gaining material welfare, which does not harm others it is the opposite of barbarism. Culture refers to human appreciation, expression and development of reason, ideas, education and all branches of the arts that elevate the sense of happiness and spiritual fulfilment.

Before we embark on specific issues of the turbulent history of the Third Reich, a few words of caution by an amateur historian might be apposite. Historians create images of the past and impart knowledge and perception of the actions of our predecessors. Historians think of themselves as protectors of collective memory, protecting it from legends and manipulations. There are great dangers of manipulating public memory, historical arguments, using false analogies and tempering with truth. However, it is not uncommon to differ in interpreting the evidence as exemplified by two of the great British historians. Edward Gibbon and Arnold Toynbee on the "Decline and Fall of the Roman Empire". According to David Cannadine, Gibbon believed that Rome had conferred on humanity civilization that is civic virtue, freedom, order, justice, prosperity, culture, poetry, philosophy, and art. Gibbon argued that 'Christianity' vanquished not only 'Paganism' but also 'Barbarism', which then triumphed over 'Civilization'. He believed that the Roman Empire fell victim to the brutal Germanic tribes which destroyed the Graeco-Latin civilization and ushered in a dark age, which took centuries to recover. Toynbee, however, did not share Gibbon's admiration for Rome's imperial civilization, nor his disregard of the Christian faith. Toynbee argued that Christianity did not destroy Rome, as the Greek civilization was by that time dead, and the new Western civilization arose through Christianity. Nonetheless, Toynbee is considered as one of the greatest historians of his age. This fundamental disagreement between two eminent historians poses the problem for the general reader, who is left to sort out the facts, without having the background knowledge or inclination to sift through the evidence.

II. EARLY HISTORY OF THURINGIA

The rolling plains of Thuringia are bound in the west by the Werra River in the east by the Saale, in the north by the Harz Mountains and in the south by the Thuringian Forest. The Thuringian tribes occupied the territory about 300 AD, the kingdom of Thuringia existed from 400 to 531, and in the 6th century, it came under Frankish domination, forming later a part of the Holy Roman Empire. The Ludovingian dynasty was established in the 12th century with the principal residence at the Wartburg Castle above Eisenach, which played a crucial role throughout the history of Thuringia and Germany. The House of Wettin inherited Thuringia by marriage and generated sovereign rulers up to recent times.

Thuringia was incorporated within the Napoleonic Confederation of the Rhine in 1806, and the Congress of Vienna in 1815 included the state in the German Confederation. During the Prussian-led unification of Germany in 1871, the Thuringian duchies, with that of Saxe-Weimar-Eisenach, became part of the German Empire. In 1920, after the First World War, the eight small states and principalities merged into the state of Thuringia, with Weimar becoming its capital.

Christianity spread through Thuringia during the 8th century and the Gospel was preached by the Apostle St. Boniface, an emissary from Rome. In about 740 AD, he established Erfurt as the See of Thuringia. A number of monasteries were established and in the 11th and 12th centuries, Benedictine and Cistercian Abbeys were founded by the Landgraves. However, with the advent of Martin Luther in 1520, the Catholic faith was abolished, loyal priests were driven away, and churches and monasteries were largely destroyed, especially during the Peasant's War of 1525. After this, the Catholic faith has mostly disappeared, except for a few pockets in Erfurt and Eisenach.

The prevailing theological concept that the natural world could only be understood or accounted for by sinfulness was sorely tested by an unprecedented disaster in Thuringia. In the book by Philip M. Soergel, 'Miracles and the Protestant Imagination', he describes the Thuringian flood in 1643, recalling the tragedy of the biblical flood. On the 29th May 1613 "the clouds broke forth with the long-awaited rain, the force of the storm was of a scale that all observers agreed was unprecedented. Within a short time, the spring planting had been destroyed[.] Then the hail began, a phase of this cyclonic storm that reportedly lasted up to five hours in many places that soon killed hundreds of head of livestock standing in the fields. Flooding soon broke out, and the River Ilm and all other small tributary streams throughout the region soon overflowed their banks. Many parts of the province's largest and most important cities – Gotha, Weimar, Erfurt, and Jena – were soon under water."

The small principality of Saxe-Weimar that has been most directly affected by the catastrophe, was recorded by the local court preacher and church superintendent, Abraham Langen in his book 'Historische Relation'. Surprisingly, rather than concentrating on the great damage as a sign of God's anger on account of the sins of Thuringian people, he presented a systematic account of the disaster. The total estimated damage in the province was over 2,000 head of livestock drowned and killed by lightning and hail, more than a thousand houses, barns and churches, and the loss of about 320 people. However, another local pastor, Bernard Schilling stressed that God himself sent the great disaster on Thuringia, "to teach true contrition and repentance, respect for God's fatherly goodness, and awe before his wondrous works."

Whereas to-day, freak weather conditions are interpreted in the context of available scientific knowledge, in the 17th century, sin and human moral transgressions were at the forefront accounting for natural disaster. What effect the catastrophe may have had on the character of Thuringian people is open to conjecture. It may be reasonable to ask whether the religious views of sinful humanity, or natural forces prevailed. However, there is no doubt that the future development of Thuringia, basking in the glory of 'Kultur', with Goethe, Schiller, and Bach among others, was followed by the Nazi order ending in the ultimate evil of Buchenwald concentration camp (see p.102).

III. WEIMAR CLASSICISM

At the time when Johann Wolfgang Goethe was born in Frankfurt on the Main in 1749, Germany was not a defined country, with natural borders or national ethos. It had a common language, though not thought to be fit, by no lesser individual than Frederick the Great, to be used in writing literature. Germany claimed to have descended from the Holy Roman Empire of the German Nation of Charlemagne, which covered the wide territory of the present day Austria, Belgium, Germany, and part of the Czech Republic. The empire consisted of a loose federation of states, princes, counts, and Imperial knights. The country lacked unity, a system of taxation, currency, or an Imperial army, and each territory had its own established religion, Lutheran, Calvinist, or Catholic, largely dependent on the local sovereign. Nonetheless, the Holy Roman Empire provided historical and legal framework, and importantly, a common language. Art was almost wholly dependent on princely patronage and there was limited evidence of great German literature by the early 18th century. Friedrich Klopstock (1724-1803) was the author of the religious epic 'The Messiah', who argued with Gotthold E. Lessing (1729-1781) and others of the role of the poet as an aesthetic experience. In philosophy, the outstanding individual was Gottfried W. Leibniz (1646-1716), who was also a mathematician discovering calculus, and this led to the famous dispute with Sir Isaac Newton who independently discovered calculus and accused Leibniz of plagiarism.

A critical change occurred about the mid-18th century when theological studies underwent a transition towards Romantic thinkers, such as Novalis (Friedrich von Hardenberg (1772-1801)). According to the scholarly account of 'Goethe the poet and the age' by Nicholas Boyle, Goethe was almost alone among literary men of his age, owing nothing to the Church or the University; this distinguishes him from the formal tradition of German culture. He was free of any ties to the Church or State, so he did not have to ingratiate himself with either institution and was able to retain complete personal integrity. Poetry was Goethe's way of expressing his freedom. The mid-18th century is also the period of Enlightenment ('Aufklärung'), dissociating the predominantly religious thinking from that of reason to attain truth. The major figures at the time were Gotthold Lessing, Moses Mendelssohn (1729-1786), and Immanuel Kant (1724-1802). It is noteworthy that Lessing's last play 'Nathan the Wise' (1779), the first German classical drama, was prescient of present-day drive towards inter-faith understanding. Lessing presents the case that the three major Abrahamic religions – Judaism, Christianity, and Islam – share a basic belief and think alike. However, Lessing adds his personal belief in 'agnostic humanism', which has not been readily recognized in the play.

In Goethe's time, Frankfurt was a prosperous, cosmopolitan free city, with three Christian denominations; the Catholics – they had most churches, the Calvinists – mostly immigrant Dutch and Huguenots – had the money and the Lutherans – had the power. There was a large Jewish population and they lived in a ghetto up to 1796. The fully-fledged citizens were eligible to sit on the Council, which was presided over by the chief justice, and between 1747 to 1771, this position was held by Dr. Johann Wolfgang Textor, Goethe's maternal grandfather. By contrast, his paternal grandfather was a Thuringian tailor of peasant stock who, after years of wandering, settled in Frankfurt and made a great deal of money especially by his second marriage to the widow of an innkeeper. Thus, establishing a family link with Thuringia, Goethe's father Caspar was the only surviving child of the marriage who inherited this fortune. Caspar Goethe belonged to the highest social class of Frankfurt because he had studied law at several universities and acquired a doctorate in 1738. He was frustrated in not gaining a post in the Imperial administration, as he made a fatal political error in aligning himself with the Emperor's rival Maria Theresa. Caspar Goethe's frustrated ambitions were transferred onto his son, with Wolfgang having no fewer than eight private tutors. The first one at the age of three in a kindergarten, followed by Latin taught by a Turkish Christian, Italian by a Dominican from Naples, French by an émigré and a Jewish municipal clerk who taught Yiddish and then Hebrew. English was taught by another teacher, as was Greek, history, geography, handwriting, drawing, piano, and then the cello. It was evident that Wolfgang was a very gifted child, with a good memory, writing poems and making good progress in languages, except for Hebrew. Although father placed all his hopes on Wolfgang, by closely following his progress and very generous financial support, the relationship between them was tense, no doubt due to excessive attention and his father's rigid preconceived ideas.

In contrast, Wolfgang's relation with his mother was a loving one, with her story-telling ability, common sense, practical attitude to life, and trust in Providence. She was welcoming to Wolfgang's friends, especially at the period of 'Storm and Stress', with unending debates in the house between him and his friends. Goethe described accurately what he received from his parents in the short poem:

"My father gave me his build,
His earnest conduct of life,
From mummy her happy nature,
And fondness for story-telling."

His father had laid down Wolfgang's future, to study law in Leipzig, a doctorate at one of the other universities, although in his autobiography he expressed the desire to study history and philology at Göttingen. However, he reconciled himself to his father's wishes and embarked on legal studies in 1765 at the age of sixteen in Leipzig, though it is doubtful if he was fully committed to this course. As is usually the case in university life, he encountered a great many influences as diverse as attending lectures on literature and writing, mathematics and physics, with classical experiments in Newtonian optics, quite apart from his legal studies. Clearly, literature and writing eventually proved to be Goethe's making, whereas he developed an intense animosity to Newtonian optics, because he failed to appreciate the rigors of science in standardising experimental conditions. He had his amorous affairs with loose women, but experienced his first serious love affair at the age of seventeen with Kätschen, the inn-keeper's daughter. When it came to religion, Goethe questioned the basic tenets of religion, Christianity, God, and the bible. An intriguing throwback to Spinoza's ideas, Goethe claimed that in his childhood he had set up in his room an altar of mineralogical specimens to a nature deity. In his third year in Leipzig he fell ill, probably with pulmonary tuberculosis and returned to Frankfurt without a degree. By all accounts he was seriously ill but managed to pull through in his home, with loving attention by his mother and his younger sister Cornelia to whom he was always closely attached. However, the relationship with his father worsened, presumably due to the frustrated expectations of Caspar that his son would redeem the ambition in which his father had failed.

Caspar Goethe prevailed once again and Wolfgang enlisted in 1770 for the doctorate in law at the University of Strasbourg. He passed the oral examination for the licentiate in law with distinction and started working on the dissertation. Perhaps the most significant event in Strasbourg was his encounter with Johann Herder, five years older than Goethe and by that time a well-recognized literary figure, emphasising the importance of language, especially the mother tongue. Goethe introduced himself to Johann Herder who made a deep impression on Goethe's open mind by his concepts of the unity between humanity, nationality, and language. Goethe had good judgment in following some of Herder's concepts and he became Goethe's mentor. Herder suffered at the time with an eye disease and Goethe's almost daily attendance on the sick man turned into a course in modern literature and criticism from a well-informed teacher. Herder's ideas agreed with Goethe's thoughts that God and Nature or body and soul are the same, reminiscent of Spinoza's concept. Goethe was heading towards a secular literary existence, distancing himself from Christianity, and pursuing Herder's ideas of being a poet in the German language, assimilating national culture, secularised religiosity and sentimentality.

However, Goethe's dissertation was rejected by the University, so he had to be content with the licentiate in law, giving up the prospect of proceeding to the doctoral degree. He returned to Frankfurt in 1771 and applied to the bar, though evidently a career in law was less important to him than that of writing. He made the acquaintance of a literary circle among whom J. M. Merck, mostly an essayist, who had extensive experience and understanding of literature. He had great influence on Goethe's confidence in pursuing a literary career, unlike Herder who was hypercritical and kept on delaying publication of Goethe's play by suggesting constant revisions. Merck was encouraging, and advised him to get on with the publication of 'Götz von Berlichingen', which proved a great success.

At that time, there arose a German patriotic group of passionate young writers adopting the name 'Storm and Stress' ('Sturm und Drang'). The main aim was to develop a national literature out of a spirit of opposition to the prevailing life and thought. Most of them were of minor significance, except for Friedrich Klopstock, though Goethe and later Friedrich Schiller joined it. Some of Goethe's poems were suggestive of pantheism, invoking nature or God. These ideas were attributed to Spinoza's philosophy, and although at the time Spinoza was read privately, few admitted publicly any adherence to his largely banned political and religious, though highly rational, ideas. This applied equally to Leibniz, who would not publicly acknowledge the heretic, excommunicated by the Jewish religious authorities in Amsterdam and banned by the Christian authorities. However, in private, Leibniz actually took the trouble of visiting Spinoza and ostensibly had a high opinion and some say jealousy of the pure reasoning power of Spinoza.

Goethe's career was sealed with the writing of 'The Sorrows of Young Werther' (1774) that became a national and European success. The theme is about an accomplished young lawyer by the name of Carl Wilhelm Jerusalem, whom he had known earlier. Jerusalem's social failures and unhappy love had driven him to commit suicide. Goethe tried to comprehend what had moved the young man to sacrifice his entire future life. Goethe does this by Werther's letters to a friend and these disclose Werther's turmoil and frustration, indeed his inner life. The epicentre is Werther's love for Lotte a lively, down-to-earth, practical girl, the daughter of a bailiff. Werther is well aware that Lotte is entirely committed to Albert, a sensible, active, and friendly man who befriends Werther. On the advice of a friend, Werther takes up a diplomatic post in another part of Germany, following the adage 'out of sight out of mind'. This does not work for him, as he is totally obsessed by Lotte, despite the fact that by then she has been married to Albert. Werther's love for Lotte is hopeless and after a great deal of introspection, he concludes that the only way out of this situation is to do away with himself. On some pretext, he borrows Albert's pistols and shoots himself. It seems that Goethe identified himself with the suicidal hero, as he acknowledged his concern that with Werther he might relapse to the pathological condition from which it originated. Werther is the first novel of youth, unconcerned by rules and conventions of manners or sexuality. The book became a classic of the 'Sturm und Drang' movement and a hallmark of modernity. Even Napoleon at his meeting with Goethe in Erfurt apparently told him that he read the novel seven times and supported his claim by profound analysis of Werther.

IV. GOETHE IN WEIMAR (1775-1832)

'Goethe is the centre of attraction and admiration of all intelligent people' *Paul Valéry's eulogy, 1932*
'Goethe is the most un-German of all Germans' *André Gide, c.1910*

Soon after the publication of Werther and being idolized by the public, Goethe struck up a relationship in 1775 with Anne Elisabeth Schönermann. She was sixteen, the daughter of a Calvinist banking family in Frankfurt and Goethe called her 'Lili'. She was serious minded, attractive, and intelligent, and the love affair was mutual, without any of the handicaps encountered by Goethe in his previous amorous liaisons. Lili was not committed to another man and she was socially and financially compatible with Goethe's circumstances. Indeed, an informal engagement took place. Goethe admitted that she was the first woman he really loved, yet he eventually rejected marriage, largely because he felt that his life would have to conform to certain norms expected by the family, incompatible with his life.

At about this time in 1775, Goethe received an invitation from the young Duke Carl August of Weimar, whom Goethe had briefly met on a previous occasion. Carl August was keen to get Goethe to visit Weimar. Goethe's decision to accept the invitation turned out to be the most significant move in his life, as Weimar became Goethe's home and existence for the rest of his long life. Carl August the Duke of Saxe-Weimar-Eisenach was eighteen, had only just come of age and was due to marry Princess Louise of Darmstadt. About 6000 people lived in the town of Weimar, which had developed a reputation as a centre of culture under the patronage of the Dowager Anna Amalia, the duke's mother and regent during his minority. His father had died during his infancy. Goethe was only twenty-six on arrival at Weimar where he was received as a literary celebrity and one of the outstanding members of the 'Storm and Stress' movement. Wieland, a well-respected writer, whom Goethe had satirised in the past, had come to Weimar three years earlier as tutor to the teenage duke and his brother. Nonetheless, he praised Goethe as intelligent, charming, full of vitality, and altogether a fine human being.

Carl August was a coarse, self-confident, young man, engaged mostly in horse riding, hunting, ordering his small army, and having sex with peasant women, which resulted in many illegitimate children that were not acknowledged by the ducal family. Goethe, though formally his function was to refine the undisciplined young duke, went against the received wisdom and instead played along with the duke's whims and follies to gain his trust. This policy paid dividends, as Goethe became a confidante of the duke, he was rapidly promoted, exercised a good influence on him. He was involved in the affairs of the duchy, as well as the nearby University of Jena.

Soon after his arrival, Goethe was introduced to a woman of thirty-three, Charlotte von Stein who proved to have exerted great influence on Goethe's future. She was the wife of the Chief Equerry, intelligent, pretty, sensible, and well versed in courtly manners, without affectation. John Armstrong describes the emerging relationship between them; "Once in Weimar Goethe quickly drew close to Charlotte; she was quite different from the other women to whom he had been passionately attached. They were not only much younger, but they were also pleasing in their simplicity, in their innocent good nature. Lili had been worldly and flirtatious but hardly Goethe's match in culture or experience. Now Charlotte, at thirty-three, was seven years older than Goethe. She was well educated, knowledgeable about art and the ways of the aristocratic world – and not available for marriage. This must have helped, for if Goethe had learned anything from the episode with Lili it was that he shouldn't be thinking of marriage. Charlotte became Goethe's mentor and their relationship was platonic. It was almost certainly so in the relatively trivial sense that they didn't sleep together. This was a matter that deeply interested the local gossip and has preoccupied a few literary historians as well."

Although under Charlotte's guidance, Goethe became more statesmanlike, he remained ill at ease and awkward in courtly company, lacking aristocratic mannerism. Goethe had been able to organise his time to enable him, in addition to his duties with the duke, conversations and walks with Charlotte, to write a play about the 16th century Italian Poet

Torquato Tasso. He had also taken considerable interest in the administrative affairs of the duke and exercising power seems to have agreed with him. The duke discussed with Goethe the affairs of the State, such as the roads, forests, pensions, a disused silver mine, and appointments. Goethe was gradually asked to take on responsibilities for the roads, then the small army and finally the finances. When a new superintendent of the clergy was to be appointed, Goethe was instrumental in proposing his former mentor Herder, who joined the Weimar intellectual circle in 1776.

The friendly relationship and trust established between Goethe and the duke paid off, as the duke created a permanent position for Goethe. He decided with Anna Amalia's approval, to make him one of the four members of the cabinet of advisors, with whom he discussed all matters of State. Goethe was granted a substantial salary, a charming little house with a substantial garden, a short walk from the palace. Clearly, the duke and the duchess were anxious to retain Goethe in Weimar and made the offer that was difficult to refuse. Retrospectively, it is tempting to speculate that what made Goethe such a unique personality in the literary world was the manifold aspects of his experience and encounters with the real world of administrative, governing, and political dealings with people. His intellectual and creative nature must have been influenced by these somewhat mundane matters for a poet, which by all accounts may have enriched the totality of his outlook on life. He certainly demonstrates an exceptional integration of art and worldly issues, which are manifested in his plays.

Goethe did not write any treatise on philosophy, sociology, psychology, religion, or ethics, and his views on these issues have to be derived from his literary works. Briefly, 'The Sorrows of Young Werther' dealt with love, its frustrations when it is unrequited, ending in suicide. 'Tasso' is concerned with the conflict between freedom of the artist and the constraints of the politicians, whereas 'Egmont' presents largely a conflict between the power of evil and justice. 'Wilhelm Meister' described education and development of the individual, and in 'Elective Affinities', Goethe suggests the natural forces that attract and bind individuals in permanent relationships. His masterpiece Faust is a well-known personality who sells his soul to Mephistopheles – the Devil, in exchange for worldly pleasure and power, perhaps the two most compelling human attributes. The Faustian bargain leads to redemption of the pledge of claiming the soul of Faust that ends in Hell.

At the age of sixty, Goethe wrote the novel 'Elective Affinities' (Wahlverwandtschaften). 'Elective Affinity' has a long pedigree, dating back to Greek antiquity, notably Hippocrates, referring to 'like draws to like'. The term was coined in the 18th century by German, Dutch, and French alchemists or chemists to mean 'mutual attraction or reciprocal affinity' between two chemical substances. The Swedish chemist Torbern Olof Bergman used the term 'elective attraction', which was rendered into German as 'Wahlverwandtschaft' (elective affinity) in about 1782. This term was adopted by Goethe. The concept of 'elective affinity' advanced through Goethe in German culture to an innate bond between two soul-mates. Max Weber later adopted the term in social science. According to Michael Löwy in his book 'Redemption and Utopia' (A study in elective affinity) (1992), Weber applied the concept to three sociological aspects. First, the special relationship between different religious forms; second, a person's adherence to another world-view (Weltanschauung), and third, the relationship between religious belief and economic issues. Thus, Weber has extended 'elective affinity' to unite socio-cultural, economic, and religious matters into a new entity, reinforcing the characteristics of each component. Thomas Mann was singularly aware of the significance of the concept of 'Wahlverwandtschaften' in human interactions. In a letter to a friend, Mann wrote "what I was trying to achieve was an equilibrium of sensuality and morality, such as I found realized in Goethe's novel 'Elective Affinities' which if I remember rightly, I read five times, while I was writing 'Death in Venice."

Goethe presented the concept in his novel based on preferred chemical attractions, which we now know extends to interactions between living cells (receptor molecules and their specific ligands). Here, Goethe displays again an innate propensity to appreciate the significance of a natural phenomenon and applies this concept to human relationships and love through an innate bond between two individuals in his novel 'Wahlverwandtschaften'. The central characters, Eduard and Charlotte, a middle-aged couple each having been married before to a rich partner they respected but did not love. Death or divorce has left them free to marry, and it transpires that they were in love before, but pragmatic considerations kept them apart. The happy relationship of the couple, however, is disturbed when Eduard invites an old friend (a captain), who found himself in dire circumstances, to live in their house and manage their country estate. Charlotte happens to be the guardian of Ottilie, a young woman who is unhappy at boarding school, so she is invited to stay with them. A compatibility becomes evident between Eduard and Ottilie on the one hand, and Charlotte and the captain on the other. Whilst there is a great deal of discussion about marriage as a permanent bond of happiness, the emerging 'elective affinities' take charge of the situation and the two new couples get married. However, fate stands in the way and instead of living happily, there is an accident and the baby of Eduard and Charlotte is drowned when Ottilie rows with the baby across a lake. There is a moral discussion about punishment due to Charlotte's and Eduard's divorce and adultery, Ottilie feels guilty and she dies. One tragedy is followed by another and ends with Eduard's death. In this novel, Goethe presents a spiritual relationship based on affinity, reciprocal attraction and interaction, combining the partners in a new intimate union, referred to by some as 'chemical wedding'.

According to the historian James Hall, Goethe believed that by running his hands down the naked body of his Roman mistress, he could better appreciate classical sculpture. Goethe's erotic life in the form of epigrams remained unpublished for a century, because as Boyle writes, "direct treatment of such unacceptable subjects as nudity, erection, masturbation, both male and female, prostitution, sodomy and venereal disease." However, this scholarly account is brought down to earth by John Armstrong in 'Love, Life, Goethe', which describes the real feelings and emotional overtones that Goethe must have experienced, bringing down the poet from the Olympian heights to the level of the common man that is the overall strength of Goethe's character. In the Venetian Epigrams, Goethe's visit to Venice revealed his erotic life. As he strides along the narrow alleys of the city, he meets a prostitute and says, "I decided to explore; but what's this – she's as wide as a river. In Venice there are as many prostitutes as there are canals, they've got it all wrong; they need to model their c***s on the tight little lanes, not on the Grand Canal."

In many other poems from this sequence we encounter a breezy, obscene, and witty, erotic philosophy. Jesus, he notes, would have liked it here; the place is full of the sinners and whores with whom the Good Lord liked to pass the time. So, Goethe reflects, perhaps I'm a decent Christian after all – since I love that kind of company, too. We learn more about the kind of company he liked when he gives – as in all areas of life Goethe was so keen to do – some advice about sexual satisfaction. "Learn from me: I've tried it with boys; interesting, but not as much fun as it is with girls. However, should you find you're getting bored of sex with your woman, just turn her over and try her backside for a change." There are plenty of useful tips on the argot of the Venetian prostitutes: 'coffee' means she'll masturbate you. And on the topic of masturbation, how could God have made such a mistake? If He was so keen on us having children and getting married and all that why did God make it so easy to enjoy yourself on your own? And, on top of that, to make masturbation a sin! No, really we need a new religion: couldn't Jesus come back to earth and found one – a sex-creed in which wanking would be a moral obligation. I'd join that Church, he says; in fact, I'd be an apostle; I'd be the first martyr." In the early twentieth century – following the publication of the more explicit verses – there was a good deal of anxious scholarly debate about their significance.

Altogether, these epigrams, Goethe's many involvements with women, 'living in sin', though later marrying Christiane Vulpius, a down to earth woman, not the society lady expected of a man of Goethe's cultural stature has alienated a small part of German society, especially women, from Goethe. Although 'poetic license' has often been invoked to dismiss these confessions, they represent as Freud later argued the dark, primitive, prurient thoughts of men, irrespective of culture, religion, or moral upbringing.

The pre-eminence of 'Kultur' in Germany owes to a large measure to Goethe, whose iconic relation to the German people has withstood the test of time. Goethe has been epitomized as 'the bedrock of German culture', especially during stressful times when the nation's morale was at a low ebb. In times of war, and there have been two world wars since Goethe's death, quite apart from the Napoleonic war during Goethe's lifetime, the cry 'back to Goethe's Germany' acted as a balm to the people's ruffled sensitivities. Lepenies relates Thomas Mann's lecture in Weimar on 'Goethe's career as a man of letters', one hundred years after Goethe's death. "Mann now spoke of an Olympian as a human being, a citizen and a man of letters who had stubbornly resisted the two main tendencies of his epoch, the nationalistic and the democratic. … Goethe's conception of the German people, as an unpolitical, intellectual nation, centred upon human values, receiving from all and teaching all, will it not always have its profound justification, even in times of violence, over-compensation, and national self-correction?"

André Gide called Goethe 'the most un-German of all Germans', because he did not retreat into inwardness and distance himself from politics. This echoes Goethe's meeting with Napoleon in 1808 in Erfurt, the capital of Thuringia, when Napoleon said, "You and I, Monsieur Goethe, possess the strange virtue of completeness." Whilst Napoleon might have thought that his reputation in posterity might well be in the hands of this man of literature, Goethe's completeness owes a great deal to his life and function in Weimar. Quite apart from his writing, Goethe had extensive administrative duties in the Duchy, as well as the education of the young

Duke Carl August. The day to day responsibilities of running the Weimar Duchy, his dealings with labourers and the Court endowed Goethe with the remarkable completeness of a unique personality. Goethe ran the Weimar theatre for twenty-five years and was involved in the nearby Jena University. Goethe was a genius and therefore unrepresentative of his age. Nietzsche, in his perceptive way, described Goethe, as not just a good and great man, but as an entire culture – Goethe is an episode without consequences in the history of the Germans. This was clearly expressed one hundred years after Goethe's death in 1932 by Paul Valery's eulogy at the Sorbonne. "Goethe is a courtier, confident, minister, a diligent official, a poet, collector, and naturalist at the same time; the great, in Germany perhaps the greatest, apologist of the world of appearances ... In the evening of his days, in the heart of Europe, himself the centre of attraction and admiration of all intelligent people".

Goethe and Schiller statue in front of the theatre in Weimar (and Author)

After the Prussian victory over France in the war of 1870-1871, the Reich was founded by Bismarck. Whereas Berlin became the political centre, Weimar assumed the mantle of Culture. However, after the defeat in 1919, when the Weimar Republic was declared, with the constituent assembly in Weimar, the centre of political gravity also moved to Weimar. The president of the Republic of course called upon Goethe when he addressed the German people and asked them to abandon imperialism and adopt Goethe's 'Spirit of Weimar'.

After the Second World War, the demoralized people of Germany were urged by the historian Friedrich Meinecke to form Goethe communities to achieve spiritual redemption. However, Karl Jaspers and Richard Alewyn urged not to use Goethe, as an excuse or justification for the misdeeds perpetrated by the Nazi regime. Goethe seems to have been called to the rescue of the damned German soul. Lepenies referred to this as "politics finds its welcome substitute in culture: the moral masterpiece". 'Wiedergutmachung' (compensation) and repentance was argued by Konrad Adenauer, and partition of Germany was seen as a punishment – divine justice – for the Holocaust. Günter Grass argued that since the horrors of Auschwitz cannot be undone, Germany had to remain divided. He advocated to follow Goethe and Herder's example and to turn to a cultural nation within a political federation. With German reunification, the writer Martin Walser, in a speech on receiving the prestigious German Peace Prize in 1998, asked that remembrance of the Holocaust to be reduced if not terminated outright. The abrogation of moral responsibility was predictable, as no people wants to be burdened with the memory that their grandfathers and/or grandmothers were mass murderers. The evil perpetrated by a people at the height of Western culture is arguably open to redemption by long term contrition, empathy, and support of the mortally injured victims.

V. FRIEDRICH SCHILLER (1759-1805)

'To be happy and free, live and let live, safety and peace, order and freedom' *Schiller's annotation of Goethe's 'Egmont', 1778*
'Schiller was a liberal [.] freedom of thought, tolerance and freedom from prejudice [.] a cosmopolitan'. *David Pugh, 2006*
'For generations of Jews within Germany [.] Schiller was spokesman for pure humanity, lofty poet of the highest ideals of mankind, represented everything they thought of or wished to think of, as being German' *Gershom Sholem, 1976*

The most significant addition to the literary figures in Weimar and Jena was the arrival of Friedrich Schiller in 1787. He was ten years younger than Goethe and probably moved to Weimar because of him, Herder, and Wieland. Schiller appeared to be envious of Goethe because he suffered considerable hardship, ill-health, and difficulties in writing. He compared his predicament with the ease of Goethe's genius, financial security, and national prestige. The two men seemed to have avoided each other, creating an awkward situation in the small community of Weimar, where they had mutual friends. Carl August arranged for Schiller the appointment of professor of history at the University of Jena, to solve the social embarrassment in Weimar. In fact, Schiller trained as a doctor and was awarded the doctorate in medicine, so his qualifications to a chair in history were questionable. He was by then the acclaimed writer of 'The Robbers', 'Don Carlos', and other dramas and fiction, but the appointment in Jena was the first move towards some financial stability.

Goethe was by that time appointed, in to-day's terms, Chancellor of the university, and was very supportive of the appointment. This was appreciated by Schiller, though concerned about inadequate time to prepare himself, to which Goethe responded, 'The best way to learn is to teach'; this might be arguably the first time that this oft repeated advice has been given. Quite apart from this, Schiller's university degree was in Medicine, which was not apparent in his writing. Goethe disliked the violence of the 'Robbers', but was enthusiastic about Schiller's 'The Gods of Greece', in which they shared a common hatred of Christianity, which they believed destroyed the humanism of antiquity. Schiller was influenced by Goethe's classicism, and he adapted the text of Goethe's 'Egmont' for a production in Weimar, which was not really approved by Goethe. Steffan Davies argued that the theme of freedom ('Freiheit') in Egmont was a "watchword of 'Sturm und Drang' but largely rhetorical. 'Froh und frei sein' (to be happy and free), 'leben und leben lassen' (live and let live), 'Sicherheit und Ruhe, Ordnung und Freiheit' (safety and peace, order and freedom) were allowed to stay, but not 'das freie Leben' (the free life)." Schiller qualified and adopted a rather cautious attitude towards 'freedom', such as 'patriotism and emergent nationhood'. Goethe expressed the notion in the correspondence with Schiller that he was an intuitive thinker with spontaneous ideas whilst Schiller was a speculative thinker.

Maike Oergel writes in 'The German Querelle and the ideal state', a fresh look at Schiller's fragment 'Deutsche Grösse' (German Greatness), that Schiller expresses the idea of German hubris, which may originate from a national inferiority and was not published. He firmly believed in culture which for Schiller was the defining feature of humanity, and calls it modernity. The German language lends itself to express modern ideas, which is contrary to Fredrick the Great's view that the German language is not fit for literature or cultural exchanges. Schiller disparages the success of British and French achievements as being political and material, even illegitimate, quoting British stealing of artistic treasures from all over the world, as part of power politics, materialism, tyranny, even national decadence. On the other hand, the German 'Kaiserreich' is transformed into a 'Spiritual Reich' (Geisterreich), with culture and a struggle for justice, truth, and reason. Schiller ascribes this difference to the Reformation, with its intellectual and moral liberation, and moral responsibility. German people have been involved in identity-building in contrast to the French. Schiller's views have a fairly nationalistic outlook. Indeed, he argues with Fichte in Jena the superiority of the German language, which predestines Germans for world cultural and moral leadership. Nonetheless, he expressed the view that States must be integrated into the whole of humanity, perhaps following Goethe's concept of 'World literature' (Weltliteratur).

David Pugh in 'Schiller and the crisis of German Liberalism' (2006), states that "Schiller was a liberal, in the meaning of the 18th century, that is freedom of thought, tolerance, and freedom from prejudice. He was also a cosmopolitan ('Weltbürger'). Schiller's philosophical thought also has a dramatic quality in its debate between the constructs of the beautiful and the sublime. There is thus something peculiarly German in the adoption of Schiller, a creative writer, as the inspiration for a political movement. The ease with which a nationalistic and militaristic image of Schiller was constructed and propagated in Germany's bad half-century should perhaps deter us from trying to reconstitute him as a liberal icon now. Drafting writers of the past into combat in modern culture wars is always a suspect and opportunistic game."

Boyle refers to Schiller's appraisal and jealousy of his rival Goethe: "Iphigenia has given me another really good day – although I have to pay for the pleasure that it gives me with the depressing feeling of never being able to produce anything similar". Eventually, an arrangement was made for the two great poets to meet, and in Schiller's words: "The first sight of him considerably lowered the high estimation of this attractive and handsome figure that had been instilled in me. He is of medium height, his bearing is stiff and so is his walk; his face is sealed, but his eye very expressive, lively, and one lingers with pleasure in his glance. For all its gravity, his countenance has much benevolence and kindness. He is *brunette* and seemed to me to look older than by my calculation he can be. His voice is altogether agreeable, his speech fluent, intelligent and vivacious; it is altogether a great pleasure to listen to him; and when he is in a good humour, as on this occasion he was, more or less, he speaks readily and with interest. We made each other's acquaintance quickly and without the least constraint."

However, for six years, there was little real contact between the two men until Goethe's involvement with plants in Jena broke the ice and a close relationship developed. This came about after Goethe's lecture on plants, when he raised an idea, which excited him about 'the primal plant' (Urpflanz). Schiller engaged him after the lecture, suggesting that Goethe had really perceived the ‘essence of plants’. Goethe resented this and pointed out to Schiller that this was not an idea but a visual experience. This was hardly an opportune moment to begin a friendship, yet both great men must have realised deep down that they had a common objective. Goethe’s starting point is to visualise (or sense) the original plant that leads to the idea of the primal plant, whereas Schiller’s thinking was reversed, from the idea to the object. There was a meeting of minds, with different but complementary intellectual approach that seems to have overcome envy, fear, and distrust, and progressed to a memorable friendship. Schiller persuaded Goethe to join him in a new enterprise of launching an exclusive cultural journal (‘Die Horen’), with contributions from the best writers on philosophy, history, science, and classical literature. Goethe agreed and they were engaged in a common task, which unfolded between them a deep instinctive affinity. Schiller referred to Goethe as a Genius, capable of instinctive creativity and their attachment lasted for the next ten years, until Schiller died.

Schiller described Goethe’s personalities in his books that may have influenced the educated Western European to be a human being (‘Mensch’). Schiller alludes to the ideal of a man that we all should aspire to, a whole, well-rounded individual. The combined forces of Goethe and Schiller advanced a concept of art that is to create a thoughtful, rounded individual, and to enable us to engage rationally in political dialogue. Alas, this proved to be a chimera, wishful thinking of well-meaning individuals, living on a different level of humanity.

The two outstanding men of literature – Goethe and Schiller – created a cultural centre unprecedented in any other state in Germany. This was supported by a local theatre in which Goethe was actively involved and staged some of his plays. The nearby University of Jena was a cultural asset that Goethe initially neglected, until about 1780 when he expressed interest in science, arguably associated with reading Spinoza and his overarching concept of God as the works of nature. He received a great deal of support from the scientists in Jena in mineralogy, anatomy, and botany, all of which were of interest to Goethe. From then on, he took an active part in supporting the university and was responsible for establishing the botanical garden. Goethe’s ‘romantic’ approach to science failed to receive much, if any recognition, which he resented and found frustrating. Whilst he appreciated the systematic description and classification of plants by the Swedish botanist Linnaeus, Goethe was unreasonably hostile to Sir Isaac Newton’s demonstration of light consisting of spectrum of colours when split by a prism under controlled conditions (in a dark room). Because

Goethe was unable to reproduce Newton's experiment in broad daylight, he considered those findings to be invalid. The disparity of these two views can be reconciled by attributing to Goethe direct observations as he and others experienced, whereas Newton dealt with natural science of reproducible observations under standardised conditions. Indeed, Newton's fame irked Goethe to an extent that made him hate the 'competing' scientist. This dichotomy between the disciplines of science and art might well be the critical manifestation of C. P. Snow's 'Two Cultures', expressed by these two respective giants of science and art.

VI. JOHANN GOTTFRIED HERDER (1744-1803)

At a young age of seventeen, Herder entered the University of Königsberg, where he became a favourite student of Immanuel Kant. He introduced Herder to the writings of Hume, Montesquieu, and Rousseau. He also came under the influence of Johann Georg Hamann, imbued with German patriotism, hatred of the French, and preferring emotions to reason. These thinkers exerted a life-long influence on Herder's ideas. He was ordained in 1765 as a Lutheran pastor, but abandoned this vocation at the age of twenty-five. He identified himself with the 'Volk', or part of the German community which shared ethnicities, life-style, customs, but especially the German language and 'Kultur'. Herder was a highly cultured person, with strong convictions concerning beauty and individual artistic originality. He was part of the Enlightenment movement and is considered to be the founder of German Nationalism. Indeed, he coined the term 'Nationalism', which was used and more often misused, out of bounds of Herder's ideological interpretation. He believed that every nation has equally valid nationalism with a common language, social cohesion, and identity. However, he had a visceral hatred for French vanity, grotesque mode of life, language, and aristocracy. Herder considered it a 'cultural crime' to borrow another language (such as French). He felt that as the era of Montesquieu, Voltaire, and Rousseau was declining, German renaissance was emerging. He was passionate about the German language, that it should not be confined to common conversation, contrary to Frederick the Great who argued that only French was a fit language for great literature and poetry. Indeed, as T. C. W. Blanning pointed out, "Germany's linguistic confusion was exemplified by Leibniz who had written in French to nobles, in Latin to scholars and in German to his relations".

Herder advocated 'back to the roots' of the common people of the native soil and history, as manifested by Folk art, songs, and poetry. He expressed these ideas as 'Volksgeist' (national spirit), which encompassed culture, history, and language. Herder was five years older than Goethe and he advised him to study poetry of the people. Goethe followed the advice and found it extremely helpful in consolidating his thoughts and writing. Altogether, he had a high regard for Herder's intellectual clarity of purpose, when he first befriended him whilst studying at the University of Strasbourg. In 1776, Herder moved to Weimar through the good offices of Goethe as Councillor of the Duchy of Weimar and his close relation with

Duke Karl August. Goethe and Herder were involved in establishing the movement of 'Sturm und Drang' (Storm and Stress) that had a profound influence on German literature.

For Herder, the world was connected between individuals creating communities, and a common language was the prime factor in their interactions. His Volk of German people were, in addition, linked by common ethical and cultural ties, and he was a vocal advocate of the national unity of Germany. Paradoxically, despite being Prussian, he hated Prussian nationalism. Herder's concept of 'Volksgeist' also significantly influenced Slavic intellectuals and he had a high regard for Slavic people and their culture. Indeed, he is regarded as the ideological godfather of Pan-Slavism.

VII. WEIMAR REPUBLIC

The sudden and unconditional surrender of Germany at the end of the First World War in 1918 was followed by recrimination and claims of "stab in the back", especially by the military and the conservative-nationalist faction of the German population. The establishment of a democratic government was counter to German history, but emerged as a result of political pragmatism. The economy was under enormous stress through the cost of the war and the Versailles treaty enforced vast compensations demanded by the victorious allies. Germany lost about 13% of its territory; Alsace Lorraine was ceded to France, with the industrial Ruhr occupied by the allies. Parts of West Prussia were given to Poland, with Danzig being made a free city. Furthermore, Memel was given to Lithuania, and northern Schleswig was ceded to Denmark. Sizeable German-speaking populations amounting to about six million people, were transformed into minorities in these four countries.

Demobilization of around six million servicemen, without available jobs, created unrest in the streets. The right-wing seized the opportunity and joined the 'Freikorps', illegal paramilitary organisations, using brute force to air their grievances and suppress left wing activities. The Weimar Republic was a dramatic change from monarchy to republic, by a demoralized and humiliated nation, having lost the war and two million men, vast casualties, losing sizeable areas of land, and facing a formidably restrictive treaty of compensation.

The National Assembly was convened in 1919 in the small Thuringian town of Weimar, arguably chosen to reassure the nation with its uniquely priced classical culture ('Kultur'). Weimar, under the influence of Goethe, Schiller, and the associated University of Jena with its famous philosophers (Fichte, Hegel, and others) was considered to be the intellectual capital of Europe. Weimar, the symbol of the 'Kulturnation' (Nation of Culture), with Goethe's timeless pronouncement that the art is 'profound and good', has been a consolation that German people always perceived as a fall-back position in bad times. After the transition from monarchy to republic following World War One, the 'free state' of Thuringia was established in 1920.

The new progressive Constitution was written and passed by the Assembly, which determined the political future of the republic. Proportional representation was subsequently deemed to have been responsible for parliamentary instability, and a presidency, which created a dual model of authority. A striking flaw in the constitution was Article 48, which arrogated extraordinary powers to the executive, at the expense of parliament. A strong president, supposedly tempered by parliamentary checks was eventually agreed, but Article 48 was increasingly applied by each successive executive, which ended up in almost exclusive use by Chancellors Brüning and then von Papen, leading to the dictatorship of Hitler.

The Weimar Constitution was approved in 1919, which stated explicitly that the German people are united in all their racial elements and inspired by the will to renew and strengthen their Reich in liberty and justice, to preserve peace at home and abroad, and to provide social progress. The Constitution has 153 Articles, which define the basic structure and function of the Reich and some of the articles specifically relevant to the present narrative are quoted here.

General Principles: Article 1- The German Reich is a republic. Political authority emanates from the people.

Article 4 – The generally accepted rules of international law are to be considered as binding components of the law of the German Reich.

Basic Rights: Article 114 – Personal liberty is inviolable. Curtailment or deprivation of personal liberty by a public authority is permissible only by authority of law. Persons who have been deprived of their liberty must be informed at the latest on the following day by whose authority and for what reasons they have been held. They shall receive the opportunity without delay of submitting objections to their deprivation of liberty.

Article 115 – The home of every German is his sanctuary and is inviolable. Exceptions are permitted only by authority of law.

Article 118 – Every German has the right, within the limits of the general laws, to express his opinion freely by word, in writing, in print, in picture form, or in any other way. Censorship is forbidden.

Article 54 – The Reich Chancellor and the Reich ministers require for the exercise of their office the confidence of the 'Reichstag' (Parliament). Any one of them must resign if the Reichstag by formal resolution withdraws its confidence.

Article 56 – The Reich Chancellor determines the political program of the Reich and assumes responsibility to the Reichstag.

The escape clause was of critical importance: Article 48 – If any state does not fulfil the duties imposed upon it by the constitution of the laws of the Reich, the Reich President may enforce such duties with the aid of the armed forces. In the event that public order and security are seriously disturbed or threatened, the Reich President may take the measures necessary for their restoration, intervening, if necessary, with the aid of the armed forces. For this purpose he may temporarily suspend, wholly or in part, the basic rights laid down in seven Articles. The Reich President must without delay inform the Reichstag of all such measures. The text of this article failed to define precisely the sort of emergency that would justify the use of Article 48. However, the Article was used to declare 'emergency decrees' (Notverordnungen). The President was bound directly to inform the Reichstag, which had the power to invalidate the decree by a majority vote. The President could then dissolve the Reichstag and call for new elections.

The escape clause of Article 48 was used or misused by a series of chancellors, from the very first one, Friedrich Ebert, on 136 occasions, which included that of the government of the State of Thuringia. During the economic crisis in 1930, President Paul Hindenburg and his Chancellor Heinrich Brüning used Article 48 for the financial reform bill in 1930 and this was rejected by the Reichstag. Parliament was dissolved and the new elections produced a significantly increased representation in the Reichstag for the Nazis, as well as to a lesser extent, the Communists. Brüning found it difficult to conduct normal parliamentary business and had to invoke repeatedly Article 48 between 1930 and 1932. The power to rule by decrees to respond to emergencies became a substitute for parliamentary consent.

This problem was similarly encountered by subsequent Chancellors, Franz von Papen and Kurt von Schleicher. The excessive use of Article 48 by successive chancellors, bypassing the Reichstag, led to loss of confidence in democracy and paved the way for President Hindenburg, on the advice of Papen to appoint Hitler as Chancellor of Germany in January 1933. Hitler, under President Hindenburg, just carried on with promulgating new decrees. With the 'Reichstag Fire', a new decree was issued under Article 48 'curtailing most of the constitutional rights', passing the 'Enabling Act' by parliamentary majority, abrogating the Reichstag authority and subjugating it to the cabinet, effectively to Chancellor Hitler. Indeed, Hitler used Article 48 throughout his twelve-year Dictatorship, as a legal tool. Thus, the great divide between Article 54 – the rule of parliamentary law and Article 48- rule by Hitler.

The complex history of the Weimar Republic is outside the remit of this account and only a brief description of the milestones leading to the collapse of the republic and the assumption of power by Hitler in 1933 will be presented. Germany became polarised between the revolutionary left wing insurgency led by Karl Liebknecht and Rosa Luxemburg and the right-wing nationalist movement. The two leaders of the Sparticist group took part in an uprising and were murdered by the Freikorps soldiers. The Beer Hall Putsch in Munich in 1922, led by Hitler and Ludendorff, resulted in Hitler being imprisoned, where he wrote his infamous 'Mein Kampf', declaring his expansionist policy towards the East and threatening war against the Jewish people.

Walther Rathenau was the major architect of the war economy, an exceptionally capable intellectual, politician, and industrialist. He served as foreign minister in the 1st Weimar government and was responsible for the 'Rapallo Treaty' with Russia in 1922, which established German-Soviet cooperation. Rathenau pursued a moderate policy towards the victorious powers and was assassinated in 1922 by the nationalist, anti-Semitic group that was also responsible for the murder in 1921 of the centre party politician Matthias Erzberger, who had signed the armistice in 1918. The great inflation and depression led to the Mark having sunk by 1923 to an insignificant low level ($1/10^{10}$) of its pre-war value against the dollar. Hyperinflation was generally attributed to the Central Bank (Reichsbank) getting it wrong, believing that the response to the fall of the currency was to print more money. The economic collapse, loss of confidence, and being ostracised by much of Europe, with Einstein as the only acceptable German abroad, was not lost on the Nazis who claimed that Weimar was a 'Jewish Republic' ('eine Juden republic').

Despite the hardships, theatre, opera, ballet, and symphony orchestra, mostly highbrow culture, was subsidized by the local governments and widely available not only in the large cities, such as Berlin and Hamburg, but also the provinces. 'Art for the people' was a widely held aspiration as it would improve human beings, offer moral education, and heal social problems. The moral and spiritual power of art was well expressed by Arthur Menges on the occasion of the 75th anniversary of the Hanoverian Opera House. "Artistic endeavour is the divine spark which rests in each person's heart is awakened and maintained, a liberating uplifting feeling is given to the people, which in the festive evening mood transforms an individual whose life during the day is determined by his work 'Arbeitsmenschen' are transformed into a person of culture 'Kulturmenschen'. And thus for the recovery of our nation". Thomas Mann also emphasized culture and theatre as Germany's great tradition, of which he was immensely proud and appreciative. Regrettably, despite the high hopes, the cultural accomplishments contributed little tangible to the moral fibre of the German people, with some notable exceptions, such as the four Protestant theologians with the 'White Rose' students and Professor Huber.

By 1930, the Reichstag was dominated by Nazis and Communists and the Centre held by Chancellor Heinrich Brüning had little support from them. Brüning relied on President Hindenburg signing an increasing number of emergency decrees, by-passing the Reichstag, which became irrelevant to governing Germany. By 1932, Hitler's NSDAP for the first time became the largest party. Brüning was dismissed from office and Germany slipped into 'legislative dictatorship' under the brief administration of Franz von Papen, which spelt further departure from democratic cabinet government. The new Chancellor was an aristocratic, calculating, ruthless political operator, who utilized the law to break with the Constitution and to restore the status quo before 1918. The infamous Article 48 was also Papen's favourite tool (see Weimar constitution, p. 48).

With Hitler's increasing representation in Parliament, the industrial magnates, such as Fritz Thyssen favouring a Hitler cabinet and Papen actively working to include Hitler in the government, President Hindenburg appointed Hitler to lead a government of 'national unity', the republic's last cabinet. It is remarkable that at Hitler's first cabinet in January 1933, it was von Papen who proposed to introduce an 'Enabling Act', which would allow cabinet to govern without the approval of the Reichstag. According to Anthony McElligott, "The following day, during the discussion of Göring's earlier proposal to dissolve the Reichstag and call new elections, von Papen went further, stating that 'it is for the best to fix now that the coming elections to the Reichstag shall be the last, and that a return to a parliamentary system is to be avoided for ever." This time, von Papen got his way. The (heavily compromised) Reichstag dismissed itself on 23 March, initially for four years (to be recalled only on those occasions when Hitler needed it for acclamatory purposes). Meanwhile the idea of cabinet dictatorship was taken a step further by Hitler who, as 'Führer' from 1934, came to embody the state as its 'plebiscitary dictator'. Looking back at the Brüning and von Papen chancellorships, it is clear that they paved the way from parliamentary democracy to dictatorship and Hitler took full advantage to impose his 'Thousand Year Reich'. He withdrew from the League of Nations, reintroduced conscription by unilateral renunciation of the Versailles Treaty of 1935, followed by remilitarization of the Rhineland in 1936, all of which was accepted by the Western powers.

VIII. THURINGIA – A PROTOTYPE OF A NAZI STATE

"Sauckel was the greatest and cruellest slave owner since the Egyptian pharaohs"

Nüremberg chief prosecutor, 1946

Thuringia was the first German state (Land) in which the NSDAP was elected in significant number to the parliament in Weimar in 1924. Later, they gained a majority and Thuringia assumed a prototype role of a Nazi state in the new government, headed by Wilhelm Frick (1877-1946).

Wilhelm Frick, born in March 1877 in Alsenz Bavaria, was the son of a Protestant schoolmaster, studied jurisprudence at the University of Munich, Göttingen and Berlin, and gained the doctorate in Law in 1901 at the University of Heidelberg. He worked as a lawyer at the police headquarters in Munich and took part in the 'Beer Hall' putsch, when he was director of Munich Criminal Police. Frick was arrested, tried, imprisoned, and dismissed from the police job. Despite this, Frick was elected to the Reichstag in 1924 and joined the NSDAP in 1925. He was the first Nazi to be elected to a ministerial post as Minister of the Interior and Education in the government of Thuringia in 1930-1. His first act was to carry out a cultural purge of the 'Kulturnation'.

When Hitler assumed power in 1933, Frick was appointed as the Reich Minister of the Interior, in the first Hitler cabinet of only three ministers. He was responsible for drafting some of the laws of the Nazi regime ('Gleichschaltung') and the Nuremberg laws in 1933-1935. He also drafted the laws for introducing universal military conscription, extending this to Austria after the Anschluss and to the annexed part of Czechoslovakia. Frick appointed in 1936, the Gestapo chief Heinrich Himmler to be the Chief of the German Police, which was in addition to his command of the SS and made him, after Hitler, the most powerful and ruthless leader that Germany has ever seen. He was the controlling authority over concentration camps and in 1943, Himmler also replaced Frick as the Interior Minister. Frick was appointed 'Reich Protector of Bohemia and Moravia', where he was ruthless in countering dissent, until the end of the war. He was indicted at the Nuremberg Trial with War Crimes, and Crimes against Humanity committed in concentration camps in the Protectorate. Frick was found guilty after due legal process, which he denied to thousands of individuals, and hanged in Nuremberg in October 1946, at the age of sixty-nine.

Fritz Sauckel (1894-1946) dropped out of school at the age of fifteen and joined the merchant navy. At the outbreak of World War One, he was on a German vessel in Australia, captured by the allies and he was interned in France up to 1919. After the war, he studied engineering in Ilmenau (Thuringia) in 1922-1923, joined the NSDAP, married and had ten children. Sauckel was appointed in 1927 Gauleiter (Nazi leader) of Thuringia and member of the regional government. In 1933 he became a Reichstag member, and a year later, he was given the honorary rank of 'Obergruppenführer' (General) in the SS. He was the only one of the thirty-one Gauleiters in the Reich to be elevated by Hitler to the title 'Gaufürst' (Gau-prince). He encouraged the link between cultures of Weimar-Jena with the ideology of the NSDAP, despite boasting that he never read a single book. During the war in 1942, he was appointed "Plenipotentiary for Labour", directing German labour and later forced recruitment of labour from the occupied countries. He was responsible for about six million forced workers, mostly from Eastern Europe, who were worked to death, ostensibly part of the policy of 'extermination by labour'. Sauckel was indicted at the Nuremberg Trial, accused of War Crimes and Crimes against Humanity. The chief prosecutor referred to Sauckel as "the greatest and cruellest slave owner since the Egyptian Pharaohs". Sauckel was found guilty and hanged in October 1946.

IX. ANTI-SEMITISM IN THURINGIA

"Anti-Semitism in Thuringia became part of the state doctrine before any other German states" *Steffen Raßloff, Historian of Thuringia, 2011*
"The Jewish minority in the Weimar Republic was unique in that many of the conflicts emblematic of the time, conflicts between visionaries and pragmatists, between reformers and traditionalists, between fundamentalists and pluralists, existed here in magnified form" *A.D. Kaunders, 1996*
"In the face of inhumanity, Humanist classicism proved powerless. Weimar became a suburb of Buchenwald" *George Steiner, 2005*
"The 'stab in the back' myth was a cowardly cry by the very people responsible for the collapse. The historical scapegoat was at hand and needed little persuasion from a population nurtured on anti-Semitism for two millennia" *Author*

The enlightenment in Europe in the 18th century led to granting citizenship with legal rights to Jews, which varied from 1812 to 1869 between the different German states. It is noteworthy that this historical development started before the unification of Germany in 1871. They were released from centuries of isolation, persecution, religious intolerance, and economical exclusion from trades and their guilds, owing land and property, except money-lending. These restrictions and the enormous regard that Jews had for learning ('people of the book') in relation to religious practice, laws of the Bible, and the extensive literature of interpretations of the Bible, seems to have made them particularly suitable for the professions. There was an outburst of suppressed ideas by intellectuals, and they became successful physicians, lawyers, businessmen, and financiers. By 1933, some 16% of all lawyers and 11% of all doctors were Jewish. Their upward mobility was astonishing and many Jews became visibly affluent. Indeed, Hugo Preuß, a lawyer, is regarded as the father of the constitution of the Weimar Republic and he became the Minister of Interior in the Weimar Republic in 1919. Walter Rathenau was the Foreign Minister and Walter Loeb was the director of Weimar State Bank in 1924. All three were of Jewish heritage, presenting the Nazi party further fuel to disparage the Weimar Republic. Rathenau was assassinated and Loeb resigned within six months because of lack of support. Even preservation of 'German Culture' against 'Jewish cultural bolshevism' became an issue of contention. Steffen Raßloff, a historian of Thuringia, has comprehensively dealt with anti-Semitism and argues that it became part of the state doctrine in Thuringia, much earlier than in any of the other German states.

The outstanding success of the German Jews was unpopular with the host communities at large and led to a new type of anti-Semitism, often referred to as 'modern anti-Semitism' that was related to the 'newcomers' competing successfully in business, the learned professions and politics. To start with, the Jena jurist Edward Rosenthal of Jewish origin wrote the Thuringian constitution in 1920-21. In industry, the highly successful vehicle and weaponry manufacture was founded by the Simson family, a leading department store chain in Gera was run by Hermann Tietz. In Erfurt, Benary established a horticultural business, Hess, a shoe factory, and Moos, a financial enterprise. The economic boom, however, was followed in 1873 by an economic crash, with serious hardship felt by all strata of the population. The Jews were made responsible for the calamity, by introducing capitalism and industrialisation and later communism, of which the ideological basis was established by Karl Marx, of Jewish heritage and had considerable Jewish following.

The general prejudice was propagated by anti-Semites that the Jews were too powerful, economically, professionally, and politically, despite representing less than 1% of the population. Similar trends in the rest of Europe evolved into the idea that the Jews strive for world domination and that they live as parasites at the expense of the host nations. Hostility towards the Jews was boosted by the loss of the First World War, for which Jews were blamed by Sauckel, Frick, and their Nazi supporters. The demobilized, unemployed soldiers felt betrayed, and it was most gratifying for them to pour all their anger and frustration onto a familiar scapegoat. Among a number of extreme right-wing organisations, the NSDAP evolved into the leading anti-communist and anti-Semitic party. They, and a number of nationalist parties, used the Eastern Jews who were traditional in their habits to attack Jews at large. They were an ethnic minority, less than 0.01% of the Thuringian population, and they did not fit the perceived 'German identity'. They were also identified with the 'Weimar Spirit' and were concerned with the survival of the republic.

According to Anthony D Kaunders (2011), "the Jewish minority in the Weimar Republic was unique in that many of the conflicts emblematic of the time, conflicts between visionaries and pragmatists, between reformers and traditionalists, between fundamentalists and pluralists, existed here in magnified form. It is not only that a history of the Jews resembles a 'micro'-history of the period, it is that the Jews were Weimar Germans with all their problems and on top of that Jews whose status within society was being increasingly questioned. Their lot, in other words, was symptomatic of what Detlev Peukert has called 'signature of the epoch', insecurity – only doubly so." Overall, there was gentile indifference to the growing anti-Semitism or worse, hostility. Whereas non-Jewish Germans faced periods of insecurity, Jewish Germans faced the evils of anti-Semitism even in times of security.

For the first time, right-wing extremists gained entry into the Thuringian parliament and Artur Dinter became the first Gauleiter (1925-1927). He used the prevailing prejudice to pass the law that the government had to be formed of German blood and of non-Marxists. This excluded the prominent Jewish democratic candidate Eduard Rosenthal from the government. In 1929, Wilhelm Frick became Minister of Interior and of Education in Thuringia and from then on he implemented radical Nazi political and 'cultural' ideology to make Thuringia a model Nazi state. In 1933, Sauckel was appointed governor for Thuringia and he exercised fully his hatred against Jews. Before the Nazis came to power, there were about 4500 Jews in thirty-seven parishes in Thuringia. Sauckel banned their Central Association, Aryans expropriated their businesses, so that by 1939, Thuringian economy was expropriated from Jewish ownership. The aim was to eradicate alien racial/foreign influence on German culture. The 'Bauhaus' and art in Weimar was cleansed of 'degenerate art'. By the end of the war, only 400 German-Jewish citizens survived in Thuringia.

Thuringia was the breeding ground for National Socialist activities, as can be seen from the article written by Professor Otmar von Verschuer for the Thuringian newspaper, 'Soziale Arbeitsgemeinschaft evangelischer Manner und Frauen Thuringens'. This emphasized education and training, tax legislation, control of immigration and emigration, genetic biological stock-taking, and marriage counselling for prospective parents, but also indirectly demanded bars to marriage for 'those of alien ancestry, ill and deformed persons and genetically ill from encumbered families'. He mentioned sterilization, but 'only in passing'. Between Frick and Sauckel, they achieved their major objectives to create Thuringia in a fully-fledged Nazi State. They took advantage of the epicentre of German Culture in Weimar and the great University in Jena, by attempting to link them with Nazi ideology, appointing like-minded University Rectors and Professors and establishing the Institute of Theology in Eisenach associated with the University of Jena. True to their ideology, they also built the Buchenwald concentration camp next door to Weimar, thereby associating symbolically the high culture of Goethe and Schiller with the criminality of Buchenwald. Over 50,000 innocent lives were lost and horrendous medical experiments were perpetrated in Buchenwald.

It has not escaped the vigilant mind of the Führer to be associated with the greats of Weimar. Indeed, Hitler loved Weimar, and kept visiting it from 1925, the Weimar inhabitants reciprocated the sentiments, as illustrated in the photographic album 'the Führer in Weimar 1925-1938'. Not surprisingly the people in Weimar now complain that the world tends to recognize Weimar in terms of Buchenwald, which is certainly unfair and unjust to the great cultural individuals, who through literature hoped to make the world a better place. The fatal link between Weimar and Buchenwald will have left an inextricable historical legacy of the Nazi horrors, which classical Weimar does not deserve and is intrinsically unjust to the legacy of its classical culture. The Weimar phenomenon also raises the critical relationship between culture and civilization, the significance of which extends well beyond Weimar to the foundations of Western Christian Civilization and the Enlightenment.

X. CLAIMS OF NATIONAL SOCIALISTS ON GOETHE, SCHILLER, AND HERDER

The Nazis sought the approval of the learned class of society and Weimar classicism was at the epicentre of German culture. Goebbels had, in addition, a critical personal interest at stake as his mentor at Heidelberg University was Professor Friedrich Gundolf, a celebrated German-Jewish literary scholar and poet, especially in his publications on Goethe. Gundolf declined to supervise Goebbels's thesis on account of his heavy commitments (or prescience), but advised Goethe to approach his colleague professor Max von Waldberg who happened to be of Jewish origin, and agreed to supervise Goebbels's thesis. It is noteworthy that on my careful inspection and that of two senior librarians of Goebbels's PhD thesis at the University of Heidelberg library, there was no 'Acknowledgement' of von Waldberg or Gundolf (see p.140). What effect these two eminent Jewish literary figures may have had on the twenty-four year old Goebbels is open to conjecture, and there is no evidence that at the time he had any anti-Semitic feelings. One of the Heidelberg librarians wondered if Goebbels may have developed a grudge due to being rejected by Gundolf. However, there can be little doubt that Goebbels had a personal interest and knowledge to misappropriate Goethe to the Nazi cause.

Although Jews in Goethe's time had been oppressed, and in Frankfurt like other cities they lived in ghettoes until 1796, there is little evidence of anti-Semitism in Goethe's writing. Indeed, among the many languages he studied in his youth was Hebrew. More surprisingly was that during congratulations at Goethe's uncle's wedding, a poem was read out in Yiddish. At a meeting of the Weimar Council, a heated discussion occurred and insults were hurled at travelling Jews, and Goethe took the part of Jews. It appears that Goebbels had little to go on directly, but found an ally in Hans Wahl who became the director of the Goethe National Museum, and of the Goethe and Schiller Archive in 1928. Wahl was an active anti-Semite and was the co-founder of the Weimar group of the 'Militant League for German Culture' under the leadership of the notorious Alfred Rosenberg. Wahl denied claims that Goethe was a friend of Jews and even that he had Jewish heritage. This allegation was further refuted by Professor Franz Koch of the University of Berlin in his publication, "Goethe and the Jews", in which he presents Goethe as an anti-Semite. Yet, another Nazi writer who considered Goethe a friend of Jews, indeed to be himself a Jew, a Freemason and to have many other 'moral failures'.

The conundrum was further marred by Wahl's confusion with his predecessors as the head of the Archive, Professor Julius Wahle, who served the Goethe Society for twenty-five years, but had to resign in 1938 because he was a Jew. The similarity between Wahl and Wahle, the outspoken anti-Semite and Jewish guardian of Goethe's literary wisdom, led to further confusion. Wahl's distortion of Goethe as an anti-Semite was of the essence for the Nazis to claim Goethe to their cause. Julius Petersen, professor of German literature at the University of Berlin, President of the Goethe Society (1926-1938), went even further than Wahl to compare Goethe to Hitler. It was Thomas Mann who repudiated these insinuations upon Goethe's integrity when in 1939 he wrote the novel, 'Lotte in Weimar', in which he used his knowledge of Goethe to attribute to him his own interpretation of Goethe's thinking of the German people that someday fate "would strike them because they betrayed themselves and did not want to be what they are. It is sad that they do not know the charm of truth that mist, smoke, and berserk immoderation is so dear to them, pathetic that they ingenuously submit to any mad scoundrel who appeals to their lowest instincts, who confirms them in their vices and teaches them to conceive nationalism as isolation and brutality." Goethe also spoke on the danger of anti-Semitism. Indeed, some inmates of Nazi concentration camps were able to keep up their spirit and morale by thoughts of Goethe's writing.

Whereas the claim of Goethe to the Nazi cause was muted, that of Schiller was enthusiastic, with Goebbels, Professor Julius Petersen and Hans Fabricius misappropriating Schiller to the National Socialist cause. They extracted from the large selection of Schiller's plays certain sound-bites that fitted the Nazi rhetoric, such as struggle ('Kampf') sacrifice ('Opfer') soul ('Seele') character, pathos and death ('Tod'). Schiller was exploited by Goebbels to lend respectability and historical legitimacy to the Nazi cause, especially with the influential middle class, as here they had arguably for the first time a Minister who supported a great German cultural figure. The dates of Schiller's commemorations happened to suit the purpose, as in 1934 at the 175th anniversary of Schiller's birth, Goebbels organised an extraordinary celebration. Goebbels and the Nazi establishment encouraged the notion that Schiller was a forerunner of the National Socialist revolution. Nicholas Martin writes in 'Images of Schiller in NS Germany' (1968), "Schiller's moral courage and powers of physical endurance are matched, Goebbels asserts, only by National Socialists and hence only they have a legitimate claim to his legacy [...] Goebbels immediately reinforces this claim in a fourteen-word sentence which, with ingenious sleight-of tongue, manages to combine allusions to Goethe, Schiller, the Bible, and Nazi racial ideology. 'Er war einer der Unseren, Blut von unserem Blut und Fleisch von unserem Fleisch' (He was one of us, blood of our blood and flesh of our flesh).

It becomes clear that there was a far more powerful and immediate reason for choosing Weimar's 'Nationaltheater', as the venue for this 'Schiller-Gedächtnisfeier' (Memorial festivity), a reason which had more to do with events in 1918-19 than in 1794. The Nazis had come to gloat over the demise of the Weimar Republic, in the very theatre where that republic's National Assembly had first met in 1919 and where its constitution had been ratified. The 'Reichsschillerwoche' (Schiller's Reich-week) was intended to combine a celebration of Schiller's birth with a symbolic laying to rest of the Weimar Republic." Furthermore, Martin argues that "the Nazis sought the blessing of a cultural saint for their own disreputable ends [...] The need to give the appearance at least that National Socialism belonged to the mainstream of German social and cultural tradition, in which veneration for Schiller still had an important place. While the 'Schillerhuldigung' (homage to Schiller) in Marbach contained many elements borrowed from earlier Schiller celebrations, its witches' brew of religious and shameless ideological manipulation marked a new low in the already chequered history of 'Schillerverehrung' (honouring Schiller)."

Schiller's poems were adapted for music by a number of composers, the best known is Beethoven's ninth symphony, in which the fourth movement has the vocal part of Schiller's 'Ode to Joy'. Whilst some parts have been altered by Beethoven, the repeating four lines are by Schiller "Be embraced, millions! / This kiss for the whole world! / Brothers, above the starry canopy / Must a loving father dwell". It is unlikely that these sentiments were greatly aired by Hitler, Goebbels, or the other Nazis.

It is somewhat amusing that Hitler, "as a sixteen-year-old schoolboy in Linz, took part in the 1905 Schiller festivities and during his time as a semi-vagrant in Vienna before the First World War he took a dim view of Schiller, regarding his dramas as the opium of the bourgeoisie, particularly the assimilated Jewish bourgeoisie." Later in 1942, during one of Hitler's monologues, "he suddenly attacks Schiller for dramatizing the wrong historical events. Rather than a cowardly Swiss sniper, Hitler exclaims, Schiller should have chosen as his subject matter the history of the medieval German emperors". Apart from this, Hitler may have had genuine reason to fear the anti-tyrannical sentiments in Schiller's Wilhelm Tell who was anyway an unknown Swiss. Martin concludes that “the worst academic writing about Schiller in Germany between 1933 and 1945 used the apparatus and appearance of scholarship to perform conjuring tricks with literary and intellectual history. It was characterised in large measure by an elastic interpretation of sources, in order to arrive at predetermined conclusions. A combination of perceived political necessity, opportunism, misplaced loyalty and genuine conviction created the conditions for the profusion of such writing – not only on Schiller – during the Nazi period.” Indeed, in theology, Grundmann and some thirty-five theologians at the ‘De-judeising Institute in Eisenach’ linked to the University of Jena have similarly spent many years to ‘prove the unprovable’ that Jesus was not a Jew, though even they realised that the Jewish St Paul could not be divorced from the Christian narrative.

George Steiner, in a lecture at the National Schiller Museum ‘Say it loud – it’s Schiller and it’s proud’ (2005), presented an anthology of praise and criticism, in which he summarised some of the major attainments of Schiller. “In 1934, Schiller Festivals were already taking on a nationalistic and quasi-religious character. Thousands of Hitler Youth marched through Marbach. Schiller was declared to fight at Hitler’s side (‘Schiller als kampfgenosse Hitlers’) [...] Between 1933 and 1945, the German Reich saw 10,600 productions of Schiller’s plays.” The ease of politically encouraged manipulations of ‘isms’ is clearly demonstrated by Steiner. “This ubiquity pales in comparison with Schiller’s role in the GDR. By 1960, there were already three million copies of works by Schiller on the East German book market [...] Schiller was considered the finest of the classics, not only as the embodiment of poetic genius, but also as a fighter in the name of progress in the Marxist sense.” Thus everyone claimed Schiller, professing one and all ideology by cherry picking the ideas to fit the claimant’s ideology. Both Hitler’s fascists and the East German Communists misappropriated Schiller’s ‘Ode to Joy’ and Beethoven’s 9th symphony, discarding the very essence of ‘We are all brothers’.

Steiner continued, in the ninth of his letters ‘On the Aesthetic Education of Man’, and Schiller states his credo: “If humanity has lost its dignity, then it has been saved by art [...] Through art, the human individual becomes an ethical being [...] For us today, however, the proud innocence of these views is no longer convincing. Benjamin was right when he said that the works of high culture stand proud on a foundation of barbarity and injustice. We know that they can even serve as ornaments to inhumanity […] We trust these voices that speak in short, naked sentences as in Kafka or Beckett, or who, like Wittgenstein, advise us to keep quiet[...] The notion of the 'classical' is rooted in the history of western culture. With Europe's descent into the barbarism of the 20th century, this concept forfeited its credibility to a large extent. In the face of inhumanity, humanist classicism proved powerless. Weimar became a suburb of Buchenwald." Steiner finished his lecture on the poignant tragic note, "In 1938, when the Nazis took over Vienna, the 72-year old collector Max Berger reported to the Office for Jewish Emigration. As a ransom, he brought with him one of Schiller's letters, a valuable manuscript. The letter was taken from him, and then the old man was beaten to death. I am not capable of thinking through the ontological and formal involvements of this event."

Herder's emphasis on the 'Volk' gained considerable support from the Nazis who believed in the Aryan race being superior to other races. Further evidence of Goethe's fine judgment is evident, whilst learning a great deal about the character of German people, he did not follow Herder's Völkisch-nationalist views. Herder is considered by some as an early exponent of modern understanding of racism, with some affinity to Nazism. However, he was less of a popular literary figure, so the Nazis did not use him for their propaganda. Herder considered Jews as a Volk, alien to the people of Germany and other countries, distinguishable from and living at the expense of the indigenous population. He had harsh racial anti-Semitic views, and denied the biblical designation of Jews as the Chosen people. On the other hand, he argued that Jews in Germany should be granted the rights and obligations of Germans.

CHAPTER 2: UNIVERSITY OF JENA

I. **Introduction to German Universities**
II. **University of Jena, Philosophy and Literature**
III. **Faculty of Theology**
IV. **Faculty of Medicine**
V. **Science, Eugenics, Racial Hygiene, Anthropology**
VI. **Patrons of Art in Jena**

UNIVERSITY OF JENA

'I am always a happy man when I am in Jena, because no place on earth has given me more productive moments'

Goethe wrote to Schiller

'Freedom and self-assertion imposition of the will upon others, revival of obstacles'

Johann G Fichte (1762-1814), professor of Philosophy, Jena

'The mystical impulses instilled by a few adventurers into the soul of the people … Anti-Semitism, about which no-one actually knows its purpose in these times of equal rights'

Herman Helmholtz referring to anti-Semitism in 1893

'The physician must and may do nothing else but maintain life. Whether this is bliss or calamity, is not for the physician to decide. If that ever becomes a consideration, in the practice of medicine, then the consequences are monstrous, and the physician becomes the most dangerous person of any nation. Should this line be crossed once it merely takes stepwise progression to extend the decision on the worthlessness and consequently the uselessness from the life of one person to the lives of others'

Dr. Christoph Wilhelm Hufeland, Professor of Medicine, University of Jena, 1762-1836

‘The new theology was to equate the ‘Christenkreuz mit Hakenkreuz’
(Christian Cross with Swastika)

Walter Grundmann, Professor of New Testament and ‘Völkiche’ Theology in Jena (1936)

I. INTRODUCTION TO GERMAN UNIVERSITIES

This is based on the extensive studies edited by Walter Rüegg in the book 'A History of the University in Europe' (1800-1945), published in 2004. Most universities started as ecclesiastical institutions which began to be secularised during the Enlightenment. Direct control by the Catholic and later Protestant Churches of Universities had undergone transformation into lay institutions during the nineteenth century. The German University model was established in 1810, according to ideas of liberal education, which were formulated by Wilhelm von Humboldt. He argued in favour of establishing common humanity, striving to remove the barriers of prejudice and to treat all mankind without reference to religion, nation, or colour, as one fraternal community. These were based on the liberal ideas of the philosopher and theologian Friedrich Schleiermacher, who had remarkably advanced views. Humboldt proposed that the functions of universities were not to pass on established and directly utilitarian knowledge, such as imparted by schools, but to demonstrate how knowledge is discovered. Schleiermacher advocated in 1808 "to stimulate the idea of science in the minds of students, to encourage them to take account of the fundamental laws of science in all their thinking". This principle is equally valid to-day and marked a significant change in the nineteenth century, creating the modern university applying new scientific methods, which in time most universities adopted. Thus, students were introduced to research, laboratory work, doctoral theses, specialisation, writing papers, and contributing at international conferences. Germany had surpassed France and Britain in medical and scientific research, largely because scientific research became a professional, strictly regulated activity. Indeed, research contribution in Germany was a pre-condition for academic advancement. In Britain and France, however, science at the time was still the preserve of private initiatives or amateurs, outside the university. A brief account is presented of two outstanding scientists who were also significant liberal politicians.

Rudolf Virchow (1821-1902) developed the 'cell theory' and made enormous contributions to the new field of pathology. He paraphrased the progress in terms "the passage from the age of Philosophy to the age of Natural Sciences". Virchow also stated that "academic education of students offered a great deal of freedom, which assigned and conceded responsibility without restriction, in order that each became independent in his own way". German universities enjoyed extraordinary academic freedom, despite the State being far from liberal. The German language was extensively used in scientific writing and German science enjoyed great prestige. However, by 1914, a tide of nationalism changed all this and university lecturers railed against the enemies of Germany, especially England.

Herman L. F. Helmholtz (1821-1894) was a great scientific innovator. He made significant contributions in physiology to the theories of vision and perception of sound. In physics, he studied thermodynamics and conservation of energy, among other themes. Helmholtz was also acknowledged as a philosopher, writing about the civilizing power of science and the laws of nature. Like Virchow he was a liberal politician. As Rector of the University of Berlin "he warned of the power of 'the mystical impulses instilled by a few adventurers into the soul of the people' and referred to anti-Semitism as a current example; 'no-one actually knows its purpose in these times of equal rights, and despite perhaps because of this fact, it fascinates even educated youth". Helmholtz's prescience materialised with the National Socialist gaining power in 1933, and one of the early moves was to expel leading scholars and scientists on racial and on political grounds.

A general analysis of the Universities in Germany in comparison to those in five large European countries from year 1200 to 2000 suggests that the largest number of universities between 1200 and 1500 appeared in Italy and France, followed in 1600 to 1900 by Germany, and to lesser extent Spain and Britain. Russia, however established its first universities only from 1600 to 1900, with a surge of large number in the 20th century. Thus, by the end of the 20th century, Germany, Italy, France, and Russia had between twenty-six and thirty-one universities, whereas Britain and Spain each had eighteen (Table 1). The other European countries had between one and five universities, except for Poland with eleven and the Netherland with seven universities.

Table 1 Universities established in 6 European countries

Years	Germany	Italy	France	Britain	Spain	Russia
1200-1500	8	15	10	5	7	-
1600-1900	15	9	16	8	10	8
2000	5	7	0	5	1	21
Total	28	31	26	18	18	29

It is difficult to draw any conclusion from the number of universities, as some universities were small and others large. This variation is most likely to have been associated with the philosophy of critical mass of the number and size of the faculties, but there is no way of determining the quality of education except by the problematic criterion of 'reputation'. Perhaps the only significance one can ascribe to this analysis is the time these seats of learning were created. Similar findings apply to other European countries not presented in the Table.

Arguably, a more informative analysis as to the creative side of the universities, which is difficult to differentiate from its national culture and propensities, is the number of Nobel Prizes awarded. The data for the same six countries are presented as the total number and the per capita percentage of Nobel Prizes awarded from 1905, when the awards were started, up to 1945 a period of forty-one years, and then up to 2013, a post-Second World War period of sixty-seven years.

Table 2 Total number of Nobel Prizes awarded

Years	Germany	Italy	France	Britain	Spain	Russia
1905-1945	46	7	31	32	3	4
1946-2013	58	13	28	89	5	19
1905-2013	104	20	59	121	8	23
% per capita*	12.6	3.3	9.2	19.2	1.7	1.6

*laureates from 1905 to 2013, according to the population recorded in 2013.

This table shows that the largest number of Nobel Prizes from 1905 to 1945 were awarded to German men and women, followed by Britain and France. After the end of the Second World War, Britain with 89 laureates has overtaken Germany (58) and France (28). The total number of Nobel Prizes won by Britain (121), Germany (104), and France (59) were well ahead of Italy, Spain, and Russia. This 'league table' is also reflected in the percentage of laureates per capita over the entire period of 108 years, with Britain (at 19.2%) well ahead of Germany (12.6%) and France (9.2%), followed by a considerable drop off in Italy, Spain, and Russia.

It is evident that Germany has been in the forefront up to the Second World War, but was then overtaken by Britain, though still well ahead of France. These data are consistent with the high standing of German science and literature before Hitler came to power, and by 2013, Germany must have regained its wartime losses. It should be noted that at the time German universities represented the establishment and the privileged classes, politically mostly on the right, with a nationalistic bent, harking back to the 'golden age' of Kaiser Wilhelm II.

II. UNIVERSITY OF JENA – PHILOSOPHY, LITERATURE AND SCIENCE

The University has a special place in the academic life of Germany. Quite a part of its many celebrated alumni, it is linked with the high culture of Weimar, established by the towering personalities of Goethe and Schiller. Indeed, the University has been named the Friedrich Schiller University of Jena and is one of the two universities in Thuringia, the other being in Erfurt. It was founded in 1558 by the elector John Frederick the Magnanimous, when Jena was regarded as a significant centre of the Reformation. Four classical colleges were established in theology, philosophy, law, and medicine. Initially, there were two professors and 171 students and they gradually developed into a renowned centre of learning, later greatly enhanced by Goethe. As the privy councillor of the Duchy of Weimar, he had considerable power to support financially the University and attracted eminent thinkers and researchers to the University. He was instrumental in establishing libraries, the botanical garden, a natural history archive, laboratories, an observatory, and mineralogical collection, in all of which he had personal scholarly interest.

The classical romantic period was well in evidence as the University attracted great minds – Friedrich Schiller, Johann G Fichte, G W Friedrich Hegel, and K W Friedrich Schlegel. Others drawn to Jena included Novalis, Hölderlin, and the Humboldt brothers. Goethe wrote to Schiller "I am always a happy man when I am in Jena, because no place on earth has given me more productive moments". Indeed, Weimar-Jena under the influence of Goethe became the intellectual capital of Europe.

The first student fraternity was founded in Jena, with the democratic spirit of unity, justice, and liberty, formulated in 1817 at the first meeting in the historical Wartburg Castle in Eisenach. Some of the major figures in the four university faculties, to which later the various science faculties were added, will be described briefly, with an emphasis on the eminent scholars and any link with nationalism and racism.

Friedrich Schiller was appointed professor of History (1789-1793), although he is generally recognised as a poet and dramatist and his doctorate was in medicine. His first lecture was entitled 'What is the purpose of studying history', a question that is equally pertinent to-day. A more extensive account on Schiller is presented on p. 43. The History Institute was established by Johann Gustav Droysen (1851-1859), and greatly gained in its reputation as a seat of scholarship. However, in 1935, Erich Muschke was appointed with strong Nazi connections. He was joined by Hans Günther in 1936, who was an outspoken racist and anti-Semite. He purged historical writings associated with Jewish scholars.

Towards the end of the 18th century, the University excelled in philosophy, largely due to the presence of K.L. Reinhold (1757-1823). He was followed by Johann Gottlieb Fichte (1762-1814) of modest, peasant stock. Because of his exceptional ability, Fichte was enabled to attend a famous monastic school at Pforta, associated with many German writers and philosophers. At the age of eighteen, he joined the theology seminary in Jena, but he did not finish his studies due to dire financial circumstances. After a decade of hardship, he broke through with his first publication on the connection between the divine revelation and Kant's critical philosophy, which met with public acclaim and Kant's praise of the work. At the age of thirty-one, he was invited to the chair of Critical Philosophy at the University of Jena. He founded the German idealism movement and was greatly influenced by Kant's ethical writing. Fichte demonstrated that practical reason is the basis of all knowledge and humanity. He was a great patriot and followed Herder in actively supporting German nationalism. The foundation of his philosophical ideas is based on Spinoza's pantheism, Kant's concept of duty, and Lessing's concept of striving. However, after six years in 1799 he was dismissed from the university, being accused, probably wrongly, of atheism. He moved to Berlin and was appointed professor, as well as Rector of the new university.

Fichte's most important work was 'Foundation of the doctrine of scientific knowledge' ('Wissenschaftslehre') in 1794-95, which presents a system of philosophy. He started this work in Jena and followed it up later with 'philosophy of nature, practical philosophy and that of postulates'. This is not the place to discuss the difficult arguments proposed by Fichte, but I will confine the account of his influence on freedom and its betrayal as analysed by Isaiah Berlin. He refers to the essay on liberty by John Stuart Mill that was endorsed by many Western European thinkers, and was to guard the liberty of individuals against encroachment by other individuals, in other words non-interference. Berlin followed the views of Kant, who argued that the most sacred object in the universe is the free moral and spiritual self, which governs our conduct. Kant believed "the only ultimately valuable thing in the universe is the individual human being … and the ultimate sin is to degrade or humiliate another human being … to deceive somebody, to enslave him the doctrine according to which I must respect other human beings".

These are Kant's 'categorical imperative' moral goals, which are ordered and discovered by the right use of reason. The compelling declaration of liberty of the individual is worthy of being hard-wired into the brain of every citizen and the oath taken by politicians elected to the government of a democratic country. Although Fichte was influenced by Kant, he seemed to have moved away from Kant's ideas concerning the sanctity of the individual. Fichte argued that the individual is nothing without society, that 'man becomes man only among other men'. Berlin stated "there is a direct line, and a very curious one, between the extreme liberalism of Kant, with his respect for human nature and its sacred rights, and Fichte's identification of freedom with self-assertion, with the imposition of your will upon others, with the removal of obstacles to your desires. These are two notions of liberty which were spread over Europe at the beginning of the nineteenth century; to ask which of them is true, and which of them is false, is a shallow and unanswerable question". Fichte lectured on 'Address to the German Nation', espoused nationalist sentiments, and was considered by many as one of the fathers of German Nationalism. Under French occupation, he urged his people to be German in language and character, recalling the much disputed writing of Tacitus on 'Germania'. Associated with nationalism were strong anti-Semitic statements, arguing against giving Jews German citizenship and civil rights, as Jews did not have a single sound idea in their heads. He referred to Jews as a 'state within a state' and believed that this could undermine the German nation. Indeed, Robert Nisbet, professor at the University of California, Berkeley, referred to Fichte as 'the true author of National Socialism'.

It is in order to recall the German Jewish poet Heinrich Heine's prescient thoughts on the force of ideas, written in 1834 just about 100 years before Hitler and the Nazis seized power in Germany. "The idea tries to become action, the word desires to be made flesh. The world is but the outer manifestation of the word. Thought precedes action as lightning precedes thunder. German thunder too is a German, and not in a hurry, and it comes rolling slowly onward; but come it will, and once you hear it crashing, as nothing ever crashed before in the history of the world, then know that the German thunder has finally hit the mark. At that sound the eagles will fall dead from the air and the lions in the remotest deserts of Africa will creep to their royal lairs. A drama will be performed in Germany in contrast with which the French Revolution will seem a mere peaceful idyll".

Karl Wilhelm Friedrich Schlegel (1772-1829) was a poet and the real founder of the German Romantic School. Born in Hanover, he studied first law, but devoted most of his time to literary studies. He lectured in Jena

University, but his career ended in Jena following a publication in which he wrote enthusiastically about the union between sensual and spiritual love. Novalis, the pseudonym of Friedrich von Hardenberg, was born in 1772 in Thuringia near the Harz Mountains. His parents were pious Lutherans and he was educated among other schools in the ducal gymnasium in Eisleben, the birth place of Luther. There, he learned theology, biblical exegesis, mathematics, and German essays. The most significant influence was Schiller in Jena, where he joined the inner circle of students around Schiller. Indeed, Novalis credited Schiller with inspiring his poetic development. Later, he met up with Fichte and Hölderlin in Jena, which led to significant involvement in German idealism. At the death of his fifteen-year-old unofficial fiancée, he wrote his most celebrated poem 'Hymns to the night' (Hymnen an die Nacht). Of an entirely different nature was a significant essay he wrote and presented at the meeting of the entire Romantic circle in Jena in 1799, entitled 'Christianity or Europe (Christenheit oder Europa).

Friedrich Hölderlin (1770-1843) is considered to be one of the greatest German lyric poets. He was born near Württemberg. His father worked in a monastery and died when Friedrich was two years old. He first studied theology at the Tübingen seminary where he befriended the fellow student G. W. F. Hegel. Hölderlin became disillusioned with the Christian faith and declined to become a minister of religion. He met Schiller and Goethe and later entered the University of Jena, where he attended Fichte's philosophy classes.

Hölderlin started writing poetry at the age of fourteen. He was strongly opposed to the oppressive regime at Württemberg and expressed his revolt in poetry. "And if the rabble, a thousand strong, droned their warnings and tried / To throttle us with their thousand tongues of priestly rage / Banning all that's new, we'd laugh them off the stage / We sons of the daughter of God, Justice." Hölderlin's major writing was his novel 'Hyperion or the Hermit in Greece', published in 1797 and 1799 (in two volumes). It deals with young Greeks fighting for independence, the conflicts and hope. His hero in Hyperion is disillusioned and is forced to leave his home country because of its despotic ruler. He writes about Germany as a broken homeland. "Craftsmen you see, but not humans, thinkers, but no humans, priests, but no humans, lords and servants, boys and established people but no humans – is this not like a battlefield, where hands and arms and all limbs lie chaotically in pieces, while the spilled blood of life runs into the sand?" Despite this prescience, he was celebrated in the Third Reich. He was in love with ancient Greece and the wife of one of his employee's, both unattainable, and the latter apparently drove him to insanity. He wrote, "I am mortal, born to love and to suffer." Hölderlin had a miserable life, suffering poverty, schizophrenia, and total separation from his mother and family. His poems were rendered to music, among others by Brahms and, he influenced many writers and philosophers, especially Nietzsche and Heidegger in the early twentieth century.

Georg Wilhelm Friedrich Hegel (1770-1831), German philosopher, was born into a family of public servants. He studied philosophy and theology in the Tübingen seminary. Hegel was appointed professor of philosophy at the University of Jena at the age of thirty-five, but had to leave two years later at the time when Napoleon fought the battle of Jena. After a number of appointments, he secured the chair of philosophy in Heidelberg and soon after, he moved to the University of Berlin, as professor of philosophy and later Rector of the university. His major works were 'Phenomenology of Mind (or Spirit)', 'Science of Logic', 'Philosophy of History', and 'Encyclopaedia of the Philosophical Sciences'. Hegel developed a dialectical scheme of investigating the truth of opposing ideas, the first he called thesis, the opposing idea he termed antithesis, and the result synthesis. Throughout history, opposing forces are at play, which are responsible for progress in all human activities, including culture, philosophy, or spiritual development. Indeed, conflict for Hegel is of the essence in humanity making progress. The individual is subservient to the society, of which he is only a cog in the wheel, and the power of authority determines the good of society.

The demands of history have been a constant theme in Hegel's arguments. As Isaiah Berlin expounded in 'Freedom and its betrayal', "Hegel seemed to place immense stress on history and the value of history, and the fact that everything in it matters and nothing else matters at all. … There is in Hegel perpetual talk about what history demands and what history condemns. This is the imagery and worship of power, of the movement of force for its own sake. The force is, for him, the divine process itself, crushing whatever is meant to be crushed. Hegel is very strong about the necessity for violent action. Progress is the work of heroes; heroes who stand above the conventional morality, because they embody the human spirit at its highest; This identification of what works with what is good, of what is right with what succeeds, with that which crushes resistance, this is the sure hallmark of the Hegelian system, whenever it is applied to politics. In spite of all his vices Hegel created an immense system which for a long time dominated the minds of mankind. As for liberty, there can be none in a tight pattern."

"The most significant application of Hegel's dialectical system of progress was made by Marx but using materialist rather than idealist approach. Civilization is most readily appreciated by the opposite, namely barbarism, so it is also with liberty and freedom. One needs only experience life under the Führer, or Comrade Stalin to recognize the inherent necessity of any individual of freedom of thought and action within the confines of society. The only barrier to this is formed by the need to protect the common security of them all." According to Karl Popper (1945), Hegel advocated disastrous political conceptions of the state and its relation to the citizens, possibly pre-dating 20th century totalitarianism, both fascism and communism. Isaiah Berlin, in accord with Popper, names Hegel as one of the major architects of authoritarianism who undermined democracy.

Although Karl Marx (1818-1883) enrolled first at the University of Bonn, he then transferred to the University of Berlin, because his father thought it to be more academically oriented and in Bonn, young Karl had poor grades. He was engaged in writing his doctoral thesis on 'The difference between the democritean and epicurean philosophy of nature', which he completed in 1841. This was an original but controversial thesis proposing that 'theology must give way to the superior wisdom of philosophy'. Marx thought that the work would not be well received by the conservative professors of the University of Berlin, so he decided to submit it to the more liberal University of Jena, which awarded him the PhD. Marx was greatly influenced by Hegel's philosophy, though critical of it, Ludwig Feuerbach's concept of dialectics, Adam Smith and David Ricardo on economics, socialist thoughts, especially of Jean-Jacques Rousseau and long-term association with his friend and socialist revolutionary, Friedrich Engels.

Marx was one of the great German philosophers, considered by some as one of the most influential figures in history. He made very significant contributions in history, economy, social sciences, and politics. His theories, referred to as Marxism, postulate that all societies progress through a class struggle that is a conflict between the ownership class, controlling production and the lower class, which through labour produces the goods. He investigated the truth of opposing opinions by logical discussion, commonly termed as 'dialectic'. Marx was in essence a revolutionary philosopher, critical of the 'dictatorship of the bourgeoisie', run by the wealthy class of capitalists for their selfish benefit. He foresaw that internal tension will develop, which will destroy capitalism and replace it by socialism, what he called 'dictatorship of the proletariat'. This in turn will be replaced by a classless society of communism. He anticipated that the socialist revolution will first take place in the most highly industrialised countries, though the reverse was true, as Russia and then China were at the helm of the communist revolution, without going through the intermediate stages of industrialisation and socialism. It would be futile to attempt to describe all his achievements but among Marx's outstanding publications were 'Das Kapital' (1867-1894) and 'The Communist Manifesto' (1848).

Marxism has been appropriated by some political forces to promote intolerance and this was particularly evident in the totalitarian state of Stalinist Soviet Union. After the demise of communism in the USSR and Eastern Europe, there was a backlash against Marxism, though he is still considered as one of the most influential thinkers interpreting the significance of economical and sociological forces.

Anti-communist sentiments in Germany had been also utilised to demonise Jews. Although Marx's father converted to Lutheranism and Karl was baptised, his Jewish heritage was a convenient stick to beat down the Jews. Indeed, both paternal and maternal grandfathers of Karl Marx were Rabbis and Karl's father Herschel (changed to Heinrich) Marx was the first in the family to receive a secular education, and became an assimilated, fairly wealthy lawyer. He read Voltaire and Kant and was involved in constitutional reforms in Prussia. The Jewish attachment to learning and thinking in depth may well have been passed down to Karl. A further intriguing point in Marx's personal life was that he married the daughter of Baron Ludwig von Westphalen, 'breaking the social taboo of the time' a marriage of a woman of a noble background and a man of Jewish origin with both grandfathers being rabbis. They had seven children together, but only three survived. Marx moved to London in 1849 at the age of 31 and remained there for the rest of his life.

Wilhelm von Humboldt (1767-1835) had not been part of the University, but he lived in Jena in 1794, when the University became the centre of German idealist philosophy and the Romantic Movement, and will have greatly influenced it. According to the Stanford Encyclopaedia of Philosophy, Humboldt had close contacts with Fichte and Schlegel. Most important was his role as philosophical adviser and critical collaborator of Goethe and Schiller. He advanced both Goethe's and Schiller's works by his discerning criticism. Humboldt and his brother collaborated with Goethe in the emerging discipline of comparative anatomy at the University. He was engaged in the theory of arts, culture, and his major work was on language and education.

Humboldt made a lasting impression on University education, arguing that liberal education is the right of all citizens, combining University teaching with research. Indeed, the Berlin University was established in 1810 based on Humboldtian principles and the whole of Germany and Western world followed this University model. His liberal views and defence of the rights of the individual were greatly admired in England by Matthew Arnold and John Stuart Mill. Not surprisingly, he rejected the conservative, nationalist view of the German historian Treitschke, and he defended Jewish rights at the Congress of Vienna.

III. THE FACULTY OF THEOLOGY

The University of Jena was arguably the most Nazified university in Germany, on account of its location in the State of Thuringia, which was the first state to elect a largely National Socialist governing body. This applies even to a greater extent to the Faculty of Theology, which was before the Nazi era, the smallest theological faculty in Germany, with liberal Protestant scholarship in New Testament and Church history. In the latter part of the 19th century, theological studies were taught by Karl von Hase (1800-1890), who was highly regarded as a biblical scholar of liberal theology. However, the faculty was transformed into a bastion of German Nazi policy, under the influence of Wilhelm Frick, an ardent Nazi who was appointed as Minister of Interior in 1930. The Thuringian church was largely taken over by 'Deutsche Christen' (German Christians) from the traditional 'Confessing Church', with right-wing and anti-Semitic activities. Julius Leutheuser became the leader of the Thuringian German Christians. Siegfried Leffler was appointed to be in charge of theological activities and was responsible for changes in the Jena theological faculty. He replaced one of the members of faculty with his old friend Wolf Meyer-Erlach, whose theological background was limited, but he was involved in many right-wing activities. Gerhard von Rad was apparently mistakenly considered to be a member of the NSDAP and appointed to a chair in Theology. He proved to be the only member of the faculty with allegiance to the Confessing Church and was mostly ostracized by his colleagues.

Walter Grundmann's appointment was the turning point in the outlook of the faculty. He completed his doctorate in 1932 at the University of Tübingen, two years after having joined the NSDAP. Grundmann was appointed in 1936 to the professorship of New Testament and 'Völkische' Theology, at the University of Jena, which was signed by Hitler himself. Grundmann became the lynchpin of the German Christian movement and a supporting member of the SS. He edited the Church journal appropriately named 'Christenkreuz und Hakenkreuz' (Cross and Swastika). Grundmann's aim was to combine theological scholarship with Nazi ideology. The appointment to the chair in Systematic Theology of Heinz Eisenhuth in 1937 was also linked with his membership of the NSDAP and the SA (1933). He was strongly supported by Meyer-Erlach, by then Rector of the University, by assuring the Thuringian Ministry of Eisenhuth's total commitment to Nazi ideology but with hardly any reference to his theological qualifications. He studied theology in Rostock, Tübingen, and Berlin and received the doctorate in philosophy at the University of Frankfurt in 1929. The triumvirate in Jena of Grundmann, Meyer-Erlach, and Eisenhuth established a Nazi-dominated theology faculty in the University. Their first act was to change the status of Hebrew studies by making it optional.

The most significant development for the University and German Christians was the establishment in 1939 in Eisenach of the 'Institute for the study and eradication of Jewish influence on German religious life.' A comprehensive and most informative study was carried out by Susannah Heschel, who published her research findings in "The Aryan Jesus" (2008). A great deal of the following section is based on Dr. Heschel's book. The most prominent person of the Institute was Walter Grundmann, the academic director of the Research Institute, with over forty university professors, students of theology, and bishops. In 1940, it published a dejudaized version of the New Testament and hymnal, and in 1941, its own catechism, which declared that Jesus was an Aryan. A large number of publications and conferences followed. The University of Jena was used for doctoral thesis biased towards radical and religious anti-Semitism. A doctoral candidate who argued in his dissertation that Jesus's ideas must be understood within the context of the Old Testament was failed, as Meyer-Erlach reported that "the theologian lacks the understanding of National Socialism, that the racial question is the basic question for everything". In contrast, a thesis on Chamberlain's theory of the Aryan origin for Christianity was recommended to be awarded a prize. The German Christian church of Thuringia required its candidates for the ministry to study in Jena and the students attended classes dressed in SA uniforms.

The theological faculty in Jena after 1945 did not change greatly, except for the professoriat. Grundmann and Eisenhuth remained active in Thuringian, but not Jena university affairs, lecturing and teaching during the DDR period. They were Thuringia's most distinguished theological scholars and later it transpired that Grundmann worked actively for the Stasi, which enabled him to travel abroad to scholarly meetings. His commentaries on the Gospels, published in 1960, became the theological best-sellers and standard works consulted by pastors in East and West Germany. Grundmann and his fellow-travellers presented themselves as victims of National Socialism. They claimed to have struggled against the claims of ideologues, such as Alfred Rosenberg, who argued that Christianity is in essence Judaism and cannot be dejudaized or nothing would be left of it. This raises the most intriguing controversy between the two German Nazi ideologues and arguably the only instance in which the protagonist of medieval Christian argument that Jesus was not a Jew but an Aryan and that he fought to eradicate Judaism led to the claim that Christian goals were essentially those of the German Nazis. Although both the German and Confessing Church fought for control of the Church, they were equally inclined towards anti-Semitism. The Jena faculty of theology, with its closely associated Eisenach Institute, reflected the extreme wing of theological 'scholarship', even to the point where its principle ideologue and spokesman, Grundmann, was equally accommodating to the Nazi and Stasi Christian apostasy and brutality.

IV. THE FACULTY OF MEDICINE

Christoph William Hufeland (1762-1836)

This was one of the four founding faculties of the University in 1558 and its first Rector, Johannes Schröter (1518-1593), was a physician. Christoph Wilhelm Hufeland (1762-1836) was educated in Weimar, where his father was the court physician to the grand duchess. In 1780, he entered the University of Jena, and the following year, went to Göttingen where he graduated in Medicine in 1783. Ten years later, he was appointed to the chair of medicine at Jena. Later, Frederick William III of Prussia granted him the position of director of the medical college and of state medical affairs at the Charité, in Berlin. Hufeland became Physician Royal to the King of Prussia, as well as giving medical advice to Goethe, Schiller, and Herder.

Hufeland's astonishing prescient statement published in his paper 'The physician's relationship' 135 years before his warning was not heeded and became a reality. "The physician should and must not do anything but maintain life, irrespective whether it is happy or miserable, worth living or not, is not for the physician to decide. If that issue were ever to be considered, then the consequences are unpredictable and the physician becomes the most dangerous person in the land. Should this line be crossed and the physician decides on the life of his patient, then all it takes is stepwise progression to extend the decision on the worthlessness and uselessness of human life to apply to the lives of others."

Hufeland writes passionately on the art of healing as one of the most rewarding, indeed holy vocations. The physician should be a highly moral individual, with no regard to his comfort, monetary gain, or prestige in society. He emphasises that the physician should consider the most important objective in his profession is "to preserve life, to restore health and relieve suffering also to ease suffering of the patient with incurable disease and death should be made as comfortable as possible". The latter echoes modern day's palliative medicine, though without the help of any effective drugs and having to rely on one's empathy and offering creature comfort. Hufeland's total commitment to the art of medicine is also illustrated by his attitude to monetary gain when he writes, "What is a fistful of gold compared to a tearful appreciation of a poor patient unable to pay but who remains for ever indebted to his physician". These memorable instructions, especially to young physicians practising in the 18th century, have been expressed by the Physician Royal to the King of Prussia, who was among other accolades director of the most prestigious 'Charitè' medical college in Berlin. Moreover, he was born, bred, and educated in Jena, the University of which was reputedly the most Nazified University in Germany, where as described below, children and adults unworthy of life were killed.

Among the outstanding medical innovators, Hans Berger (1873-1941) studied first mathematics and them medicine in Jena and served as a psychiatrist during the First World War. He was the first to record electrical activity of the human brain in 1929 and coined the term electroencephalography (EEG). However, he had no knowledge of electrophysiology and it was only in 1934 that E.D. Adrian confirmed and interpreted the significance of the original findings. Berger was elected Rector of the University in 1927 and retired in 1938 as Professor Emeritus in Psychology. It transpired later that Berger was a member of the SS, and that he served on the 'Court of Genetic Health', which was responsible for forced sterilization and that he was an anti-Semite. After clinical depression, he committed suicide in 1941.

Max Henkell (1870-1941) qualified in Medicine at the University of Würzburg and Freiburg. He was appointed Professor of Gynaecology at the University of Jena and carried out abortions as early as 1914 on thirty-three patients with TB, nine with heart disease, and six with mental illness. This lead to widespread debate about the place of eugenic abortions. At the time, Henkell was largely condemned by his colleagues. The rationale of terminating these lives is obscure, but illustrates the laxity of ethical norms that were applied by some gynaecologists. Despite having been involved in a scandal because of high frequency of infections and post-operative mortalities in 1911, as well as unethical behaviour, he became Rector of the University in 1923. Henkell joined the NSDAP in 1933.

Yusuf Ibrahim (1877-1952) was a highly respected paediatrician of Turkish origin, and his name was attached to the clinic for child and adolescent medicine at the University, named 'Kinderklinik Yusuf Ibrahim' (Children Clinic of Yusuf Ibrahim). Despite this reputation, he participated in the euthanasia programme, killing children defined as 'unworthy of life'. Ibrahim was investigated by the medical historian, Dr. Susanne Zimmermann, who reported on his active personal involvement in the euthanasia programme. He sent children to the killing centre where even the Institute's paediatricians did not obey his signed demand to murder some of the children. Dr. Zimmermann had to fight the Jena Medical establishment before her well-researched revelations of Ibrahim's Nazi practices were accepted. He was succeeded by Erich Hässler (1899-2005) to the chair in paediatrics who was a member of the 'Office for Racial Policy', a broadly based organisation. In his book on childcare, he called Jews 'rootless parasites'. Hässler was a member of the Jena student fraternity, 'Sängerschaft zu St. Pauli', and he was ostensibly rewarded with longevity, as he survived to the age of 106.

Karl Astel (1898-1945) was already a fanatical Nazi during his student days in the medical school in Munich. He joined the 'Freikorps' in 1919, and participated in street fights and most right-wing upheavals. After graduation, he worked as a 'sports physician' in Munich and in 1932, he became head of the 'Hereditary Counselling Centre' in the main SS office, as well as director of the 'Office of Racial Hygiene School of SA' in Munich. Evidently, Astel was in great demand, as among other high offices he was elected as a judge at the Hereditary Health Court in Jena. He was responsible for thousands of forced sterilizations between 1933 and 1945. Astel came to the attention of Fritz Sauckel, who appointed him in 1934 to the full professorship in the medical faculty in Jena. Indeed, a novel Institute was created to fit Astel's and Sauckel's interests, coined 'Institute for Teaching Human Genetic Research and Breeding', which was renamed after being advised of the rather inappropriate title to the 'Institute of Human Genetic Research and Racial Politics', which was perhaps more suitable to the know-how of the sports physician.

Astel's stratospheric promotion reached unprecedented heights when in 1939 he was made SS-lieutenant colonel and Rector of the University of

Jena, a marriage that did not bode well for the University. He was supported by no lesser authorities than Hitler and Himmler and was free to teach and commit crimes against humanity under the august umbrella of the Friedrich Schiller University. Astel became the leading Nazi racist, he utilized and adapted the politicized Darwinian concept developed by Ernst Haeckel of 'survival of the fittest' to his racial prejudice, as a pseudo-scientific programme of eradication of the racially unfit people. In one of his keynote university speeches in 1936, he called for Jena to be a model SS University, in which he was largely successful. It is somewhat reassuring that in 1945 Karl Astel was committed to a mental hospital and shot himself on 3rd of April 1945, thus ending a most 'illustrious' career in the annals of medical history.

It has to be pointed out that after the war, German physicians were in denial about their part in the atrocities of the profession during the Nazi era. They closed rank and argued that these deeds were perpetrated by a few psychopathic individuals. Indeed, most of these 'psychopaths' went back to practice medicine and some who were active in pursuing Nazi policies even reached high office after cessation of hostilities.

Dr. Benno Müller-Hill, professor of Genetics in the University of Cologne writes in his book 'Murderous Science'. "When I started talking to these people, I knew them only from their publications or from files in archives. Sometimes, I expected to talk with a living agent of evil – after all, they had once been involved in the most evil events. But these old ladies and gentlemen in whose homes I sat and whose hospitality I accepted did not at all correspond to the images which I had formed of them. Most of them had declared that they had not known anything of the mass murders of mental patients, Jews and Gypsies; that they had not known anything of the events which had linked their academic institutions with the murderers; that there were no traces of anti-Semitism in their field of work; that either they had not joined the Nazi Party at all, or that they had been forced to join; that their best friends were Jewish or half-Jewish; that, as pure scientists, they had never handled expert reports on racial origins; and that they had given little or no thought to the general context of these events". Müller-Hill then reflects, "For what would I have done in their place? But in science there can be no appeasement. No man has the right to forgive in the name of the dead. And the memory of the dead should be revered. Reconciliation is only possible between living people who have equal rights."

V. SCIENCE- BIOLOGY – EUGENICS – RACIAL HYGIENE – ANTHROPOLOGY

Ernst Abbe (1840-1905) is closely linked with the future of the University of Jena, as with Carl Zeiss and Otto Schott, they founded the modern optical industry in Jena, renown throughout the world. This was probably the first serious link between University and Industry. Abbe was born in Eisenach to a humble working class family. His father's employer supported Ernst to attend secondary school and eventually he studied at the Universities of Jena and Göttingen. Abbe was awarded the PhD in Göttingen in 1861, and a few years later, he was appointed to the extraordinary professorship in Physics at the University of Jena. He made highly significant contributions to modern optics, especially greatly enhancing the power of resolution of microscopes.

Goethe had considerable influence on the development of Biology in Jena, as he was greatly interested in Botany and admired the work by the Swedish botanist Linnaeus. He pursued himself detailed description of plants and was associated with the Botany and Anatomy Departments at the University of Jena. Indeed, he was responsible for establishing the botanical garden in Jena. After Goethe's death in 1832, Biology, Anatomy, and Physiology were supported by the University, largely following Darwin's theory of evolution. Karl Gegenbaur (1826-1903) was appointed to the chair in Anatomy in 1855. He published critical work on structural similarities among different animals, emphasising common evolutionary origin. He was a student of Virchow among others, collaborated with Ernst Haeckel, and was a strong supporter of Darwinism. William Thierry Preyer (1841-1897), an English physiologist, was appointed in 1869 as professor and director of the Physiology Institute at the University of Jena. He was also greatly influenced by Darwin's theory of evolution and published work on developmental physiology. The same year, Edward A. Strasburger was appointed Professor of Botany at the University. He postulated the concept that nuclei of cells can arise only from division of other nuclei and introduced the terms cytoplasm and nucleoplasm. Oscar Hertwig (1849-1922) was a student of Haeckel and Gegenbaur, and he pursued comparative animal development and Darwin's theory, but refuted Darwin's belief that chance plays an essential role in evolution. Gustav A. Schwalbe (1844-1916) was appointed Professor of Anatomy at Jena in 1873, with interest in the anthropology of primitive man. He was the first to demonstrate that cerebrospinal fluid is drained through the lymphatic system.

It is evident that Jena was a centre of advanced biological research in the late 19th and early 20th century. The most influential scientist in Biology, however was Ernst Haeckel, (1834-1919) and he was the foremost exponent of Darwin's theories in Germany. He studied Zoology at the University of Jena, was awarded the doctorate, promoted to the professorship of Comparative Anatomy in 1862, and worked in Jena for forty-seven years. Haeckel visited Darwin as a young biologist and was immensely struck by the theory of natural selection. He believed that the fundamental point of the theory was animal ancestry of humans, overthrowing the anthropocentric idea that humans are the centre of the universe. This concept had the revolutionary force similar to that proposed by Copernicus, discarding the Ptolemaian and religious dogma that the earth is the centre of the universe in favour of the heliocentric concept.

Ernst Haeckel viewed matter and mind as one substance, called his philosophy 'monism', and considered it to be synonymous with pantheism, which he admitted to be equivalent to atheism. This notion is rather reminiscent of Baruch Spinoza's (1632-1677) philosophy, rejecting Descartes's dualism of mind and body in favour of a single matter and finding God in all nature. It is not known if Haeckel acknowledged Spinoza, as many philosophers shied away from referring by name to Spinoza's 'dangerous concepts'.

There was almost complete agreement among Darwinists that natural evolution may account for all aspects of human society and behaviour, including ethics and altruism, and denied divine intervention. Indeed, Darwin argued that human social moral instincts, reason and group selection led naturally to the rule of, "Do unto others as you would have them unto you", encompassing the central teaching of Judaism by Hillel and that of Christianity by Jesus. Nonetheless, Darwinism changed the long-standing understanding of the value of human life, not least because they evolved from animals, instead of the Judeo-Christian concept of being made in the image of God. Darwinism also denied the existence of immaterial and immortal soul, as an essential tenet of the sanctity of human life, in Judeo-Christian teaching. Extinction of less-fit organisms was argued to be beneficial and to foster progress. As stated by Richard Weikart, "Darwinian theory was thus not just about biological change, it was a matter of life and death." Indeed, Haeckel advocated killing of the 'unfit' individuals, as a logical consequence of his Darwinian monistic view.

Moreover, he seemed to have approved infanticide of congenitally handicapped infants. Although Darwin's theory overturned many religious doctrines, including the nature of ethics, moral codes, the value of human soul, life, and death, many Christian and Jewish religious thinkers have now accepted some aspects of Darwinism. No doubt, this has been due to the overwhelming evidence not only from research on fossils over the past 150 years, but also the recent robust evidence derived from DNA studies on evolution.

Surprisingly, Haeckel opposed militarism and war on the basis that the weak and sick were not allowed to fight, so they would have more children, whilst the strong may be killed, contrary to his eugenic principles. Thus, Haeckel joined the peace movement before World War I and promoted pacifism. Hitler adopted Darwinism that provided for him justification for infanticide, euthanasia, and genocide. The Judeo-Christian morality was superseded by an 'atavistic retro-evolutionary move'. Hitler found in Haeckel's Darwinism the justification to select the fittest Nordic German race for expansion and the less-fit for extinction, thereby 'speeding up the evolutionary process'. Many Darwinian biologists argued that racial extinction was inescapable and even beneficial for it brought about evolutionary progress for the human species. Otherwise, Haeckel was a liberal, promoting the peace movement and homosexual rights. He linked Virchow's concept of cell biology with Darwinism and argued that the laws of evolution may be applied to solve ethical and social problems. Indeed, biology was to be used as a basis for nationalism, but without the prevailing anti-Semitism. He believed that Anthropology was a branch of Zoology, whereas psychology was to be studied in comparison with differences in development among animals and humans. Haeckel and his colleagues argued that in the wake of the enlightenment, science, tolerance, reason, culture, and truth will thrive and discard all the irrational, superstitious, and backward religious beliefs. Regrettably, this was not to be. Despite volumes of philosophical and literary treatises endorsing and expanding the humanitarian concept of the enlightenment, human nature failed to translate the reasoned arguments into the communal psyche. Evil prevailed, tainted with modern, pseudo-scientific arguments, largely based on the evolutionary animal past, protecting its territorial integrity – 'us and them'. He was not a proto-fascist, though significantly influencing Hitler's ideology. There is no evidence that Hitler would have met Haeckel, who died in 1919. His legacy in Jena has been profound, for quite apart from having been the leading Darwinist in Germany, he was a highly rated zoologist. Haeckel's French edition on 'Monism as Connecting Religion and Science' was published in 1897, and Georges Vacher de Lapouge used the expressed view, to overturn the French revolutionary cry 'Liberty, Equality and Fraternity' to 'Determinism, Inequality and Selection'. He opposed protection of the handicapped individuals as it perpetuates the unfit at the expense of evolution of superior people. Lapouge's views were more in accord with those in Germany than France. Darwinism was adopted avidly by German biologists and young people were largely converted by Ernst Haeckel.

In the past, biology was commonly studied by medically qualified scientists and this applied also to Anthropology (study of man). Eugenics or Social Darwinism was introduced by Francis Galton, a half cousin of Charles Darwin, after reading the evolutionary theory of Darwin "Origin of Species", which appeared in 1859. "The Descent of Man" was published by Darwin twelve years later. Alfred Ploetz (1860-1940) founded the first eugenic society in the world, the "German Society for Race-Hygiene", which was entirely influenced by Haeckel through his exposition of Darwinism. From the very start, the Church voiced robust criticism, and there were serious moral concerns voiced, among others by Adam Sedgwick, Darwin's former mentor in natural science at the University of Cambridge. He feared that Darwinism may have brutalising and degrading effect on people. With remarkable prescience, a German Protestant pastor, in 1876, expressed serious concern about the negative effect of Darwin's theory on the cultural achievements of the past century. Indeed, in 1880, Robby Kossmann, a German zoologist stated that the Darwinian theory might lead the State to preserve "the more excellent at the expense of the less excellent life". This view has spread widely, and there were philosophers and bioethicists who referred to "Darwin's Dangerous Idea", that Darwinism discredits the Judeo-Christian idea of the sanctity of human life, and potentially justifying euthanasia and infanticide.

Racial hygiene, a term used in Germany instead of eugenics, became a new province of anatomists, which underpinned Nazi policies, that led to racial discrimination forced sterilization and mass murder. As reported by Michael H. Kater in 'Doctors under Hitler', "Between 1933 and 1939 positions in 'Rassenkunde' were launched in most medical facilities. Berlin, Greifswald, Munich, Halle, and Leipzig had their own chairs or university institutes in 1933. Frankfurt received one in 1935 (Otmar Freiherr von Verschuer) and Giessen in 1938 (Heinrich Wilhelm Kranz). In Tϋbingen, faculty members Wilhelm Gieseler, Heinrich Hoffmann, and Otto Stickl, everyone a staunch National Socialist, looked after the needs of Rassenkunde". The most prominent exponent of this pseudoscience was

Professor Eugen Fischer (1874-1967), who became the director of the Kaiser-Wilhelm Institute for Anthropology, Heredity, and Eugenics. He applied Mendelian laws to physical traits of a population of offspring of intermarried white men and black women in German South West Africa (now Namibia) and claimed that they followed Mendelian laws. This questionable research established Fischer as the founder of 'racial biology' and played a central role in German racial hygiene.

Fritz Lenz (1887-1976) became professor of eugenics for racial hygiene at the University of Munich in 1923. In an early article in 1917 and later, he argued that culture, evolution, personality, and redemption are all dependent on race. He claimed that race is one of the most decisive factors in the entire course of the history of a people. He considered the Nordic race intellectually superior, and denied Jewish intellectual contributions. He was probably right to claim that his article in 1917 on race and ethics contained all the criteria of Nazi ideology. Many of the racist ideas of National Socialism, Hitler adopted from scientists and scholars dealing with the social, ethical, and moral implications of Darwinism. Lenz's prestige as a medical professor, may have lent scientific respectability to his racial views, which were integrated in the text-book on human genetics co-authored with Fischer and E. Bauer. Lenz emphasized, however, that his views were not based on science, but were postulates, incapable of proof. Nonetheless, he advocated restriction of reproduction of inferior individuals and supported infanticide of disabled infants. Max Nordau interpreted the welter of racist views by stating that "Evolution acted as a cover for natural barbarism, allowing people to cover their instincts with the last word of science".

Hitler's deputy Rudolf Hess declared National Socialism to be 'applied biology' and racial hygiene as the treatment of German people threatened by degeneration. This enabled the National Socialists to advocate the removal of 'diseased' people, in order to save the health of German people ('Volksgesundheit'). "Genetic Health Courts" were formed to identify the genetically, racially, and socially unfit people; mentally ill, children with malformations, homosexuals, political opponents, Jews, Sinto, Roma, and some Christian groups. Many anatomists and physicians sat on these courts, making far-reaching decisions on sterilization, euthanasia, and murder, using all the finesse of Western culture and science. Special mention has to be made of the racial hygienist Otmar von Verschuer (1896-1969) who became the director of the Kaiser Wilhelm Institute for Anthropology in Berlin. He was a religious Christian belonging to the Confessional Church in Frankfurt, and after his move to Berlin in 1942, he joined the Niemöller's congregation, by which time Niemöller was imprisoned. Verschuer attempted to define Jewish racial characteristics, and his infamous post-doctoral student Josef Mengele followed up Verschuer experiments on twins in concentration camp in Auschwitz and supplied eyes, organs and skeletons to Verschuer. Mengele became the ultimate icon of evil in transforming the noble healing profession to medical torture and mass murder, as he decided in Auschwitz life or death of innocent victims of German racial hygiene.

Johann Paul Kremer (1883-1965) was Professor of Anatomy at Münster University. Kremer worked in Auschwitz as an SS doctor at the ramp, selecting people for life or death. He participated in a large number of mass killings by Zyklon gas, as well as public executions. His medical interest was the effect of starvation on the human body and selected starved inmates of interest before killing them by intra-cardiac injection of phenol, 'for good fixation of organs such as liver, spleen and kidney'. Dr. Kremer was sentenced to death in the Auschwitz Trial, based on his diary and own confessions, but the sentence was later commuted and he was released in 1958. Kremer shares with Mengele a double doctorate by the great German universities and murderous medical experiments.

Julius Hallervorden was a psychiatrist and neuropathologist also at the Kaiser Wilhelm Institute, but that of Brain Research in Berlin. He studied 697 brains from euthanasia centres and instructed in the methods of removing and fixing the brain for microscopical examination. Heinrich Gross physicians at the Vienna psychiatric hospital received training at the German killing centres, and 336 children under his care were murdered and their brains studied for many years, regrettably up to 1978.

Hans F. K. Günther (1891-1968) was an outspoken racist. He studied first comparative languages at the University of Freiburg and was awarded the doctorate in 1914. He was a social anthropologist and followed the racial theories of Arthur de Gobineau and Houston S. Chamberlain. His first book, 'Short Ethnology of the German people', was widely read and was followed by a polemical book on 'Biological Nationalism of German Pagan Nationalist Romanticism', which raised a great deal of interest especially by Heinrich Himmler. He defined the racial 'ideal type' of Nordic Aryan, based on appearance, skull measurements and 'historical creativity'. He taught racial theory and Nordic roots of German people at the Universities of Jena, Berlin, and Freiburg, and published a large number of books on the subject. In 1931, he was appointed to the new chair of Social Anthropology in Jena, which was one of the earliest acts of the Nazi Minister, Wilhelm Frick in Thüringen. Even Hitler attended Günther's inaugural lecture 'The

Lesson of Social anthropology' (Die Aufgabe der Socio anthropologie), arguably the only University lecture Hitler ever attended. By this time in 1932, he joined the NSDAP and was known as 'Race Günther and Race Pope' (Rassen Papst).

Günther had a major influence on Nazi racial thought. He was in great demand, and by 1935, he moved to a chair in Berlin, followed in 1940 to the chair of Racial Science at Freiburg, teaching race theory and eugenics, and publishing books on these subjects. He recognized that there were no pure races, that not all Aryans were Nordic, and that Jews belonged to a racial mixture of non-European people belonging to Asiatic and Oriental stock, responsible for degenerate ideas on liberalism, democracy, and socialism. Günther considered the Nordic race as the great creative force in history which has to be guarded against mixing with other races, to prevent endangering the future civilization. He advocated eugenic measures to purge Germans of all degenerate influences, foremost the Jews. Günther's race theories were adopted by the Hitler regime as a central plank in the struggle for civilization by eliminating and finally murdering the Jews in Europe. This was a novel German Nazi concept of 'civilization', which Günther pursued after the war unhindered by his record.

Thus, Hitler utilized the ideas of reputable scholars of the prestigious German academic community, including professors of medicine, biology, anthropology, theology, and philosophy into his racial, anti-Semitic world-view. The concepts of leading academic personalities played a significant role in the willingness of the ordinary Germans to support Nazi atrocities, leading to mass murder. A great deal of 'Anti-Semitic Catechism' was assembled by the writer-publisher Theodor Fritch (1852-1933) in 'The Handbook of the Jewish Question', which appeared as early as 1893, went through forty-nine editions, and was read by millions of Germans, including, of course, Hitler.

Most anatomists had a medical degree and their involvement in perpetrating medical atrocities was both active in procuring or ordering organs of interest to their particular area of research, and passive by availing themselves of the unprecedented opportunity of obtaining "fresh well preserved material" of all ages and a variety of diseases. Most of the corpses were delivered from concentration camps and prisons, and were victims of starvation, disease, hanging, shooting and the results of lethal medical experiments. The cadavers were used for teaching medical students, and by racial hygienists, neuropathologists, and anthropologists.

Whilst 70% of chairmen of Anatomy Departments from 1941-1944 held a Nazi affiliation, only one anatomist, professor Günther Hertwig of

Rostock openly voiced opposition to the regime, and he lost his position in the University. According to Hildebrandt, all anatomical departments in Nazi Germany, without exception, used bodies of German Nazi victims; Jews, Poles, and Russians. However, all contributors to Nazi policy and those taking advantage of the opportunities of studying the unique human material at their disposal, made the common excuses that they did not know and showed no evidence of guilt or contrition. Whilst Eugen Fischer was retired by the end of the 2nd World War, Otmar von Verschuer was appointed to the chair in Münster and Fritz Lenz in Göttingen.

The Anatomical Institute at the University of Jena played a major role in using 2224 corpses during the Nazi rule (1933-1945). Hans Böker headed the Institute from 1932 to 1938 and his successor was Rüdiger von Volkmann, who actively supported the National Socialist policy. The Anatomy Institute received corpses from 200 executed individuals convicted for minor crimes by the special Nazi Courts in Weimar, Jena, Erfurt, and other Thuringean cities. The accused were German citizens and they were stripped of all their rights to defend themselves. A number of documents appear to have been removed from the archives after the war, making it impossible to ascertain the cause of death of most of the prisoners, who presumably were supplied from the Buchenwald concentration camp. Many corpses were received through the euthanasia programs (Aktion T4), from nursing homes and mental hospitals, and this included children who were transferred from the University Children's Hospital in Jena to the killing centre of handicapped children. The cause of death was fictitious, so these doctors were guilty of both medical perjury and murder.

Eugenicists were concerned with the so-called biological degeneration threatening the health and vitality of Germans by non-European or non-Germans. Some eugenicists argued that human racial competition and war is part of the Darwinian struggle of survival of the fittest. Hitler and his cohort adopted Social Darwinism, which helped in formulating Nazi ideology and linked it with extreme nationalism, anti-Semitism, and finally mass murder. According to Steven Ascheim, the path from Social Darwinism, Wagnerism, Nietzscheism to racism, anti-Semitism, and Nazi ideology, may have paved a complex way to Auschwitz. Darwinist eugenics smoothed the path for Nazi ideology in territorial expansion, war, racial fight, and extermination. In addition to eugenics, German anthropology provided theories and ideologies to legitimize 'scientific racism' on Darwinian grounds. This was applied to atrocities in South West Africa and Nazi genocide. Michael Burleigh, in 1991, and others have argued that Nazism attempted to fabricate new men and women by transforming the Judeo-Christian ethical values in favour of some ill-defined primitive civilization supported by Darwinian and Nietzschenian ideas. According to Fritz Lenz, Hitler stated in 1917 that "With every deed and with every inaction, we have to ask ourselves; does it benefit our race? And then make our decision accordingly."

VI. PATRONS OF ART

Eduard Rosenthal studied Law at the University of Heidelberg and Berlin, and was appointed to the Chair in Law at the University of Jena. He was father of the constitution of the state of Thuringia and also held the post of Dean of the University of Jena. He and his wife were a highly cultured Jewish couple who founded the reading society and were co-founders of the 'Kunstverein' (cultural society). Their son died fighting in the 1st World War, and Rosenthal himself died in 1920. After the Nazis came to power, Clara Rosenthal was ostracized in Jena, prohibiting her from subscribing to newspapers, attending any social or university functions, and listening to radio, all of which drove the seventy-year-old leading cultural lady of Jena to commit suicide.

Felix Auerbach (1856-1933) came from a highly educated Jewish family in Breslau, where he was educated. He studied at the Universities of Breslau, Heidelberg, and then Berlin, where he was a student of the renowned physicist Hermann Helmholtz; in 1875 he was awarded his doctorate. The subject of his dissertation was 'The nature of vowel sounds', reflecting his early talent and love for music. Auerbach, arguably pioneered a novel branch of physics, with research papers published in the Annals of Physics and Chemistry, among others on 'Pitch of a tuning fork' and 'Grassmannschen vocal theory'. In 1889, he succeeded to Abbe's chair in Theoretical Physics at the University of Jena, but he was denied the full professorship on account of his Jewish origin, which was granted thirty-four years later in 1932, and four years before his retirement as Emeritus Professor of the University. Auerbach made significant contributions to theoretical physics and his life-long commitment to the arts motivated him to study the physical basis of the Arts. This brought him in contact with Paul Klee, Wassily Kandinsky, Ludwig Kirchner, Edward Munch (who painted a portrait of Auerbach), and Walter Gropius (who built him the house), among a host of other artists.

He and his wife were great patrons of the Arts in Jena, following in the footsteps of Edward Rosenthal and his wife. The anti-Semitic climate in Germany, which was more intense in Jena than other universities, and Hitler gaining power in 1933, drove Felix Auerbach at the age of seventy-seven, and his wife, to commit suicide. In his farewell letter, he wrote that his life was full of joy, after nearly fifty years of living with his wife, and now they are leaving this earthly existence.

The Auerbach and Rosenthal families in Jena raise a most painful and difficult question. Here we have two acknowledged, great academic personalities of the University of Jena, making outstanding contributions to the University and its national fame, one in jurisprudence and the other in science. Both have established and maintained the cultural life of Jena to a standard that even Goethe and Schiller would have approved. Yet, both the Auerbachs and Clara Rosenthal (blissfully Edward died in 1920) took their lives. The Auerbachs and Rosenthals were highly civilised individuals, but anti-Semitism at the University and upper echelons of Jena society prevailed. Had they received any support from their intellectual friends whom they nourished over decades with culture, remains to be explored. Is there any correlation between high culture, ostensibly ennobling the spirit, and lack or loss of empathy and support for one's friends and fellow human being in time of need? This is a critical moral issue that has not been adequately explored. One can surmise from the suicide of the Auerbachs and Clara Rosenthal, as well as the diary of Victor Klemperer, that it is unlikely that his colleagues and friends offered much support. The uncomfortable and disturbing association between high culture and low moral and ethical behaviour of an educated community is a serious indictment of Western Civilization. It seems to endorse the thesis of Professor John Carey, that the traditional notion, probably starting with Aristotle, that Art is character-forming, lifting the spirits, enhancing morality, and has a civilizing effect is wishful thinking. The arts are beautiful, and they may elicit great aesthetic pleasure, but their influence on morality, humanity, and fellowship that defines civilization is at best doubtful and at worst divisive of communities.

As a postscript, the 'Auerbach House', built by Gropius, used to be a cultural centre for scholars and artists up to 1933, has recently been declared a 'German Foundation Monument for Protection'. Similarly, the 'Rosenthal Villa' has been restored and scheduled to be used as originally stipulated in the Rosenthal's will for cultural functions, conferences, and for scholarship holders in the arts and culture. Thus, the Auerbach and Rosenthal Houses remain cultural monuments of two great Jewish intellectual families, victims of the 'Model National Socialist University'. This brings hope for the future that in the final analysis, culture has triumphed over the vicissitudes of barbarism, though at what cost. There remains the bitter memory of perverted scholarship, not least in re-writing the theological basis of monotheism, and postulating a vile concept of racism that denies the worth of human beings.

CHAPTER 3: BUCHENWALD CONCENTRATION CAMP

I. **Life in the camp**
II. **Medical experimental atrocities and advances in killing technology**
III. **Prominent personalities**
IV. **Liberation of the concentration camp**

BUCHENWALD CONCENTRATION CAMP

"Concentration camps are essential institutions, maintaining totalitarianism by eliminating opposition and insure fear" *Adapted from Hannah Arendt, 1950*
"In the face of inhumanity humanist classicism proved powerless. Weimar became a suburb of Buchenwald" *George Steiner, 2005*
"A new link arose between Weimar's classical culture and Buchenwald's unlimited brutal power" *Eugen Kogon, Austrian Diplomat in Buchenwald, 1946*
"That a policy of steady starvation and inhuman brutality was carried out at Buchenwald for a long period of time; and that such camps as this mark the lowest point of degradation to which humanity has yet descended. The memory of what we saw and heard at Buchenwald will haunt us ineffaceably for many years." *British parliamentary report on the Buchenwald Concentration Camp in 1945*

"Kadish for the unborn child" *Book by Imre Kertesz, 2004*
"One who remains silent instead of preventing sin becomes partner in crime" *Interpretation of 'Job' by Chief Rabbi Israel Meir Lau, 2011*
"And the world remained silent" *Elie Wiesel's Memoirs, 1995*

Fig. 1 *Aerial view of* Buchenwald *Concentration Camp following liberation, end of April 1945. Photo: U.S. Air Reconnaissance. National Archives Washington.*

I. LIFE IN THE CAMP

The location of the first major concentration camp adjacent to Weimar, the jewel in the crown of German and European culture, was one of the most unfair strokes of National Socialism, bordering on cultural vandalism by the sick mentality of the SS "Übermensch" (Superman). Weimar and its culture remain victims of the legacy of the "Thousand Year Reich". The contribution of Weimar, its University of Jena, and the neighbouring Eisenach to Western Christian Culture is unique. Johann Wolfgang Goethe and Friedrich Schiller in literature and poetry, Johan Sebastian Bach and Liszt in music, Martin Luther in religion, and Fichte and Hegel in philosophy have all made monumental contributions to the spiritual and cultural life, in the small Duchy of Weimar.

Buchenwald (Beech Forrest) is five miles from the town of Weimar, where Goethe settled down in 1775 at the age of twenty-six and made it into a place of cultural pilgrimage of Europe. There was a justified pride of the Thüringian people to have a God-send in Goethe, identified by the Dowager Anna Amelia as an appropriate person to educate her son August, the future Duke of Saxe-Weimar-Gotha. It is a mystery that Goethe and Schiller, two paragons of freedom, idealism, and spirituality spent their lifetime in late eighteenth to the nineteenth century Weimar and yet within about a century, the people of Thuringia elected a government, opposed to freedom, declared themselves to be 'Übermenschen' and introduced barbarism and murder on the doorsteps of hallowed ground. This was the grotesque turning point of everything that Weimar classicism stood for.

The following brief description of the Buchenwald concentration camp is based on 'The Buchenwald Report' prepared in 1945 by a special intelligence team from the Psychological Warfare Division of the US army, with active collaboration of prisoners. It was translated and edited by David A. Hackett in 1995. Buchenwald was one of the first major camps built in July 1937, among the other camps in Germany and Austria. The report demonstrates the clear division between the measured tone of the scholars and enquiring personnel, in contrast to the emotional and poignant witnesses of suffering humanity. This barrier between the victim and even the empathetic individual is palpable up to this day, some seventy years after the Holocaust, when most of the surviving victims have died. Buchenwald, in contradiction to Schiller's 'Ode to Freedom and Universal Brotherhood', tried to establish the ideology that all men are not brothers, not created equal, many are unworthy of life, according to criteria laid down by university educated 'racial hygienists', and have to be exterminated.

By 1940, when concentration camps became a growing industry, they were classified into three categories. Category 1 were work camps, the mildest form of loss of freedom. Category 2 indicated harsher living and working conditions. Category 3 were death camps ('Vernichtungs-lager') of which the most notorious was Auschwitz. Buchenwald was to start with in category 2, later category 1, and ended up as category 3, though all camps seemed to have an 'extra-territorial' legal status, that is life and death was at the whim of the SS and Gestapo. The Buchenwald camp was initially built, mostly by German political prisoners held in 'protective custody'. As soon as Hitler came to power in January 1933, the Gestapo was permitted by an 'emergency decree' to imprison for indefinite period, without a trial, persons deemed dangerous to the state.

Fig.2 *The symbolic 'Goethe Oak' in Buchenwald after it was bombed.*

The prisoners had to clear parts of the forest on the Ettersberg Mountain. Allegedly at the behest of the camp commander SS major Karl Koch, they spared the legendary 'Goethe Oak' as an island of culture in the sea of barbarity. Indeed, Goethe must have taken walks in that forest with Frau Charlotte von Stein discussing poetry, literature, and philosophical themes on humanities that left a lasting imprint on the culture of Germany and the world. The irony of retaining the semblance of culture of the most revered man in Germany in the midst of hell met its nemesis during an air-raid, through a direct hit of Goethe's Oak by the US Air Force, thus ending the charade of culture; perhaps Goethe screaming from his grave "not in my name". The pebbles on the tree stump (Fig. 2) suggest that Jews must have paid homage to Goethe, as it is the Jewish custom to place pebbles on Jewish graves, in memory of the destroyed Temple in Jerusalem. However, the stump of the 'Goethe Oak' acquired a symbolic link between the greatest German writer-poet with the ultimate barbarity. Weimar people rightly complain about visitors being preoccupied with Buchenwald, forgetting the local architects of this regrettable association, Wilhelm Frick and Fritz Sauckel. Indeed, the Weimar people benefitted economically from the trade and services provided for the SS personnel in the camp.

The camp commandant was SS Major Karl Koch, the first deputy commandant SS Major Artur Rödl (recipient of the Blood Order) and a second deputy commandant SS Captain Weissenhorn. They were previously prison guards and even the SS were amazed by the bestiality of the latter with graffiti "God in his scorn created SS captain Weissenhorn". A number of SS guards were exercising their power by inflicting maximum pain and suffering on the innocent victims. The living conditions were appalling; work lasted from morning light until twilight, the food was unfit for human consumption, hygiene facilities were minimal, and a great deal of any free time was taken up by several daily roll calls ('Apell').

The aim of this chapter is not to narrate the atrocities perpetrated by the Germans under the cover of a nationalist and racist ideology, with Himmler's delusion of the superior ancient Nordic race, the history of which was untraceable. The purpose is to highlight the utter divide between the classical culture of Weimar-Jena-Eisenach and the inhumanity of Buchenwald. It is also to emphasise the role of the university-educated, ostensibly the most highly principled medical men, whose standards fell well below the lowest common denominator, exercising their base emotions with the encouragement and connivance of their superiors.

Fig. 3 *Gate into the Buchenwald concentration camp, with the notice 'Arbeit macht frei' (Work sets you free) and the author*

A total of about a quarter million individuals passed through the infamous gates of the camp with the welcoming motto, 'My country right or wrong!' ('Recht Oder Unrecht mein Vaterland!'). That Fichte or Hegel in the neighbouring Jena might have approved, probably in theory only. The bars of the gate had inscribed another warning citation, 'To each his own due' ('Jedem das Seine'), cited among others by Tacitus, at times describing the Germans in unflattering terms. The brutal SS welcoming party for the unfortunate individuals at the camp gate, was from the very start determined to break the will and dehumanize them. Goethe's prescience is clearly seen when on one of his walks through the Ettersberg woods, as they were known in his time, he dictated to Johann P. Eckermann his poem 'Freedom is a wonderful thing'. The early intake of mostly German political and Jewish prisoners, was followed by every nationality occupied by German forces and especially their Jewish inhabitants. A rough division of the inmates can be made according to their treatment by the SS hierarchy. (1) The prevailing harsh treatment was meted out generally to the political, criminal, antisocial, homosexual prisoners, and Jehovah's Witnesses. (2) Jews were singled out for the worst treatment in the kind of work schedule, food and living conditions, with the object of extermination. (3) Liquidation of Russian prisoners of war. The total number of Russians killed in Buchenwald was between 7000 and 9500 men. (4) Prominent personalities were isolated from the other inmates and their treatment was significantly better.

The plenipotentiary of categorical evil was the head of the SS supermen, Heinrich Himmler who ordered the following notice to be displayed in the camp. "There is one path to freedom. Its milestones are called obedience, industry, honesty, order, discipline, cleanliness, sobriety, willingness to sacrifice, and love of the fatherland". In Buchenwald, indeed as in other camps, Himmler's advice was the path to the crematorium, after which the anguished souls gained freedom and catharsis from Himmler's unsolicited advice.

In 1938, Ernst vom Rath, a German Embassy secretary, was assassinated in Paris by a young Pole, Herschel Grynszpan, whose parents were killed by the Germans. The reprisal on 'Kristallnacht' ('the night of broken glass'), with attacks on synagogues took place throughout Germany. Over 10,000 German Jews were arrested and sent to Buchenwald, where sixty-eight were beaten to death by the SS. They packed 2000 persons, in each Block, with a normal capacity of 400 to at most 500 people, with complete breakdown of the sanitary conditions. SS sergeants pushed people's heads into overflowing toilet bowls until they drowned. In a few weeks, hundreds of these 'action Jews' had died. Later, most of them were released – after the SS and some of the prisoners robbed them of all their money and jewellery.

Bruno Bettelheim, an Austrian child psychoanalyst was a prisoner at Buchenwald during this period. He published one of the first scholarly articles on the concentration camp. The next action against the Jews followed after the assassination attempt against Hitler in the 'Bürgerbräukeller' in 1939. Jews were seized at random (three men from each of the seven Jewish blocks) and shot. All the others were locked in darkened blocks for three days without any food. In October 1942, Jews began to be transported out of Buchenwald to death camps and that lasted until summer 1943. Up to 200 Jews who passed themselves off as skilled construction workers (among them lawyers, authors, doctors, and artists) were held back by the camp administration. The number of Jews in the camp rose again for the first time towards the middle of 1944, because of a large number of new prisoners from Hungary.

In the narrative of The Buchenwald Report: "To fall sick in the concentration camp was a catastrophe from the outset. And when they were torn from their normal living situations and suddenly plunged into this vale of misery, with all its horrible concomitant circumstances, thousands fell ill. At any moment sickness could result in a death sentence, coming from the person who for the rest of the world brought cure to the sickbed: the physician!" The infirmary called 'Revier' was a place associated with fear of the whim of the SS 'doctors' who despised the dirty business of treating inmates. The medical administration was under the command of the Waffen SS Weimar doctor under who was the camp doctor. The entire network of concentration camps was directed by SS colonel Dr. Enno Lolling. Subordinate medical corps worked under the instructions of the camp doctors and the most notorious was 60-year old master sergeant Friedrich Wilhelm, whose duty was to administer lethal injections. Of at least eight camp doctors, SS Lieutenant Colonel Dr. Werner Kirchert and SS First Lieutenant Dr. Hans Eisele excelled themselves with the worst mistreatment that neither Hippocrates nor presumably the German or Austrian Medical Schools could have foreseen. Fortunately, the shortage of SS doctors led to the employment of prisoner's doctors of whom there was a surplus of Jewish doctors. By 1945, there were 70 prisoner doctors of all nationalities. Outpatient care was performed by prisoners and the most commonly applied Pharmaceutical Formulary was "above the navel aspirin, below the navel castor oil". The estimated death rate was an average of 7,300 per year, and as the population was less than 10,000 up to 1943, the "camp would have been a pile of corpses", unless the SS had ensured continuous delivery of new prisoners, which was achieved through their efficiency.

Dental treatment was directed by SS oral surgeons and dentists and the work performed by trained prisoners. With some exceptions, the dental care was reasonable, but all the decisions were taken by the SS dentist and the patient was not allowed to protest, even when a healthy tooth was removed. The ever watchful Reichführer SS Himmler decreed that any gold teeth or fillings of dead prisoners should be removed, as well as those from healthy people which were not repairable. The camp Commandant Koch utilized some of this gold for his own benefit.

From 1943, the prison population increased to 86,000 of innocent human beings, and the death toll increased as the camp accommodation and sewage system was designed only for 20,000 people. Corpses of prisoners were disposed of in the crematoria in Weimar and Jena until 1940, and no doubt the civilian population was aware of the increasing traffic utilising these facilities. By 1941, Buchenwald built its own large ovens with big chimneys and an adjacent morgue, autopsy room, and rooms for personnel, to cope with the enormous demand of mass murder. The knowledge, indeed connivance of the Weimar civil population of the conditions in Buchenwald, will be referred to later.

The infirmary was also used for grossly unethical experiments on humans who acted as guinea pigs, without any human rights. Vivisection was performed by Dr. Hans Eisele, graduate of Freiburg Medical School, with only a single surviving individual. Dr. Wagner studied tattooing, which also fascinated Commandant Koch and his wife. The best examples of tattooed skin of inmates were then prepared for "artistic" displays in the pathology department and admired by SS visitors. Koch had a table lamp made from human bones, stretched over with tattooed human skin. Hundreds of tattooed human skins were sent by order to SS Colonel Dr. Enno Lolling for his aesthetic appreciation.

II. MEDICAL EXPERIMENTAL ATROCITIES AND ADVANCES IN KILLING TECHNOLOGY

The greatest medical atrocities were perpetrated in the "Isolation Block 46" from 1941 to 1944 by SS Major Dr. Erwin Ding-Schuler with the expressed approval of the medical establishment of the German army; the general staff chief doctor Lieutenant General Dr. Siegfried Handloser trained at the Kaiser Wilhelm Academy for Military Medicine, the Reich Health leader SS Lieutenant General Dr., Leonard Conti, with involvement of Professor Hans C J Reiter qualified in Tübingen, Eugen Gildemeister, graduate of the Universities of Greifswald and Breslau and Dr. Joachim Mrugowsky of the Halle Medical School. The diary entry on the findings of the clinic stated, "Since animal experiments do not permit sufficient evaluation of the typhus immunization, experiments must be carried out on humans."

Experiments were made on hundreds of inmates to test the efficacy of "vaccines" against typhus, yellow fever, smallpox, paratyphoid, cholera, and diphtheria. They also experimented with materials for chemical warfare and other poisons. This amoral offer by the SS was taken up with alacrity by the major German pharmaceutical firms, who were prepared to set aside the ethical code of human experimentation. Among the firms lacking moral scruples were I.G. Farben, Höchst, Behringwerke, all of which collaborated with SS Brigadier General Professor Joachim Mrugowsky, director of the Hygiene Institute of the Berlin Waffen SS. Altogether, 158 people died from a cohort of about 450 and this does not include those deliberately infected with the highly contagious blood from typhus patients, serving as hosts to keep the bacteria alive. These were attending the centre almost monthly for the purpose of 'passage' of the organisms, and most of them eventually died. The lucky ones who survived these extreme human experiments were damaged for life, with heart trouble, paralysis, loss of memory, and other problems.

To recount the gruesome punishments that the prisoners had to undergo at the hands of German 'supermen' is an insult to decent German men and women and hurts the conscience of Western Civilization. However, Buchenwald has excelled in its ingenuity for murder, in maximizing the efficiency of techniques of killing to unprecedented heights. Murder by starvation and work under atrocious conditions was a 'passive' method of getting rid of the undesirable individuals. Clubbing a person to death was practised only when by mischance a person on the way to the crematorium, believed to have been killed, gets up among a pile of dead people. Hanging people by the neck needed individual attention and some of the emaciated bodies, especially of children, had insufficient body weight for gravity to pull them down and needed assistance by the ever helpful SS men. Shooting people one by one was equally inefficient when the objective was to go for mass murder. It also had an adverse psychological effect on some of the more tender hearts among the SS men, well recognized even by Himmler who shied away at executions, probably afraid to be contaminated by splattered brain fragments. Gassing was not yet developed, but Buchenwald was not designated as an extermination centre. Faced with a technical problem of murdering between 7000 and 9500 Russian prisoners of war, they refined the method by ushering groups of six men to small shower rooms with sound-proof walls; the door had a slit and the SS shot the men with an automatic pistol. This procedure enabled the slaughter of 500 prisoners of war from 9.0pm to 5.0am, with the Geneva Convention of conduct of Prisoners of War ignored in the extra-territorial universe of the concentration camp.

Another deception exercised by Himmler's gallant gentlemen serving the German Volk was by 'Genickschuss', shooting through the base of the skull. On the pretext of measuring the victim's height, an ingenious device propelled a firing pin at the measuring stand. Thus, an inanimate third party delivered the 'coup de gras', but on occasions, the machine malfunctioned and the SS man administered a 'mercy blow' with a club, which directly smashed the skull. Commando 99 was responsible for these sophisticated murders and all members were rewarded by the Military Service Cross. Finally, medicalised murder was meted out to some individuals by 'Abspritzen' or lethal injection, using barbiturates. 'Special treatment' (Sonderbehandlung) became a code word for murder, particularly of Jews. Nazi jargon for torture and murder were described by Joseph Wulf 'Aus dem Lexikon der Mörder' (From the Lexikon of Murder, 1963). Despite all the contrived methods of killing, they still could not cope adequately with the number ordained to meet their maker and these people were transported to Auschwitz, the ultimate sophisticated German centre of mass extermination by gassing using Zyklon B. Thus, Reichführer SS Heinrich Himmler will be remembered as the icon of evil in the annals of Western civilization, a latter-day Genghis Khan, yet functioning in the midst of one of the most cultured people of Europe in the years 1937-1945 of *Ano Domini*. The legacy of Himmler's perverted, target-orientated reasoning shows that there are no limits of men's inhumanity to men, irrespective of their cultural attainments.

Fig. 5 *Crematorium in Buchenwald concentration camp, with multiple ovens (Author)*

There were, however a few exceptionally decent individuals that demonstrated empathy and goodwill, despite the dehumanizing effect on the enslaved inmates. An SS doctor who chose to serve on the eastern front rather than the camp's annihilation machine. An SS corporal smuggled mail out for the prisoners. Some SS gave prisoners timely tips about forthcoming 'selections', saving lives. A number of nameless Catholic clerics, Pastor Paul Schneider and Jehovah's Witnesses have taken courageous stands of conscience and many have suffered as a result and even lost their lives. These righteous men and women must always be honoured and remembered, as many were unsung martyrs of humanity and recognized by 'Yad Vashem' (The Holocaust Memorial) in Jerusalem

III PROMINENT PERSONALITIES

Hardly any nationality escaped being represented in Buchenwald, though by far the largest numbers were from Germany and the occupied countries under German forces, with a predominance of Jewish people. Mostly, the Europe-wide diligence of the German authorities is truly astonishing, some would claim credit to the efficiency of the individuals who had to identify, transport, and select the poor victims for life or death at the ramp of the camp. And all this whilst fighting a heroic war on two fronts for the glory of the Thousand Year Reich.109, 121, 143, 168, 180, 241, 242, 245, 261, 387, 401, 402, 472, 473,

Nations Represented in Buchenwald

Germans, Austrians, French, Spanish, Italians, Swiss, Czechs, Yugoslavs, Croats, Albanians, Greeks, Bulgarians, Romanians, Poles, Russians, Belgians, Dutch, Luxemburg, Latvians, Lithuanians, Estonians, Danes, Norwegians, English, Americans, Mexicans, Brazilians, Chinese, Egyptians, Canadians, Africans

It is of interest that anti-fascist forces were formed among the inmates, of which the most organised were the German communists, accustomed to strict party discipline. Internal camp leadership was initially under the control of professional criminals, but the political camp inmates managed to take over control by exploiting the basic tendency of the SS towards corruption, despite Himmler's claim of the incorruptible, disciplined, SS supermen. They managed to persuade the SS to create a police force of inmates, which they allowed and that determined the conditions in the camp.

A large number of prominent politicians were imprisoned in Buchenwald, among whom only a few will be noted:

- Leon Blum – former French prime minister and his wife
- Paul Reynaud – former French prime minister
- Pierre Bloch –former French justice minister
- Kurt Schuschnigg – former Chancellor of Austria
- Konrad Adenauer – former Mayor of Cologne and first post-war Chancellor of Germany.

Among eminent writers, Elie Wiesel, Jean Amery, Jorge Semprún, and Imre Kertész were incarcerated in Buchenwald and some of their writings are presented in chapter. Elie Wiesel (1986) and Imre Kertész (2002) were each awarded the Nobel Prize for literature. Remarkably, Meir Lau, a seven-year-old child, became the future chief Rabbi of Israel. Dietrich Bonhoeffer, the well-known anti-Nazi Lutheran pastor, who called the 'Führer, Verführer' (misleader) was an active member of the anti-Hitler resistance movement. He was imprisoned by the Gestapo, moved to Buchenwald and executed in Flossenbürg, two weeks before liberation (see p. 380). Bruno Bettelheim, the Austrian-born American child psychiatrist, was imprisoned in Buchenwald in 1939 and then released after an amnesty. The fourteen-year-old Ben Helfgott was transported to Buchenwald and became the future captain of the British Olympic team in weight lifting.

Elie Wiesel, born in 1928 in Sighet, Romania, was a survivor of Auschwitz and Buchenwald concentration camps. As was the current practice in the shifting borders of that part of Romania, Wiesel and many other Jewish people, spoke Yiddish, Romanian, Hungarian, and German. Wiesel stated that reason came largely from his father and faith from his mother, both of whom perished in the Holocaust. Wiesel was liberated by the US Army in April 1945. It was Francois Mauriac the Nobel Laureate in Literature who persuaded Wiesel to write about his experiences, resulting in one of his most tragic and most likely recognised books. He first called the memoirs 'And the World Remained Silent' written in Yiddish and then re-wrote it abridged in French with the less poignant title 'Night' (La Nuit). It has now been translated into thirty languages and sold several million copies.

Jean Améry was born in 1912 to a Catholic mother and Jewish father in Vienna as Hans Chaim Meier. He was raised in the Roman Catholic faith, and studied philosophy and literature at the University of Vienna, but did not complete his studies. With the Nüremberg Laws passed in 1933-1935, Améry believed that Germany passed the death sentence on Jews. With the German 'Anschluss' (Annexation) of Austria, Améry fled to France and then to Belgium with his Jewish wife. He joined the resistance movement in Belgium, was captured and tortured by the Gestapo, and sent first to Auschwitz, then Buchenwald, and finally to Bergen Belsen, where he was liberated by the British army. After the war, he changed his name to Améry to dissociate himself from German culture. He wrote about his experiences of torture by the Gestapo and the German death camps about twenty years after liberation in a book entitled 'Jenseits von Schuld und Sühne' (Beyond

Guilt and Atonement), which was later translated into English 'At the Mind Limits: Contemplation by a Survivor of Auschwitz and its Realities'.

Jorge Semprún was born in 1923 into a Spanish bourgeois political family. Indeed, his grandfather served as Prime Minister to King Alfonso XIII. His mother died when he was seven, and at the outbreak of the Spanish Civil War, his father was appointed ambassador for the Spanish Republic to the Netherlands. With Franco's victory, the family moved to France where Semprún studied philosophy at the Sorbonne. During German occupation of France, he joined the Communist Revolutionary movement in 1942 and was arrested by the Gestapo in 1943. He was sent to Buchenwald concentration camp, losing his identity as prisoner No. 440.409.

Israel Meir Lau was a seven-year-old Polish Jewish boy, who was nicknamed 'Lulek' in Buchenwald. His history is unique as he survived Buchenwald at a tender age by his brother bribing the German warden with a gold watch, so as to ignore his presence. He lost both his parents during the Holocaust, left for Palestine at the age of eight with his older brother who also survived. In the midst of the horrors of the camp was Feodor, a Russian prisoner of war, whose humanity broke through the hell of camp existence. At considerable risk, Feodor looked after Lulek, he was his guardian angel and probably saved his life. Lau refers to the vicissitudes of his life experience as a time of ten miracles (Mishpacha Magazine 2006). Israel Meir Lau, the eight-year-old survivor of Germans' attempts to dehumanise the child, became the Chief Rabbi of the State of Israel. 'The Children of Buchenwald', by Judith Hemmendinger and Robert Krell (2000), describes the post-war lives of some of the children, and Lau gives a poignant account of his experience. "I was born twice, first biologically in June 1937 in Piotrków, and then spiritually upon my arrival in the Holy Land on July 17, 1945, the day of Tisha B'Av. I was eight years old then. I speak of a second birth because it is hard to conceive that after experiencing Buchenwald, the long marches, the hiding and the cold, that such a little orphan could become a little boy wearing blue and white shorts, playing soccer and marbles. I had walked among the dead and had helped push carts piled high with corpses to the crematoria. And yet, the same little boy had learned to sing again and to recite the alphabet. Could I actually be the same person?"

Lau excelled in Jewish studies at Talmudic colleges and in due course wanted to marry and bring up a family. He met the daughter of Rabbi Yitzchak Yedidya Frankel the Chief Rabbi of Tel-Aviv. However, the time-honoured custom was for the father to make the request on behalf of his son, but he was an orphan. He was unsuccessful in arranging to meet the father of the girl he met secretly, but in the end, the father agreed to see him and spoke to him. "After three sons, God blessed us with a girl. My wife and I love her dearly. I was told that you are a very talented student, but I must be honest with you and will explain the reasons why I hesitated to give my only daughter to a man who is alone in the world, who never had a family life and does not remember his parents. How can such a man raise a family? Will he make our daughter happy? I would like to cite a verse of the Torah: For this (marriage), a man will leave his father and mother, (Genesis II, 24). I believe that because of her education, our daughter has what is needed to create the basis for a solid and genuine Jewish family, and I trust you to make her happy. From that day on my life has been different. I am received like a son in the rabbi's family and my wife and I now have eight children". Rabbi Lau's three sons and five sons-in-law became rabbis in Israel, some running large Talmudic colleges in memory of their grandfathers all who were murdered by the Germans. Their commitment to the God is steadfast, absolute, and perpetuates the Jewish tradition.

Imre Kertész was a Hungarian writer born in 1929 of an assimilated Jewish family. He was imprisoned and transported to Buchenwald at the age of fifteen. He survived the camp, and after returning to Budapest, he worked as a journalist and playwright before turning to writing novels. His masterpiece "Fatelessness" describes a Jewish boy of fifteen in Budapest, who is puzzled to find himself separated from his family on the way to Auschwitz and subsequently to Buchenwald. As a child, he seems to accept the atrocities witnessed as part of a strange reality devoid of sentiments of the 'concentration camp world'. The novel is likely to be based on Kertész's experience in the camps though the author does not admit it. Among a number of books, he wrote, 'Kaddish for an unborn child', about a man who could not bear to bring into the world a child, following the end of humanity he experienced in Auschwitz. In 2002 Kertész was awarded the Nobel Prize in literature. The Swedish Academy citation states, "In his writing Imre Kertész explores the possibility of continuing to live and think as an individual in an era in which the subjection of human beings to social forces has become increasingly complete. [He] upholds the fragile experience of the individual against the barbaric arbitrariness of history."

Ben Helfgott, a Polish Jew at the age of fourteen, was deported with his father to Buchenwald. He lost his father but survived after being transported to Theresienstadt concentration camp. After liberation, Ben returned to his home town to learn that his mother was shot and he was an orphan with a surviving sister. To his consternation, he was racially abused in his hometown by some Polish army officers. However, he was one of the lucky 'Boys' who were brought to England. Despite all the suffering of a child, he proved himself in weight lifting and captained the British Olympic weight lifting team in 1956 in Melbourne and 1960 in Rome. He is a happily married man with three sons and succeeded in business. Helfgott was awarded the MBE by the Queen and is the only known survivor of German concentration camps to compete in the Olympic Games. It proves the indestructible tenacity of human nature over adversity. Ben Helfgott had the immense satisfaction that he was able to repay, in a unique way, the welcome and opportunities he received in England.

IV. LIBERATION OF THE BUCHENWALD CONCENTRATION CAMP

The high point in the life of the surviving prisoners was when American troops entered the camp. The event really deserves a full description, but here I will confine the narrative to the words of General Eisenhower and Prime Minister Churchill and their associates.

On April 13, less than forty-eight hours after its liberation, Eisenhower, along with Bradley and Patton, toured Buchenwald camp. That evening in Marburg he discussed Ohrdruf, Buchenwald, and Nordhausen-Dora with Hodges and Bradley in the presence of his son, Captain John Eisenhower. "The only speck of optimism I can see," he said, "that I really don't think that the bulk of the Germans knew what was going on." After relating that Patton had told him that the mayor of Gotha and his wife had committed suicide after seeing Ohrdruf, he added, "Maybe there is hope after all." Captain John Eisenhower left by jeep the next day to make his own visit to Weimar and Buchenwald. Eisenhower was still so disturbed by what he had seen that the atrocities again became the major topic of conversation when he met Prime Minister Churchill in London a few days later. Eisenhower spent a long evening with Churchill discussing the state of the war and visited him the next morning at the annex to 10 Downing Street (the War Rooms). Eisenhower promised to send photos of the camps to Churchill, who apparently shared his outrage. He urged Churchill to send a group of members of Parliament and journalists to tour the camps at once. An American delegation, Eisenhower feared, "might be too late to see the full horrors, whereas an English delegation, being so much closer, could get there on time." On April 19, General Walter Bedell Smith relayed a report to Churchill through Lord Ismay that "the German concentration camps which have recently been overrun by the Allied armies are even indescribably more horrible than those about which General Eisenhower spoke to you yesterday." With fresh reports appearing about British discoveries at Bergen-Belsen liberated on April 15, all London was talking about German atrocities. John Carlisle, Churchill's private secretary, wrote in his diary, "The papers are full of [reports], with stomach-turning photographs, consequent on the Allied armies overrunning Buchenwald and other German concentration camps. Proof is now supplied that the stories of the last ten years have not been just propaganda. On the day after Eisenhower's visit, April 19, Churchill delivered a short but moving speech to Parliament in reply to a member's question. E. P. Smith had asked whether steps would be taken to maintain 'the captured prison camp of Buchenwald as a memorial to German methods.' Although refusing to commit himself to specific steps, Churchill stated: 'No words can express the horror which is felt by His Majesty's Government at the proofs of these frightful crimes now daily coming into view. I have this morning received an informal message from General Eisenhower saying that the new discoveries, particularly at Weimar, far surpass anything previously exposed. He invites me to send a body of Members of Parliament at once to his Headquarters in order that they may themselves have ocular and first-hand proof of these atrocities.'"

Calling the matter one of "urgency", he arranged for the appointment to a special team of ten members of Parliament 'for this extremely unpleasant but none the less necessary duty' of investigating the camp. A carefully balanced delegation of four Conservatives, three Labour members, one Liberal, one Liberal National, and one Independent left London, within twenty-four hours. Among them were one woman and one Jewish member; two of the ten were from the House of Lords. The delegation arrived at Eisenhower's SHAEF Headquarters in Reims the evening of April 20. The next morning, the group flew on military Dakotas into Weimar and reached Buchenwald at 11 A.M. on Saturday, April 21, just ten days after liberation. The committee's brief, factual report, published by His Majesty's Stationery office in May 1945, concluded, "That a policy of steady starvation and inhuman brutality was carried out at Buchenwald for a long period of time; and that such camps as this mark the lowest point of degradation to which humanity has yet descended. The memory of what we saw and heard at Buchenwald will haunt us ineffaceably for many years."

Meanwhile, on April 19, Eisenhower also cabled Marshall in Washington to arrange a visit of a U.S. congressional delegation. In his telegram he stated: "We continue to uncover German concentration camps for political prisoners in which conditions of indescribable horror prevail. I have visited one of these myself and I assure you that whatever has been printed on them to date has been understatement. If you would see any advantage in asking about a dozen leaders of Congress and a dozen prominent editors to make a short visit to this theatre in a couple of C-54's, I will arrange to have them conducted to one of these places where the evidence of bestiality and cruelty is so overpowering as to leave no doubt in their minds about the normal practice of the Germans in these camps."

At the liberation of Buchenwald American soldiers were horrified to find thousands of wretched-looking men. To their total astonishment they also found about 900 children, all Jewish boys from the age of eight onwards. It appears that the most painful experience was the separation from their mothers. They faced their fate with total incomprehension, some acquiescing with the situation, others pledging to fight the perpetrators of their fate. Surprisingly, there is very limited information available about their life and survival in Buchenwald. For many or most of them, Buchenwald was their second camp as they had already experienced all the horrors of Auschwitz. They were malnourished and the misplaced kindness of the American military who provided high-calorie food resulted in many deaths. Most of them lost their parents, and an appeal was made to countries to take in the orphans. Indeed, France accepted 480, Switzerland 280, and England 250 children. Their physical convalescence was fairly rapid, but the psychological effects were often long lasting. However, after they were resettled in various countries, many had distinguished careers – including Bruno Bettelheim and the many cited in Martin Gilbert's book 'The Boys: Triumph over Adversity'. Elie Wiesel and Imre Kertész were awarded the Nobel Prize for literature and Israel Lau became the Chief Rabbi of Israel.

On that occasion, a poignant, personal point was made by Rabbi Meir Lau in his book 'Out of the Depth'. "After the liberation, General Patton decided to invite the residents of Weimar to the camp, insisting that they view the horrors with their own eyes. I was wandering around the camp, free and fearless, when I saw the Weimar residents, mostly women and elderly men. Suddenly, a command car stopped next to me, and a giant American soldier lifted me. Gripping my heels in one hand and my shoulder with the other hand, he raised me high in the air, and shouted in German to the Weimar residents: "Do you see this little boy? This is who you have been fighting for the past six years. Because of him you started a world war. He is the enemy of National Socialism, the Nazis' archenemy. A little Polish boy! You murdered his father and mother, and you almost murdered him as well! You followed the Führer – for this? You followed him in blind faith – for this?!' He spoke on behalf of me, my parents, and indeed the entire Jewish people."

These words are reminiscent of Yevgeny Yevtushenko's reaction after visiting the 'Babi Yar' Nazi massacre in the suburb of Kiev.

"And I myself am one massive, soundless scream
Above the thousand thousand buried here

I am each old man here shot dead. I am every child here shot dead
Nothing in me shall ever forget!
The 'Internationale,' let it thunder
When the last anti-Semite on earth is buried forever."

Dmitri Shostakovich was so touched that he wrote his 13th symphony to the poem.

The Buchenwald concentration camp atrocities hit the Weimar inhabitants after the camp was liberated by the US forces. The good people of Weimar were obliged to visit the camp three days after it was liberated. They were astonished by the hell they found at the doorsteps of their rightly beloved 'Kulturstadt'. They denied any knowledge of what was happening in the camp. And the insouciant Burghers of Weimar bemoaned: 'we did not know, we were not told. We did not ask, we minded our own business.'

At the following Sunday service at the Evangelical Church, the Weimar 'Superintendent' Kade delivered during his sermon a response or interpretation of the activities the inhabitants discovered in the camp, of which they were totally unaware. He and the people of Weimar condemned these activities, sadism and torture that led to the death of these people. He stated that this was possible only because of 'Geisteshaltung', which broke away from Christianity and under which the Church suffered. So they can admit before God that they do not share any blame for these atrocities. A defence of the 'Innocent Bystanders'.

The newly elected mayor of the town, Fritz Behr, Superintendent Kade, the Roman-Catholic deacon, Breitung, and the Director of the Goethe National Museum, Hans Wahl, wrote a letter to the American Military Governor concerning Weimar and the Buchenwald camp. They appealed to the world's sense of justice that the 'Kulturstadt' Weimar does not deserve to be besmirched with the stain of Buchenwald. Evidently, the reputation of Weimar was at stake, as the inhabitants were accused of knowing what was happening in Buchenwald and keeping quiet, thereby sharing moral responsibility. Whereas they were right in protecting the classical reputation of the giants of German culture, they cannot claim the status of innocent bystanders of the depth of depravity their countrymen practised at their doorsteps. Their knowledge, and economic benefit has been amply documented by Jens Schley in business, transport, publishing, pharmaceuticals, butchers, bakers, grocers, and all requirements of the SS. The heavy traffic from the camp to the crematorium had not been lost on the Weimar public and became the subject of endless talk when on an occasion the dead bodies fell out from their wooden boxes on the way to the crematorium.

As the prisoner Rolf Weinstock wrote in his reminiscences of the informal visit by the Weimar inhabitants of the camp in April 1945: "Repeatedly they asked the question, facing each other. How could such a thing happen within a few kilometres from Weimar?" Despite the question being repeated over the years, it still remains an open question to this day. The Nobel Prize winner in literature, Imre Kertész, who was enslaved in Buchenwald during the last year of the war, wrote years later "that the Weimar burghers at the visit of the camp indicated with their hands and feet to the American officers that they did not know anything about the camp. During the eight years of the camp's existence, they must have seen the prisoners daily on the way to their forced labour, they could see their wretched appearance, so they must have known it all, but simply opted not to acknowledge the uncomfortable truth."

Jens Schley concludes in his book, 'Buchenwald neighbours' (1999), supervised by Professor Ludolf Herbit, "Without the collaboration of the majority of inhabitants of Weimar, Buchenwald, as all other concentration camps could not have existed for any length of time". Eugen Kogon, an Austrian diplomat, imprisoned in Buchenwald, wrote after the war, 'The Theory and Practice of Hell', "Thus arose a new link between Weimar and Buchenwald. On the one hand a well-nurtured culture, and on the other an unlimited brutal power. Weimar and Buchenwald were two neighbours that differed in nature and meaning, both were used to enforce National Socialism over the entire society". Indeed, barbarism and classical culture, Buchenwald and Weimar were unlikely partners, yet partners they were. The cultural legacy of the Nazi regime has been expressed by some Germans, "Between us and Goethe lies Buchenwald", yet another nail in the ideology of the Supermen from Austria.

A trial of the Buchenwald staff and Frau Ilse Koch took place before a U.S. Military tribunal at Dachau in 1947. Thirty-one members of the staff of the Buchenwald camp were found guilty of atrocities and twenty-two were sentenced to death, eight being subsequently commuted, the rest to various terms of imprisonment. Twelve of the defendants were executed.

CHAPTER 4: UNIVERSITY OF HEIDELBERG

I. **Brief history of the University**
II. **Heidelberg University during National Socialism**
III. **Academics who did not support National Socialism**
IV. **Joseph Goebbels, PhD student at the university**
V. **Philipp Lenard, Nobel Prize winner who later discovered**
VI. **'Racial fission'**
VII. **Martin Heidegger, the renowned philosopher but flawed human being**
VIII. **Are the narratives of Jena and Heidelberg representative of other German universities?**

UNIVERSITY OF HEIDELBERG

"A strong wave of nationalism swept in the early 20th century and the 'Heidelberg Spirit' mutated into 'Heidelberg Myth" *Paraphrased from, Stephen Remy, 2002*
'The whole function of education is to create Nazis' *Bernhard Rust, Reich education Ministry, 1934*
'Einstein's Jewish Physics is the Jewish Fraud of relativity' *Professor Philipp Lenard, 1933*
'Freedom and liberal education is the right of all citizens, combining University teaching with research.' *The guiding spirit of education of Wilhelm von Humboldt 1767-1835*
'At the 50th anniversary of Heidelberg University in 1936, the Journal Nature published: "Heidelberg; Spinoza and Academic Freedom", whilst Spinoza, the Jewish philosopher was invited to the chair in philosophy in 1673 this would be impossible in 1936 under the Nazi treatment of scientists of Jewish descent' *Journal Nature 1936*

'Professor Alexander Mitscherlich published the horrific medical experiments disclosed at the Nüremberg Trial against Nazi physicians in his book 'Medicine without humanity' (1960). He was ostracised by senior medical establishment and later dismissed from the Chair in Psychology.'

Author

I. BRIEF HISTORY OF THE UNIVERSITY

Universities in Europe have largely evolved from a religious order. In addition to theology, they taught philosophy, logic, and Latin and Greek classics. The pride of place of these early centres of learning were the Italian Universities in the 13th century (Padua, Naples, Siena, and Bologna) and almost simultaneously or followed by French, Portuguese, Czech-German, and Polish Universities. Among these, Heidelberg was the oldest of the twenty-three Universities in Germany and three in Austria. Established in 1306, by permission of Pope Urban VI to create a school of general studies. Papal approval was necessary to ensure recognition of a University degree throughout Christendom. The University was founded by 'Rupert I Count Palatine of the Rhine', between the Neckar, a tributary of the river Rhine, and the wooded mountain with the ruins of the castle, giving the place a tranquil, romantic feeling. Initially, the University consisted of four faculties; theology, philosophy, jurisprudence, and medicine and later natural sciences, followed by social sciences.

Generally, the prevailing religion of the time influenced Heidelberg University, starting with Roman Catholicism (1386-1556), followed by the reformation brought forth by Martin Luther in the 16th century, when it became a Protestant University. The counter-reformation brought in by the Jesuits turned it again into a Catholic University. By the late 18th and 19th century, liberalism prevailed and the University developed into a cultural and academic centre of excellence (1803-1933). Despite the religious upheavals, the University evolved in the spirit of liberty and tolerance, best illustrated by the invitation in 1673 of Baruch du Spinoza, an excommunicated Jew, considered by the Church as a most dangerous atheist, to the professorship in Philosophy, which he declined. Indeed, as early as 1652, the University appointed Jacob Israel as Professor of Medicine and he became the first Jewish Rector of the University, arguably an unprecedented situation for its time in any other University. The liberal attitude of scholarship must have been maintained up to the 20th century, with the appointment of the eminent German Jewish philosopher Emil Lask to a full professorship in 1913. He left an enduring legacy on the synthesis of Greek with Kantian philosophy and the logic of philosophy.

Among the famous alumni of the University were the composer Robert Schumann, philosopher Ludwig Feuerbach, writer Somerset Maugham, psychologist Wilhelm Wundt, discoverer of the periodic table of chemical elements Dimitri Mendeleev, and political philosopher Hannah Arendt. Among its professors were the philosophers Friedrich G. W. Hegel, Emil Lask, and Karl Jaspers, the scientists Hermann von Helmholtz, Gustav R. Kirchhoff, and Robert W. Bunsen, and the social scientist Max Weber. Another measure of status of the University is that nine scientists were awarded the Nobel Prize during their tenure at Heidelberg, whilst thirty Nobel Laureates were associated with the University. As the objective of the brief description of this most prestigious University is to compare it with the University of Jena during the National Socialist era, the overall intellectual contributions of the above eminent individuals will not be discussed.

During the Weimar Republic after the First World War in 1919 up to 1933 when Adolf Hitler was appointed Chancellor of Germany, Heidelberg University had a reputation as a stronghold of liberalism, the republic's model University and referred to by some as the 'Heidelberg Spirit'. However, a strong wave of nationalism swept in the late 19th and early 20th century and the 'Heidelberg Spirit' mutated into the 'Heidelberg Myth'.

The irony of Heidelberg University's existence is that it was first erected on the site of Jewish quarters from which the Jews were evicted, their land expropriated and the University established. The site was very near the present day Church of the Holy Spirit and the University was partly financed from the proceeds of the seized real estate. With some interruptions due to wars and the plague, the University prospered and developed an international reputation for learning. Its pride of place was the great library, which fell victim to the 30 Year War, when Pope Gregory XV 'persuaded' the Emperor and Maximilian I to transfer to Rome the valuable contents from the library. These included about 2800 Latin, Greek, Oriental, and German manuscripts, and 5000 books were removed in 1622 and only thirty-eight were returned to Heidelberg two centuries later. Losing the library, in Detlef Junker's words, is tantamount to 'losing the university's memory'. Worse was to come when about seventy years later, Louis XIV laid claim to the whole of the Palatinate and the French troops destroyed the city, including the University with its library.

The Weimar Republic lasted fourteen years, and it was plagued with the depression, economic hardship, devaluation with loss of money by the middle classes, and political unrest of the nationalists caused by signing the Locarno treaty. The left wing revolt, and general distrust of the imposed democracy, lead to calls for the old, trusted 'strong man' leadership. All this was reflected in the University by a decline in liberal forces and the anti-republican, nationalist, and anti-Semitic professors, as well as junior instructors gaining strength. Jewish and socialist professors were harassed by nationalist professors and radical students. By 1932, the eminent statistician and socialist Emil Gumbel, a Jew, recorded the violence committed by both the right and left, with the judiciary demonstrating leniency towards the former. The controversy resulted in Gumbel being dismissed and this marked the end of liberal Heidelberg and start of the third Reich at the Heidelberg University. A novel subject, 'racial science', emerged, with the objective of creating a racially pure Germany, resulting in dismissing all Jewish Professors, staff, and remaining students after 1933. The regime defined 'German Spirit' in scholarship in opposition to the 'Jewish Spirit', claiming that only Aryan scientists were capable of understanding nature.

II. HEIDELBERG UNIVERSITY DURING NATIONAL SOCIALISM (1933-1945)

With the advent of National Socialist takeover of Germany, by gaining majority in the Reichstag with 37% voting for the party, the old President Paul von Hindenburg appointed Adolf Hitler Chancellor of Germany on the 29th January 1933. The first direct effect was to subordinate public life to the authority of the new regime by passing the 'Law of the Restoration of the Professional Civil Service' known as coordination (Gleichschaltung). The Universities belonged to the civil service and the doctrines of Nazi policy were enacted. The party proceeded to control the University partly through the Reich Education Ministry (REM) of which the head was Bernhard Rust, who stated among other pronouncements "The whole function of education is to create Nazis". Thus, a Nazi University was created with the 'Instructors League' (Dozentenbund), to which about half of all the professors belonged. The 'Führer principle' was imposed by the Rector of the University, following the example of Martin Heidegger, recently elected Rector of Freiburg University. However, the Nazis had little regard for intellectuals and considered Universities as institutions, which should propagate the Nazi Aryan ideal of the 'Volk'. Wilhelm Groh, a legal scholar, was elected Rector of the University in 1933, resulting in dismissal of a third of the staff, among them forty-nine Jews for political but mostly racial reasons. These were filled with Nazis or their sympathizers, which probably sums up the Rector's academic contribution to the law faculty. It is of considerable interest that the influence exerted by the student body imbued with radical nationalism and anti-Semitic doctrine, were at the vanguard of agitation in removing non-Aryan and Marxist professors. They were led by Gustav A. Scheel, disrupting and boycotting lectures delivered by 'unacceptable' Professors, burning books in the University square, and playing an active role in the faculty purges.

The professorship accepted the dismissal of their Jewish colleagues in almost total silence, as was the case throughout German Universities. In Heidelberg, the general notion was that there were too many Jews among the University staff and there was no collective protest by professors against the draconian Nazi party's policies. However, the honourable exception was the Medical Faculty's appeal to the Ministry of Culture on behalf of Jewish scholars, arguing that Jews made substantial contributions to Medicine and it would be a great loss if they were to be removed from the

University. The professors could be divided into two ill-defined groups: (1) those that accepted the status quo, continued their scholarly pursuits, and acted as 'innocent bystanders'. (2) Supporters of the new regime, with long- or short-term membership of the Nazi party.

Among the fascists was the professor of theoretical physics Philipp Lenard, born in Bratislava (formerly Pressburg of the Austro-Hungarian Empire), now the capital of Slovakia. He was an assistant to the professor of physics, Heinrich R. Hertz, investigating cathode rays, for which Lenard was awarded the Nobel Prize. Lenard became an ardent nationalist and anti-Semite, denounced Einstein's theory of relativity, claimed that all great investigators were exclusively of Aryan-Germanic origin, and that scholarship is conditioned by race and blood. Indeed, he espoused the notion of 'Aryan physics', among the many followers of whom was Johannes Stark, another Nobel Prize winner in physics. Indeed, the Heidelberg Physics Institute was renamed in 1935 as the Philipp Lenard Institute.

Carl Schneider, professor of psychiatry, published highly regarded work on schizophrenia. He joined the Nazi party in 1932, became the chairman of the Medical Faculty in 1934 and the head of the Baden's Racial Policy Office. Several instructors were dismissed and Schneider replaced them with like-minded assistants, and later, he would promote a number of professors with strong Nazi and anti-Semitic views. He supported the new sterilization law of the mentally ill and advocated that psychiatrists should provide proof of health of every patient and that German doctors should secure the 'racial health' of the Volk. He identified in Hitler 'the teacher and advisor of Germans in all questions of people's health'. Schneider became one of the leading directors of the euthanasia programme (Action T4), resulting in the death of tens of thousands of mentally ill and handicapped people. According to Henry Friedlander, use of electric and insulin-induced shock provided the model experience and some personnel for the murder of Jews. Schneider taught on 'race and racial hygiene', and at the Heidelberg clinic, 285 sterilizations were carried out in 1934-1935, justified by the 'hereditary protection law'.

In the philosophy faculty, six professors were dismissed on racial grounds by Rector Groh who appointed pro-Nazi Hermann Güntert as faculty chairman, and Ernst Krieck to the chair of pedagogy and philosophy. The philosopher Karl Jaspers, who was not Jewish but his wife was, lost his position. Eugen Fehrle was appointed to a new chair in folklore, created for him in 1936, and later he served as chairman of the philosophy faculty. He joined the SS and became advisor in ideological instruction.

The faculty of theology suffered disruption. Its members did not join the NSDAP with the exception of its chairman, Robert Jelke, and was not involved in the conflict between the small Confessional Church and the large Nazi-supported German Christians. However, it was the only faculty to offer overtly anti-Semitic courses, such as 'The Jewish Question and World-Historical Problem'. When Theodor Odenwald replaced the previous chairman, he was an active member of the 'Institute for the Study and Eradication of Jewish Influence in German Church Life', based in Eisenach and Jena University.

The Law faculty dismissed about one third of its staff with eight professors, including Gustav Radbruch and Gerhard Anschütz who supported the republic and a law-based state. The majority, however, linked conservative views with Nazi ideology, rejecting the concept of individual rights protected by law, accepting the law excluding 'non-Germans' from civic life, which led to a stream of anti-Semitic laws. A number of legal scholars, such as Ernst Forsthoff and Eduard Wahl belonged to the NSDAP, SA, and the 'Dozentenbund', supported the Nazi legal system and yet after the war, became prominent members of the legal profession.

The University Rector wielded considerable power and was designated as the 'Führer' of the university. The first Rector (1933-34) was the historian Willy Andreas, a conservative nationalist, though he never belonged to any of the Nazi parties. He requested that the state formally confirm that it upheld the freedom of research and teaching. Yet he praised Hitler and declared that the time for academic intellectualism is over and knowledge will be translated into action. Accordingly, he was responsible for the first wave of dismissals. Wilhelm Groh (1934-1936) was a legal scholar who succeeded Andreas as Rector of the University. He taught that foreign ideas were incompatible with German nature and professors and teachers should toe the line of the National Socialist revolution. He even acted as an informer on Professor Jaspers who was Aryan but his wife was Jewish. He declared that the university should provide the shock troops for National Socialism.

Ernst Krieck (1937) was professor of pedagogy and philosophy and called for a radical overhaul of the university, with the total focus on the ideology of the state and uniting scholarship with politics. He requested the Ministry of Culture to erase the names of the American donors, some of whom were Jewish, from the new university building, and permission was granted. Krieck was appointed Dozentenbundführer of Baden and he advocated special indoctrination camps for young university instructors. He referred to England as “the vampire of the people, the exploitative initiator of all disorder and strife and all injustice in the world for 300 years”.

Paul Schmitthenner (1938-1945) replaced Jaspers and the chair was renamed as the professorship for military policy and science. For him, the university was a place of military and political education, and the nature of modern war was ‘total war’. He conducted seminars on expansion of Germany’s borders, first on the west and then the east borders. He was a high-ranking SS officer and strived to link the University to the party. Schmitthenner became the most powerful figure in academia in south-west Germany, being elected as Culture Minister of Baden. His anti-Semitism went as far as advising the removal of Jewish names from the war memorials. Even Hitler did not go along this route and the names of the war dead were not removed. According to Remy, Nazification was driven from below, involving most faculties of humanities and sciences, lending intellectual power for the Nazi regime.

Karl Heinrich Bauer was a capable surgeon who was appointed in December 1942 by Bernhard Rust to head the Heidelberg University surgical clinic. This was despite his wife coming from a mixed Aryan and non-Aryan marriage. However, Bauer had special ‘racial dispensation’ from Hitler, allowing him to serve as a surgeon to the army and having operated on several of Hitler’s generals; indeed, he was awarded the first class War Merit Cross. Bauer was an authority on ‘Racial Hygiene’, ranking races, and he became a supporter of the Nazi sterilization law in 1933, though he was not a Nazi and indeed could not join the Nazi party because of his marriage to a non-Aryan. He advocated a war of racial expansion, forced sterilization, and other measures of ‘racial protection’. Despite these activities, after the war he claimed that he rejected Nazism and developed a reputation of being an anti-Nazi. He became the most influential figure in 1945, working effectively to reopen the University in 1945 and indeed serving as its first post-war Rector. He was at the helm of protecting former Nazis and even excluding those with anti-Nazi credentials.

III. ACADEMICS WHO DID NOT SUPPORT THE NATIONAL SOCIALIST POLICIES

Whilst concerted opposition to the Nazi takeover did not exist, the legacy of Weimar liberalism and 'Heidelberg Spirit' was maintained by individuals of high moral, intellectual, and scholastic principles. Most of them were elderly individuals, educated during the Wilhelmine and Weimar period. Alfred Weber of the Institute for Social and Political Sciences pursued his brother, Max Weber's new discipline of sociology. He was consistently anti-Nazi by conviction and resisted the SA flying the swastika flag over his Institute for which he was pilloried in the press, leading to his resignation. Martin Dibelius, a highly regarded theologian both in Germany and abroad, was not a Nazi, though a nationalist, disillusioned with Weimar. He signed a petition in 1934, calling for the resignation of the 'Reich Bishop' Ludwig Müller, a former army chaplain appointed by Hitler as bishop of the German Protestant Church. However, he defended the Jewish Boycott in 1933 and advocated the need to solve the 'Jewish problem'. He was largely enthusiastic about Hitler's rise to power. Nonetheless, Dibelius's post-war career rose to becoming president of the Council of German Protestant Church and leader of the World Council of Churches.

Karl Jaspers, a highly regarded scholar and exponent of 'Existential Philosophy', failed to appreciate in 1933 the new regime's destructive nature. His wife was Jewish and he encountered serious difficulties with his colleagues and administration, though he was allowed to teach. However, Jaspers was dismissed in 1937 after a critical report by the Rector Ernst Krieck. Gustav Radbruch, a legal scholar and Minister of Justice in the Weimar government and then professor at Heidelberg University, was dismissed on political grounds. He was a supporter of the Weimar Republic and did not support the Nazi cause. Walter Jellinek was another legal scholar who initially appeared to support some of the ideas of the regime, and he belonged to the anti-republican faction of the law faculty. However, he was dismissed as he was defined as a Jew by the regime.

In common with all other German universities, there were no collective protests against the illiberal, anti-intellectual policies, or the dismissal of their erstwhile colleagues, mostly for religious (quasi-racial) reasons of the dictatorship of the regime. The student body at large played a dastardly role in pursuing Nazi policies, acting as a vanguard in hounding out professors and instructors they considered unsupportive of Hitler's policies; their venom was, especially directed against Jewish scholars.

The shining exception was Dr. Alexander Mitscherlich (1908-1982) who deserves special mention. He was a product of Weimar Republic's culture and modernity. The political violence of the Nazis repulsed Mitscherlich. He was first interested in history and the humanities, which he studied at the University of Munich from 1928. However, in 1933 he changed to studying Medicine at the University of Heidelberg. He was arrested by the Gestapo in 1937 and spent eight months in prison. Mitscherlich qualified in Medicine at the University of Heidelberg in 1941 and gained research experience in anthropology and psychotherapy, and then worked in the hospital as a neurologist. After the war, Mitscherlich was an observer at the Nuremberg Trials of Nazi physicians, who were found guilty of inhumane medical experiments perpetrated on the inmates of concentration camps. He published with Fred Mielke, in 1960, the first exposure of these experiments in the book entitled 'Medicine Without Humanity'. Mitscherlich established the clinic in psychosomatic medicine at the Heidelberg University in 1949, and later, in 1953, was promoted to the chair in this speciality. From 1966 to 1973 he was professor of psychology at the University of Frankfurt.

Mitscherlich was one of the few psychiatrists analysing the Holocaust, war crimes, and the lack of any sense of culpability and guilt by the German society in his book, 'The Inability to Mourn. Principles of Collective Behaviour' (1967). According to Hartmut Hanauske-Abel, he encountered great hostility from the senior medical establishment after he published the proceedings of the Nüremberg trial, though they instigated his attendance at the trial. Among these, Dr. K. Haedenkamp, who was the most powerful person in charge of the Federal Chamber of Physicians, suggested that Professor Mitscherlich should be dismissed. It is noteworthy that Dr. Haedenkamp had been a 'Storm Trooper' and was decorated by the Nazi regime for organising 'de-Judaisation' of the German profession. Mitscherlich was then attacked by the largely intact German Medical hierarchy who actively supported Hitler. Among them were Professors F. Sauerbruch and F. H. Rein, outspoken supporters of the racial policies and education; they served as consultants to the notorious medical experiments of Professor Karl Brandt who was hanged for his inhumanity and misdeeds. Professors Büchner, who directed the lethal altitude and freezing experiments on camp inmates of the 'Luftfahrtmedizinische Pathologie' (Airforce Medicine and Pathology), and Professor W. Heubner, who designed the lethal experiments in Dachau concentration camp. Thus, a group of prominent and powerful professors involved in medical atrocities ganged up against one of the most honourable members of the German medical profession and branded him an 'unpatriotic scoundrel, psychopathic hater of Germans.' They succeeded in denying Mitscherlich support for research, and he was deemed not to be fit to teach and was dismissed by the University of Frankfurt. The salary was diverted to Professor Otmar Verschuer, the racial geneticist of Aryan supremacy, who with his assistant Mengele, procured human tissues from Auschwitz victims for 'genetic' investigations.

After the war, some universities made an attempt to recall the academics expelled during the Nazi period, but very few returned. They maintained the 'Heidelberg Myth' that the University was the victim of Nazi Dictatorship, backed only by the Nazi students within the university. The professors closed ranks, opposed denazification, supported each other often by spurious evidence and all of them ostensibly helped their Jewish colleagues. Indeed, not only did they believe in their innocence, but have convinced themselves that they too have been the victims of Nazism. The immediate post-war history was polarized by two diametrically opposite accounts. Gerhard Ritter in his 'Der Professor im Dritten Reich' (The Professor in the Third Reich – 1945) claimed that the vast majority of professors wanted nothing to do with the regime. Max Weinreich in 'Hitler's Professors' (1946) concluded that 'Scholarship' provided the ideas, which led to the murder of millions of innocent people in the Holocaust. Whereas Ritter's view prevailed over twenty years after the war, as the general amnesia wore off, mounting evidence favours Weinreich's conclusion.

It is, however, important to appreciate that the chauvinism expressed by the 'German Spirit' pre-dated 1933 and the principal advocates were university professors and right-wing individuals. Völkich nationalism, anti-Semitism, and biological and cultural racism were all products from the same source, which was opposed largely by foreign academics, well-illustrated in the columns of Nature (the most prestigious scientific journal in the world). Hitler declared the 550th anniversary of the University of Heidelberg to be of national significance, to demonstrate to the world the achievements of German science, culture, and the close connection between the University and the 'Volk'. A report was published in February 22 1936 in Nature entitled 'Heidelberg, Spinoza and Academic Freedom'. "An event of a different kind may be remembered, the anniversary of an important historic gesture by the University of Heidelberg. On February 16, 1673, a letter was sent from Heidelberg to the philosopher Spinoza, inviting him to occupy the chair as "Ordinarius" in that university. This appears to have been the first occasion on which a university called to a professorship one who was known not to profess its prevailing religion. The opinions of Spinoza were at that time widely known. The relevant parts of the letter of invitation had been translated as follows:

"To the Very Acute and Renowned Philosopher, Benedict de Spinoza
Most renowned, Sir

His serene Highness the Elector Palatine, my most Gracious Master, has commanded me to write to you, who are yet unknown to me, but most highly commended to His Serene Highness the Prince, and to ask you whether you are willing to accept an Ordinary Professorship of Philosophy in his Illustrious University. You will not find anywhere a Prince more favourable to distinguished geniuses, among whom he reckons you. You will have the utmost freedom of philosophizing, which he believes you will not misuse to disturb the publicly established Religion."

There follow a few compliments and directions and the letter ends:

"I will add only this, that if you come here, you will live pleasantly a life worthy of a Philosopher. So Farewell and Hail to you, most honoured Sir, from your most devoted, J. LOUIS FABRITIUS, Professor in the University of Heidelberg, Heidelberg, 16 February 1673."

The report in 'Nature' continues, "It is just ten years since the definitive edition of the works of Spinoza was published by the University of Heidelberg. Had Spinoza himself been living today, it would be quite impossible for him to occupy a position at Heidelberg. That university has dismissed or forced into retirement more than forty-five of its staff on the ground either of their opinions or of their Jewish descent. Spinoza would have come under the ban on both of these counts. Nevertheless, Heidelberg is deeply indebted to men who have had a similar history to Spinoza. Emil Lask, a thinker of Jewish origin, was perhaps the most important philosopher that Heidelberg had produced for half a century. He was, moreover, the only member of the Philosophical Faculty of Heidelberg who fell on active service in the War. Yet it was in the very building where Lask had held his seminars that there appeared in 1933 the well-known notice of the 'Deutsche Studentenschaft: *Wenn der Jude Deutsch schreibt, lögt er'*. (When a Jew writes in German, he is lying.). No member of the faculty protested."

Furthermore, the 'Nature' report notes that, "On the façade of one of the great university edifices at Heidelberg – built largely by the help of benefactors of Jewish origin – there stands the inscription 'DEM LEBENDIGEN GEIST' (To the Living Spirit). The new regime does not approve this formula and the discussion still rages as to whether it should not be changed to 'DEM DEUTSCHEN GEIST!' It is an indication of the atmosphere in which teaching is now carried on in Germany that the distinguished physicist, Philipp Lenard of Heidelberg, has just issued the first of the four volumes of his great treatise on physics with the title 'Deutsche Physik'. It bears a dedication to Dr. Frick, Minister of the interior, 'dem Förderer grosser Forschung im Dritten Reich!' (The supporter of advanced research in the third Reich) and the opening sentences of the preface may be translated thus:

'German Physics?' one asks. I might rather have said Aryan Physics or the Physics of the Nordic Species of Man ('der nordisch gearteten Menschen'), the Physics of those who have fathomed the depths of Reality, seeker after Truth, the Physics of the very founders of science. But I shall be answered 'Science is and remains international'. It is false. Science, like every other human product, is racial and conditioned by blood."

Lenard was supported in his tirade against 'Jewish Physics' by Johannes Stark, another professor of physics and Nobel Laureate. When the renown British physicist Professor A. V. Hill of University College, London condemned the Nazis' treatment of German scientists in an article in the journal 'Nature', Stark replied that Hill was entirely wrong and that Germany was entitled to protect itself against disloyal citizens. As Hill by that time raised substantial sums of money in aid of the refugee scientists, he responded in 'Nature' that he was uncertain whether his fundraising success was due to his own advocacy or to Stark's, but anyway he thanked Stark for his help. It is uncertain whether Stark appreciated this English sense of irony.

After the war in 1945, there was no concerted action by the university to apologize, to invite the dismissed scholars to their former positions or indeed to pay compensation or pension. Nonetheless, among the professors restored to their previous posts were notably Karl Jaspers, Walter Jellinek, and Gustav Radbruch.

IV. JOSEPH GOEBBELS, PHD STUDENT AT THE UNIVERSITY

Goebbels was born in 1897 to a devout Catholic family of working class in Rheidt, a small town in the Rhineland. His father was a factory clerk, narrow-minded, pedantic, money conscious and tyrant in the house. His mother, originally a farmhand, was a god-fearing and loving person. He attended a Franciscan brother's boarding school and completed the 'Abitur' at a Christian Gymnasium. Goebbels suffered a deformed right leg, the cause of which is uncertain but could be club foot (a congenital condition) or osteomyelitis. He was short (5'5) with dark hair, brown eyes, and walked with a limp, hardly a paragon of Aryan manhood; indeed, he was rejected for military service in World War One.

Goebbels was bright and cultured. He read Russian (Dostoyevsky, Tolstoi, Gogol), Scandinavian (Strindberg), and German literature, including Houston Stewart Chamberlain's extreme nationalism and anti-Semitism, Oswald Spengler's philosophy and criticism of liberalism, which disagreed with Nazi ideology and anti-Semitism and the will to power by Friedrich Nietzsche. He was enthusiastic about art, especially Expressionists, such as Van Gogh, Emil Nolte, and Ernst Barlach, and attended classical concerts. This was at a time of depression, economic hardship, unemployment, dissatisfaction with the Weimar government democracy, and agitation by Hitler and his cohort, blaming Jews for betraying Germany and losing the First World War. Goebbels was a womaniser, with some just a passing lust or infatuation. However, he had a serious, fairly long-lasting liaison with a young Jewish teacher Else Janke from his home town in Rheidt, until one day she told him that her mother was Jewish and he noted in his diary that her charms were destroyed for him.

Goebbels studied literature and philosophy at the Universities of Bonn, Würzburg, Freiburg, and Heidelberg. He hoped to write his doctoral thesis under the supervision of Professor Friedrich Gundolf, a German-Jewish literary scholar and poet, considered to be one of the most respected scholars during the Weimar Republic. His most famous book was on Goethe, the last edition of which was published in 1930. Gundolf declined Goebbels's application to supervise his PhD thesis because of a great many commitments, but advised him to approach his colleague Professor Max von Waldberg, who indeed became Goebbels's supervisor or 'Doctorvater'

(Doctoral father). Waldberg was a scholar of German literature, also of Jewish origin, and he advised Goebbels to write the doctoral thesis on Wilhelm von Schutz, a relatively unknown German romantic dramatist. The thesis starts with a citation from Dostoyevsky's 'Lacrimae', the English translation from German is as follows.

"In the life of people, however, reason and knowledge have only ever played a secondary, a subordinate, a service role – and that will always be so! The people are formed and driven forwards on their way by quite a different force, by a commanding and compelling force, whose origin is perhaps unknown and remains inexplicable, but which nonetheless exists."

It is significant that Goebbels, as early as 1921-22 whilst writing his PhD thesis after years of studying a German romantic dramatist, cites a quotation from Dostoyevsky's 'Lacrimae', which suggests that reason and knowledge play a minor part in people's lives. Instead, obscure but powerful natural forces drive people in their lives. This may have been Goebbels 'leitmotiv' in his future dealings, discarding reason and playing on people's irrational, emotive impulses.

There was no evidence that Goebbels had any anti-Semitic feelings towards either Gundolf or Waldberg. It is noteworthy that on examination of the original thesis at the Heidelberg library, I failed to find an acknowledgement to the supervisor and this was confirmed by two of the senior librarians. As it is a well-accepted custom in Heidelberg, in common with other universities to acknowledge one's supervisor, there remains the suspicion that the thesis may have been 'doctored' during the Nazi regime. As a postscript to Waldberg's supervision of Goebbels's doctorate, he was obliged to give up teaching in 1933, and two years later was dismissed from the University of Heidelberg and died in 1938. His wife committed suicide in 1942 when faced with deportation. Gundolf was 'luckier', he died from cancer in 1931, and his works were banned by the Nazis in 1933, including his masterpiece on Goethe.

After completing the doctorate, Goebbels wrote some poetry and literature, which failed to bring him personal satisfaction that he so craved. His novel 'Michael' was partly autobiographical, and made little impact. Goebbels felt unfulfilled in his artistic endeavours, altogether lacking confidence and being short of money, all of which drove him to depression. About 1923, he came into contact with the Nazi party, following the 'Beer-Hall Putsch' and a year later, at the age of twenty-seven, Goebbels joined the Nazi party. He was associated with Gregor Strasser, the leader of the social-revolutionary, proletarian, anti-capitalist wing of the party. However, his shrewd instincts and opportunism made him change to

Hitler's more accommodating wing of the NSDAP. As Robert Wistrich aptly described, "It was in the Nazi Party that Goebbels's sharp intelligence, his oratorical gift, flair for the theatrical effects, uninhibited opportunism, and ideological radicalism blossomed in the service of the will to power." Demonising the enemy has always worked in expressing self-identity, superiority and xenophobia. Indeed, Goebbels recognised the traditional scapegoat, the Jew, and used it to depersonalise him, and simultaneously engendering national superiority and the pleasure and material benefit resulting from hatred.

Goebbels made rapid progress, and by 1925 he was made business manager of the NSDAP in the Ruhr district and he founded and edited the National Socialist letters of the Strasser brothers. Hitler rewarded Goebbels by appointing him in 1926 as NSDAP leader of Berlin-Brandenburg. A year later, he founded and edited his own newspaper 'The Attack' (Der Angriff). From then on, his flair for propaganda, rhetorical skill, appealing to primitive instincts, slander and insinuations became evident, and resonated with the unemployed masses of the Great Depression. He demonized the international Jewish financiers in Washington and London with equal vehemence as the Jewish-Bolsheviks in Moscow. In 1933 at the celebrations of Nazi Party victory, Goebbels attacked Jewish penetration of the professions, especially law, medicine, property, and theatre. He became a rabid Jew-hater and following the 'Kristallnacht', which he may have instigated, Goebbels unleashed a rabble-rousing rant, with the attendant atrocities against the Jews. He demanded that Jews should be exterminated in Europe.

Goebbels was on intimate terms with Hitler, and was his spokesman and the appointed propaganda minister. He was one of the first politicians to realise the value of radio broadcasts – thanks to the discovery of radio waves by the Jewish physicist Heinrich Hertz – in reaching the great masses of German people. His anti-Semitic, racially-based polemics played an important role in estrangement of Jews from the 'Volk', playing on their basic anti-Semitic sentiments, depriving Jews of any human qualities and rights and finally deporting them to concentration camps and their death.

Goebbels's first of ten rules noted in his diary was "Be good to all people, especially Mother, Father and Else." Both, his 'Doktorvater' and Else were Jewish whom he greatly admired, respected, and Else, he loved. These people he subsequently called 'Unmensch' (subhuman) and to be 'ausgerottet' (exterminated). This goes beyond the notion of love-hate relationship between two individuals, who were his loyal supporters at a critical time in his life. Perhaps it is wrong to apply the term morality to his type of 'Weltanschauung' (World View), of a 20th century, Doctor of Literature, a product of Western Christian Culture and the Enlightenment, which played a significant role in inciting wholesale murder of millions of children, innocent civilians, as well as infanticide of his own children for the sake of an evil racial ideology.

How was it possible for a man highly educated at the Universities of Bonn, Würzburg, and Freiburg, with a doctorate in literature from the most celebrated University of Heidelberg and educated in the Western Christian tradition, to mutate into a hate-spewing monster? It is unlikely that there is any one trigger that made Goebbels to become, next to Hitler the most outspoken exponent of racial prejudice, fascism and anti-Semitism. His failure as a writer, lack of confidence, gummy leg, short stature and shortage of money drove him into a depressed state of mind. However, then he discovered a niche in hatred and jealousy, and giving went to character assassination of the very people who nurtured and supported him. For the German Nazis, he was the right man at the right time, who mastered and exploited the new media of radio and cinema beyond all expectations. Goebbels craved for recognition and overnight became a celebrity of the new order. Joachim Fest has a point, when he attributes Goebbels's physical deficiencies, coupled with intellectual prowess, to self-hatred; over-compensating these traits by extolling the Nordic-racial physical ideal and hatred of intellectuals and Jews who mentored him.

V. PHILIPP LENARD (LÉNÁRD FŸLÖP), THE NOBEL LAUREATE AND DISCOVERER OF 'RACIAL FISSION' BETWEEN GERMAN ARYAN AND GERMAN JEWISH PHYSICS

I have selected Lenard as the second case study, because he was a renowned scientist, who was awarded the Doctorate of Philosophy at the University of Heidelberg and was a rabid anti-Semite. Lenard was born in Bratislava in 1862, now the capital of Slovakia. He had a Roman Catholic upbringing and from the age of nine, he attended a church school. A year later he was enrolled in the Bratislava 'Real Gymnasium' (High School), where the major emphasis was on science subjects. Lenard was fortunate to have a gifted physics teacher by the name of Virgil Klatt, who had a well-equipped physics laboratory and carried out fairly advanced experiments with cathode rays and electrical discharge in gaseous environment. Klatt must have influenced young Philipp to study physics and he also had to persuade his father to allow his son to study physics at University, instead of joining his wine business. At the time, the teaching was carried out in Hungarian, which was Lenard's preferred language. He became an ardent Magyar nationalist and objected violently to exchanging German names for Hungarian places.

Lenard studied physics at the University of Budapest, Vienna, and Berlin, and in 1883, he moved to Heidelberg working under Georg. H. Quincke and he was awarded the doctoral degree in 1886. He then joined as an assistant to Heinrich Hertz in University of Bonn who discovered electromagnetic waves, later known as radio waves. Hertz called Lenard one day to show him the discovery he made with cathode rays. As Hertz was too preoccupied to pursue the experiment himself, he advised Lenard to take over the investigation and even suggested the method how to study cathode rays in a pure state. Indeed, by 1894, he published what became to be known as the 'Lenard window', which enabled physicists to study cathode rays under well-controlled conditions. Later Lenard extended the work of Hertz on the photoelectric effect by demonstrating that when ultraviolet light falls on a metal it takes up metal electrons, which can be accelerated or retarded by an electric field. He was awarded the Nobel Prize in Physics in 1905 mostly for the cathode ray tube experiments. Two years later, he was appointed Professor and Director of the Physics Institute at the University of Heidelberg. Altogether, Lenard was an outstanding experimental physicist, though not a great theorist, as he lacked adequate knowledge in mathematics. It was largely Einstein who interpreted some of Lenard's findings, which may have injured his inflated ego.

There is a consensus that Lenard suffered from a personality defect, which tended to repel people, though he felt a deep need for friendship. He was paranoid about not receiving adequate credit and recognition for major discoveries in physics. He apparently locked his laboratory when having visitors, afraid that they might steal his ideas, and he ran the Institute as a dictatorship. When J.J. Thomson discovered the electron in 1897, he was generous in acknowledging Lenard's experimental contributions. However, Lenard found this inadequate and may have prompted him to write to a fellow Nobel Prize winner who was fighting in the trenches: "we should especially beat the Englishmen because they had never quoted me directly". This was compounded by blaming the British for his twenty-two-year-old son's death, because of the shortage of food and due to the wartime blockade, although his son died of kidney disease. Lenard's Nobel Prize money lost much of its value due to the rampant inflation in the Weimar Republic, and he blamed this on the Jews.

When Germany's foreign minister, Walther Rathenau of Jewish persuasion, was assassinated, the government ordered that all offices should be closed and university classes cancelled. Lenard, however, was not prepared to honour a Jew and kept his Physics Institute open. This led to a group of workers and Heidelberg students to charge the building, dragged Lenard out and threatened to throw him into the River Neckar. He was saved by the police, who kept him in jail overnight in protective custody. This humiliating experience must have had a lasting effect on Lenard's deplorable personality.

There can be little doubt that Hertz inspired Lenard in the cathode ray experiments and fired his interest in the photoelectric effect. At that time, the relationship between the very modest Hertz and the egocentric Lenard was harmonious. Indeed, in his publication in 1894, Lenard thanked Hertz profusely for encouraging his work and for all the help he had received. Moreover, in his private letters from Bratislava to Hertz, Lenard expressed great respect for his mentor and sincere sympathy for Hertz who was seriously ill and died within a few months. As J. F. Mulligan wrote in the 'Physical Perspectives' (1999), "Lenard's deep respect and admiration for Hertz at this time may be found in the tribute he published in August 1894. Lenard writes, "The portrait presented to the reader today is that of the man with whom science at the commencement of this year buried its best and richest hopes." The article continues in the same vein for three pages, including the following statements about Hertz's scientific papers: "His work reflects his own character, which was as simple and straightforward, as true and steadfast as the operations of Nature itself," and about Hertz's personality: "To describe fully this noble character would be beyond my feeble powers." Certainly, there is no evidence of the slightest trace of disaffection. One last revelation of Lenard's gratitude for his relationship with Hertz in Bonn may be found in a letter sent by Lenard on January 27, 1894, to his former colleague, the astronomer Max Wolf. "For myself I must be happy that my wish has been fulfilled in that I have come to know intimately a truly great spirit, if only for a very short time".

Later, Lenard gradually changed his attitude toward his former mentor, whom he greatly admired and expressed such gratitude for his guidance. With time, he forgot or denied his debt to Hertz, and in 1929, in his book of 'Grosse Naturforscher', Lenard's aim was to prove that all great physicists were of Aryan-Germanic racial stock. Hertz's contribution was negligible, presumably because his father was Jewish. Later, he stated that Hertz's early experimental success were due to his Aryan stock on his mother's side, whilst the 'Jewish Spirit' came from his father on "Principles of Mechanics". This was demonstrable nonsense as Hertz's early papers and doctoral thesis were entirely theoretical. Just as well that he failed to acknowledge later that he was once a devoted assistant to Hertz in Bonn, so as to avoid further embarrassment to Hertz. Another significant Jewish adviser, especially during the early stages of Lenard's academic career was Leo Königsberger, professor of mathematics at the Heidelberg University. Lenard's paranoia knew no bounds and he even resented Röntgen's Nobel Prize in 1901 for the discovery of x-rays, as he apparently failed to acknowledge Lenard's help. In his lectures Lenard would never mention Roentgen's name in relation to x-rays. At the beginning of the First World War he indulged in propaganda of German science, by claiming that British physicists have plagiarized the work of Germans.

Finally, Lenard greatly admired Einstein as a physicist when he discovered the theoretical law of the photo-electric effect in 1905 and referred extensively to Lenard's prior work. Indeed, some years later, Lenard had written to Einstein that he considered him a "deep and far reaching thinker". However, with time, politics and the national and international attention paid to Einstein transformed Lenard's admiration to hatred of Einstein. He disliked Einstein's theory of relativity, which led to intense disagreements between the two physicists, in which the German Physical Society supported Einstein's theory. Lenard's hatred for Einstein's contributions, which he coined maliciously the term 'Jewish Physics' reached a point by 1925 that he displayed a sign outside his Heidelberg office that read: "Entrance is forbidden to Jews and members of the so-called German Physical Society". By that stage, Lenard refused to acknowledge Einstein's equation, which included the light-quantum hypothesis that agreed with the results of Lenard's photoelectric experiments. At the same time, Einstein published three papers, each one worthy of a Nobel Prize. Lenard seems to have replaced his commitments from physics to political nationalist propaganda and anti-Semitism. Paranoia among scientists is well known, and intense personal enmity often develops as a result of not quoting a colleague's contribution. Equally, patriotism towards great scientists, or for that matter, artists or literary figures, is fairly common and well tolerated. However, to condemn a whole nation or religion based on the notion that one's contribution has not been adequately recognized is strange and unprecedented.

By 1924 Lenard joined the NSDP and from then on his increasingly nationalistic and anti-Semitic fervour dominated all his activities. He retired from the chair of physics in Heidelberg in 1931 and devoted all his time to the Nazi cause and support for Hitler. He became the leader of 'German or Aryan Physics', in contrast mostly to Einstein's 'Jewish Physics' and the 'Jewish fraud' of relativity. He also despised 'English Physics', which he considered as plagiarized from German physicists. Regrettably, he was joined in this irrational pursuit by many German physicists, including Professor J. Stark, another Nobel Prize winner. Indeed, he became more of a political agitator and less of a physicist. The US army liberated Heidelberg in 1945 and Lenard, at the time eighty-three years old, fled the city but shortly gave himself up. The military were at a loss to know what to do with the old man and sought advice from Samuel Goudsmit, a Dutch-American physicist. Knowing Lenard's past, Goudsmit advised "Ignore him", as this would be greater punishment for Lenard than standing trial. He was not arrested, but ordered to leave Heidelberg. He died in a small village in 1947. At the 1st Physics symposium in 1947, Max von Laue announced the death of Philipp Lenard in the following words: "We cannot and will not hide or excuse the failures of the pseudo-politician Lenard, but as a physicist he belongs among the great". Joseph Mulligan, in a footnote, remarked, "No definitive biography of Lenard exists in any language because he would have presented a better subject for a physician than for a biographer".

As a postscript to the Lenard affair, the centre of physics teaching and research at the University of Heidelberg, hitherto known simply as the 'Physikalisches Institut', has been solemnly renamed the 'Philipp Lenard-Institut'. At the dedication ceremony, Dr. Wacker, the Minister of

Education proclaimed "The problems of science do not present themselves in the same way to all men. The Negro or the Jew will view the same world in a different way from the German investigator." Prof. J. Stark, the president of the 'Reichsanstalt', who followed him, was, according to the German report, "particularly zealous against the followers of Einstein and attacked with the greatest frankness the scientific methods of Prof. Planck, who even to-day stands at the head of a celebrated learned institution!"

The next day, a number of German physicists assembled to make public declaration of their union against the 'Jewish evil' (Jüdischer Ungeist), from which German science must be completely freed. Party-member Prof. Dr. Tirala (Munich) spoke on 'Nordic Race and Science', to which race we owe the great series of discoveries. Prof. Dr. Krieck (Heidelberg) pursued the arguments of the understanding of science within the National-Socialist world philosophy (*Weltanschauung*). Professor Dr. I. Stein stated that under National Socialism the medical man realises his high responsibility for blood and race, health and potency of his people. Prof. Dr. Tomaschek (Dresden) discussed the 'abstract mathematical junk' of the Jewish physicists who opposed the living conception of the 'Holy Laws of Nature', such as the Nordic investigator wins for himself in reverence before the logic and greatness of Nature.

'Geheimrat' Lenard delivered the concluding words, and expressed his approval of these addresses. He exhorted all to continue energetically the fight against the Jewish spirit, which had by no means vanished from the German universities. He recounted many examples of Jewish arrogance (Einstein), supported by the Jewish publishing house (Springer), and expressed his confidence that this movement for German co-operation would embrace all our centres of higher learning. The ceremony concluded with Sieg Heil and the Horst Wessel song.

The most famous equation defining the three parts of nature by Einstein:

Energy (E) = Mass (M) x Speed of Light (C^2); $\mathbf{E=MC^2}$ was dubbed by Lenard, Stark, and other German physicists as 'Jewish Physics'. The irrational cannot be countered by the rational. Instead, I suggest that the true upholders of German-Aryan physics might have preferred their equation of 'blood and race': Energy of Genocide (E) = Mass Murder (M) x degree of Barbarity (B^2); $\mathbf{E=MB^2}$.

VI. MARTIN HEIDEGGER, THE RENOWNED PHILOSOPHER BUT FLAWED HUMAN BEING

Although not directly part of the 'Heidelberg Myth', Martin Heidegger (1889-1976) has been greatly influenced by Emil Lask, Professor of Philosophy at the University of Heidelberg. Heidegger illustrates the complex link between a great philosophical mind, the author of 'Being and Time' (Da sein) succumbing to the Nazi lure, the 'Führer Principle'. Heidegger was born in the village of Messkirch in Germany to poor devout Roman Catholic parents, father was a sexton in the village church. Martin was sent to a Jesuit seminary, where he stayed only a few weeks, on account of a 'psychosomatic heart condition'. Although seemingly he abandoned Catholicism as he thought it was incompatible with his philosophy, he went on to study theology, but after about two years, he switched to philosophy at the University of Freiburg.

Heidegger was a student of Edmund Husserl (1859, 1938), Professor of Philosophy at the University of Freiburg (1916-1928). He completed his doctoral thesis in 1914, served in World War 1, and his first salaried job was as Husserl's assistant. Husserl was born in Czechoslovakia of a Jewish family. He considered philosophy to be complementary to science and attempted to link mathematics to philosophy. He was Heidegger's mentor and it appears that they may have developed a reciprocal influence on their understanding of the concept of phenomenology. The two philosophers' ideas became fairly intertwined, with a tendency to read the older Husserl through Heidegger more recent writings. A somewhat similar relationship may have existed in their interpretation of the concept of intentionality that is perceiving, believing, desiring, fearing, or doubting. The emphasis on the relation of practice to theory may well have differed between the two philosophers. Husserl was instrumental in appointing Heidegger to the Chair in Philosophy at Freiburg University.

Heidegger's most original work was the philosophy of 'Being and Time' (Da Sein), first published in 1927. According to Michael Inwood, Fellow in Philosophy at the University of Oxford, the central question for Heidegger was "What is being? What is it for something to be? ... The essence of the human being lies in its existence.... Our existence is temporal, as we are aware of the inevitability of one's own death; reaching back into the past and anticipating the future".

Another influence on Heidegger's philosophy was that of Emil Lask (1875-1915), professor of Philosophy at the University of Heidelberg (1913-1914). Lask was born in Austria of Jewish parents and his aim was to synthesize Greek with neo-Grecian philosophy. In depth scholastic research suggests that Heidegger's major concept of 'Being and Time' owes a great deal to Emil Lask's writing, which has not been fully acknowledged. Heidegger regarded, however, Soren Kierkegaard as the greatest influence on his own concepts of 'angst' (anxiety), mortality, existence in the face of death, and the temporal nature of existence. He considered Nietzsche's 'Will to Power' as the ultimate expression of Western philosophy of existence and knowledge.

Heidegger had at least twelve gifted PhD students who developed into prominent philosophers and probably six of them were of Jewish origin. He had a serious love affair with one of his students, Hannah Arendt, who had to flee the country because of her Jewish origin. She established herself in the United States as one of the most influential political philosophers of the 20th century. Heidegger had another extra-marital affair with Elisabeth Blochmann, also a student of his and of Jewish parentage. However, he helped her to leave Germany before the start of the war.

Although a controversial subject, a consensus has emerged that Heidegger actively supported the fascist movement and Hitler's policies. The only controversy remains whether his philosophy had any influence on the fascist ideas. He formally joined the Nazi party in 1933, four months after Hitler became Chancellor of Germany and one month after being elected Rector of the University of Freiburg. He directly implemented the 'Gleichschaltung' totalitarian policy promoted by the Nazi government. All Jewish professors and lecturers were dismissed and that included Husserl, who was born Jewish and converted in his adulthood to Lutheran Christianity. Although Husserl was informed of his 'enforced leave of absence' by the previous Rector a week before Heidegger was installed as Rector, there is no evidence that he made any effort to help Husserl. Indeed, Heidegger had by then broken off any contact with Husserl, and in 1941, apparently under pressure, he removed the dedication to Husserl from his book on 'Being and Time', which was restored in the post-war edition. Heidegger endorsed the 'Führer Principle' well before Hitler came to power. Later in his speeches, he stated "The Führer alone is the present and future Germany and its law". However, within a year, in 1934, he resigned from the rectorship, possibly being disappointed that most Nazis were unable to comprehend his ideas and he became frustrated with academic policies.

After the war, the Denazification Committee published its report on Heidegger and he was charged on three counts: (1) his official position in the Nazi regime, (2) his introduction of the 'Führerprinzip' to the University, (3) engaging in Nazi propaganda and incitement of students against reactionary professors. He was dismissed from the University and in 1949 declared a fellow traveller of Nazism by the State Commission. However, in 1951 he was re-appointed and given emeritus status, which enabled him to teach up to 1976.

It is significant that Heidegger failed to utter a single word about the Holocaust or the extermination camps. However, in a public lecture he stated, "Hundreds of thousands die en masse. Do they die? They succumb. They are done in. Do they die? They become mere quanta, items in an inventory in the business of manufacturing corpses. Do they die? They are liquidated inconspicuously in extermination camps. And even apart from that, right now millions of impoverished people are perishing from hunger in China. But to die is to endure death in its essence. To be able to die means to be capable of this endurance. We are capable of this only if the essence of death makes our own essence". Here Heidegger callously but correctly stated that the victims of the death camps were deprived not only of their lives but of the dignity of an authentic death, since they were 'liquidated' and not killed in a combat as one would kill an enemy in war. In an answer to a question by Herbert Marcuse, a former student of Heidegger, concerning his silence about Nazi racial policies, Heidegger countered by comparing the 'same terror' of expulsion of 15 million East Germans by the Allies.

Heidegger never apologised for his support of the Nazi murderous regime and implied that the Allies pursued similar policies. He refused to understand the historical mass murder committed by Germans on unarmed civilians, most if not all of whom have supported Germany. His former friend and colleague Karl Jaspers, Professor of Philosophy at the University of Heidelberg testified against Heidegger during the hearings of the Denazification Committee. Hannah Arendt first suggested that Heidegger's behaviour precipitated Husserl's death and called him a 'potential murderer'. Later, however she recanted, stood by him, and testified on his behalf, despite her suffering and her people's near demise. This may have been some primitive, visceral loyalty bond with her former mentor, lover, and 'Doctorvater'. It is noteworthy that according to Michael Inwood, Heidegger also expressed Anglophobia, blaming England for the pitiful state of the world. Apparently besides engineering, paving the way to socialism, commonplace thinking and tastelessness, England had made few contributions to culture. He also raises the all too common paranoia among academics that England has rejected his thoughts and his writing have not been translated into English. Perhaps the English philosophers saw through the shallow nature or make-belief of the paradox between 'Da Sein' and 'Führer Principle' advocated by Heidegger.

In an attempt to interpret these three diverse but related case histories, there is a common thread running between the three individuals. Lenard a great physicist, Goebbels an infamous politician, and Heidegger considered to be a great philosopher of the 20th century, each of them leaving an indelible mark on history in their specific fields. They share two principle features, (a) the division between culture and civilization and (b) affinity towards Jewish mentors, ideas and emotional links by Goebbels and Heidegger to Jewish women. All three were products of great German Universities, arguably the pinnacle of Western Culture. Yet the downfall into the abyss of Dante's inferno was facilitated by their incitement directly or indirectly of hatred, racism, vilification, and extermination of the self-proclaimed 'Untermensch' (though the latter does not apply to Heidegger). These are examples of the chasm between culture and civilization at the individual level.

The prevailing anti-Semitism may have contributed to the attitude of these three highly educated and cultured individuals. There is no evidence that Goebbels held any anti-Semitic feelings towards his two Jewish intellectual mentors, though he was affected by Else, arguably his dearest and most supportive girlfriend, on telling him that her mother was Jewish. Lenard must have imbibed anti-Semitism during his youth, when he became an enthusiastic Magyar nationalist in his native town of Bratislava (Pozsony). There was no compelling evidence that Heidegger was an anti-Semite, despite his intellectual support and membership of the Nazi party. However, recent publication of his 'black notebooks' released by the philosopher and director of the Heidegger Institute, Peter Trawny, suggests otherwise. In excerpts published in the 'Frankfurter Allgemeine Zeitung' in 2014, Heidegger wrote in 1939, "With their special computational talents, Jews have lived longest according to the racial principle which is also why they are most vehemently opposed to the full application [of this principle]." In 1941 he wrote, "World Jewry, spurred on by emigrants who were allowed to leave Germany, is ungraspable wherever it may be, and, with all its unfolding power, does not need to participate in war." The 'Black Notebooks' also reveal that 'World Judaism' was a driving force in dehumanisation of the modern world; this involved Bolshevism, Americanism, and Fascism itself. These utterances leave experts in no doubt about his overt anti-Semitic views. The question remains whether one can differentiate between one's conduct and views as an individual and his philosophy. Some believe that he dishonours philosophy.

Whether Heidegger's anti-Semitism was a resentment of his debt to his Jewish mentor Husserl and the ideas developed in concert with those of Lask or his encounter with Ernst Cassirer at the meeting in 1929 at Davos, cannot be resolved. Intellectual debates often become heated, one's ego is touched, especially in an open forum and resentment of the opponent's contrary views are then targeted to a culturally accepted undesirable trait – that he is a Jew, which may determine one's emotional response. It should be remembered that Heidegger was brought up by poor Catholic parents, he was educated in strict Catholic schools, was a Jesuit novice, and studied theology at the University of Freiburg. However, he had undergone a 'crisis of faith', broke with Catholicism, and turned to philosophy. Nonetheless, when Heidegger became a lecturer in philosophy, his major topics were St. Paul, St. Augustin, and Martin Luther, all of who were very critical of Jews. Despite this anti-Jewish influence during his developing years, he was greatly influenced intellectually by Husserl, Lask, and his Jewish PhD students. At the emotional level, he had a life-long liaison with Hannah Arendt, all of which must have affected his attitude to Jews.

The complex intellectual and emotional relationships between these personalities and their Jewish mentors and lovers (at least with Heidegger and Goebbels) is intriguing and would require expert psychological analysis. However, during their formative years, they seem to have had high regard for their Jewish mentors who played a seminal role in their development. Lenard was an assistant of Heinrich Hertz who gave him the idea and support to pursue the photo-electric effect and electro-magnetic waves. Leo Königsberger, professor of mathematics, advised and supported Lenard during his early academic career. It was mostly Albert Einstein who provided the interpretations of Lenard's findings, for although a supreme experimentalist, Lenard was poor in theoretical physics and mathematics. Goebbels, had been taught and mentored by the Jewish professors Gundolf and his 'Doktorvater' (PhD supervisor) von Waldberg. In addition, his girlfriend Else supported him emotionally and spiritually, possibly as few or none of his many other girlfriends. Heidegger had not explicitly expressed an opinion about his Jewish mentor Edmund Husserl or link with Emil Lask's philosophical concepts. However, his two love affairs, especially that with Hannah Arendt are unlikely to be manifestations of shear lust and altogether suggest a love-hate relationship between the intellect and emotion of Heidegger's personality.

In spite of or perhaps because of the closeness to their Jewish mentors, they gradually loosened and then cut their ties and eventually repudiated often in an irrational way any Jewish contribution to science and culture. These self-righteous individuals advocated eradication of any Jewish influence in German affairs, ignoring their own involvement. Whether these were manifestations of self-hatred, translated to their intellectual and emotional Jewish ties, is difficult to establish. Perhaps the German name of supervisor of a doctoral thesis of 'Doktorvater' might in these case histories manifest a novel type of 'Doktorvater Oedipus complex'. The derogatory term 'Doktormord' was used by some students when they violently disagreed with the views of their supervisor. It is noteworthy that there is a literature on an alternative interpretation of the Oedipus complex that is having one's own mind and being an ardent seeker of truth (W. Bion). Whatever the interpretation of these individuals' admiration, debt of gratitude for the contribution to their intellectual make up that eventually turned into hatred may have been, this phenomenon was not unique to the selected individuals.

VII. ARE THE NARRATIVES OF JENA AND HEIDELBERG REPRESENTATIVE OF OTHER GERMAN UNIVERSITIES?

Active political opposition to the racist policies of the Universities of Jena and Heidelberg were almost unknown. Collaboration with Nazi policies was the norm, as was also concluded by Stephen Remy in his extensive study of the Heidelberg University. He referred to the 'Heidelberg Myth' of purity of the professors and lecturers who went along with the dismissal of their colleagues with equanimity and some even aggressively supported racial theories of the 'supermen'. Recent studies by Robert Ericksen of the University of Göttingen strengthens the conclusion that there was no real opposition, indeed extensive collaboration with the ideology of the regime, irrespective of the discipline or the field of science and humanity. Ericksen states that the University clinic in Göttingen performed about 2000 forced sterilizations for 'racial improvement' and a 'care facility' responsible for 200 victims of 'euthanasia – the Nazi experiment in culling'.

Ericksen also drew attention to Edward Y. Hartshorne who spent a year in Germany (1935-1936) and reported his findings in 'German Universities and National Socialism'. There was no outright opposition to the Nazification of the universities, and professors participated in creating 'political universities'. Hartshorne reports the five standard arguments by many professors defending the new regime. "(1) Universities had become 'rotten inside,' with too much specialization, too little care for teaching, too much privilege. (2) Universities had become 'hot-beds of radicalism.' (3) Universities had become 'hot-beds of Judaism.' (4) University faculties had 'degenerated into a nest of quarrelsome cliques or schools'. (5) For those who criticize the loss of 'scientific objectivity' in bowing to the Nazi Weltanschauung, these professors were now simply being more honest in openly proclaiming their allegiance to a set of worthy values, a strong and resurgent Germany based on commitment to the German Volk." He concludes that most of the professors supported Hitler and the 'Führer Principle', as declared by the Rector of University of Freiburg, Martin Heidegger. The diaries of Professor Victor Klemperer of his bitter experiences at the University of Dresden are equally revealing and damning of his academic colleagues. Nazification of the University of Jena has been presented in chapter three. One is bound to conclude, despite all the claims of innocence and opposition by university professors, that Max Weinreich's view is vindicated in his book, ‘Hitler’s Professors’, of collusion and collaboration with Nazi policies. Many Germans with any lingering doubts about the regime must have been influenced by the highly educated classes, which were their role models, to participate in the Nazi crimes.

CHAPTER 5: GOD, MONOTHEISM, EARLY JUDAISM AND CHRISTIANITY

I. **Monotheism**
II. **Early Judaism**
III. **Rabbinic Judaism**
IV. **The Chosen People**
V. **Early Christianity – Jesus**
VI. **Paul of Tarsus**
VII. **Gospels and Acts**
VIII. **Early break between Judaism and Christianity**
IX. **Constantine's conversion to Christianity**
X. **Anti-Jewish polemical writing 'Adversus Judaeos'**
XI. **Peter Abelard, a true Catholic theologian with human frailties**
XII. **Thomas Aquinas**
XIII. **Philo and the Greek Culture**
XIV. **A tragic ecclesiastic mistake – fatal split between Christianity and Judaism**
XV. **Reformation – Martin Luther**
XVI. **Faith**

GOD – MONOTHEISM – EARLY JUDAISM AND CHRISTIANITY

<table>
<tr><td>‘That which is hateful to you do not unto others’.
Rabbi Hillel, 1st century BCE</td><td>‘Do unto others as you would do unto yourself’.
Jesus Christ, 1st century CE</td></tr>
<tr><td colspan="2">‘Three major propositions for the existence of God. 1. The innate idea of the perfect being (St Anselm). 2. The cosmological argument that as everything has a cause, so must the universe; the Cause of causes is God. (St. Aquinas). 3. The Great Designer – God the evidence of design in the universe is the life of plants and animals (Socrates and Plato)</td></tr>
<tr><td colspan="2">‘Monotheism, the belief in One God was the defining characteristic of Judaism.’
The One God had entered into a covenant with Abraham, the ancestor of the Jews and with the descendants
the people of Israel. And later the law of Moses’.
Defined by James C. VanderKam, 2001</td></tr>
<tr><td colspan="2">‘Nation shall not lift up sword against nation, neither shall they learn war anymore’.
Isaiah</td></tr>
<tr><td>‘Not the God of the philosophers but the God of Abraham, Isaac and Jacob’.
Pascal, 1628-1662</td><td>‘Divine elective affinity between God and his people’

Modified from Goethe</td></tr>
</table>

I. MONOTHEISM

Western Civilization is largely the product of Christian Culture, hence it is well-nigh impossible to delve into the highly contentious issue of culture and civilization without an introduction to the history of early

Judaism, and its relationship to early Christianity. According to Geza Vermes in 'Christian Beginnings', "In the early stages of biblical history Judaism represented not so much monotheism, the claim that there is only one God, but monolatry, which means practically ignoring the pantheon of the other peoples, the Jews revered only their own God Yahweh. The Genesis Apocryphon from Qumran Cave I, dating from the second century BC, presents the patriarch Abraham as a charismatic controller of demons. When his wife Sarah was taken to Pharaoh's harem, the patriarch's prayer rendered the king and all his male courtiers impotent to safeguard Sarah's virtue".

The third/second-century BC Hellenistic Jewish historian Artapanus presents Moses too as a miracle-working agent of God. We learn from him that "Moses was thrown into prison by Pharaoh when the king heard his intention to liberate the Jews, but at nightfall a series of miracles happened: the gates of the jail opened; some guards fell asleep while others died, and all their weapons fell to pieces. Thus Moses was able to walk out of the prison." It was only under the influence of the prophets of the exilic and post-exilic periods in the sixth century BC that proper monotheism, the idea of a single God responsible for the creation of the world and mankind, entered Jewish consciousness together with the conviction that only this God would ultimately be duly recognized by the whole human race.

There has been a great deal of speculation about the major evolutionary forces in the momentous transition from polytheism to monotheism probably about three millennia ago. One proposition is that Elijah arranged a public showdown in which El won over Baal in sacrificing a bull by igniting it from heaven. Thus, Yahweh was superior and Baal was vanquished. Elijah's support of Yahweh in countering the influence of King Ahab's wife Jezebel, who was loathed because she and Ahab supported the Canaanite god Baal, may have had crucial political and economic influence. An alternative rather attractive idea of transition to monotheism is later in the Babylonian exile when Cyrus of Persia conquered Babylon and allowed Israelites to return to Jerusalem. The dominant Persian religion at the time was Zoroastrianism, which believed in a creative and protective god, in conflict with a bad god. The dualism has been manifested in Abrahamic monotheism in the one God and the antithesis – the devil or Satan.

According to Yehezkel Kaufmann, however, "It had come to the Hebrews as an insight, an original intuition." Yahweh showed no tolerance to any competition from other gods and allegedly instructed Elijah to kill all Baal worshippers, resulting in thousands of dead Syrians. Josiah's policy towards people that practised polytheism and threatened to corrupt the Israelite religion was explicit in Deuteronomy. "As for the towns of these peoples that the LORD your God is giving you as an inheritance, you must not let anything that breathes remain alive. You shall annihilate them – the Hittites and the Amorites, the Canaanites and the Perizzites, the Hittites and the Jebusites – just as the LORD your God has commanded, so that they may not teach you to do all the abhorrent things that they do for their gods, and you thus sin against the LORD your God". The origins of monotheism, did not auger well, like most other "isms", it was associated with intolerance and murder, no doubt emulated throughout history and zealously practised up to the present day. William F. Albright believed "the Canaanites with their orgiastic nature worship, cult of fertility and their gross mythology were replaced by Israel, with its pastoral simplicity, purity of life, lofty monotheism and its code of ethics".

Robert Wright argues in 'The Evolution of God', that the transition from polytheism to monotheism was a milestone, a cultural revolution in the history of mankind. He suggests a series of changes in Yahweh from an anthropomorphic polytheism towards an abstract monotheism. Yahweh had no single function as ascribed to the other deities, but emerged as a single almighty, wise and transcendent God, who ordered absolute obedience of his laws, ethics, and morality as described in the scriptures. This belief has been maintained by the followers of three Abrahamic religions up to the present.

The existence of God has been the subject of numerous learned tracts by theologians and philosophers that is beyond the scope of this account. In Christianity, there are three major propositions for the existence of God. 1. Anselm's 'ontological argument' of the innate idea of the existence of the perfect being. 2. The 'cosmological argument' postulates that since everything has a cause, so must the universe as Acquinas stated, "The Cause of causes is God". 3. The 'teleological argument' states that the evidence of design in the universe is the life of plants, animals, and the human mind points to the great designer – God. According to Rabbi Louis Jacobs, Jewish authorities generally prefer the cosmological and teleological arguments. An alternative proposal is Kierkegaard's 'leap of faith', in which the human will has a role to play. He argues that Jews do not seek the "abstract God of the Final Cause but the God who gave the Torah to his people Israel and through them to all mankind". In Pascal's famous phrase, "not the God of the philosophers but the God of Abraham, Isaac and Jacob".

Israel, after prolonged conflicts with other nations and being exiled, because they did not live up to Yahweh's expectations, were then entrusted to become "a light unto nations that my salvation may reach to the end of the earth". Israel is the only God's covenanted people, to bring peace to other people of the universe. As proclaimed by Isaiah, "they shall beat their swords into ploughshares and their spears into pruning hooks; nation shall not lift up sword against nation, neither shall they learn war any more". Yahweh's final judgment, after pursuing Israel's enemies, would bring freedom from affliction and salvation to all. The Hebrew Bible often demands decent treatment of foreigners and states "you shall love the alien as yourself, for you were aliens in the land of Egypt". Ethnic purity has been of importance up to the present day, so it is of particular interest that Ruth, the great-granddaughter of King David was a foreigner, hailing from Moab with whom Israel had much trouble.

II. EARLY JUDAISM

During an early period of Judaism, according to the John Collins Eerdmans Dictionary, between the conquest of Alexander the Great in the 4th century BCE and the last Jewish revolt against Rome in the early 2nd century CE, the Judeans (Joudois) were given the right to live according to their ancestral laws by the Persians as well as by the Greek rulers. Regrettably, the rabbis did not preserve the literature from that period and much of the Diaspora is to be found in the Greek literature, written to a large extent by Philo of Alexandria and later Josephus. The Ptolemy and his counsellors were impressed by the wisdom of Jewish sages and thought that they worship the same God known as Zeus to the Greeks. However, a false history arose about Moses, the origin of Jewish people and their social life, which was attributed to some Egyptian historians giving rise to a negative Jewish stereotype. Some writers consider this to be the roots of anti-Semitism.

Judaism, as defined by James C. VanderKam, "is the designation of the entire Jewish way of living and believing. It is related to the name for the land where many Jews lived – the land of Judah or Judea. The scriptures repeatedly mention God's promise that the descendants of Abraham and Sarah would possess the land, and the book of Joshua shows how that promise has been fulfilled. The people of Israel lived in the Promised Land for centuries, but finally their sins, according to the Deuteronomic History, so sorely tried the divine patience that "God (Yahweh) invoked the curses of the covenant upon them, and passed them unto the power of their enemies". Jerusalem and the first Temple built by Solomon around 960 BCE were destroyed by the Babylonian forces in 586 BCE, and the Jewish people were exiled to Babylon. About five decades later Cyrus, the Persian ruler, allowed them to return to Judea, Israel.

The 2nd Temple was rebuilt by them and rededicated in 515 BCE. It was desecrated by Antiochus Epiphanes in 167 BCE and destroyed by Titus, the military leader of the Romans, in 70 CE. By this time, a large number of Jewish people were dispersed in the diaspora, yet the land of Israel remained a powerful symbol. The Temple became a centre for pilgrimage and sacrifices were being offered. To this day, Jews pray to return to their home, to Jerusalem. VanderKam continues with the fundamental characteristic of Judaism. "Monotheism, the belief in One God was a defining characteristic of Judaism. Jews confessed that God was one and that he was the creator and sustainer of all, and non-Jews recognized monotheism as a trait that made Jews different from most others. The one God had entered into a covenant with Abraham, the ancestor of the Jews and, later, with his descendants, the people of Israel. The covenant remained valid and binding; it not only defined a relationship between God (Yahweh) and his people but also. That the descendants of Abraham were to follow the Law of Moses. Among the laws that regulated the conventional behaviour of Jewish people, worship of the one God, Sabbath observance, circumcision, food laws, festivals, and separation from others because of the theological danger of intermarriage and impurity."

Violation of the Covenant was regarded as the root cause of catastrophes such as the destruction of Jerusalem and the Temple. This heralded a new era in Jewish history. They placed all their hopes to the coming of the Messiah (in Hebrew 'Mashiah'), meaning the anointed and noted in the Septuagint by the Greek word Christos. They envisaged a leader from King David's line, according to the Psalms of Solomon. However, whilst Maimonides made the Messiah a principle of faith, Nahmanides taught that the Messiah was not fundamental to the Jewish religion, unlike for Christianity having declared Jesus Christ the Messiah.

According to Professor James Kugel, the Scripture, Torah (Pentateuch; five books of the Old Testament), was of great interest in the 2nd Temple period, with arguments about the meaning of each verse. The most striking archaeological evidence of the importance of the Scripture comes from the Dead Sea Scrolls found in Qumran, in the Judean desert in 1947 by a Bedouin shepherd searching for a stray goat. The library consisted of 800 manuscripts dealing with the Hebrew Bible, Psalms, Deuteronomy, or interpretations of biblical themes, mostly written in Hebrew and about 10% in Aramaic. Studying the Torah in Qumran was an active ongoing activity concerning the right conduct of man, the law and blessings in the mid-3rd and 1st century BCE.

Altogether, ten additional caves with scrolls were discovered, written between 200 BCE and 70 CE, a critical period in the history of Christianity and Judaism. There is compelling evidence that the scrolls refer to a Jewish sect known as the Essenes, referred to by the Roman Pliny the Elder and corroborated by the Jewish writers, Philo and Josephus. However, they were ascetic Jews, withdrawing from prevailing Jewish life into the desert, abstaining from marriage and renouncing sexual intercourse, more akin to Christian than Jewish attitude to sex. Indeed, there is some resemblance between the Aramaic speaking Christians in Mesopotamia, with ethnic and cultural ties to Judaism and the Essenes. The major issue that set them apart was the belief in Jesus as the Messiah. Despite the rivalries, the two communities lived side by side and recognized their common patrimony, revealed by the Dead Sea scrolls.

After the exiled Jews in Babylon returned to Israel, and the only point of reference with their past some 50 years earlier were passages written centuries earlier, the laws of the Torah played the most important role in restored Judea. These covered civil and criminal law, ethical behaviour, ritual purity, diet, and temple procedures, all of which were considered to come from God. To break the law, which 'is free of any error or defect', was not only committing a crime but also a sin. Thus, even the Babylonian exile was explained not by the superior power of Babylonian forces, but by God allowing His people to be conquered as a punishment for the failure to keep the Laws of the Torah, the covenant He concluded with their ancestors.

The Torah had to be interpreted and so a new class of biblical interpreters emerged who played a most significant role in post-exilic society. The Levites were involved in reading and interpreting the Law of God. The success of interpretation of the Bible of ancient Israel established the basis of Judaism and later Christianity, both of which persisted for the next two millennia. Interpretation of the Jewish Bible reached its height at about the 3rd century BCE to the 2nd century CE and created the mode of interpretation up to the present day. The enormous literature that arose from the ancient interpreters has been classified, according to James Kugel, by modern scholars into four postulates. "1. All ancient interpreters assumed that the Scriptural texts were cryptic [metaphorical]. 2. Whilst the Scriptures were written hundreds of years earlier the message was equally valid to the interpreter's own days. The instructions about correct conduct, the prophesies and laws were timeless guides to the people. 3. The Scriptures were written by different prophets and sages at different times and different levels of society. Nonetheless, these diverse writings were considered to be harmonious in all details, to be true, perfect, without any error and without any redundancy. 4. Some parts cite directly the words spoken by God, others refer to the court history of King David, King Solomon or book of psalms. All scripture was considered to be of Divine origin, guidance or inspiration and all was sacred."

A large proportion of early Jewish literature was written in Greek, and much of what survived are excerpts quoted by the Church Fathers, so what was transmitted may have been biased in favour of their own agenda. Philosophical treatises are rare with the exception of Philo of Alexandria. Faithfulness to God's laws and Jewish readiness to die for the law has been emphasized by several authors, including Philo and Josephus. This may have reached martyrdom, as exemplified by the Maccabees. Indeed, the Torah was considered by some Jewish authors writing in Greek, as a universal law that would appeal to every human being through reason. Although this was not a missionary endeavour, Israel was reaching to the rest of humanity, as perhaps part of the mission to be "the light unto the nations".

There is archaeological and documentary evidence of inscriptions, papyri, coins, and other artefacts of Judaism embracing Greek culture, yet maintaining its Jewish identity. This applies especially to the Jewish elites, best seen with Philo. Generally, their cultural identity was bipolar, that is, the relationship to Hellenism was selective, but retaining the commandments of the Torah. It is noteworthy, as mentioned earlier, that the Greeks might well have considered the God of Israel what Zeus represented in Greek culture. There was no evidence of syncretism by Jewish thinkers, but the Greco-Roman period enabled them to explore and express their Jewish identity in a novel way.

Palestine during the Hasmonean Period (164-40 BCE) was established by an overthrow of the Seleucid rule. The Hasmoneans were a priestly family from rural Judea and they retained Hellenism that became indigenous in Jewish Palestine. They pursued territorial expansion and built strongholds, such as Masada. The Herodian Period (40 BCE-39 CE) followed historically, during which a number of building projects and palaces were erected, and the Western Wall was added to the 2nd Temple in Jerusalem. All the architecture was based on the Greek decorative patterns, though blending with indigenous tradition.

The Book of Esther is pertinent within the present narrative in that it was probably the first recorded threat of total destruction of the Jewish people over two thousand years ago. The 'Book of Esther' was probably written between 400 and 300 BCE, towards the end of the Persian period, and there is no agreement as to the date of the book's canonization. It is noteworthy that Esther is the only biblical book of which no remnant has been found in the Qumran Dead Sea Scrolls. The essential feature of the narrative is that the Persian King Ahasuerus fell in love with Esther and made her Queen. The king's most senior official Haman was incensed with Mordecai, the uncle of Esther, because he refused to bow to Haman, unlike all the people. He found out that Mordecai was a Jew and prevailed on the King to ordain extermination of all Jews in the land. However, Esther pleaded with the King on behalf of her people and the King rescinded the order. On finding out that Mordecai previously denounced people who had plotted to kill the King, and had not been rewarded, he ordered the execution of Haman and his replacement with Mordecai. The King also permitted the Jews to fight and kill Haman's supporters, including his ten sons.

This redemption from extermination of the Jewish people is celebrated on the Holiday of Purim, the name derived from 'par' (the 'lot') that Haman cast to exterminate the Jewish people. Even if the authenticity of the book is debated, the notion that total destruction of the Jewish race was conceived by Haman about 2000 years before the Holocaust, shows a prescience that is hard to dismiss from Jewish history. It is worth noting that this attempt and that of Exodus to eliminate the Jewish people, which turned out to be triumphs of victory and survival are commemorated, whereas the disaster of the Holocaust that has paralysed Jewish minds and exegesis, is imprinted on every Jewish mind largely in silence.

III. RABBINIC JUDAISM

Rabbinic Judaism, according to Philip Alexander, is the form of Judaism, which emerged out of the Second Temple period led by the Pharisees who rebuilt Judaism in Palestine after the destruction of the Temple by Titus in 70 CE. This ended the Jewish way of life, including the priesthood, ritual, festivals, and animal sacrifice. The rabbis filled this vacuum by creating an authoritative body of Jewish belief, prayers, festivals, laws, and the overarching importance of the Sabbath and dietary restrictions; these tended to isolate Jews from non-Jews. Judaism became a religion of the book, the scrolls of the Torah, open to endless debates about interpretation, but no room for doubt of their authenticity or Greek ways of philosophical thoughts.

By the third century CE, it was probably the dominant force in Palestinian Judaism and was carried to Babylonia by Palestinian scholars. It is the form of Judaism followed by most Jews to the present day. There is evidence that competition for converts between Christianity and Judaism continued until the conversion of Constantine in 312 CE. The fundamental rabbinic principle that the law of the state is to be followed, demonstrates the ability of Jewish people to accommodate to the customs of the host culture. The guiding principle is the written Torah found in the five books of the Old Testament, which is embodied in the Mishnah. This comprises the rabbinic laws from the early third century CE, which formed the basic text of the Talmud. Other key texts include the Talmud, law codes, and Bible commentaries known as the Midrashim. Rabbinic Judaism survived almost 2000 years of dispersion and persecution world-wide, a testimony to its resilience and ability to adapt to any adverse situation though at a terrible cost of suffering.

The most prominent rabbi during early Judaism in the 2nd Temple period was Hillel. According to Paul Mandel, he arrived in Israel from Babylon during the 2nd half of 1st century BCE and died in the 1st half of the 1st century CE. He was one of the most highly regarded Jewish religious scholars, with powerful authority, leaving an indelible impression on Jewish religious culture, oral law, purity, civil, matrimonial and sacrificial law, ritual, and finances. He played a critical role in the propagation of legal exegesis of the Scripture (Midrash). He expressed the Torah in the Golden rule "that which is hateful to you do not do unto others", adding that "all the rest of the Torah's laws are specifications of this principle." It is significant that Jesus may have paraphrased this dictum in his famous statement, "Do unto others as you would do unto yourself", and passed this fundamental moral law to the rest of the world. Hillel's disciples referred to as the 'House of Hillel', which is noted for its leniency in its ruling, as opposed to the greater stringency of the 'House of Shammai', followers of his former student. Hillel left for posterity a number of oft-quoted anecdotes which provide a true, if idealized portrayal of the legal authority of Second Temple Judaism with authoritative knowledge of the ancient oral traditions. Hillel's character as a popular teacher is also evident in his many epigrammatic sayings which have become bywords of Jewish culture.

Shammai, like Hillel, was an eminent scholar in the 1st century BCE. Little biographical detail is available, but he studied with Hillel. Indeed, Hillel was the president of the legal counsel, whilst Shammai was the vice-president. His legal opinions tended to be conservative and severe, dealing with the laws of Sabbath, Day of Atonement, purities, and civil and criminal laws. A number of disputes arose between the two rabbis and their disciples, leading to separate schools of law, ultimately resulting in great many controversies, splitting the Torah, according to the 'House of Hillel', noted for leniency, and the 'House of Shammai', for greater stringency.

According to Ra'anan Boustan and Shaye J. Cohen, Yohanan ben Zakai lived through the Jewish Revolt against Rome (66-74 CE). He followed the traditions of Hillel and Shammai and was a bridge between them and the rabbis of the 2nd century Palestine. He was a leader of the Pharisees, actively opposing the teaching of both Sadducees and priests with cultic practices. With loss of the Temple, he enacted a number of rulings altering Jewish ritual and Temple practices. Yohanan ben Zakai, according to rabbinic narrative, was carried out of the besieged city in a coffin by his disciples. He meets up later with Vespasian and makes the prophesy that he will become the next emperor. The flattered general gives him permission to establish an academy in Yavneh under Roman auspices. The academy is credited with Yohanan ben Zakai and Rabbi Gamaliel who was his likely successor transferring the Oral Torah to the written word. Rabbi Gamaliel, thought to be the grandson of Hillel, was highly respected by all people and according to Acts 22.3, he was the teacher of St. Paul in the 1st century CE. The sages of Yavneh established the basis of a new Judaism, without the Temple, and canonisation of the Hebrew Bible. About a century later, the Mishnah was produced, which is the basis of the new Judaism that led to its survival to the present day.

IV. THE CHOSEN PEOPLE

The Jewish people have been chosen by God to worship only him, to proclaim his truth among the nations of the world and to abide by the Laws of the Torah. According to Rabbi Jacobs, the two passages in the Bible pertinent to this are as follows.

(1) From Deuteronomy 10:14-15, "Mark the heavens to their uttermost reaches belong the Lord your God, the earth and all that is on it. Yet it was to your fathers that the Lord was drawn in His love for them, so that He chose you, their lineal descendants, from among all peoples – as is now the case. God so loved the patriarchs, Abraham, Isaac, and Jacob, who were faithful to Him and obeyed His word, that He made a covenant with them and chose their offspring who themselves became bound to the ancient covenant." It is not entirely clear why God has chosen Israel, but the most plausible interpretation has been that the Hebrew people, the Israelites and later the Jews, among all the people in the land were the only monotheists.

(2) From Exodus 19:5-6, "Now then, if you will obey me faithfully and keep My Covenant, you shall be my treasured possession among all the peoples. Indeed, all the earth is mine, but you shall be to me a kingdom of priests and a holy nation". Rabbi Jacobs sees a conflict in this declaration, because God's care and providence extends equally, to all human beings He has created in His image. Furthermore, this raises the vexed problem of selecting a small group of people for favoured treatment, though coupled with heavy responsibilities. The Book of Amos even goes so far as to say: "You alone have I singled out of all the families of the earth. That is why I call you to account for all your iniquities" (Amos 3:2). Another aspect of election for their function (or ordeal) is that the Israelites were given the Torah by Moses on Mount Sinai. Indeed, Jews recite the blessing before reading the Torah during services, "Praised are you Adonai our God, Ruler of the World, for choosing us from all the nations and giving us God's Torah".

However, Maimonides (Rambam) did not pay much attention to this motif, and does not list it in his foundational 13 Principles of Jewish Faith. Nonetheless, Orthodox Judaism views the concept of the Chosen People as a spiritual calling that ties Jews to God through the Torah and 'Mitzvot' (blessings). Conservative Judaism views the idea of being chosen as a unique heritage wherein Jews are able to enter into a relationship with God and effect change in the world by helping to create a compassionate society.

There is no racism in the notion of 'Chosen People', indeed there is no pure Jewish race, as anyone who "embraces the Jewish religion is a child of Abraham and hence a full member of the Chosen People."

V. EARLY CHRISTIANITY – JESUS CHRIST

'Do not think that I have come to abolish the law of the prophets; I have come not to abolish but to fulfil. For truly I tell you, until heaven and earth pass away, not one letter not one stroke of a letter, will pass from the law'. *Matthew 5:17-18 quoting Jesus*
'According to the book of Genesis God created man in his own image. According to Aristotle men created Gods after their own image'. *Robert Wright, 2009*
'Today it is a commonplace to acknowledge that Jesus and his followers were Jews thoroughly embedded in the Judaism of their day [...] Well into the twentieth century, New Testament scholarship tended to separate Jesus from his Jewish milieu'. *Professor Daniel Harlow, 2012*
'Marcion's and Tertullian's Jews are a construct. They are 'rhetorical not historical Jews''. *Pauline Fredriksen in St Augustine and the Jews, 2008*
'Christocentricity does not stem from the historical Jesus' *Geza Vermes in 'Christian Beginnings', 2012*
'Jesus felt purely and thought only of the One God in silence; whoever makes him into God does outrage to his holy will'. *Goethe in 'Poems of West and East 1819*

Of the three Abrahamic religions – Judaism – Christianity, and Islam – Judaism was established after God revealed himself to Abraham who recognised Yahweh as the one and only God. Christianity emerged two millennia, and Islam about one and a half millennia ago. Unfortunately, the great religious triad, instead of embracing their common ancestry, fought each other, ostensibly each safeguarding the greatness and holiness of one and the same God. First came the Christian crusades against Muslims and Jews, followed by the Inquisition, and Pogroms culminating in the Holocaust against the Jews, and now we have Jihads against both Christians and Jews. The Jews carry the burden of having discovered the one and only God among numerous other gods, and every theological, intellectual, artistic device and polemic has been employed to deny them the accolade. According to the doctrine of supersession, the Prophets chastised and then condemned the people of Israel for not abiding by God's commandments. They were thought to be unworthy of being the chosen people of God and they were superseded by the newly chosen people of Christianity. About three billion Christians and Muslims worship the Abrahamic God of the Hebrews, but the diminishing number of Jews (less than 20 million) have been the common scapegoat. The Muslim religion will not be pursued in this book as its people had not been a significant party to the genocide.

The most significant episode following the emergence of monotheism in Judaism is the entry of Jesus as a critical figure in monotheism, establishing Christianity, through Paul and the Gospel writers. The gap between the historical and later Jesus is due to lack of any written word and everything appears to be related by word of mouth of the later redactors. Jesus (Greek for the Hebrew Joshua) was the Jewish founder of Christianity. Mary (or Miriam in Hebrew) was a Jewish woman who conceived Jesus through the Holy Spirit as a virgin and is said to fulfil the prophet's prediction (Matthew 1:18-22). Joseph the Jewish father was presumably not the biological father, though Matthew and Luke present genealogies to prove Jesus's descent from King David. To establish the connection between Joseph and David is important, because of the Jewish belief that the Messiah will be a descendant from the Davidic dynasty.

Geza Vermes, in his life-long studies of early Christianity, with unique knowledge of the 'Dead-sea Scrolls', has recently summarised authoritatively his understanding in the book 'Christian Beginnings. From Nazareth to Nicaea (AD30-325)'. Vermes responds to the question posed whether Jesus started a new religion, substituting his inherited Judaism. "Whether we judge by the general description of the cultic and cultural context presented by the evangelists, or by the actual teachings ascribed to Jesus, his religious conduct appears to have coincided in all the essentials with that of his Jewish contemporaries in the Holy Land. We are told that he was circumcised when he was eight days old, and his mother presented him in the Temple of Jerusalem and offered the sacrifice prescribed by the Law of Moses forty days after his birth (Lk. 2:22-4; cf. Lev. 12:1-8). Furthermore, he was quoting verses from Deuteronomy, and instructing his followers to obey commandments in the Decalogue. According to the Synoptic Gospels, he regularly attended the local synagogue on the Sabbath, where he often taught the assembled gatherings, healed the sick, and practised exorcism. He was a popular, much sought-after religious figure who attracted large Jewish crowds and his charismatic nonconformity was criticized by the synagogue and Temple authorities.

The infancy Gospel of Luke ends with the episode of the thirteen-year-old, legally adult, Jesus making his pilgrimage to the Temple with other members of his family in conformity with the prescription of the Torah." (Presumably his 'Bar Mitzvah'). "Jesus is portrayed as respecting various external observances: for example his cloak had tassels attached to it (Mt. 9:20; Lk. 8:44; Mt. 14:36; Mk. 6:56) in conformity with the law of Numbers 15:38. In other words, he behaved and looked as an ordinary Jew of his age. It has been argued that Jesus discarded the biblical dietary laws (Mt. 15:10-11; Mk. 7:15-20). In his figurative speech, Jesus maintained that the true cause of uncleanness was not external, but internal. Its source was the heart, out of which sprang thoughts leading to fornication, theft, murder, etc. – every breach of the Law. They caused sinfulness much more than food that entered through the mouth and ended up in the latrine. Jesus's words were misinterpreted by a glossator who inserted for the benefit of the later non-Jewish church the phrase 'Thus he declared all foods clean' (Mark 7:19). No evidence suggests that Jesus intended to annul the distinction between clean and unclean food.

Did Jesus oppose any of the tenets of the Torah? Some Jews, who disapprove of Jesus, say so, as do some Christians who disapprove of Judaism. However, two statements of Jesus survive in Matthew and Luke that demonstrate that the religion preached by him derived from the Law of Moses and was not a negation of it. For Jesus, Judaism and the Torah were not a passing phase in the divine plan, but a religion destined to remain 'until heaven and earth pass away'. 'Do not think that I have come to abolish the law of the prophets; I have come not to abolish but to fulfil. For truly I tell you, until heaven and earth pass away, not one letter not one stroke of a letter, will pass from the law' (Mt. 5:17-18). Jesus celebrated the

Jewish festivals of lights (Hanukkah) and Passover in Jerusalem. This has been viewed by some as not the teaching of Jesus, but that of the likely Jewish Mathew, though the non-Jewish Luke advocated the same view, in fact more emphatic on the lasting tenets of the Torah.

Jesus was not against the Mosaic Law. Rather he tried, like other Jewish teachers before and after him, to summarize and abridge the Torah and help his disciples to concentrate their minds on the essentials. He selected the Ten Commandments as the kernel of Judaism as did his contemporary, Philo of Alexandria (*Special Laws* I.I). Like Rabbi Hillel among others, Jesus also proposed the so-called Golden Rule as his one-article code of morality: 'Whatever you wish that men would do to you, do so to them; for this is the Law and the Prophets'. Jesus disclosed the great commandment, the combination of two fundamental precepts of the Torah, 'Hear O Israel, the Lord our God, the Lord is one and you shall love the Lord your God with all your heart', and 'You shall love your neighbour as yourself'. Nothing stands closer to the heart of Judaism. In short, the religion of Jesus was the religion of Moses and the biblical prophets, but a religion adapted for the requirements of the final age in which he and his generation believed they found themselves. Jesus preached care for the poor, orphans, widows, prisoners, the sick, and a social responsibility that is wholly admirable, especially for its time."

Vermes sums up, "The religion proclaimed by Jesus was a wholly theocentric one in which he played the role of the man of God par excellence, the prophet of prophets, the shepherd of the flock, the leader, revealer and teacher without being himself in any sense the object of worship as he later became in the fully fledged Christianity created by Paul and John, and especially from the second century onwards. In the Synoptic Gospels, unlike the rest of the New Testament, the focal point of reflection and teaching is God, and not Jesus or Christ [...] The religion practised and preached by Jesus was meant to be a passport allowing the holder without let or hindrance and without the need for other go-betweens to enter directly into the Kingdom of God. Christocentricity does not stem from the historical Jesus." Furthermore, there is no evidence that Jesus spread the 'good news' to the other nations.

A very similar conclusion on Jesus has been drawn by the Orthodox Rabbi Schmuley Boteach in his "Kosher Jesus". He argues cogently that "Jesus lived, taught and died as a Jew. He conducted himself as a devout rabbi and Pharisee. He wore a Jewish head covering, prayed in the Hebrew language, ate only kosher food, honoured the Sabbath, had the mezuzah parchment on the doorpost of his home, celebrated all the Jewish festivals and studied Torah regularly. Jesus has emerged as yet another in a long and great chain of prophets and sages who predicted the Temple's destruction and its rebuilding". Boteach argues passionately that there is the historical Jesus, "the soft shepherd of Israel with no interest in proselytising gentiles and the anti-Semitic firebrand condemning Jews to hell [...] One is authentic and the other manufactured". He believes that Pauline editors and, one must add, writers of the Gospels, are responsible for the transformation, in order to substantiate their claim that Jesus Christ came to replace Judaism. He quotes Dr. Michael Brown the world's leading Jewish-Christian missionary-scholar in his book, 'Answering Jewish Objections to Jesus', "Our Jewish people have been persecuted, abused, expelled, and even killed for rejecting a counterfeit message of a counterfeit Christ preached by a counterfeit church – and there is blood on the hands of the Church."

Rediscovery of Jesus's Judaism is disconcerting and dare I say embarrassing, when for 2000 years the greatest minds in Christianity were at best ignoring or at worse not knowing a crucial fact about Jesus, that he was a Jew, especially as it was obvious to people with limited vision, such as Hitler and his cohort. Indeed, as we have seen a newly created Institute was established in Eisenach, linked to the University of Jena, with the sole objective to dejudaize Jesus and Christianity. The rediscovery was highlighted in 2008 by the 'Time Magazine', as one of their top ten ideas changing the world. "This is seismic", the editors exulted. "For centuries the discipline of Christian 'Hebraics' consisted primarily of Christians cherry-picking Jewish texts to support the traditionally assumed contradiction between the Jews – whose alleged dry legalism contributed to their fumbling their ancient tribal covenant with God – and Jesus who personally embodied God's new covenant of love. But today, seminaries across the Christian spectrum teach, if you get the [Jewish] context wrong, you will certainly get Jesus wrong."

Mark, Luke, and Matthew quoted Jesus reciting one of the most significant of the affirmation of the unity of God in Deuteronomy the 'Shemah' (6:4-5), though Matthew and Luke omitted the first line: "Hear O Israel: The Lord our God is one. And you shall love the Lord your God with all your heart, with all your soul, and with all your might."

According to Professor Daniel C. Harlow, "Today it is a commonplace to acknowledge that Jesus and his first followers were Jews thoroughly embedded in the Judaism of their day. But this has not always been the case. Well into the twentieth century, New Testament scholarship tended if not to separate Jesus from his Jewish milieu then at least to view him as transcending its 'legalism' and 'ritualism'. Only in the post-Holocaust era have Christian scholars overcome the negative caricature of ancient Judaism and reckoned with the essential Jewishness of Jesus. For much of the first century CE, the term 'Christianity' is inappropriate if taken to suggest a non-Jewish religion. The term itself (*Cristianismos*) was invented in-house in the early second century. Initially, though even 'Christian' did not designate adherents of a non-Jewish faith but followers of partisans of *Christos* the Jew." These points are well in accord with the above authenticated scriptural arguments of Geza Vermes.

Harlow argues that it is not necessarily the substance of Jesus's teaching that the Pharisees and Sadducees found objectionable, but more the authoritative pronouncements in his own name, without reference to the revered rabbis and that was not in keeping with tradition. Even in contemporary parlance, Jesus's behaviour would suggest a lack of respect for the views of the learned elders ('der cheretz') and arrogance ('chutzpah'). In addition, Jesus was critical of the Jerusalem priesthood, as is commonly observed in most religious sects with regard to one's establishment. These differences and polemics would not endear himself with the authorities, though certainly not to get him killed.

The principal source for Jesus of Nazareth are the four Gospel writers, between 50 and 120 CE of the Second Temple period of Judaism. Jesus regarded himself as God's final envoy to the people of Israel, calling on them to follow him. Jesus's proclamation of the coming 'Kingdom of God' might have been regarded by Pilate to be subversive as it challenged the 'Kingdom of Rome'. Of even greater importance was probably the messianic enthusiasm of large crowds that greeted him in Jerusalem and his attack on the Temple that concerned the Romans and the chief priests. The motivation of Jesus's opposition to the affairs in the Temple may be associated with the impending destruction of the Temple. According to Mark, Jesus is accused by Caiaphas of blasphemy, after confessing to be The Messiah, and the 'Son of Man', suggesting that Jesus arrogated divine power to himself.

The most significant reason for Jesus's crucifixion by the Roman executioners was that Pilate added to Jesus's cross 'King of the Jews', suggesting that he was executed on grounds of political sedition. Pilate was concerned that Jesus's demonstration in the Temple might create serious disturbance in Jerusalem during the tense atmosphere of the Passover, whereas the chief priest sought to avoid police action by the Romans, risking destruction of the Holy place. Thus, the chief priest may have worked with Pilate to preserve public order, and arrested Jesus with Pilate's approval. The decisive judgment by Pontius Pilate, the Roman Governor, was death by crucifixion. The Gospel writers shifted all the blame on the Jews and exonerated Pilate and the Romans who were in power. There are countless accounts of this event with every conceivable interpretation, but the result was that the Jews were accused of 'Deicide'. So were their descendants in perpetuity for all times by Matthew (27.25) and had the Jews invoke the guilt upon themselves; 'Let his blood be on us and on our children'.

Modern studies by Christian theologians of the historical Jesus and the Gospel writers, in relation to the Jewish authorities and their revolts against the brutal Roman reign in Palestine has resulted in questions about the historical account of the 1st century CE. As James Carroll has stated in his book, 'Constantine's Sword; The Church and the Jews' – "It cannot be overemphasized that the texts of the New Testament were being written at one of the most violent epochs in history, with the twin assaults on Jerusalem, in 70 and 135 CE serving as a rough bracket within which the composition occurred. The events of those years, and in particular the destruction of the Temple in 70 CE, marks a watershed". Israel refused to yield to Rome in 66-73 CE, when Jerusalem was destroyed and according to Josephus and Tacitus 600,000 Jews were killed in the 1st and 850,000 in the 2nd Jewish war, decimating the population. Under these circumstances, Rome defining Jews as its enemy, will have proved useful for the Church to declare the Jews as its enemy, 'an enemy of an enemy becomes a friend'. This might have been the root cause of the break and hostility between Judaism and Christianity, so the 1st century needs to be considered with great care.

Boteach also emphasises the church fathers' accommodation with Rome. "Perhaps the biggest concession of the New Testament authors to Rome was the favourable portrayal of the Romans – that is, when they are mentioned at all. Despite their positively brutal occupation of Judea, the Romans are hardly featured in the Gospels. When they are, they function as benign onlookers, or else, in Jesus' Passion, as hapless tools of the manipulating Pharisees. All things considered, the Romans come across as almost gentlemanly, simply doing their best to keep things running in an orderly manner. They appear to be a civilizing force amidst a tribe of primitive, stubborn Jewish extremists and zealots. Aside from the obvious injustice of this portrayal, it is, as Hyam Maccoby emphasizes, utterly unhistorical [...] Romans cherished war and domination. The axiom by which they prospered was 'might makes right'. They lived by the sword, ruled by the sword, and made sure that others died by the sword [...] The real Rome was to be found not in the carved images of the Arch of Titus, but in the thousands of captured slaves that were dragged in chains through its marble.

Worst of all, early Christian Gospel editors provided the spiritual underpinnings for hatred of Jews, turning Jesus against his people and making him the archetypal anti-Semite. In their hands, Jesus is made to affirm that the Jews will be punished by God for killing their prophets. He derides and denounces them saying: "You snakes! You brood of vipers! How will you escape being condemned to hell? Therefore I am sending you prophets and wise men and teachers". It is utterly inconsistent with the beautiful teachings on ethics in the Sermon on the Mount about the meek and humble inheriting the earth. Was Jesus really prone to such vulgar outbursts and temper tantrums? There are many other such passages of Jesus spewing hateful invective against his people, all added long after Jesus' death and all designed to distance Jesus from his people, making him more Roman than Jewish. These verses abound especially in the Gospel of John [...] You belong to your father, the devil, and you want to carry out your father's desires. He was a murderer from the beginning [...] These verses constitute some of the most poisonous attacks on Jews ever written. They would later be used throughout the centuries to justify the most grisly crimes against the Jews."

VI. PAUL OF TARSUS

Paul was born circa 5 CE in Tarsus (present day Turkey) as a Jew of the tribe of Benjamin. His Hebrew name was Saul, sharing it with King Saul, the first King of Israel. He had a Jewish upbringing and was well thought of within Judaism and the Jerusalem Temple authorities. Paul's dramatic experience was on 'the Road to Damascus' where God 'was pleased to reveal his son to me' (Gal. 1.15.16). Paul's conversion has been dated c.33-36 and he died c.67, so his recorded Letters and Acts are likely to have been written well before the Gospels, with the first written by Matthew c.70. He worshipped God, who revealed himself through the death and resurrection of his son Jesus, and was the fulfilment of God's promises to Israel. Paul wrote thirteen pastoral letters (Epistles) of which 'Romans, Corinthians, Galatians, Philippians, and Thessalonians' are especially well known and frequently quoted, as well as a number of Acts.

Paul's theology is most complex in the New Testament and there are at least three portrayals of Paul.

(1) The Acts describe him as an observant Jew and even after he became a believer in Jesus, he continued to follow the Jewish laws and observe Jewish customs. He attends synagogues, goes to Jerusalem to give alms and offer sacrifices, and undergoes ritual purification in the Temple. To Luke, Paul was a Jew with the additional faith in the Messiah Jesus.

(2) In the letters to Romans (his last), Paul confirms most of the points made in the Acts by calling himself a born Hebrew, having been circumcised on the 8th day and a descendent of Abraham. He refers to the Jewish people that "to them belong the adoption, the glory, the covenants, the giving of the Law, the worship and the promises" and that they are beloved for the sake of the patriarchs and to them belongs the Messiah (Rom. 9:3-5; 11:28). He also states that the election of Jewish people is "irrevocable, all Israel will be saved", and that the Torah is "holy, just and good".

(3) In stark contrast to both the Acts and the letter to the Romans, in the letter to the Galatians, Paul refers to the Jews "killed both the Lord Jesus and the prophets and drove us out; they displease God and oppose all people. But God's wrath has come upon them at last!" (1 Thess. 4:15-16). Paul writes, "Circumcision counts for nothing, and real circumcision is that of the heart, spiritual and not literal. The Torah presided over a ministry of condemnation, as an ally of sin that brought only deaths all who rely on

works of the Law, especially circumcision, are under God's curse". For Paul, Jesus is more than just the Messiah "there is one God, the Father, from whom we are all things and for whom we exist, and one Lord, Jesus Christ, through whom we exist (1 Corr. 8:6). Covenant election and salvation being possible only in Christ". Clearly, this epistle is incompatible with that to the Romans and the Acts, as it exchanges Christ for the Torah. Nonetheless, this may not signify, at least to Paul, conversion from Judaism to Christianity, but a move from one form of Judaism (Pharisaic) to another form of Judaism (Christian).

According to Hyam Maccoby, Paul was incapable of reading Hebrew, so when he quotes the Hebrew Bible in the epistles, he uses the Greek Septuagint translation rather than the Hebrew version. These differ considerably, inviting a number of errors, and one of these is quoted by Boteach. "Paul's mistakes make parts of the Christian doctrine he devised problematic. For example, one of Paul's most monumental claims is that Jewish law is no longer applicable after Jesus. He argues in Galatians that the Law of Moses has been rendered obsolete by Jesus' death on the cross. Jesus has fulfilled the law and atoned for the sins of mankind. This is an astonishing claim given that Jesus himself said, as we quoted earlier, that anyone who doesn't keep every last letter of the law will be last in the kingdom of heaven."

Paul regarded faith in Christ as the fulfilment of Judaism, and his Gentile mission to be the prophetic vocation within Judaism. So far, one might argue that Paul fulfils Isaiah's prophecy that Israel will be the "light unto the nations" acting as spiritual mentors and offering guidance to the world (42:6, 49:6, 60:3); the letter to the Galatians and the Acts may have been written later. In the process of transmission, the theological basis of Judaism has undergone a significant mutation, abandoning among others the dietary laws and circumcision, as well as in a sense monotheism. Abrahamic monotheism and the Sinai covenant have been redefined, and they may have been considered to be rather demanding and perhaps difficult to fulfil, as demonstrated by constant chastisement of the Jewish people by the Prophets. The change from historical Jewish covenantal religion to that proposed by Paul -supersession- and the writings of the Gospels created Christianity, an offspring of Judaism, with attendant, recriminations, hostility, polemics, strife, ending in the accusation of deicide by the Jews.

Paul's leadership created communities of gentiles that adhered to Judaic moral code, but not to the ritual obligations, such as the dietary laws or the need to be circumcised. Paul's exegesis of the scripture (Gen. 15.6), referring to Abraham's faith in God, implied not only the descendants of

Abraham but all who trusted God would share the covenant between Abraham and God. Furthermore, he wrote that faith in Christ was decisive in salvation of both Jews and Gentiles. Paul believed that Jesus will return in the 'Second Coming' and the Christians will be resurrected to share in God's Kingdom. Paul became the apostle of Love and a symbol of universal brotherhood in the quest to spread Christianity across the Roman Empire. His organisational skills, fired by absolute belief in Jesus, made him the most critical and significant individual in establishing and spreading universal Christianity. However, love and intolerance are two human attributes even in an individual like Paul, for woe to those who disagree with him about the Gospels, as they will be condemned by God to Eternal suffering.

Robert Wright, in 'The Evolution of God', writes "Leviticus 19.18 'love your neighbour as yourself' applied initially only to Israelites, but in the post-biblical period, it became the cornerstone of world brotherhood. Hillel would paraphrase the Torah, 'Do not do to others what you would not wish to do to yourself', Confucius said, 'Love your fellow man', and the Buddhist scripture also proclaimed, 'let none wish others harm. An all-embracing love for all the universe. Love unmarred by hate within, not rousing enmity.' The most quoted aphorism is that by Jesus that goes further than all the above, 'Love your enemies and pray for those who persecute you'." All are universal poetic words, which alas fell on deaf ears.

Whilst many Jewish followers of Jesus wanted to retain the dietary laws and the Abrahamic contract of circumcision, Paul perceived the disincentive of these measures and ordained that these are not required and that the only thing that matters is faith through love. It was a pragmatic and strategically successful move that conquered the Roman Empire, but alienated the Jews. It is noteworthy that Matthew tried to convert devout Jews to the Jesus movement, stressing its compatibility with traditional Judaism. However, Luke most likely a gentile targeted mostly pagan converts.

The Resurrection after the crucifixion and burial was an immensely powerful symbolic event and both are critical in the theology of Christianity. Indeed, all sins can be wiped off by God's sacrificing his only son. Unfortunately, there is scanty evidence of the historical Jesus and accounts of the four Gospels have been written 35-70 years after his death. Their provenance is shrouded in uncertainty and some of the writers did not even live in Israel. According to the prevailing understanding, the Messiah did not die before accomplishing his mission, so the death of Jesus was inconsistent with the general expectations.

Wright argues that "As stories spread orally, from person to person, an overarching dishonesty can take shape without a conscious attempt to mislead [...] By the time that the Gospels were written the evidence about the 'historical Jesus' were scanty, stories then circulating about Jesus in oral or written form, had no doubt been shaped by the psychological and rhetorical needs of his followers. Consider the problem of Jesus being from a humble village, Nazareth, The Hebrew Bible had said that the Messiah would be a descendant of King David and, like David, would be born in Bethlehem. Mark never addresses the question of how 'Jesus of Nazareth' could have been born in Bethlehem. But by the time Matthew and Luke were written, an answer had emerged – two answers even. This contradiction between Luke and Matthew suggests that in this case, Mark, the earliest Gospel, is the place to find the awkward truth: Jesus of Nazareth was Jesus of Nazareth (and not Bethlehem). As the decades go by – 70, 80, 90 CE – the Jesus story gets less constrained by historical memory and more impressive. In no previous Gospel does Jesus equate himself with God. But in John he says, 'The Father and I are one'. Christian legend and theology have by this point had sixty or seventy years to evolve, and they are less obedient than ever to memories of the real, human Jesus."

James Carroll, in 'Constantine's Sword', questions the responsibility for the crucifixion "In the original version of this pivotal profession of faith (at the Council of Nicaea), not only is the death of Jesus not mentioned, neither is the crucifixion. In the second version, means of death – the only concrete, historical detail in the entire formulation – is given as 'crucified under Pontius Pilate.' Explicitly holding the Roman procurator responsible contrasts with Gospel accounts that emphasize his reluctance before Jewish bloodthirst, a change that may reflect the Church's new status in the empire as favoured instead of persecuted. But the introduction of the phrase 'in fulfilment of the Scriptures' makes an affirmation of the supersessionist pattern of 'prophecy historicized.' We have seen how easily the proclaiming of the story of Jesus as 'fulfilment' opens into anti-Judaism."

Paul's influence on the beliefs of Christianity has been fundamental in creating Christianity as a religion, indeed he was one of its principal architects. Paul was arrested in Jerusalem in 57 AD on a charge of treason, but on claiming Roman citizenship, he was taken to Rome where he was martyred c.67. Paul was convinced that he has been sent to evangelize Gentiles and his missionary travels are recorded in the Acts. He initiated the idea that Gentiles would acknowledge Israel's God and pursue worship in Jerusalem, without becoming Jews.

VII. THE GOSPELS AND ACTS

The attitude of the Gospels writers to early Judaism varies greatly. According to Harlow, the Gospels of Mark is the earliest Gospel, written about 70 AC, in the parable of the 'Vineyard and the Tenants' indicates suppression of Judaism by Jesus and his followers. Mark shows Jesus dismissing central religious traditions of Jerusalem like 'Shabbat, food, Temple offerings'. Nonetheless, with the Luke – Acts they are the least negative towards Jews and Judaism, whereas paradoxically Matthew and John appear to be most Jewish and yet expressing the most anti-Jewish views.

The Luke-Acts were written around 80-90 AC, apparently using Mark and other sources. The account emphasises the historical continuity of salvation between Israel and Christian movement. Jesus does not abandon the Temple, but after cleansing it, he and the apostles continue to worship and teach within it. As with Joseph and Moses, Jesus is at first rejected by his brethren but eventually vindicated by God to empower him to save the ones who rejected him. The history of Israel is continued and fulfilled in Jesus, but is now open to anyone in every nation who abides by him; by "believing in Jesus and receiving forgiveness of sins through his name". The inclusion of Gentiles in the restored people of God does not replace Israel but extends its membership to the nations, without following their customs and circumcision. However, the Luke-Acts describe the response of Jews to Paul's message about Jesus as mixed, some accept it, but most reject it and even accuse Paul of defiling the Temple, and threaten his life.

The Gospel of Matthew was written about the same time as the Luke-Acts (80-90 AC) and draws on Mark and others. It was addressed to believers in Jesus who considered themselves otherwise Jewish in ethnic, cultural, and religious respects. They observed the Sabbath, alms giving, prayer, fasting, ritual purity, and dietary laws unlike that of Mark. Matthew traces Jesus's genealogy to Abraham and comparative narrative to Moses. According to Matthew, Jesus did not want to abolish the Torah, but is its true and final interpreter. Jesus, like Moses, is the liberator who has come to set his people free from bondage. Like Luke, ethnic Israel does not hold exclusive elect status, as God's salvation now includes the Nations at large. In the most damaging anti-Jewish pronouncement made ostensibly as a Jew, Matthew tells Pilate, "His blood is on us and on our children' (27:25)." Even if the Jews were to be responsible for Jesus's death, Jewish teaching does not advocate responsibility of children for their fathers' guilt or sins. Matthew's pronouncement, as a Jew or by any member of the Jewish community, would not have made the future generations carry the burden of their fathers' actions.

The Gospel of John written 90-100 AC, broke from the synagogue and its formative roots in Judaism, calling Jesus's opponents 'the Jews'. They are portrayed as representing ignorance, unbelief, and rejection of Jesus. Despite this, its Jewishness is evident in regard to the Torah, Temple, Sabbath, and Festivals. However, John's Gospel alone demonstrates an explicit Christology of divinity and incarnation. Jesus pronounces "No one has ascended to heaven except the one who descended from heaven. Before Abraham was I. The Father and I are one. Whoever has seen me has seen the Father (3:13; 8:58; 10:30; 14:9). Jesus is the one and only path to God and to eternal life: 'I am the way, the truth, and the life; no one comes to the Father except through me' (14:6)." John does not relate in parables or aphorisms but in long monologues. The total break becomes clear when the Jews assert their Abrahamic paternity and deny this to Jesus, John responds, 'You are of your father, the Devil'.

VIII. THE EARLY BREAK BETWEEN JUDAISM AND CHRISTIANITY

Harlow is explicit. "Without question the Christian movement began as a messianic renewal movement within Judaism and for several generations retained much of its Jewish character. Yet the seeds for a gradual distancing and eventual separation from Judaism were planted early on with the movement's high Christology, which led to veneration of Jesus in a way that infringed on Jewish monotheism, and in its outreach to Gentiles, which led to a demotion of the Torah and a dismantling of covenant election by descent or conversion.... In the last two decades, the leading metaphor for Christianity's separation from Judaism has been the 'parting of the ways'. The metaphor is salutary insofar as it grants Judaism its own integrity, but it is also problematic because it conjures up images of two neat and tidy religious groups who began as happy siblings but ended completely estranged. When, why, and how the separation took place remains contested".

Among many suggestions, is the destruction of Jerusalem and the Temple in 70 CE, failure of the Bar Kokhba Revolt in 135 CE, the law-free Gospel of Paul, and the Christology in the New Testament. It has also been suggested that a formal curse ("Birkat Ha-Minim"), was designed to expel believers in Jesus from synagogues. Harlow suggests three likely factors account for the break.

1. Ethnic-demographic: the Jesus movement by the end of the 1st century was largely non-Jewish and hence a Gentile religion.
2. Sociological-cultural: Pauline congregations towards the end of the 1st century were separated from those of the synagogues and the two social groups were moving away from each other. Generally the rabbis ignored Christianity, whereas the church Fathers, like Justin, Origen, Jerome, and Chrysostom had scholarly exchanges with learned Jews but later expressed polemics against Judaism.
3. Theological-religious: early Christianity is heavily dependent on Jewish scripture, theology, and ethics, but it diverged from Judaism in covenant election and monotheism. Gentiles were welcomed without having to adopt the Jewish rituals and circumcision or keeping to the laws of the Torah. The critical issue of Jesus being identified so closely with God in prayer and worship, Christian

> messianism was irreconcilable with Jewish monotheism. This theological division has been dated to 30-40 CE."

It is extremely difficult to summarise a complex period of transition from Judaism to Christianity, but the more knowledgeable, though not necessarily universally accepted view will be quoted from Geza Vermes's 'Christian Beginnings' (2012). Vermes recapitulates the evolutionary process in two phases: "the short Jewish opening period from AD 30 to circa 100 is followed by the Gentile development through the second, third and early fourth centuries up to the Council of Nicaea in 325 and beyond." The Jewish phase – "The religion reconstructed from the Synoptic Gospels, a renewed version of prophetic-charismatic Judaism of the Old Testament age, is wholly devoted to preparing Jesus' Jewish followers for entry into the imminently expected Kingdom of God. In this eschatologically inspired religion attention is focused not on Jesus, but on God. For example, in the Synoptic Gospels Jesus never calls himself 'the Son of God'; he does not even appear to be keen on being designated as 'the Messiah'. His followers see in him a man of God, the miracle-working prophet and sage of the end time [.] After Jesus' death his disciples proclaimed Jesus 'a man attested by God with deeds of power, wonders and signs' (Acts 2:22), that is to say, a charismatic prophet, who was recognized also as the crucified, risen and glorified Messiah. The Didache or The Teaching of the Twelve Apostles is the only early literary witness of this exclusively, or almost exclusively, Jewish-Christian outlook outside the books of the New Testament. He is never described as the 'Son of God'. In the Didache, as in the Acts of the Apostles, Jesus simply remains 'the Servant', who ministered to God and men as instructed by heaven [...] Casting of Jesus in a new mould began with Paul."

The Gentile-Christian phase – "This was initiated by the Apostolic Fathers in the first half of the second century. The trend is characterized by the reshaping of the image of Jesus following non-Jewish patterns, by the allegorical interpretation of the Greek Old Testament, which Christianity took over from Hellenistic Judaism, and by a growing theological, as distinct from concrete historical, anti-Judaism. Such a transfer of a doctrinal message from one civilization into another, known as acculturation, may be successful if it avoids a fundamental distortion of the original ideas [...] The new perception within Christianity first manifest itself in the Epistle of Barnabas. Written for Gentile Christians, The Jesus of Barnabas, like the Jesus of John, has ceased to be Jewish; indeed, 'the Jews' are his enemies. He is simultaneously the earthly Son of Man and the eschatological as well as celestial Son of God, who participated in the work of creation long before his descent to earth. The Apostolic Fathers affirmed that the incarnate Christ was God and man, but did not try to show how those two notions could hang together.

A Christian theology formally linked to Platonic philosophy, a system totally different from Jesus's non-speculative mode of thinking, was born with the apologist Justin Martyr. He was a professional philosopher and expert in the Greek Bible. Who elevated Jesus to divine status with eternal pre-existence and participation in the work of creation? Furthermore. He presented the prediction by Isaiah of what Christians understood as a virginally conceived Emmanuel of 'God with us' [...] By the mid-third century the summit of pre-Nicene Christian thought was reached with Origen, the sage whose work epitomized all existing philosophical, scriptural and theological knowledge. His assumption of the Father to humans, and through his suffering, death and resurrection to achieve their redemption [...] By the start of the fourth century the church. the divine quality of Christ, the Son of God, his closeness to God the Father, his pre-existence and role in the creation of the universe were generally agreed by all the leading thinkers. They also agreed on a lack of equality between the Father and the Son. Even Origen was adamant: the Father was 'the God', the Son was only 'God'; he was 'second God', placing himself below the Master of the universe. However, the dogma of consubstantiality triumphed, no doubt thanks to the clever politicking of the party led by Bishop Alexander and Athanasius, which succeeded in winning over to their side the all-powerful emperor. After 325 the claim of inequality between Father and Son amounted to heresy.

However, by the sixteenth century the rediscovery by Renaissance scholars of the ancient sources of classical civilization forced Christians to return to the Bible for a revitalization and purification of their faith. Creating Protestantism. It would seem that by now it has reached, or will soon reach, a stage when a fresh revival will be called for, a new 'reformation', zealous to reach back to the pure religious vision and enthusiasm of Jesus, the Jewish charismatic messenger of God, and not to the defying message Paul, John and the Church attributed to him." Perhaps Aristotle may have been prescient in stating "according to the book of Genesis God created man in his own image, according to Aristotle men created Gods after their own image." In a final thought-provoking citation, Vermes quotes Goethe's moving lines, echoing Judaism, Jesus, and pre-Nicene Christianity, as well as the theology of Islam, in the 'Poems of West and East (West-Őstlicher Divan 1819)'. "Jesus felt purely and thought/ only of the One God in silence; / whoever makes him into God/ does outrage to his holy will.’

IX. CONSTANTINE'S CONVERSION TO CHRISTIANITY

The critical milestone in the history of Christianity was the conversion of Emperor Constantine to Christianity in 312. The legend has it that Constantine, through a miraculous vision of a cross in the sky, and the inscription 'By this conquer' he won the battle against Maxentius. This led Constantine to convert to Christianity and he used the new faith to conquer the Roman Empire. By the end of the 4th century, Christianity was the official religion of the Roman Empire and paganism was banned. Orthodoxy was now defined by the Emperor who found it expedient to ban other religions to rule over his Empire by proclaiming 'One Empire – One Religion'. Constantine ordered the Council of Nicaea in 325, attended by 250 Bishops. The God-based ethnicity was replaced in explicit terms how Jesus is God. According to the evidence presented by Carroll, the Bishops agreed unanimously, and a few who did not were exiled. "The heart of the Christian message is that God sent his son to lay out the path to eternal life. Jesus is a heavenly being who controls access to heaven. And will judge the living and the dead." The 'Nicene Creed', a statement of belief, is being recited up to the present day and functions as a loyalty oath fulfilling a political necessity as much as a religious one.

A critical point in the shifting sands of responsibility is seen in the Nicene statement described by Carroll: "In the original version of this pivotal profession of faith, not only is the death of Jesus not mentioned, neither is the crucifixion. In the second version, equal emphasis on incarnation, suffering, and resurrection has been replaced by a strong emphasis on death, with the elaboration 'suffered, died, and was buried.' That strong emphasis is redoubled when the means of death – the only concrete, historical detail in the entire formulation – is given as 'crucified under Pontius Pilate.' Explicitly holding the Roman procurator responsible contrasts with Gospel accounts that emphasize his reluctance before Jewish bloodthirst, a change that may reflect the Church's new status in the empire as favoured instead of persecuted."

Further theological shifts evolved through a series of subsequent councils, finally in the Council of Constantinople (381) "the Son of God became Man in order to be crucified. The crucifixion takes the place of the Resurrection as the saving event, and Christ the victim takes the place of Christ the victor as the symbol of God's love for the world. This shift has important implications for relations between Christians and Jews. With the cross at the centre of a theology of salvation, it becomes the means of salvation. In this altered context, the Gospel slander that shifts chief responsibility for that cross from the Romans to the Jews – the creed's indictment of Pilate notwithstanding – sets in motion a dynamic that will keep Jews at the heart of a quickened, and quickly armed, Christian hatred.

'Tell me, do you praise the Jews for crucifying Christ', Saint John Chrysostom will ask, around 387, 'and for, even to this day, blaspheming Him and calling Him a lawbreaker'? Chrysostom (c.349-407), the bishop of Antioch, still revered as the patron saint of preachers, was the master of the sermon genre known as *Adversus Judaeos*." In another sermon, he says, "I know that many people hold a high regard for the Jew, and consider their way of life worthy of respect at the present time. This is why I am hurrying to pull up this fatal notion by the roots. A place where a whore stands on display is a whorehouse. What is more, the synagogue is not only a whorehouse and a theatre; it is also a den of thieves and a haunt of wild animals. No better disposed than pigs of goats, [the Jews] live by the rule of debauchery and inordinate gluttony. Only one thing they understand: to gorge themselves and to get drunk. When animals have been fattened by having all they want to eat, they get stubborn and hard to manage. When animals are unfit for work they are marked for slaughter, and this is the very thing which the Jews have experienced. By making themselves unfit for work, they have become ready for slaughter. This is why Christ said, 'As for my enemies, who did not want me to reign over them, bring them here and slay them before me'."

This is the most insulting narrative in the history of theological polemics of a man who, through hatred, seems to have lost any sense of propriety. Shortly after these sermons were preached, there were several violent outbursts against Jews in Antioch, with its great synagogue destroyed. Jews were excluded from holding public office and many were expelled. "Antioch is the site, in this period, of a first draft of the 'ritual murder' charge brought against Jews. In 414, what might be termed history's first large-scale pogrom occurred, that savage assault, referred to earlier, on the large, ancient, and prestigious Jewish community in Alexandria. A historian of the time says the Jewish settlement there was destroyed."

The Nicaean Creed can be explained by Constantine's speech given at the conclusion of the Council as reported by Eusebius, the Bishop of Caesarea. He describes Constantine's dream in which God's Christ appears to him with the cross in the heavens he had seen it before, and to use this sign in all his battles. Carroll refers to this 'mythmaking' by the emperor himself, evoking the four directions of his empire. Constantine's cross has been used till this day in Churches and as personal ornaments. The legend is later completed by Helena, Constantine's mother, who found the 'True Cross', during her pilgrimage to Jerusalem, apparently hidden by the Jews.

At this point of history enter two critical individuals in the pantheon of Christianity, Saint Ambrose (339-397), the bishop of Milan and his disciple Saint Augustine (354-430), the bishop of Hippo. Both were cultured, educated men; Ambrose the son of a Roman official, serving as an imperial governor in Milan. When he became bishop he was a powerful preacher, following in Christian tradition against the Jews, as summarised by the scholar J. W. Drijvers. "They thought they had defeated Christianity by killing Christ, but through the finding of the Cross and the nails, as a result of which Christ and Christianity had come to life again, they themselves were defeated. Now, even the emperors recognize Christ and they have made themselves subservient to his power. Ambrose evidently presents Judaism as a force of nature opposed to Christianity. And is undoubtedly of the opinion that the emperors should combat Judaism and that the Church and the secular authorities should consider the ruin of Judaism their common cause." Ambrose declared Jews as the Church's last problem, reminiscent of some 1500 years later, the National Socialist ideology propitiated by Hitler and his intellectual friends proposed the "final solution" on similar lines. Carroll argues that the legend of the 'True Cross' starts a new period of contempt for the Jews, directly linked to the cross, in the name of Helena, the saint, the devoted mother of the emperor. It should however, be born in mind that on account of a dynastic intrigue, Constantine killed his first born son and his wife, which hardly demonstrates true Christian love and charity by the man who led Christianity's conquest of the Roman Empire.

X. ANTI-JEWISH POLEMICAL WRITING 'ADVERSUS JUDAEOS'

To recapitulate the extensive anti-Jewish writing, it is likely to have begun in the first century when Christianity separated from Judaism, with Paul a key figure in this momentous event. Paul, an observant Jew, after his vision and conversion through the death and resurrection of Jesus, wrote the letters ('epistles'), well before the four Gospels were written. In these he extols the Jewish people, God's Covenant, the Law, and the Torah given to the Jews. However, Paul honestly believed in Jesus as the Messiah and this was in direct opposition to most of the Jews and their rabbis. Strongly held beliefs and ideas lead to theological conflicts, which progress to hostile rhetoric verbal abuse, slander, and culminating in extreme language. He eventually denies any validity of the basic Jewish teaching, the laws, and the Torah, accuses Jews of killing Jesus, and had probably initiated the historical process of hatred of Jews and their religious obligations, though adhering to the Judaic moral code.

The Gospels have largely pursued an anti-Jewish polemic written between 75 and 100 years CE, by the parables depicting Jewish laws, morals and people in an adverse light and repeating the curse of deicide. This theme has been pursued by Marcion (c.140), Justin Martyr (c.150-160), Tertullian (190), Origen (220-250), Chrysostom (c.380), Ambrose (c.390), and Augustine (c.400). According to Blumenkranz and Simon's analyses of Christian and Augustine's works, the amount of Christian anti-Jewish invective was a measure of the younger Christian community's insecurity in relation to the much older Jewish rival.

St. Augustine (354-430) was a writer of letters, sermons, and books. 'The City of God' was his masterpiece, a narrative on the relationship between the Church and Empire, politics and virtue. Augustine applied Platonic ideas to Christian theology, reminiscent of Philo's link of Greek philosophy with Jewish thoughts. Augustine was well read and sensitive of the Jewish root and branch of the Christian faith, as espoused by Paul. Following the 'Adversus Judaeos' of Chrysostom and Ambrose arguing that "Jews continued existence cannot be justified", Augustine tows a more tolerant line. He expresses Christian contempt for the Jews, for their rejection of the obvious testimonies of the prophets that God has cast them off. Augustine calls on Jews to repent and join the Church of Jesus.

However, he rejected Chrysostom and Ambrose's arguments that Jews were enemies of Jesus, in the light of Jesus's own Jewishness, and that they should be spared. He writes, "the Jews who killed him and refused to believe in him, to believe that hc had to die and rise again, suffered a more wretched devastation at the hands of the Romans, and were utterly uprooted from their kingdom, where they had already been under the domination of foreigners. They were dispersed all over the world and thus by evidence of their own Scriptures they bear witness for us that we have not fabricated the prophecies about Christ. A continuing Judaism would serve as a source of authentication for the prophecy-based claims of Christianity. As long as Jews existed, with their ancient texts, the ancient – and therefore noble – character of Christianity was apparent, because those texts 'foretold' Christ. The dispersion of Jews helps with this, and so it is God's will – Scatter them! – That they be allowed to live as exiles everywhere. They must be allowed to survive, but never to thrive; their 'backs' must be 'bent down always.' Their homelessness and misery are the proper punishments for their refusal to recognise the truth of the Church's claims." Thus, they were to be tolerated and not killed, as witnesses to Christ, though kept under miserable conditions.

Carroll then shows the legacy spawned by Augustine's edict. "Let them survive, but not thrive! – would underlie the destructive ambivalence that marked Catholic attitudes toward Jews from then on. Ultimately, history would show that such double-edged ambivalence is impossible to sustain without disastrous consequences. For a thousand years, the compulsively repeated pattern of that ambivalence would show in bishops and popes protecting Jews – but from expressly Christian mobs that wanted to kill Jews because of what bishops and popes had taught about Jews. This is the legacy that haunts the Catholic Church into the twenty-first century, a perverse legacy from which, despite the twentieth-century's jolts, the Church is not yet free." Jews were ostracised, denied owning land and entering professions and crafts, and were excluded from all professional guilds. They were isolated from the population at large, living in ghettos and praying, studying the Torah and living by God's precepts, waiting for the Messiah to come and liberate them. They were permitted, indeed encouraged to deal as money-lenders, because this was prohibited for Christians. Undoubtedly, they developed great skills individually or by networking, which led to further friction, and often expelled from countries when the ruler borrowed money and could not or did not want to repay his debts.

A recent scholarly account of 'Augustine and the Jews' by Paula Fredriksen, professor of Scripture at Boston University, draws attention to the contemporary thinking of Augustine and his reading of the Bible. By Augustine's time, the anti-Jewish polemics were well established and he argued against them. Fredriksen states that "the Jews and of their arguments are a construct: they are 'rhetorical Jews,' not historical Jews." St. Augustine's well known 'witness doctrine', according to Fredriksen's interpretation, argued "that the Jews, alone of all the religious minorities within the (newly) Christian state, should be unimpeded in their religious practice. Why did the Jews merit this unique exemption? Because, said Augustine, their religious practices devolved from a unique author: God the Father. The same god whom Christians worshiped was himself the source of Jewish scripture, Jewish tradition, and Jewish practice. Thus God himself, Augustine insisted, wanted the Jews to remain Jews. Let them preserve their ancient books, he urged; let them live openly according to their ancestral practices while scattered among the Christian majority. In so doing, Augustine taught, the Jews performed a valuable service of testimony for the church. Jews, uniquely, were 'a community set apart from the other nations' and the agent of their separation was God himself. Pagans and heretics thus were the church's responsibility; the Jewish community, God's. No one should forcibly separate Jews from Judaism, Augustine taught. To do so, he insisted, was to contravene God's will.

The 'scattering' of fleshly Israel was never solely a divine punishment for the Jews, but it was always, also a providential divine gift to the nations, or more precisely to the church, to aid in her mission to turn the nations from their idols and demons to the true god, Israel's god."

Despite Augustine's wisdom and immense influence on Catholic teaching, the treatment of Jews and Judaism has on and off changed only in one important aspect, their survival. Throughout the middle ages, the Jews were prime targets for conversion by missionaries and often when voluntary conversion was denied they were either burned at the stake or forcibly converted. Large scale murders were carried out in the first crusade in 1096 of thousands of Jews in the Rhineland. The Church defined violence as a sacred act. Many Jews chose to die than to convert. This pattern was repeated in subsequent crusades, satisfying both spiritual fervour and earthly requirements of looting, raping, and wanton destruction.

To stop the unholy carnage, Pope Callixtus II (1119-1124) issued the papal bull in defence of Jews (Sicut Judaeis), which does not seem to have inhibited people's appetite for killing the deniers of Christ. Indeed, over the next four centuries more than twenty popes re-issued the papal bull. The attitude of the Church oscillated between those who preached Christianity in its noble way, not to commit brutal death, as counselled by Abelard.

The next accusation against the Jews were the "Blood Libels", which originated in 1144 in Norwich, England, when a dead body was found in the woods. The false charge of ritual murder was made against the Jews during Holy Week, that blood from the murdered boy was used in a ritual that ridiculed the Eucharist. A retaliatory murder of a Jew was perpetrated on Good Friday. The blood libel was repeated in Gloucester twenty-four years later and spread all over Europe up to the 20th century, despite rejection of blood libels by the Vatican.

The prejudice spawned by the teaching that Jews killed Jesus led to the belief that they are out to kill Christians. They were accused of poisoning wells in Bohemia in 1163 and as a result, twenty-seven Jews were executed. Well poisoning rumour spread to Germany, Austria, and France, resulting in executions and the Jews of Paris were expelled from the city. The Black Plague in 1348 was blamed on the Jews, as a continued poisoning of the wells, with anti-Jewish violence that wiped out entire communities in Germany. The Jews were believed to be murderers, and the insinuation against the Jews in the Gospels, by priests in the pulpit and confirmed by the institutional meaning of "Jew the anti-Christ" were not prevented by formal ecclesiastical repudiations.

Saint Anselm (1033-1109) was an English monk, bishop, theologian, and philosopher of great significance in the development of the Church. Anselm provided the theological justification for the veneration of the Cross. He provided the proof of God's existence through an ontological argument. He advocated application of reason in place of superstition and attempted to explain the doctrine of Incarnation by reason. Equally, he applied reason to focus against the Jews as being the infidels, and tried to persuade them to accept the Christian faith, that God needs a human blood sacrifice for redemption. Pinchas Lapide, a Jewish writer, argues "that the ruler of the world cannot justify anyone without a blood sacrifice is as incomprehensible to Jews as it is contrary to the Bible." Carroll draws attention to the glaring paradox "that Jesus' death was freely chosen by Jesus himself and that Jesus' death was caused by the Jews. A new and pernicious layer is added to the Augustinian framework of ambivalence. When Jews are blamed for the event that makes possible Christian salvation."

By the early 13th century, Innocent III (1198-1216) took on the title of Vicar of Christ. He would also require England's King John (1208) to accept him – the pope – as England's feudal lord. He would declare null and void the baron's Magna Carta (1215). Nonetheless, it survived the pope's dismissal, and it became the foundation of constitutional government. Innocent convened the Lateran Council in 1215, which proved to be the most important ecumenical gathering of hundreds of bishops, priors, abbots, and ambassadors from Europe's kingdoms, but not the Byzantine Church. According to Carroll, "Innocent established with final clarity the papacy's claim to monarchical authority. The pope was the feudal overlord of the world and at last Europe's emperors, kings, and barons by and large agreed. The legislation passed by the Fourth Lateran Council put in place the main elements of the Catholic culture as we know it. The council was the first to promulgate crucial Church resolutions designed to isolate, restrict, and denigrate Jews. What had until then been merely local indignities were now made universal."

The importance of the Fourth Lateran Council for the future of Jewish-Catholic relations cannot be over-emphasized. "It was not the riots in connection with the First Crusade in 1096," Hans Küng writes, "but this council which fundamentally changed the situation of the Jews, both legally and theologically. Because the Jews were 'servants of sin,' it was concluded that they should now be the servants of Christian princes. So now, in Constitution 68 of the council, for the first time a special form of dress was directly prescribed for Jews, which would isolate them; they were banned from taking public office, forbidden to go out during Holy Week, and had a compulsory tax imposed on them, to be paid to the local Christian clergy".

XI. PETER ABELARD, A TRUE CATHOLIC THEOLOGIAN WITH HUMAN FRAILTIES

Peter Abelard (1079-1142) was a devout Catholic and brilliant teacher of theology, though not a priest, in a cathedral school in Paris in 1118, with thousands of students. Abelard followed Anselm of Canterbury's method of applying reason to faith. He expressed a scientific paradigm that is relevant to all inquiries "by doubting we come to questioning and by questioning we learn truth". He falls in love with Heloise, a beautiful and brilliant young pupil, who is the niece of the powerful abbot Fulbert of Notre-Dame. This happens frequently to charismatic young teachers, when the special relationship between the knowledgeable teacher and the young female student imbibing his knowledge, in the process of which she develops an attachment, wanting him as much as his knowledge and the teacher reciprocates in giving it all. As Carroll says, "Still it is a grave violation when Abelard and Héloïse fall passionately in love. 'Under the pretext of work we made ourselves entirely free for love and the pursuit of her studies provided the secret privacy which love desired. There was more kissing than teaching; my hands found themselves at her breasts more often than on the book. And the more such delights were new to us, the more ardently we indulged them. 'Whatever you wished,' Héloïse would write 'I blindly carried out.' The two exchange a lifelong correspondence to which Abelard would refer in his *The Story of Calamity*." Predictably, the love affair takes its tragic turn when Héloïse becomes pregnant. Secretly they marry, but her uncle learns what has happened and takes mortal offense. Fulbert orders thugs to cut off his genitals, justice by 'paying back in kind.' He is banished, and so is Héloïse. They enter separate exiles, he becomes a monk, she a nun and share an unprecedented Christian spiritual love.

Abelard attempted to end Christian hatred of Jews, to respect them and to choose the way to Jewish-Christian mutual understanding. Carroll explains, "Abelard seems to have been influenced by the intellectually vital centres of Spanish Jewry, and through them, by newly translated works of ancient Greek thinkers. This contact would make Abelard aware of Judaism as a living tradition, not simply an Old Testament caricature, and it would prompt him to respond to it. Eventually he would portray the Jew in his writing in a unique way: respectfully. In his *Exposition of the Epistle to the Romans*, written around 1130. Abelard roundly rejected the idea that 'the death of the innocent Son was so pleasing to God the Father that through it he would be reconciled to us. Christ came to show us how to live, not to die in submission to the brutal power of the Father."

In a uniquely rare expression of empathy from a leading Christian theologian, Abelard expresses poignant sentiments in his "*Dialogue of a Philosopher with a Jew and a Christian*, as he puts these words in the mouth of the Jew: "To believe that the fortitude of the Jews in suffering would be unrewarded was to declare that God was cruel. No nation has ever suffered so much for God. Dispersed among all nations, without king or secular ruler, the Jews are oppressed with heavy taxes as if they had to repurchase their very lives every day. To mistreat the Jews is considered a deed pleasing to God. Such imprisonment as is endured by the Jews can be conceived by the Christians only as a sign of God's utter wrath. The life of the Jews is in the hands of their worst enemies. If they want to travel to the nearest town, they have to buy protection with high sums of money from the Christian rulers who actually wish for their death so that they can confiscate their possessions. The Jews cannot own land or vineyards because there is nobody to vouch for their safekeeping. Thus, all that is left them as a means of livelihood is the business of money-lending, and this in turn brings the hatred of Christians upon them." These words expressed by a devout Christian reverberate with deep appreciation of humanity in distress.

Abelard's assertions set off a great debate. Many support him, and many others condemn him. No one has forgotten Héloïse, least of all Abelard. She has by now become one of the greatest abbesses of Europe, whereas Abelard is condemned as a heretic. Yet their letters have never stopped. Carroll writes, "In Abelard, the Church is offered the antidote to the poison of ambivalence toward Jews that had found its highest expression in Anselm, for in Abelard's view the 'deicide Jew' will be unnecessary, and the 'witness Jew' will be released. The Jew's difference from the Christian will be a measure of human tolerance." No reasonable explanation seems to have been advanced why Jews should be held responsible for killing Jesus when it was ordained by God, as a function necessary for the salvation of the world. Pope Innocent III must have perceived a weakness in his missionary policy of conversion by commissioning two new religious orders – the Dominicans and the Franciscans.

XII. THOMAS AQUINAS

Thomas Aquinas (1225-1274) was the greatest Dominican and thinker in Christianity 900 years after Augustin. He was first trained in Cologne, followed by Paris at the school where Abelard taught previously. He wrote two influential summaries (Summas). The 'Summa Theologica', using Aristotelean logic and concepts to define Christian belief, and 'Summa Gentiles', encompassing Christian faith to engage in debates with unbelievers. He argued that using 'natural reason', all are compelled to agree. This is unlikely to be compelling as 'natural reason' is fundamentally open to conjecture.

Thomas overturned arguments held by previous Christian authorities for over a millennium of Judeo-Christian narrative that it was Jewish ignorance, stupidity, being blind, and stiff-necked that prevented them seeing the truth. He concluded that Jews confronted with the truth of Jesus, had not been ignorant at all. They knew very well that Jesus was the Messiah, Son of God, but they murdered him anyway. The disbelief of Jews derived, therefore, not from ignorance, but from a deliberate defiance of truth. This value judgment was potentially more damaging than the earlier interpretation which Thomas knew only too well was demonstrably untrue and insulting. Carroll points out that "Dominicans and Franciscans were inevitably directed to preach to Jews. It was necessary to forcibly require Jews to listen to the preachers by an edict, issued in 1242 by King James I of Aragon. If they do not wish to come of their own will, our officials shall compel them to do so, putting aside all excuses. Jews were herded into churches and preached at. Disputations were arranged, great debates at which Jews were allowed to rebut the arguments of the preachers. The movement of organized anti-Jewish polemic would grow throughout the thirteenth century. Friars would enter synagogues uninvited. However, despite the staggering intellectual achievement of the new Christian scholarship, Jews remained, by and large, unmoved."

When the authorities realised that the vast majority did not convert, they sought for reasons and 'discovered' that rabbinic Judaism had been codified, interpreted, and published in 'sacred scholarship' as the Talmud. They seized on the Talmud as the secret source of all the evil that prevented Jews to see reason. Pope Gregory IX in 1227 ordered investigation of the Talmud. "A convert of Judaism, one Nicholas Donin, testified in 1236 before the pope himself about the blasphemous and heretical content of this compilation of writings. Gregory ordered the archbishops and kings of Europe, as well as the Franciscans and Dominicans, to expose the secrets of the Talmud, 'the chief cause that holds the Jews obstinate in their perfidy.

The faculty of the University of Paris, had held its trial in the form of a debate, with conscripted Jewish sages speaking for the Talmud and Dominicans speaking against. The faculty rendered its verdict: The Talmud was a work of heresy. The Talmud was the reason Jews were refusing to convert. Destroy the Talmud, and the truth of 'fulfilment' arguments from the Old Testament, rationally offered, would be clear to them at last. Up to twenty-four cartloads of books, something like twelve thousand volumes, were dumped onto the pavement near Notre-Dame. Those books were all the known copies of the Talmud to be found in Paris and its environs, brought here by the soldiers of King Louis IX. His men had invaded and ransacked Jewish homes and synagogues to get at the books. The king's men took their stations around the mountain of books, to keep back the Jews as torchbearers approached. The King carried out the physical sanction decreed by the spiritual court. The bonfire was lit. The Talmud burned." Carroll points out that in 1942, 700 years later in the same place, 13,000 Jews of Paris were rounded up and deported to German extermination camps. We can see here the prescience of Heine when he wrote in Paris, 'First they will burn books and then people.' A new stage in the history of cultural vandalism was reached in Paris in 1242 in that the assault on the books of Talmud was by intellectual and ecclesiastical bodies and not by an illiterate mob. "The public burning in the great square of Paris was a first indication that a living, growing Judaism would not be allowed to survive in a Europe ever more under the sway of the sword-perverted cross."

Most of the major religions are unanimous in universal love of all, yet in reality, these are symbolic, religious, and rhetorical pronouncements saying 'see how good, moral and spiritual my teaching is; be reasonable and follow me.' The absolute conviction of each religion in the only path to God, Nirvana and heaven on earth has not lead tolerance towards fellow men. On balance, most if not all religions carry a heavy burden of guilt by desecrating the image of their God by stoning, the sword, crucifixion, hanging, the guillotine, and finally gassing their innocent brothers and sisters. It seems to have never occurred to those God-fearing individuals that they are blaspheming and desecrating their God, and preventing good times, harmony, and happiness on this earth.

XIII. PHILO AND THE GREEK CULTURE

> 'God designed the divine algorithm
> to create the earth, animals and people'
>
> *Paraphrased from Philo, 25BCE-50CE*

Athens represented secular philosophy, reasoning, and art, whereas Jerusalem divine morality, ethics, laws, and precepts. These two ideologies differed also in believing in many as compared to one almighty God. Their co-existence caused a great deal of friction, but Philo of Alexandria was able to reconcile the two cultures and showed that the revealed religion could not only resist the challenge of Greek logic but be nourished by intellectual reasoning. In some ways he foreshadowed by a millennium the great Maimonides (Rambam) who applied Greek logic to the interpretation of scriptures. However, whilst Maimonides emerged as one of the greatest and certainly the most intellectual sage in the exegesis of Judaism, Philo had little or no following within the Jewish religion. The reason for this is that he engaged in a Greek lifestyle, despite being an observant Jew. He was one of the most important thinkers, in antiquity, reading Plato in terms of Moses and vice versa, and his biblical interpretations were often steeped in platonic logic. Indeed, Robert Wright states in the 'Evolution of God', "If people of any Abrahamic faith – Judaism, Christianity, or Islam – are looking for the most ancient Abrahamic theologian whose language lends itself to a modern sensibility, Philo may be their man. For that matter, if they are looking not for the oldest science-friendly theological language, but just for the best science-friendly theological language, Philo may still be their man [...] While Jesus was preaching in Galilee, Philo, over in Alexandria, was laying out a world-view with key ingredients, and specific terminology."

Philo discarded the anthropomorphic description of God by arguing that it was allegorical. He applied the word 'Logos', which was variably interpreted as 'reason, order, wisdom and computation' among others. The more one's rational mind dominates the base impulses, the more one is in harmony with the divine. According to Erwin Goodenough (historian of religion, 1986), Logos is the 'reasoning principle in the universe and

Natural Law for all men and matter.' In that sense, it was what modern scientists would call the basic laws of physics, chemistry, and biology – the rules that keep the world operating and intact. The Logos, wrote Philo, was conceived in God's mind before all things and is manifest in connection with all things. Prior to creating the universe, God formulated the Logos the way an architect might conceive a blueprint or the way a computer programmer might design an algorithm. Long before modern science started clashing with the six-day creation scenario in Genesis, Philo has pre-empted the conflict by calling those six days allegorical: they actually referred not to God's creation of the earth and animals and people, but to his creation of the Logos, the divine algorithm, which would bring earth and animals and people into existence once it was unleashed in the material world – that is, once the material world was created to serve as its medium. Then God's plan could tangibly unfold. Philo felt that the Torah was explicit and he summarised it in one of the most humane and memorable statements. "This is what our most holy prophet through all his regulations especially desires to create, unanimity, neighbourliness, fellowship, reciprocity of feeling, whereby houses and cities and nations and countries and the whole human race may advance to supreme happiness." It is intriguing to note that Philo's theology written during Jesus's lifetime had a greater impact on Christianity, by interpreting 'Logos as flesh or the son of God' which might have influenced the writing of the Gospel of John.

XIV. A TRAGIC HISTORICAL MISTAKE – FATAL SPLIT BETWEEN CHRISTIANITY AND JUDAISM

Jesus, the 'Messiah – Son of God' was born as a Jew (Joshua), to a Jewish mother (Miriam) and father (Josef). Paul was born as a Jew (Saul) and probably two of the Gospel writers were Jews. The Ten Commandments were passed on from God to Moses, a Jew leading his people to the 'Promised Land.' With such an illustrious pantheon of Jewish origin of Christianity, in addition to which the covenant between God and his chosen people, the Jews, why has there developed the greatest and longest hatred and fratricide in the history of mankind. As a non-theologian in Judaism or Christianity, and not having read volumes of learned writings, arguments and polemics, I dare to suggest that the umbilical cord between the mother and its offspring has never been completely severed and kept on festering for the past two millennia. The Jews were chastised by the prophets for not adhering fully to the Torah. It is doubtful if any people bar a few saintly individuals and heavenly angels could abide by the rigid prescribed lifestyle of 613 commandments, from daybreak to night, from cradle to grave. Humans were given free will, a brain capable of reasoning, memory and seemingly unlimited power of evolutionary advances.

The Jews declined to accept Jesus as their Messiah and from then on, they were accused of killing Jesus, of being the Devil's children, the Torah is all lies, and the Jews blasphemed against God. Love and hate are kindred spirits, readily changing from one extreme to the other. Paul, following in Jesus's footsteps was preaching to the Jews to accept Jesus as the promised Messiah. When they largely ignored or rejected Paul's teachings, he turned to the 'other' – Gentile world, reforming Judaism into a sect, which made it easier to accept and follow, by dropping the painful process of male circumcision and the cumbersome dietary restrictions. The competitive nature of what became Pauline Christianity gradually turned into hostility and marked the beginnings of the 'longest hatred and intolerance'.

Luther was also first looking up to the Jews, as their elder brethren, having been chosen directly by God to receive the covenant. However, when the Jews refused to adopt Luther's Reform Christianity in the 16th century, a flurry of invectives were thrown at them, with accusations, harassment, isolation, loss of freedom and civil rights, potentially paving the way to Hitler's atrocities in the 20th century and the near demise of

European Jewry. Historical longevity of anti-Jewish atrocities have been recently documented for over six centuries (see Ch. 12).

Whereas the covenant between God and Israel was direct, the covenant claimed by the early Christians to acquire by supersession was based on Paul's interpretation of the prophets' chastisements of the Israelites. Paul argued that through Jesus his followers have now become the 'rightful chosen people'. Jacob Neusner's narrative is enlightening, "The Christian habit of offering derogatory definitions of Judaism for the express purpose of highlighting a more benign Christianity. 'For I tell you,' Matthew has Jesus say 'unless your righteousness exceeds that of the Scribes and Pharisees, you will never enter the kingdom of heaven.' At the risk of overemphasizing the point, but also, familiar as I am with what is still routinely preached in Church pulpits, I repeat: This slander of the Pharisees originates not in Jesus' contest with them but in the conflict of the second generation of his followers with the Pharisees. From the denigration of the Pharisees, to the delegitimizing of Israel's right to exist, to the implicit supersessionist division between old and new, false and true. At its most basic level, this polemic violates everything Jesus can be presumed to have taught about love."

Indeed, Marcion in the 2nd century rejected the Hebrew 'wrathful creator God' supplanted Jesus's loving God, raising the question whether this was a new different God or more likely a God conceptually more acceptable to the new Church. Marcion expressed very strong anti-Jewish polemics and some consider him to be one of the early anti-Semites. He was followed by an avalanche of concerted anti-Jewish writing. St. Ambrose, the Bishop of Milan, the greatest theologian of the age would use the True Cross against the Jews and urged violence as the proper response to their denial of Christian claims. However, the Mishnah, in the words of the Christian scholar Clemens Thoma, "does not contain a single passage clearly denouncing Jesus or Christianity. At a time when the Church Fathers loudly and aggressively preached and wrote against the Jews, such refraining from polemics is proof of considerable inner strength. It is also an indication that rabbinic Judaism had no need to define itself against what could be dismissed as a minority breakaway sect. In this it was unlike nascent Christianity, which of necessity defined itself against a Jewish negative. The Harvard professor and world-renowned Scripture scholar, Helmut Koester is a Lutheran pastor. He quotes with approval, a statement by a Harvard colleague that the New Testament is "a tragic historical mistake. Reconciliation of the two heirs of the tradition of Israel was no longer possible."

Saint Augustine's attitude towards the Jews has been critical to trace their fate over the next millennium and half. He argued that as the Jews were scattered among the nations where Christianity thrives, they should not be slayed, as they are witnesses to the prophecy-based claims of Christianity. Was this a self-fulfilling prophecy instigated by the reasoning of St. Augustine to have witnesses of Jewish fallacy and by default Christian truth spread throughout the world, culminating in Hitler – Himmler – Goebbels radical 'solution'. Mass killing the Jews, and with them witnesses to the Christian vision deals a double blow, extermination of Jewish people and with it weakening Christianity by eliminating their living witnesses to authenticate the mission. According to Fredriksen, Augustine protected Jews, because their religious practices were passed on directly by God, who wanted the Jews to hold to their beliefs. She argued that the 'historical Jews' are under God's jurisdiction, they are scattered in all places, and serve to authenticate and spread the mission of Christianity.

The tragic historical mistake of Christianity is to have defined itself against the tenets of Judaism, instead of accepting the one God first declared to the people of Israel and then reformed to suit other people according to the teachings of Jesus. A common propensity of intellectuals, theologians, philosophers, or scientists is to feel strongly about an ideology, concept or whatever they perceive to be the truth. The reasoning portion of the cerebral cortex after intense study of a concept, interacts with the emotive and instinctive older limbic region, resulting in 'fighting for one's principles'. This scenario may well apply to most intellectual activities and is greatly enhanced when it concerns God, whom one serves, obeys, prays to and believes in owe of one's entire existence. Instinctively, there is a desire to convert friends and enemies to the 'one and only truth' of their belief and if that does not succeed, competition, hostility and polemics are commonplace, leading to physical ways of persuasion and finally extermination.

XV. THE REFORMATION – MARTIN LUTHER

"The Jews drink out of the original spring. The Greeks drink out of the stream flowing out of the stream, The Latins, however, out of the puddle" *Martin Luther, 1543*
"I would advise and beg everybody to deal kindly with the Jews and instruct them in the Scripture [...] How can we expect them to improve if we prohibit them to work among us and so force them to usury" Martin Luther 1543
"The obdurate Jews, whom it was a matter of great urgency to expel from all German territory [...] unless they desisted from their calumny and usury and became Christians" *Luther's last sermon, 3 days before he died in 1546*
"The synagogues are burning in Germany as an homage to the greatest anti-Semite of his time, the warrior of his people against the Jews" *Martin Sasse, Lutheran Bishop of Thuringia on 'Kristallnacht', 450 years after Luther's birth.*

The critical moment in the history of religion in Germany and the spread to Europe and the world was the emergence of Martin Luther on the religious firmament (1483-1546). Luther started the Protestant Reformation, ostensibly by nailing 95 theses on the church door in Wittenberg in 1517. Luther was born in Eisleben, a town 80 miles north-east of Eisenach, and he was baptised as a Catholic. Within a year, the family moved to Mansfeld, where his father was a leaseholder of copper mines and sat on the local council. His mother was a hard working woman of humble origin. Martin was given a solid education at schools in Mansfeld, Magdeburg, and Eisenach. These schools focused on grammar, rhetoric, and logic, and later Luther referred to his education as "purgatory and hell". He entered the nearby University in Erfurt, Thuringia in 1501 and was awarded, the Bachelor (1502) and then the Master degree (1505). Martin described the University as a 'beerhouse and whorehouse'. To please his father, Martin enrolled in the Law School of the same University. However, the legend has it that on returning home from the University, he experienced a severe thunderstorm and cried out for help from St. Anne, pledging to become a monk if saved from the storm. He left the Law school to enter an Augustinian friary, but even there he was a restless spirit, and despite long hours of prayer, fasts, pilgrimages, flagellations, and constant confessions, he was not close to God. He was ordered by his seniors to engage in an academic career and was ordained as a priest in 1508. He taught theology in Wittenberg, was awarded the Bachelor degree in biblical studies a year later, and the Doctorate in Theology in 1512 by the University of Wittenberg.

Luther was an avid scholar of the Holy Scriptures and concluded that the Roman Catholic Church has lost the central truth and trust in Christ's teachings. He wrote 95 contentious heretical theses and crimes of the Roman Catholic Church. This was triggered in response to the selling of indulgences by Dominican priests. The theses were translated from Latin to German and spread within weeks in Germany and then in Europe. This heralded the start of the Reformation, condemned as sacrilegious by Pope Leo X in an edict in 1520. At the Diet of Worms in 1521, he was given a choice, either renouncing or carry the consequences of his beliefs. In front of the assembly, Luther stood by his writings and as a result, he was excommunicated and declared an outlaw and a notorious heretic by the Emperor. However, Frederick the Wise arranged for Luther's abduction on his way from the Diet and was hidden in the Castle of Wartburg, above Eisenach under the pseudonym of Jörg. There he translated the New Testament into German, published in 1522, whilst the Old Testament he translated with his collaborators and published in 1534. His marriage introduced the novel clerical practice of Protestant priests.

The reformation originated in the Renaissance, with critical examination of traditional doctrines. Luther argued that the Bible alone is the infallible source of divinely revealed knowledge. He considered the

Catholic Church corrupt and had lost the central truths of Christianity, the doctrine of justification that is God's act of declaring a sinner righteous, by faith alone in Jesus the Messiah. He condemned the notion that mass is a sacrifice, arguing that it is a gift to be thanked for by the whole congregation. Luther also rejected compulsory confession and encouraged private confession and absolution.

Luther studied Hebrew throughout his life. He is quoted, "If I were younger I would want to learn the language, for without it one can never properly understand the Holy Scripture. For that reason they have said correctly: The Jews drink out of the original spring, The Greeks drink out of the stream flowing out of the stream, The Latins, however, out of the puddle." He followed the writings of Rabbis, especially David and Moses Kimhi and Solomon (Rashi) whom he considered best. Luther followed the Hebraist Johannes Reuchlin who found a great deal of Christianity in Jewish writings and did not end up, as many Reformers, despising the people while using their insights. Reuchlin was active in saving Jewish literature from being burnt especially by the Dominicans in 'The Battle of the Books'.

Luther's attitude towards the Jews can be clearly divided into two periods. In the early period before 1537, he speaks highly of Jews, as a people having been chosen by God to transmit his message to the world. He says "the Jews are the best blood on earth" (Luther, L.C. xxv.409); "through them alone the Holy Ghost wished to give all books of Holy Scripture to the world; they are the children and we are the guests and the strangers; indeed, we should be satisfied to be the dogs that eat the crumbs which fall from the master's table" (xxv.260). He was compassionate to their misery and enthusiastic for their conversion to Christianity. Remarkably, the Catholic Church accused Luther of being a Jew at heart because he denied the supernatural birth of Jesus. He states, "our fools the popes, bishops and monks, these ruffian blockheads" dealt with the Jews in a way that any Christian would have preferred to be a Jew. Luther published an entire pamphlet in 1543 (That Jesus was born a Jew i.b. xxix 45-74) and closes it with the following appeal "I would advise and beg everybody to deal kindly with the Jews and instruct them in the Scripture; in such a case we could expect them to come over to us. Finally, how can we expect them to improve if we prohibit them to work among us, to have social intercourse with us, and so force them to usury. We must deal with them not according to the law of the pope but according to the law of Christian charity. We must allow to compete with us in earning a livelihood, so they may witness

Christian life and doctrine, and if some remain obstinate, what of it? Not every one of us is a good Christian (i.6xxix.74)."

Luther expected general conversion of Jews to Christianity and when this did not happen his attitude changed dramatically, and became incensed at Jews for their refusal to become Christians. When Duke John Frederick of Saxony, a supporter of the Reformation ordered the expulsion of Jews from his country, Luther refused to intercede with the Duke. He published a vitriolic attack in 1541, in a book entitled "About Jews and their lies", referred to in the chapter on 'Lutheran Church and the Holocaust' (p.368). Luther had been suffering from ill health for years, with vertigo, fainting, tinnitus, and cataract in one eye. His poor health may have made him short-tempered and harsh in his writings. His last sermon was delivered in Eisleben, his place of birth, in February 1546, three days before he died. It was entirely devoted to "the obdurate Jews, whom it was a matter of great urgency to expel from all German territory". James Mackinnon writes that it concluded with a "fiery summons to drive the Jews' bag and baggage from their midst, unless they desisted from their calumny and their usury and became Christians. We want to practice Christian love towards them and pray that they convert but they are our public enemies." When at last Luther was dying, in bed during the night, after having complained of chest pains, he declared that Jews had done this to him.

Carroll argues with his customary perceptiveness that "the personal venom of Luther's hatred of Jews, and his perhaps psychotic experience of the Jew as standing between him and salvation – the Jew makes death absolute – are what separates Catholic anti-Semitism from that inspired by Luther. The shadow cast by Luther fell in a particular way over Germany, over Hitler, obviously, and perhaps over Marx." A great deal has been written about Luther being credited with reviving anti-Semitism in Germany. There is no doubt that the Nazis found Luther's statements, music to their ears, as Bernard Rust, Minister of Education in Nazi Germany stated, "I think the time is past when one may not say the names of Hitler and Luther in the same breath. They belong together; they are of the same old stamp." Martin Sassed, the Lutheran Bishop of Thuringia 450 years after the birth of Luther and on the 'Kristallnacht' declared with joy, "The synagogues are burning in Germany as an homage to the greatest anti-Semite of his time, the warrior of his people against the Jews." Carroll says, "Luther's hatred of the Jews is a sad and dishonourable part of his legacy, and it is not a fringe issue. It lay at the centre of his concept of religion. 'The unmentionable odour of death' that W. H. Auden sensed above Europe in September 1939, he traced back to something rotten in the great reformer’s program, the madness, as Auden put it, ‘from Luther until now’.”

XVI. FAITH

'The most profoundly spiritual and passionately religious people in the world's history, the people who produced Moses and the prophets and Jesus and Paul, were a people whose history was conspicuous by the most terrible suffering, the cataclysmic traumas of slavery, wanderings in the desert, a homeland marked by the ever- present threat of war and annihilation, brutal captivity, exile, ruthless suppression and control by a series of imperial subjugators' *John Cottingham on religious faith, quoted by Jonathan Sacks, 2002*
'Theology is faith in search of reason. Faith does not owe apology to the intellect' *St. Anselm's statement, 1033-1109*
'I have found it necessary to deny knowledge, in order to make room for faith' *Kant in his 'Critique of Pure Reason', 1781*

Faith, as stated in the Bible, means 'Trust in God'. The prophet Habakkuk based the whole of the Torah on one principle, 'But the righteous shall live by faith.' For Judaism and Christianity the prime confession of Faith is "Hear, O Israel, the Lord our God, the Lord is one" (in Hebrew the 'Shema'). Rabbi Jacobs argues that with the onset of atheism 'Trust in God' was modified to 'Belief in the existence of God'. St. Anselm, however, in a memorable admission, states that "theology is faith in search of reason" but paradoxically he also argues that "faith does not owe apology to the intellect". Hans Küng also believes in a "rationally justified faith" but quotes, "Faith is the assurance of things hoped for, the conviction of things not seen" (Heb. 11:1), which takes faith into ill-defined territory. Kierkegaard's 'leap of faith', in which the human will has a role to play" has attracted considerable support. A particularly intriguing argument is that 'faith is higher than reason', treating it almost as a divine gift given to those who seek God with all their heart, mind, and will. In a sense, this mood is closer to the biblical insight into the nature of faith than is the rationalistic approach of the medieval thinkers. However, the Roman Catholic interpretation of to-day states that faith is "holding true all the doctrines which the church presents for belief". Nonetheless, the common faith of Jews, Christians, and Muslims is in "God as creator of heaven and earth".

These views are consistent with the neurobiological division between the emotional limbic system and the rational pre-frontal cortex. However, whether faith is higher or lower than reason is not a point of contention, suffice to say that the two functions are different, though usually interactive. Polarisation towards the rational or emotional pole is evident throughout the spectrum of every religion. The appeal of faith to tradition is that human beings in the past have claimed to have met a Being who endowed their lives with moral worth and significance. They hear God speaking to them when, for instance, they read of how he had spoken to Isaiah, Jeremiah, or Micah.

Aristotle understood the innate curiosity of mankind about the wonder and misery of nature. It led most people to religion and later others to science. Thomas Hobbes (1588-1679) had no interest in theological puzzles and argued that men invented gods only for solace to cope with hardship of everyday life and from our fear and ignorance. In the 'Leviathan', Hobbes denies Christian appeal to conscience and refers to it as a convenient means to be manipulated by priests. Indeed, Hobbes courageously stood for atheism and rejected Christian theocracy with questionable motives of the clergy. With the onset of the enlightenment, Jean Jacque Rousseau (1712-1778) attacked Christian policies in his short treatise on religion in 'Emile', his masterpiece. The book was condemned by the Church and burned; Rousseau had to flee persecution the rest of his life. Sober consideration of Rousseau's concept of man clearly shows him having conscience, virtue, charity, empathy, and wonder of God's creation. It seems that the 'sin' Rousseau committed was not to attribute these human qualities to divine grace, but to the natural goodness of man, and that in itself was arguable. He suggested that as long as men are social beings, religion will exist, though the naïve faith in God will be feeble, as long as it is tied to external authority instead of their moral needs.

Kant wrote in his "Critique of Pure Reason" (1781), as reported by Küng, "I have found it necessary to deny knowledge, in order to make room for faith". Indeed, both for Kant and Rousseau, "faith is a truth of the heart or conscience", beyond all philosophical reflections. There is clearly a conflict between faith and reason. The latter being the contingency of people who firmly believe that everything must be open to logical understanding, whereas faith is more inclined to be in the domain of religious belief. It is therefore interesting that some mystics refer to 'faith higher than reason', as it is a divine gift of the Bible.

Tradition plays an important part in faith and is rooted in historical events of encounter with God, especially in Judaism. For both Jews and Christians the Shema ('The Lord our God, the Lord is One') is the fundamental confession of faith as declared in Deuteronomy, as well as in the Gospel of Mark. Moreover, Paul speaks of 'justification by faith apart from works of the law', which differentiated between Christian faith and the legalistic Jewish alternative. This became a critical issue in Christian anti-Judaism, although Paul affirms that God's covenant is the basis of Jewish justification and this extends to the Gentiles. Rabbi Sacks argues rationally in his 'Dignity of Difference' "God no more wants all faiths and cultures to be the same than a loving parent wants his or her children to be the same. That is the conceptual link between love, creation and difference. We serve God, author of diversity, by respecting diversity." These words of ecumenical wisdom propose a mission statement that men of reason should have no difficulty to accept. Human diversity, like God who created diversity is there for all of us to see, and is biologically an essential feature of the evolutionary process. Sachs also quotes Einstein who had something profound to say about faith. "But science can only be created by those who are thoroughly imbued with the aspiration toward truth and understanding. This source of feeling, however, springs from the sphere of religion. To this there also belongs the faith in the possibility that the regulations valid for the world of existence are rational, that is, comprehensible to reason. I cannot conceive of a genuine scientist without that profound faith".

Modernity brought with it citizenship and civil rights for Jews and first time after the French revolution in 1789 that Jews were free to move out of imposed isolation in Ghettoes. They could join the mainstream of European society, and an increasing number became emancipated. As rabbi Sacks argued in his Reith Lecture in 1990 on 'The Persistence of Faith', "The cost of emancipation was that Jews would have to undergo the most characteristic change of modernity; the privatisation of faith". Sacks also writes elsewhere of the great dilemma of the Holocaust "the absence of a shared set of Jewish meanings which alone might have allowed the Holocaust to be incorporated into collective Jewish memory. For the religious believer, the Holocaust confirms his faith; for the unbeliever, it confirms his lack of faith. He quotes the philosopher John Cottingham on religious faith in the moving words: "The most profoundly spiritual and passionately religious people in the world's history, the people who produced Moses and the prophets and Jesus and Paul, were a people whose history was conspicuous by the most terrible suffering, the cataclysmic traumas of slavery, wanderings in the desert, a homeland marked by the ever-present threat of war and annihilation, brutal captivity, exile, ruthless suppression and control by a series of imperial subjugators. This is the people who reflected endlessly on *chesed*, the loving kindness of God, who produced the immortal lines, 'surely thy goodness and loving kindness shall follow me all the days of my life".

Mark Lilla argues, "For a moral faith to be truly moral it must also be a rational faith – that is, consistent with reason in its practical employment. He attributes to Rousseau and Hegel that every civilization known to us developed out of religion, which has the power to forge social bonds that no other force seems to possess. That this truth caused his readers to forget another truth – that religious passions can violently break those same social bonds – does not make it less true." Liberal theologians hoped that the moral principles expressed in biblical faith will be reconciled with modern political life. They taught morality, tolerance, progressive politics, and patriotism, and were imbued with faith in the natural goodness of man. However, they failed to recognise the all too emotional make up of man as envisaged by Hobbes, Locke, and Hume. As William James noted, human beings need faith and religion as much as they need to eat and drink. It is ironic that as much as some scientists are distancing themselves from God, they instinctively refer to him, and the latest is the 'God's particle' – Higgs boson.

Nietzsche also refers to faith, "It is still a metaphysical faith upon which our faith in science rests – that even we seekers after knowledge today, we godless anti-metaphysicians, still take our fire, too, from the flame lit by a faith that is thousands of years old, that Christian faith which was also the faith of Plato, that God is the truth, the truth is divine." Kant suggested that "while fear may have given birth to ideas of demons, and while the heart may beat to vague religious notions, our noble ideas of God could have arisen only from our highest faculty, our reason. That is why there is no shame in saying that God is something man needs. Religion has roots in needs that are rational and moral, even noble. Once we see that, we can start learning how to satisfy those needs rationally, morally and nobly."

The loss of faith creates a void in some people without spiritual nourishment that human beings need to feel good about themselves and the world. There is no effective secular body at large that can fill the vacuum that loss of faith creates. The spiritual support that faith can offer, irrespective of the rational basis, is a fundamental social phenomenon that is likely to have an ontological basis in the distant past.

CHAPTER 6: ENLIGHTENMENT, CIVILIZATION, CULTURE

I. **Introduction**
II. **Enlightenment**
III. **Morality and Conscience**
IV. **The Church, Jews and Enlightenment**
V. **Civilization versus Culture**
VI. **Do Humanities Humanise?**
VII. **Germany's Special Culture Path ('Sonderweg')**
VIII. **People of the Book; Burning Books**
IX. **German-Jewish Affinities**

ENLIGHTENMENT, CIVILIZATION AND CULTURE

'Thinking for oneself at all times is Enlightenment'

Immanuel Kant, 1724-1807

'Death and life are in the power of the tongue'

Proverbs 18:21, adopted by Goebbels, 1897-1945

'I disapprove of what you say, but I will defend to the death your right to say it'

Voltaire 1694-1778

'Power regardless of its nature...
Is naturally the enemy of enlightenment...
Truth is at once the enemy of power
and those who exercise it.
Truth is above laws'

Condorcet's philosophy 1743-1794

'Nüremberg trial struck a blow to complaisant Christianity and Enlightened humanity, which to this day failed adequately to explore, explain or deal with the radical evil, to which they were a party, however indirectly, and cannot be exonerated'.

Lawrence Douglas in 'The Memory of Judgment', 2001

I. INTRODUCTION

Light has enormous significance in the religious, metaphysical, physical, and biological sense. God created light before everything else and the greatest scientists from Galileo, Copernicus, and Newton to Einstein, were studying the sun, stars and the physical properties of light, which marked the renaissance of science. In the biological sphere, energy from light is absorbed in photosynthesis by chlorophyll in plants, eventually to produce oxygen, which is largely its sole source in the Earth's atmosphere.

The Hebrew Bible declares 'Let there be light' at the very beginning of the creation of heaven and earth. Nathan Aviezer, professor of physics equates the creation, the sudden emergence of an enormous ball of light, named by scientists 'Big Bang', with Genesis (1:3). He argues that the discovery of light at the very beginning of time is consistent with the written word in the Bible. The discovery of the 'primordial gravitational waves' by the Harvard-Smithsonian Centre for Astrophysics suggests to scientists 'instant creation'.

The great significance of light versus darkness, good versus bad, has been the motif of many ideologies throughout history and not least that of the enlightenment. Among the prophets, Isaiah states, 'light unto the Nations' (42:6, 49:6, 60:3), which designates the Jewish people as spiritual mentors, giving guidance to the world. There is no indication whether this is to be direct or through an intermediary prophet. However, a critical paradigm to be considered is whether the Jewish Jesus may have been ordained to pass the teaching of one and only God to the Nations. Indeed, in the Acts 13:47 "Jesus is the 'Light' unto the Gentiles". Whether this was done by Jesus alone or more likely through the Jewish Paul, does not change the basic notion. Paul reached non-Jews by his pragmatic approach, shedding disincentives, such as circumcision of males and restrictive dietary laws, thereby easing conversion and emphasizing love instead of law. Rabbi David Kimhi comments, "And unto your light, nations shall walk (Book of Isaiah, 60:3), and the light, is the Torah that comes forth for them from Zion, and Israel shall be the maintenance of the nations [...] There shall be peace for them among all nations, as is stated of the Messiah: 'He will judge among the nations and they shall beat their swords into plowshares' (Book of Isaiah, 2:4)".

Jews have introduced novel ideas, which invariably disturbs the harmony of the established views. The first unique concept was of course, the 'single omnipresent, omnipotent invisible God' and his rigid laws and ethics. The 'Ten Commandments' have largely been absorbed into the jurisprudence of most nations. God's 'Word' of creation, logos, spirit, or reason of the Septuagint, the Greek translation of the Pentateuch and later referred to as the 'Old Testament', has resonated up to the present time. Indeed, Philo applied Greek philosophical reasoning to Logos as the link between God and the universe. Philo was an observant Jew, living within a large Jewish community in Alexandria. However, his writing had a greater impact on Christianity than Judaism. It is challenging to speculate whether Philo influenced some twelve centuries later the Jewish sage Maimonides (Rambam), who settled in Cairo and also used Greek philosophy in many of his interpretations of Judaism. He wrote extensively on theology, law, medicine, and though initially his writing was viewed with suspicion by the rabbis, because of using alien Greek reasoning, his wisdom prevailed and he became one of the greatest Jewish thinkers of all time. His 'Guide of the Perplexed' was written for Jewish intellectuals, whose confusion stemmed from apparent contradiction between faith and reason. It is equally uncertain if Philo may have influenced Spinoza sixteen centuries later, equating God with Nature.

Menorah – The seven-branched candelabrum became the centrepiece of Jewish culture and identity. The earliest appearance of the Menorah was on minted coins of the last Hasmonean king, tombs, and walls of houses. Indeed, the Menorah became a generic symbol of the Jewish religion. It was present in the Second Temple and is found on the Arch of Titus in Rome (81 CE). The Menorah was selected as the emblem of the State of Israel, derived from the vision of the prophet Isaiah as the 'Light unto the Nations'. Hanukkah, the Jewish 'Festival of Lights', is a holiday commemorating rededication of the second Holy Temple in Jerusalem after the successful revolt by Judas Maccabeus against Antiochus. The festival is observed by kindling the lights in an eight-branched Menorah over eight days, reciting blessings and singing a hymn.

Arguably the earliest and most important scientific discoveries dealt with proving that the earth rotates around the sun by Copernicus and Galileo, with Newton's robust demonstration of the force of gravity. Newton then demonstrated the detraction of light by a prism into the spectrum of colours. These pioneers of science changed the world outlook and largely introduced science as the most powerful force for discovering the truth about the workings of nature. Some two centuries later Einstein, established the speed of light as a constant that led to the theory of relativity, gravity, space, and time, and changed our understanding of the universe.

The two cultures, Art and Science, and the inevitable failure to unify them is well illustrated in the Goethe – Newton Conundrum. The giant literary figure, placed among the three greats – Dante – Shakespeare – Goethe, had great admiration for Linnaeus's orderly classification of plants. Goethe himself had shown a great deal of interest in plants, indeed he established the Botanical Garden at the University of Jena. However, he showed uncharacteristic animosity towards Newton, who by the time of Goethe was greatly revered for his experiments, demonstrating the diffraction of light under defined experimental conditions. Goethe argued that because light cannot be split into its component colours under natural but only the 'artificial conditions' used by Newton, it cannot be a true interpretation. Here, we have a demonstration of both great men seeking verifiable natural truth, but Goethe in the 18th century was not aware of a basic rule of scientific investigations, that the conditions under which an experiment is carried out must be standardized to exclude variable factors that may affect the results. Nonetheless, Goethe demonstrated the quest of an artist to understand interactions with science, in biology, geology, physics, and human relationships. The latter was expressed in Goethe's novel 'Wahlverwandtschaften' (elective affinities), applying the chemical concept of preferential interaction between elements to human attractions and bonding between men and women.

The unfortunate divide between Church and Science, which initially led to burning at the stake of scientists stepping out of line with the principles of the Church, has harmed the Church and antagonised scientists up to the present day. The case of Galileo having to recant his scientific belief that the earth moves around the orbit of the sun is well known. It took the Catholic Church almost half a millennium to admit the truth of the heliocentric nature of the cosmos; Luther also failed to accept the scientific truth. Under these irrational circumstances, many scientists ignored the teachings of the Church on Nature and surged ahead with unprecedented success in discovering Nature's laws both in the physical and biological world. Nonetheless, the two cultures, Religion and Science, need to be harmonised perhaps by faith not only in the teaching of the Church but also in the verifiable truth of science. I believe this is an objective that religious faith might aim to develop in a revival of its significance for the welfare of humanity.

II. ENLIGHTENMENT

Light – Enlightenment in French (Lumières), is a term applied to reasoned propositions, coined in the 18th century in France, and was based largely on reason, truth, and science. It was the most important intellectual, cultural, social, and scientific transformation of the Western world since the Renaissance. The Enlightenment is seen by some as 'the revolution of the mind'. The principal exponents were men of great intellect and logical thinking; Jean-Jacques Rousseau (1712-1778), Voltaire (Francois-Marie Arouet, 1694-1778), and Marie J. A. N. Condorcet (1743-1794). The British Enlightenment also acknowledged reason as of the essence, but argued that it is associated with emotion, empathy, and is guided by realism and historical precedent. Conceptually this attitude lacked the attraction of unity of concept that is human reason alone, but acknowledged the reality of human endeavour and judgment, which is governed by both reason and emotion. The distrust of the abstract intellectual concepts and favouring instead the pragmatic well tried experience has been at the forefront of British thinking; common sense and exemplary tolerance. The men responsible for this concept were the Scot, David Hume (1711-1776), the Irishman, Edmund Burke (1729-1797), and the Englishman, Adam Smith (1723-1790). The German view, led by Immanuel Kant (1724-1802), was broadly following the French concept and perhaps even more rigid. Kant advocated the faculty of pure reason, detached from emotion, expressed in his celebrated 'Categorical Imperative'; unconditional, rule of moral behaviour. As Churchland argues, "Kant's conviction that detachment from emotions is essential in characterizing moral obligation is strikingly at odds with what we know about our biological nature. Basic emotions are Mother Nature's way of orienting us to do what we prudently ought. The social emotions are a way of getting us to do what we socially ought, and the reward/punishment system is a way of learning to use past experiences to improve our performance in both domains."

Freedom of speech is a categorical imperative of the Enlightenment as stated by Voltaire, 'I disapprove of what you say, but I will defend to the death your right to say it'. This statement has become the Gospel of democracy, with qualification that free speech should not incite or threaten violence against people, especially the minorities, which exist in every country. The universities are particularly vulnerable to abuse by students, testing newly acquired ideas that may excite their as yet uncritical and inexperienced minds and can lead to violence by engaging others with different or opposing ideas. Some lecturers may take the lead in ideological polemics, usurp their status, and threaten liberal democracy. Extremists have recognised the soft option of the Universities, and under the protective cloak of free speech, they have promoted intolerance and even terrorism. Safeguards of free speech must go hand in hand with safeguards of liberty, free from threats, abuse, and coercion. The biblical proverb (18:21), 'Death and life are in the power of the tongue', is a powerful counter-argument to safeguarding civil liberties, epitomised in the mouth of a Goebbels or the author of the 'Protocols of the elders of Zion'. University Vice-Chancellors have a problem, which they have not addressed adequately. Although Voltaire's absolute dictum is right, it must be qualified not to incite physical harm, so as to prevent future bloodshed. Incidentally, if Voltaire were to be challenged 'to defend to the death the right to say it', there can be little doubt from his character that he would not exercise his principle. Jeffrey Collins, professor of History at the Queen's University, Ontario, refers to Voltaire as a "Sycophant to enlightened despots". With the exception of Kurt Huber of the 'White Rose', no other philosopher has opposed the National Socialist and some, such as Heidegger, were active collaborators of the Nazi ideology.

It is noteworthy that the neurobiological discoveries of the interactions between the pre-frontal cortex of reasoning and the 'limbic system' of emotion argues in favour of the British view of the enlightenment. Rousseau declared 'Good and Evil flow from the same source'. Indeed, the lofty ideals of the enlightenment were perverted by the free will, giving individuals the power to subjugate others to their persuasion and ideals displaying intolerance to any dissent. One of the indictments of the enlightenment is that despite its worthy ideals, it brought about or at least failed to prevent totalitarian regimes in the 20th century, with suffering, loss of liberty, imprisonment, and, finally, extermination of millions of people. The assumption was made by some theologians that God has been rejected and with it, the shackles of Judeo-Christian morality resulting in new criteria of good and evil.

An insightful analysis of the Enlightenment by Tzvetan Todorov points out a rare consensus between Diderot, Condorcet, and Kant that the enlightenment endorsed criticism of all facts and that moral and political views must be also open to examination and discussion. Indeed, Kant expressed, "the maxim of thinking for oneself at all times is Enlightenment." A distinction has been drawn between two types of activities, one is to promote good and the other to aspire to truth, in order to remove knowledge from the control of religion.

Condorcet was a materialist, eliminating divine providence from its role in history and human affairs. He was a proponent of universal education and the universality of humanity. Condorcet identified a significant distinction between "the sphere of the will, which aspires to good, and the sphere of knowledge, which focuses on truth. The former is exemplarily embodied in political acts: the latter in science. The two follow different lines of reasoning, and Condorcet went so far as to maintain that 'generally speaking, power, regardless of its nature, regardless in whose hands it has been confided and regardless of the manner in which it has been conferred, is naturally the enemy of enlightenment'. The reason for this conflict seemed simple to him: the more enlightened people are, the more capable they are of deciding for themselves and the less they will tend to submit blindly to power. 'Truth is at once the enemy of power and of those who exercise it'. The political authority must not teach its choices disguised as truths. 'Truth is above laws' and the conflict between their criteria and those between individuals, communities and governments creates complexities that have not been resolved."

Rousseau argued in favour of an inbuilt continuity between accumulated knowledge and moral and political perfection, as opposed to many contemporary philosophers. 'We can be men without being scholars' is obviously true, but the increase in our knowledge has not improved the moral and political status of humanity. Indeed, the immense progress made through education, science, communication and every field of human endeavour in the 20th century has been associated with two bloody world wars, two deadly dictatorships and the pinnacle of evil – the Holocaust.

The changes wrought by the Enlightenment were running in parallel and some would suggest as cause and effect of a transition from God to humanity. Todorov argues persuasively that, "Whatever contributes to the welfare of human beings was deemed good. Such an assertion represents not so much a rejection of the Christian doctrine as a revision thereof. Christianity posited the equivalence of two loves, the love of God and the love of one's neighbour. St Paul proclaimed many times that 'one who loves another has fulfilled the law'. All that Enlightenment thinkers did was to affirm that for them one of the terms of this equation was good enough. 'It's enough to hold to Christian love,' Lessing declared in 1777, 'what happens to the Christian religion does not matter'. Benjamin Franklin illustrated this ten years later, when he maintained that 'the most acceptable service to God is doing good to man'. With the Enlightenment, the pursuit of happiness became a legitimate objective, replacing that of salvation of the soul, and was endorsed by European thinkers, poets, philosophers and artists. Voltaire declared, 'The best citizen is the one who contributes to the happiness of the world' and a most poignant and brief line was expressed by Alexander Pope in his 'Essay on Man' – "Oh happiness! Our beings end and aim".

Rousseau, in 'The Social Contract', drew the conclusion of strict equality before the law of every citizen. The social contract theory of Edmund Burke stated "a partnership in all science; a partnership in all art; a partnership in every virtue and in all perfection". He wisely stated that legitimate politics secured rights, while civilized religion promoted community. It was the New World of North America that expressed human rights in the common law of the 'Declaration of Rights' in 1776. Only thirteen years later in the French Revolution (1789) was this established in France, though blacks in America and women in Europe had to wait over a century and a half to be granted the right to vote? The Enlightenment was a Western European movement and demonstrated the interactions between otherwise warring states of Europe. Hume explored this issue as early as 1742, arguing in 'Of the rise and progress of the arts and sciences', that plurality of states in Europe seems to favour the development of culture. He stated that "plurality fosters a critical spirit, whereas unity tends to stifle it", a judgment that might be heeded by the advocates of a United Europe. Plurality encourages tolerance, it protects the critical spirit and enables us to see things from different points of view.

III. MORALITY AND CONSCIENCE

Moral philosophers have been arguing about the basis of morality, what is right and wrong in social relationship. Robert Solomon asserted that, 'Morality is a set of fundamental rules that guide our actions', whereas John Rawls, like many other moral philosophers, tried to formulate rules of fairness that ought to govern policy and legislation. The definition of morality is of considerable significance and this was given by Bernard Gert in the entry of the Stanford Encyclopaedia of Philosophy as either (1) descriptively to refer to a code of conduct (a) put forward by a society or some other group, such as a religion, (b) accepted by an individual for his or her own behaviour, or (2) normatively to refer to a code of conduct that given specified conditions, would be put forward by all rational persons."

John Stuart Mill (1806-1873) showed profound insight into social life by proposing that "the only thing that is desirable as an end in itself is happiness". It is a view that echoes Aristotle's much earlier claim that the highest good is happiness, in the ancient sense of living well and flourishing. For Mill, "the moral sphere is fundamentally about conduct that injures, damages or harms others or their interests [...] In Mill's considered opinion, the sole end for which liberty may be restricted is self-defence". Recently, Thomas Scanlon reiterated the thesis that "all that counts morally is the well-being of individuals, no one of whom is singled out as counting for more than others." Further analysis of the French versus British views of the enlightenment by Friedrich Hayek in 'The Constitution of Liberty' and J. L. Talmon in 'The Origin of Totalitarian Democracy' are highly pertinent. They reiterated the French revolutionary philosophical approach, relying on reason only. In contrast to the British evolutionary, well tried progress by small incremental steps, bearing in mind the interaction between reason, emotion, and experience. The French way was to enforce freedom and human rights by revolution and political means, which resulted in large number of victims and finally consumed the children of the revolution. The English approach defined the limitations of the power of the state, safeguarding the freedom of the individual.

The relationship between conscience, morality, and religion is a complex issue. Whether human conscience is a guide to moral decision or conversely morality arises from conscience, is debatable. Furthermore, is morality a gift from God and involves the natural law that he wishes man for his own good to follow, with threat of punishment if disobeyed.

Alternatively, is it a result of genetic, neuronal, and/or environmental interactions that develop from birth and onwards in social life. As with many similar questions and dilemmas, both viewpoints accept that conscience and morality are closely linked and form the basis of civilised behaviour of a good society. Whether one derives this point of view through faith in God's moral laws or by the interaction of the above factors remains an open question. Perhaps the only compliment that Hitler paid to the Jews was to state that "Conscience was a Jewish invention". As the neurobiological and genetic evidence become more compelling and tracing of our neurological and genetic codes are presently making astonishing advances, the question might be resolved.

IV. THE CHURCH, JEWS AND THE ENLIGHTENMENT

From the very emergence of Christianity, the 'Christian Fathers' were hostile to Jews who rejected Christ, and even advocated extermination of Jews unless they accepted Jesus Christ, first as a prophet, later as the Messiah, and finally as the son of God. It was St. Augustine who argued that they should be allowed to live under dire conditions to act as witnesses to the Christian truth. The principle taught by the Christian fathers that the Jews should be eliminated for the 'glory of God', as the absolute truth was possessed only by Christianity, unlike Hitler's genocide, which was for the untainted purity of the 'Volk'. Love and morality fall victims to any dastardly act under the banner of the 'glory of God'. This was well expressed by Pierre Bayle, a French Protestant persecuted by Catholics in an attempt to 'save the souls of Protestants'. Bayle quoted the injunction from the Gospels (Luke 14:23) to justify persecution: 'Beat, whip, imprison and kill the obstinate and take away their women and children'. Todorov argues, "A noble end cannot be achieved by ignoble means because the end will be lost on the way." He cites John Paul II who accuses, "the morality that resulted from the Enlightenment of being purely subjective, depending on will alone, and susceptible to pressure from those in power, unlike Christian morality, which he deems immutable because it is objectively based on God's word. There is reason to ponder whether the Pope's objectivity is real since no one can claim direct contact with God. The principles of good and evil are the subject of a consensus: this consensus is potentially that of all of humanity, and it is established through an exchange of rational arguments. The morality of the Enlightenment proceeds not from egotistical self-love but from respect for humankind." It might be argued that the 'light of Isaiah' is the light of morality and religion, whereas that of the Enlightenment is the light of reason, and the interaction between these two complementary, long established ideals is a highly desirable goal.

Isaiah's prophecy was that Israel will be 'The light unto the Nations', acting as a spiritual mentor and offering guidance to the world (42:6, 49:6, 60 :). The fulfilment of this has been open to interpretation. There is little doubt that Jews through Paul carried out this mission to the Gentiles, though greatly revised by introducing Jesus as the Messiah. Perhaps the fact that 1.5 billion Christians have been converted to the God of Abraham, as were another billion of Muslims speaks for itself. Not surprisingly major differences developed, especially in interpretations, exegesis, prophets, prayers and festivals to suit the vast diversity of humanity.

Jewish Enlightenment ('Haskalah') emerged in the late eighteenth century. It is astonishing that despite being oppressed, isolated, and prevented from joining educational and professional institutions on and off until the Enlightenment, when Jews were let out from their ghetto existence and gained civil rights, almost overnight they excelled in the arts, literature, music, law, medicine, science, and economy. They attempted to integrate Judaism with Kantian philosophy of Rationality, Justice and Learning. Prayer became a cultural affirmation of one's faith. Karl Marx wrote his masterpiece on 'dialectical materialism', a scientific method of understanding history and economics, ushering in egalitarian principles of communism, not entirely out of tune with those of Jesus and this led to world revolutions. Freud explored the subconscious, stumbling onto sexuality linked to the selfish gene, which shook the religious establishment. Einstein presented novel concept of gravity, light and relativity which revolutionised our understanding of the physical world. Recent discovery of the 'primordial gravitational waves' confirms yet another prediction of Einstein's – a scientist of prophetic insight into the universe. Jews have been credited paradoxically with both communism and capitalism, presumably not entirely because of their talent in economy and finances. Jews have been awarded 193 out of a total of 855 Nobel Prizes, which amounts to 22% and does not bear comparison with representing less than 0.2% of the world population. Overall they have won 41% of all Nobel Prizes in economics, 28% in medicine, 26% in physics, 19% in chemistry, 13% in literature, and 9% of all peace awards. Steiner refers to "some primal force is at work", but whether this is the continuation of 'light unto the nations', a hereditary trait or some socio-economic factor is open to speculation.

V. CIVILIZATION VERSUS CULTURE

'Civilization was the principal victim of Nazi ideology' Justice Jackson, Nüremberg Trial, 1946
'The Holocaust was not only a political crime, it was also a moral failure' Wolf Lepenies, 2006
"The Holocaust is a rupture with civilization" Hannah Arendt, 1943
'The National Socialist regime demonstrated all the instincts of barbarism, repressed by centuries of civilization, but always present in the innermost nature, all the negations of the traditional values of humanity' François de Menthon, Nüremberg Trial, 1946
"The most organised cultural violence was anti-Semitism and the most extreme was human sacrifice. The two merged in the Holocaust" Adapted from G. Didi-Huberman 'In Spite of it all', 2008
'During Hitler's reign great art was allied with great evil' Thomas Mann, 1996

In an extensive study, "A History of Civilization", Fernand Braudel discusses the origins of the terms civilization and culture and their interchangeable usage since the early 19th century. The term civilization emerged in the 16th century in France and by the next century, it was applied only in jurisprudence to indicate an act of justice or judgment. However, there are two essential aspects of civilization. First the moral values endorsed by the 10 Commandments, Hillel-Jesus dictum 'Do unto others as you would do unto yourself', then the proclamations of human rights in the Babylonian Cyrus cylinder (c.578 BC), England's Magna Carta (c.1215), the American Declaration of Independence (1776), and the French Declaration of the Rights of Man in 1789 are landmarks in the history of freedom, liberty, and the development of Civilization. These liberal ideas invoked the notion of freedom, tolerance, and respect for the individual. The second are material values of civilization, which apply to technological, economic, and biological factors. These include human endeavours in basic conditions of land, climate, vegetation, animals, agriculture, food, shelter, clothing, communications, and industry. The opposite of civilization is barbarism that refers to regression to primitive unruly practices of early human beings or atavism. Indeed, Claude Lévi-Strauss considers civilization as the difference between primitive and modern societies.

Culture, in contrast, denotes human intellectual appreciation, development of education, rationalism, ideas, customs, and all aspects of arts, commonly associated with spiritual matters; literature, poetry, music, paintings, and sculpture. The confusion between culture and civilization may be ascribed to the notion that culture has a humanising effect on the development of civilization. In Germany, Poland, and Russia, a division between the two concepts has been maintained with emphasis on culture, at the expense of civilization, including democracy, whereas in Britain, U.S., and France, culture has conventionally implied civilization, politics and democracy. Religion spans across both, civilization by its moral values, and culture in all aspects of art and education throughout the history of Western civilization. Faith in God has a significant civilizing effect on millions of people and is a powerful force that many intellectuals are prone to ignore at their peril. Nonetheless, religious wars have led to some of the worst atrocities in the annals of warfare by religious fanatics, who convince themselves and then force it on others, that they are doing God's will. Toynbee, in his book, 'Civilisation on Trial' (1948), defined civilisation as a field of study, that is a people living within reasonably definable borders, with a complex culture of political, ethical, religious and other beliefs that are so intertwined that it is difficult or impossible to dissociate them. This is the most common understanding, which integrates culture within the concept of civilisation and does not differentiate between them. Toynbee emphasized that Civilization is the fundamental form of human society, though later in life he downgraded civilizations and promoted religious identities above them.

However, throughout history a reversal into barbarism has been manifested by each religious faction, when extreme fanaticism of belief in and access to God takes over the existence of an individual and all reason and restraint are lost. Hence, in the major religions we can observe the extremes of civilization linked with culture on the one hand and culture linked with barbarism on the other, which tends to demean the institution of religion. The recurring theme of religious oppression has not received adequate attention by theologians, despite its critical significance, and raises the disturbing question if it has a survival value for religion. Nonetheless, Western civilization is to a large measure, a product of Western Christianity. Braudel makes a fundamental point in arguing that "a European, even if he is an atheist, is still a prisoner of an ethic and mentality which are deeply rooted in the Christian tradition. He remains, one might say of Christian descent".

The working definition of civilization used in this book is based on the principle of natural justice, by reasoning humanity, abiding by individual freedom, and gaining material welfare, which does not harm others – it is the opposite to barbarism. Culture refers to human appreciation, expression and development of education, reason, ideas, and all branches of the arts that elevate the sense of well-being, happiness, and spiritual fulfilment.

Friedrich Nietzsche has probably come nearest to the essence of German spirit. In writing on "Kultur contra Zivilisation", he distinguished between the two. He thought it possible that Zivilisation is the converse to Kultur and that the former was inferior to Kultur. By the twentieth century, the British and French claimed to defend the Christian European civilization from the aggression of the Austrian and German barbarians, the descendants from the Goth and Huns. On the other hand, the Germans, especially during the Great War, claimed to defend European culture.

The concept of 'civilization' served at the Nüremberg Trial to refer to 'natural law or natural justice'. Justice Jackson pointed out that 'civilization was the principal victim of Nazi ideology', indeed the practice of civilized – not cultured – nations was a recurrent theme in the Nuremberg indictment. According to Lawrence Douglas in his book, 'The Memory of Judgment' (2001), the concept of civilization served as a bona fide source of international law, which could have alternatively referred to natural law or natural justice. François de Menthon declared that The National Socialist regime demonstrated 'all the instincts of barbarism, repressed by centuries of civilization, but always present in men's innermost nature, all the negations of the traditional values of humanity.'

VI. DO HUMANITIES HUMANIZE?

The fundamental question, whether art raises the spirit of man and heightens his civil behaviour towards fellow beings has usually been taken for granted, yet never resolved. The development of visual art from the early times of cave paintings, to the figurines worshipped by some believers or the golden calf worshipped by the ancient Hebrews, raising the wrath of God, are clear manifestations of human desire and need to express aesthetic feelings linked to spiritual matters. The illumination of bibles and learned books further links art to spiritual appreciation, which persisted during the medieval period. Indeed, the arts have been supported by the Church in painting, sculpture, and music, expressing the Bible stories and teachings of Moses, Christ, and the Apostles. Great architecture of churches and cathedrals again associated art with homage to the creator and teachers of religion. With the renaissance in the 16th century and later the enlightenment in the 18th century, a transfer of art occurred from the sacred to the secular sphere. Great art received patronage from wealthy individuals and in modern times, art has ceased to be the province of the rich and has been popularized with a diversity of expressions and tastes.

Indeed, as early as the classical Greek period over 2000 years ago, the significance of art has been controversial. Aristotle believed that art, especially music, was character forming and improves moral qualities, unlike Plato who believed that art has no rational basis, enhances emotional expression and does not aim to reveal truth. In the 18th century, Goethe visiting an art gallery wrote, "the emotion experienced upon entering a House of God. The objects of adoration consecrated to the holy ends of art". Rather similar thoughts were expressed by William Hazlitt on visiting the National Gallery that it was akin to going on a pilgrimage to the "holy of holies". John Keats perhaps made the most profound statement, "Truth is beauty and beauty is truth", which endorses the unity between the aesthetic and rational spheres of humanity.

There have been many studies of the effect of art on other human activities and all that could be concluded, not surprisingly, is that the study of art refines appreciation of art. The great surge by some of the American fine art museums spending millions of dollars on art from Europe in the belief that it will change people's material to more spiritual endeavours has not accomplished its objective. In fact, mostly the educated and middle classes took full advantage of these developments.

A salutary lesson may be learnt from Frank Palmer's plausible view that literature can strengthen our moral imagination by entering the mind of the reader. He gives us Shakespeare's Macbeth as an example of understanding murder. Nonetheless, Palmer concedes when considering Tolstoy or Delius that "a man of fine artistic sensibilities may in other respects remain a swine". Marghanita Laski, among others, addressed the question whether arts improve our humanity and whether they elicit any distinct quality in our existence. She devised a table of criteria for kindness and altruism to define the goodness of a person. The result failed to support the make-belief that the arts make people better. Goering and Hitler competed in stealing Jewish art collections, but dozens of Rembrandts, Rubens, Leonardos, or Cranachs did not make either of them less than pre-meditated murderers. George Steiner consistently raised the issue of concentration camp commandants and personnel, listening to Mozart, Bach, or Beethoven failed to deter them next day from killing hundreds of men, women and children, possibly still humming some of the tunes. There is little or no evidence that arts equate with or enhance civilization, though they may elicit spiritual well-being, happiness, and diversion from common material issues that confront people in everyday life.

Hitler may well be considered as the ultimate in Evil for whom even Genghis Khan was no match, so his appreciation of the arts is surprising and pertinent. Despite Hitler being generally dismissed as an artist, Frederic Spotts in his book, 'Hitler and the Power of Aesthetics', has convincingly presented Hitler having serious interest in paintings, sculpture, architecture, and music. According to John Carey, Professor of English Literature at the University of Cambridge (in 'what good are the arts?'), apart from Wagner, Hitler admired Bruckner's symphonies, he was an admirer of classical Greek art, and was apparently capable of discussing the philosophies of Kant, Schopenhauer, and Nietzsche. Hitler's interest in art was further manifested by bringing culture to the masses through music festivals, art exhibitions, and funding grants to support artists. Indeed, after becoming Chancellor in 1933, the first building to be erected was the House of German Art in Munich. Beauty mattered more than people, but what is beautiful or degenerate art ('Endartete-Kunst') was the Führer's prerogative. Goebbels was a writer of plays and a novel, Rosenberg studied architecture, Goering was an art collector, Hans Frank was cultured and university educated. Dr. Mengele with a double doctorate was the product of German University education, he was the arbitrator between life and death of thousands of innocent men, women and children at the selection ramp of concentration camps. He was a lover of classical music,

Schumann's 'Träumerei' was his favourite piece. Indeed, in Thomas Mann's succinct statement, "During Hitler's reign great art was allied with great evil".

Despite all the evidence that the humanities may not humanise or have moral and educational values, Robert Hewison in his otherwise powerful book, 'Culture and consensus, England, Art and Politics since 1940', maintains that "culture is the shaping moral medium for all society's activities". One of the most insightful analysis of the divide between culture and civilisation has been presented by Wolf Lepenies, formerly Rector of the 'Wissenschaftskollegium' of the German Institute for Advanced Study in Berlin and Professor of Sociology at the Free University in Berlin. In his book 'The Seduction of Culture in German History', Lepenies argues persuasively that the Germans claimed to be the only nation to possess and value culture – they are a 'Kulturnation' whilst the rest of the West are merely 'Civilised'. The overestimation of cultural achievements might have facilitated the coexistence of humanism and bestiality, as characterised by the proximity of Weimar classicism – Jena University with the Buchenwald concentration camp. By the same token, the destruction of the famous Louvain Library by the German army, twice within thirty years, was an act of barbarism, which contradicts the German love for art and knowledge unless it is confined to everything German and the rest, with some notable exceptions, is of little interest or better destroyed. Leonardo's Mona Lisa or Michelangelo's 'Pietas' evoke spiritual sentiments, but as to having any effect on the person's empathy, altruism, or morality, there is little evidence, despite long-standing wishful thinking in favour of these qualities. Indeed, Carey (2005) quotes Browning that art destroys its admirer's human core and leaves a monster. "The bishop of St Praxed's church combined art-worship, cruelty, holiness and racism, Christianity and paganism, impotence and lust in a single poisonous amalgam, when planning the decoration for his tomb:

Some lump, ah God of lapis lazuli
Big as a Jew's head cut off at the nape,
Blue as a vein o'er the Madonna's breast
Saint Praxed in a glory, and one Pan
Ready to twitch the nymph's last garment off
And Moses with the tables.

Carey points out that literature may also fail in affecting moral behaviour but it differs from music or visual art, in so far that it is subject to reason, arguments, qualifications, reappraisal, and criticism. Most importantly, literature deals with concepts and language and it is the medium that explores concepts. An intriguing point to consider is that some literature, especially Shakespeare's, leads to creative reading, because it is written in a way open to individual interpretation. Creativity is a very human characteristic, which greatly uplifts the spirit and happiness, and can manifest itself in small matters of 'discovery' of an original meaning in a text or in writing a successful book.

George Steiner, in 'Bluebeard's Castle', argues that after the Holocaust we cannot assume that 'the humanities humanize', as aesthetic appreciation can co-exist with extreme evil: "A fair proportion of the intelligentsia and of the institutions of European civilization – letters, the academy, the performing arts – met inhumanity with varying degrees of welcome. Nothing in the next door world of Dachau impinged on the great winter cycle of Beethoven chamber music played in Munich [...] Why, demands Steiner, should we labour to elaborate and transmit culture if it did so little to stem the inhuman? Great art and music have flourished under totalitarian regimes, and this suggests that culture has always been 'tautological with elitism'. Are not the elevation and transcendence that culture induces essentially irresponsible?"

John Drummond, in his memoir 'Tainted by Experience: A Life in the Arts', recounts how, in 1963, he was making a BBC documentary about Georg Solti's Decca recording of Wagner's 'Götterdämmerung' in Vienna, a commission which brought him into close contact with members of the Vienna Philharmonic Orchestra. 'The orchestra was riddled with anti-Semitism. When he [Solti] later received the Gold Medal of the 'Gesellschaft der Musikfreunde' for the 'Ring' and other opera recordings, practically no one from the professors of the orchestra committee turned up. They all had their excuses – teaching, travel, or prior engagements. On the morning of the presentation day, Solti was telephoned in his room at the Imperial Hotel and a woman's voice said, 'They are not coming because you are a dirty Hungarian Jew.' After receiving the award, as Solti walked along the corridor, the door of the office of Ernst Vobisch, the orchestra's chairman, was open, and all the missing committee members were sitting there having coffee. Vienna doesn't change."

Carey argues, "if western culture truly had the effect Steiner claims, then here at its very heart, among gifted practitioners who are devoted to its daily perfection, in the very country where the Holocaust was engendered, and within two decades of its horrors becoming common knowledge, we should surely find, if anywhere, some evidence of remorse. Drummond's story, on the contrary, shows hatred festering on, unrepented, unassuaged."

VII. GERMANY'S CULTURAL 'SONDERWEG' (SPECIAL PATH)

German historians have often been concerned in the past with the special path 'Sonderweg' that the German people have selected. Hans-Ulrich Wehler carried out an extensive historical study in 2003 and argued that Germany's 'descent into barbarism' in 1933 was not caused by being threatened by the neighbouring countries, as suggested by other historians, but taking the wrong path as it evolved into a modern state. This is not the place to discuss the historical nuances that have led to the adoption of the 'Sonderweg', but briefly, these involved the fragmented Germany of the middle Ages. Martin Luther's bloody confrontation with Rome and the subsequent struggle between Catholics and Lutherans, created a further split in German society. Germany suffered greatly from the 'Thirty Year War' in the seventeenth century and lost a third of its population, which took a long time to recover. Later, Wehler turned to political issues which differentiated Germany from other European countries. These concerned the power of the aristocracy, army, legislature, civil service, and labour movement, encompassing most of the activities of the nation. Germany's late unification in 1871 through war and Prussian leadership by Bismarck resulted in an authoritarian Prussian military tradition. According to Norbert Elias in 'The Germans', "Germany's unification thus involved brutalization of large sections of the middle classes, a process in which the student fraternities in the universities played a critical role". Defeat in the First World War, with its attendant hardships, had a devastating effect on the morale of the population. The demobilized soldiers found themselves without jobs and were readily recruited into private armies (Freikorps). These emerged as nationalist, anti-democratic movements with the objective of undermining and ousting the newly formed Weimar Republic. The 'Freikorps' paved the way to Hitler's power, and was able to break through all barriers and transform the people into a mass movement.

The influence of philosophy on the German people has been pervasive, beginning with Gottfried W. Leibniz (1646-1716), followed by Immanuel Kant (1724-1804), Friedrich Nietzsche (1844-1900), and later Martin Heidegger (1889-1976). Leibniz was a polymath who excelled in mathematics, philosophy, logic, and history. He discovered calculus at the same time as Newton, who accused him of plagiarism, though there was no evidence for this. Leibniz argued that there were two major problems in philosophy; the relationship between the individual and the world at large, and the other is free will. The ultimate constraints of the world were forces, which he called monads, the example of which was the soul. These monads have an innate harmony, which ensures that they fit together. Kant's romantic ideology considered freedom and political expression in an intellectual and somewhat cavalier way. 'Kultur' (Culture) as opposed to democracy and parliamentary government, has been the byword of the aristocracy that appealed to the newly created industrial middle classes. The German historian Thomas Nipperdey (1927-1992) argued that by the 19th century, music, scholarship, and science were great achievements that changed Germany from being the poor relation among the Western nations to becoming a dominant intellectual force.

The concept 'Kultur' as compared with 'Zivilisation' has been explored by many historians. Norbert Elias differentiates between German and French national understanding especially by the middle classes. The French "claim 'la civilisation française est la civilisation humaine' was, on the one hand, undoubtedly an expression of French nationalism and expansionism. But it expressed at the same time the belief that the French national tradition embodied and represented moral and other values and attainments valid for humanity as a whole [...] the German term 'Kultur' in the late nineteenth and early twentieth centuries was increasingly used in the sense of 'national culture', the humanist and moral connotations associated with it at an earlier stage in its career faded into the background and finally disappeared." Elias then points out a crucial difference between German and British moral codes that it is wrong to kill, maim, attack physically or steal, and cheat, but it is permissible if found necessary in the interest of the society at large. This dual and contradictory moral code of conduct is common to both countries, but in Britain, a compromise between these has been wrought. The German view has been rigid to apply the concept culture or civilisation, consistent with the French concept of enlightenment.

Wolf Lepenies discusses in his book the contribution of the history of German ideas current mostly in the 19th and 20th century, to the development of the National Socialist state. He emphasises Elias's argument that the Germans have become obsessed with the appealing notion of being a cultured people ('Kulturnation'), in contrast to the political and civilized France and Britain. It is likely that this concept may have developed as a compensation for being looked down on by the West. Even Frederick the Great denigrated the German language, stating that literature could not be written in German but only in French. The British Empire stretched over large parts of the world, with the confidence of the upper classes educated to lead and govern. Arguably the greatest scientist of its time, Sir Isaac Newton, and the greatest literary figure, William Shakespeare, were the envy of Germany. By the late 19th century, the small insignificant Duchy of Weimar, prompted by the discerning eye of the Dowager Anna Amelia, appointed Goethe as tutor to the Duke Carl August. This single inconspicuous move paved the way for German entry into the European cultural club. In a small but important political gesture, even Napoleon at the height of his conquest acknowledged Goethe's cultural status by inviting him to a meeting and by all accounts it turned out to be a mutually successful exchange of literary ideas.

Lepenies argues that "Seeing culture as a substitute for politics has remained a prevailing attitude throughout German history – from the glorious days of 18th and 19th century Weimar [...] And even for members of the intelligentsia in exile, the attitude of playing off culture against politics remained [...] The Nazis were brought to power not so much by the aesthetic appeal of their rituals as by their pledge to restore German pride, their promise to limit the power of big corporations and to create jobs, and their appeal to widespread anti-Semitic feelings, among other reasons. Ideas either originate from intellectuals or are firmed up into a coherent narrative, which then carries the insignia of authority that the general public is more readily prone to accept, most likely through an intermediary".

Weimar classicism, of Goethe and Schiller, with music by Bach and later Beethoven and Mozart among others, has moved the European cultural centre of gravity to Germany and in a large measure to Weimar. Certainly, culture has received the support of the vocal majority at the expense of political movement towards democracy, which was an inevitable loser of the 'Sonderweg'. The cultural elite of Germany consisting of ninety-three intellectuals, writers, artists, and scientists published in October 1914 a manifesto addressed to the civilized world. They denied German responsibility for the war and condemned the West. Indeed, the First World War was considered by some to be between British civilization and German culture ('Kultur'). 'Kultur' was defended by German militarism and they claimed that not only German but the entire European culture depended on the victory of German militarism. Schiller in a poem entitled 'German Greatness', claimed that "German dignity resides in the culture and character of the nation and that both are independent of the political vicissitudes. While the political Empire has tottered, the spiritual realm has become all the firmer and richer". The view prevailed among German elite that democracy was alien to the German spirit and that the Weimar Republic had no real chance of succeeding.

After the founding of the Reich by Bismarck in 1879, Nietzsche argued that no true poet or philosopher could be found in Germany. Furthermore, he attacked German patriotism and predicted that for cultural renaissance, Germany needed a political or military disaster. The tension between politics and culture may have contributed to the rise of National Socialism and the collapse of the Weimar Republic. Although the Nazis burnt books, spurned art they proclaimed degenerate, which included most modern painters, as well as Goya and of course Jewish art, Hitler was a frustrated painter, Goebbels a failed novelist, and Speer an average architect. The studies by Frederick Spotts suggest that Hitler had serious designs in supporting the fine arts, theatre, literature, and music.

Lepenies emphasizes the German illusion that Culture comes first and politics follows. On the contrary "To survive the rupture of civilization it had inflicted upon Europe, Germany would have to give up the most German of all ideologies; the illusion that culture can compensate for politics ... The Holocaust, the great divide of Western civilization should have marked the point of no return, after which the exultation of culture over politics was no longer possible in Germany. The Holocaust was not only a political crime, it was also a moral failure of a magnitude that could no longer be compensated by any artistic achievement". In Theodor Adorno's words, "there cannot be any poetry after Auschwitz".

George Steiner in the T. S. Eliot Memorial Lecture in 1971 perhaps expressed the most cogent thoughts, which he calls 'post-culture' published in 'Bluebeard's Castle'. "We now realize that extremes of collective hysteria and savagery can coexist with a parallel conservation and, indeed, further development of the institutions, bureaucracies and professional codes of high culture. In other words, the libraries, museums, theatres, universities, research centres, in and through which the transmission of the humanities and of the sciences mainly takes place, can prosper next to the concentration camps [...] We know also – and here is knowledge thoroughly documented but in no way, as yet, incorporated in a rational psychology – that obvious qualities of literate response, of aesthetic feeling, can coexist with barbaric, politically sadistic behaviour in the same individual. Men such as Hans Frank who administered the 'final solution' in Eastern Europe were avid connoisseurs and, in some instances, performers of Bach and Mozart. We know of personnel in the bureaucracy of the torturers and of the ovens who cultivated a knowledge of Goethe, a love of Rilke [...] One of the principal works that we have in the philosophy of language, in the total reading of Hölderlin's poetry, was composed almost within earshot of a death camp. Had the Enlightenment and the nineteenth century understood that there could be no presumption of a carry-over from civilization to civility, from humanism to the humane, the springs of hope would have been staunched and much of the immense liberation of the mind and of society achieved over four generations been rendered impossible. No doubt, confidence should have been less. Perhaps the trust in culture was itself hubristic and blind to the counter-currents and nostalgias for destruction it carried within".

Thomas Mann's revulsion towards the Nazi regime developed early after Hitler and his cohort gained power in a democratic election by the Germans. Even after leaving the country in 1937, Mann was puzzled by Hitler's speeches on culture. As quoted by Lepenies of Mann's response "Astounding. This man, a typical product of the lower middle class, with a limited education and an acquired taste for philosophizing, is truly a curious phenomenon. No doubt at all that for him, in contrast to types like Göring and Röhm, the main concern is not war but German culture". However, with increasing atrocities marking out the Third Reich, Mann's views hardened. Whilst in Princeton, Mann wrote in 1944 'Lotte in Weimar' (The Beloved Returns) a tribute to German culture. Mann said that his new novel was "the most consciously, emphatically and deliberately Germanic he had ever undertaken, a mixture of theology, music and genius that continuously suggested the term 'German' with the words 'tragic' and 'demonic' [...] To speak of a pact with the devil that had caused the German catastrophe was not an explanation but an obfuscation of the Nazi period".

Max Weber, the great German sociologist was consistently arguing since the end of the First World War that present political problems could not be solved by harking back to past intellectual achievements. People should engage in culture for its own sake and cultivation of the mind but not for political guidance. The division between culture and political activity was most cogently expressed by Percy Bysshe Shelley that "poets are the unacknowledged legislators of the world – but only the Germans had taken it seriously". In contrast, Friedrich Meinecke the greatly respected German historian, who by that time was eighty-four years old, wrote the widely read 'The German Catastrophe'. He advocated reliance on well-rehearsed German virtues of high culture (music and poetry), religion and elective affinities ('Wahlverwandschaften') among German people, and the formation of 'Goethe communities' all over the country. At least in some respects the clarion call of 'back to Goethe legacy' was also called for by Thomas Mann. This call to moral and cultural roots may well be a manifestation of repentance.

It is noteworthy here to consider the views of the political philosopher Hannah Arendt, whose emotional relationship with Martin Heidegger, her 'Doktorvater' was alluded to earlier. Arendt's other teacher was Karl Jaspers, professor of philosophy at the university of Heidelberg (see p.131). Following the publication of Jaspers's book after the war in 1946 on 'The question of German guilt' (Die Schuldfrage), Lepenies refers to their correspondence, that Arendt was troubled by the book, because Jaspers was speaking of Nazi crimes as if they could be dealt with in court: "Your definition of Nazi policy as a crime ('criminal guilt') strikes me as questionable. The Nazi crimes, it seems to me, explode the limits of the law; and that is precisely what constitutes their monstrousness. For these crimes, no punishment is severe enough. It may well be essential to hang Göring, but it is totally inadequate. That is, this guilt, in contrast to all criminal guilt, oversteps and shatters any and all legal systems. That is the reason why the Nazis in Nuremberg are so smug".

After the war a controversy developed between the emigrant writers such as Mann and Adorno and those that stayed behind and had taken refuge in 'Inner Emigration'. These were led by Frank Thiess, a mediocre writer who stated in his 'Return to Goethe' that they suffered more than the émigrés and by their very presence and reading of Goethe contributed to the survival of the German spirit. This was in response to Mann's outspoken accusation that those who stayed behind helped by their presence to legitimize the Nazi regime and the books written were stained with blood and shame.

VIII. THE 'PEOPLE OF THE BOOK', BURNING BOOKS

The Jewish people are frequently referred to as "The People of the Book", because they adhered rigorously to the Hebrew Bible (Old Testament). This Book was carried by them everywhere in the diaspora and sustained them for several millennia of persecution. The accolade has also been applied to Christians who cherish the New Testament and the old one. The critical difference has been that Jews were strictly prohibited to paint or sculpt any celestial or earthly representation, from the time they venerated the 'Golden calf', when they had to wait for a long time for Moses to come down from Mount Sinai with the Tablets of 10 Commandments. Thus, Jews were limited to the word of the Bible. In contrast, the Catholic Church made it a distinct feature of visual representation of Jesus, the Apostles, and the Gospels on the walls of churches, to enable people to follow the stories of the scriptures.

Throughout history of the past two millennia, burning books has been a demonstrative way to show hatred, disdain, and denial of religious, ideological or cultural pursuit, especially of minorities. Fire, initially illuminates and soon laps up in flames the sacred words of the book. One of the earliest recorded milestones was the fire of the great library in Alexandria (642 AD), which was the repository of the wonders of the ancient civilization though the cause of the fire has not been established. The early Church Fathers in the 5th century committed to flames large numbers of 'forbidden books'. Burning the Talmud has been a favourite pastime during the medieval period in Europe. According to Matthew Fishburn, in his comprehensive account 'Burning Books' (2008), "Religious censorship had dire consequences for the Jewish populations of Europe. Twenty-four cartloads of Jewish writings were burned in Paris in 1288, and many books were burned in England in 1299. In the 1240s the Talmud was regularly burned as it 'threatened and insulted' Catholicism, and expurgations of the text were ordered in Spain in the 1260s. The real mechanism for censorship began with the papal bulls regarding the mass conversion of the Jews, most famously in the early fifteenth-century *Etsi doctoris* of Benedict XIII. Once again the main target of these attacks was the Talmud, culminating in its burning by the Inquisition in 1554."

Savonarola and his disciples in Florence urged the citizens to rid the city and its homes of smut, vanity and frivolity. In the 'Bonfire of Vanities' in 1497, a great pyramid of books, said to have included Ovid, Dante and

Boccaccio was set alight in the town square. French censorship during the Enlightenment, involved burning books of Voltaire, Rousseau, culminating in the destruction of 4 million books by the 18th century. England did not fare better, as books were burned as rituals in the 16th and 17th C, with Luther's works being burned in London. Astonishing as it seems a few years later Tyndale's New Testament was burned publicly by the church leaders.

Goethe, as ever a man of wisdom and judgment, disapproved of book burning, and by the 18th and 19th C, this practice was considered to be barbaric. Yet, students and German nationalists gathered in Wartburg Castle in Eisenach, about 20km west of Goethe's abode in Weimar and burned those books they considered un-German. This act in 1817 indicated not only a break with the past but also a prohibition of future memory. In Nathaniel Hawthorne's story, 'Earths Holocaust' (1844), pilgrims erect a pyre in order to burn the chattels of civilization. Here the Holocaust refers to books but within a century, German 'supermen' of culture burn men, women, and children of civilization, as predicted by Heine.

One of the cultural losses in the First World War was burning the famous Louvain University Library by the German armed forces. The infamous burning of books written by Jewish, socialist, and other authors in 1933 by University students and the SA took place in front of the Opera House in Berlin in a torchlight parade, a great favourite of the fascists. The sequence of 'the people of the book, from burning their books, to burning the people of the book' sadly has proved to be real. Dr. Joseph Goebbels, the propaganda minister, spoke of his hope that from the ashes of the un-German books, the phoenix of the new Reich would rise. The doctor of literature got his metaphor misplaced, as the Thousand Year Reich ended after twelve years in ashes, including Hitler, Goebbels, and his innocent six daughters whom he murdered prior to his well-earned demise.

Following the "Reichstag fire in 1933, student organisations announced burning of Jewish and decadent literature, which was planned in considerable detail. They were greatly encouraged by the German philosopher and Nazi member Alfred Baeumler at his inaugural address as Rector of the University of Berlin. He exhorted the students to pursue book burning directly after his lecture. To Heidegger's credit, the newly appointed Rector of the University of Freiburg, banned these activities.

Fire was the dominant metaphor of Nazi iconography and one of the consolations of swastika is a fire symbol. The Manchester Guardian ridiculed the ceremony of 'Brown shirt brigades of witless students', and concluded that "the German fires were one of the most unedifying examples of mob psychology that can be found in history from the days of Alexandria's library onwards". The Time magazine carried the event as 'Bibliocaust', and Walter Lipmann referred to the 'moral and intellectual character of the Nazi regime', whilst Echo de Paris commented that 'burning books in front of the University was one of the saddest expressions of the new German spirit'. H. G. Wells, at the launch of his latest utopian novel 'The Shape of Things to Come', described National Socialism as 'the clumsy lout's revolution against civilization', though book burning is futile because books 'have a vitality exceeding any human being'. George Orwell called book burning 'the most characteristic activity of the Nazis'.

A most telling argument was advanced by the novelist Joseph Roth, based in Paris by stating "Let me say it loud and clear: The European mind is capitulating. It is capitulating out of weakness, out of sloth, out of apathy, out of lack of imagination [...] Now, as the smoke of our burned books rises into the sky, we German writers of Jewish descent must acknowledge above all that we have been defeated [...] The event is an exercise in the political development that had begun with Bismarck, followed by Hitler, to burn books, to murder Jews and revise Christianity". A unique counterintuitive venture was hatched in 1934 in Paris by German anti-fascists named "Deutsche Freiheitsbibliothek, better known in English as the 'Library of the Burned Books'. Alfred Kantorowicz was its head and among other literary figures was Arthur Koestler, H. G. Wells and Romain Rolland.

The Austrian novelist Erwin G. Kolbenheyer was one of many writers and intellectuals in Germany who aggressively embraced the fires and reforms they had heralded. German attack on its own literature, written by the 'wrong people' or contrary to the perverse ideology of the governing Nazis is one of the lasting memories of the cultural holocaust. In the words of C.E.M. Joad, the Nazis have "exorcised culture, burned books, exiled artists, scientists, writers and philosophers and made war upon the mind of man." Later in the war, slogans were evolved, such as 'books cannot be killed with fire' and especially forcibly 'books are weapons in the war of ideas'. The far-reaching effect of German thoroughness was an attempt to extend their 'Judenrein' (free of Jews) empire to that of books.

In East Europe, especially Poland, destruction of Institutions and burning of libraries were linked with eradication of Jewish communities. German thoroughness was again evident by the creation of special "Brennkommandos" (arson squads). Czechoslovakia lost over 100 libraries with an estimated 2 million volumes, Romania 300,000 volumes, and in Vilna Lithuania, 80,000 books were sold for pulp at RM 19 per ton. Systematic looting was perpetrated not by illiterate people, but even by celebrated Hebrew scholars, such as Dr. Johannes Pohl. His collection of some 550,000 books would create a centre in Frankfurt for research into the Jewish question not only for Europe but for the world. He boasted that for the first time in history, Jewish studies will be done without Jews. This was part of the 'Hohe Schule' (High School) a pre-war initiative for an institution designed to promote National Socialist ideological research on communism, racial hygiene, Jewish question, freemasonry, and other subjects. The leading philosopher of the Third Reich, Dr. Alfred Rosenberg pursued the most sustained cultural looting, with established offices in twenty-four European cities. This was a systematic, government sponsored endeavour of cultural rape, depriving Europe of its historical heritage by a man of Latvian and Estonian parentage, who claimed that Western Civilization, including Greek sculpture and Italian Renaissance, was the product of the Aryan race.

A joint Anglo-American Monument, Fine Arts and Archives Office (MFAA) was created to protect cultural property from acts of war, to conserve such monuments and ultimately restitution or reparation of these. The most sensational finds of the MFAA were in Hungen, a small town with hundreds of thousands of volumes destined for the 'Hohe Schule' in Frankfurt, as reported by Janet Flanner in the New Yorker. "In a brick kiln in the town of Hungen was the most insultingly cache of all. Here were hidden the most precious Jewish archives, tomes and synagogue vessels from all over Europe, including the Rosenthalian collection from Amsterdam and that of Frankfurt Rothschilds. In the kiln, the repository for the Jewish material Rosenberg planned to use in his projected post-war academy, where anti-Semitism was to be taught as an exact science, priceless illuminated parchments of Torah were found cut into covers for Nazi stenographers' typewriters or made up into shoes. Here, too were thousands of Jewish identity cards, marked with a yellow 'J,' all that remained of Jews here, no emblems of dynastic Teutonic history. There was nothing in the ugly rooms except the rubbish and mean utilities to which these remnants of Jewish lives, identities and God-loving faith had been finally reduced."

The Offenbach Archival Depot was the greatest warehouse of looted books and religious items in occupied Germany, and a temporary home for several million volumes, housed in the completely undamaged former IG Farben building in Frankfurt am Main. Alfred Kantorowicz wrote the appropriate anthology 'Verboten und Verbrannt' (Forbidden and Burnt). Sadly amusing was the publicity of Ray Bradbury's novel 'Fahrenheit 451', in which the book was protected by asbestos. Cultural destruction went hand in hand with physical genocide. And yet there was no expression of collective feeling of guilt in Germany.

An artistic expression of book-burning practised from the time of books having been introduced into the literary world is the recent exhibition of "Diabolus in Vitro" by Antonio Riello. He produced with Massimo Lunardon a 'Venetian Glass Library' of 100 Riello's favourite books, each having a unique design and encapsulating ashes of the book in the stem or base of the glass chalice (Fig. 1 with kind permission of Antonio Riello). He attempted to express his feelings of revulsion at the cultural vandalism practised throughout the ages up to the present time. Riello's love for books has immortalised them symbolically in glass, as vestiges of sacred literary knowledge. Among the 100 reliquaries are books by Plato, Goethe, Kafka, Proust, Freud, Wells, Joyce, Arendt, Primo, Levy, and Bradbury, spanning the pantheon of literary culture and brutality. The artistic representation of this symbolic act of homage to great writers and their ideas can be interpreted in many ways. One that particularly lends itself to the theme discussed in this book is the fragility of glass that encloses cultural expression. Indeed, a regrettably close association between culture, civilization, and brutality is a symbolic expression of humanity that the artist succeeded to impart. The 'Cultural Holocaust' endorses Heine's prescient statement "When one burns books one will soon burn people."
Bertolt Brecht's poem entitled 'The Burning of Books' is a witty repose to cultural vandalism (translated by Michael R. Burch).

When the Regime
Commanded the unlawful books to be burned,
Teams of dull oxen hauled huge cartloads to the bonfires.

Then a banished writer, one of the best,
Scanning a list of excommunicated texts,
became enraged – he'd been excluded!

He rushed to his desk, full of contemptuous wrath,
To write a fiery letter to the morons in power –
Burn me! He wrote with his blazing pen
Haven't I always reported the truth?
Now here you are, treating me like a liar!
Burn me!

The most poignant story I have heard was citing Rabbi Jack Riemer of 'The Book – The Holocaust – The Outer Space'. "I want to say Kaddish for a 'Sefer Torah' (prayer for the Bible) today, that lived for a fairly long time, and then disappeared in the sight of all the world. It is the story of a Sefer Torah that made its first appearance in the very depths of Hell in the Bergen Belsen concentration camp, and that made its last appearance in the heights of heaven. Rabbi Dasberg heard that Joachim Joseph was becoming 13 years old, the age of 'bar mitzvah', he asked if he could teach him. They studied together secretly at night [...] The bar mitzvah (coming of age at 13) took place before dawn on a Monday in March, 1944, inside a barrack of the camp. Those men who were strong enough covered the windows and doors with blankets and stood watch to make sure that no SS guards were coming. Four candles, scrounged from somewhere, gave off enough flickering light for Rabbi Samuel Dasberg, the former Chief Rabbi of the Netherlands, to unfurl this tiny Sefer Torah--the five books of Moses, handwritten by a scribe, on a parchment scroll that was just four and a half inches tall. Thirteen year old Joachim Joseph chanted the blessings just as the rabbi had taught him from the ancient scroll in the singsong Hebrew melody that has been passed down for hundreds of years. People were listening in the beds all around."

Joachim Joseph, who is now a seventy-one year old Israeli physicist, recalls, "Afterwards everybody congratulated me. Somebody fished out a piece of a chocolate bar that he had been saving and gave it to me. Everybody told me, 'now you are bar mitzvah, now you are an adult. We are so very proud of you. Mazel tov!' And I felt very good. Rabbi Dasberg also gave Joseph a gift that day. He gave him the miniature Torah scroll that they had used, covered in a red velvet wrapper and tucked into a small green box. He said: This little Sefer Torah is yours to keep now, because I am pretty sure that I will not get out of this place alive, but maybe you will. At first, I didn't want to take it, but he insisted. He convinced me. And the condition was; *I had to promise that if I ever got out of there, that I must tell the story*, the story of my bar mitzvah." Joachim Joseph hid the Torah in his backpack.

After liberation, Joseph eventually sailed to Palestine and despite the loss of early education, he studied atmospheric physics, and got a doctorate in 1966 from UCLA. He pioneered experiments how dust particles in the atmosphere affect the climate. And that is how he came to meet Ilan Ramon, the first Israeli astronaut. When Ramon saw the miniature Sefer Torah on the shelf in Joseph's home, he asked about it, and Joseph told him the story. A few months later, Ramon called from Houston, Texas and asked him for permission to take the Sefer Torah with him up into space and Joseph reluctantly agreed. The story of that Sefer Torah was told to the world in January 2003 when Ilan Ramon held the scroll aloft during a live teleconference from aboard the space shuttle Columbia. “This Torah scroll was given by a rabbi to a young, scared, thin, thirteen year old boy in Bergen Belsen,” Ramon said from inside the space shuttle. “It represents more than anything the ability of the Jewish people to survive. It represents their ability to go from black days, from periods of darkness, to reach periods of hope and faith in the future.” And then, eleven days after that interview, the space ship Columbia disintegrated on its way back to earth, and Ilan Ramon and the other members of the crew were killed. But the Bible, the Old Testament may have been scattered to the four corners of the world, certainly not envisaged by the Rabbi when he entrusted his most cherished possession to the thirteen-year-old boy. Joseph said that he had no regrets in sending the Torah into space, commenting that “It did what perhaps it was destined to do.”

My irreverent and almost certainly impertinent interpretation or speculation is that God’s Bible may have landed in His ‘Holy of Holies’, by a pre-destined route, via Bergen Belsen from the Rabbi to the Bar Mitzvah boy. Perhaps it serves to remind Him of the fate of His Chosen People with whom He seems to have lost direct contact after passing on the Tablets of the Ten Commandments to Moses, which were recited even under the ultimate evil conditions of the concentration camp.

Fig. Symbolic representation of 'cultural vandalism' of book burning by Antonio Riello and Massimo Lunardon. The ashes of each of some 100 books were enclosed in the stem or base of individually designed delicate glass chalices. What was 'Verboten und Verbrandt' (Forbidden and Burnt) is re-created as symbols of memory of what is good in humanity, its fragility and evil counterpart. Goethe's 'Wahlverwandschaften' is included for he opposed book burning.

Johan Wolfgang
Goethe
'Wahlverwandschaften'

Marcel Proust
'Les Plaisirs Et
Les Jours'

Franz Kafka
'Der Process'

Hannah Arendt
'The Origins of
Totalitarianism'

Primo Levi
'Se Questo È
Un Uomo'

Ray Bradbury
'Fahrenheit 451'

IX. PARADOX OF GERMAN-JEWISH AFFINITIES

"Jews administer the spiritual patrimony of a people, who deny us the right and ability to do so"

Moritz Goldstein, German Journalist, 1912

'Spiritually we are Jews [...] through Christ and in Christ we are Abraham's descendants'

Pope Pius XI declaration, 1938

"In their self-discipline, their quiet civility and unsentimental brilliance, they had really been the last Prussians... The embodiment of all that was good and right about Germany"

Joachim Fest of his father's account of his Jewish friends, 2012

"Cut off from their own religious traditions, yet denied full participation in civic life, assimilated German Jews embraced their host nation's philosophy, literature and music with a fervour rooted in anxiety German philosophical culture had become the preserve of Jewish intellectuals"

Michael Löwy, 1992

"Not least in their love of knowledge, the Germans had a Jewish-Talmudic inventiveness and skill at categorizing, Jewish toughness, indestructibility, a Jewish sense of envy and private quarrels"

Bogumil Goltz, 1801-1884

After the Second World War Thomas Mann posed the question how the Defeated and humiliated Germans would be able to survive as a second class people. "Perhaps history has in fact intended for them the role of the

Jews, one which even Goethe thought befitted them: to be one day scattered throughout the world and to view their existence with an intellectually proud self-irony". Mann, an émigré himself from Nazi Germany, presented these thoughts with a degree of irony, the connection through a common fate that could please neither the Germans nor the Jews. Indeed, Mann argued that one reason for the chronic German anti-Semitism was the fact that Germans and Jews resembled each other. At a sad and paradoxical moment in history Germans and Jews, the murderers and their victims, resembled each other more than ever before. They resembled each other because both, members of the cultured nation and the 'people of the book' took refuge in a religion – like reverence for culture. He stated "We poor Germans! We are fundamentally lonely, even when we are famous! No one really likes us." These were Mann's thoughts that apply with equal force to Jews.

In an engaging section of the book entitled 'The Seduction of Culture in German History', Lepenies also drew attention to the German-Jewish affinities. He points out that Goethe was not alone in drawing an analogy between Germans and Jews. Bogumil Goltz, the 19th century scientist studying people and cultures, claimed "that not least in their love of knowledge, the Germans had a Jewish-Talmudic inventiveness and skill at categorizing, Jewish toughness, indestructibility, a Jewish sense of envy and private quarrels". Similar sentiments have been expressed by Theodor Adorno. In an interesting analysis written by Hermann Cohen during the First World War on Germanism and Judaism, he argued that "the German idealist tradition and pre-eminence in European higher education may have enabled Judaism to thrive and develop within a gentile environment." This was echoed by Fritz Stern in suggesting that the German 'Kultur' was the main reason why Germany was such an attractive place for Jewish intellectuals. Indeed, Michael Löwy went further by suggesting that the 'Bildungsideal' (Cultural ideal) of Kant, Goethe, and Schiller assured German Jews an indissoluble bond between the Enlightenment, ethics, art, and reform monotheism.

Ernst Cassirer (1874-1945) supported the integration of philosophy and culture in the liberal tradition of Humboldt, Goethe, and Thomas Mann, and ignored political and economic questions. In a recent appraisal of the legacy of 'Ernst Cassirer, the last philosopher of culture', Dr. Edward Skidelsky (2009) makes a critical point in the intellectual development of Cassirer. "Cut off from their own religious traditions, yet denied full participation in civic life, assimilated German Jews embraced their host nation's philosophy, literature and music with a fervour rooted in anxiety."

Indeed, Skidelsky argues that German philosophical culture had become the preserve of Jewish intellectuals. This analysis of the assimilated Jews may explain the resentment towards them by the non-Jewish intellectuals.

Ruth Klüger, in 'Landscapes of Memory', argues that "language is the strongest bond there is between an individual and a place, German, strange as this statement may sound, is a Jewish language. Consider that until the Holocaust, most of the world's prominent secular Jews spoke and wrote it: Kafka, Freud, Einstein, Marx, Heine, Herzl and Arendt." However, all except Kafka were German or Austrian-born Jews, whereas Kafka was a German-speaking Czech Jew. It is remarkable that during the Habsburg monarchy the classical German culture was spread to remote eastern towns by German-speaking Jews.

Paul Celan, born in Czernowitz, Bukovina, is an outstanding example of a poet who struggled after the war, when almost his whole family was murdered by Germans and he was taken to 'work camps' to use their language for his poetry. Indeed, he said of the German language "through the thousand darknesses of death ringing speech". Paul's mother, as many Jews, spoke at home German, read German classics, and she passed his mother language to him. Paul recalled his first encounter with poetry at the age of six, when he learned to recite Schiller's 'The Song of the Bell'. Moritz Goldstein wrote prophetically in 1912, "Jews administer the spiritual patrimony of a people, who deny us the right and ability to do so".

Even the Yiddish language of the Ashkenazi Jews originated about the 10th century in Rhineland. It is based on Middle High German spoken in that region and was fused with Hebrew and Aramaic. As it spread East to Poland, Russia, Latvia, and neighbouring countries, the language acquired a large vocabulary of Slavic words, but the German origin is clearly evident. However, the written language is in Hebrew alphabet and there is an extensive literature with a Nobel Prize awarded to Isaac Bashevis Singer in 1978. Yiddish is now mostly spoken by Orthodox Jews in the United States, Israel, Britain, Europe, and other parts of the world with observant Jewish communities.

Pope Pius XI declared in 1938 during the anti-Semitic attacks in Italy, "Spiritually we are Jews. Through Christ and in Christ we are Abraham's descendants". Pius XI kept up his attacks on Fascist and Nazi racism until he died late in 1938 when Cardinal Pacelli succeeded him as Pope Pius XII, who signed the concordat with Hitler in 1941. These astonishing views of no lesser individuals than Pius XI, Goethe, and Mann over the last two centuries were either dismissed or ignored during the National Socialist period by the German Christian movement. This was headed by Professor

Walter Grundmann, Director of the 'Institute for the study and eradication of Jewish influence on German Church life'. A large group of theologians were working on purging any Jewishness out of Christianity. Thus, a spiritual 'Juden-frei' Bible was forged in parallel with Germany being made free of Jews; a parallel double endeavour of physical and biblical murder. This applied also to the German Protestant hymnals used in Churches. They examined over 2300 hymns of which they denounced 1971 as Jewish in language or thoughts, as well as dogmatic, sentimental, tasteless, self-denigrating, or poetically unacceptable. Really a sad reflection on the Church using such 'deplorable material' for centuries of spiritual fulfilment of its worshippers. The Institute was located in Eisenach, with its Wartburg Castle, where some four centuries earlier Martin Luther was hiding from the Catholic Church and translated the Bible into German. There is an irony in the juxtaposition of Luther labouring to achieve great accuracy in translating the Bible, only to be revised by the 'Institute' removing any reference to Judaism and de-Judeising it. However, even the learned men of the 'Institute' could not get round the conundrum of Paul's rabbinic Jewishness, so they erased him altogether from the Christian canon.

Christianity's supersession of Judaism has been based on the proclamations, critique, and chastisement of the Jewish people by the prophets. Susannah Heschel, in her comprehensive investigation of 'The Aryan Jesus', described the 'Nordic Ring' consisting of anthropologists, racial hygienist, and other scientists studying Teutonic ideology. They claimed the ultimate supersession by the 'Aryan Teutons' of being the 'real chosen people' of the Bible. According to Heschel, other 'völkich circles' argued rather cynically that once Christianity is dejudaized, there would be nothing left of it. Indeed, some claimed that the Institute's work could only reveal that Christianity was nothing more than a form of Judaism or that Christianity was Judaism for non-Jews. The final stroke was by Willy Staerk, a theologian with a double accolade of being an anti-Semite as well as anti-Nazi, who claimed that both Nazism and Judaism were rooted in blood, flesh, and soil, unlike Christianity, a spiritual religion. There we have it, almost any theological permutation can be made to fit a pre-conceived idea.

Gershom Scholem was a German-born Jewish philosopher and historian (1897-1982) who immigrated to Palestine in 1923. Scholem argues that following the struggle of Jews for civil rights, facilitated by the French Revolution and German Enlightenment, a relationship was initiated between the Germans and Jews. Scholem highlights the significance of Friedrich Schiller as a bridge between the Germans and Jews, within as well as outside Germany. "Schiller, spokesman for pure humanity, lofty poet of the highest ideals of mankind, represented everything they thought of, or wished to think of, as being German. Here they found what they were most fervently seeking [...] After all, Schiller, to whom their love clung so passionately, was not just everybody; he was the national poet of Germany. He was a factor in the Jewish belief in mankind. Schiller provided the most visible, most impressive, and most resounding occasion for the idealistic self-deceptions engendered by the relations of the Jews to the Germans." Scholem argued in 1962 against the myth of a German-Jewish dialogue. It was a passionate attempt on the part of assimilated Jews to embrace German culture, but was not reciprocated by the Germans. Although the Jews contributed whole-heartedly to creativity in literature, art, music, and science, Germans as a whole did not respond favourably, there was no dialogue.

Scholem does not see the attempt as early as 1673 to invite Spinoza to the prestigious Professorship of Philosophy at the University of Heidelberg as a milestone in German-Jewish relationships. He does admit to the German language as his mother tongue and the remarkable development of Yiddish in the Rhineland in the tenth century, based on Middle High German. However, Scholem argues "As a price of Jewish emancipation, the Germans demanded a resolute disavowal of Jewish nationality – a price the leading writers and spokesmen of Jewish avant-garde were only too happy to pay. What had begun as furtive glances turned into a passionate involvement with the realm of German history. The German elite demanded of the Jews that they give up their heritage." This is consistent with Heine's "conversion being a ticket to join the cultural club of Europe", which was followed by Gustav Mahler to take charge of the Vienna Opera. It must be remembered that Scholem expressed these views with the hindsight of the Holocaust. However, they do not invalidate the thoughts expressed above, characterising important manifestations shared between Germans and Jews.

The oft hailed German affinity to 'blood and soil' ('Blut und Boden') has become perhaps real, as German soil has now been soaked with Jewish blood. Ironically, the Nazi ideology has received its posthumous blow, by Jewish and German Aryan blood, that of victim and perpetrator being mixed in the sacred German soil, and their ashes in German sky, as an unpredicted reality inflicted by National Socialism on the Fatherland. This was up to now a theoretical postulate, turned into reality. Heinrich Müller, the head of the Gestapo and one of the principal organisers of the Holocaust, was last seen alive in Hitler's bunker on May 1 1945 the day after Hitler committed suicide. According to Professor Johannes Tuchel, Müller's body was interred in 1945 in a mass grave in the oldest Mitte Jewish cemetery in Berlin. A further irony is that the cemetery happens to be the resting place of the celebrated 18th century philosopher Moses Mendelssohn. Although there is no forensic verification, the gravedigger had allegedly confirmed the identity of Heinrich Müller. Thus the architect of mass murder found his safe haven among his victims, a 'final obscenity' to the 'final solution'.

At one pole of the historical spectrum of German-Jewish affinities, we have the historical Christian-Jewish relationship, and at the other, the process of learned professors, pastors, and theologians attempting to remove any traces of Judaism from Christian teaching and eventually removing the Old Testament from the Christian Canon. The length to which the human mind and logic distorted by prejudice and hatred is capable to go defies comprehension.

CHAPTER 7: THE LEGAL SYSTEM, HITLER, RACIAL HYGIENE, AND NÜREMBERG TRIAL

I. **Introduction**
II. **National Socialist interpretation of the Law**
III. **Adolf Hitler, stateless person acquiring German citizenship**
IV. **Nüremberg Laws**
V. **Eugenics mutated into 'Racial Hygiene'**
VI. **Nuremberg trial**
VII. **Genocide terminology**

THE LEGAL SYSTEM, HITLER, RACIAL HYGIENE, AND THE NÜREMBERG TRIAL

'Bad Laws are the worst sort of tyranny' *Edmund Burke, 1729-1797*
'The final solution was the greatest crime in history. A crime that left the imagination and intellect shattered' *Sir Hartley Shawcross, the British prosecutor of the Nüremberg Trial, 2016*
'The Nazi crimes, it seems to me, explode the limits of the law; and that is precisely what constitutes their monstrousness. For these crimes, no punishment is severe enough [...] This guilt, in contrast to all criminal guilt, oversteps and shatters any and all legal systems' *Hannah Arendt's 'The Question of German Guilt' (Die Schuldfrage)*

I. INTRODUCTION

German constitutional law had a challenging task to deal with the changes since the unification of Germany in 1871 under Bismarck, the powerful Federal Chancellor. The second German Reich was formed (1871-1918) and King William the First of Prussia was proclaimed German Emperor. Following the defeat of the First World War in 1918, the young William II resigned and the democratic Weimar Republic was established (1918-1933), which lasted only fifteen years. This was followed in 1933 by Hitler's dictatorship (1933-1945), which he proclaimed to be the third German Reich that will last 1000 years. Truth, providence, or good fortune prevailed and the tyrant and his executioners lasted twelve years, with over 20 million people killed, many more injured and countless millions uprooted and destitute. He precipitated the Second World War in 1939, resulting in the defeat of Germany in 1945. The West German Federal Republic was created in 1949 and in 1990 united with the East German Democratic Republic.

Thus, over a turbulent period of eighty years the legal system in Germany had to be adapted four times to suit the challenging political changes. During this epoch in German legal history, administrative law followed the changes wrought by the constitutional law. Here we shall consider briefly some pertinent issues regarding the three aspects of jurisprudence – constitutional law, administrative law, and the executive arm in the transition from the Weimar Republic to the Nazi dictatorship. When Germany changed from monarchy to republic, the structure of the legal system that evolved between 1871 and 1918 was essentially retained, with the law codes remaining in force. The three levels of courts consisted of the highest appellate court, the middle Federal State courts, and the lower regional courts. There were also Administrative Courts. According to professor Michael Stolleis, most of the judges were politically conservative, appointed before 1914 and some were nationalistic and anti-parliamentarian in their outlook. Although the Weimar constitution was not formally abrogated, giving rise to the notion of continuity with the Nazi system, this is not a true reading of the situation. It is more correct as Knut Noir has asked whether we "might not be better advised to regard the Third Reich as essentially a space devoid of law" or another German historian argued that "constitutional history ends with 1933". The Weimar Constitution is briefly described on p.52.

II. NATIONAL SOCIALIST INTERPRETATION OF THE LAW

> 'Protesting the illegality of the law made no sense in Germany'
>
> *Alan Beyerchen, Professor of German History, 1977*

Law was interpreted according to the racist Völkisch precepts or 'Völkisch natural law'. The Nazis created gradually a more pervasive extra-judicial system that invoked incarceration and killing in concentration camps, killing by Special Forces (einsatzgruppen) or 'protective custody' by the Gestapo. Special 'People's Courts' were also established staffed by reliable followers of Nazi policy. Altogether, the older law had to be interpreted under the guidance of National Socialist ideology. Finally, there were 'arbitrary measures or terror' (Massnahmen) and 'Führer's orders' that had to be obeyed. The principles laid down by Hans Frank, the 'Reichsjuristenführer' (Reich leader of jurists): "The basis for the interpretation of all legal sources is the National Socialist ideology, as expressed in the party programme and the Führer's statements". A judge was bound by all Führer's decisions, using the ideology of the Führer's will, needs of the 'Volk' community, loyalty, and faith.

Younger jurists invoked concepts or sound-bites, which were too vague to define in legal terms, such as community, nation, race, honour, blood and soil, and overall obedience of the Führer. Especially, community (Volk) was arguing against individualism and given an anti-democratic meaning. Again in the words of Hans Frank, President of the Academy for German Law in 1934, "We start from the law of the community, and this communal law is the real inner reversal of our legal point of view and our legal system". The concept of 'Community' was never defined precisely and was used in so many diverse ways that it became doubtful if it carried any legal value in the final analysis as Hitler pronounced, "The health of the German nation is more important than the letter of the law". At the same time, freedom of the press was extinguished, as Hitler believed that it was 'objective lunacy'.

During the final years of the republic, a group of young right-wing individuals were imbued by National Socialism. The most significant among a number of lawyers were Carl Schmitt, Reinhard Höhn, Rudolf Huber, and Otto Koellreutter. As soon as the NS gained power in January 1933, basic legal rights were denied, many people were arrested, political parties and trade unions were broken up, and a wave of emigration started. Carl Schmitt was a leading scholar of considerable intelligence to be converted to National Socialism; he was an early critic of the parliamentary democracy and advocate of dictatorship of the Reich President. He was rewarded by Göring to a number of important positions and functions, including that of Prussian Councillor of State (Staatsrat). His notorious article, 'The Führer Protects the Law', was music to the ears of Nazis and he also indulged in anti-Semitic polemics, all of which belittled his reputation. Otto Koellreutter supported National Socialism as early as 1930, and wrote in 1933 the first Nazi constitutional theory, its law in 1935, and administrative law a year later. The new Nazi constitutional and administrative law was advanced by a group of individuals who moved into the newly vacated professorial chairs; Ernst Rudolf Huber, Theodor Maunz, and Gustav Adolf Walz to mention only some of them. Wilhelm Frick, the minister of the Interior helped to draft and to administer the laws (see p.55). Reinhard Höhn was a young constitutional lawyer turned to National Socialism in 1933. He opposed all liberal thinking, individualism, and the traditional doctrine of constitutional law. He claimed that "the state as a legal person and the concept of community are mutually exclusive". The law Höhn advocated was ostensibly opposite to "Roman-Jewish" thinking, which he characterised as "liberal, rational, abstract, individualistic materialistic, alien to the people, nihilistic and corrupting".

Theodor Maunz was a highly regarded professor of German Constitutional law, who wrote the most important textbook on the subject. He was esteemed for his admirable qualities of courtesy, kindness, discipline, and scholarly attitude to law. He joined the Nazi party and the SA in 1933. Stolleis writes "whilst waiting for a chair (Maunz) emphasised the political nature of law and the totalitarian nature of the Führer's will. As though to prove his absolute devotion to the party line, Maunz – a student of Hans Nawiasky, whose Jewish background had already embroiled him in one of the largest anti-Jewish hate campaigns – appeared as a speaker in 1936 at the conference on 'the Jews in jurisprudence'. There he expounded on the 'fatal predilection of Jewish theorists of administrative law for the liberal doctrine of the 'Rechtsstaat'. In 1935 he received an appointment in Freiburg, and in 1937 he was made full professor." In a lecture he declared the "end of subjective public right, and he pronounced arrests by the Gestapo sovereign acts outside the judicial realm." The fact that he did not break off his ties with the church and attended Sunday mass in a village in the Black Forest, away from the public limelight of Freiburg, proved a farsighted insurance strategy. After the demise of the Nazi system, "Maunz was able to join the Christian Socialist camp, become an expert adviser, participate in the deliberations over the Basic Law, write the textbook 'Deutsches Staatsrecht' (German constitutional law), and was soon after appointed Bavarian Minister of Culture. Thus he had returned to where he had begun, with parliamentary democracy and the Rechtsstaat", a state founded on the rule of law for which he criticized 'Jewish theorists' and thereby his Jewish mentor.

It is noteworthy that in 1933, Heidegger was appointed Rector of the University of Freiburg and endorsed the dictum, 'Führer alone is the present and future Germany and its law.' Maunz was at that time the candidate for the chair in law and it is unlikely that the Rector's view on law has escaped his attention. It transpired almost fifty years after the end of the war, as pointed out by Stolleis, that Maunz has been a "wonderful companion, an important adviser for twenty-five years, writing hundreds of anonymous articles, advising on the programme and giving legal opinion to the far-right 'Deutsche Volks union (DVU) party." The very fact that a stalwart democrat and legal authority like Maunz gave advice and support to the DVU, made the party respectable. Indeed, the neo-Nazis may well have benefitted from the close links with such a reputable personality.

These disclosures by Stolleis elicited angry responses from some of the members of the 'Association of Constitutional Lawyers', rather reminiscent of the medical doctors being similarly accused of disloyalty to their profession. Stolleis also echoes the lack of any disclaimer or apology for the moral and ethical stance by the professional legal body or academic institutions. As he states no "association has dared to open Pandora's box, except for some embarrassed whispering a brooding silence is likely to descend once again on the profession."

There was no resistance to the NS constitutional theory, as the older individuals retired or became bystanders. Emigration was the only option for Social Democrats or lawyers of Jewish descent. As Stolleis wrote, "The balance sheet at the end is depressing. A theory of constitutional and administrative law ... no longer existed ... The National Socialist state had no need for a theory of constitutional and administrative law. Hitler did not think much of Professors"; for a change he may have been right, dated for his Reich).

III. ADOLF HITLER A 'STATELESS' PERSON ACQUIRING GERMAN CITIZENSHIP

'The irony of the man who alleged to have epitomized the 'Ur-German' was a stateless man of Austrian provenance. A sham naturalised German of dubious legality, with a police record and imprisonment. One might conclude that Hitler was not a Kosher German'

(Author)

'Hitler was the mirror of every German unconscious. The loudspeaker, which magnifies the inaudible whispers of the German soul'

Professor Carl Jung, 1947, quoted by M Gallard 1994

Hitler was an Austrian citizen, but gave up his citizenship in 1925. The stated reasons were that he lived in Germany since 1912 and served in German armed forces over six years, of which four and a half years were at the front and he will be applying for German naturalisation. He indulged in racist, anti-Semitic activities, and in 1924, Hitler was convicted for leading with Erich Ludendorff the 'Beer-Hall Putsch' and imprisoned for high treason. By 1932, he was the leader of the National Socialist party and there was an urgent need for Hitler to be naturalised as a German citizen, for it was a year before the Reichstag election, and as a stateless person he could not stand for election. Leaders of the NSDAP were anxious for Hitler to be naturalised, as according to the Weimar Constitution of 1919 (Act. 41 Abs. 2) only a German citizen can be elected to become the President of Germany.

A total of seven authenticated attempts were made to procure Hitler German nationality. Hitler instigated himself the first attempt to gain citizenship in 1925 in Thüringen, which would automatically entitle him to German citizenship, but this attempt failed. From this time onwards, his political friends pursued Hitler's naturalisation. These attempts were largely pursued secretly, so as not to alert the public. In 1929, his NSDAP comrades in the Bayern State, led by Wilhelm Frick the first NSDAP Member of Parliament, applied for naturalisation, which failed for reasons of Hitler's past political activities. When in 1930, Frick was declared Minister of culture in the State of Thüringen, he attempted to appoint Hitler to the State High School for handicraft and building linked to the Weimar 'Bauhaus' movement. However, even this move failed for constitutional, political, and financial reasons. The next move by Frick was in summer 1930, when there was little political activity, and Frick was deputising for the head of the Thüringen government, to appoint Hitler as police commissioner in Hildburghausen, a small place in Thüringen. Despite all the precautions and subterfuge in selecting the right time, the proposal failed.

By 1931 the NSDAP participated in the government of the Free State of Braunschweig, which like Thüringen had large NSDAP representation. The Minister of Interior was Dr. Dietrich Klagges, a member of the NSDAP, and he was requested directly by the party's central office in Berlin to appoint Hitler as 'Professor in Organic Sociology and Politics' at the Braunschweig Technical College. This patently obvious attempt to get 'Professor Hitler' naturalised by the back door failed and became a 'cause celebres' of a 'drop out' kid from school to be nominated to a professorship. The next plan for Hitler's naturalisation was to appoint him to a position in the office of the Mayor in Stadtoldendorf, a small place in the State of Braunschweig and this was also turned down. All these failed attempts to procure Hitler German nationality, alerted the public, and both the National and foreign newspapers had a heyday. The newspaper 'Tempo' wrote "As of yesterday the whole of Europe laugh about Adolf Hitler". The 'Berlin Daily' wrote "All the comical papers in the world are well supplied with material". The paper 'Germania' commented "It is a national Comedy, which will find later the way on to the theatrical stage"; indeed, some theatre, some stage, with 40 million killed and more injured!

The secret shenanigans concerned with appointing Hitler as a State employee of the Hildburghausen police commission led to a parliamentary enquiry, which Hitler had to attend as witness to explain how it was that the Thüringen government was unaware of his application. Hitler was accompanied by many Nazi luminaries, including Rudolf Hess, Joseph Goebbels, Baldur von Schirach, Gregor Strasser, Wilhelm Frick, Fritz Sauckel, and Fritz Wächter. Hitler's response to most of the questions, was that he was unable to remember. Throughout the proceedings, the NS members attending the enquiry created an uproar and Hitler turned into one of his hysterical outbursts. However, the committee members of different political parties were unable to reach a clear majority vote on the issue and concluded that a further judicial proceeding will be required. The affair left many unanswered legal questions, whether Hitler has perjured himself, in order to acquire German citizenship, which might have been a punishable offence.

By 1932, the leadership of the NSDAP were anxious to solve discretely the problem of Hitler's German nationality in time for the presidential elections. The issue was now handled directly by Berlin, with the aid of Hans Frank's legal mind and a large number of politicians in Braunschweig, to solve this thorn in the NSDAP leadership. After considering a number of proposals, Klagges was entrusted with the task of Hitler to apply for the post of 'Regierungsrat', official advisor of the Braunschweig Embassy in Berlin. Not to leave any loophole, arrangements were made to register Hitler's place of residence in Braunschweig. This move succeeded and in March 1932, Hitler was formally appointed as 'Regierungsrat' of Braunschweig, which solved the problem as this entitled him to German nationality. As a postscript, it transpired that Hitler never worked in the Berlin Braunschweig Embassy, nor did he take up residency in Braunschweig. The same year he stood in the Reich presidential election, and within less than a year, in January 1933, he became Chancellor of the Reich.

The general perception that Hitler was welcomed by Germany with open arms is not entirely true, as is evident from the reluctance to grant him citizenship on six separate occasions. As pointed out by Michael Stolleis, the political parties were still free to express their views, the liberals, social democrats, and the communists voted against the motion, which was supported by the NSDAP, 'German Nationals' (Deutschnationale), as well as the Catholic party, that was aware of the imminent signing of the 'Concordat' between Hitler and the Vatican. Was Hitler a bona fide government official ('Regierungsrat') of Braunschweig or was this a deceitful ploy, the 'original sin' of the doomed 'Thousand Year Reich'? The legality of Hitler's nationalisation process remains open to legal opinion. As late as 2007, seventy-five years after Hitler was naturalised as a German citizen, the State of Lower Saxony was asked "to establish formally the way whereby the State of Lower Saxony as judicial successors of the State of Braunschweig could formally withdraw Hitler's German citizenship". This followed a long debate throughout Germany concerning the possibility of such a posthumous move, which would be of historical significance. However, the Ministry of Interior of Lower Saxony declared that it is legally impossible to withdraw the appointment, as the official is dead.” Furthermore, that would have made Hitler ‘stateless’, which for a German is forbidden by law. Stolleis considers this move “as a piece of absurd theatre and part of a political show. The wish to extinguish symbolically ‘Hitler’ hoping that history could be redressed – is in my eyes senseless. We have to accept the past with all its cruelties.”

The irony of the man who alleged to have epitomised the ‘Ur-German’ was nothing more than a sham-naturalised German of dubious legality, with a police record, imprisonment, and stateless, with previous Austrian provenance. One might conclude that Hitler was not a ‘Kosher German’. Friedrich Meinecke quoted the historian Otto Hintze that Hitler “did not belong to our race at all. There was something wholly foreign about him, something like an otherwise extinct primitive race that is completely immoral in nature”. There we have the absurdity, the glaring injustice, whilst thousands of German Jews, some living in Germany for many generations were disenfranchised of their German nationality, at the same time the stateless Hitler, with a serious police record, acquires German nationality by subterfuge, becomes the ‘Führer’ of the Third Reich and even posthumously his German nationality cannot be abrogated.

IV. THE NŰREMBERG LAWS

These were aimed specifically against the Jews to deprive them gradually of citizenship, isolate them from the general population, and eventually remove them from Germany by deportation to killing centres. The first law passed in 1933 'Gleichschaltung' (Law to Restore the Professional Civil Service), dismissed all individuals of Jewish descent and that included university staff. The 'Reich Citizenship Law' deprived German Jews of citizenship rights and redefined them as Subjects of the state; this also revoked exemption of Jewish veterans of the armed forces granted in the earlier 1933 Law. Then followed the 'Law for the protection of German blood and honour', which outlawed marriage between Jews and non-Jews. A number of other regulations were attached to these two main statutes, which provided the basis for removing Jews from German, political, economic, and social life. Senior Jewish doctors had to resign from hospital appointments, followed by suspension to award doctoral degrees to Jews. Overall, about 250 decrees removed Jews from professions and economic life and made them outlaws in Germany. The progressive deprivation of liberty was most poignantly described by Victor Klemperer, professor of romance languages, in his book, 'I Shall Bear Witness', based on his diaries. He lost his university job, livelihood, and even his cat. He suffered humiliations, was abandoned by his friends, and escaped deportation to concentration camp largely due to his marriage to an Aryan.

Among the chief architects of Nüremberg Laws was Wilhelm Stuckart (1902-1953), who studied law in Munich and Frankfurt. He fought in the "Freikorps" and joined the NSDAP in 1922. From 1930, he served as a district court judge, and joined the SS in 1933. At the age of thirty-one he became State Secretary of the Prussian Ministry of Education, followed two years later by becoming State Secretary of the Reich Ministry of the Interior. He co-authored the Nuremberg anti-Jewish racial laws and was a leading constitutional expert and loyal member of the SS. Stuckart attended the Wannsee Conference in 1942, where he proposed compulsory sterilization of non-Aryans. He was also chairman of the 'Commission for the Protection of German Blood'. Stuckart was arrested in 1945 and at the Nuremberg trial, he testified falsely that he knew nothing of the extermination programme and was sentenced to four years' imprisonment. Stuckart was killed in a car accident in 1953 under suspicious circumstances.

Hans J. S. Globke (1898-1973) was educated at the Catholic Kaiser Karl Gymnasium and then studied law at the Universities of Bonn, Cologne and Giesen. He served in 1929 in the Weimar Republic as an administrative councillor to the Prussian Ministry of the Interior. Although he did not join the NSDAP, Globke applied his legal skills to formulate the emergency legislation that gave Hitler dictatorial powers. He co-authored with Stuckart the Reich Ministry's official commentary on the Nuremberg Citizenship Law introduced in 1935 and the basic laws of persecution of Jews. Despite his dismal record of providing a legal basis for Nazi laws, he was appointed State Secretary to the Chancellery in 1953 under the anti-Nazi Chancellor Konrad Adenauer and served until his retirement in 1963. The communist regime tried Globke in absentia and pronounced a life sentence, which he most likely deserved.

V. EUGENICS MUTATED INTO 'RACIAL HYGIENE'

'The rational neo-cortex of the brain fails to control the more ancient emotion-ridden thalamus and amygdala'

Arthur Koestler, Neuro-functional interpretation, 1967

'The sociological counterpart to the atomic chain reaction in Nazi Germany; Eugenics → Racial Hygiene → Sterilisation → Euthanasia → Gnadetod→ Genocide'

(Author)

Well before the National Socialists gained power in Germany, 'Social Darwinism', introduced by Darwin's half cousin Francis Galton (1822-1911) in England, was applied in Germany as a way of improving the 'Volk' (people). Galton coined the term 'Eugenics' in 1883 which deals with influences that improve the inborn qualities of a race. In Germany, Social Darwinism caught on initially because it was argued that the poor and weak survived through welfare, lack of fitness for war, and they multiplied faster than the talented, fit individuals who excelled in war and were lost in greater numbers.

Alfred Ploetz (1860-1940), Germany's leading Social Darwinist, called attention to this social 'counter selection' that will lead to racial degeneration and must be prevented. Robert N. Proctor, in his book 'Racial Hygiene' (1988), points out that Ploetz argued that medical care should be denied to the 'weak', for this encourages their survival and is counterproductive for natural evolution. Indeed, he coined the term 'Rassenhygiene' (Racial Hygiene) and argued that help for these individuals will endanger the quality of the race. According to Proctor, these theoretical discussions led Ploetz to the dangerous concept that "If negative qualities of the race could be located and eliminated in the germ cells, then the need for a Darwinian struggle for existence would be eliminated. A kinder and more 'humane' form of selection might thereby replace the brutal force of natural selection; indeed, intelligent racial hygiene might eliminate the need for a struggle for existence altogether." Phrases such as 'the struggle for existence' and 'the survival of the fittest' became catchwords for the new Social Darwinism that reflected the broader social and economic structure of the times.

Ploetz founded with others, as early as 1905, the Society for 'Racial Hygiene' to further racial improvement. Up to 1920, racial hygienists were mostly concerned with the declining birth rate and an increase in mentally ill in state institutions. The ideology of racial hygiene was to improve the human race, especially the Western 'cultured races' (Kultur Rassen). Ploetz, in his founding treatise, was against anti-Semitism, ranked Jews along with Aryans as two of the world's best cultured races, quoting the achievements of Jesus, Spinoza, and Marx. Indeed, he rejected the notion of pure races, arguing that they were mixed since time immemorial and this applied both to Aryans and Jews. He also believed that interbreeding of races not too far apart was well recognised as a way of improving fitness and variation. He warned against 'vulgar race propaganda' of the like of Gobineau's vision of superiority of the Nordic race. A comprehensive program of health care included racial hygiene, along with social and personal hygiene. Although Ploetz belonged to a secret Nordic club, he adhered to the notion that most Jews should be classified as Aryans. Nonetheless, the Nazis have appropriated Ploetz into their fold and hailed him as preserving not only the health of the general population but especially the 'Nordic race'. They subverted Ploetz's concepts to have underwritten the 'biological foundations' of the Nazi racial state. He was showered with honours and in 1936, he became an 'honorary professor of racial hygiene' at the University of Munich and was awarded the Goethe Medallion (Germany's highest honour in science and arts). A year later at the age of seventy-seven, Ploetz joined the Nazi party – the jewel in the crown – No. 4, 457, 957.

Some philosophers attempted to distinguish between the local German 'racial hygiene' and the more international 'eugenics'. By 1932, before Hitler gained power, 'racial hygiene' was accepted as a medical discipline and taught at most German medical faculties. It is important to appreciate that 'racial hygiene' emerged from the German medical academics and was not imposed by the state. With the Nazis consolidating their power, it became more obvious that racial hygiene was closely linked to the 'Jewish question'. Financial support for research also played a disproportional role, as can be seen in the case of the psychiatrist Ernst Rϋdin who became head of the Society for Racial Hygiene in 1933. His institute was awarded, in 1935, a total of 300,000 RM, more than that given to the combined Physics and Chemistry Kaiser Wilhelm Institutes. This indicates the importance the Nazis gave to Race – proving their superman status – in comparison with the basic sciences. Perhaps what they gained in self-glorification, they lost in scientific know-how, which may have contributed to their final demise, the 'Endlösung' (Final Solution) of the Nazi terror.

Fritz Lenz (1887-1976) had the honour of being awarded in 1923 the first Chair in 'Racial Hygiene' at the University of Munich. By 1933, he declared, "It is the will of the Führer, that the demands of racial hygiene should be put into practice, without delay." There was no limit to which glorification of Hitler would not go, including 'the greatest doctor of the German people', being guided by biology as the basis of National Socialism ideology. Proctor quotes Hitler's speech in 1923 to the Physicians League: "You National Socialist doctors, I cannot do without you for a single day, not a single hour. If not for you, if you fail me, then all is lost." And the doctors did their damn best to oblige the 'great doctor'. According to Michael H. Kater, 45% of all doctors eventually joined the Nazi party. By 1943, about 46,000 of the total of 90,000 physicians joined the league of Nazi physicians, some were also in the SA and members of the SS, greatly in excess of other professions. The reason for the medical profession joining the Nazi party in such disproportionally large number can be ascribed to the large number of Jewish doctors (almost 50% in Berlin), who were deep down considered to be aliens, within the systemic anti-Semitism in Germany, professional opportunism by filling the vacated posts, as well as the traditional conservative character of doctors of medicine.

Eugen Fischer (1874-1967) was the director of the 'Institute for Anthropology, Human Heredity and Eugenics of the Kaiser Wilhelm Institute' (KWI) in Berlin. He established his reputation by studying the mixed races of white men with black women and their children in South West Africa. Fischer was an ardent exponent of 'racial hygiene'. In 1933 he was elected Rector of the University of Berlin, and according to Müller-Hill, he declared in his inaugural address: "The new leadership, having only just taken over the reins of power, is deliberately and forcefully intervening in the course of history and in the life of the nation, precisely where the intervention is most urgently, most decisively, and most immediately needed. This intervention can be characterized as a biological population policy, biological in this context signifying the safeguarding by the state of our hereditary endowment and out race, as opposed to the unharnessed processes of heredity, selection, and elimination." In a lecture in 1939, Fischer states, "When a people wants, somehow or other, to preserve its own nature, it must reject alien racial elements, and when these have already insinuated themselves, it must suppress them and eliminate them. The Jew is such an alien and, therefore, when he wants to insinuate himself, he must be warded off. This is self-defence. In saying this, I do not characterize every Jew as inferior, as Negroes are, I do not underestimate the greatest enemy with whom we have to fight. But I reject Jewry with every means in my power, and without reserve, in order to preserve the hereditary endowment of my people." Later in 1943, Fischer writes in the 'Deutsche Allgemeine Zeitung', "It is a rare and special good fortune for a theoretical science to flourish at a time when the prevailing ideology welcomes it, and its findings can immediately serve the policy of the state." Finally, in 1944, Fischer writes in accepting to chair a workshop at an Anti-Jewish Congress convened in Cracow: "Dear Reichsminister! That you intend to create a scientific front line for the defence of European culture against the influence of Jewry, and to call together for that purpose scientists from all the nations fighting Jewry, seems to me a very good idea and absolutely necessary. I am delighted to accept your invitation."

Otmar von Verschuer (1896-1969) was a graduate of Medicine from the University of Marburg. His interest developed mostly in eugenic studies of 'racial hygiene' and twin research, later collaborating with Mengele. He worked at the KWI of anthropology, human heredity and eugenics in Berlin from 1927, and was appointed its first director of human genetics and later research in twins. Verschuer succeeded Fischer as director of the KWI in Anthropology in 1942. E. M. Zimmer Lederberg, a biologist, stated that Verschuer did not formally join the Nazi party until 1940, but he participated in activities that strongly advanced the Nazi agenda to protect Nordic people (Aryans) from 'contamination' by 'inferior races'. Then at the close of the war, he hid or destroyed the records of these activities and other activities carried on by KWI personnel. Verschuer supported eugenic sterilization of subjects with a variety of mental diseases, including epileptics and 'serious alcoholism'.

As a devout Christian, he advocated eugenic sterilization based on the Christian concept of sacrifice. "It is demanded of us Christians, who follow the example of our master, that we be willing to sacrifice our lives in the service of Christian charity. Christian charity extends to children who will be born. We are therefore obligated to extend the circle of humans to those who are not yet born, and I believe it is justified to demand from people a lesser sacrifice than the sacrifice of life, namely to forego having children, for the love of children that are expected to be diseased, so that from the perspective of Christian charity sterilization must be regarded as justified." After the sterilization law was passed, an Institute for Hereditary Biology and Racial Hygiene was set up at the University of Frankfurt, and Verschuer became its first director in 1935, while still working with the KWI. Verschuer stated that, "The National Socialist State with exceptional energy has assumed [the responsibility] for the practical administration of hereditary and racial care. The first goal was the fight against racial alienation through the Jews. The second deed is [sterilization] of those with hereditary illnesses through the Law for Prevention of Congenitally Ill Progeny. In the two years since [this law] has been in place, approximately 100,000 sterilizations have been carried out."

According to Zimmer Lederberg, Verschuer generally opposed euthanasia or the idea of breeding supermen, though he supported 'positive eugenics to favour propagation of Aryans. His involvement in twin research and medical atrocities in 1944 were linked primarily through collaboration with his assistant Mengele in Auschwitz, as noted in the following report "My assistant, Dr. Mengele (M.D., PhD) has joined me in this branch of research. He is presently employed as Hauptsturmführer and camp physician in the concentration camp at Auschwitz. Anthropological investigations on the most diverse racial groups of this concentration camp are being carried out with permission of the SS Reichsführer [Himmler]; the blood samples are being sent to my laboratory for analysis." Mengele and his Jewish slave assistant Dr. Miklos Nyiszli sent other 'scientific materials' to the KWI, including the bodies of murdered Romani people, internal organs of dead children, skeletons of two murdered Jews, and blood samples of twins infected by Mengele with typhus."

Whilst there is no direct evidence that Verschuer supported Genocide, it is revealing that with Fischer he was the guest of honour in March 1941 to a working congress at the inauguration of the 'Frankfurt Institute for the Investigation of the Jewish Question'. The objective of the meeting was the "total solution to the 'Jewish question', bluntly stated the 'Volkstod (death of the nation)." This may have been one of the first open reference to annihilation of the Jewish nations as early as March 1941.

Verschuer escaped prosecution as a war criminal, as no hard incriminating evidence was found. He certainly removed secret files from the Institute and destroyed them. A commission set up by Otto Hahn at the KWS to investigate Verschuer concluded that his link with Auschwitz was established and that he was judged to be a 'racial fanatic'. During the denazification hearings, Verschuer countered every witness denouncing him as a 'communist agent'. He had the temerity to claim that 'Mengele had excellent relations with his patients in Auschwitz'. Indeed, Dr. Mengele was plying children with sweets before removing their eyes and killing them. Finally, Verschuer was judged by the denazification authorities to be a 'Nazi fellow traveller' (Mitläufer), a mild category. Later, in 1946, a commission in charge of rebuilding the KWI in Frankfurt decreed that "Verschuer should be considered not as a collaborator, but one of the most dangerous Nazi activists of the Third Reich." Nonetheless, in 1951, Verschuer was appointed to the chair of human genetics at the University of Münster.

It is intriguing to hear from no less a person than Gertrud Fischer, the daughter of Professor Fischer, when asked by Müller-Hill if Verschuer was anti-Semitic, she replied, "No certainly not. He supported segregation ('Trennung') of the Jews." Remarkably this applied to Verschuer, the guest of honour at the 1941 Frankfurt congress of the 'total solution of the Jewish question, stated as 'Volkstod – death of the nation'.

Ernst Rüdin (1874-1952) was one of the fathers of 'racial hygiene'. He co-founded the 'Society for Racial Hygiene' to promote eugenics in 1905, and by 1931, he was the Director of the KWI in Psychiatry in Munich. His interest was in the psychiatric aspects of population genetics. According to Katrin Weigmann, in 'In the Name of Science' she writes, "In a research proposal to the Reich Research Council, Rüdin wrote 'what is important to safely and humanly antagonise counter-selective forces in the German society would be to research the question: which children can, already as children, be undoubtedly characterised as inferior and worth eliminating, so that they can be suggested for euthanasia'. With this goal, Rüdin initiated a collaboration with the University Hospital in Heidelberg, where Carl Schneider was conducting experiments to differentiate between inherited and acquired mental retardation. The patients, mainly children, were subjected to a series of examinations to investigate their learning abilities, and results were compared with the pathology of their brains after their murder". The indications for compulsory sterilisation were extended to 'morally feeble and other psychopaths'.

Rüdin stated shortly after Hitler assumed power that, "The importance of racial hygiene has only become known to all intelligent Germans through the political work of Adolph Hitler, and it was only through him that our more than thirty-year-old dream has become reality and racial hygiene principles have been translated into action". He trained psychiatrists to decide the fate of people with disorders that were to be eliminated in courses at the KWI for psychiatry. James Watson, the co-discoverer of the structure of DNA, dubbed it 'Elimination by scientific selection'. Weigmann states that, "Just as anthropologists reigned over the lives of despised races, it was the psychiatrists who decided the fate of people with neuropsychiatric indications."

Paul Weindling, in his book 'Health, Race and German Politics between National Unification and Nazism, 1870-1945', presents a comprehensive and extensively researched account of the history that lead to eugenics, racial hygiene, sterilisation, euthanasia, and finally genocide. Eugenics was not inherently a Nazi ideology, indeed it was expounded by the English scientist John Galton, but as with Darwinism, it was misinterpreted, adapted, and appropriated to serve the Nazi ideology. Weindling argues that as early as 1890, the movement for 'biological purity' gathered strength. "Moral decadence, chronic diseases like tuberculosis, venereal diseases and alcoholism, crime and deviant social behaviour were diagnosed as symptoms of hereditary degeneration [...] By 1932 sterilization legislation was prepared, and accepted by a wide range of Catholic, Jewish and socialist eugenicists [...] The concern with the economic burdens of the racially degenerate intensified; the category of the degenerate was enlarged to include 'races' such as Jews, gypsies, and slavs, social 'problem' groups such as criminals or the feeble minded and homosexuals. Biology justified the subordination and mass killing of the greater proportion of the population. Compulsory sterilization and 'euthanasia' of congenitally disabled children and mental patients were instituted".

Thus, health care was divided into promoting Nordic elite superman at the expense of eliminating those people the Nazis considered inferior, degenerate undesirable elements that endanger the purity of the Volk. Weindling quotes the estimates of Eugenicists that 1.2 million Germans should be sterilised, and that between 1934 and 1945, 360,000 persons were sterilised under the law, though an unknown number of foreign workers, Jews, gypsies, and mulattos were illegally sterilised. Among the Germans, the most common sterilisation was carried out for 'hereditary feeble-mindedness' – the diagnostic criteria for which must have been equally feeble and one-quarter were for schizophrenia. To the credit of the Catholic church, family members, individuals with moral values, and a few doctors, there was resistance to this inhumane measure carried out by the medical profession.

Whilst there were arguments within the Nazi hierarchy about this unpopular measure, a new and even more sinister phase of Nazi 'health measure' appeared on the horizon – euthanasia. This meant murder of the individual and thereby any future offspring. Weindling stated that, "The SS represented the ultimate extreme of Nazi medicine, with the polarity of positive eugenic selection and negative eugenic extermination [...] The SS made racial biology the basis of their social policy and military strategy. Himmler favoured polygamy to ensure that women of racially high quality should have as many children as possible so as to make up for war losses." He contributed by having two extramarital offspring.

By 1943, Karl Brandt, who was Hitler's personal physician assumed the leading role in medical killing. Weindling points out that Hitler empowered administration of 'Gnadetod' (mercy killing) in 1939, after advice received from representatives of most medical specialities. These healers of individual patients, were transformed to 'healers of the Volk', by exterminating all new-borns and children with congenital diseases, 'idiots, Mongols, and incurable conditions'. The order was not dependent on law, but on the supreme power of the Führer over life and death. To play God over innocent children and then adults was a highly contested privilege, fought out between Conti, Brack, and Bouhler. The latter won this desirable trophy and carried out the task with the assistance offered by the psychiatrists, Dr. Carl Schneider of Heidelberg and among others by the paediatrician Dr. Ibrahim of Jena.

The code name 'T4', after the administrative office in Tiergartenstrasse 4, was given to the killing, which was planned to be secret. Drs Karl Brandt graduate of the Munich and Leonardo Conti of the Berlin University Medical Schools had the privilege of starting the killing orgy by lethal intra-cardiac injection. Reputedly, they swabbed the skin with alcohol before inserting the needle, so as to symbolise a medical procedure, albeit medicalised murder. This procedure was not efficient enough for the large number of patients, and killing by gas was started on Jewish mental patients. 'Extermination of valueless life' was the reasoning extended to incurable mental disorders. According to Weindling, some 6000 children were killed at special children departments, administered by paediatricians and medical staff. A number of euphemisms were applied to these actions, such as 'special treatment', 'disinfection', 'cleansing', 'cleansing the body politic', as well as 'preventive detention', the excuse to imprisonment and that of concentration camp. It is noteworthy that despite the threats of the Gestapo and SS, the T4 programme was at least formally ended due to public pressure and that of the Church.

Medical Murder (MM) or euthanasia served as training ground to Mass Medical Murder (MMM) of the Holocaust – the 'Mother of all killing fields in the history of mankind'. After the invasion of the Soviet Union, mass killing by hanging, shooting, and vans adapted with internalised exhaust fumes were all inadequate to cope with thousands committed to death, in addition to the great 'psychological strain' on the perpetrators of these foul deeds. The final stroke or Mother of MMM was by introducing gas chambers, using Zyklon B in Auschwitz in 1941 on Soviet prisoners of war; Geneva convention of war perhaps did not envisage such an eventuality. The horrendous totality of the 'MMM' was the agony of millions who were killed and millions of their suffering family members, based on the racial narrative of academia, the willing executioners of law and the eager medical doctors for the benefit of the 'Volk', which we know has no scientific validity and is the figment of imagination of depraved pseudo-scientists, who brought only shame to the high standing of science.

VI. THE NÜREMBERG TRIAL

> 'Nazi atrocity, crimes against humanity was a State-Committed Crime: genocide, murder or any other crime become anonymous when it is committed by the State. Nobody bears the responsibility. Everybody shares it [...] those who support the administration, those who conceive the crime and who ordained it.'
>
> *Summary by Charles Dubost, Nuremberg prosecutor, 1946*

Nazi individuals and organizations were tried on four counts: crimes against peace (waging war), war crimes, conspiracy (to commit crimes), and crimes against humanity. Here we shall focus mostly onto crimes against humanity under the National Socialist regime. This included murder, extermination, enslavement, deportation committed against civilian population, before and during the war; persecution on political, racial or religious grounds, whether or not in violation of domestic law. Justice Jackson expressed a fundamental and far-reaching view that civilization was the principal victim of Nazi pathology. The use of legal language is an attempt to respond and condemn the unprecedented Nazi crimes against the Jews and express a robust concept of humanity. It is wrong to refer to the mistreatment of the Jews as a case of 'persecution' (to afflict, harass, annoy), as the ultimate aim was to annihilate the Jewish race.

American prosecutor – William Walsh argued that the final solution was premeditated by the leading Nazis before they came to power. Jackson elaborated on the Nazi plan to annihilate all Jewish people, as a measure of preparation for war. This is, in concert with Himmler's speech to SS major general in October 1943, identifying Jews as a potential military adversary a fifth column. "We know how difficult we should have made it for ourselves if with the bombing raids, the burden and deprivations of war, we still had Jews today in every town as secret saboteurs, agitators and trouble mongers". This underlined intentionality was the 'ultimate premeditated crime' argued by Lucy Dawidowicz in her book 'The War against the Jews 1933-1945'. The alternative view was proposed that this was not a premeditated goal, but an unplanned evolution, such as reaction to bombing, or response to increasingly serious defeats on the Eastern front. They also failed initially to differentiate between concentration camps and secret extermination camps (such as Treblinka and Chelmno), pointed out by the Russian prosecutor Smirnov. Altogether, the murder of Jewish people was kept secret, because of possible repercussions, both abroad and at home, being aware of the immorality of the action and fear of reprisal, all of which were not considered. Shawcross (British prosecutor) described the final solution as 'the greatest crime in history', a crime that left the 'imagination and intellect shattered'.

The Nuremberg trial was based on documentary evidence, mostly by non-Jews, paper over people, and preferred testimony by perpetrators, in contrast to the Eichmann trial which was mostly by Jews, predominantly with survivor testimony, moving from perpetrator, to bystander, to victim. Thus, the Nuremberg prosecution failed to honour obligation to survivors, which was a contentious issue.

The French prosecutor, Francois de Menthon initially equated 'Crimes against Humanity' as perpetration of common law crimes (such as theft, enslavement, murder) not mentioning specifically Jews. However, despite Menthon's statement, there was agreement between the British and Americans that the practices of civilized nations were violated. Jackson pointed out that civilization was the principal victim of Nazi ideology, indeed the practice of civilized – not cultured – nations was a recurrent theme in the Nuremberg indictment. According to Lawrence Douglas, in his book, 'The Memory of Judgment' (2001), the concept of civilization served as a bona fide source of international law, which could have alternatively referred to natural law or natural justice. Menthon declared that the National Socialist regime demonstrated "all the instincts of barbarism, repressed by centuries of civilization, but always present in men's innermost nature, all the negations of the traditional values of humanity". The shrunken head of Buchenwald was symbolic of the Nazi atrocities as a crime of atavism or rebirth of savage and primitive impulses.

The greatest historical paradox, arguably of the most cultured people in Europe who valued 'Kultur' above everything else, was that a significant proportion of Germans have been judged to act as savages with primitive impulses. This may resonate with one of the views about Germans expressed in ancient times by Tacitus. In contrast, Richard Rubenstein and John Roth asserted that "civilization now includes death camps and emaciated inmates among its material and spiritual products". This view suggests that the Holocaust is an act of civilization, whereas the Nuremberg prosecution attributes it to acts against civilization. Bauman challenges the concept of a “failure of civilization to contain the morbid, primitive nature of man”. He argues that modern civilization is not a moral force that is “a system of institutions that cooperate to impose a normative order and the rule of law, which safeguards social and individual security”.

The legal difficulties, in contrast to humane perceptions arose from indictments to criminalize entire organizations such as the SS and Gestapo cannot be discussed here. However, the notorious and unprecedented atrocities perpetrated in the name of these organizations are widely recognized. Barbarism can thrive by exploiting modern, industrialized, science-assisted procedures of research and development, in order “to quantify the killing efficiency from single individuals to thousands and millions made possible by University educated medical men and women”. The American, British, and French prosecutors largely agreed “that twenty centuries of civilization was almost destroyed by the return to ancient barbarism in a new guise all the more brutal because it was more scientific”.

The concluding arguments at Nuremberg were impressively summarised by Charles Dubost, the French prosecutor, as described by Douglas. Nazi atrocity was a “State-Committed Crime: Genocide, murder, or any other crime becomes anonymous when it is committed by the State. Nobody bears the responsibility. Everybody shares it – those who by their presence maintain and support the administration, those who conceived the crime and those who ordained it, as well as he who issued the order. As for the executioner, he says to himself, ‘Befehl ist Befehl’ (order is order) and carries out his hangman’s task”. Thus, crimes against humanity are state-sponsored crimes.

The British prosecutor, Sir Hartley Shawcross focused his summation upon the crimes of the Holocaust and transformed the Nuremberg trial into the crimes against Jews. He changed the weight of documentary evidence, largely written by the perpetrators, to that of the testimony of victims by presenting a personalized account of a German engineer through the eyes of a bystander. Mr. Gräbe happened to be an eyewitness of mass execution against the Jewish population in the Ukraine (Dubno) and gave the following testimony: “Without screaming or weeping these people undressed, stood around in family groups, kissed each other, said farewells, and waited for a sign from another SS man who stood near the pit, also with a whip in hand. During the 15 minutes that I stood near I heard no complaint or plea for mercy. I watched a family of about eight persons .... An old woman with snow-white hair was holding the one-year-old child in her arms and singing to it and tickling it. The child was cooing with delight. The couple were looking on with tears in their eyes. The father was holding the hand of a boy about 10 years old and speaking to him softly; the boy was fighting his tears. The father pointed to the sky, stroked his head, and seemed to explain something to him. At that moment the SS man shouted something to his colleague. The latter counted off about 20 persons and instructed them to go behind the earth mound. Among them was the family I have mentioned".

Douglas pointed out, "by this account Shawcross invited the court to see the victims in a manner almost entirely overlooked by the prosecution – as people". He also brought his summation to a close by these words: "You will remember not in vengeance – in a determination that these things shall not occur again". Throughout the trial, the Jews remained abstract victims and it was only during the Eichmann trial that the victim's voice was heard and expressed as a symbol of martyred humanity. The Nuremberg trial demonstrated, in Douglas' words, "the limits of the law to speak adequately on behalf of humanity's most traumatic history. Altogether, it is fair to conclude that the trial struck a blow to the complaisant Christianity and Enlightened humanity, which to this day failed adequately to explore, explain or deal with the radical evil to which they were a party, however indirectly, and cannot be exonerated."

Robert Conot, in his book 'Justice in Nüremberg' (1983), reported on Thomas Dodd's summary for the prosecution, "It is a strange feature of this trial that counsel for the respective organizations have not sought to deny these crimes but only to shift responsibility for their commission. The military defendants blame the political leaders for initiating wars of aggression the SA blames the Gestapo for concentration camp murders; the Gestapo blames the leadership corps for anti-Jewish pogroms; the SS blames the cabinet for the concentration camp system; and the cabinet blames the SS for the exterminations in the East. The fact is that all these organizations united in carrying out the criminal program of Nazi Germany. They are to blame. When the membership of these organizations swore an oath of obedience to Hitler, they united themselves for all times with him, his work, and his guilt." Complementing Dodd, Telford Taylor concluded: This was not war; it was crime. This was not soldiering; this was savagery."

When the court adjourned for Christmas, some of the individual actions and observations made by the defendants, as narrated by Conot, are noteworthy. "Hess seldom spoke, but intimated that he was now in communication with mysterious forces that would abort the trial; certainly, none of the defendants would be executed. Jodl occupied his time mapping out military campaigns that would have won the war. Schacht wrote an indictment of Adolf Hitler. Streicher, like Rosenberg a primitive artist, drew. Speer decorated his cell walls with red and blue crayons. Goering was called by Schacht a 'born criminal,' exuded an air of confidence, delighted in the exposure of the atrocities, and considered his presence among the defendants an accident and miscarriage of justice that would be rectified by the verdict.

Ribbentrop tried his misjudged diplomacy and asked: "Why can't the victors accept this as a historical tragedy that was inevitable, and try to work toward a peaceful solution? It is no use heaping hatred upon hatred. All the persecutions and atrocities are revolting to all of us, I assure you. It just isn't German. Can you conceive of me killing anybody? Tell me frankly, do any of us look like murderers?" Frank, more realistic, suggested that Hitler had been a genius at cultivating the evil in men: "Just imagine – I was a minister at thirty; rode around in a limousine! I sit here among such repulsive characters as Streicher, Goering, Ribbentrop." Kaltenbrunner was ignored by the other defendants, who shrank away from him as if he were the ghost of Himmler. Even his defence attorney, Kurt Kauffmann, a staunchly Catholic former party member, declined to shake hands with him."

Conot continues, "Goering always led the way to the chapel, though Rosenberg, Streicher, Jodl, and Hess did not attend. Usually separate services were held for the four Catholics, Frank, Schirach, Seyss-Inquart and von Papen. On Christmas Eve Catholics and Lutherans together stood before the tiny Christmas tree with its flickering candles, and sang the traditional hymn 'Silent Night, Holy Night' and other carols. It was a poignant moment. Frank was quite certain that it was his last Christmas, and his thoughts were shared by a number of the other defendants. Goering continued his bravado: "If I've got to die, I'd rather die as a martyr than a traitor". He crushed a capsule of cyanide between his teeth, went into a convulsion, and the world was a better place. Before the executions "Tod durch dem Strang!" (Death by hanging), the condemned men prayed with the reverend Gericke and father O'Connor who were rejected only by Rosenberg, Streicher, and Jodl. The others were leaders of the Third Reich who made peace with the world and Christ, though previously denied to belong to the Christian faith".

VII. GENOCIDE TERMINOLOGY

Raphael Lemkin was a Polish Jewish lawyer who managed to escape the Holocaust and travel to America. He engaged single-handed with no support to investigate the legal issues of German action against European Jewry. Lemkin concluded as early as 1941 that the intention of the Nazi government was to exterminate all Jews, using the euphemism of 'Final Solution'. He perceived the idea that this should be interpreted as a 'crime against humanity', that goes beyond the selected victims, but affects all human beings. Thus, 'Endlösung' (Final Solution), what Churchill called 'crime without a name' or Lemkin's 'crime against humanity' emerged in 1943 as 'Genocide', a crime in international law and was formally adopted by the United Nations General Assembly as late as 1948. Michael Ignatieff delivered a lecture on Raphael Lemkin in 2001 to the US Holocaust Memorial Museum on the struggle and frustrations that Lemkin had to suffer before his vision of the enormity of the Nazi threat of extermination of European Jewry became evident to the world at large. Ignatieff argued that the objective of genocide was to create a world without enemies, a crime in the service of a utopia, which can be extended to any other group. He raised the spectre of humanity that does not aim for the Judeo-Christian world of brotherhood, but a world without enemies, thereby exterminating targeted groups of people. We owe a great debt of gratitude for the forlorn, unloved, unsupported Raphael Lemkin for pursuing this critical concept of jurisprudence, one that affects the entire civilized world.

CHAPTER 8: "THE THOUSAND YEAR REICH" FOUGHT ON THREE FRONTS; THE THIRD FRONT – SWASTIKA VERSUS STAR OF DAVID

I. Introduction
II. The cold war against the Jews
III. The Wannsee Conference
IV. Development of efficient techniques of mass murder
V. Good Times
VI. Involvement of the Wehrmacht in the murder of civilians
VII. Resistance on the Jewish front
VIII. Nuclear fission between German-Aryan and German-Jewish physicists
IX. Meitnerium (Element 109)
X. Atomic war against Nazi Germany
XI. Sociological aspects of the Nazi war against Jews
XII. Evil in civilised societies

THE 'THOUSAND YEAR REICH' FOUGHT ON THREE FRONTS; THE THIRD FRONT – SWASTIKA VERSUS STAR OF DAVID

I. INTRODUCTION

<table>
<tr><td colspan="2">'The formal decision was taken in January 1942 to exterminate 11 million Jewish people at the Wannsee Conference by 15 senior officials, 9 of them had doctorates from the Universities of Jena, Tübingen, München, Frankfurt, Leipzig, Breslau and Halle; 2 had legal qualifications. The conference was presided by Reinhard Heydrich.'

Wannsee conference, based on minutes written by Adolf Eichmann, 1942</td></tr>
<tr><td>'If international finance Jewry were to bring about a world war, it would mean the destruction of the Jewish race in Europe'.

Hitler's public statement, 1939</td><td>'Intellectual disgrace' stares from every human face, and the seas of pity lie locked and frozen in each eye.'

W H Auden, following burning synagogues on Kristallnacht 1938</td></tr>
</table>

Over the period of twelve years, the National Socialist regime fought on three fronts. The Western front was established following years of preparations, first occupation of the Ruhr territory, then the 'Anschluss' of Austria, and Hitler's 'final demand' of Sudetenland from Czechoslovakia. When granted by the British and French allies, Hitler proceeded to break up Czechoslovakia, by annexing the Czech past as a 'German protectorate' and granting Slovakia independence under the puppet government headed by the nationalist Roman Catholic priest Father Jozef Tiso. The Second

World War was finally precipitated by Germany invading Poland in 1939. The 'blitzkrieg' by German forces defeated the French and British armies, within about three weeks, leaving Britain after successful evacuation of the bulk of British forces at Dunkirk to fight Germany. The invasion of Poland was carried out with the connivance of Russia, Hitler's principal declared enemy, after signing a non-aggression pact with Stalin's Russia. This gave Hitler a free hand in Poland, where the territorial plunder was shared with Russia and allowed time for Germany to re-arm for the Eastern theatre of war against Stalin. The spectacular successes of Hitler's victories, 'Germany the master of Europe', sealed the Faustian pact between the Volk and the Devil. Without a formal declaration of war in May 1941, Hitler's forces invaded Russia, under the 'Operation Barbarossa', initially again a spectacular success in Germany's 'blitzkrieg', followed by stalemate, reversal and finally defeat of Germany.

The third front, against the Jews, started shortly after Hitler seized power in 1933, unlike the brief interlude of Chamberlain trying to negotiate with Hitler and waving the infamous piece of paper with Hitler's signature 'peace in our time'. The third front was not the radio and cinema propagated 'blitzkrieg' of the heroic Wehrmacht, SS, Luftwaffe, and Marine. It started as a cold war with a series of anti-Jewish laws, followed by secret progressive life-destroying measures, culminating in mass murder of an innocent, defenceless, civil population of children, women, and men on an unprecedented scale, perfected by German specialists, developing increasingly efficient methods of mass killing.

Hitler's political aim to destroy Jews in Germany had been described in 'Mein Kampf'. In January 1939, he stated in public that "if international finance Jewry, were to bring about a world war, it would mean the destruction of the Jewish race in Europe", a prophecy he repeated later. Lucy Dawidowicz, in her book, introduced the term 'The War against the Jews 1933-1945', and analysed comprehensively his arguments. She writes that "war against the Jews fitted into Clausewitz's classical definition of war as a political act, the continuation of politics by other means. This was National Socialism's innovation, having transformed conventional anti-Semitism with its metaphoric imagery of combat into a literal war of annihilation. 'True wars', said Himmler, 'wars between races', are merciless and fought to the last man, until one side or the other is eliminated without trace." This view is supported by correspondence between officers on the Eastern front, as well as private letters by soldiers to their wives in Germany who refer to 'the war against the Jews'.

A formal meeting considering the extermination of the Jews took place in March 1941 at the inauguration of the working congress of the 'Frankfurt Institute for the Investigation of the Jewish question.' According to E. M. Zimmer Lederberg, the aim of the meeting was to discuss the "total solution to the Jewish question". Bluntly stated the 'Volkstod' (death of the nation). The guests of honour were professors Otmar von Verschuer and Eugene Fisher, the two principal architects of racial hygiene, both highly regarded German academics, with impeccable university qualifications. According to Peter Padfield, in his book 'Himmler' (1990), he gave instructions to Heydrich in July 1941 to use gas for the implementation of the programme of genocide, and this may mark the organisational beginning of the genocide. Himmler made it particularly clear to his party comrades when he stated, "The Jews must be exterminated. How is it with the women and children? Allowing the avengers in the shape of the children to grow up for our sons and grandsons. The difficult decision had to be taken, to cause this 'Volk' to disappear from the earth." At the time when the Allies landed in France in 1944, and three months later when Italy fell, Frank declared, "The ultimate lines of combat have been clearly drawn: on the one hand, the swastika, and on the other the Jews." More recently, the Hamburg Institute for Social Research reported the crimes of the Wehrmacht under the title 'Vernichtungskrieg' (Extermination War). The notion of Germany fighting the war on three fronts, the third one a unique cowardly war against peaceful, unarmed civilian Jews, having no hostile intentions towards German people will be argued in the following account.

However, the concept of a world 'Jewish conspiracy' bent on domination of Germany, defined the Jew, indeed any enemy of Germany as Jews or tools of Jews. Hitler preached a programme of anti-Semitism, by first depriving Jews of all rights as German citizens, followed by expropriating their property and finally eliminating them from Germany. Under the influence of Rosenberg (originating from Estonia), and other Russian and Ukrainian émigrés who collaborated with the Nazis, they schemed to liberate Russia and the East from the 'Jewish-Bolsheviks'. At the same time it would create the much needed 'lebensraum' (living space) and restore the land to its original German owner. Except for the anti-Semites, neither the bulk of German people nor the Jews took Hitler's arguments seriously. "The Jew would really devour the people of the earth, would become their master, the international world Jew slowly but surely strangles us, the Jew destroys the racial foundations of our existence and thus destroys our people for all time." Speeches or writings of the 'mythic Jew' and programme of annihilation were discussed as ravings of a lunatic.

In ‘Mein Kampf’, the central idea was ‘the war against the Jews that would end in their annihilation and the world supremacy of the Germans.

II. THE COLD WAR AGAINST JEWS

> 'This was not war; it was crime.
> This was not soldiering; this was savagery.'
>
> *Telford Taylor, Nüremberg trial, 1946*

After assuming power in 1933, the first phase in the cold war was to enact the law ('Gleichschaltung') to remove Jews from all state, educational, and cultural appointments. In the second phase, at the 1935 Nuremberg party congress, Hitler introduced further anti-Jewish legislation, depriving German Jews of their rights and protection, but legislation of losing the German citizenship was instituted later in 1938, thus reversing some sixty years of progress. A further law for 'The Protection of German Blood and Honour' was to prevent Gentiles having sexual intercourse with Jews. By the summer of 1936, that is within three and a half years of gaining power, the Nazi lawyers completed a programme of identifying, disenfranchising, and isolating Jews from the rest of society. Another mile-post was the assassination of Ernst vom Rath a third secretary in the German embassy in Paris by a seventeen-year-old Polish Jewish student Herschel Grynszpan whose parents in Hanover were expelled with about 50,000 Polish Jews from Germany. This was a pretext for the 'Kristallnacht' (night of glass) in November 1938, allegedly orchestrated by Goebbels, for the Nazis to perpetrate arbitrary violence against the Jews, their businesses arresting many and destroying synagogues.

By the beginning of 1939, German Jews were effectively placed at the mercy of the Nazis, and removed from the judicial due process. By the time of the German invasion of Poland in 1939, Goebbels almost achieved to dehumanise Jews, using every expletive in the German vocabulary, without any public outcry. The cold war was over, with Hitler's declaration of war against the Jews, and destruction of the Jewish race in Europe. Planning of the 'final solution' begun shortly before Keitel invaded Poland in September 1939. 'Einsatzgruppen' (death squads) were set up, consisting mostly of the ethnic German minority and police. They were assigned to the combat troops and their task was to deal with elements hostile to Germany. Heydrich ordered them to 'liquidate' (a term commonly used to kill) Polish ruling circles, intelligentsia, the clergy, Jews, and others. They murdered tens of thousands of innocent people as a matter of policy decided between Hitler, Himmler, and Heydrich with the military (Keitel and Brauchitsch), though the latter abstained from murders during the early phase, yet tacitly accepting the ideological campaign of annihilation of civilians. The Nazis shunned every moral code of conduct and may have adopted the Roman principle, which distinguished between war against civilized people that obeyed certain rules of honour and mercy, as applied to the Western front, and war against barbarians, which was conducted without any restraint, as was pursued on the Eastern front and the war against the Jews.

Jews were herded into ghettos, conditions which resulted in 'natural' high death rates caused by hunger, cold, disease, and exhaustion as a preliminary to starting the wholesale murder of the 'final solution'. With the invasion of Russia, the 'murder machinery' was well oiled and the function of the 'Einsatzgruppen' was intensified and enlarged. Mass murder of Jewish men in 1941 in German-occupied Russia, escalated to extermination of whole Jewish populations, children, women, and men. The propaganda machine alleging 'Jewish power and Jewish conspiracy', succeeded with people conditioned by systemic anti-Semitism of Christian age-old teaching of the New Testament. The men waging war against the fighting Russian enemy and the unseen enemy behind the scene, responsible for the war, had to be destroyed. Linking the war against the Russian Bolsheviks with that of the Jews was achieved by referring to 'Jewish Bolsheviks', who jointly were all out to annihilate the peaceful, decent German Volk. Dawidowicz points out that the German war against the Jews was consistent with Clausewitz's classical definition of war as a political act. He also introduced the concept of 'total warfare' backed by the will of the people.

The National Socialist objective of making first Germany and later, when much of Europe was conquered, extended to the rest of Europe 'Judenfrei' (free of Jews). Increasingly large number of Jews emigrated, but most Jews still believed in the myth that the 'Cultured German' people would not endanger their lives. However, no country was willing to accept large numbers of refugees. Several hair-raising plans by the Nazis of dumping Jews in Madagascar, Africa, or Siberia were abandoned.

III. THE WANNSEE CONFERENCE

The formal decision was taken most likely in January 1942 at the Wannsee Conference (a suburb of Berlin) to exterminate the Jewish people. However, as Longerich writes in his book, 'Holocaust', Hitler made a speech to the 'Gauleiters' and Reich leaders, in which he "once again returned to his 'prophecy' of 30 January 1939 [repeated since, of exterminating the Jewish people], as revealed in Goebbels's diary. As regards the Jewish question, the Führer is resolved to make a clean sweep. He prophesied to the Jews that if they were to bring about another world war, they would bring about their own destruction as a result. This was not empty talk. The world war is here, the destruction of the Jews must be the necessary consequence [...] We are not here to show sympathy with the Jews, we must sympathize with our own German people. If the German people had once again sacrificed around 160,000 fallen in the Eastern campaign, the authors of this bloody conflict will have to pay with their lives."

Indeed, extermination of European Jewry began as early as 1939 after invasion of Poland, and was accelerated after the invasion of the Soviet Union in June 1941. 'Einsatzgruppen' were assigned to follow the army, round up and kill Jews, Polish leaders, and intellectuals, and in the USSR, leading members of the communist party and partisans. However, it was in July 1941 that Göring gave written authorization to Heydrich to prepare a plan for the 'total solution of the Jewish question in territories under German control and to coordinate with the relevant government organisations". Heydrich wanted the commitment of all the relevant ministries and individuals to the task and thus share the burden of responsibility, arguably of the first coordinated, scientifically planned and executed mass murder by a modern, cultured West European state. Furthermore, as noted above in March 1941 the 'Frankfurt Institute for investigation of the Jewish Question' discussed, 'Volkstod' (Death of the Nation), with Otmar von Verschuer and Eugene Fischer.

The pre-requisite to the fatal decision was established, as discussed in the next chapter ('Complex academic structure of genocide'), by academia, legal authorities, the medical and allied professions and orchestrated by all the media under the efficient direction of the propaganda minister. The Jews were the pariah, caused the present and World War One, and all the problems of the German 'Volk'. They were depersonalised at home, schools, and universities to the point that a broad consensus may have been reached for 'trennung' (separation) of Jews. This seemingly benign move was of course going back to medieval times of creating ghettos. However, the real agenda of extermination was not made public, though clearly understood by the Nazi hierarchy.

At the Wannsee Conference were fifteen senior representatives of the ministries of Interior, Justice, Propaganda, the Reich 'Four Year Plan', and occupied Eastern Territories. The conference was presided by the 'SS-Obergruppenführer' Reinhard Heydrich, responsible to 'the Reichsführer SS', Heinrich Himmler, in turn responsible to the 'Führer' Adolf Hitler. The minutes of the meeting were formally written by the 'SS-Obersturmbannführer' Adolf Eichmann, responsible to the head of Gestapo 'SS-Gruppenführer' Heinrich Müller. Nine of the fifteen members had doctorates from the great German Universities of Jena, Tübingen, München, Frankfurt, Leipzig, Breslau, and Halle (two were not identified), in addition, two members studied law and were certified by the relevant bar councils. Altogether, eleven of the fifteen members of the Wannsee Conference had a doctorate or legal qualification, leaving four non-professionals which included Heydrich and Eichmann.

The meeting lasted altogether ninety minutes, which was to seal the fate of 11 million people. The efficiency of mass murder by the stroke of fifteen signatures surpasses even the proverbial German efficiency. Hitler and Himmler were given a wish list by Heydrich and the senior officials of 'Gnadetod', not only of Jews within the occupied territories, but it extended beyond to England, Ireland, Switzerland, Sweden, Hungary, Spain, Portugal, and Turkey. According to Eichmann, after the meeting, cognac was served and a frank discussion ensued, without euphemisms, about exterminating millions and the technique of mass killing. Apparently Heydrich was pleased with the meeting, as he expected some resistance and instead found all round agreement and support for the fate of European Jewry. Heydrich made it clear what was to be understood by the phrase 'Final Solution'; the Jews were to be annihilated by a combination of forced labour and mass murder. Indeed, all those present at the meeting became accomplices to the subsequent mass murders. Eichmann, the official scribe, was given firm instructions to render the discussion into 'office language', which he duly obliged. Of the fifteen participants at the Wannsee Conference, only one, the lawyer Wilhelm Kritzinger, stated publicly that he was ashamed of participating at the conference, which led to the atrocities.

IV. DEVELOPMENT OF EFFICIENT TECHNIQUES OF MASS MURDER

The most explicit extermination policy was declared by Her Himmler, the head of SS, Gestapo and concentration camps, in Posen, Poland in October 1943 to his inner circle of SS 'Gauleiters'.

> **"The question which you 'meine Parteigenossen' (my party comrades), have all taken for granted, but which has become for me the most difficult question of my life, the Jewish question. You all accept it as self-evident and agreeable that in your 'Gau' there are no longer any Jews. The maxim with its few words, 'the Jews must be exterminated', is 'meine Herren' easily spoken. For he who has to execute its demands it is the hardest and most difficult task there is [...] I ask of you that what I say in this circle you really only hear and never speak of. We come to the question: how is it with the women and children? I have resolved even here on a completely clear solution. That is to say I do not consider myself justified in eradicating the men – so to speak killing or ordering them killed – and allowing the avengers in the shape of the children to grow up for our sons and grandsons. The difficult decision had to be taken, to cause this 'Volk' to disappear from the earth. To organise the execution of this mission was the most difficult task we had hitherto. It was accomplished without – as I believe I am able to say – our men or our officers suffering injury to spirit or soul."**

Deportations started of complete families to concentration camps, some of which were specially constructed for extermination. The technique was improved, to enable efficient killing of large masses of people, as train-loads of people arrived from all European countries conquered by the German armies. In Poland, which had the largest Jewish population of some 3.5 million people, they were first isolated in ghettos and then taken to killing grounds, where men, women, and children were made to undress, marched to the edge of dug up trenches and shot, so the victims fell into mass graves. The clothes were collected and sent to Germany to be used by the 'Volk'; presumably nobody asked where the millions of clothe came from. It must have been a god-send to the poor and needy people. The method of killing was deemed inefficient and bad for the morale of German soldiers, "some of them did not enjoy killing, especially children". The technology of mass murder – a new speciality for which the Nazis were ill-prepared – had to be improved.

The entry of doctors of medicine into the gruesome 'Healer-Killer' paradox has an ancient precedent in Germany. In the late 16th century, Master Frantz Schmidt, a highly respected citizen of Nüremberg, was a physician and claimed to have treated over 15,000 patients, including imperial emissaries and a Teutonic knight. Despite this honourable activity, he also acted as a Master Executioner, and according to his count, he performed 228 executions and many floggings. He specialised in the subtle art of torture before killing. The 'Gnadentod' (merciful death) started at the top with the head, so that the culprit was already dead when the limbs were broken by the wheel. However, if the offence was severe, the 'physician-executioner' began with the feet and worked his way up, with the 'coup de gras' when the cart wheel was slammed down on his head.

The difference of 300 years of progress, Protestantism, Enlightenment, Science, Art, and Civilisation at large between Master Schmidt and Dr. Dr. Mengele is that the former killed 228 judicially convicted citizens of Nüremberg openly for the merriment of the 'Volk', whereas Dr. Dr. Mengele dispatched to the gas chambers thousands of totally innocent children, women, and men in sworn secrecy. Unlike Master Schmidt, he specifically selected twin children, removed their eyes and some brains and sent these to his Master Professor Verschuer at the Kaiser Wilhelm Institute in Berlin.

Although German medical practice of euthanasia on a large number of German individuals with ill-defined congenital and other diseases was carried out in dedicated killing centres in Germany, the techniques were inadequate for mass killing. Furthermore, face to face or close proximity of killing defenceless human beings had created psychological problems even in some indoctrinated Germans. The technical ingenuity of German engineers rose to the challenge and devised 'gas vans', in which the exhaust pipes expelling carbon monoxide were placed inside the van. Human beings were loaded into these vans and when the engines were switched on, people were suffocated after a few minutes. As related by Bauman, the engineer Willy Just reported on the problems encountered with the technology, entirely detached from the suffering of the victims. This is illustrated by Christopher R. Browning's excerpt from Just's report on the efficiency of the technology. "A shorter, fully loaded truck could operate much more quickly. A shortening of the rear compartment would not disadvantageously affect the weight balance, overloading the front axle, because actually a correction in the weight distribution takes place automatically through the fact that the cargo in the struggle toward the back door during the operation always is preponderantly located there. Because the connecting pipe was quickly rusted through the 'fluids', the gas should be introduced from above, not below. To facilitate cleaning, an eight- to twelve-inch hole should be made in the floor. The 'thin fluids' would exit even during operation, and the 'thicker fluids' could be hosed out afterwards".

The concern is not about the 'cargo' – men, women and children – who during the struggle for air lose control over their bodily functions, but the cold-blooded technical improvements of mass killing. The next and final achievement of German mass murder technology was to use Zyklon B in specially built gas chambers, which were camouflaged as 'shower rooms', so the people ushered into these chambers, should be under the misapprehension that they are having a shower after a long miserable journey to the concentration camp.

The final road to oblivion was paved with the deception by the honest, German National Socialist, so as to achieve a fast, cheap and disciplined murder, out of sight of the murderer, who can return with a peace of mind to the warm bosom of his wife and children. The words of the mastermind of the unimagined horror inside the gas chamber were uttered by Her Himmler, the head of SS, Gestapo, the greatest exterminator of humanity the world has ever seen and the chief of staff of the war against the Jews. The extermination policy was clearly presented without the usual euphemisms by Himmler's talk to his inner circle of Gauleiters in Posen. The speech is presented verbatim above, the complete admission by the greatest exterminator of humanity, Anno Domini 1943. The criminal action of the German Nazi government has been commonly ascribed to a small number of criminals, psychopaths, sadists, or amoral individuals. This view has been refuted in the report by George M. Kren and Leon Rappoport. "By conventional clinical criteria no more than 10 per cent of the SS could be considered 'abnormal'. This observation fits the general trend of testimony by survivors indicating that in most of the camps, there was usually one, or at most a few, SS men known for their intense outbursts of sadistic cruelty. Our judgement is that the overwhelming majority of SS men, leaders as well as rank and file, would have easily passed all the psychiatric tests ordinarily given to American army recruits."

It is even more disturbing to think that the genocide was perpetrated by normal individuals, referring again to Arendt's 'banality of the individuals involved in the genocide'. In the comprehensive sociological analysis of the Holocaust, Zygmunt Bauman asks, "How were these ordinary Germans transformed into the German perpetrators of mass crime?" In the opinion of Herbert C. Kelman, moral inhibitions against violent atrocities tend to be eroded once three conditions are met, singly or together; the violence is authorized (by official orders), actions are routinized (by exact specification of roles), and the victims of the violence are dehumanized (by ideological indoctrination)."

The Germans were anxious that the killing should take place in an orderly, disciplined way, unlike the programs instigated by the 'uncultured' Russian counterpart. The civilised superiority of the Germans was manifest by the rationally organised executed mass killing, in place of an orgy of killing by the Slavs. Most of it was at a distance from the victims, by lawyers, and bureaucrats sitting behind a desk and passing orders, so that murder was pursued by proxy, at the stroke of a pen. Furthermore, by establishing a chain of activities – passing the command centrally, identification, concentration and transport of the victims is done by people, each of whom may not experience direct involvement or responsibility, but the combined effect of the separate activities resulted in mass extermination. This may occur in a 'moral vacuum', promoting indifference without recognition of the evil perpetrated to human beings. Commandant Rudolf Höss of Auschwitz even boasted over the superior efficiency of the technique of mass murder by Zyklon B compared with the exhaust-filled vans used to suffocate people in Treblinka.

The more sophisticated SS general Otto Ohlendorf studied law at the Universities of Leipzig, Göttingen, and Pavia and he gained a doctorate in Jurisprudence. Ohlendorf joined the SS in 1926, gained rapid promotion and was appointed commander of 'Einsatzgruppe' D. He was a man of considerable intelligence expressed pride and satisfaction in the 'humane' way he ordered mass killing of 90,000 Jewish children, women, and men in the Ukraine and Russia. The civilised German murder under his jurisdiction adhered to four principles: "1. Exclusion of the public; 2. Military execution by a firing-squad; 3. Arrival of the transport and carrying out the liquidation in a smooth manner to avoid unnecessary excitement; 4. Supervision of the property to prevent looting". According to Lawrence Douglas, Ohlendorf even revealed a competitive attitude towards his rivals in extermination by saying "I believe that to a large extent the figures submitted by the other Einsatzgruppen were exaggerated". And these were the German supermen at the cutting edge of 'Kultur'. Hans Mommsen the distinguished German historian in the 'Adam von Trott Memorial Lecture' had clearly interpreted and expressed the significance of the Holocaust to Western civilisation. "While German civilization has developed the means for unimaginable mass-destruction, the training provided by modern technology and techniques of rationalization has produced a purely technocratic and bureaucratic mentality, exemplified by the group of perpetrators of the Holocaust, whether they committed murder directly themselves or prepared deportation and liquidation at the desks of the Reich Main Security Office ('Reichssicherheitshauptamt'), at the offices of the diplomatic service, or as plenipotentiaries of the Third Reich within the occupied or satellite countries."

The biblical tragedy of enslavement of Jews by the Egyptian Pharaohs was re-visited upon them some three millennia later, enhanced by the German scientific and technical advances, as well as the modern governmental support. However, murder of all the male children by the Egyptians merged into murder of all and every born and unborn member of 'the enemy of the German Volk'.

V. GOOD TIMES

A most revealing book written in 1988 by Ernst Klee, Will Dressen, and Volker Reiss 'Schöne Zeiten', ('Those were the days') or more literal translation ('Good Times'), was the caption of the photo album of Kurt Franz, commandant of Treblinka extermination camp. This is a unique account of 'The Holocaust through the Eyes of the Perpetrators and Bystanders'. In the 'Foreword' Lord Dacre writes, "How did the ordinary Germans look upon these grisly killings which they carried out or watched? At first there was some apprehension: if the war should be lost, it was said, surely there would be a heavy price to pay. But that stage soon passed: the war was not going to be lost – indeed, it seemed, it had already been won. Individually, some men were disgusted or ashamed, or suffered psychological stress. The strain on the nerves of the killers, it was said, was unimaginable and led to terrible nightmares; so many of them took to drink, and some even went mad and shot all around them, indiscriminately. Even Standartenführer Paul Blobel, who had carried out the Babi Yar massacre, went off his head for a time; but he soon recovered and went on with the work [...] Some were positively addicted to it and 'could not have enough of it'. There were also special inducements: extra rations of schnapps, cigarettes and sausages as reward for a hard day's butchery. That was for SS men only, as others complained. But some of the others needed no inducement.

Ordinary soldiers of the Wehrmacht who came to watch would sometimes ask to join in, borrowing guns to share the sport and shooting Jewish children as they ran, 'like hares'. Within the party there was one interesting case of dissent. Wilhelm Kube, Gauleiter of White Russia insisted that he was as 'hard' as anyone: had he not liquidated all the Jews in his Gau? But he believed that there were Jews and Jews, and that German Jews, having imbibed something of German culture, were a cut above East European Jews and should not be indiscriminately exterminated with them. What a torrent of denunciation this heresy would bring on him from the former theology student and commander of Einsatzkommando 2, now head of the SS in White Russia, Obersturmbannführer Dr. Eduard Strauch." Among the commanders of 'Einsatzgruppen' were medical doctors, such as Dr. Thomas, lawyers, Dr. Stahlecker and Dr. Ohlendorf, and an academic, Professor Dr. Six.

As is evident from briefing of a number of heads of 'Einsatzgruppen' those that were unwilling or unable to carry out these frightful acts of murder were able to opt out for other duties, without suffering serious consequences. A representative report is that from Gebietskomissar Gerhard Erren when he arrived in the small town of Slonim on 25 January 1942. "Upon my arrival there were about 25,000 Jews in the Slonim area, 16,000 in the actual town itself, making up over two-thirds of the total population of the town. First of all, property was expropriated and all the German official buildings, including the Wehrmacht quarters, were equipped with the furniture and equipment that had been made available [...] The Jews were then registered accurately according to number, age and profession and all craftsmen and workers with qualifications were singled out and given passes and separate accommodation to distinguish them from the other Jews. The action carried out by the SD on 13 November rid me of unnecessary mouths to feed. All Jews will be eradicated with the exception of all but the most essential craftsmen and skilled workers, after auxiliary work for the east-west movement has been carried out [...] I was holding a whip or a pistol. I was loading or unloading. The men, children and mothers were pushed into the pits. Children were first beaten to death and then thrown feet [first] into the pits [...] There were a number of filthy sadists in the extermination Kommando. For example, pregnant women were shot in the belly for fun and then thrown into the pits. Before the execution the Jews had to undergo a body search, during which anuses and sex organs were searched for valuables and jewels".

Daniel J. Goldhagen, in his extensively researched book 'Hitler's Willing Executioners – Ordinary Germans and the Holocaust' (1996), studied especially the police battalions, part of the 'Einsatzgruppen' as they were a representative cross-section of Germans to draw conclusions about the genocidal mentality of the ordinary man. He argues that the German political situation produced voluntary killers that must have been a product of the society, which radically lost its moral bearing towards humanity. Indeed, Goldhagen states that the Nazis wrought a revolt against civilisation. "It was above all a cognitive-moral revolution which reversed processes that had been shaping Europe for centuries. It was a peaceful revolution willingly acquiesced to by the German people. The Nazi German revolution was the most brutal and barbarous revolution of modern Western history for those who would be excluded from the new Germany and Europe, namely the tens of millions whom the Germans marked for subjugation, enslavement, and extermination, As a world of unrestrained impulses and cruelty, the camp system allowed for the expression of the new Nazi moral dispensation, one which was in its essential features the antithesis of Christian morality and Enlightenment humanism – 'those stupid, false, and unhealthy ideals of humanity,' as Göring called them [...] In the Nazi German cosmology, some humans, by reason of their biology, ought to be killed; others were fit for slavery, and they too could be killed if the Germans deemed them to be superfluous."

Himmler declared in his idiosyncratic jargon, "Whether nations live in prosperity or starve to death interest me only insofar as we need them as slaves for our 'Kultur', otherwise it is of no interest to me. Eastern Europe would become a German colony populated by German settlers and Slavic slaves." The camp system was revolutionary because it was itself already a microcosm of the new world. Indeed, the ever-growing camp system was the embryo of the new Germanic Europe, which essentially would have become a large concentration camp, with the German people as its guards and the remaining European peoples (with the exception of the 'racially' privileged) as its corpses, slaves and inmates." The camp – Germany's distinct, indeed perhaps, central institution – was the training ground for the masterly conduct of the ordinary new German 'superman', and it revealed his nature. The camp reveals that Himmler's 'Kultur' had, to a great extent, already become the Culture of Germany. The German mass murder, their reintroduction of slavery on the European continent, their adoption of free license to treat 'subhumans' however they wished, without any restraints – all suggest that the camp was the emblematic institution of Germany during its Nazi period and the paradigm for the Thousand Year Reich. There was no limit to the slaughter and barbarism that ordinary Germans were willing to perpetrate, in order to save Germany and the German people from the ultimate danger – 'Der Jude'.

A secret document to 'Eliminate the Jews once and for all' was made by 'Generalkommissar' for White Russia, Wilhelm Kube, 31 July 1942, to the 'Reichskommissar' for the Ostland, Heinrich Lohse concerning 'combating partisan and Judenaktion in the White Russia Generalbezirk'. This is of particular significance because of the alleged lack of any resistance by Jews to the German onslaught. "It has become apparent during the course of all clashes with partisans in White Russia, in both the former Polish and former Soviet parts of the Generalbezirk, that the Jews, together with the Polish resistance movement and the Moscow Red Army in the east, are the principal supporters of the partisan movement. Consequently, the question of how the Jews in White Russia should be handled is a political matter taking priority over all considerations about risks to the economy as a whole [...] During the course of extensive discussions. It was established that we have liquidated about 55,000 Jews in the past ten weeks. In the Minsk area ['Gebiet Minsk-Land'] the Jews have been completely eradicated, without any negative effect on the workforce. In the mainly Polish area of Lida 16,000 Jews have been liquidated in Slonim 8,000 Jews. On 28 and 29 July about 10,000 Jews were liquidated in the city of Minsk, 6,500 of them Russian Jews – for the most part old people, women and children – and the rest Jews unfit for work, who had mostly been sent from Vienna, Brünn, Bremen and Berlin in November of last year to Minsk on the Führer's orders. There are still some 10,000 living in the city of Baranovichi alone, of whom 9,000 will be liquidated next month."

Report by SS-Obersturmführer August Häfner on the killing of children. "Then Blobel ordered me to have the children executed. I asked him, 'By whom should the shooting be carried out?' He answered, 'By the Waffen-SS,' I raised an objection and said, 'they are all young men. How are we going to answer to them if we make them shoot small children?' To this he said, 'Then use your men.' I then said, 'How can they do that? They have small children as well.' This tug-of-war lasted about ten minutes. I suggested that the Ukrainian militia of the Feldkommandant should shoot the children. There were no objections from either side to this suggestion. I went out to the woods alone. The Wehrmacht had already dug a grave. The children were brought along in a tractor. I had nothing to do with this technical procedure. The Ukrainians were standing round trembling. The children were taken down from the tractor. They were lined up along the top of the grave and shot so that they fell into it. The Ukrainians did not aim at any particular part of the body. They fell into the grave. The wailing was indescribable. I shall never forget the scene throughout my life. I find it very hard to bear. I particularly remember a small fair-haired girl who took me by the hand. She too was shot later. Many children were hit four or five times before they died."

Letters of SS-Obersturmführer (first lieutenant) Karl Kretschmer "My dear Soska, I am in a very gloomy mood. I must pull myself out of it. The sight of the dead (including women and children) is not very cheering. But we are fighting this war for the survival or non-survival of our people [...] As the war is in our opinion a Jewish war, the Jews are the first to feel it. Here in Russia, wherever the German soldier is, no Jew remains. You can imagine that at first I needed some time to get to grips with this. Please do not talk to Frau Kern about this." A report from the priest Jonas Gylys: "Like executioners they beat innocent people, punching elderly and pregnant women. Innocent people suffered like Christ at the hands of Judas. Before their blood had even had time to dry they robbed them of their property. The priest's words were apparently directed at those who had been involved in liquidating the Jews. Characteristically, G. went to visit the Jews held in the synagogue, without any authorization, to give them solace and courage." From: Ereignismeldung UdSSR, No. 130, 7 November 1941).

The litany of murder goes on and on and it needs to be re-emphasized that this is not from the victims but German perpetrators of systematic genocide, later extended over the entire European continent. A further source of evidence confirming the less than honourable discipline of the German soldiers has been published recently in (2012) 'Soldaten – On fighting, killing and dying – The secret World War II transcripts of German POWs' by Sönke Neitzel and Harald Welzer. Surreptitious recordings of POWs revealed sexual violence; "We drove past a village in Russia, simply pulling them into the armoured car, raped them and threw them out again." They were well aware of the mechanism of the holocaust, with mass executions of Jews, asphyxiation vans, de-lousing centre where 200 Jewish men were dissolved in a vat of acid. Quite apart from these gruesome reports, the historian Ernst Klee wrote about hordes of German soldiers, taking photographs at mass executions of Jews and other civilians; he called them "Execution tourists".

With the striking success of the German war machine in most of the West and East Europe, the entire Jewish population of the European continent became hostage of the Nazi government under the extra-judicial mandate of Himmler's SS 'final solution'. According to Longerich, a day after declaration of war on the United States (on the 13th December 1942) Hitler made a speech to the Gauleiters, reiterating his prophecy of 1939, as noted in Goebbels's diary "As regards the Jewish question, the Führer is resolved to make a clean sweep. He prophesied to the Jews that if they were to bring about another world war, they would bring about their own destruction as a result. This was not empty talk. The world war is here, the destruction of the Jews must be the necessary consequence. The question must be seen without sentimentality. We are not here to show sympathy with the Jews, we must sympathize with our own German people. If the German people has once again sacrificed around 160,000 fallen in the Eastern campaign, the authors of this bloody conflict will have to pay with their lives." It appears that the Nazi hierarchy attributed even the chain reaction that was triggered by the Japanese attack on Pearl Harbour, followed by the United States declaration of war against Japan that brought Germany into the war against the United States onto the Jews. Thus, the infinitely powerful Jews had willed Hirohito's generals to attack the United States.

Here we have the declaration of war of extermination of the Jewish people by Hitler himself. Following the Wannsee Conference in January 1942, according to research by Longerich, Heydrich outlined the aims of the future 'Jewish Policy' as follows, "After appropriate prior approval by the Führer, emigration as a possible solution has been superseded by a policy of evacuating the Jews to the East. These 'actions' (the deportations that had already begun) were to be regarded merely as 'temporary solutions' (Ausweichmöglichkeiten), nonetheless 'practical experience would be accumulated' which would be 'of great importance for the impending final solution of the Jewish Question'. The impending 'final solution' was envisaged as involving 11 million Jews, a figure which was broken down by country in a statistical addendum to the minutes. This list not only includes Jews living in areas under German control, but also those of Great Britain, Ireland, Portugal, Sweden, Switzerland, Spain and Turkey [...]. Those Jews fit for work will be led into these areas as road-builders, in the course of which, no doubt, a large number will be lost by natural wastage. The fate of those 'unfit for work', children and mothers in particular, was not further elucidated by Heydrich. It is clear that they too were to be killed, because Heydrich wanted to prevent the survival of the 'germ cell of a new Jewish regeneration' at all costs." This is reinforced by the Governor General Frank before the conference "We can't shoot these 3.5 million Jews, we can't poison them, but we will be able to intervene in a way that will somehow lead to their successful extermination. The General Government must become just as free of Jews [Judenfrei] as the Reich. Where and how that happens is a matter for the official bodies that we must set up and deploy here, and in due course I shall let you know how effective they are."

The well tried practice in Germany was now applied with greatly improved efficiency by the SS Adolf Eichmann to the European states. Isolation of the Jews, expropriation all their properties, deportation to the killing centres in concentration camps scattered in Poland, Germany, and Austria. Despite enthusiastic collaboration in the genocide by the Austrians, they claimed to be 'the first victims' of the Nazi regime. The narrative of Austrian total involvement in the atrocities against Jews requires another book. However, according to Peter Watson in 'The German Genius' (2010), Hitler and Eichmann were Austrians, most of the commandants of the death camps at Belsen, Sobibor and Treblinka, as well as 40% of the personnel were Austrians, as were 80% of Eichmann's staff. The 'Anschluss' was hailed by the Austrian population and the SS was swamped with Austrian applicants.

VI. INVOLVEMENT OF THE WEHRMACHT IN THE MURDER OF CIVILIANS

As the 'Blitzkrieg' gradually changed into a defensive war, the increasing German military bravery and failures in both the Eastern and Western fronts seemed to parallel an increasing cowardice manifested in mass killing of the unarmed Jewish civilians. According to Longerich, whilst initially the Wehrmacht abstained from killing civilians, as early as 1941, they joined in the fray that included the upright aristocratic sons of the German military establishment. The honour of the Wehrmacht has been jealously guarded as the last bastion of German decency and all atrocities against the civilian population (especially Jews) has been attributed to the SS. However, recent studies have disclosed crimes of the Wehrmacht, demonstrated by the Hamburg Institute for Social Research, under the titles 'Vernichtungskrieg' (Extermination War) and another named 'Verbrechen der Wehrmacht' (Crimes of the Wehrmacht).

Another study of the military by Longerich shows that the Wehrmacht has been implicated directly or indirectly in the war against the Jews. "The Commander of the 6th Army, Walther von Reichenau, spoke in an order dated 10 August of the 'necessary execution of criminal, Bolshevist, and mainly Jewish elements' that would have to be carried out by the orders of the Reichsführer SS. The Commander of the 11th Army, Erich von Manstein, described 'Jewry' in an order of 20 November as 'the middle-man between the enemy at our backs and the remains of the Red Army that are still fighting on and the red leaders'. The Commander of the 17th Army, Karl Heinrich von Stülpnagel, gave an order on 30 July not to take indiscriminate reprisal against the civilian population but – if the deed could not be pinned on the Ukrainians – to concentrate on 'Jewish and Communist inhabitants' [...] Christian Gerlach has provided a number of examples that prove how, during the conquest of Belarus in the summer of 1941, front-line troops made attacks on Jews that sometimes involved carrying out shootings." Among the horror accounts revealed by eavesdropping on POW officers, the historian Helen Fry reports that General Dietrich von Choltitz, the former military governor of Paris, said "the worst job I ever carried out – which however I carried out with great consistency – was the liquidation of Jews, The Jews were lined up in pits in the woods and shot, and children thrown in."

In his conclusion Longerich writes "because the Wehrmacht leadership declared itself satisfied with the basic principles of the ideological war and permitted a second war against the civilian population behind its front line, it too, bears the responsibility for implementing the Holocaust". The fate of Jewish soldiers in the Russian army has also been studied by Longerich: "From the very early stages, the policies for annihilating the Jewish population of the Soviet Union particularly affected the Jewish soldiers of the Red Army. They were amongst those groups of prisoners who were separated out in the camps and liquidated as a matter of course."

The war against the Jews was the only success that could be claimed by Hitler and Himmler, as 'their willing executioners' were able to murder 6 million Jews. As shocking and incomprehensible such a vast number is to the civilised men and women, this fell short of the 11 million targeted by Heydrich. His dearest soul-mate, Hitler, did not think the task was completed, because in his last testament dictated to his secretary hours before he committed suicide, his main message to the 'Volk' was again his obsession with continuing the fight against the Jews embedded in his pathological mind.

VII. RESISTANCE ON THE JEWISH FRONT

The possibilities for a peace-loving civilian population to resist an armed, trained, disciplined, and brain-washed Gestapo and SS is difficult to envision. Nonetheless, a large proportion, and some estimate up to 40%, of partisans actively resisting the German army in Poland and Russia were Jewish men. In France, a fair proportion of the resistance ('maquis') were Jews. The heroism of the 'Bielski brothers' in Poland, living in forests and protecting over 1000 Jewish civilian men, women, and children with armed resistance to German attacks has become a legend. In Treblinka, the mass extermination camp in Poland, where some 800,000 Jews were murdered, an uprising took place in August 1943 by a substantial number of inmates under the leadership of Rudy Masaryk. A number of inmates escaped, but most were captured and shot dead, but a few survived and two of them were witnesses at the Jerusalem trial of Adolf Eichmann, the SS officer in charge of collecting and deporting Jewish people from all over Europe to the extermination camps.

The major uprising against the German had occurred in the large ghetto in Warsaw. The Jews were aware of their fate when they were due to be sent to concentration camps. After several failed attempts by the German authorities and even an earlier armed attempt to liquidate the Ghetto with some 200,000 surviving people, the fight began. According to the detailed account of Dawidowicz, "on Monday 19 April 1943 armed German, Lettish and Ukrainian patrols began to be deployed around the Warsaw ghetto. By daylight ZOB (Jewish Combat Organisation) units were mobilized. At 6.00 a m, a contingent of 2,000 heavily armed SS troops entered the central ghetto, with tanks, rapid-fire guns and three trailers loaded with ammunition. The civilian ghetto population was underground, hiding in their bunkers. ZOB attacked the entering German columns. With incendiary bottles mass-produced in a secret ZOB laboratory, they blew up German tanks and German troops. By 5.00 p.m. the Germans, surprised and shocked by Jewish resistance, withdrew from the ghetto, having lost some 200 dead and wounded.

'We were happy and laughing' said a ZOB combatant. 'When we threw our grenades and saw German blood on the streets of Warsaw, which had been flooded with so much Jewish blood and tears, a great joy possessed us.' Everyone knew that the Germans would return, that the Germans would ultimately defeat ZOB, that the Jews would soon be annihilated; yet after that day's fighting in the ghetto, people embraced and kissed each other." On that very day in the Rabbi's room the first Passover night ('seder') was celebrated when God liberated his chosen people from Pharaoh's slavery. "The reading of the Haggadah was punctuated by gunfire and shell-bursts. The assembled Jews wept when the rabbi intoned: "Pour out Thy wrath upon the heathen nations that do not acknowledge Thee and upon the kingdoms that do not call upon Thy name; for they have devoured Jacob and laid waste his dwelling place." And God was there or 'hid his face' as his chosen people were being murdered for one reason that they declared their belief in him.

Next day, "Lettish Waffen-SS reinforcements entering the ghetto were received with grenades and explosives. An electric mine killed about 100 Germans of a 300-man force. Then the Germans brought in tanks and field artillery. Occupying several roofs, they set up heavy machine-guns [...] SS again demanding that ZOB units lay down their arms. If not, the entire area would be bombed. Once again, ZOB's reply came from its guns [...] The Germans began setting fire to Ghetto buildings. ZOB countered by igniting the warehouses of the 'Werterfassung', the agency in charge of expropriated Jewish property. Pillars of smoke began to rise over the ghetto. The Germans cut off the supply of electricity, gas and water from the ghetto streets. ZOB fighters remained exultant, their morale high. On one roof they flew the red-and-white Polish flag alongside the Jewish blue-and-white banner. On another roof a ZOB banner proclaimed: 'We shall fight to the last.' By Thursday 22 April the ghetto was enveloped in dense smoke. To dislodge the tens of thousands of Jews hidden in bunkers and underground shelters, the Germans brought in flame throwers. Emerging from their smoke-filled burning hide-outs, the Jews, hands held over their heads, were marched to the Umschlagplatz. There the Ukrainians, beating and bullying them, loaded them on the waiting freight trains. On Friday 23 April Mordecai Anielewicz, ZOB commandant, sent a letter to his friend Zuckerman, then on the 'Aryan' side. 'The last wish of my life has been fulfilled. Jewish self-defence has become a fact. Jewish resistance and revenge have become realities.' No one had hoped to hold out that long. They numbered about 1,000 combatants. According to the Home Army estimates, the Germans had some 5,000 men and officers, massively equipped. On 8 May the Germans surrounded the hide-out of ZOB head-quarters. The civilians in the bunker surrendered, but the ZOB fighters entrenched themselves, ready to fight the Germans. Instead, the Germans stopped up all the entrances and sent gas into the bunker. Over 100 fighters were inside. One of them called out, 'Let's not fall into their hands alive!'

They began to kill themselves and each other, in a scene that must have rivalled the mass suicide at Masada. Mordecai Anielewicz was among them. On 10 May about seventy-five ZOB survivors made their way through the slime of Warsaw's sewers to escape, with the help of comrades on the Aryan side. The Warsaw ghetto became one huge cemetery." The fighting resisting the Germans lasted twenty-one days, with hundreds of Germans killed and compares well with the fully equipped Czech, Polish and French armies fighting German invasions. It is noteworthy that the 'Polish Home Army' was reluctant to help the Jewish rebels, because the situation was hopeless, and the Polish nationalists had their own long-standing history of anti-Semitism before and indeed after the war. However, it is uncertain if many of them were aware that the German policies towards the Jews was a foreplay of future actions against the Poles.

A large number of Jews fought in the British, American, and especially the Russian forces, who, as described above, were sufficiently large to merit 'special attention by the Germans. The Jewish contributions to the war effort was considerable and included a special unit assembled by the British in Palestine.

The undoubted heroism of the publicised German forces on the Western and Eastern front, must be viewed against their cowardice of the war by stealth, the third front, the war against the peace-abiding, unarmed German and European civilian Jewish populations. Whereas Germany lost the war on both the Eastern and Western fronts, it gained a resounding victory in the unilateral war of cowards at a price of thousand years of history of genocide by the Reich. Germans murdered systematically innocent civilians over twelve years of categorical evil, whilst sheltering under the umbrella of Goethe, Schiller, Kant, Bach, and Beethoven. Every one of them would if they could declare "not in my name", unlike the university academics, law-makers, and doctors of medicine. Dismal failure of the conventional war on the two fronts and unmitigated tragedy of victory on the third front, has left the 'Thousand Year Reich' with the memory of – Shame, Betrayal of 'Kultur', Cowardice, Spiritual Barbarity – The Holocaust – the Ultimate Sin of humanity.

VIII. THE NUCLEAR FISSION BETWEEN GERMAN-ARYAN AND GERMAN-JEWISH PHYSICISTS

<table>
<tr><td colspan="2">German and Allied scientists worked for the military, but the difference, which it will never be possible to forgive, is that the [German physicists] worked for the cause of Himmler and Auschwitz, for the burners of books and the takers of hostages'.

Phillip Morrison, Professor of Physics c. 1950</td></tr>
<tr><td>'Hitler's providential refusal of Planck's request to exempt Jewish scientists from being dismissed from their Universities, might have denied Germany producing the atom bomb, winning the war and the SS ruling over Europe'.

Author's interpretation of Planck's meeting
with Hitler in 1933</td><td>'The decision by Fermi and Szilard not to publish the discovery that pure graphite, free from impurities absorbed neutrons, which induce uranium fission may have saved the world'.

Max Perutz, 2002</td></tr>
<tr><td colspan="2">Professor David Hilbert of Göttingen University was asked by Minister Bernhard Rust in 1940 "How is mathematics in Göttingen now that it has been freed of Jews", Hilbert replied: "Mathematics in Göttingen? There is none any more".</td></tr>
</table>

The policy of Nazi Germany to make Germany and then Europe free of Jews started with the 'Law for the Restoration of the Professional Civil Service', within three months of gaining power on the 30th January 1933. Universities and educational authorities were the very first to be affected with the result that a total of 1,145 university teachers in all faculties lost their posts or about 14% of the educational staff in 1933. This was proportionally much greater for nuclear physicists as 50% emigrated in 1933. The most celebrated case was that of Albert Einstein, who resigned in 1933 from the post of president of the Kaiser Wilhelm Institute of Physics in Berlin and left for Britain and subsequently to the United States. In addition, twelve physicists and chemists left Germany: Hans Bethe, Felix Bloch, Max Born, James Franck, Dennis Gabor, Fritz Haber, Gerhard Herzberg, Victor Hess, George de Hevesy, Erwin Schrödinger, Otto Stern, and Eugene Wigner, and in 1938, Lise Meitner. A further group of ten scientists and colleagues left Europe, such as Enrico Fermi of Italy whose wife was Jewish, and Niels Bohr of Denmark, whose mother was Jewish. Most of them joined the Manhattan Project for the development of the atomic bomb: Enrico Fermi, James Franck, Maria Goeppert-Mayer, Robert Oppenheimer, Edward Teller, Victor Weisskopf, John von Neumann, Otto Frisch, Rudolf Peierls, Felix Bloch, Emilio Segrè, and Leo Szilard.

A significant episode of the Third Reich was the meeting in Berlin in May 1933 between Max Planck and Adolf Hitler, president of the prestigious 'Kaiser Wilhelm Society'. Planck pleaded with Hitler to exempt Jewish scientists and he mentioned Fritz Haber whom Hitler would recognise, as he invented the process for producing ammonia from nitrogen in air, essential in the production of both explosives and fertilizers. Hitler responded that he must act against all Jews, as "a Jew is a Jew". "He ignored my comment that forcing worthy Jews to emigrate would be equivalent to mutilating ourselves outright, because we need their scientific work and their efforts would otherwise go primarily to the benefit of foreign countries". Hitler said, "People say I suffer occasionally from nervous debility. This is slander. I have nerves of steel." As he said this, he pounded his knee, spoke faster and faster, and whipped himself up into such a fury that I was left with no other choice than to remain silent and to take my leave." It must be said that the Planck-Hitler encounter was written up in 1947, fourteen years after the event, just a few weeks before Planck's death, when he was very frail and with the help of his wife Marga.

There are many and diverse accounts of this meeting. One account suggests that when Planck pleaded for exempting very capable Jewish scientists from dismissal from the Kaiser Wilhelm Society, Hitler flew into a rage and Planck made a hasty retreat. Allegedly, Einstein heard that Hitler threatened the seventy-five year old Planck with the concentration camp. A very different narrative was that the meeting was business-like – reminiscent of Pope-Pius XII 'concordat' – in that Planck was assured of autonomy and support for 'German physics', as long as the Society follows the Nazi doctrine. The latter view was supported by the historian Helmuth Albrecht that Planck brokered a deal, if he goes along with the declared laws, he will be left to get on without interference. This interpretation is consistent with subsequent funding of the KWG, as well as with a letter from Heisenberg to Born.

Jewish physicists who faced dismissal by the anti-Semitic laws were: Albert Einstein, Max Born, James Franck, Hans Bethe, Felix Bloch, Otto Stein, Rudolf Peierls, Lise Meitner, and Samuel Goudsmit. This is a roster of the great and the good in German physics in the first half of the twentieth century. Planck saw clearly not only the loss to Germany but also the gain of scientific knowledge by other countries.

Another issue entered the narrative of the German nuclear programme early in 1930's the nationalist, anti-Semitic division of Physics into 'Deutsche Physik' (or Aryan Physics) and 'Jewish Physics' (or Einstein's Physics). The instigators of this movement were Johannes Stark and Philipp Lenard, both being Nobel laureates in Physics. The controversy emerged well before Hitler appeared on the political scene. The anti-Semites were jealously watching the unprecedented international admiration for Einstein's intellectual leap in physics. A cohort of non-scientists and physicists attacked the theory of relativity, targeting Einstein and dubbed it 'Jewish Physics', as early as 1920. Paul Weyland denounced the theory on the one hand as an 'enormous bluff', and on the other hand as 'plagiarism' in itself a contradiction.

These anti-Semitic attacks would not have stirred up the scientific world, if the two Nobel Prize winners, in physics, Johannes Stark and Philip Lenard were not to have been at the helm of the movement. Lenard was dealt with in the chapter of the University of Heidelberg. Suffice to say, that both older scientists, though outstanding experimental physicists, felt slighted by the public acclaim of Einstein's achievements. They were unable to understand the new theoretical physics encroaching onto their territory and a mix of incomprehension, jealousy, and the feeling of lost esteem led them to accuse Einstein and his followers as dealing in 'theatrical speculations without experimental substance'. To this was added a hefty dose of anti-Semitism and the ever-ready prejudiced public accepted the new racial concept of 'Jewish Physics', which of course was bad science and 'German or Aryan Physics' was pure science only capable of being generated by the Aryan race. By 1924 Lennard and Stark, harked back to the 'Asian people that brought Christ to the crosses and the racially alien spirit that has been hovering since over the honest Aryan-German people'. Ludwig Bieberbach, professor of mathematics at the University of Berlin, in a chain reaction differentiated between German and Jewish mathematics. The great liberator of German science, Adolf Hitler, endorsed the 'racial fission' of science into German and Jewish science, to restore the purity of science and to free it from Jewish influence.

Later, an example of vicious denunciation of 'Jewish Physics' is evident in the writing of Ludwig Glaser, a physicist who studied at the polytechnic of the University of Berlin and was a protégé of Stark and Lenard. Although he had difficulties with the 'Habilitation' exam at the University of Würzburg, he eventually qualified and later was appointed professor at that University. Glaser was an opponent of the theories of relativity and quantum physics. He joined the NSDAP in 1932 and wrote 'Jews in Physics and Jewish Physics' in 1939, that Germany has the "sorry distinction of producing a Jew like Einstein. This German citizen, expatriated in 1933, was revealed to be not simply the docile scholar his numerous followers passed him off as, but a Jewish politician, who in gratitude to the host country that had taken him in, denounced, scorned and abused it throughout the world, in true Hebraic style." Glaser castigates the great theoretical physicist Hermann Helmholtz for having granted 'the Jews admission to physics'. "The part-Jew (Jüdische Mischling) Heinrich Hertz, the Jew Wertheimer, the Jew E. Goldstein, the Jew Grunmuch and many others are students of Helmholtz. The Jew Emil Gabriel (!) Warburg – offspring of the race of second-hand dealers and money-changers in Hamburg – was brought in from Freiburg to succeed Helmholtz at Berlin University. He worked there from 1895 to 1905 and finally occupied the highest position the German Reich can offer in physics: This very Jew assumed Helmholtz's place as President of the Reich Physical and Technical Institute from April 1905 until March 1922. Warburg made a thorough job of it for Jewry. Then the Jews R. Börnstein, James Franck, Peter Pringsheim, Max Born, F. Reiche, A. Korn, F. Grünbaum and many others followed later." In this vein, Glaser continues to present a further list of eminent 'Jew Physicists'.

Ball writes that Einstein declared in public "as long as I have any choice in the matter, I shall live only in a country where civil liberty, tolerance, and equality before the law prevail. These conditions do not exist in Germany at the present time. He was talking not just about the Nazis but also his former friends and associates, who had decided that Einstein's refusal to come back to a country that excluded Jews from full citizenship was an act of gross treason. The Prussian Academy of Sciences was outraged." The vendetta against Einstein knew no limit by Rust and of course Goebbels. After Einstein tendered his resignation from the Academy the statement of one of the secretaries, the orientalist Ernst Heymann, reflects the attitude of the scientists in the academy: "The Prussian Academy of Sciences heard with indignation from the newspapers of Albert

Einstein's participation in the atrocity-mongering in France and America. The Prussian Academy of Sciences is particularly distressed by Einstein's activities as an agitator in foreign countries, as it and its members have always felt themselves bound by the closest ties to the Prussian state and, while abstaining strictly from all political partisanship. It has therefore no reason to regret Einstein's withdrawal." Einstein responded to Heymann's accusation in a public statement "The primary duty of an academy is to further and protect the scientific life of a country. And yet the learned societies of Germany have, to the best of my knowledge, stood by and said nothing while a not inconsiderable proportion of German scholars and students and also of academically trained professionals have been deprived of all chance of getting employment. I do not wish to belong to any society which behaved in such a manner."

Mark Walker commented on the exchange between Einstein and the Academy. "The academy scientists surrendered their independence and became accomplices by helping the National Socialist state force the Jewish scientists out of the academy. No 'Aryan' scientists resigned in protest. Indeed, there is no record of a scientist even considering resignation. There seems good reason to suppose that many others in the academy did not just acquiesce in the anti-Semitic purge but actively approve it". It is likely that the conclusion might be drawn in general about the attitude of scientists during the early days of Nazi Germany, before hostilities of world war two started and there is no reason to believe that after nineteen thirty-nine their views have changed. The denunciation of Einstein by his erstwhile colleagues gained momentum after Haber and the third Nobel laureate in physics James Franck resigned, from his chair of physics at Göttingen in protest to the Civil Service law.

Although he was exempted from the law as a veteran, having fought in the First World War and had been awarded two Iron Crosses, he felt it his moral duty to resign. His reasoning was that he could not work for a state that made his children second-class citizens. Neither could he stand back and watch others to be unjustly dismissed. Many academics labelled this a 'political act' and forty-two members of Göttingen staff signed a petition calling Franck's resignation 'equivalent to an act of sabotage'; a term akin to that of 'gross treason' used in Einstein's case. Here we have another celebrated university body which not only failed to support their colleague, but throw at him a vicious accusation. A post-script to this has been related by the mathematician David Hilbert, when he was asked at a social occasion by Minister Bernhard Rust, "How is mathematics in Göttingen now that it has been freed of Jews", Hilbert replied "Mathematics in Göttingen? There is really none any more".

Werner Heisenberg, one of the most eminent German physicists, was initially harassed by the SS as he used 'Jewish Physics', but through friendly family connections, Himmler stopped further harassment and wrote to Heisenberg that he could discuss 'modern physics', as long as he does not name Einstein. This is reminiscent of Heine's famous 'Lorelei' being recited at school by 'Author unknown'. The net result was that many German physicists were deprived of the scientific knowledge required for the development of atomic energy, which may have contributed to the failure of Germany producing the bomb, but success of the Manhattan project. Whilst Planck lost his cause, Hitler's refusal may well have saved Europe from SS domination, as will be argued below. The Jewish scientists, with appropriate incentives would have most likely joined forces with the German physicists and develop the atom bomb before 1945 and win the war for Germany. Did Hitler's gift of Jewish science 'Untermenschen' to the US, and the ignoble 'Deutsche Physik' movement save Europe from ultimate SS barbarism? To justify this bold claim, I shall present the German and American nuclear weapon programme in some detail.

The German 'Uranprojekt' started in 1939, soon after Otto Hahn and Fritz Strassmann observed in December 1938 that the collision of neutrons with uranium produced barium. This was interpreted, and the mathematical basis calculated by Lise Meitner and Otto Frisch, concluding that uranium nuclei had been split and coined the process 'nuclear fission'. The programme was to produce uranium and separating the isotope, as well as producing heavy water, used in nuclear reactor as a coolant and optimising neutron activity. However, when it became apparent in January 1942 that the nuclear energy project is not a short-term policy in ending the war, it was broken down into nine main areas and a number of Institutes. The principal scientists involved were: Walther Bothe, Klaus Clusius, Kurt Diebner, Otto Hahn, Paul Harteck, Werner Heisenberg, Hans Kopfermann, Nikolaus Riehl, and Georg Stetter. Altogether there was a lack of scientists, as well as concerted activity between them. The most successful team in Leipzig was led by the theoretical physicist Werner Heisenberg with the experimental knowledge of Robert Döpel. The critical experimental proof of increase in neutrons was demonstrated by the German team in April 1942, but in June 1942, Döpel's reactor was destroyed by an explosion which largely terminated the project in Leipzig – 'Deus ex Machina'. Nonetheless, the Berlin group pursued the work with increased expenditure but failed in getting the reactor working until the end of the war. The plant in Oranienburg in 1944 had produced about twenty-five tons of uranium oxide and this was of a sufficient threat to the commander of the United States Manhattan project general Leslie Groves to ask the Air Force to destroy it, which was duly accomplished.

In the United States, six months after the report of uranium fission early in 1939 by Hahn, Strassmann, Meitner and Frisch, Leo Szilard, and his colleagues were seriously concerned that Germany might develop an atomic bomb. He approached Albert Einstein, the most prestigious authority in physics, to write a letter to President Franklin D. Roosevelt. The letter was written by Szilard and Einstein and finalised under Einstein's name on the 2nd of August 1939, informing the president of the immense power of destruction of an atomic bomb and the danger of it being first developed by the Germans. The letter was delivered to the President through an intermediary by hand on 11th October 1939 (see below). The president appointed a 'Uranium Committee' with a small budget of $6,000. The project met considerable scepticism over two years but a serious atomic project began on December 1941, curiously a day before Pearl Harbour was bombed. At a meeting between President Roosevelt, Vannevar Bush, and Vice President Henry A. Wallace in October 1941, the President approved the atomic program. To control it, he created a top Policy Group consisting of himself – although he never attended a meeting – Wallace, Bush, Conant, Secretary of War Henry L. Stimson, and the Chief of Staff of the Army, General George Marshall. He also agreed to coordinate the effort with that of the British, and on 11 October 1941 he sent a message to Prime Minister Winston Churchill, suggesting that they correspond on atomic matters. However, at that time the British did not seem to be keen and it was only in August 1943 that Churchill and Roosevelt negotiated the Quebec Agreement of cooperation between the United States, Britain, and Canada.

Unlimited manpower and industrial resources were made available for the Manhattan project under the command of Major General Leslie Groves who organised the science establishment at Los Alamos in New Mexico and imposed almost a military discipline and strict censorship on the relevant scientific community. The key scientists assembled for the Manhattan project under the leadership of Robert Oppenheimer to accomplish the secret mission, to name just some, were Leo Szilard, Otto Frisch, Rudolf Peierls, Enrico Fermi, Felix Bloch, Edward Teller, Niels Bohr, David Bohn, James Franck, Victor Weisskopf, John von Neumann, Eugen Wigner, Maria Goeppert-Mayer, Klaus Fuchs, and Emilio Segre. By July 1942 Fermi's team in Los Alamos demonstrated the critical experimental proof of increase in neutrons (three months after the Germans) and had succeeded by December 1942 to develop an effective reactor.

It would be invidious and highly technical to delve into the contribution of each individual scientist, as this was a team effort, held together by Robert Oppenheimer, quite apart from the immense contribution by many scientists in industry. However, a most unusual role was played by Leo Szilard who studied in 1919 under Laue, Planck, and Einstein. He acted as a catalyst, stricken by the fear that the Germans will get the bomb first. He got the ball rolling by approaching Einstein and writing a letter to President Roosevelt, as noted above. Indeed, Szilard could be considered as the initiator of the Manhattan Project. Szilard and Fermi demonstrated that only pure graphite free from impurities absorbed neutrons which induce fission in other uranium atoms to emit more neutrons. Fermi wanted to publish this critical data, but Szilard restrained him. The Germans used impure graphite in the same type of experiment and failed to sustain a chain reaction, which led them to use heavy water instead. Had Fermi and Szilard published the results, the Germans would have realised their mistake. In Perutz's words, not having published the paper on the necessity of using pure carbon "may have saved the world".

Whilst Szilard was full of ideas, he lacked the discipline of applying his ideas to systematic research, except when he was driven by the fear that the Germans might get the bomb first. He was constitutively unable to tolerate authority and was in constant conflict with General Groves, who considered Szilard an undisciplined man, without discretion and a risk to the Manhattan Project. Szilard, on the other hand, considered Groves an ignorant fool and did not bother to hide it. Indeed, Szilard failed to be appointed to any paid employment and was extremely hard up financially, unlike von Neumann, Teller and Wigner, his old friends from school days in Budapest.

It would be inappropriate to discuss the complex scientific technology and design studies carried out, suffice to say that work was carried out to separate uranium^{235} from uranium^{238}. Natural uranium consists of 99.3% uranium^{238} and 0.7% uranium^{235} and only the latter is fissile and has to be separated from the predominant isotope. This required a number of experimental trials by several industries, at an enormous cost until the optimum purification was achieved. There were five major project sites with Los Alamos as the principle research and design laboratory. By July 1945, 50kg of 89% enriched uranium^{235} was delivered to Los Alamos, which was used in the 'Little Boy' bomb. The Manhattan project reached its objective in producing the first atom bomb after the end of hostilities in Europe and was dropped on Hiroshima in Japan on 6th August 1945 with devastating effect. The bomb was estimated to be equivalent to 13 kilotons of TNT. An area of approximately 4.7 square miles (12km^2) was destroyed. Japanese officials determined that 69% of Hiroshima's buildings were destroyed. About 70,000 to 80,000 people, or some 30% of the population of Hiroshima was killed immediately, and another 70,000 injured. Long-term sequelae of radiation damage were studied over many years.

According to a report by Samuel A. Goudsmit, a Dutch physicist who emigrated to the United States, wrote in, 'Nazis' Atomic Secrets', two years after the war ended that the Germans were not advanced enough to produce the atomic bomb. They were still discussing the 'uranium problems' they had not appreciated the necessity of freeing graphite of impurities, they failed to calculate the correct amount of uranium required for a bomb, and failed to produce a chain reaction. The chief architect of the German atomic project was thought to be Werner Heisenberg. He suggested that he and his colleagues deliberately slowed the pace of research to deny Hitler the ultimate weapon of war. Goudsmit disputed this construct of Heisenberg's and insisted that if German scientist would have made the bomb if they had the knowledge and had they not been under Nazi political rule. It is also evident that the Nazis were never persuaded by the scientists of the reality of this theoretical super-weapon to allocate vast financial and labour investment, unlike that for their Peenemünde rocket programme, which cost a comparable amount to the Manhattan Project.

Heisenberg's true views became clear when he heard about the Hiroshima atom bomb, whilst detained with other scientists at Farm Hall in Cambridgeshire where the place was bugged and all conversations recorded. According to Ball's account of the conversation when Heisenberg heard on the radio the news "he could not believe that the Allies could have produced several tons of pure uranium-235. To this, Hahn responded, 'I thought that one needed only very little '235'. If they have, let us say, 30 kilograms of pure '235', couldn't they make a bomb with it?' Heisenberg replied that 'it still wouldn't go off': he didn't believe it was enough. 'This statement', comments Jeremy Bernstein, 'shows that at this point Heisenberg has no idea how a bomb works.' 'But tell me why you used to tell me that one needed 50 kilograms of '235' in order to do anything', he demanded. 'Now you say one needs two tons.' Heisenberg went away and made a better calculation deciding that indeed only a few tens of kilograms would suffice." The historian Paul L. Rose argued that Heisenberg misunderstood the physics involved, greatly overestimated the critical mass of uranium 235 in 1940, unlike the calculation made directly by Frisch and Peierls in 1940 on learning Hahn's data from Meitner. Both Heisenberg and

Weizsäcker claimed to have deliberately deceived the authorities and this claim made after the war has been disputed and certainly does not accord with the 'Farm Hall' disclosures.

The German bomb was formally not developed. However, from the documents recently released by the Russians of the documents from the 'Kaiser Wilhelm Institute of Physics', the Germans did succeed to build some sort of atomic bomb. Apparently Diebner's team working in Gottow conducted successfully the first nuclear weapon test in March 1945 in Ohrdruf, Thuringia. The bomb killed hundreds of prisoners of war and concentration camp inmates. The documents also revealed that Heisenberg advocated in 1942 the development of a nuclear weapon and this was corroborated by the 'Luftwaffe' Field Marshall Erhard Milch.

As with medical doctors, who perpetrated extreme atrocities in concentration camps were labelled psychopath, so in German physics, incompetent Nazi physicists were identified by Heisenberg and colleagues, such as Bagge and Diebner. However, there was little recrimination after the war, denazification was perfunctory, because of professional allegiance, solidarity and a reluctance to 'soil one's own nest'. The so called 'Persilschein' (whitewash certificates) were issued by colleagues even for serious offenders. By and large, the scientists failed to feel guilty about any of their activities under the Nazi regime. According to Ball, "To feel no responsibility at having worked under, and in some sense for, a racist, genocidal gang of criminals seemed to indicate a sheer absence of moral reason." He considers that Heisenberg was in denial of the past. "He was apt to refer to 'the bad side of Nazism', with the implication that there was a 'good' side too. He seemed, even after the revelations of Auschwitz, to remain stubbornly blind to the character of the leaders, insisting that if Germany had won the war then in time – he gave it fifty years – the Nazis would have become civilized. 'He still goes on defending all the evil things in Germany as being the normal by-products of any social revolution', wrote Goudsmit to Rosbaud in 1950 after meeting Heisenberg in the United States. That Heisenberg could peddle this naively optimistic line in 1947 even to one refugee physicist in Britain who had lost his job and then friends and relatives in the concentration camp makes it clear that there is something to be explained in Heisenberg's character."

The physicist, Philip Morrison, a scientist of wisdom and humanity wrote in a review of the book by Goudsmit in response to the distortions propagated by German physicists. Both the German and Allied scientists worked for the military, "but the difference, which it will never be possible to forgive, is that they worked for the cause of Himmler and Auschwitz, for the burners of books and the takers of hostages." Laue arguably the only physicist who was respected outside Germany for his integrity responded with a sort of apology, stating the difficulties in non-compliance and that most of the work was "honest, solid scientific investigation." Morrison replied that he appreciated Laue's arguments "But it was sentiments like theirs, weaknesses like theirs, and fears like theirs which helped bring Germans for a decade to be the slaves of an inhuman tyranny, which has wrecked Europe, and in its day attacked the very name of culture. It is not Goudsmit, Morrison wrote, who should feel an unutterable pain when the word Auschwitz is mentioned, but many a famous German physicist in Göttingen today, many a man of insight and of responsibility, who could live for a decade in the Third Reich, and never once risk his position of comfort and authority in real opposition to the men who could build that infamous place of death."

Whatever might be the truth of these claims, one point is clear that the Germans were pursuing the atomic weapon project. It gives credence to the oft repeated claim, wishful thinking or yet another 'Big Lie' by Goebbels and others, that a secret weapon will soon dramatically turn the tide of the war in Germany's favour. There can be little doubt that if the nuclear option had become available, Hitler would have had no hesitation to use it as a last resort, to save German and European 'Kultur' from its enemies. He would not concern himself with the likelihood that in the process he would kill a vast number of his own citizens, who he believed in his last utterances failed him as they had not the will to fight for the glory of the German spirit. Indeed, Hitler's response in 1945 to Speer's objection to the order to destroy Germany's infrastructure if the war is lost was, "It is not necessary to worry about what [the people] will need for survival. On the contrary, it is best. To destroy even these things. For the nation has shown itself to be the weaker, and the future belongs to the stronger Eastern countries. The garbage left over after this struggle will anyway be only the inferior ones, because the good ones will be dead." (Related in Joachim Fest's book 'Inside Hitler's Bunker'). After twelve years of adulation of the Führer by the people of Germany, Hitler was bent on taking the German people with him to their death. Perhaps, this was his subconsciousness 'final will', emulating the Masada spirit of mass suicide by the embattled Jews facing the inevitable defeat by the Roman army. There should be no Germany after the 'great Führer', total apocalypse. Germans should be scattered over the world like the Jews, as was suggested by Thomas Mann recalling Goethe's wish for a German diaspora.

IX. MEITNERIUM (ELEMENT 109)

'Adolf Hitler, the defender of German science activated the chain reaction of racial fission' into German science and Jewish science'. *Author*	'A physicist who never lost her humanity'. *Motto on Lise Meitner's tombstone, 1968*

Lise Meitner deserves a special notice in this short treatment of science – gender – racism – atomic energy saga. She was an Austrian-German physicist born in 1878 into a well to-do assimilated Jewish family in Vienna. Her father was one of the first Jewish layers in Austria, who supported Lise, the third of eight of his children, to obtain private education as she excelled in mathematics. In those days, women were not allowed to attend higher education, but Lise gained an 'External Matura', which enabled her to enter the University of Vienna at the age twenty-three. She was the first woman admitted to lectures on physics to the laboratories. She studied under Anton Lampa, Stefan Meyer, and later the famous theoretical physicist Ludwig Boltzmann between 1901-1906 and was the second woman to gain the PhD in Physics in 1935 from the University. Remarkably, three of Lise's sisters also gained the PhD degrees. Meitner went to Berlin in 1907, where Max Planck exceptionally permitted her to attend his lectures, and after one year, she became Planck's assistant. At about that time in 1908, at the age of thirty, she converted to Lutheran Christianity. She worked with the chemist Otto Hahn, which started a scientific collaboration and lasted thirty years. She worked as a 'guest' in Hahn's department of Radiochemistry in the Kaiser Wilhelm Institute in Berlin-Dahlem without a salary until the age of thirty-five, when she got a permanent position at the Institute. The collaboration between the physicist (Meitner) and chemist (Hahn) was very productive and among other discoveries was the first long-lived isotope of the element protactinium, for which she was awarded the Leibniz Medal by the Berlin Academy of Sciences. In 1917, Meitner was given her own laboratory at the institute. After a number of significant scientific breakthroughs, in 1926 Meitner was the first women in Germany to be awarded the full professorship in Physics at the University of Berlin. She was highly regarded by physicists and Einstein dubbed her as the 'German Marie Curie'. By the 1930s, Meitner had been well recognised by her major publications with Hahn in the top ranks of physicist, taking part in the Solvay conference in 1933 (see photograph p.159).

When Hitler became chancellor in 1933, Meitner was acting director of the Institute of Chemistry. Nonetheless, she was dismissed from her position at the University, barred from speaking at scientific meetings and her joint findings with Hahn were published under his name alone. As an Austrian citizen, however, she was able to carry out research at the Institute till 1938, though without recognition. By 1934, Meitner and Hahn begun to investigate neutron bombardment of uranium, following Fermi's experiments using neutron irradiation of uranium and finding potential new elements. Hahn and Meitner were then joined by a young chemist named Fritz Strassmann who joined the institute in 1929 and was an avowed anti-Nazi. The three worked on generating new radioactive substances from uranium. However, after the Anschluss, and although Hahn had no sympathy for National Socialism, after some consultation with the Institute, he informed her in March 1938 that she must leave. Apparently Meitner recorded in her diary that "He has in essence thrown me out." By June 1938, all Jewish academics were prohibited from leaving Germany. Meitner was lucky as Kurt Hess, a chemist and Nazi informed the authorities that she was about to flee. With the help from Dutch physicists however, she escaped to the Netherlands in July, without her possessions and 10 Marks in her pocket. Meitner secured a post at Manne Siegbahn's laboratory, though not supported because of his prejudice against women in science.

After Meitner's escape, Hahn and Strassmann continued with the neutron bombardment and consistently came up with Barium, which they were unable to interpret. Hahn wrote to Meitner in December 1938 "Perhaps you can suggest some fantastic explanation [...] If you can think of anything that might be publishable, then the three of us would be together in this work after all." A few days later at Christmas, Meitner discussed Hahn's finding with her nephew, Otto Frisch, also a physicist exiled from Germany. They came to the momentous conclusion that the uranium nuclei had been split and used the biological term 'nuclear fission'. The significance of this interpretation was enormous as Frédéric Joliot demonstrated early in 1939 that more neutrons are emitted when uranium is bombarded with neutrons. The released neutrons during fission will split more uranium nuclei, thereby releasing more neutrons and so on, as long as fissionable uranium is available, resulting in a 'chain reaction'. A great deal of energy is released and this was calculated by Frisch and Peierls, another exiled physicist from Germany who by that time became Professor of Mathematical Physics at the University of Birmingham. They worked out that to construct an atomic bomb a small amount about 1 kg of fissionable uranium 235 would be needed, unlike the prevailing assumption that tons of uranium might be required for a bomb and hence was an impracticable proposition. They wrote the Frisch-Peierls memorandum for the British government, the basis of an influential MAUD Committee report which started work on atomic research in Britain and later was also important in triggering off the Manhattan Project.

The political conditions in Nazi Germany forced Hahn and Meitner to publish the data in separate papers; the Hahn-Strassmann paper described the experimental process in the journal 'Naturwissenschaften' early in 1939, whilst the Meitner-Frisch paper on the interpretation and mathematical basis of nuclear fission was published in the journal 'Nature'. These two papers with that of Frisch and Peierls's calculations were critical in getting Szilard and colleagues to persuade Einstein to write to President Roosevelt, which led later to the Manhattan Project. Meitner was invited to join the project at Los Alamos, but her prescience made her refuse, declaring, "I will have nothing to do with the bomb."

The posthumous saga to the discovery of nuclear fission was the 1944 award of the Nobel Prize in Chemistry to Otto Hahn. The omission of Meitner for her contribution in nuclear fission and the collaborative work over decades with Hahn has been the subject of many comments of the injustice by the Royal Swedish Academy of Sciences. The historians Elizabeth Crawford, Ruth Lewin Sime, and Mark Walker documented the history of this discovery in a paper, "A Nobel Tale of Postwar Injustice". Meitner herself had not expressed any reproach about it, though it became a 'cause celebre', somewhat reminiscent of another Jewish female physicist – Rosalind Franklin, with the discovery of the structure of DNA shared between Watson, Crick, and Wilkins, though she died before the Nobel Prize was awarded and therefore was not eligible for the prize. However, she was honoured for her contributions to science by very many awards, naming element 109 'Meitnerium', as well as science institutes, astronomical findings, and streets after her.

She was honoured in the USA in 1946 'Woman of the Year', had dinner with President Harry Truman who remarked "So you are the little lady who got us into all of this!" Like Einstein, Meitner refused to return to Germany, though offered a prestigious position. In one of her reproaches to Hahn, after she heard on the radio the conversation of the German scientists interned in Farm Hall in 1945: "Someone should force a man like Heisenberg and many million others to look at those camps and at the martyred people [...] It was clear to me that even people like you and Laue had not grasped the real situation. This is, of course, Germany's misfortune, the fact that all of you had lost your standard of justice and fairness. You have all worked for Nazi Germany as well and have never even tried to put up a passive resistance either. Certainly, to buy off your consciences you have helped a person in distress here and there, but you have allowed millions of innocent people to be slaughtered without making the least protest [...] You did not have any sleepless nights. You did not want to see it; it was too inconvenient."

It took Hahn many years before he saw the enormity of the catastrophe of millions of individuals when he wrote to Meitner in 1958 on her eightieth birthday. "We all knew that injustice was taking place, but we didn't want to see it, we deceived ourselves. Come the year 1933 I followed a flag that we should have torn down immediately. I did not do so, and now I must bear responsibility for it." Meitner's science, combined with innate feeling of humanity, despite the vicissitudes of being persecuted and uprooted from her country, friends and colleagues found its resting place in Hampshire, England near Cambridge, where her nephew Otto Frisch lived. She died on October 1968 and the motto on her tombstone says it all. "A physicist who never lost her humanity."

X. THE ATOMIC WAR AGAINST NAZI GERMANY

We can discern six mileposts and the critical corollary in the development of the atom bomb.

1. Hitler's refusal of Planck's request to retain Jewish scientists in their research posts.
2. 'Deutsche Physik' movement led by the two Nobel Prize winners, Lenard and Stark, to deprive German physicists the scientific knowledge of theoretical 'Jewish Physics' to develop the atomic bomb.
3. Meitner and Frisch recognising that Hahn's and Strassman's experiment, following thirty years of collaboration with Meitner, demonstrated 'nuclear fission'.
4. Frisch and Peierls calculating the critical mass of uranium required and writing the 'memorandum' of the feasibility of producing an atom bomb, predicting the effects of such an explosion, which formed the basis of the British and later contributed to the US project of building the bomb.
5. Einstein's letter drafted by Szilard and Wigner to President Roosevelt, drawing attention to the potential danger of an atom bomb, which the Germans might develop and the advisability of initiating a nuclear programme in the United States.
6. Oppenheimer leading the Manhattan project of scientists to a successful conclusion.

The corollary of the above points is that Germany's effort to produce the atom bomb was thwarted through Hitler's refusal to grant Planck's request not to dismiss Jewish scientists. As Planck predicted, by forcing these scientists to leave, the country had significantly tipped the balance in favour of the United States atomic project. The irrational proscription of 'Jewish Physics', led by Lenard and Stark, deprived young German physicists of essential scientific knowledge.

It is evident that German Jewish scientists were responsible for the initial five steps and played a significant direct role in the 6th, ensuring success of the Manhattan Project. Indeed, Hitler and his cohort providentially signed their own death warrant. The Jewish physicists had been greatly motivated not only by the hardship suffered but also by having been deserted by the country they felt strong loyal ties, by their science colleagues with whom they collaborated and some even educated, and by the Church, as some were Christian converts of the second generation. It could be argued with considerable justification that in the intellectual war between Germany and the Allies, there were at least two outstanding factors working in favour of the Allies. Firstly, breaking the German 'Enigma Code' by a group of brilliant individuals led by Alan Turing at Bletchley Park. Secondly, the role of the emigrant mostly non-Aryan physicists developing the atomic bomb, and as important, depriving Germany directly and indirectly in getting the bomb before the Allies, has not been fully acknowledged.

The question of morality of scientists producing the ultimate weapon of destruction has been the subject of heated debate after the danger of the Nazis winning the war had been removed. Their overall plan besides murdering the entire Jewish people was to murder, displace, and enslave millions of Slavs. All these actions were in place by the SS claiming Germans to be a superior race ('Übermensch'), the need of more space ('lebensraum') and considering the Slav people as primitive hordes, lacking culture who are only fit to be slaves to the German Volk. Europe and no doubt extending to the Middle East, Africa, and parts of Asia and South America would come under the sway of the SS-Gestapo-Racist ideology of the 'Übermensch'. The enthusiasm with which the SS and Gestapo practised 'mercy killing' ('Gnadetod'), was regrettably matched by the passive 'innocent bystanders', both among the Volk and academia, as they were better off to close their eyes and ears to the suffering of the rest of humanity. Superiority over other people is an age-old aphrodisiac, one which few people can resist when the entire government apparatus constantly dehumanises 'the other'.

Throughout times, science has proved an unstoppable human endeavour. Atomic fission, the chain reaction, and emerging energy were discovered, irrespective of their applications to the war effort, though under peaceful conditions it would have taken a few more years. The Hiroshima-Nagasaki atom bombs were used ostensibly to stop the Pacific War with Japan, but there was, in addition, the motivation to find out in a real terms the capacity of the weapon. The bomb has not been employed since 1945, but as a source of energy, it is of increasing importance. Once natural gas, oil, coal and shale have been exhausted, atomic energy may well be the only real source of energy to maintain the global requirements for this basic commodity. Acquiring this double-edged weapon by rogue elements is a constant danger, as indeed are microbiological and chemical weapons.

The letter from Albert Einstein to President Franklin D. Roosevelt

Albert Einstein
Old Grove
RdNassaPoint
Peconic
Long Island
August 2nd, 1939

P.D. Roosevelt,
President of the United States,
White House
Washington, D.C.

Sir,

Some recent work by E. Fermi and L. Szilard, which has been communicated to me in manuscript, leads me to expect that the element uranium may be turned into a new and important source of energy in the immediate future. Certain aspects of the situation which has arisen seem to call for watchfulness and, if necessary, quick action on the part of the Administration. I believe therefore that it is my duty to bring to your attention the following facts and recommendations:

In the course of the last four months it has been made probable – through the work of Joliot in France as well as Fermi and Szilard in America – that it may become possible to set up a nuclear chain reaction in a large mass of uranium, by which vast amounts of power and large quantities of new radium-like elements would be generated. Now it appears almost certain that this could be achieved in the immediate future.

This new phenomenon would also lead to the construction of bombs, and is conceivable – though much less certain – that extremely powerful bombs of a new type may thus be constructed. A single bomb of this type, carried by boat and exploded in a port, might very well destroy the whole port together with some of the surrounding territory. However, such bombs might very well prove to be too heavy for transportation by air.

The United States has only very poor ores of uranium in moderate quantities. There is some good ore in Canada and the former Czechoslovakia, while the most important source or uranium is Belgian Congo.

In view of this situation you may think it desirable to have some permanent contact maintained between the Administration and the group of physicists working on chain reactions in America. One possible way of achieving this might be for you to entrust with this task a person who has your confidence and who could perhaps serve in an inofficial capacity. His task might comprise the following:

a) to approach Government departments, keep them informed of the further development, and put forward recommendations for Government action, giving particular attention to the problem of securing a supply of uranium ore for the United States.

b) to speed up the experimental work, which is at present being carried on within the limits of the budgets of University laboratories, by providing funds, if such funds be required, through his contacts with private persons who are willing to make contributions for this cause, and perhaps also by obtaining the co-operation of industrial laboratories which have the necessary equipment.

I understand that Germany has actually stopped the sale of uranium from the Czechoslovakian mines which she has taken over. That she should have taken such early action might perhaps be understood on the ground that the son of the German Under-Secretary of State, von Weizsäcker, is attached to the Kaiser-Wilhelm-Institut in Berlin where some of the American work on uranium is now being repeated.

Yours very truly,

(Albert Einstein)

XI. SOCIOLOGICAL ASPECTS OF THE NAZI WAR AGAINST JEWS

'Humans and animals discriminate between 'us and them' members of out-groups, who elicit fear and prejudice, which stem from deep evolutionary roots'. *Elizabeth Culotta, "Roots of Racism" 2012*	'The overall ethical rules that apply to individual violence are erased from group violence and become an abstraction'. *Robert Toscano, 2009*
'The Holocaust may be manifestation of the predisposition to primeval aggressive instincts as expressed by Konrad Lorenz'. *Zygmunt Bauman, 1989*	'Man is born for happiness and freedom, yet everywhere he is unhappy and enslaved. *Jean Jaque Rousseau, 'Social Contracts', 1762*

"The Holocaust is not an exclusively Jewish problem of history", Zygmunt Bauman wrote in 'Modernity and the Holocaust'. "The Holocaust was born and executed in our modern and rational society, at the high stage of our civilization and at the peak of human cultural achievement, and for this reason it is a problem of that society, civilization and culture". It is evident that religion did not prevent the ultimate desecration of humanity, despite the denial of Christianity's involvement in the Nazi regime, as discussed later. The ideology of the enlightenment elevating human rationality to new heights also failed, despite freedom of expression and liberty, to prevent the massacre of the innocents. The pursuit of culture, a significant feature of the German people has not been a moderating force but was co-existent with mass murder. Anti-Semitism has been pervasive in its intensity, long-standing among most if not all social classes, underpinned by the Church with its teaching and preaching the Gospel and ancient prejudices. The 'otherness' of some Jews in their habits, appearance, interests, religion, and competitive nature, often very successful both in trade and the professions, with a flair for innovative ideas, may have contributed to lack of empathy, prejudice or outright hatred.

In a recent paper in the journal 'Science' (2012), Elizabeth Culotta writes on the 'Roots of Racism' and considers the evidence in humans and indeed animals discriminating between 'us' and 'them'. The fear of 'them', members of outgroups who can elicit implicit prejudice, which "stems from deep evolutionary roots and a universal tendency to focus coalitions ('ingroups') and favour our own side". According to the Harvard psychologist, James Sidanius, people think that those in their ingroups are smarter, better, more moral and more just than the members of outgroups. Some psychologists refer to 'ingroup love' and 'outgroup hate', and cruelty to 'them' starts with kindness to 'us'. It is generally recognised that 'we' are more peaceful, trustworthy, friendly, and honest than 'they'. The so-called 'Implicit Association Test' to reveal bias in recognising faces showed that outgroup faces are rapidly associated with negative responses, such as 'hatred' both with adults and children. Moreover, the prejudice against 'outgroups' has been demonstrated in non-human primates, such as chimpanzees, and rhesus monkeys, whose lineage diverged from humans 25-30 million years ago, suggesting that the outgroup bias is 'core to our species'. Sidanius concludes that "what we are arguing is a natural preference for drawing ingroup-outgroup boundaries. It can be race, religion, nationality, dialect or arbitrary set differences, but once those boundaries are drawn, people like to discriminate across them."

Bauman notes that the Holocaust may be a manifestation of the predisposition to primeval, aggressive instincts as expressed by Konrad Lorenz. An equally valid and neuro-functional interpretation might be that of Arthur Koestler that the rational neo-cortex of the brain fails to overcome or control the more ancient emotion-ridden thalamus and amygdala. He was well ahead of his time in grasping the significance of the two fundamental interacting divisions of the brain. Bauman quotes the succinct views of the eminent sociologist Everett C. Hughes. "The National Socialist Government of Germany carried out the most colossal piece of 'dirty work' in history of the Jews. The crucial problems concerning such an occurrence are (1) who are the people who actually carry out such work, and (2) what are the circumstances in which other 'good' people allow them to do it? What we need is better knowledge of the signs of their rise to power and better ways of keeping them out of power".

In a well-conducted research, Helen Fein studied the correlation, if any, between local anti-Semitism, degrees of Jewish acculturation and assimilation, and communal solidarity. The only significant results were the absence of solidarity and possibly lack of moral constraint. Bauman concludes that it is likely that the Holocaust was a failure, not a product of modernity. The reverse type of sociological study was pursued by Nechama Tec by exploring rescuers who were prepared to help the victims. She studied correlation between the readiness to help and those of social class, education, denomination, and political allegiance only to find that none of these were correlated. Tec could only conclude that "These rescuers acted in ways that were natural to them – spontaneously they were able to strike out against the horrors of their times". There were no detectable social determinants of moral behaviour, which is all the more surprising, as the questions asked were most pertinent, yet not related to the moral stance demonstrated by these good people. Nonetheless, the findings of both Fein and Tec leave open a critical question of what moral force makes individuals act with such empathy and altruism. Is this a counterpart of innate, archetypal characteristic co-developed with animal brutality of survival value or a more recent development? Finding individuals of high moral standing in a sea of immorality leaves real hope for humanity and deserves the most thorough investigation with a new insightful set of questions. These may identify and characterise the great divide between the defensive-cowardly actions of some and those with empathy and altruism, which so far neither psychology nor sociology have been able to solve.

Bauman refers to the insightful lesson of the Holocaust by the theologian Richard L. Rubenstein. "The world of death camps and the society it engenders reveals the progressively intensifying night side of Judeo-Christian civilization. Civilization means slavery, wars, exploitation, and death camps. It also means medical hygiene, elevated religious ideas, beautiful art, and exquisite music. It is an error to imagine that civilization and savage cruelty are antithesis. In our times the cruelties, like most other aspects of our world, have become far more effectively administered than ever before. They have not and will not cease to exist. Both, creation and destruction are inseparable aspects of what we call civilization."

Another interpretation by Henry Feingold suggests that the Holocaust was a new development in the history of modern industrial society. "Auschwitz was also a mundane extension of the modern factory system. Rather than producing goods, the raw material was human beings and the end-product was death, so many units per day marked carefully on the manager's production charts. The chimneys, the very symbol of the modern factory system, poured forth acrid smoke produced by burning human flesh. The brilliantly organized railroad grid of modern Europe carried a new kind of raw material to the factories. It did so in the same manner as with the other cargo. In the gas chambers the victims inhaled noxious gas generated by prussic acid pellets, which were produced by the advanced chemical industry of Germany. Engineers designed the crematoria; managers designed the system of bureaucracy that worked with a zest and efficiency more backward nations would envy. Even the overall plan itself was a reflection of the modern scientific spirit gone awry. What we witnessed was nothing less than a massive scheme of social engineering."

The concept of 'sanctity of human life' was politically unacceptable, strictly prohibited, and supplanted by the 'sanctity of the German soul', which licensed murder if any real or perceived danger to that objective was suspected. A number of individuals argued that cruelty is social in origin and that a little SS man might live in most of us, waiting to come out. The Milgram and Zimbardo's experiments on normal people, though in an artificial setting, suggest that most individuals can become cruel if fortified and legitimized by superior authority and given total power over their victims. An explanation of the unprecedented massacre carried out in a country priding itself on high culture has been generally ascribed to anti-Semitism. However, an alternative interpretation has been proposed by Bauman. "The perpetration of the Holocaust required the neutralization of ordinary Germans' attitudes toward the Jews, not their mobilization; that the 'natural' continuation of the traditional resentment towards the Jews was much more a feeling of revulsion for the 'radical actions' of the Nazi's thugs than a willingness to co-operate in mass murder; and that the SS planners of the genocide had to steer their way toward the 'Endlösung' (Final Solution) by guarding the job's independence from the sentiments of the population at large". The lack of support for anti-Jewish activities by the population paradoxically occurred at the same time as the keen approval of anti-Jewish legislation with legal prohibitions and eviction of Jews from the German 'Volk'.

These views are largely in agreement with the conclusion reached by Ian Kershaw. "Where the Nazis were most successful was in the depersonalization of the Jews. The more the Jew was forced out of social life, the more he seemed to fit the stereotypes of a propaganda which intensified paradoxically, its campaign against 'Jewry' the fewer actual Jews there were in Germany itself. Depersonalization increased the already existent widespread indifference of German popular opinion and formed a vital stage between the archaic violence and the rationalized 'assembly line' annihilation of the death camps. The 'Final Solution' would not have been possible without the progressive steps to exclude the Jews from German society which took place in full view of the public, in their legal form met with widespread approval, and resulted in the depersonalization and debasement of the figure of the Jew."

Furthermore, Bauman emphasises that physical and mental distance between the designated victims and perpetrator or population at large made the genocide possible. Moral inhibitions are less likely to act at a distance, as is evident with administrators and law makers and can be dubbed as 'murder by proxy'. This does not include the two extreme poles of German Society in direct proximity with the innocent captives; the camp guards, many exercising their brutality in the newly acquired power over captive victims. At the other pole of social class were doctors of medicine who personally face-to-face inflicted the most horrendous experimental torture in the annals of medicine, under the protective umbrella of 'scientific investigations'. These were not hooligans of the beer halls enjoying power, but the cream of German Society graduating from illustrious universities of Jena, Heidelberg, Tϋbingen, Berlin Leipzig, Vienna, Hamburg, Frankfurt, and the rest of the academic firmament. Morality and ethical norms were subjugated by opportunism of self-abasing individuals, so called 'doctors of death'. Raul Hilberg raised the sensitive question in his book 'The Holocaust, Ideology, Bureaucracy and Genocide'. "Whether any other Western civilized nation, could be capable of such a thing. And then, soon after 1945, we see the query turned around totally as one begins to ask; 'Is there any western nation that is incapable of it? [...] In 1941 the Holocaust was not expected and that is the very reason for our subsequent anxieties. We no longer dare to exclude the unimaginable."

Bauman also raises the question of 'shame' by bystanders not willing (or able) to help the victim out of fear of becoming a victim, that is self-preservation and that of the family. He argues, "The inhuman world created by homicidal tyranny dehumanized its victims and those who passively watched the victimization by pressing both to use the logic of self-preservation as absolution for moral insensitivity and inaction [...] The Holocaust can be interpreted] as an eruption of pre-modern, barbaric, irrational forces, presumably long ago suppressed in 'normal' civilized societies." Dare we conclude that modern civilization is also a regrettable triumph of evil over reason?

David J. Goldhagen, in 'Hitler's Willing Executioners', argues that virtually the entire German elite-intellectual, professional, religious, political and military people accepted 'eliminationist antisemitism' and they largely failed to express dissent from the inhumane anti-Jewish measures. Goldhagen focussed especially on the 'police battalions' involved in mass killings of Soviet Jewry. "These were made up of men who seemed by their backgrounds to be the least likely candidates for becoming willing executioners [...] many of which were composed of 'ordinary Germans' [...] They had no special ideological training, no particular military background, who were often older, in their mid-thirties, and who were family men. Furthermore, these units ended up in killing operations not by design, but by chance [...] It is these people, and not Hitler's most fanatical followers, whose actions are most difficult to explain [...] They were engaged in repeated face-to-face killings, where they confronted their victims and were parties to unspeakably gruesome scenes of spattered blood, bone, and brain matter, over an extended period of time […] In sending these units to kill, the regime proceeded as if any German was fit to be a mass executioner."

The final episode of extermination of the Jewish people took place in the last months, weeks and days before the end of the war, when the surviving, emaciated, starving men and women were taken on 'death marches', eventually to nowhere. Goldhagen has elected to analyse "The death marches of 1945, when Germans marched Jews around the European and German countryside in flight from allied armies, among other things, allow the perpetrators' actions to be examined at a time when, because they were under virtually no supervision, they could choose most freely to act as they wished [...] The death marches are therefore subject to the hypothesis that the perpetrators were motivated by their own anti-Semitism, by their attendant belief in the justice of the slaughter of the Jews. Indeed, beating, deliberate starvation and even forceful denial of any food, which German civilians were offering to the emaciated prisoners passing through villages, were inflicted by the guards of the death march".

A remarkable prescience of Nietzsche's expressed the horrifying but likely paradox of our civilization in his 'Basic Writings'. "The same men who are held so sternly in check '*inter pares*' by custom, respect, usage, gratitude, and even more by mutual suspicion and jealousy, and who on the other hand in their relations with one another show themselves so resourceful in consideration, self-control, delicacy, loyalty, pride and friendship – once they go outside, where the 'stranger' is found [...] emerge from a disgusting procession of murder, arson, rape, and torture, exhilarated and undisturbed of soul, as if it were no more than a student's prank, convinced that they have provided the poets with a lot more material for song and praise."

An interesting difference has been drawn by Roberto Toscano between individual and group violence. In the latter category, the individual is erased and becomes an abstraction. The overall ethical rules that apply to individual violence do not interfere in the abstraction of group violence. Nazi legislation and propaganda converted the concrete Jewish neighbour into the abstract idea of a Jew and according to Toscano only this made the genocide possible. What is clear about the Holocaust is that there was a chain of perpetrators, directly or indirectly involved in the machinery of genocide, there were the innocent victims, 6 million of them, and there was the third party of bystanders; these were innocent, indifferent, minding their own business. Alternatively, as Carroll argues there were no innocent bystanders. A broad consensus may well have been reached on these arguments, except for the lunatic fringe of holocaust deniers, such as the anti-Semitic historian, David Irving, and the Iranian politician Ahmadinejad.

However, it is not clear what lessons, if any, have been learned, what are the objectives of maintaining the memory of arguably the greatest evil perpetrated by humans upon their neighbours, business and professional colleagues, many speaking the same language by and large sharing and contributing to the same culture – yet being different in religion and 'Wahlverwandtschaften' (elective affinity). Christianity, common religion to almost all the perpetrators has been dilatory in dealing with the legacy of their sons and daughters and distancing themselves from the Nazis, because Rosenberg, Himmler, and a few others had pagan ideas does not absolve them from two millennia of anti-Jewish indoctrination.

Jewish religious thinkers and rabbis proposed a diverse set of answers, few, if any, have been universally acceptable. The central question, where was God? Some even argue that he was in Auschwitz suffering with the Jews, which certainly would not make him omnipotent. The orthodox answer that Jews have sinned and they have been punished, presumably applied also to the one and a half million infants and children who could hardly know the meaning of sin, which is not traditionally inherited in the Jewish religion. If a fraction of the time spent on perfecting and interpreting further the dietary laws, prayers, keeping the Sabbath, and the Festivals were to be devoted by the Jewish sages and their students to the existential question of the 'longest hatred', then at least there would be a hope that future generations might live a life devoid of hatred, harassment, and extermination.

XII. EVIL IN CIVILISED SOCIETIES

<table>
<tr><td colspan="3">‘Hitler has been a genius at cultivating evil in men’.

Hans Frank after the verdict of the Nüremberg Trial, 1946</td></tr>
<tr><td>‘Political situations are evil only because evil people have created and sustained them’.

The philosopher John Kekes ‘The Roots of Evil', 2005</td><td>‘The evildoers were quite capable of judging the moral significance of the suffering they caused their victims but their judgements were depraved’.

John Kekes, 2005</td><td>‘Evil is the dark shadow that the light of reason cannot banish’.

Terry Eagleton, 2010</td></tr>
</table>

Evil is the most critical aspect of civilization and therefore will be given further attention. Evil is an abstract term referring to serious harmful, painful, and cruel activity, divorced from moral feeling and violates their victim’s freedom, physical security and well-being. It is the antithesis of what is considered to be good. For both Judaism and Christianity, the existence of evil has been a problem, given the belief in a benevolent God. In the insightful analysis of ‘The Roots of Evil’, the philosopher John Kekes argues that evil is the most basic and most serious problem, as “it is an attack on the fundamental conditions of human well-being [...] Mass murder of innocent people is not an unprecedented event but part of a historical pattern [...] It threatens the very conditions of civilized life.” He analysed diverse case histories of evil activity by individuals acting alone or with the encouragement of an evil government or political group, two of which are summarised here, and three cases added from the Third Reich.

Albigensian Crusades against the Cathars about 1200 AD were instigated by Pope Innocent III. The Cathars were largely simple people, rejecting the corruption of many priests, not unlike Martin Luther three centuries later. However, they had no theological or political interest and lived in preparation of a better life in a spiritual world. The ecclesiastic authorities saw the Cathars as subverting the foundation of Christianity, so they were maligned by lies, as Devil worshippers, practising sexual excess and other absurd lies. Finally, Pope Innocent III declared Catharism to be a heresy, which was a sin meriting not only excommunication but also death. Indeed, as early as the 12th century, persecution was socially sanctioned violence through established governmental, judicial, and social institutions. 'The Army of God' massacred about 20,000 men, women, and children.

The French Revolution was one of the most potent forces of the Enlightenment, with its clarion call for 'Liberty, Equality and Fraternity.' Unlike the crusades against the Cathars, the revolution in 1789, over half a millennium later, was generated by a call of reason, with a great deal of blood-letting, culminating in Robespierre's assuming power and the beginning of the 'Terror State'. Arrests, show trials followed invariably by the guillotine, as well as lynching of thousands of people whose policies differed from those of Robespierre. 'Fraternity' was the first victim of the revolutionary call and after some time both 'Liberty and Equality' were eroded and never really accomplished. The power of the revolutionaries laid in the legislative forum of the 'Convention' seized by Robespierre, and followed by the slaughter of the innocents. The guillotine was found to be messy and inefficient to deal with the victims and the ingenuity of the mass killers devised a method of tying up by ropes 60 prisoners at a time and shooting them with cannon. Another advance in mass killing was by punching holes in the sides of barges, with naked young men and women tied together in the boats and then towing them to the centre of the river. There were endless massacres of women and children and old people kneeling in front of a pit they had dug, so that when they were shot, they tumbled into their grave and some were buried alive. In Paris, kangaroo courts known as the Revolutionary Tribunals were ordered by Robespierre and the invariable death sentence was declared within hours.

There we have an ideology that dehumanized its adversaries. Robespierre rejoiced that 'a river of blood would now divide France from its enemies'. Kekes quotes from a historian, "There are only two parties in France: the people and its enemies. We must exterminate those miserable villains who are eternally conspiring against the rights of man. Robespierre became incapable of distinguishing right from wrong – not to say cruelty from humanity." He was driven by his passion, which became his standard of reason, morality and truth. All the atrocities for which he was responsible were set aside, because they were at variance with his passionately held views. The remarkable paradox about Robespierre was that he followed Rousseau's concepts, as instanced in his Declaration of Rights from the

Social Contract, "Man is born for happiness and freedom, yet everywhere he is unhappy and enslaved". Kekes concludes that evil has many causes, one of them being ideology, which however, requires political opportunity, which fails to protect the requirements of reason and morality.

Franz Stangl was born in Austria (1908) into a Catholic family. He worked in the Austrian police, which was incorporated after the 'Anschluss' into the Gestapo. Stangl eventually became the Commandant of the Treblinka extermination camp, which was responsible for mass murder of men, women, and children. Gitta Sereny, who interviewed Stangl, described him as one of the people closely associated with 'total evil'. When he took over the command of Treblinka, he reported to Odilo Globocnik – the SS general in charge of all the extermination camps. "Treblinka is the most awful thing I saw all during the Third Reich. It was Dante's Inferno. Dante come to life. The hundreds, no, the thousands of bodies everywhere, putrefying, decomposing. It is the end of the world. He (Globocnik) responded 'it is supposed to be the end of the world for them.' And Stangl brought order to the camp, increasing the efficiency of killing and disposing of 900,000 innocent beings in a disciplined manner, for which he was awarded the Iron Cross of the Third Reich, declaring him to be "the best Kommandant in Poland".

Sereny asked Stangl the critical question, "You had acknowledged that what was committed was a crime. How could you, in all conscience take part in the crime?" The gist of his answer was "It was a matter of survival. What I had to do, while I continued my efforts to get out, was to limit my actions to what I – in my conscience – could answer for." He was taught at police training school that one of the definitions of crime is 'intent' and he had no intent. It defies reason to believe that Stangl's supervision of the beating, deprivation, starvation, and ultimately murder by gassing can be divorced from 'intent'. He claimed, "I have never intentionally hurt anyone". To Sereny's question, "What was the worst place in the camp for you? The undressing barracks. I avoided it from my innermost being: I couldn't confront them; I couldn't lie to them; I avoided at any price talking to those who were about to die: I couldn't stand it. He agreed with Sereny that 'you had acknowledged to yourself that what was being committed here at Treblinka was a crime'."

Here we have an average man, he attended an Austrian school, up to the age of fifteen, and did very well after being apprenticed in the textile industry. He then joined the police, where he was trained in the police academy and made very good progress. By all accounts, he was hard working, disciplined, showed respect for authority, love of his family and intelligent, indeed he was able to quote 'Dante's Inferno'. Above all, he was ambitious. His wife was aware of his "wild ambition" and said "I am very proud of him, he was constantly being promoted, praised and decorated for this and that achievement." The facts assembled by Sereny suggest that Stangl's SS superiors were able to make him Commandant of Treblinka by rewards, status, comforts and power he enjoyed, knowing his ambition to get on and be recognized. He has overcome a degree of empathy, as noted by his observation about the undressing barracks prior to murder, that 'his conscience' found objectionable, but he became desensitised to the evil by the 'superman's courage' in the face of human suffering, so authoritatively preached by Himmler and his comrades.

Adolf Eichmann was born into a Catholic lower-middle-class German family in 1906. After an unremarkable early life, in 1932 he joined the Nazi Party and the SS, and in 1934 he applied to and was accepted into the SD, the section of the SS in charge of the Final Solution, that is, the extermination of the Jews. He eventually rose to a rank equivalent to lieutenant colonel and was given the job of arranging the transportation of Jews from all over Europe to forced labour and death camps. He was responsible for the murder of millions of innocent people. After the collapse of Nazi Germany, he escaped to Argentina. He was traced and caught by Israeli security forces in 1960, brought to Israel, tried, sentenced to death, and hanged in 1962. "This mass murderer turned out to be a very ordinary bureaucrat who, although showing extraordinary diligence in looking out for his personal advancement', was not the blood-thirsty, sadistic monster many people expected. That his job involved the killing of millions was a matter of indifference to him. He just wanted to be good at whatever task he was given [...] He was not stupid. It was sheer thoughtlessness that predisposed him to become one of the greatest criminals [...] That such remoteness from reality and such thoughtlessness can wreak more havoc than all the evil instincts taken together which, perhaps are inherent in man – that was, in fact, the lesson one could learn in Jerusalem. Eichmann 'acted not as a man but as a mere functionary [...]

He did his duty, as he told the police and court over and over again; he not only obeyed orders, he also obeyed the law [...] He declared with great emphasis that he had lived his whole life according to Kant's moral precepts, and especially according to a Kantian definition of duty [...] To the surprise of everybody, Eichmann came up with an approximately correct definition of Kant's categorical imperative [...] 'The principle of my will must always be such that it can become the principle of general laws' [...] His supposed duty happily coincided with his supposed self-interest.

Their combined motivational force, relentless Nazi propaganda, the authority of his superiors, and his physical distance from the murder of his victims were strong enough to silence any qualms he may have had about doing his share in murdering millions. This seems to me a good explanation of the evil Eichmann did".

Josef Mengele (1911-1979), of Roman Catholic parents, had a doctorate in anthropology from the University of Munich and another doctorate in medicine from the University of Frankfurt. He was a mass murderer responsible for thousands of death sentences on totally innocent civilians at the selection ramp in Auschwitz, and Ravensbrück, and no doubt well-qualified with a double doctorate to dispatch human beings right or left, life or death. He also carried out experiments on twin children and then had them killed to carry out thorough pathological and microscopical examination of their organs. He apparently was nice to the children whilst he used them for his experiments and even plied them with sweets. Dr. Mengele has written a new chapter in the annals of medical history, the seriousness of which has as yet to be fully comprehended; by all accounts he was not insane.

These five cases of Evil manifest diverse motivations and basic causes or associations; the Albigensian Crusaders – Faith and religion, Robespierre – Ideology and reason, Stangl, Eichmann, and Mengele– ambition and opportunism. Kekes argues that the motives that have led to evil actions in the first two cases, are those that provide an ideal and give meaning to one's life [...] Faith and ideology may have built-in prohibitions of evil. However, they have not been realized for reasons that the existing prohibitions of evil were weak, the circumstances favoured evil actions." Whether the Crusaders, Robespierre, Eichmann and Mengele recognized that in normal circumstances their actions would have been evil is questionable. They believed, however, that their circumstances were not normal, that they are serving a cause and they have the sanctions of their leaders or established authority, their actions were morally justified. They believed otherwise, and inflicted horrendous suffering on innocent people, while feeling righteous about it. What made this possible was the crusader's extremist faith, their belief that they are God's servants and unscrupulous leaders seeking glory, recognition from the people and power. Robespierre's ideology, Stangl's, Eichmann's, and Mengele's ruthless ambition, doing their duty, zero degree of empathy and moral baseness may explain how they could have directly or indirectly murdered thousands of innocent beings.

The 'apologists' of religion used the time honoured biblical argument 'that we are all sinners as a result of the fall'. This has been reinterpreted by the evolutionary view, of our primitive past, which can emerge from our limbic system of the brain, given the appropriate conditions. The liberal attitude emerged from the Enlightenment, that we are basically good and do evil only because of bad, immoral, or evil governing powers that mislead us. Neither standpoint is tenable in the face of the crusaders, Robespierre, or Stangl murdering children, women and men, burning alive, hanging, drowning or gassing, after denying them justice, freedom and carrying out torture and cruelties that cannot and must not be the justification of any ideology. Evil actions must be condemned, without exempting the evildoers, especially by those who were either fortunate not to be targeted or did nothing when their neighbours, friends, or colleagues were desperate for help or support. Basically, evil violates all precepts of religion and the ideas of the Enlightenment, and yet fails to protect the individual from murder, torture, and denial of basic human rights. It is imperative that we acknowledge that evil exists, both within Religion and Enlightenment and that learned tracts of principles are woefully inadequate to deal with the problem of evil.

Religious faith, ideology, or science without or with ambition and honour did not prompt directly the evil actions but abuse of these ideals. As Kekes points out, "faith tends to spurn reason and anything is acceptable in the name of God or ideology, because it dehumanizes and demonizes the real or imagined opponents [...] However, Nietzsche is a critic of the religious tradition and does not share the Enlightenment illusions about human reason and goodness. His view about evil is inseparably connected with his criticism of the Judeo-Christian approach to morality. It is a value constructed by the weak to resist the power of the strong. True morality, Nietzsche thinks, rejects these notions of good and evil as pernicious shams, and recognizes that good is what contributes to the creative activities of the strong, and bad is what stands in their way. As a result, he denies the reality of evil; it exists only as a product of resentful weak minds."

Kekes then moves to classify evil into: (a) external causes which are natural influences or metaphysical, such as God's design or human injustice, and (b) internal causes are psychological, such as ignorance or cruelty. External causes of evil are commonly political injustice, created and maintained by people through their own evil actions. Internal causes following Platonic explanations is that evil is caused by ignorance of the good and has been adopted in Christian theology through the work of Augustine and Aquinas. "Evil is the effect of original sin, the propensity of human beings to malfunction, choose evil over the good, and thereby pit themselves against God's morally good order. This type of Christian thinking about evil dominated Western thought until the Enlightenment." According to Kant, "Enlightenment is man's emergence from his self-imposed immaturity. Immaturity is the inability to use one's understanding without guidance from another."

Philippa Foot attempted to explain "evil as a natural defect that leads evildoers to act contrary to the human good. Human beings are basically good. And acting morally is part of practical morality." Kekes countered this argument by saying, "that some of our natural propensities are good, others are evil and neither is more basic than the other." He rejected Foot's view as it fails to account for evil, which is widespread, recurring throughout history and is detrimental to human life. Furthermore, the secular optimism of the Enlightenment is unfounded because both good and evil propensities are basic to human nature." Regrettably, reason did not prevent the actions of the five evil individuals, indeed they used reason to justify their evil actions.

It is morality that humanity has developed whether by evolutionary forces or religious teaching, most likely by both, which prohibits evil actions. Morality is one of the strategies man has developed to guide our judgment and control our primordial evil propensities. It is likely that evolution was the driving force in the development of our vices, such as aggression, selfishness, cruelty, envy and hatred, as much as the conduct of kindness, love and altruism. Quite apart from the evil discussed, if pleasure is derived in the infliction of pain by physical violence, this type of evil deals with sadism, which is likely to represent a pathological form of evil and may well involve some perpetrators of torture, without consciously admitting it. Stangl and Mengele may have been sadists, both acting face to face with their victims, exercising the ultimate power of life and death, the former through obeying orders from his superiors, whilst the latter serving Nazi ideology or inhumane science in his pursuit of human experiments.

Arendt dealt with evil in at least two books, 'Origins of Totalitarianism' (1951) and 'Eichmann in Jerusalem' (1963). In the latter, she described the trial of Adolf Eichmann, who served in the SS section, in charge of the 'Final Solution', exterminating the Jewish people. Arendt concluded with the most often quoted words of Eichmann's evil that it shows the 'banality of evil.' Arendt, however, distinguishes between limited and radical evil. "Murder is only limited evil, the murderer who kills a man [...] Still moves within the realm of life and death familiar to us. In contrast, 'the real horror of the concentration and extermination camps lies in the fact that here murder is as impersonal as squashing a gnat [...] There are neither political nor historical nor simply moral standards. This is the appearance of radical evil. Limited evil serves the purpose of an individual. Evil is radical because it destroys the possibility of civilized life. If everything is possible, then there are no limits, no rules, no laws [...] Concentration camps are essential to the preservation of power and totalitarian regime more than any of its other institutions. The ordinary man came to do extraordinary evil."

Arendt then argues "imagine Robespierre if the French Revolution had not occurred or Stangl, Eichmann and Mengele in an Austria and Germany without Nazism. Robespierre might have spent his life as a provincial lawyer, Stangl and Eichmann might have been officials in some office. Mengele would become a conventional doctor, as his inhumane experiments would not have been possible. Evildoers do not just violate moral limits, but reveal a depraved attitude toward them [...] To think of such evildoers as enemies of humanity is not too strong a condemnation [...] The manner in which evil actions harm their victims undermines the foundation on which the society rests [...] That is why their society held, or should have held, them morally responsible and severely condemned them. A central task of morality is to prevent this from happening."

Tolerance is favoured by most reasonable people and requires that we should not judge and condemn others. Kekes rightly states, "There can be no morally acceptable reason for violating elementary decency and causing evil [...] That is why evil actions are much worse than simply morally bad why they provoke outrage for transgressing limits in a manner that threatens the very possibility of civilized life [...] The illusion that human beings are basically good and they do evil only because unjust political arrangements corrupt them has been propagated by the Enlightenment [...] However, political situations are evil only because evil people have created and sustained them." It is significant that after their evil activities, most of the individuals considered here were dissatisfied with their lives and considered to be failures. "Robespierre saw his fellow Jacobins reject his ideology and have him executed. He realized that the Revolution had lost its momentum, his ideology was being repudiated, his murder of thousands was for naught, and none of his important goals had been achieved." Stangl, after years of prevarication and denial, came to the conclusion in the jail to which he was sentenced for life that, "I should have killed myself in 1938' rather than accept the inducements he was offered to become a mass murderer. Before he died he repudiated his life and was wracked by guilt for the way he lived during the crucial years". Both Eichmann and Mengele were on the run in foreign countries, separated from their kith and kin. Eichmann was caught by Israeli forces, tried in Jerusalem and sentenced to death by hanging. Mengele managed to survive and after collapse of the

‘Thousand Year Reich’ and out of his SS uniform, he still tried to justify to his son his actions, had apparently no moral scruples over his past existence, despite being wanted for murder and medical torture.

It is remarkable that after presenting a most comprehensive insight into the nature of evil, Kekes still falls back on the time-honoured role of the humanities, which cultivate moral imagination that enables one to cope with evil. All the evidence from the time of the extermination of the Cathars by the educated ecclesiastic hierarchy, Robespierre, with the ideals and culture of the enlightenment, Eichmann, familiar and correctly citing Kant, Mengele with the best education that 20th century German schools and universities could offer, and even Stangl able to quote Dante in describing Treblinka, probably saw their radical fallacy. Humanities have raised men and women from the state of primitive existence to great spiritual heights, without denting the hard-wired primal memory, urging man to its atavistic activity.

In his concluding notes, Kekes states that “elementary decency, therefore, marks the boundary within which civilized life can be lived and on the outside of which barbarism reigns. The evildoers were clearly not insane, or irresistibly stressed, they had no acceptable excuse. That they were blinded by faith, ideology or ambition is a psychological explanation of the causes of their evil actions, not an excuse for them. They were quite capable of judging the comparative moral significance of the justification they believed they had and their immediate experience of the suffering they caused their victims. And they did judge, but their judgments were depraved [...] Evil has the following general characteristics: it is mixed because it involves the combination of internal and external conditions, multicausal because the conditions that jointly cause it vary with individuals, societies, times, and places.”

CHAPTER 9: COMPLEX ACADEMIC STRUCTURE OF GENOCIDE

I. **Introduction**
II. **Thuringia (Thüringen)**
III. **Christianity**
IV. **Academic anti-Semitic agenda**
V. **Legal profession**
VI. **Medical profession**
VII. **Enabling trigger of genocide**
VIII. **Turbulent flow of rivers of dark dreams of history**

THE COMPLEX ACADEMIC STRUCTURE OF GENOCIDE

"Of all religions, the Christian is undoubtedly that which should instil the greatest toleration, although so far the Christians have been the most intolerant of all men"

Voltaire, 1763

"The basis for interpretation of all legal sources is the National Socialist ideology, as expressed in the party programme and the Führer's statements"

Hans Frank, Reich Leader of Jurists, 1936

"We should abandon the notion to pick a single decision that led to the 'Final Solution'. The National Socialist regime was already considering genocidal projects against the Jews in the years 1939 to 1941."

Professor Peter Longerich, 'Holocaust', 2010

"The forces of Law linked with those of Medicine forged the notion of 'Gnadetod' (compassionate death) meted out to children and adults judged to have life unworthy of living"

Professors Karl Binding and Alfred Hoche, 1920

"It is not only what we do, but also what we do not do, for which we are accountable"

Molière, 1622-1673

"Nazi Germany rested on the temporary alliance between the elite and the mob"

Hannah Arendt, 1973

I. INTRODUCTION

Any interpretation of events in the history of Germany leading to the Genocide is fraught with difficulties. This is an attempt at 'meta-analysis', that is gathering the elements that form part of a complex whole of basic studies, interpretations, and views of historians, theologians, sociologists, and intellectuals. History recalls a succession of wars involving the German people. The religious strife and bloody wars after the Lutheran reformation of Christianity in the 16th century divided the country into the largely Catholic south and Protestant north. There was no respite in the 17th century, with the 'Thirty Year War' which decimated the German population, losing about a third of its people. The Napoleonic wars followed in the late 18th and early 19th century. Unification of Germany from twenty-seven States to the Reich was achieved under the Prussian Bismarck as late as 1871, with Wilhelm I being declared Kaiser. The declaration of Pope's infallibility in 1870 was greeted by Germany embarking on a series of wars against the Roman Catholic Church, the enemy of liberalism, in contrast to 'Bildung', cultivation of the spirit by the Protestants. Rudolf Virchow, the great medical scientist and liberal thinker, coined the term 'Kulturkampf' (Culture War). The middle classes were brutalized and a development of nationalistic student fraternities followed.

A comprehensive analysis of the sociological aspects in Germany, leading to genocide was written by Norbert Elias in 'The Germans; power struggles and the development of habitus in the 19th and 20th centuries'. He refers to the shock suffered by the self-image of the highly cultured Western European Christian civilization by an abrupt breakdown of highly cherished norms of civil society, resulting in unrestrained barbarity. Social Darwinism in the late 19th and early 20th century of the human struggle for existence in war and peace was enthusiastically embraced in Germany. A number of anthropologists, historians, scientists, and physicians had been engaged in a programme of eugenics, later termed 'racial hygiene'. The basic argument ran along the lines that the 'lower races' stood in the way of advances in culture and civilization, because of their innate mental inferiority, incapable of adopting 'higher culture' and morality. Some of these 'high cultured' learned individuals argued that racial extermination is justified as it would result in moral progress of humanity. The intellectual-driven premise was argued among others by Alfred Kirchhoff of the University of Leipzig, that Darwinian survival of the fittest makes it a categorical scientific imperative for racial extermination of crude, immoral hordes.

The opportunity to take these academic polemics into practice came sooner than expected in German Southwest African (renamed Namibia), during the Herero tribe revolt in 1904-1906. The German military commander, General Trotha, ordered the annihilation of all Herero men, women, and children in what was generally considered to represent a Darwinian 'Rassenkampf' (racial war). Most Germans considered black Africans little more than animals and murdered some 80% of the Herero people. This represents the first genocide by Germans, though affecting non-European Africans. The massacre aroused considerable controversy in Germany and the Chancellor voiced criticism that general Trotha's actions were contrary to all Christian and humane principles. Mary Fulbrook also cites the suppression of the Maji-Maji rebellion in German East Africa, in which some 250,000 people or half to three-quarters of the Vidundi, Matumbi, and Pangwa tribes lost their lives through fighting, deliberate starvation by destruction of agriculture, and causing famine as a matter of German policy.

By the 20th century, the Kaiser and his entourage were restless and the assassination in Sarajevo of the crown prince Archduke Franz Ferdinand triggered off in 1914 the First World War. The Germans unexpectedly signed the armistice in 1918 in Compiegne, the treaty of Versailles in 1919, and later had to agree to Allied Reparations bill of 132 billion gold marks. All this did not augur well for the newly established Weimar Republic as a democratic state during such a perilous time. It was unpopular, not least with the 6 million demobilised servicemen, many of whom joined illegal paramilitary organisations.

The Great Depression, following the stock-exchange crash in 1929, with mounting unemployment, loss of the value of pensions, all added up to a socio-economic crisis. The Mark lost its value, the Weimar democracy lost any support it might have retained, and communist agitation frightened the upper and middle classes. The 'stab in the back' myth current among the multitude, blamed Jews for loss of the war. Furthermore, millions of demobilised unemployed servicemen lead to unrest and agitation. The timing for a demagogue who would solve all problems was ripe and Hitler was the man to fulfil the task. Hitler and his supporters promised strong rule, to which Germany was accustomed, mixed with a large dose of nationalism and anti-Semitism, both of which fell on receptive ears. The emerging formula of gaining power was the cry for Germany to regain its former glory and 'Kultur', purifying German 'blood' and spiritual revival from the pollution of 'Jewish-Bolshevik' influence. Regaining lost territory from the 'perfidious French' and gaining 'lebensraum' (living space) in the East was claimed by the National Socialists. All was orchestrated with marches, a great deal of flag waving, and not least, street fighting, with physical threats and abuse of any individual daring to disagree or oppose the Nazi policy. Hitler's promise of creating a 'Thousand Year Reich', was initiated through democratic elections, so the German electorate handed over ruling the country to a 'Stateless Austrian', who, despite a police record for 'high treason' was naturalized as a German citizen by subterfuge and of questionable legality.

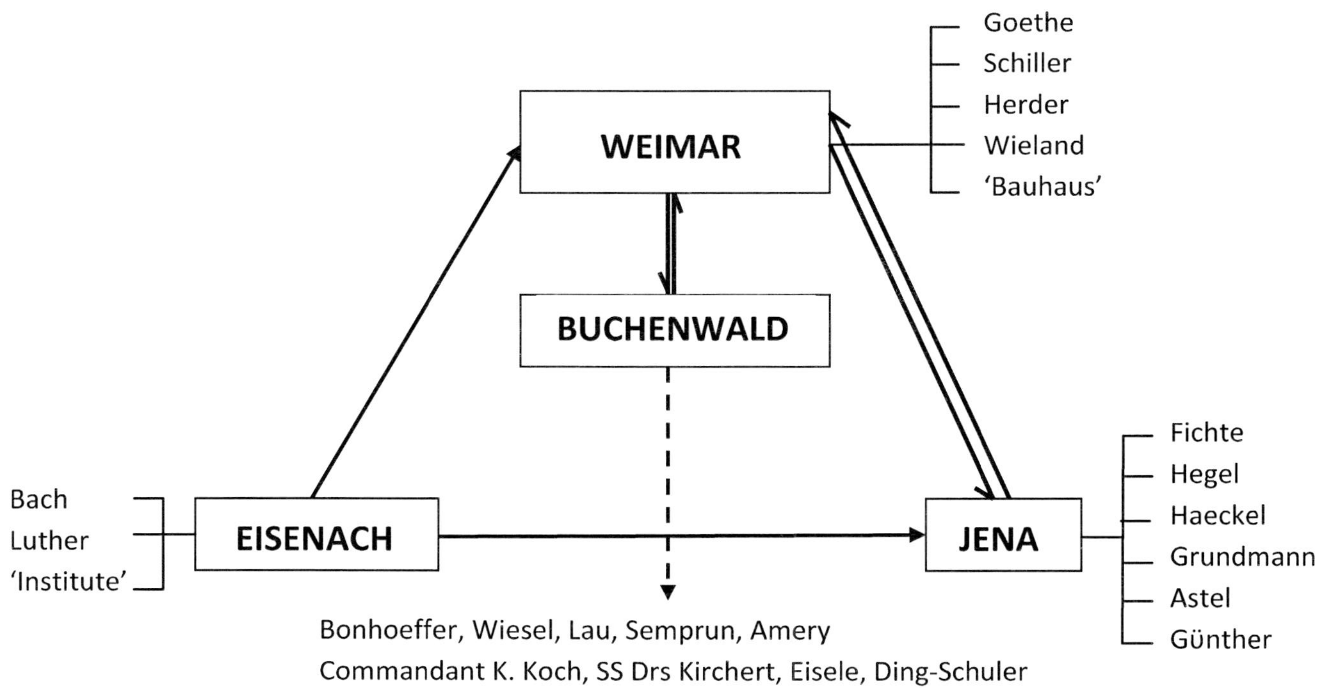

Fig. 1 *A diagrammatic illustration of the 'Microcosm of Culture versus Barbarity' in the state of Thuringia, in the centre of Germany.*

II. THURINGIA (THÜRINGEN)

This is a small State in the centre of Germany, Fig. 1. With Weimar, Jena, and Eisenach, the state represented the high point of German and Christian culture in Western Europe. Goethe, and Schiller in Weimar, the humanities, theology and sciences at the linked University of Jena, with the historical influence of Bach and Luther in the nearby Eisenach, were tragically situated in the proximity of the notorious concentration camp of Buchenwald. The epicentre of European culture adjacent to the unprecedented mass killing and barbarity in Buchenwald is a reality that should be the concern of all who value Western Civilization and Culture.

Weimar, Jena, and Eisenach were centres of Culture, Art, Religion, Philosophy, Law, Music, Biology, and Medicine, in juxtaposition to the notorious Buchenwald concentration camp. The key persons are given for each place. 'Institute' stands for the 'Institute for the study and eradication of Jewish influence on German religious life'.

Despite its enviable history, Thuringia was the first State to elect a National Socialist government (see Chapter 1). Long standing reflections and reading the ever-increasing literature lead to the paradigm of 'the complex academic structure of genocide'. This enormously complex historical development over two millennia consists of four essential theological, academic, legal and medical parts, which was triggered off by the prevailing socio-economic conditions and contributed to the physical and cultural genocide (Fig. 2).

III. CHRISTIANITY

Christianity has evolved from Judaism and its very existence from the first century after Jesus was conditioned by supersession of God's Covenant and the status of the children of Israel as the 'Chosen People'. The arguments of the replacement theology were based on the writings of the Prophets addressed to the Jews in an effort to make them obey all the commandments of the law written in the Torah. These chastisements were no more or less to teach a community some four thousand years ago, with prior polytheism and pagan culture to obey the one and only true God. There are no directly written words by Jesus and most of the information about him originate from Paul, the Gospels, and the Christian Fathers, written years and centuries after his death. A 'historical Jesus' has now emerged, well summarised by the life-long studies of Géza Vermes in the previous chapter (p.159). When the Jews rejected Jesus as the Messiah, a wave of anti-Judaism was initiated by Paul (circa 5-67 CE), the Gospel writers, and the Christian Fathers from the second century CE onwards. They were accused of not following the teaching of Jesus, their own Prophet, later to be declared the Son of God, and they were also cursed with alleged deicide.

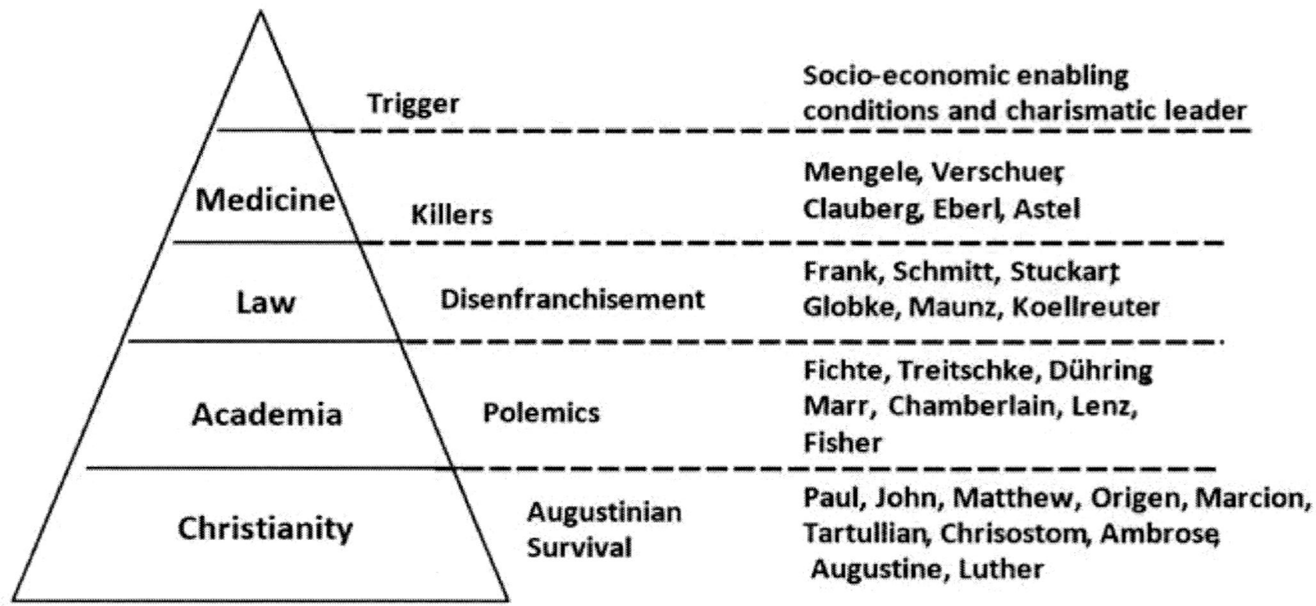

Figure 2 *The Complex Cultural Construct of Genocide*

Jews were threatened with extermination by the 'Christian Fathers' – Origen, Tertullian, and Chrysostom from the 2nd century onwards. It was St. Augustine (354-430 CE) who's teaching largely prevailed up to the 18th century, 'to let Jews survive but never to thrive, so as to witness the righteousness of Christianity'. Martin Luther in the 16th century similarly turned against the Jews after they rejected conversion to what became Lutheran Christianity.

Both the Catholic and Protestant churches inculcated from infancy at home, school and church anti-Jewish teaching, albeit initially on religious grounds and invoking the ultimate curse of having killed Jesus, the son of God. The basis of religious anti-Semitism has been established by Paul, the Gospels, the Christian Fathers, two millennia of preaching against the Jews, and in the 16th century by the Reformation reviving anti-Jewish prejudice by Martin Luther. Faith in the teaching of the Churches has pre-conditioned people to consistent prejudice entering all spheres of culture, literature, music, visual art, and the notion of a dark side of Judaism.

Martin Niemöller, in a lecture in 1946, stated, "Christianity in Germany bears a greater responsibility before God than the National Socialists, the SS and the Gestapo. Are not we Christians much more to blame, am I not much guiltier, than many who bathed their hands in blood?" James Carroll argues cogently as a devout Catholic that Augustine's edict 'let them survive but not thrive' has been a thousand-year legacy practised by the Catholic Church towards Jews. An ambivalent attitude of Popes and Bishops would protect Jews from Christian mobs that wanted to kill Jews, because of what the Popes and Bishops had taught about Jews. He states that "this is the legacy that haunts the Catholic Church into the twenty-first Century, a perverse legacy from which, despite the twentieth century's jolts, the Church is not yet free [...] In silence the sin of the Church is acknowledged as the sin that was part of what led to genocide. There is no more talk that exempts 'the Church as such' from this judgment." However, recently, Paula Fredriksen, in a scholarly book entitled 'Augustine and the Jews' (2008), argues that the 'rhetorical Jews should be differentiated from the historical Jews' on theological grounds; "God himself wanted the Jews to remain Jews".

On similar lines but different rationale, George Steiner wrote, in 1971 in 'Bluebeard's Castle', "It seems to me incontrovertible that the holocaust must be set in the framework of the psychology of religion". Later, in 1996, he argued, "We will not be capable of thinking the Shoah, albeit inadequately, if we divorce its genesis and its radical enormity from theological origins”. Steiner quotes Professor Donald MacKinnon, Fellow of Balliol College, Oxford, “There could be no justifiable future for Christianity so long as Christian philosophy and practice had not faced up to, had not internalised lucidly, its seminal role in the millennial torments of Judaism and in the Holocaust.” Peter Pulzer, Professor of Government in Oxford stated, in 1988, “I am more strongly convinced than I was when I wrote the book that a tradition of religiously-inspired Jew hatred ... was a necessary condition for the success of anti-Semitic propaganda. These statements were endorsed by Gregory Baum, Professor of Theology and adviser to Vatican II: “The theological negation of Judaism and the vilification of the Jewish people that were part of the Christian tradition were translated into genocidal action of monstrous proportions, not indeed by Christians themselves, but by a political party that used for its own purposes a heritage built up by Christianity and counted on a good deal of Christian cooperation.”

IV. THE ACADEMIC ANTI-SEMITIC AGENDA

Anti-Semitism was propagated by some University-trained academics and intellectuals, who saw in Jews a different race and developed theories, largely based on crude nationalism, and a weird concept of 'Übermensch' ('Superman') of the German Volk. This involved historians, anthropologists, and biologists adapting Social Darwinism and Eugenics to their own end, to eliminate the 'other' and weaker in society. Publications by learned Professors offered an intellectual basis underpinning coercion, depriving people of liberty, incarceration, and finally leading to mass murder. Johann Gottlieb Fichte (1762-1814), Professor of Philosophy in Jena, argued vociferously against the Jews, against giving them German civil rights and citizenship, that they do not have any sound ideas in their head and would undermine the German nation. Heinrich von Treitschke (1834-1896), Professor of History in Munich, stated, "Jews are Germany's misfortune. The Jew belonged to a rootless, inferior species of humanity." Eugen Dühring (1833-1921), a lawyer, lecturer at the University of Berlin and writer of philosophical tracts, denounced Jews, Greeks and the 'Cosmopolitan Goethe'. He argued in his book, 'The Jewish question as a racial, moral and cultural question' (1881), that the Jews, despite being an inferior race, were taking over Europe. They should be forced back into the ghettos and their property confiscated. Wilhelm Marr (1819-1904) founded the influential 'Anti-Semitic League' in 1879 and the 'Pan-German League' in 1891. Marr argued that the Jews were a race, so assimilation into the German Volk would not mitigate the conflict between German and Jewish races. He publicised his views in the pamphlet 'The way to victory of Germanicism over Judaism' (1879). Although not an academic, his views were a link in the German anti-Semitic chain, following Treitschke, and they were adopted in Nazi ideology. It is worth noting that of his four marriages, two of his wives were of Jewish origin. Towards the end of his life, he renounced his anti-Semitism and allegedly apologised for his prejudice. Houston S. Chamberlain (1855-1927) was a vicious anti-Semite, arguing in his book that Germany upholds the European Christian culture against the corrupting influence of the Jews. It is likely that some of the expressed views may have been influenced by the theories of the French racist Arthur de Gobineau, author of 'An essay on the inequality of human races, 1853-1855)'.

Fritz Lenz (1887-1976), Professor of Eugenics for Racial Hygiene in Munich, stated that evolution and redemption are dependent on race and he advocated eliminating the inferior races – the Jews (Ch. 2). Eugene Fisher (1874-1967) was the director of the 'Institute for Anthropology, Human Heredity and Eugenics at the Kaiser Wilhelm Institute'. He studied mixed races of white men with black women and their children in South West Africa. He argued that mixing the lesser 'Negro blood' with 'White blood' would bring about destruction of the European culture. After Hitler gained power in 1933, the Institute dealt with Nazi racial policy, teaching SS doctors, the members serving on the judiciary of Berlin's Hereditary Health Court and passing judgments on 'racial purity'. Dr. Paul Nitsche was a founding member of the 'German Racial Hygiene Society'. He was a member of the Nazi Party since 1933, served as the head of the T-4 division involved in selecting patients for transfer to the killing facilities.

Hans F. Günther defined the racial 'ideal type' of Nordic-Aryan, based on appearance and skull measurements. He was appointed in 1932 to the new chair of 'Social Anthropology' in Jena and became the most outspoken racist, to the extent that he was nick-named 'Rassen Papst' (Race Pope, Ch. 2). Perhaps the most surprising individual to become a card-carrying member of the Nazi party was Martin Heidegger (1889-1976), a professor of philosophy. When Hitler came to power in 1933, he became Rector of the University of Freiburg. Heidegger was and still is regarded as one of the most important philosophers of the 20th century and he was of immense value to Hitler and Goebbels to gain support from such a prestigious authority. Among his many pro-Nazi statements, he endorsed the 'Führer Principle' and was helpful to the party by attracting further academic support.

Steiner, in 'Language and Silence' (1967), was most explicit when he wrote, "The blackness of it did not spring up in the Gobi Desert or the rain forests of the Amazon. It rose from within, and from the core of European civilization. The cry of the murdered sounded in earshot of the universities; the sadism went on a street away from the theatres and museums. The high places of literacy, of philosophy, of artistic expression became the setting for Belsen. We know now that a man can read Goethe or Rilke in the evening, that he can play Bach and Schubert, and go to his day's work at Auschwitz in the morning. It is almost axiomatic from the time of Plato to that of Matthew Arnold, that culture is a humanizing force, that the energies of spirit are transferable to those of conduct [...]The universities, the arts, the book world failed to offer adequate resistance to political bestiality.

Why? What are the links, as yet scarcely understood, between the mental, psychological habits of high literacy and the temptations of the inhuman?"

Steiner pursues, in 1984, the gnawing question, which has made an indelible impression on his psyche in the introduction to another of his books, 'A Reader'. "Instead of being an insurance against inhumanity, the humanities and the ideals of disinterested abstraction taught by the humanistic and scientific disciplines might, in fact, make us more prone to political-social indifference – are we not accomplices to all that leaves us indifferent? – and might, in fact, make us fellow-travellers to barbarism." Steiner consistently and emphatically poses over the past half a century the critical question that concerns European Civilisation, without an adequate answer as yet been forthcoming.

V. THE LEGAL PROFESSION

The legal profession was willing to follow the National Socialist doctrinal ideology by enacting anti-Jewish laws, which deprived them of statehood, liberty, freedom, and economic existence. Whilst knowing fully well that they have made life for Jews well-nigh impossible and that judicial proceedings against Jew-baiters were flouted, they fell short of enacting legal edicts to murder men, women, and children for reason of race or religion. But they legalized murder of people with disabilities, under the euphemism of euthanasia. The Wannsee extra-judicial body has filled the gap that even Nazi lawyers could not openly sanction by the resolution of the 'final solution' – extermination of the Jewish people (see p.290).

Hans Frank, the 'Reichsjuristenführer' (Reich leader of jurists), laid down the principle that, "The basis for the interpretation of all legal sources is the National Socialist ideology, as expressed in the party programme and the Führer's statements." Carl Schmitt was a knowledgeable legal scholar who converted to Nazi ideology, advocating dictatorship and anti-Semitism, and wrote 'The Führer protects the law'. Wilhelm Stuckart was a lawyer who joined the SS in 1933 and was appointed 'State secretary of the Reich Ministry of the Interior' at the age of thirty-three. He co-authored the Nüremberg anti-racial laws and was one of the legal representatives at the Wannsee Conference, where he advocated compulsory sterilisation of non-Aryans, in effect extermination of the entire people of a different religion, re-classified as race. Hans I. Globke was also an eminent lawyer who formulated the emergency legislation that handed over to Hitler dictatorial powers. He co-authored with Stuckart the basic laws of persecution of Jews. Theodor Maunz, professor of German constitutional law, joined the Nazi party and SA. He was critical of 'Jewish theorists' of law and among other pronouncements, Maunz declared 'arrests by the Gestapo are sovereign acts outside the judicial realm'. Otto Koellreutter and Richard Höhn were constitutional lawyers supporting the Nazi laws and overriding personal law. These activities by respected, eminent lawyers gave Hitler and his supporters a free hand to deal with Jews without recourse to due judicial process and they have fully availed themselves of the extra-judicial system, practised by the Gestapo and the SS in concentration camps.

VI. THE MEDICAL PROFESSION

The Medical profession had the largest membership of the Nazi party (44.8% of all the licensed physicians). Doctors were the arbiters of life and death, as many advocated and pursued euthanasia or legalized murder, initially of their own German people with certain disabilities. Unlike the other contributing professions to the Holocaust which acted indirectly, Christianity through its traditional anti-Jewish doctrines, academia by its anti-Semitic prejudice, and law by enacting anti-Jewish laws, depriving a section of the German community of basic human rights, doctors of medicine were the only professional individuals in face-to-face contact with their victims. They selected for life or death at the 'ramp' or for lethal work and some for experimentation. 'Healer – turned killer' was a new phenomenon in the history of medicine, clearly defying the Ten Commandments, the Hippocratic Oath, Civil Law of the country, and Natural Law of humanity. All laws were abolished in Dante's underworld of concentration camps, ruled by the pure Aryan culture, discovered from pre-history by Himmler, Rosenberg and their acolytes. Those that were lucky to be selected by Dr. Mengele and his medical colleagues to live were then selected either for death by well-tried formula of exhaustion by work and starvation or for medical experiments. These 'Aryan Medical Scientists' availed themselves of a new code of ethical approval to torture, mutilate, and then to record at post-mortem the end results of their misdeeds. All for the glory of the Reich and its Volk, not to mention personal gratification in contributing to 'medical science', that heretofore no medical man would have dared to pursue. The German Medical profession carry the heavy burden of being the willing executioners of the Nazi regime.

Of the multitude of doctors of medicine who were willing to act as mass murderers and pursue inhumane experiments on captive people, only a few will be considered here. Josef Mengele first studied anthropology in Munich and was awarded the doctorate in 1935, his major subject being racial differences between people. He followed this up with a doctorate in Medicine in Frankfurt in 1938 under Professor Verschuer. In 1943, he was posted to Auschwitz, where with a double doctorate, he was well qualified to carry out selection at the ramp of continuous new transports of people for life or death by simply looking at them for a few fleeting moments. He was more attentive looking out for 'experimental material', especially children and adult twins on whom he perpetrated frightful experiments concerning hereditary factors, eyes being of special interest to him. Many were killed for post-mortem examination of their organs.

He collaborated with his mentor Professor Verschuer, head of the 'Human Heredity Department' at the Kaiser Wilhelm Anthropological Institute in Berlin, and supplied him with the autopsy material from Auschwitz. Otmar Von Verschuer came from an aristocratic family. He fought in the First World War, joined the 'Freikorps' after the war, and as a student at Marburg University, joined the extreme anti-Semitic student fraternity. He qualified in Medicine in 1923 and became interested in genetics. Verschuer examined hundreds of twins to find out if conditions, such as criminal behaviour, mental disorders, cancer, and tuberculosis were inherited. He advocated forced sterilisation of the 'mentally and morally subnormal'. Verschuer was appointed to the professorship and head of the new 'Institute for Hereditary science and race hygiene' at the University of Frankfurt in 1935.

Dr. Carl Clauberg was professor of gynaecology at the University of Königsberg, joined the Nazi party in 1933 and became an 'SS Gruppen Führer'. On his own initiative, he carried out sterilization experiments on women in Auschwitz and Ravensbrück concentration camps. He sterilised 700 women, many of whom died. Clauberg was an outright sadist, and it is regrettable that Königsberg University have not investigated his case history. Dr. Irmfried Eberl was an Austrian who studied medicine at the University of Innsbruck, joined the Nazi party, qualified in 1933, and trained in psychiatry. By the age of twenty-nine, he became the medical director of the T-4 Euthanasia Programme of murder of mentally ill people. He was well qualified to become the only medically qualified person to be appointed to command the extermination camp in Treblinka. Eberl established an efficient killing machine, but was hopeless at disposal of 'mountains of bodies'. He was dismissed by his SS superiors for 'incompetence' and for stealing valuables from his murdered victims. Dr. Karl Astel was a fanatical Nazi and joined the 'Freikorps' in 1919. He worked as a 'sports physician' in Munich and in 1932 he became director of the 'Racial Hygiene School of SA'. Astel was responsible for numerous forced sterilisations and became professor and head of the new 'Institute of Human Genetic Research and Racial Politics' at the medical school in Jena. There was no limit to his promotion; SS lieutenant colonel and then 'Rector' of the University of Jena. Astel was supported by Hitler and Himmler and contributed to 'Jena becoming a model SS university'.

It is surprising and disappointing that the renowned Medical Schools responsible for the university education of these individuals and many other doctors lacking humanity, felt no compulsion to investigate their school curriculum, unless they have not considered that there was anything wrong in the activities of the end products of their institutions. Neither is there any evidence that the Medical Schools attempted to revoke the degrees from any of these individuals.

Each of the four highly regarded institutions and professional bodies contributed to the complex enabling academic structure. The sum of the whole was greater than the individual parts, enabling the ultimate evil of a modern, cultured, science-driven, enlightened nation, to mass murder on an unprecedented scale of innocent, unarmed, and defenceless people. Robert Ericksen stated explicitly that "One of the most distinctive features of the Holocaust – its modern, technologically sophisticated nature – is rooted directly in German Universities. University-trained technicians, engineers, architects, doctors, and lawyers assisted at various stages in the process, helping make it possible to kill so many people so efficiently in such a short period of time. Here the universities can be seen to have. Provided training necessary for experts to do their jobs. It is impossible to imagine certain specific horrors of the Holocaust [without] the training and expertise provided by German universities." Konrad Jarausch – writing about German lawyers, teachers, and engineers (1900-1950), argues that these professional experts have perpetrated crimes leading to death, for their personal benefit and are accessories to Nazi crimes. The oft repeated Hannah Arendt's observation of Eichmann at his trial 'the banality of evil' is echoed by Ericksen that "the killers look very like us, but were given a licence to kill by their churches and universities, as both institutions endorsed the Nazi regime. Shortly after 1945, the terms Nazi and German were mutually exclusive: The Nazis committed crimes, and the Germans could not stop them. This was an early defensive ploy, which was later corrected by the shameful reality that "Nazis were Germans".

George Steiner expressed it succinctly in 'My unwritten books' (2008): "Twentieth-century barbarism burst from within the heartland of European civilisation. And when barbarism challenged, the humanities, the arts, much of philosophic inquiry, proved impotent. There was many a lover of fine arts and classical music among the butchers, many a teacher of great literature among the sycophants."

VII. THE ENABLING TRIGGER OF GENOCIDE

Once the infra-structure was in place and the population was pre-conditioned by the four enabling institutions of religion, academia, law, and the trusted medical guardians of life and death, a powerful trigger was required to set off the complex enabling act of genocide. The trigger was the prevailing condition after the First World War. The shock of losing the war, with hardly a family not having lost a loved one, the Versailles Treaty with its heavy reparations, global depression, unemployment, economic hardship, political dissatisfaction with the Weimar regime, and distrust of the imposed untried democracy, were all contributing to the crisis. The people called for strong traditional German leadership and the need to vent one's anger on a well tried historical scapegoat. The uneducated, deprived, dissatisfied, unemployed, and misled people took over, let loose their frustrations onto a target of hatred that their elders have approved.

Hitler, the half-educated, failed artist, charismatic demagogue, and his acolytes assumed power of dictatorship. The categorical evil and shame are the only lasting memories of the 'Thousand Year Reich', threatening to destroy the well-deserved admiration for the classical Weimar culture of Goethe and Schiller. Aarne Sürala, concluded after he visited the death camps that "Auschwitz has a message that must be heard: it reveals an illness operative not on the margins of our civilisation but at the heart of it, in the very best we have inherited. The Holocaust challenges the foundations of Western Society." Does it also question the fulfilments of two thousand year ideals of Christianity and almost two centuries of the Enlightenment? The crooked cross and sword of Genocide is depicted in Fig. 4.

'The Heavenly Way to Mercy Killing'
(Die Himmelfahrtstrase auf Gnadetod)
The Crooked Cross and Sword of Genocide

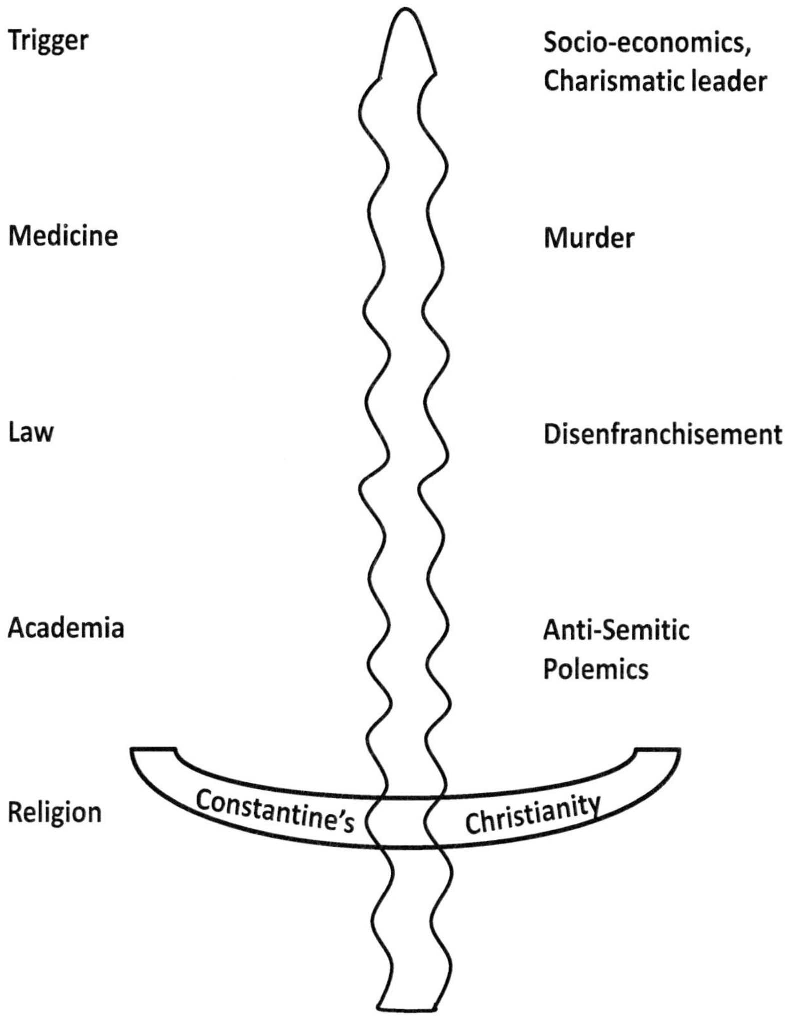

CHAPTER 10: THE CATHOLIC AND PROTESTANT CHURCHES AND THE HOLOCAUST

I. **The Catholic Church and the Holocaust**
II. **The Lutheran Church and the Holocaust**
III. **Christianity during the National Socialist Period**
IV. **Was Nazism an anti-Christian ideology?**
V. **Case histories of four anti-Nazi theologians**
VI. **Jewish responses to the Holocaust**
VII. **Anti-Semitism**
VIII. **Evolutionary God**

THE CATHOLIC AND PROTESTANT CHURCHES AND THE HOLOCAUST

‘Hitler had almost as little fondness for Nietzsche as he had for Rosenberg’s ‘ersatz’ religion. Hitler derided paganism and the rubbish they dredge up from German pre-history! Then they read Nietzsche with fifteen-year old boys’

Richard Steigmann-Gall, 2003

‘The first anti-Semite for Hitler was Jesus but for Hans Schemm it was Luther, for others it was Paul, the writers of the four gospels and/or the Christian Fathers’

Author

‘Hence today I believe that I am acting in accordance with the will of the Almighty Creator:
By defending myself against the Jew, I am fighting for the work of the Lord’

Hitler in ‘Mein Kampf’, 1925

‘A European, even if he is an atheist is still a prisoner of an ethic and mentality which are deeply rooted in the Christian tradition’

Fernand Braudel in ‘A history of Civilisation, 1993

‘It is not the survivors only who should feel an unutterable pain when the word Auschwitz is mentioned, but the ‘innocent bystander’ who lived in the Third Reich in comfort unmoved by the infamous place of death’

Paraphrased from Philip Morrison, (1915-2005)

I. THE CATHOLIC CHURCH AND THE HOLOCAUST

Christianity arose from Judaism and the split inevitably engendered considerable animosity between them. Paul and the Gospel writers showed increasingly greater anti-Jewish polemic, which was embedded in the New Testament. The age-old anti-Jewish preaching from the pulpit, making the Jews responsible for killing Jesus, portrayal of Jews in visual art and literature as evil people, devoid of morality and reason, resulted in their being dubbed as anti-Christ. They were denied loss of basic civil rights, freedom, and liberty over the centuries, which had a profound effect on institutionalizing the isolation, hatred, and persecution of the Jewish people. They served as the ultimate scapegoat of any catastrophe, whether caused by natural forces, such as the plague, or man-made such as lost wars, blood libels, or conspiracy theories to rule the world. In modern times, liberal ideas, communism, or capitalism have all been blamed on Jews. When they were barred from owning land and thereby unable to be farmers, and equally prohibited from joining professional guilds or crafts, there was little opening left to them to earn a living. They could, however act as money lenders, indeed were encouraged, as in early times Christians were not permitted to lend money. With time they became good at it which led to the Shylock stereotype in infinite guises, and again Jew the usurer became a hate figure. When however, the Medicis in Italy begun lending money, this was acceptable and approved by the Church.

At the time when Martin Luther preached anti-Catholic rhetoric, the Church denounced him and his followers as heretics and Jews, and for good measure, accused Jews as instigators of the Christian Reformation. The astonishingly crude language used by both sides during the schism of the Church by the Reformation, may throw some light on the more fundamental schism of followers of the Jewish Jesus from Judaism to Christianity. This might be significant in assuaging the anti-Jewish polemic especially in the Gospels of Matthew and John.

The lack of compliance by the Jews, indeed their rejection of Jesus as their King or Messiah, with the opprobrium of deicide was the trigger for the total split, leading to hatred, invectives, harassment and murder of Jews by the Christian rulers. The crusaders on route to Jerusalem to slay the Muslim infidel ruling over the Holy Land, found it propitious to rob and kill the Jewish unbelievers, especially in Mainz and the German Rhineland. The Spanish Inquisition was ordained by the devoutly Catholic King Philip

II and Isabella in 1484, strongly supported by the papacy. The King declared in 1536 that "all the heresies which have occurred in Germany and France have been sown by descendants of Jews, as we have seen and still see daily in Spain" (quoted by Goldhagen). The Jews were given the option of conversion or expulsion from Spain and many were murdered.

In a remarkable draft encyclical written by Pope Pius XI, *'Humani Generis Unitas'*, the Church defended the persecuted Jews, condemned the Nazi regime's anti-Jewish persecution, and called for it to be halted. However, it appears to have been suppressed by the Vatican hierarchy and the succeeding Pope Pius XII began his papacy by burying this remarkable document in defence of the Jews, now known as the Hidden Encyclical, in the 'silence of archives'. The fact that the Vatican tried for half a century to hide Pius XII's act of suppression and the encyclical itself, says a great deal about Pius XII, and about the Vatican of that time that dealt with the Holocaust.

The controversy following Pacelli's Concordat between Nazi Germany and the Vatican was signed in 1933. Pacelli, later Pope Pius XII, argued that the agreement saved the Catholic Church in Germany, whilst others felt that it gave a free hand to Hitler's racial activities, denying the right of German Catholics to oppose any measures promoted by the regime. Despite many appeals to the Pope, with evidence of oppression and mass murder of the Jewish people in Europe, the Pope considered it political not to intervene on their behalf. The evidence of the Danish and Norwegian Lutheran Churches, which sent letters of protest to the German or national authorities in 1942 before the impending deportation of the Jewish populations, failed to elicit adverse action against the Churches, which was given as the main reason for the Vatican not to oppose formally the odious activities of the Nazis. Later, the Pope or Vatican wrote the encyclical 'With Burning Concern' (Mit Brennender Sorge) which objected to the violations of the Concordat, but did not mention either the Jews or Nazism by name.

The culpability of Pope Pius XII and the Catholic Church in the 'Final Solution' has been studied by the Roman Catholic historian John Cornwell of Jesus College, Cambridge. He felt honour-bound to investigate the accusation against Pius XII that he failed to oppose the ungodly activities of Nazi Germany against the Jews. Cornwell wrote in his preface to 'Hitler's Pope', "I was convinced that if his true story were told, Pius XII's pontificate would be vindicated [...] I applied for access to crucial material in Rome, reassuring those who had charge of the appropriate archives that I was on the side of my subject. Acting in good faith, two key archivists gave me generous access to unseen material: depositions under oath. And also documents in the office of the Vatican Secretariat of State. I started to draw together, critically, the huge circuit of scholarship relating to Pacelli's activities during the 1920s and 1930s in Germany.

By the middle of 1997, nearing the end of my research, I found myself in a state I can only describe as moral shock. My research told the story of a bid for unprecedented papal power that by 1933 had drawn the Catholic Church into complicity with the darkest forces of the era. I found evidence, moreover, that from an early stage in his career Pacelli betrayed an undeniable antipathy towards the Jews, and that his diplomacy in Germany in the 1930s had resulted in the betrayal of Catholic political associations that might have challenged Hitler's regime and thwarted the Final Solution. His is not a portrait of evil but of fatal moral dislocation – a separation of authority from Christian love. The consequences of that rupture were collusion with tyranny and, ultimately violence".

The direct involvement of the Catholic Church in the Holocaust is clearly seen in the State of Slovakia, which was headed by Monsignor Jozef Tiso, the President and the devout Catholic Prime Minister Vojtech Tuka. They instigated, in 1942, deportation of Jews to their deaths in concentration camps in Poland. Father Tiso preached in a mass that expelling the Jews was a Christian act, because Slovakia had to rid itself of its pests. Indeed, the Slovak bishops collectively issued in 1942 a pastoral letter justifying the deportation of the Jews as Christ-killers. However, by 1943 when the war looked less promising for the Nazis, they issued a pastoral letter against deportation, by which time three quarters of Slovak Jews were deported to their death. In Croatia, many Catholic priests themselves took part in mass murder, as well as being commanders of the death camps.

II. THE LUTHERAN CHURCH AND THE HOLOCAUST

'Our Protestant Churches have greeted the turning point of 1933 as a gift and miracle of God'

Paul Althaus, Protestant theologian, 1933

'The hierarchy of Rome was 'Jewish-clerical Christianity'; Luther's belief in the Hebrew Old Testament was an attempt in the last 500 years 'to spiritually make us Jews'

Alfred Rosenberg on the Catholic and Lutheran Churches according to Steigmann-Gall, 2003

A resumé of Martin Luther and the Reformation has been presented in the chapter on Thuringia, dividing his attitude towards the Jews into two periods. In the early period before 1537, he speaks highly of Jews, as a people having been chosen by God to transmit his message to the world. He says "the Jews are the best blood on earth" (Luther, l.c. xxv.409); "through them alone the Holy Ghost wished to give all books of Holy Scripture to the world; they are the children and we are the guests and the strangers; indeed we should be satisfied to be the dogs that eat the crumbs which fall from the master's table" (xxv.260). He was compassionate to their misery and enthusiastic for their conversion to Christianity. Luther published an entire pamphlet in 1543 'That Jesus was born a Jew.

Luther expected general conversion of Jews to Christianity and when this did not happen, he became incensed at the Jews for their refusal to become Christians. He pursued until his dying day, an emotional, crude, anti-Jewish polemic published in 1541, in a book entitled 'On the Jews and their lies'. He advocated, according to Alice L. Eckardt, "confiscation of rabbinical texts, to forbid the rabbis to teach, and burn down synagogues along with Jews' homes, so that Judaism's falsehood could no longer be taught. If these actions caused Christians to fear Jewish retribution, all Jews should be driven out of the country 'for all time'. He perceived Jews as evil 'lords of the world' and thus the most dangerous foes."

It seems that history had repeated itself after fifteen centuries, as in the original schism between Judaism and nascent Christianity. Luther's overtures to the Jews, castigating former crude attempts by the Catholics to follow their doctrine had failed. The end result was Luther's outspoken hatred against them in a language threatening Jewish existence, reminiscent of that used first by Paul in his epistle to the Galatians in total contradiction to The Acts and the epistle to the Romans. Abject hatred and threatened extermination of the Jews was voiced later by the early Christian theologians, such as Origen, Tertullian, Chrysostom, and Anselm. However, Augustine opposed killing Jews, arguing that they should be allowed to live under restricted conditions, so as to serve as witnesses to Christ.

Although the brutal, vindictive language reflects the uncompromising conviction exclusively in the light of their religious belief, this needs to be considered within the context of the middle ages. Religion, mysticism, and superstition prevailed, one manifestation of which was belief in supernatural spirits residing in witches. The pope and clergy seemed to have propagated the notion that evil, natural disasters, and other bad events not open to reasoned explanation or ascribed to God was blamed on witchcraft. This was practised usually by women, acting as intermediaries of the devil. They were thought to cast spells and observe rituals at night or the Sabbath. The solution to prevent spread of evil was simply to get rid of the witches. They were deemed to have sex with the devil on their Sabbath, with lurid notions of the size and nature of his penis. The accusation of witchcraft was brought against political enemies by Pope John XXII who had a French bishop burned at the stake. It was easy to bring a charge of witchcraft against individuals and communities entirely for religious or political transgressions. Thus, in the early 14th century, the Templars were accused of child murder, sodomy, and other trumped up charges, with financial implications, and they were exterminated. The Catholic Church used witches as useful scapegoats for all ills in the world and they were publicly burned. At the forefront of the Inquisition were the Dominicans Heinrich Kramer and Jacob Sprenger, who convinced Pope Innocent VIII of the serious threat to the Church and Civilization by witchcraft, and so obtained almost unlimited powers from him.

Sprenger was alleged to have burned over 500 witches in a single year, towards the end of the 15th century. A woman accused of witchcraft had no legal representation and confession of guilt was extracted through torture of the poor women and ended in most cases by burning at the stake. Altogether, scapegoats were used for religious, political or personal reasons to eliminate ideological or political enemies, to gain financial advantage or from hatred of another human being. Whilst relativisation of evil activities is often practised by some historians, it is generally unhelpful as it alleviates or diminishes the opprobrium of the perpetrators of harm. The scandalous practice of senseless accusation of witchcraft mostly against innocent women and the awe-inspiring public amusement of burning them alive is a manifestation of how public or private individuals utilized scapegoats to further their selfish causes. The major distinction to be drawn, however, between the different scapegoats is that once witchcraft had run its course, up to the point when reason had defeated superstition, at least in Western societies the Church yielded to the force of enlightenment and education of the multitude. Indeed, it had gradually conceded long-held beliefs about nature to the irrepressible march of science. In contrast, the persistence of anti-Judaism has been unique, as the hostility finds new ways to maintain irrational old hatreds by mutation like a virus, changing its external recognition signature. In the 20th century anti-Judaism has mutated from religious to racial and recently to the Zionist mode.

III. CHRISTIANITY DURING THE NATIONAL SOCIALIST PERIOD

The overall involvement, culpability, and conception of Christianity in the Nazi Third Reich has been subject of outstanding scholarship by the historian Steigmann-Gall, himself a Catholic. He argues against the conventional view that the Nazi movement was anti-Christian, let alone atheist. Within months of Hitler gaining power in 1933, through a democratic process by the German electorate, the 450th anniversary of Martin Luther's birth was due to be celebrated. The coincidence of the two events had not escaped the attention of the Nazi hierarchy. The two events were celebrated, for instance, in East Prussia by the Lutheran Bishop Friedrich Kassel and the Gauleiter Erich Koch who was the president of the provincial Protestant Church Synod, and member of the NSDP. In his speech, Koch drew the two propitious events together, implying that the Nazi seizure of power was an act of divine will and compared explicitly Hitler's and Luther's struggle for recognition and that the Nazis fought with Luther's spirit. Unsurprisingly, Koch, the devout Christian, later proved to be the most ruthless Reich Commissar of Ukraine, taking a leading role in the brutal murder of thousands of Jewish families and partisans.

The early Nazi ideology was preached by Dietrich Eckart (1868-1923), a Catholic journalist by training, as well as a writer and a poet. He was the young Hitler's first mentor and may have reinforced Hitler's prejudices, as he hated Jews and Marxists, whom he blamed for Germany's defeat in World War One. Eckart introduced Hitler to the Munich society and taught him social graces. In his book, 'Bolshevism from Moses to Lenin', Eckart shared with Hitler the belief that "Jews represented the occult power of revolutionary subversion throughout history and were responsible for deflecting man from his natural path … [Furthermore, he argued that] the struggle against the Jews was ontologically bound with the struggle for Christianity". Eckart was an alcoholic and morphine addict and died at the age of fifty-five.

Goebbels, writing even before 1933, presented the consistent Nazi ideology that "money is the power of evil and the Jew its servant. The Jew has his fateful mission to once more dominate the sick Aryan race The eternal quality of the struggle was intimately connected with God and Hitler as 'an instrument of divine will' shaped by history Nothing exists outside God". Goebbels, the most radical mouthpiece of Hitler and his cohort does not speak as an opponent of Christianity, though it could be argued that he is playing up to the largely god-loving German people. An influential number of Lutherans considered Jesus a model anti-Semite, contradicting the undeniable historical fact of Jesus being a Jew and centuries of theological studies to demonstrate his lineage from King David. Among these anti-historical revisionists was Dietrich Klagges, contributing to the Nazi education in his book 'Volk und Führer', declaring simple direct opposite meanings that appealed to Goebbels and the multitude: Creation-Destruction, Good – Evil, God – Satan, Redemption – Annihilation.

This resonated with Walter Buch, president of the party's Supreme Court (and Bormann's father in law), who emphasized the significance of Christ and Christianity to Nazism. Buch, unlike Eckart and Goebbels, was a Lutheran as was Hans Schemm, the head of the National Socialist Teacher's league, both of whom followed the teachings of Luther as the 'first anti-Semite'. Buch often quoted Luther's words 'The intellect is the Devil's whore'. Schemm considered Nazism as a religious revival movement with his slogan "Our religion is Christ, our politics Fatherland". According to Steigmann-Gall, Hitler's 'Mein Kampf' gave "no indication of his being an atheist or agnostic or of believing in only a remote, rationalist divinity. Indeed, he referred continually to a providential, active deity: "What we must fight for is to safeguard the existence and reproduction of our race. So that our people may mature for the fulfilment of the mission allotted it by the creator of the universe". Though elsewhere in 'Mein Kampf', Hitler intones more than a naturalist pantheism devoid of Christian content. Again, it was in the question of race and race purity in which Hitler most frequently intoned such a God: It was, in his view, the duty of Germans "to put an end to the constant and continuous original sin of racial poisoning, and to give the Almighty Creator beings such as He himself created."

In his earlier writings, Hitler concluded that the Bible had to be 'purified' of the Old Testament in line with Eckart's and others' views because of its origin in Judaism; not only Germany, but also the Bible must be made 'Judenfrei' (free of Jews). For Hitler, Jesus was not just one archetype among others, but "our greatest Aryan leader. The original anti-Semite". In this respect, the Nazis failed to follow their dear leader, as Hitler stated that the first anti-Semite was Jesus, whilst among many Lutherans, Hans Schemm claimed Luther as the first anti-Semite. However, to make Jesus into an anti-Semite is a contradiction, though he would have to be a self-hating Jew, which may have struck a common cord with Hitler who was himself concerned with his alleged Jewish ancestry. Could this be

Freudian wishful thinking, especially as Nazis in their adulation of the God-sent Führer, considered him as the Messiah?

Hitler maintained that the movement's goal was to "translate the ideals of Christ into deeds and complete the work which Christ begun and could not finish". On another occasion, Hitler proclaimed, "we are the first to exhume these teachings! Through us alone, and not until now, do these teachings celebrate their resurrection!" Hitler was not anti-Christian, let alone an atheist. He demonstrates that many participants in the Nazi movement felt a personal attachment to Christianity, and claimed that their ideology of anti-Semitism, anti-Marxism, and anti-liberalism was inspired by Christian values. In 'Mein Kampf', Hitler claims to pursue the messianic missions. "Hence today I believe that I am acting in accordance with the will of the Almighty Creator: by defending myself against the Jew, I am fighting for the work of the Lord." Even the 'Hitler Oath' calls upon God: "I swear by God this holy oath that I want to offer unconditional obedience to the Führer of the German Reich and people." Steigmann-Gall's examination centres on the concept of 'positive Christianity' a religion espoused by many members of the party leadership. He also explores the struggle that 'positive Christians' waged with the party's paganists – those who rejected Christianity as foreign and corrupting – and demonstrates that this was a conflict not just over religion, but over the very meaning of Nazi ideology itself. It is the first comparative analysis of the religious beliefs of leading Nazis and a timely reminder of the intimate relation between Liberal Protestantism and National Socialism.

Erich Ludendorff with Paul Hindenburg were two famous military leaders who won some of the great victories in the 1st World War. Ludendorff may have also been the earliest pagan among the Nazis. Ironically, he was one of the leading military men responsible for Germany's surrender and would then lead the promotion of the 'stab in the back' legend, a fiction which largely attributed the defeat to the Jews. His anti-Christian pagan ideology was expressed in the 'Blood and Soil' slogan. Despite General Ludendorff's enormous military prestige poised against the undistinguished and largely obscure corporal, Hitler succeeded in expelling Ludendorff from the National Socialist Party. This surprising coup by the corporal in the late 1920s, must have been forgotten when it came to 1933 by the aristocratic, haughty von Papen and his upper class industrial associates who thought they could control the Austrian upstart and advised Hindenburg to appoint Hitler as Chancellor. A colossal error of judgment by the aristocratic ruling class that was never acknowledged by them and thankfully they were not given another chance to rule Germany.

Alfred Rosenberg (1893-1946) was born in Estonia, though his parents were ‘Volksdeutsche’. He joined the Nazi party and his main activity was to write in the Nazi newspapers and books against Judaism, Bolshevism, and Freemasonry that were apparently threatening Germany. He became the leading pagan theorist of the Nazi movement, but it is doubtful if he was taken seriously by the Nazis. His most important book was ‘The Myth of the Twentieth Century’, which Hitler allegedly referred to as ‘stuff nobody can understand’, written by a ‘narrow minded Baltic German’. There is an obvious irony in the Austrian German dismissing a Baltic German, the two leading ‘German Germans’ into an abyss for which history has expressed its verdict (‘Urteil’). Rosenberg was rewriting even Church history, denying Jesus’s Jewishness and transforming him into a ‘slim, tall and blond’ man, in contrast to the Jewish stereotype or for that matter the physical attributes of Goebbels, Himmler, Hitler, and the rest of his inner circle (with the exception of Heydrich). Dinter similarly considered Jesus a ‘perfect Aryan’, as were the apostles except for Judas.

According to Steigmann-Gall, Rosenberg’s engagement with Catholicism was almost as close as Judaism, defining the Catholic priesthood as ‘a racially defiled mixture of Etrusev-Syro-Near Eastern Jews’ and the hierarchy of Rome as ‘Jewish-clerical Christianity’. In contrast, Luther was ‘the greatest forerunner of German nationalism, racial purity and spiritual independence.’ These views came straight from Houston Chamberlain’s books, who declared Luther ‘the greatest man in world history’, though Rosenberg admonished Luther for his belief in the Hebrew Old Testament. It was an attempt in the last 1500 years ‘to spiritually make us Jews’, and he approved the Gospels of John and Mark. Rosenberg formally left the Protestant Church in 1933.

Steigmann-Gall states that “Hitler had almost as little fondness for Nietzsche as he had for Rosenberg’s ‘ersatz religion’. Hitler derided paganists and ‘the rubbish they dredge up from German pre-history! Then they read Nietzsche with fifteen-year-old boys.” Hitler’s mentor, Dietrich Eckart, had rejected Nietzsche as early as 1917: “We Germans, who profess through and through our faith in the Christian worldview, reject this despiser of our religious foundations.”

Himmler was brought up strictly as a Catholic and in 1919, he wrote in his diary “Come what may, I shall always love God, shall pray to Him, and shall remain faithful to the Catholic Church and shall defend it even if I should be expelled from it. At that time he took great pleasure in attending church: confession and communion were important to him." When he joined the NSDAP and took part in Hitler's failed putsch, he was still attending church, though his attitude towards Catholicism began to change. His diary entries of 1923-4 criticized books on Catholicism that he read as 'too doctrinaire' or 'fanatical.' Himmler had not yet abandoned Christianity. He attacked the anti-Christian tone of a book on scientific theory by Ernst Haeckel: 'the section that concerns his suppositions and attack on, and denial of, a personal God, is just terrible.' Himmler also read Ernest Renan's 'Life of Jesus' and enjoyed it, save for one major flaw: 'Renan believed that Jesus was a Jew, and he is from all appearances a friend of the Jews.' However, Himmler the Catholic began to have high regard for Protestantism and accepted 'without comment völkisch arguments identifying Protestantism with Germandom and reserved his wrath for Catholics."

Wilhelm Frick, a member of the Protestant Church, was an active NSDAP supporter from the time of the Munich putsch. As the appointed Reich Interior Minister, he stated that the National Socialist state is prepared to work with the Christian Churches, as long as the churches are bound to the Volk and do not oppose the state. Bernhard Rust, a gauleiter and Reich Education Minister after 1933 argued in favour of unifying the Protestant and Catholic Churches with the Volk to create 'Practical Christianity'. Support for the Nazi regime came from several religious sources. The Lutheran Bishop of Mecklenburg voiced his support for the Nazi regime, before and after Hitler gained power. Paul Althaus, the theologian, proclaimed "Our Protestant Churches have greeted the turning point of 1933 as a gift and miracle of God." The newly created Reich Church was headed by Reich Bishop Ludwig Müller, a member of the German Church, despite significant opposition by a rival candidate. However, the conflict within the Protestant Church continued, especially when the synod voted for the application of the Aryan Paragraph in the Protestant Church (the new law that all civil servants and their spouses must be 'free of Jewish blood'). Ironically, Jesus, Paul, and most of the apostles would have been dismissed from the Church.

Hitler encouraged the Protestant Church to become the established church on his conditions of cooperating with National Socialism, but without success. There was a great deal of disagreement between the different factions of the Church and even here 'the Jews were behind the Church struggle' according to the Ministerpresidänt of Saxony. "There is no empirical evidence to support the claim that the Nazis tried gradually to extinguish the Protestant Church in Germany or that they secretly held off a final showdown until they were secure in their control of the state... The creation of a Reich ministry with the sole purpose of ending the Church struggle cannot be taken as an anti-Christian act. Had the Nazis wanted to destroy Christian institutions, they would have handed control of the Reich Church Ministry to a paganist or not created such a ministry at all. Only when Hitler gave up on the Reich Church did he give up on institutional Protestantism once and for all. This was the most important watershed for relations between the Protestant establishment and the Nazi State."

Herman Göring stated in 1935, "When I hear that a 'Germanic wedding' is to be celebrated, I have to ask: my God, what do you understand to be a Germanic wedding? What do you understand to be National Socialism?" He upheld positive Christianity and disdained people who overstated their 'blood and soil' connection or those of Wotan and Thor. That year, in 1935, Goering married his second wife in a Lutheran church officiated by the Reich Bishop Müller and subsequently baptised his daughter in a Lutheran church.

Baron Otto Gustav von Wächter was an Austrian lawyer who joined the SA in 1923 and the Austrian Nazi Party in 1930. Wächter defended indicted members of the Nazi party and was instrumental in organising the failed 'putsch' in 1934. He fled to Germany and joined the SS. It is remarkable that the membership of the Austrian Nazi Party was at that time higher than that of the German party, when the population of Germany was about five times greater than that of Austria. The main issue, however is that Wächter was appointed Governor of Krakow (1939-1941), Governor of Galicia (Ukraine, 1942-1944) and established the Waffen-SS Division to fight the Russians. He finished his career with the honorary rank of SS Lieutenant General. Otto Wächter was from early to the last days of the Nazi movement an active and leading member complicit with murdering Polish academics and thousands of Jews. It is significant that in accord with other leading Nazis, he professed the Catholic faith. Indeed, his son Horst Wächter treasures a photograph of his father's pilgrimage to the 'Black Madonna of Czestochowa', as he stated during an open discussion between Horst, defending loyally his father and Niklas Frank who condemns outright his father's appalling atrocities. Niklas carries a picture of his dead father after he was hanged in Nüremberg, ostensibly to reassure himself that he is dead. As with many Nazis, the Roman Catholic Bishop of Austria, Dr. Alois Hudal, accommodated Otto Wächter in his 'Teutonic College of Santa Maria dell Anima' in Rome and arguably, Otto found his well-deserved domicile among the 'Anima'.

IV. WAS NAZISM AN ANTI-CHRISTIAN IDEOLOGY?

In 'The Holy Reich', Steigmann-Gall sets out to correct the misconception that Nazism was an anti-Christian movement. Personal ties, institutional links, and ideological common ground in Nationalism, Racism, and anti-Semitism connected Nazism and Christianity, and many members of the Nazi elite considered themselves to be devout Christians. Even those espousing Nazi or Pagan rhetoric were hardly able to overcome their parental religious and school upbringing. "The part of Christianity the paganist most opposed was specifically 'Roman.' The institutional arrogance they decried was specifically 'papal.' Lutheranism, in its intent if not in its implementation, was often cast as the antidote; in contrast to Catholicism, it was national, personal, spiritual. Protestantism's renewal would be contingent on a rejection of the Old Testament and much Christian dogma, but not on a rejection of Christ himself. These paganists upheld an image of Christ the fighter, Christ the anti-Semite." Perhaps the most telling fact was that Church membership remained very high throughout the Nazi era. Thus, in mid-1920s, the Protestant church membership decreased by approximately 200,000 and 50,000 a year joined the church. However, in 1933 the reverse happened, 50,000 a year left and 325,000 joined the church.

Protestant, unlike Catholic, women were attracted to Nazism by the cultural role of women at the centre of German family, the home, and motherhood. A surprisingly large proportion subscribed to the tenets of 'Schöpfungsglaube' (spiritual belief) and the dictum 'Kinder, Kirche, Küche' (Children, Church, Kitchen). Protestant women signed a petition opposing educational reforms that would offer girls the same education as boys. A number of Protestant women organizations actively supported Nazi legislation, as stated in the book by Claudia Koonz, 'Mothers in the Fatherland'. "A new morality, a new will for purity, healthy marriages and healthy families – together with physically, spiritually, and psychologically healthy children." According to Steinmann-Gall, "The members of the largest Protestant women's organization the Protestant Women's Auxiliary (Evangelische Frauenhilfe), were among Hitler's most avid supporters at the polls", and he quotes Michael Phayer, "Protestant women liked to view themselves as the precursors of the völkisch renewal under the National Socialists."

Altogether, the Nazis expressed similar ethical values and beliefs to those of the Protestants, constantly referring to Christian traditions. Catholics were in greater conflict with the Nazis, especially in protecting human life against euthanasia. Not one Protestant churchman voiced a public protest against euthanasia, unlike the famous denunciation from the pulpit in 1941 by the Catholic Bishop C. A. von Galen that at least decreased the number of German mentally and physically handicapped people killed. However, neither Catholics nor Protestants voiced their opposition to the disappearance of Jews from German life.

There was a pagan faction among the Nazi leadership with anti-Christian beliefs, of whom Rosenberg, Heydrich, Himmler, and Bormann, head of the Party Chancellery with ministerial rank, were the principal exponents, though Hitler, Goebbels, and Goering did not take this seriously. Opposition to clericalism was greater than that to Christianity itself, especially later during the war when the regime turned against the institutions of Christianity. "Hitler's professed hatred of Christianity was shot through with ambiguity and contradiction. Even as he accused Christianity of being Jewish and Bolshevik, at all times he carefully protected the Jew Jesus from his attacks. The enduring hope among leading Nazis for a Protestant Reich Church – when all other autonomous sources of power in German society were rapidly being suppressed or banned – demonstrates the Nazi leadership's desire to cooperate with a variety of institutional Christianity in the building of a new Germany."

Steigmann-Gall concludes that "Christianity, in the final analysis, did not constitute a barrier to Nazism. Quite the opposite: for many of the subjects of this study, the battles waged against Germany's enemies constituted a war in the name of Christianity. Nearly all Nazis surveyed here believed they were defending well by waging war against evil, fighting for God against the Devil, for German against Jew. They were convinced that their movement did not mean the death of God, but the preservation of God [...] Whereas past forms of Christian politics were known to embrace nationalism, anti-Semitism, anti-Marxism, or anti-liberalism, the Nazis took these ideologies to new levels. However, this did not make them un-Christian [...] If they rejected most of Christian dogma, they elevated past Christian figures as the intellectual forefathers of their new system."

Furthermore, Steigmann-Gall raises an important issue of transition from Christian religious to racial anti-Semitism. As the liberalisation of anti-Jewish laws in the 19th century led to Jewish emancipation and some conversion to Christianity, an explosive release of repressed artistic, intellectual, and entrepreneurial energy occurred in a people who had survived adverse conditions and pursued their theological learning as a sacred religious duty, practically in isolation over the best part of 2000 years. They excelled in medicine, law, economics, and banking, and were remarkably creative in music, literature, philosophy, and academia. It was astonishing to find Friedrich Gundolf, a German Jew, professor of Literature at the University of Heidelberg to be one of the most celebrated and knowledgeable exponents of Goethe. Even the liberal Protestants saw the 'foreign' people competing effectively with the more 'gemütlich' (relaxed) host population. But these 'upstarts' were Jews, they were different and the New Testament had amply characterised them at best to be undesirable people. Thus, a racialist anti-Semitism developed in the nationalist Protestant circles.

The Nazi paganist ideology based on Nordic legends, new faith in old idols based on Wotan mystic runes and others, was never really taken seriously. However, "Among paganists and Christians Luther was cast as a great national hero and religious reformer; as the first German, the first Protestant, and implicitly the first Nazi. Many party leaders demonstrated their belief that Christianity was deeply relevant to Nazi ideology. They did so in their private conversations, their writings, and their actions, both before 1933 and after." As Steigmann-Gall points, out German Nazism now serves as a way of differentiating good from evil in the world and is unlikely to disappear.

After the war it was almost a necessity to protect the Churches from the taint of Nazi pollution and a myth was created that Nazi ideology was anti-Christian. This was part of the response to the emerging menace of the atheist Russian Communist takeover of Eastern Europe that developed into the 'Cold War'. "Nearly all Western societies retain a sense of Christian identity to this day. Moral boundaries are still in some measure drawn by biblical stricture and other forms of Christian social ethic. That Nazism as the world-historical metaphor for human evil and wickedness should in some way have been related to Christianity can therefore be regarded by many only as unthinkable. Christianity is not just a theological system: it is also a byword for moral and upstanding behaviour of any kind. But men of God have been responsible for numerous acts of aggression and murder born of prejudice. The crusades, Inquisition, and Apartheid, to name only the most obvious historical episodes, are generally regarded as 'un-Christian' moments, even though it was piously Christian men who devised them and carried them through. Of course in a Christian society, the best way to attack intolerance of any kind, most particularly anti-Semitism, is to argue that it is anti-Christian. By detaching Christianity from the crimes of its adherents, we create a Christianity above history, a Christianity whose teachings need not ultimately be investigated." Steigmann-Gall's extensive studies are more than timely to redress the myth that Christianity is absolved from any guilt in the tragedy that happened in the midst of a Western European country based on Catholic and Protestant Christian values.

V. CASE HISTORIES OF FOUR ANTI-NAZI THEOLOGIANS

A small but highly significant group of Christian theologians who opposed the German National Socialist ideology stands out from the vast majority of their brethren, with high moral, ethical and religious standards. Karl Barth, Dietrich Bonhoeffer, Martin Niemöller, and Heinrich Grüber actively opposed the Nazi regime at great sacrifice to themselves. They had no direct connection with the Institute in Eisenach, and the theological establishment, and they were outstanding men of honour of the Church.

Karl Barth (1886-1968), the Swiss Reform theologian, is considered to be the most important thinker since Martin Luther. He was professor of theology in Göttingen, Münster, and then in Bonn. Barth was largely responsible for writing the 'Barmen Declaration' in 1934, which rejected the influence of Nazism on German Christianity and argued that the Church's allegiance to the God of Jesus Christ would give strength to resist the influence of other 'lords', such as the Führer Adolf Hitler. Indeed, Barth mailed this declaration to Hitler. Inevitably, he had to resign the professorship in Bonn for refusing to swear an oath to Hitler and returned to his native Basel where he was appointed to a chair in theology. After the war, he was instrumental in the Darmstadt Statement (1947) on German Guilt and Responsibility for the 3rd Reich and 2nd World War.

Dietrich Bonhoeffer (1906-1945) was a German Lutheran pastor of a distinguished middle-class family. He studied theology in Tübingen, Berlin, and New York. He gained the Doctorate in theology at the age of twenty-one and in 1931, became a lecturer in theology at the University of Berlin. When Hitler gained power in 1933, Bonhoeffer left for London and worked as a pastor for two years. However, he returned to Germany, joined the Confessional Church, which believed that Christianity was incompatible with National Socialism and its racial doctrine. He held the view that the Church has obligations towards the victims of every social system, even if they do not belong to the Christian community. Indeed, he helped Jews to escape from Germany, at great personal peril and was virtually the only voice of the Church resistance to the persecution of Jews. In 1933, a few days after Hitler gained power, Bonhoeffer, in a radio broadcast, warned Germany against slipping into an idolatrous cult of the 'Führer' who would turn out to be a 'Verführer' (misleader). He was an active member of the anti-Hitler resistance, joining his brother in law Hans von Dohnányi. However, the Gestapo became aware of his activities and by 1940 he was forbidden to speak, preach, or publish. In April 1943, he was arrested, charged, and imprisoned first in a military prison in Berlin and after the failed plot on Hitler's life in July 1944. When his connection with the conspirators was discovered, he was transferred to the Gestapo's high security prison. Early in 1945, he was moved to Buchenwald concentration camp and executed in Flossenburg by hanging on April 9th 1945, just two weeks before the US army liberated the camp. After the war, he became a martyr of the Church and exercised great influence on Protestant thinking in Europe and America.

Martin Niemöller (1892-1984), a decorated submarine Commander during the 1st World War, studied theology after the war and then worked as a pastor in Berlin. Initially, Niemöller welcomed the Nazi rise to power, sharing anti-communism and hatred for the Weimar Republic. However, as Hitler attempted to subordinate the Evangelical Church to State policy, Niemöller became disillusioned. In 1934, he took charge of the Confessional Church and with Dietrich Bonhoeffer, and Heinrich Grŭber began resistance to the Nazi-oriented German Christians. They established an organisation to help Jews threatened with imprisonment in concentration camps to emigrate. The Church attracted thousands of pastors and Niemöller preached sermons that enraged Hitler. He ordered his arrest in 1937, was tried and found guilty of subversive activities against the State, and received a short prison sentence. However, Hitler had him re-arrested and sent first to Sachsenhausen and then to Dachau, surviving seven years until liberated by the Allied forces in 1945. After the war, he was elected President of the Protestant Church in Hesse and Nassau and became an influential member of the Church and President of the World Council of Churches (1961-1968).

Heinrich Grŭber, a less known Protestant (1891-1975), opposed the Nazi regime and joined Martin Niemöller and Dietrich Bonhoeffer in the Confessional Church, to resist the racial policies. Grŭber was arrested by the Gestapo in 1940 and sent to the Sachsenhausen concentration camp and then transferred to that in Dachau, from where he was released in 1943. After the war, he became the Dean of St. Mary's Church in Berlin.

Each of these four outstanding truly Christian individuals left a legacy of high moral, ethical, and religious values, when the vast majority of their brothers in the Churches were either passive bystanders or collaborators of the odious regime. Their memorable pronouncements will or should withstand the vicissitudes of time, however their religious or cultural anti-Semitism represents the German sentiments of the time.

Nonetheless, Karl Barth - the defender of Jews in a sermon in 1933 denounced the Jews "as an obstinate and evil people" It is particularly revealing that he writes in a private letter that "In personal encounters with living Jews (even Jewish Christians) I have always, so long as I remember had to suppress a totally irrational aversion". This argues for an innate or cultural anti-Semitism imbibed from childhood onwards in his cultural, literary and environmental encounters. Dietrich Bonhoeffer, when preparing with leading Protestant theologians and university professors the 1943 'Freiburg Circle' document dealing with resistance to Hitler contained an appendix. This was called "Proposals for a solution to the Jewish problem in Germany". It stated that a post-Nazi state would be justified in taking steps "to ward off the calamitous influence of one race on the national community". It condemned the genocide, but stated that because the Nazis had killed so many Jews "The number of Jews surviving and returning to Germany will not be so large that they could still be regarded a danger to the German Nation. During the early years of Nazi rule, Martin Niemöller stated in a sermon to his flock, "We see a highly gifted people which produces idea after idea for the benefit of the world, but whatever it takes up becomes poisoned, and all that it ever reaps is contempt and hatred because ever and anon the world notices the deception and avenges itself in its own way". Despite this, he expressed a moral dilemma when responding to Nazi coercion in the memorable lines.

"First they came for the Jews and I did not speak out - because. I was not a Jew, then they came for the communists and I did not speak out – because I was not a communist, then they came for the trade unionists and I did not speak out- because I was not a trade unionist, then they came for me- and there was no one left to speak out for me."

Heinrich Grüber was eloquent in preaching collective guilt of German people for the crimes committed; 'Every German who glosses over his past is a potential criminal of to-morrow'. Despite his commitment to fight evil, he stated that "he was convinced that most of the Jews who had lived in Germany were rootless. They performed no productive labour, but did business (probably shady dealings). The Jews from 1919 until 1932 ruled Germany financially, economically, politically, culturally and journalistically. Whoever wants to contribute to the solution of the Jewish problem should collaborate with other people of good will in facilitating the emigration of Jews to countries where they are needed".

The destinies of these honourable men were:

- Karl Barth- Swiss theologian, had to leave Germany.

- Dietrich Bonhoeffer – murdered after imprisonment in Buchenwald concentration camp.
- Martin Niemöller – survived seven years in Sachsenhausen and Dachau concentration camps.
- Heinrich Grüber – survived two years in Sachsenhausen and Dachau concentration camps.

Analysis of these four brave and honourable men is important as it may shed light on anti-Semitism at large in Germany and elsewhere. It is very likely that the anti-Semitism was inculcated early in their life through the Church's teaching of the Gospels, especially 'John and Matthew', and the extra-judicial verdict of deicide against the Jewish leaders some 2000 years ago. These four individuals demonstrate the intellectual prowess and moral fortitude that enabled them to overcome their prejudice, to which they admitted. They were exceptional individuals and to expect the general population to act in a similar way would be unrealistic. However, they teach us a critical lesson that prejudice in general and anti-Semitism in particular can be overcome. Here is a weak link in a chain that can be broken. This quartet of Godly people, three of whom shared Gestapo interrogations, concentration camps, and one of them the ultimate fate with God's chosen people, may hold the secret of solving the longest and most tragic hatred of the people with whom the God of Abraham sealed the Covenant. The search by humanity for redemption may not lie in the vast theological tracts, but in a critical analysis of what made these exceptional individuals act in a truly moral way. Whilst moral activity may be the product of the enlightenment combined with faith, there were few individuals imbued with the rationale of the enlightenment, but without a religious faith, who came forth to oppose publicly the radical evil. The individuals cited demonstrate true morality and religious faith, despite their systemic prejudice, a paradoxical phenomenon that deserves to be studied in depth.

VI. JEWISH RESPONSES TO THE HOLOCAUST

<table>
<tr><td>‘Nazis in the ‘Final Solution’ attempted to destroy the only witnesses to The God of History’

Eliezer Berkovits, 1966</td><td>‘To attribute the Holocaust to the sins committed by the Jewish people is blasphemous against the memory of the dead victims’

Lord Rabbi Sachs, 2002</td></tr>
<tr><td colspan="2">‘Nothing justifies Auschwitz and unlike when God finally revealed himself to Job, there is no such revelation in Auschwitz’

Elie Wiesel, the Shoah, 1986</td></tr>
<tr><td>‘You cannot reason someone out of something he has not been reasoned into’

Jonathan Swift, 1667-1745</td><td>‘If God exists how was Auschwitz possible, if God does not exist enlightened humanity is on trial’

The conundrum facing humanity – Author</td></tr>
</table>

A stunned silence of a paralysed religious establishment lasting two decades followed the full revelation of the ‘Hurban’ – a national Jewish tragedy. Inevitably, the traditional rabbis fell back on ample historical evidence to recycle the well-trodden grounds that God’s actions are incomprehensible to the finite human mind. Alternatively, Jews have sinned and the holocaust was their punishment. The mystery of God’s retribution using Hitler as he was going to use Haman a few millennia ago, is insulting to the morality that God has bestowed in the Mosaic Law and the human mind, freedom to reason. To separate one and a half million infants and children from four and a half million parents, grandparents, and families, to shoot, drown, burn and gas them by ostensibly ‘sin-free’ Gentiles is beyond everything that monotheism, enlightenment, and humanity stand for. In a memorable religious and humane statement, Rabbi Sacks admonished those rabbis who attributed the Holocaust to the sins committed by the Jewish people. "Rabbis Teitelbaum, Hartem and Rubenstein are significantly wrong, they have mistaken the nature of Jewish tradition and blasphemed against the memory of the dead – God forbid that we should add to their death that it was justified". This epitaph is fully deserved by those rabbis who desecrate the memory of all the innocent children and adults who have been subjected to the radical evil for the one reason only that they were born as Jews. The same children and their parents accused of having sinned are elsewhere referred to as 'martyrs' for having died for their belief in the one and only God – a paradox that defies reason.

A host of charismatic rabbis having a cohort of faithful followers sought redemption in penitence ('teshuva') and the coming of the Messiah. The prediction that the Messiah will come and alleviate all suffering is true, in terms argued by Karl Popper that 'every prediction is correct as long as it is not dated'. The prediction or hope in the coming of the Messiah has so far not materialised, and has demonstrated robust timelessness. It promises the ultimate redemption or release of humanity from suffering evil brought about by human primordial instincts that neither religion nor logic of the Greeks nor reason of the enlightenment has so far alleviated. Richard Rubenstein, a rabbi and theologian, concluded, 'There is no justice and there is no judge.'

This is the most challenging part to write for reasons that there are too many paradigms proposed, as the tragedy is unprecedented in the history of civilization. Steven Katz, director of Jewish studies at the University of Boston has compiled a scholarly account of theological arguments across the entire Jewish religious spectrum – from the ultra-orthodox to the reform views of leading rabbis and scholars. A brief outline will be presented, following Steven Katz's account and divided into (I) Biblical models and (II) Innovative and radical responses.

SIX BIBLICAL MODELS OF RESPONSES TO THE HOLOCAUST

THE BINDING OF ISAAC

('Akedah', Genesis 22:2). The biblical account of God's command to Abraham to sacrifice Isaac, the son he loves. Abraham, having total faith in God, is prepared to kill his son, but an angel intervenes, Isaac is spared, and Abraham's belief in God is vindicated. The victims of the Holocaust, as with previous Jewish tragedies, are interpreted as martyrs to God, who willingly sacrificed themselves and their loved ones in order to prove their faith in God. Thus, piety, not sin, is the basic factor accounting for the Holocaust. This classical biblical interpretation might apply to a few Godly individuals, but certainly is at best a post-hoc wishful thinking to sanctify the tragedy, to give it some meaning in the face of sheer hatred and brutality by a determined enemy, which unfortunately is the only demonstrable reality.

THE BOOK OF JOB

The comparison with the Holocaust is in Job being righteous, adhering to God's commands, pious and moral, lacking sinfulness, yet he is subjected to great suffering through death of his wife, children, and animals. Despite all the doubts engendered by the calamities thrown at him, his faithfulness to God remains steadfast and is eventually rewarded both materially and spiritually, though his innocent first wife and family seem to have been sacrificed on the altar of Job's faithfulness. The biblical parable of one individual and his family needs to be extrapolated to the six million innocent people killed in the Holocaust and to dismiss this astronomical figure in the life of a people on the basis of the 'principle' of the parable is difficult to sustain. Furthermore, Job is eventually rewarded by God with a 'double blessing', unlike the six million human beings, unless as suggested by some, the creation of the State of Israel is the reward. This quid pro quo does not strike one as a righteous ethical basis of God's action, from which one expects super-natural moral and ethical values. Of course the comparison of the suffering of Job, or the 'Binding of Isaac' with the Holocaust flies in the face of the view advocated by many orthodox and especially ultra-orthodox rabbis (such as E. Berkovits and Jacobovits) that the Holocaust has been the result of the sinfulness of the Jewish people.

THE 'SUFFERING SERVANT' (BOOK OF ISAIAH)

The righteous vicariously suffers and atones for the wicked and allays God's wrath and judgment. God suffers with his creation, so Israel, God's people must be long suffering. Supported by Hasidic rabbis, orthodox thinkers (E. Berkovits) and conservative thinkers (A. J. Heschel). A historical interpretation of the 'Suffering Servant' has been proposed by the German Reform Rabbi Ignaz Maybaum, as quoted by S. Katz "that it is a paradigm of Israel's history. First in the 'Servant of God' in *Isaiah*, then in the Jew Jesus, and now at Treblinka and Auschwitz. God uses the Jewish people to address the world and to save it: 'They died though innocent so that others might live.' The special God-given task, the 'mission' of Israel, is to foster and facilitate this relationship between God and the nations. It is they who must make God's message accessible in terms that the gentile nations will understand and respond to. Accordingly, modern Israel repeats collectively the single crucifixion of one Jew two millennia ago. The Golgotha of modern mankind is Auschwitz. The cross, the Roman gallows, was replaced by the gas chamber."

GOD HIDES HIS FACE

('Hester Panim' Deuteronomy Micah and Psalms).
God's absence from historical events of human sin; he turns away from the sinner, mankind is abandoned. This frequent absence of God when he is most needed has puzzled theologians, especially his apparent indifference in the struggle between good and evil. Modern theologians, including Martin Buber, Joseph Soloveitchik, and Eliezer Berkovits attempted to interpret his disappearances, so as to spare God from direct involvement in the evil; the Holocaust is men's 'inhumanity to men', and not Divine punishment for sins perpetrated by the Jewish people. Indeed, God apparently suffers with sinners, which contradicts the previous and the next point. A further doctrine under this rubric is 'The Burden of Human Freedom' which God has given to man and is now misused. However, God will ultimately triumph. 'His face will not hide forever', and the evidence is the creation of the State of Israel, following on the Holocaust. Of course it is open to conjecture if this explanation among others is true or was it the Balfour declaration about twenty years earlier and that the opportune time

had come for the war time allies to concede after unprecedented suffering a part of Palestine for a Jewish Homeland.

'BECAUSE OF OUR SINS WE ARE PUNISHED'

('Mipnei Chataeynu', Deuteronomy).
The traditional biblical view has been that a good moral and ethical life according to the teaching of the Torah brought forth blessings, whereas the reverse was sinful and brought retribution. This view has been held by a number of ultra-orthodox and Hasidic rabbis with emphasis on the modern life of Jews liberated from the ghettoes. Joel Teitelbaum (Satmar Rebbe) pronounced with total certainty, 'Sin is the cause of suffering'. For him and Rabbi Isaac Hutner Zionism precipitated the Holocaust, as the Jewish people broke their covenant with God that their exile should be ended by the coming of the Messiah and not hastened by their own efforts. For others of the right wing of the religious spectrum, the primary sin was Reform Judaism and assimilation, with echoes of Martin Luther denouncing the Catholic Church and the papal edict excommunicating him from the Christian Church. The onus of responsibility by this account of the Holocaust is on the victims or at least some of them. The victims are blamed for their own destruction and Hitler's cohort was presumably designated by God to execute the punishment. If this is God's justice as understood by the venerated rabbis, they are utterly wrong. As the Chief Rabbi of Britain Jonathan Sacks stated, they have blasphemed against the six million victims.

THE BURDEN OF HUMAN FREEDOM; THE FREE-WILL DEFENCE.

The Holocaust is the manifestation of man's inhumanity and the human freedom given by God has been misused for evil ends. Hence, man, not God, is responsible for the Holocaust. However, unlike in biblical times, such as the Exodus from Egypt when God intervened on behalf of his people, he refrained from interceding during the Holocaust. This narrative is pursued by E. Berkovits to defend traditional Jewish theology. Altogether, the free will argument makes better sense, especially when linked to the concept that God has completed his function sometime in the past and has left it to humans to obey his commands and blessings or carry out mutual destruction, at which they have shown remarkable ingenuity and increasing efficiency by misusing theology, science and culture, all driven largely by the human intellect.

MYSTERY AND SILENCE

The holocaust is beyond man's reason and silence surrounding the mystery is the response.

Rabbi Jonathan Sacks, in his lecture in Yad Vashem (1983) on 'The Holocaust in Jewish Theology', argued that Jews after the Holocaust are duty-bound to bear witness and meaning to the suffering. Indeed, the Covenantal duty would fail if we allow the Holocaust to be forgotten or conversely to dominate our lives. Furthermore, Sacks argues that 'the Holocaust is exempt from Divine Justice but was a deed of human injustice in exile – God had withdrawn His Providence (in biblical terms 'hiding of the face – Hester panim'). He quotes Eliezer Berkovits that the Nazis in the 'final solution' attempted to destroy the only witnesses to the God of History. The in-gathering of exiles after the Holocaust and the creation of the State of Israel testifies that God exists. "They walked through the valley of the shadow of death, the people of Israel lives' (Am Israel Chai)."

Rabbi Soloveitchik argued that there are two covenants, that of shared history and that of shared destiny. The shared history, of the biblical and rabbinical eras, and the sentence of death by virtue of being a Jew in the Holocaust are well authenticated but confound understanding. However, the covenant of shared destiny is open to hope and the coming of the Messiah, but if history teaches us anything, it is that the oldest persisting hatred and anti-Jewish prejudice is bound to re-assert itself under a new guise to result yet in another tragedy. High culture and low morality are by now unfortunately twins in arms between spiritual heights and base atavistic urges, that have bedevilled humanity since the time of Adam and Eve.

INNOVATIVE AND REFORM RESPONSES TO THE HOLOCAUST

Emil Fackenheim rejects any notion of sin. The attempt to exterminate Jewish people he interpreted by applying Buber's dialogue of revelation 'as the personal encounter of an I with the Eternal Thou (God)'. He postulates that God was in Auschwitz and he urges Jews not to hand Hitler the posthumous victory by fulfilling a sacred duty to survive, which he calls the 614th commandment (there are 613 commandments in Judaism).

Fackenheim urges to affirm the God of Sinai by denying Hitler's attempt at extermination. This concept denies the traditional repetitive response to sin of Jews who are human beings like the rest of humanity – no better no worse – but ostensibly chosen for a religious mission. If God was in Auschwitz, and we know that Hitler equates with Auschwitz, then God will have encountered Hitler. It would be less than helpful to pontificate on such an encounter, as Hitler won his war against the Jews by enforcing systematically the most draconian measures and after extreme suffering he exterminated the bulk of European Jewry. Some rabbis relish crumbs of comfort from the few that survived – at what price – and a revival in Judaism as if the Holocaust was just another Jewish tragedy in over 3000 years of its existence.

BROKEN COVENANT: A NEW AGE

Irving Greenberg argues that the obligation of the Covenant with Jews has been broken through the Holocaust and God's apparent non-interference in the slaughter of the innocent. He argues that the old era of the Jewish covenant has ended and a new era has begun. Greenberg presents three major periods of covenantal history of Israel. (1) The biblical era of the 1st Temple (586 BCE) when God was in command. (2) Destruction of the 2nd Temple by Rome in 70 CE, following which the sages argued that now Jews must take a greater role in the Covenant. (3) The Holocaust (1941-1945) has destroyed the Sinai Covenant and is now voluntary. Jews have continued to believe in the God of Israel, but the obligations of the religious commandments are open to interpretation.

REDEFINITION OF GOD – PROCESS THEOLOGY

Alfred North Whitehead and Charles Hartshorne have argued that the classical concept of the relationship between God and man needs to be redefined in order to construct a coherent theology. The existence of God is not questioned, but his attributes of omnipotence and omniscience are denied. This novel concept of 'process theology' has been further developed by the Jewish theologian Arthur A. Cohen in his 'The Tremendum: a theological Interpretation of the Holocaust'. He argues that the uniqueness of the Holocaust is devoid of any meaning. Cohen suggests that the catastrophe is incompatible with our belief in a beneficent and providential God, who is not an agent in human affairs but lets man use his or her free-will. This revised concept of God bypasses the fundamental question where was God during the Holocaust. Elie Wiesel argues that the Shoah resulted in a rupture of the relationship between the Jews and God. He states that 'nothing justifies Auschwitz', and unlike when God finally revealed himself to Job – there is no such revelation in Auschwitz. "Treblinka erases all justification and all answers." He expressed a need for new Jewish scholarship – a new Talmud.

GOD IS DEAD

The Jewish theologian, Richard Rubenstein, reached the conclusion, as have many others, that the only honest response to the absence of God in Auschwitz is that 'God is dead', that God is not concerned with human affairs. For Rubenstein, all theological interpretations are unconvincing when considering the catastrophe of the Holocaust – 'There is no God and no covenant with Israel.' However, Rubenstein argues that with the death of God, the existence of Israel as a community or people needs to be maintained. This is an extreme view, suggesting that the traditional history of Judaism should be denied but the entity of Jewry as a people or race actively maintained. The Jewish philosopher Emmanuel Levinas argues that the classical theologies that defend God and his justice 'despite the gas chambers' are untenable. Whilst he does not deny the existence of God, the major demand is the defence of the ethical obligation that humans owe to one another.

VII. ANTI-SEMITISM

Hatred of Jews has a long history, enormous literature, and failure to understand it, as it is not based on reason. This has been well expressed by Jonathan Swift in the eighteenth century "You cannot reason someone out of something he has not been reasoned into." The complexity of anti-Semitism is too great to go into here, but Sir Richard Evans described it succinctly "as a very peculiar pathology that recognises no national borders. It is a mental condition conducive to paranoia and impervious to truth. Its lexicon has no word for individuality. It is fixated on group identity. It is necessarily dehumanising when people become abstractions. Once an emotional stereotype has been created, an enduring poison distorts the perceptions of the victims."

Jews must have lived in Europe since the time of dispersion. In the Rhineland town of Worms in 1096, there must have been a substantial Jewish community, as eight hundred Jews were put to the sword and many chose suicide for themselves and their children rather than face to be butchered. Nonetheless, Jews went back, and by 1328, Worms had the most famous rabbinical school of Rashi. Sadly, the oldest and most famous German University of Heidelberg, established in 1306, was erected on the site of Jewish quarters, from which the Jews were evicted, and the University was partly financed from the proceeds of the expropriated Jewish property. Unlike other minorities like the Huguenots, the Jews were never integrated into the host societies, initially because of religious reasons. After the Enlightenment, the element of race was advanced by intellectuals, based on spurious arguments, the age-old prejudice, and the necessity of finding a scapegoat. Christian anti-Judaism turned into racial anti-Semitism.

The theological question where was God during the massacre of six million innocent human beings has been at the forefront of concern by some and silence by others. If God was with children, women, and men in Auschwitz, that is a blasphemy, if he was absent, that is also a blasphemy. The conundrum facing humanity: if God exists, how was Auschwitz possible, if God does not exist, enlightened humanity is on trial.

God must have accomplished his task of creating the universe, providing laws of ethics and morality, and giving free will to human reasoning. His abiding covenant with the Jewish people is their survival, as they bear the testimony of the existence of God; if they are exterminated then there is no God. These theological propositions by learned rabbis, finding prophetic pronouncements to fit the argument, carry little weight or comfort to counter Josef Mengele's quip that he replaced God as the judge of 'who shall live and who shall die'. The counter-intuitive proposition of Emil Fackenheim that the Shoah was not to be understood but was to be responded to by adding the 614th command of Jewish faith and its survival so as not to yield Hitler a posthumous victory. The force of the commandment is well understood but to relinquish the fundamental need to understand the Shoah begs the question, defies reason, and worse, lacks the wisdom for preventing future catastrophe. The very fact that there is not a single answer but a vast array of diverse contradictory interpretations, speculations, and dogmatic statements, based on the prior belief or non-belief of the individual, leads one to the conclusion that we have no compelling answer.

According to Berkovits, "The only meaning to be extracted from the Holocaust is that man is capable of limitless evil. The religious meaning of 6 million deaths is no more and no less than that they, as other Jews had done before them, died for the sanctification of God's name "Kiddush Hashem)". This is heartless, thoughtless, lacking any understanding of the sanctity of life, humanity, the mother-child visceral ties, or the father's helpless anguish. It is reminiscent of Heidegger's crass observation on death, ignoring that one and a half million children and 4.5 million young and old women and men suffered loss of dignity, homes, starvation, beating, deportations, separation, shootings, gassing, and burning in crematoria. One cannot believe that a just, merciful God requires, permits, or acts as an innocent bystander for the sanctification of His Name; "For evil to succeed it only takes good men to do nothing" (Edmond Burke 1796). This was the position adopted by the vast majority of 'Good Germans' and they were guilty for their uncaring attitude, lack of empathy, humanity and Hillel's and Jesus's admonition "Love your neighbour as yourself (Lev. 19:18). To wash one's hands of the greatest evil the world has ever seen is misappropriating the theology of God to that of Satan. To turn one's face, to shut one's eyes, to close one's mind to the greatest sin ever perpetrated systematically by a cultured people is evil in its own right by man or god and blasphemous of the entire concept of humanity and a just or even unjust world.

The Holocaust is the quintessential evil perpetrated by a post-enlightenment civilization manifested by religious, intellectual, legal, and medical intolerance against a defenceless minority, who declared over 4000 years ago the existence of one God, his laws and ethics and maintained their belief, without threatening the host country, despite constant harassment and persecution. The unsuccessful attempt to suppress Judaism is a supreme testimony of the validity of the Hebrew Bible and its age-old suffering people.

VIII. EVOLUTIONARY GOD

The Biblical God had been established in the Abrahamic religions of Jews, Christians, and Muslims. There is little doubt about the prime mover or the unique contribution that the Hebrew have made towards declaring a single God who created the universe. However, historical and archaeological investigation into the pre-biblical period suggests an evolutionary process from polytheism to monotheism. Initially, the existence of other gods was not denied in the belief of a single most powerful God. With time, all other Gods were banished in favour of the single God who would not tolerate any competition by lesser Gods. The Canaanite God Baal was widely admired for his earthly power and sexual prowess, attributes not emphasized with Yahweh, though procreation was of great significance to all. Gods of procreation, such as Aphrodite, were prayed to by women of antiquity. Abraham's wife Sarah was promised by Jehovah to produce a son at the unlikely age of 100, and she conceived Isaac.

However, even with firmly established Jehovah as the single deity by Judaism, followed by Christianity and later by Islam, the intolerance and struggles culminating in murder between the three religions, all believing ostensibly in the one and same God have been and continue to be the hallmark of monotheism. They deny or have lost a common language, reminiscent of the confusion in building the tower of Babel and they are blind and deaf to the predicament.

'Ehyeh Asher Ehyeh – I am who I am', alternative translation: 'I will be who I will be'

Were the words, which God told Moses to tell the Israelites if they questioned who sent him. God did not, indeed could not identify his being in words that would adequately express his existence. He leaves the interpretation of his words wide open and rather suggests to the questioner not to ask such naïve questions. Among a welter of possible interpretations, however there is the future tense 'I will be who (or what) I will be' that is open to God adapting to future circumstances or the evolution of God.

Indeed, there is some historical evidence for such a concept. God initially speaks directly to Noah, Abraham, Moses, Isaac, and Rebeka over a span of hundreds of years, though not identified in person. The progression from God speaking directly to pre-eminent biblical figures, is followed by divine intervention in freeing the Israelites from bondage and giving them the five books of Moses. In the next phase, God ceases direct communication and follows by indirect guidance, instructions, and admonitions by the prophets over hundreds of years. God then ceases to communicate directly or indirectly and there seems to be a dramatic change from revelation to interpretation by the sages who attempt to interpret both simple and complex issues in the biblical narrative, known as 'Midrash'. One may speculate that the reason might be that his work of the universe has been completed 'and He saw it was good'. However, according to Rabbi Akiva (2nd cent. CE), God deliberately left the world unfinished, so it could be completed by the work of human beings.

Men and women develop reason and exert free will. God established his identity, purpose, and eternal laws that humanity should follow. If these are not heeded or by their very nature cannot be fulfilled, despite all the pomp and ceremony of the established churches, people suffer and evil prevails. God becomes an abstract deity, all powerful and yet ceased to manifest his presence in ways readily understood by men and women. The robust evidence in favour of evolutionary forces and the descent of man might have been God's design or algorithm. According to Philo, first came the Word, Logos, and creation, within six biblical days, possibly interpreted as six chronological trilenia. God's manifestation of nature has been changing, on account of changes in climate, human development from the hunter-gatherer to domestication of animals and growing crops. Whilst God is immutable and the constant point of the universe, in the Aristotelean sense, is it nonetheless possible that God's attributes and manifestations may have adapted to the evolving dynamics of the universe.

The biblical evolutionary manifestations of God might be perceived in a survey of the multitude of names of God. Yahweh of the Old Testament is by far the most frequently used name of the God of Israel, the modern translation of which is 'Jehovah'. This name is attributed to have been given to Moses in a vision on Mount Horeb. In the Exodus, Yahweh gives assurance of his strength and love for the Israelites. Yahweh has been interpreted as the verb 'to be', meaning 'He is or He will be'. He is the living God and the future tense 'He will be' implies for all times and encompasses potential change as new circumstances arise. Elohim – is explained as majesty, excellence and greatness, commonly used, but the root-meaning of the word is unknown. Elohim is encountered more frequently in later writings and this may have been due to a broadening of the idea of God as the transcendent and universal Lord. Thus, the meaning or attributes of God has evolved significantly from the God of Israel to that of the universe. Elohim also describes God as the Creator of nature, and since nature has undergone evolutionary changes, God must be their architect. Yahweh and Elohim is often found especially in prophetic literature, and considered to be a common name. El – as a name of God appeared in many languages (Assyrian, Phoenician, Aramaic, Arabic, Ethiopian), in addition to Hebrew. El has been used mostly in poetry and usually attached to some attribute such as, 'God Almighty' (El Shaddai), 'living God' (El Hai). The Hebrew from which it may have been derived means 'to overpower' or 'overpowering in strength'. Does this imply survival of the strongest and potentially fittest? Adonai – a later name used for God. 'Zeba ot' (God of Hosts) is often used with Adonai. According to the Jewish Encyclopaedia, the Hebrew conception of the divine nature of God and the relation to his people varies with the circumstances, so that a new manifestation may elicit a new name.

The concept of an evolutionary God and his mission in accord with natural evolutionary forces might be compatible in a divine setting invoked in Charles Darwin. Natural evolution has been the driving force of every aspect of biological science and is being slowly accepted by increasing number of religious authorities. There is a progression from God speaking directly to biblical figures, to divine intervention in freeing the Israelites from Egyptian bondage and then by the 10 Commandments and the five books of Moses. In the next phase, God ceases direct communication and follows by indirect guidance, instructions and admonitions by the prophets, culminating in silence over almost two millennia. His creation has been accomplished and he will have engraved the algorithm of evolution of nature and all its living creatures. His unique work should be venerated and not usurped, fought over and destroyed. It is in that sense that Spinoza's controversial concept of equating God with Nature or his manifestations may be critical in studying God's creativity. Perhaps scientific investigations may be a form of religious study.

CHAPTER 11: PSYCHOLOGY OF LEADING NAZIS AND THEIR CHILDREN; COGNITIVE AND EMOTIONAL INTERACTIONS

PSYCHOLOGICAL MANIFESTATIONS OF LEADING NAZIS

<table>
<tr><td>"In group love, out group hate, and kindness to us, cruelty to them"

Belief by some psychologists</td><td>"Syndrome that dare not speak its name (SS-N)"

The coexistence of culture and barbarity; Author</td></tr>
<tr><td colspan="2">'You National Socialist doctors, I cannot do without you
for a single day, not a single hour...
if you fail me, then all is lost'.

Hitler's speech to the Physicians League in 1923</td></tr>
<tr><td colspan="2">'Healers became killers'

Professor Robert Jay Lifton, 1986</td></tr>
</table>

The mental state of National Socialist leaders has been the subject of a great deal of discussion and the only common thread is the narcissistic claim to racial purity and superiority of Nordic Germans. This is demonstrable nonsense, as even Ploetz rejected back in 1930 the concept of pure race. Presently, DNA studies have demonstrated the mixed origin of individuals tested, with 99.9% sharing common genes. There is the amusing case of a Scottish lady who claimed her pure Scottish pedigree, but when her DNA was tested showed African genes. Quite apart from the Nazi claims, all the physical characteristics, dwelt on by the Nazi scholars defining the Nordic type were in contradiction to the features of the prime claimants – Hitler, Himmler, Göring, Goebbels, and Rosenberg –. The only exception was Heydrich, the typical Nordic-looking German, yet mocked from early childhood, and whilst on service in the Navy nick-named 'Isi' for alleged Jewish ancestry. Indeed, Himmler created in 1935 an agency the

‘Ahnenerbe’ (ancestral heritage) to promote the study of the origins of the mystic ‘Aryan race’. Some of the leading Nazis may be classified into three putative disorders.

I. NAZI MANIFESTATIONS OF A NOVEL SOCIAL BIPOLAR DISORDER – 'SYNDROME THAT DARES NOT SPEAK ITS NAME' (SS-N)

The coexistence of primordial barbarism within a modern society that evolved over two millennia of Christianity, and over two centuries of Enlightenment, with culture and enormous strides in the sciences, calls for critical study. The National Socialist epoch is a replay of ontogeny of human development, not blunted by the duality of good and evil, ostensibly both pleasing and pleasurable to the individual and society. The Nazi period had demonstrated a novel social bipolar disorder, with manic barbarity at one end, and culture of the arts, science, music and education at the other end of the spectrum, termed, 'Syndrome that dares not Speak its Name' (SS-N; paraphrased after Oscar Wilde). Is this an evolutionary burden we all may carry and most people can control, or does it affect only some individuals and surfaces under some circumstances? The reversal of the modern cultured Western man or woman to a state of atavism and the coexistence of culture and barbarism that culminates in the SS-N may afflict some vulnerable individuals under the spell of a charismatic leader. SS-N should be distinguished from the psychiatric bipolar disease, manifested by periods of depression and mania. The short case histories of Philipp Lenard, Joseph Goebbels, Hans Frank, Reinhard Heydrich, Martin Heidegger, and Richard Wagner may illustrate some features of this syndrome.

Philipp Lenard (see p.144) had a Roman Catholic upbringing in Bratislava (Slovakia), part of the Austro-Hungarian Empire, and later studied in Budapest, Vienna and was an ardent Magyar nationalist. He gained his PhD in physics at the University of Heidelberg and then became an assistant to Heinrich Hertz, professor and director of Physics at the Institute of Physics in Bonn who discovered electro-magnetic waves (radio waves). Hertz also worked on cathode rays and advised Lenard to pursue this work, which Lenard, a brilliant experimental physicist, carried out and lead to the Nobel Prize in 1905. Lenard thanked Hertz profusely for all the help he received from his mentor. He was not a great theorist and acknowledged the help he also received interpreting the results from Albert Einstein and the mathematician, Professor Leo Königsberger. All three scientists who enabled and greatly assisted him to carry out the studies were of Jewish heritage and initially he thanked and largely acknowledged their help. Yet a few years later, Lenard expressed virulent hatred towards Jews, denigrating what he maliciously called 'Jewish physics'. By 1925, he displayed a notice outside his university office stating 'Entrance for Jews is forbidden'.

Lenard's irrational attack on 'Jewish Physics' could be interpreted as self-hatred for having to depend on the assistance of three Jewish scientists, people he must have been sensitised to hate during his youth as a Magyar nationalist, strongly associated with anti-Semitism. The coexistence of great science with rabid hatred for people for whom he first expressed high esteem and to whom he owes a great debt of gratitude, shows a dualism that fits the pattern of SS-N.

Joseph Goebbels (p.140) had a strong Roman Catholic upbringing, he completed the 'Abitur', and by all accounts, read classical literature and was enthusiastic about art and music. Goebbels studied literature and philosophy at the Universities of Bonn, Würzburg, and Freiburg, and gained the PhD in Heidelberg. Friedrich Gundolf, the foremost literary scholar during the Weimar Republic, was one of his mentors and his doctoral supervisor was Professor Max von Waldberg. One of his most devoted girlfriends was Else Janke, who supported him emotionally during frequent bouts of depression. All three individuals were Jews and here we have a man with a cultural background and accomplishments, and significant Jewish intellectual and emotional ties. Yet, he joined the Nazi party and emerged as the vilest Jew-baiter the world has ever seen, the spokesman for Hitler, Himmler, and the Nazi establishment, dehumanizing Jews and advocating their extermination. Goebbels shows clearly the duality of culture at one pole and barbarity at the other pole of SS-N.

Hans Frank also had a Roman Catholic upbringing and his father was a lawyer. Frank joined the army in 1917 at the age of seventeen and after demobilisation, he first joined 'Freikorps' and then in 1919, the predecessor to the NSDAP. He was one of the party's earliest members. Frank studied law and was granted the state examination in 1926. He became the personal legal adviser to Hitler, and later to the Nazi party. He was elected to the Reichstag in 1930, as Minister without Portfolio in 1934 and finally Governor General in occupied Poland the throughout the war. Undoubtedly, Frank was a capable lawyer, devoted to the arts, literature, and music, and was an accomplished chess player. He boasted and indeed was responsible for murdering two million Poles and one and a half million Jews. These dual manifestations are consistent with the criteria of SS-N.

Martin Heidegger (p.149) had a Roman Catholic upbringing and studied theology but then switched to philosophy at the University of Freiburg. He studied under Edmund Husserl, professor of philosophy, who was his mentor and completed his doctorate in 1914. Emil Lask, professor of philosophy at the University of Heidelberg, greatly influenced Heidegger's major concept of 'Being and Time'. Heidegger had a serious love affair with one of his PhD students, Hannah Arendt, who became a famous political philosopher. Both, Husserl and Emil Lask were Jewish, as was his lover Hannah Arendt and six of his twelve PhD students. Thus, both conceptually and emotionally, Heidegger was associated with Jews and despite this, he adopted and supported the Nazi ideology. He introduced the 'Führerprinzip' to the University of Tübingen and stated that 'The Führer alone is the present and future Germany and its law'. After the war, he showed abject insensitivity to the Holocaust and no admission of guilt, contrition, or apology for his Nazi links. Heidegger is an example of an exceptionally gifted philosopher, seemingly not burdened by close intellectual and emotional links with Jewish individuals and yet supporting an evil anti-Semitic ideology, consistent with the SS-N.

Having analysed some of the pertinent features of the Nobel laureate in Physics (Lenard), the master of propaganda and misinformation (Goebbels), a legal authority (Frank), and a highly celebrated philosopher (Heidegger), it is appropriate to complete the narrative with a renowned composer of music (Wagner), who died fifty years before Hitler gained power and was appropriated by the Nazis. Richard Wagner (1813-1883) was brought up as a Lutheran by his mother. Wagner's father was a clerk in the Leipzig police and died when his son was six months old. They lived in the Jewish quarter of Leipzig and his mother cohabited with the actor and playwright Ludwig Geyer, whom she probably married. The family moved to Geyer's home in Dresden, where Richard stayed until the age of fourteen and was known as Wilhelm Richard Geyer, the only father Richard had ever known. Geyer's attachment to the theatre and music was shared by Richard who wrote a play at the age of thirteen and then wanted to set it to music. He managed to get music lessons, and by the age of about fifteen, wrote his early piano sonatas. Wagner entered the University of Leipzig in 1831, at the age of eighteen, studying music composition, and he joined the Saxon student fraternity. Wagner composed a number of operas and became one of the world's most celebrated composers of operatic music.

Wagner's paternity has been subject to speculation, when he discovered letters from Geyer to his mother, raising the possibility that Geyer was his biological father and that Geyer was Jewish. According to Cosima's diaries, Wagner did not believe that Geyer was his real father, though she noted a resemblance between Wagner's son Siegfried and Geyer. Some of Wagner's biographers suggested that Wagner himself believed that Geyer was Jewish. Nietzsche was asked by Wagner to proof-read his autobiography, after which he believed that Wagner's father was Geyer and wrote a pun on Geyer and Adler, the latter being a common Jewish name. Despite the conjecture, there is no evidence that Geyer was Jewish.

There were a number of problematic sides to his character. He was an anti-Semite, both in his pronouncements and in writing a damaging essay on "Jewishness in Music". He was highly critical of Felix Mendelssohn and Giacomo Meyerbeer's music, and blamed them for his initial failures, despite Meyerbeer's support for Wagner's music; he even lent him money. Some experts believe that his operas depict adverse caricatures of Jews. Wagner's daughter married Houston Stewart Chamberlain, an avowed anti-Semite. Wagner enlarged his attack of alleged Jewish influence onto all German art, and advocated that Jews should convert to Christianity, though later that they should be annihilated. Despite his obsessive anti-Semitism, he liked the poet Heine and had long-lasting Jewish friends, notably Hermann Levi, an observant Jew and son of a rabbi. Levi conducted the premiere of Wagner's last opera – Parsifal. Wagner had a number of extra-marital affairs with married women and lived for years away from his wife. After she died, he married Cosima, the wife of the conductor Hans von Bülow. She was twenty-five years younger than Wagner and she bore him three pre-marital children.

Not surprisingly, Hitler adopted Wagner as the favourite composer of Nazi Germany. This handed a poisoned chalice to Wagner's standing, as he was associated with the creation of Nazi Germany. Bayreuth became a focus of German nationalists, endorsed by the violent anti-Semitism of his wife Cosima. After her death, the Festival was taken over by her English-born daughter Winifred, a personal friend of Hitler, following in her mother's footsteps.

The obvious question asked, is what made a brilliant musical composer such a vicious anti-Semite, which at the time was rife in Germany, grounded in traditional Christian demonization of Jews. When they were granted German citizenship, the Jews surprisingly took up the arts, professions, and businesses, and they proved remarkably astute and successful. An 'alien people' began to compete with the 'true Germans' and the contemporary society felt thwarted. Emerging nationalism was coupled with that of industrial capitalism, which was considered to be modernism advanced by Jews. According to Malte Fischer, the theatre and literary scholar, "Wagner had the feeling that the music business, in which he could not succeed, was in Jewish hands. But that, of course, was not true". He certainly resented the success of the Jewish composer Felix Mendelssohn and Giacomo Meyerbeer, both in music and economics during his early days when he was a failure on both counts. Wagner as a leading composer helped to carry anti-Semitism from the dirty bars to the middle class salons and to spread Jew-hatred among the cultured people, especially those admiring music, which was held in such a high regard in Germany.

Thus, we are confronted by a university graduate, brilliant composer, sharing with Hitler and Heydrich alleged Jewish ancestry, although without real evidence, yet he was caricatured for his apparent Jewish features. Even Queen Victoria, after Wagner was presented to her, remarked that he was small and had a crooked nose. He must have resented the 'stigma' and sublimated this into virulent anti-Semitism. Wagner was a musical genius coupled with intense hatred of Jews consistent with SS-N.

The five diverse individuals discussed share in common a Catholic background, university education with doctorates from Heidelberg, Freiburg, or Leipzig University, some with Jewish mentors and conceptual links, two of them having serious emotional involvement with Jewish women. Four of them became ardent Nazi followers, they appropriated Wagner into the Nazi fold, and share the manifestations of SS-N.

II. ANXIETY OVER ALLEGED JEWISH BLOOD, POTENTIALLY LINKED WITH SELF-HATRED AND ANTI-JEWISH ATTITUDE

Adolf Hitler's name and family is shrouded in mystery. His father Alois Schicklgruber (1837-1903) was the illegitimate child of Maria Anna Schicklgruber (Hitler's grandmother), whose name was recorded in the baptismal register, as the name of Alois's father was not known. However, in 1842, Johann Georg Hiedler married Anna when Alois was five years old. By the age of ten, Alois's mother died, and when he was nineteen, his stepfather died; Alois was then looked after by Hiedler's brother. It was only much later by the age of thirty-nine that Alois was legitimised and the baptismal register changed from Schicklgruber to Hitler, also spelled Hiedler or Hütter (German for hut or shepherd) or from the Slavic work 'Hidlar'. Hans Frank claimed at the Nuremberg trial 'that there were letters stating that Hitler's grandmother Anna Schicklgruber whilst working as a housekeeper for a Jewish family in Graz by the name of Frankenberger, the family's nineteen-year-old son had sex with her and was the father of Alois.' However, there is no real evidence that Alois's father and hence Hitler's paternal grandfather was Jewish. It is a matter of conjecture whether Hitler knew about his family history, but it would be very surprising if he were immune to his father's illegitimacy, his original name being Schicklgruber and the possibility that his grandfather might have been Jewish.

A genetic study had been conducted in which saliva samples were collected from thirty-nine of Hitler's known relatives to test their DNA origins and found that a chromosome called Haplogroup E1b1b1 which showed up in [Hitler] samples is rare in Western Europe and is most commonly found in the Berbers of Morocco, Algeria, and Tunisia, as well as among Ashkenazi and Sephardic Jews. Eb1b1bi accounts for approximately 18 to 20 per cent of Ashkenazi and 8.6 to 30 per cent of Sephardic Y-chromosomes, and appears to be one of the major founding lineages of the Jewish population. This study is inconclusive as to Hitler's Jewish origins; it is noteworthy that the specific haplotype was shared by Einstein, Caravaggio, St. Augustine, William Harvey, and the Wright Brothers! The self-hatred invoked by the suspicion of Jewish blood in Hitler may have developed into an Oedipus complex against his father, with whom Adolf had a strained relationship, and then projected onto the Jewish race. When the Russians liberated Berlin and carefully examined Hitler's burned body, they kept part of his skull and the lower jaw, which is a source of Hitler's DNA and might offer further evidence of his ancestry.

Hitler was better read and more cultured than is generally appreciated, as is evident from the book by Frederic Spotts. He was obsessional about his personal habits. He was a strict non-smoker, teetotaller, and vegetarian, which must have singled him out among his war-time and later 'Freikorps' comrades. Although Lothar Machtan argued in his book that Hitler was homosexual, there is no solid evidence for this view. Henry Murray, an eminent psychologist at Harvard University, suggested that Hitler was unable to come to terms with his sexuality, having homosexual tendencies that he was impotent, and a masochist, had an Oedipus complex and was paranoid. Daniel Pick, a distinguished historian as well as a psychoanalyst, quotes in his book "The pursuit of the Nazi mind" (2012), the study by the psychologist Walter Langer of Hitler's psychic development. Langer based his findings on the material collected by the "Office of Strategic Services (OSS) of the United States in 1943 and published in "The mind of Adolf Hitler" in 1963. He portrayed Hitler as a "disturbed figure, racked with fixations and fetishes, a perverted masochist, whose delusions about the Jews and whose mastery of his people were wrapped up in his own troubled childhood and subsequent self-loathing. In forming this picture Langer seized on such details as Hitler's closeness to his mother, his fear of his formidable, abusive father, his fraught, allegedly sexual relationship with his niece Geli Raubal and his lack of physical interest in women after her suicide."

Altogether, historians of fascism postulated an erotic component in Hitler's relationship to the people. There may have been some sexually pathological feature about the Nazis, their hypermasculine bonding and repressed homosexuality. Pick argued (2012) that Hitler's sexuality was important in understanding the Nazis, and even the persistent interest in Nazis and their sexuality. The multiplicity of disorders in producing a 'psychological profile', which was commissioned in 1943 and without access to Hitler must leave considerable doubt about the validity of the reports. Furthermore, there is considerable doubt whether Hitler consummated his partnership with Eva Braun, at least according to his personal butler, and he seemed to have shunned sexual activity.

Hitler preferred natural remedies and distrusted scientific medicine. Nonetheless, he tried several doctors and medicines. His personal doctor, Theo Morell administered at the time fashionable vitamins and hormones. He was a chronic insomniac, which might have been caused by amphetamine he had been taking. There was circumstantial evidence that Hitler may have contracted syphilis. He developed a tremor in his left hand and arm, apparently before the war and got progressively worse, which was treated by Morell with drugs for Parkinson's disease. According to Weindling "privately the racial hygienists suspected that he (Hitler) had psychopathic traits and classified him as an un-Nordic East Slav". Finally, a recently released secret document prepared by the Cambridge psychologist Dr. John MacCurdy suggested that Hitler believed that "the Jews are the incarnation of Evil, while he is the incarnation of the Spirit of Good. He is a god by whose sacrifice victory over Evil may be achieved". By 1942 when Hitler and his cohort faced external failure, in the War against the Soviet Union he focused his attention on a perceived enemy within, the Jews. Dr. MacCurdy carried out extensive analysis of Hitler's speeches and identified three morbid tendencies: shamanism, epilepsy, and paranoia. Shamanism, namely exploits of hysterical symptoms, working himself up in the presence of a crowd. However, later epilepsy, which in the given context implies Hitler's ruthless streak, losing heart, with failed ambition on the Russian front. Hitler's growing paranoia, exacerbated his 'Jew phobia'. Dr. McCurdy wrote, "The notion of a great, military victory has passed into the background, while he poses more as a martyr, the speech ending on the theme of death".

Although Hitler was born in Braunau am Inn, he moved in his childhood in 1898 with his family to nearby ancient Roman city of Linz and lived there until 1907, where he attended the 'Real-Schule' (secondary modern school). It is noteworthy that a number of famous personalities lived in Linz. Johannes Kepler the astronomer and mathematician (1571-1630) after whom the local Johannes Kepler University is named. Another celebrity was the composer Anton Bruckner who lived in Linz between 1858 and 1868 and was the organist in the 'Old Cathedral'. The philosopher Ludwig Wittgenstein attended the same school in Linz as Hitler and allegedly at the same time as Hitler; this is possible as both were born in 1889. It would not be surprising if Wittgenstein's brilliant mind may have brought about strong resentment and anti-Semitic feelings in Hitler. It is ironic that Adolf Eichmann, who was responsible for gathering and transporting Jews from all over Europe to the concentration camps, also spent his youth in Linz.

The third encounter with Jews is reputed to be his mother being treated for cancer by Dr. Block, a Jewish doctor, and she died in 1907, as most people would have died with cancer in those days and indeed to-day. Hitler was very close to his mother and he may have been resentful and possibly even blamed the Jewish doctor for her death. Altogether, it is highly likely that Hitler would have been troubled by the possibility of his Jewish ancestry, quite apart from the other alleged encounters with Jews. According to a report published by the London Daily Mirror in 1933, "a gravestone was found in a Jewish cemetery in Bucharest inscribed with some Hebrew characters and the name Adolf Hitler but it is now known that this Bucharest Hitler could not have been the Nazi leader's grandfather. At the time, though, this picture worried Hitler sufficiently that he had the Nazi law defining Jewishness written so as to exclude Jesus Christ and himself." His pathological hatred of Jews might be a manifestation of self-hatred by the gnawing doubt concerning his Jewish ancestry. The manic will to power associated with shear barbarity, flouting every precept of civilization and humanity, linked with real or assumed love for art (paintings and architecture) may add up to the dual burden of SS-N and Jewish self-hatred.

Reinhard Heydrich (1904-1942) was the son of a Catholic, musical family, indeed his father founded the Hallé conservatory. Reinhard himself was an accomplished violin player. There were unsubstantiated rumours that Heydrich may have Jewish ancestry, on account of his paternal grandmother's name was Süss. However, this is unlikely as it appears that after Reinhard's grandfather died, his grandmother re-married to Her Süss (who anyhow was not necessarily Jewish), so there would not be blood relationship with Reinhard. Robert Gerwarth, in his book 'Hitler's Hangman', writes that 'Hugo Riemanns Music-Lexikon' named Bruno Heydrich, his father, a Jewish composer, with the name 'Süss'. The family sued the Editor and won the case, when it was established as a malicious insinuation by a former disgruntled student. It was then made public that Reinhard's uncle Hans Krantz married a Jewish woman. At school Reinhard's schoolmates teased him by calling him 'Isi or Isidor'. Even when he joined the naval cadets, the name Süss stuck and fellow cadets called him the 'White Moses'. Paradoxically, among Hitler's leadership, Heydrich was the only one with the desirable 'Nordic-Aryan' appearance: elongated head, blond-hair, blue eyes, tall, slim, and stern hardness of Nazi mythology. Despite his appearance, he was troubled with the 'Jewish stigma'. Heydrich served as an officer in the German navy, but in 1931 he was dismissed for dishonourable conduct towards a woman. Soon after, he joined the Nazi party and with his organisational abilities, total ruthlessness, and fanatical anti-Semitism he had a meteoric rise. In 1932 he was appointed head of the SD, Himmler's deputy in 1933, and head of the 'Reich Security Head Office' (Reichssicherheitshauptamt, RSHA) in 1939. Goering ordered Heydrich to organise the 'final solution' of the Jewish problem. He was in charge of the Wannsee conference in 1942, at which the executive and administrative decisions seem to have been taken to exterminate the Jewish people. Heydrich was appointed 'Protector of Bohemia and Moravia' and the only person assassinated by order of the Allies, though at a price of the dreadful reprisals of the entire Czech village of Lidice.

As with Hitler, Heydrich most likely harboured secret fears of having Jewish blood, which will have driven him to over-compensate his demonstrable hatred for Jews. In another sense, as Wasserstein argues, self-hating Jews are really haters of other Jews. He had a neurotic temperament and was ruthless in pursuing his murderous task. At the same time, he had exceptional musical talent being a fine violinist. Thus, he shares with Hitler the dual burden of Jewish self-hatred and SS-N.

Heinrich Himmler was born in 1900 to a devout Catholic family. Father was a very ambitious classics teacher, with University degree in philosophy, who became the Rector of the Wittelsbacher Gymnasium in Munich. Heinrich was a sickly infant, developing acute lung infection at the age of two, and he was always molly coddled by his mother on account of his weak constitution. He was educated at the Royal Wilhelm Gymnasium in Munich and was described by a classmate as under-average size, plump, wearing spectacles, and hopeless at gymnastics, for which he was mercilessly teased. Father made heavy demands on him, and indeed Heinrich was a star student excelling in every subject. He is likely to have despised himself, within the overt masculine German society, by being awkward, short sighted, lacking an athletic body, and altogether physically unremarkable. At nineteen he was still a devout Catholic and there is no evidence that either Heinrich or his father was anti-Semitic. Himmler read many books, which gradually turned to anti-Semitism, such as Stewart Chamberlain. At the age of nineteen he allegedly developed paratyphus infection, probably of psychosomatic manifestations, when he was not keen attending the Technical High School. Nonetheless, he enjoyed working a year on a farm as part of the course and completed the diploma in agriculture.

After a spell of working for a fertiliser company, Himmler found his real niche when he joined the paramilitary activities, and by 1923, he became a member of the Nazi Party. His organisational abilities, natural bend to gather information and for intrigue came to the fore, and his advance in the party was rapid. From the post of 'Deputy Gauleiter' (Gau leader) of Lower Bavaria, he was promoted to 'Gauführer', and by 1929 he became the powerful 'Reichsführer SS', followed by becoming the Police

President. Himmler was responsible for establishing in Dachau, on the outskirts of Munich, the first concentration camp. Later, the network of concentration and extermination camps came under Himmler's jurisdiction, with 'extra-territorial laws' defined by the personal whims of the Reichsführer SS.

Himmler suffered from severe stomach cramps lasting days and recurred over years; his father died of stomach cancer and this may have played on his mind. The psychological state of Himmler has been debated by many and Peter Padfield, in his book 'Himmler Reichsführer-SS' (1990), argues that from his early diary Himmler may have manifested a schizoid condition, often given to explain the psyche of mass murderers. As a student of twenty-one in Munich, he notes in his diary that he constantly berates himself, talks too much, is obsessed with trivia, deals with morals and ideas rather than actual people, and works because it is his duty. All this may support the schizoid diagnosis, and according to Professor Bradley Smith, "The tone of his descriptions clearly indicates that, even though he wanted warm relations, his fears and self-doubts forced him to erect strong defensive walls." He apparently had sado-masochistic fantasies in his dealings with girls, which may be significant in his later years in power. Himmler's predilection to macabre spectacles must have been familiar to his staff, as in Sobibor the SS commandant, his staff and the 'Gasmeister', Oberscharführer Eric Bauer prepared a special demonstration in the latest advances of the technique of mass killing. They selected 300 young attractive Jewish girls. In front of Her Himmler and dozen of his SS officers and those of the camp, the girls were ordered to strip then marched up the 'Himmelfahrt Strasse' (heavenly highway) or Himmlerfahrstrasse into the gas chamber and the door was shut. It has not been recorded whether her Himmler looked into the gas chamber to ascertain the fate of the 300 girls, but he may have congratulated the staff on the disciplined and efficient way of despatching, '300 enemies of the Reich'. Himmler also witnessed the most horrific medical experiments on human beings, which he authorised in Dachau; the effect of high-altitude falls, and freezing experiments.

Padfield concludes that "it is a fact which cannot be disputed since it rests on the evidence of a thousand documents that he (Himmler) was aided in his historical exhibition of sadism not simply by silence but by the active support of thousands, indeed millions. We are looking at the characteristics not of an isolated man, nor of a monster, but of a man who came to embody the miasma rising from a nation, a man who was the focus of a national disaster as natural as an earthquake or an epidemic disease." Padfield adds that the Germans wanted to be the master race, they were half-educated, with half-truth, drunken people. Himmler fits the criteria of psychopaths laid down by Simon Baron Cohen; "zero-degree empathy, preoccupation with themselves, need to dominate, show complete detachment from other people's feelings, capable of mindless aggression, pleasure from someone's suffering and knowing right from wrong but cannot feel the difference between them". By all accounts, Himmler was a psychopath, with sado-masochistic and schizoid traits, with absolute devotion to his Führer, who in his final hour disowned him. A comparative analysis of the formative characteristics of these five evil individuals is given in the Table.

Herman Goering was known to be a habitual heroin addict. Rudolf Hess was considered by the British prison personnel to be a paranoid hypochondriac. These two, von Ribbentrop, Albert Speer, Rudolf Höess, and others during the Nuremberg trial were analysed by the psychologist Gustave Gilbert who not surprisingly found that the Nazis lacked empathy and had no feelings of guilt. Carl Jung altogether stated that "Hitler was the mirror of every German's unconsciousness. The loudspeaker which magnifies the inaudible whispers of the German soul". Robert Lifton, in "The Nazi Doctors – A study of the psychology of evil" (1986) – interviewed, among others, twenty-eight physicians involved at high levels with Nazi Medicine. He came to the conclusion that the Nazi doctors have undergone 'doubling', by which he meant a second, relatively autonomous self, which enabled one to participate in evil. Thus, they made a Faustian pact with the devil, a quintessential German theme.

III. MENGELE – CLAUBERG – EBERL – MEDICIDE SYNDROME

The introduction by German-Austrian Doctors of Medicine engaged in mass killing and/or extreme experiments deserves recognition by coining a novel anti-Hippocratic syndrome, the 'Mengele –Clauberg – Eberl – Medicide' Syndrome. Whilst there were too many doctors to honour them all, perhaps the eponym can be fairly awarded to the three men, so as to maintain within the medical fraternity a reminder what the profession is capable of, despite education at some of the most celebrated European Medical Schools. They differ in their skills and manifestations, but have in common their total abandon of Hippocratic ethics, and sinking into the abyss of medicalised mass murderers – a novel, morbid chapter in the history and practice of medicine.

Josef Mengele (1911-1984), of Roman Catholic parents, had a doctorate in anthropology from the University of Munich and a second doctorate in medicine from the University of Frankfurt. He was a mass murderer responsible for thousands of death sentences of totally innocent civilians at the selection ramp in Auschwitz and Ravensbrück, using a novel criterion of 'augenblick' (glance), which with his double doctorate empowered him to dispatch human beings right or left, life or death. He also carried out experiments on twin children and then had them killed to carry out thorough pathological and microscopical examination of the organs. Out of approximately 3000 twins selected for experimentation, about 200 survived. Dr. Mengele has written a totally new chapter in the annals of medical history, the seriousness of which has as yet to be fully comprehended. By all accounts he was not insane and apparently he had a pleasant personality.

Carl Clauberg (1898-1957) served in the First World War as an infantry man. After the war, he studied medicine at the University of Kiel, Hamburg, and Graz, and must have been fairly competent as he was appointed as Chief of the University Gynaecology clinic and later as professor of Gynaecology at the University of Königsberg. Clauberg joined the Nazi party in 1933, reaching a rank of 'SS Gruppen Führer'. On his own initiative in 1942, he asked Himmler's approval to carry out mass sterilization experiments of women in Auschwitz and Ravensbruck concentration camps. Himmler agreed and Clauberg carried out injections of acid directly into the womb or high doses of x-rays targeting the womb. Mass sterilization of Jewish women would introduce a novel advance in the technique of exterminating Jewish people. Some women died and about 700 were sterilized. Clauberg's mentality made him to inform strapped-in women that he inseminated their wombs with animal sperms and that monsters were growing in their wombs!

Irmfried Eberl (1910-1948) was an Austrian born in Bregenz, but little is known of his childhood. Eberl studied medicine at Innsbruck University, qualified in 1933, and there he trained as a psychiatrist. He joined the Nazi party whilst a medical student and later as a psychiatrist he actively supported killing of people with mental disorders. In 1940, at the age of twenty-nine, he was appointed medical director of the killing hospital in Brandenburg under the T-4 Euthanasia Programme. After the T-4 murder programme had to be formally abandoned, he was transferred to the Chelmno extermination camp and shortly afterwards in 1942, he assumed command of the Treblinka extermination camp. According to one of the SS officers describing Eberl's leadership: "He was very ambitious. It was said that he ordered more transports than could be 'processed' in the camp. That meant that trains had to wait outside the camp because the occupants of the previous transport had not all yet been killed. At the time it was very hot and as a result of the long wait inside the transport trains in the intense heat many people died. At that time whole mountains of bodies lay on the platform"

Eberl was dismissed from Treblinka for incompetence and replaced by Franz Stangl, for not killing people efficiently and for not concealing the mass murder from the local inhabitants in the villages. He was also indicted with his colleagues for stealing possessions from the murdered people. Gitta Sereny interviewed Stangl in prison describing his findings when taking over command of the Treblinka camp: "In the Treblinka station there was a train full of Jews, some dead, some still alive. It looked as if it had been there for days. Treblinka that day was the most awful thing I saw during the Third Reich. It was Dante's *Inferno*, Dante come to life [...] I went straight back to Warsaw and told Globocnik [the SS general in charge of all the extermination camps]. 'It is the end of the world', I said to him and told him about the thousands of rotting corpses. He said 'It's supposed to be the end of the world for them.'"

ANTI-HIPPOCRATIC MEDICIDE SYNDROME (1945)

Mengele, Clauberg, Eberl Syndrome

	Dr. Mengele	**Dr. Clauberg**	**Dr. Eberl**
University	Munich Frankfurt Germany	Kiel Hamburg Graz Germany	Innsbruck Austria
Religion	Catholic	?	Catholic
Selection Life/Death	Yes	No	Yes
Medical Experiments	Children Adults Twins Eyes Amputations	Women Sterilization	No, Commandant of Extermination Camp in Treblinka

Table 2 *Comparison of some formative characteristics of four prime evil movers of the Third Reich*

	Hitler	**Heydrich**	**Goebbels**	**Himmler**
Religion	Catholic	Catholic	Catholic	Catholic
Father and Family	Lower class, Father illegitimate, domineering died when Hitler was 9	Middle class, Musical	Lower class	Peasant family, father domineering. Grandfather illegitimate.
Mother, and Family	Loving, close association with mother	Middle class educated mother	God-fearing, loving mother.	Protective, loving mother.
Father's occupation	Clerk	Classical musician	Factory clerk	Rector of Gymnasium
Father's character	Obsessional, hysterical, limited education, sexuality uncertain, charismatic	Neurotic temperament, ruthless, organising abilities, great musical talent	Narrow minded, pedantic, tyrannical, short in stature, club foot	Ambitious, poor physique, organising abilities, obsessional, read extensively
Education	School drop-out	Gymnasium	Franciscan, boarding school, gymnasium, PhD, literature	Gymnasium, technical College, Diploma in Agriculture
Early life	Failed painter	Dismissed from Navy, dishonourable conduct	Failed writer	Assistant in fertilizing company
Jewish association	Grandfather suspected to be Jewish	Grandmother suspected to be Jewish	Intellectual, emotional	None

IV. CHILDREN OF PROMINENT NAZIS

The country with one of the highest educational records, where thousands of learned thesis and books were written on education, where pedagogy was developed and highly esteemed, was eventually lead and taught by a school drop-out, half-educated man who had the gift of persuasion and verbal power that moved the Volk. This is the most frightening aspect of Western Christian Civilisation. Peter Sichrovsky, in his book 'Born Guilty' (1987), wrote "what the Führer had to say about his approach to the education of German youth: my pedagogy is harsh. Weakness must be chipped away. The youth that will grow up in my fortress will frighten the world. I want a brutal, authoritarian, fearless, cruel youth. Youth must be all of this. It must be able to bear pain. It must not have anything weak and gentle. The light of the free, marvellous beast of prey must once again shine from their eyes. I want my youth to be strong and beautiful."

The second and third generation of innocent young Germans tried to come to terms with the problem, and some have recognised guilt and responsibility. Professor Michael Stolleiss expressed a view of the first post-war generation of young Germans who were neither directly nor indirectly associated with the National Socialist regimes. "While I, like most people of my generation do not have a sense of personal guilt, I do feel a sense of shared responsibility for that period and its crimes". He writes as the director of the Max-Planck Institute for European Legal History and Professor of Law and Legal History at the University of Frankfurt, but above all as a man of moral integrity and judgment. To what extent does his considered moral responsibility for this period apply to the children of academics who laid down the basis of 'racial hygiene' and of well-known Nazi leaders?

Racial Hygiene developed in Germany as a national socialist interpretation of Galton's 'Eugenics' (see chapter 7). The three leading academics Ploetz, Lenz, and Fischer, followed by Verschuer and Rüdin, collectively laid down the ideological basis for the Nazi policies of Euthanasia of the 'incurable' and then extended to that of Jews, gypsies, and homosexuals. Benno Müller-Hill, professor of Genetics at the University of Cologne, was able to interview professor Lenz's son, Fischer's daughter, von Verschuer's son, and Rüdin's daughter.

Widukind Lenz, Professor Fritz Lenz's son, became after the war himself professor and director of the Institute of Human Genetics at the

University of Münster. He was interviewed by Müller-Hill in Lenz's office and asked, "Did you know about the extermination of the Jews in the East and about euthanasia in Germany?" "My father knew about the destruction of 'lives unworthy to be lived'." "Did your father ever tell you that he participated in an advisory role in the formulation of a law on euthanasia between 1939 and 1941?" "No, I don't know anything about that." "And about the extermination of the Jews?" "We only knew about isolated cases of killing Jews in the East. That is to say, neither the whole truth nor the whole extent. That was all kept secret." "Do you know of any public references to the mass exterminations?" "Rosenberg informed representatives of the German press at a reception on 18 November 1941 that the final solution had started. He ordered them not to write about it in detail, but to use certain specific stock phrases to refer to the mass extermination of the Jews [...] "No one could be expected to understand these hints; they were ambiguous," says Lenz. "That's true, if one closed one's eyes and ears, but even ordinary people knew about the murders committed by the Einsatzgruppen." Lenz responded that, "Old Ploetz went one day to see Frick in Berlin. He protested against the killing of the Jews in the East, which he had heard about, and gave his party card back. That wasn't race-hygiene as he had conceived it." This is a significant point, implying that the academics could not have even conceived that their idea might be taken to its logical conclusions – racial-oriented mass murder. Indeed, this is consistent with Hitler's notion that professors live in 'Ivory Towers', and when someone turns their academic ideas into practice, they scream that this was not what they meant.

Lenz expanded then on the early years of National Socialism in an academic narrative, he quotes Nietzsche, forgets about anti-Semitism and the 'final solution', but admits that Hitler read his father's book 'The principles of human heredity and race hygiene' (1927) authored by Baur E. – Fischer E. – Lenz F. To the question as to how Lenz pictured his father as a scientist, Lenz replied, "My father was entirely a theoretician and, as such, was a mixture of the scientist guided by knowledge and the unworldly Utopian. However, he thought of himself as a pragmatist, in the sense of English and American pragmatism, to which he liked to refer. Thus, he saw himself as an adherent of a theory of values which holds that the practical consequences of an action are more important than the correct opinion [.] He believed, like so many others, that the race was going to rack and ruin, and that the National Socialists were the ones who could stem the tide." When asked about the law in 1933, expelling Jews from German universities, Lenz replied, "I can't remember that my father ever discussed the law in favourable terms and I do remember that he was perplexed and saddened by every injustice and by the individual suffering which resulted from it. It's true to say, and we can't spare him this reproach, just as we can't spare many others, that he didn't feel that he shared any responsibility for the law, and that he didn't foresee all the developments to which it would later lead." He also responded that it was not an important programme from his father's point of view and "please don't make a moral issue of it."

Finally, when Müller-Hill asked him how history will view the guilt of Lenz, Fischer, and von Verschuer, there was a long discourse from the son of Lenz, which is quoted here in full, as it throws light by a highly intelligent academic vacillating in admitting complicity or guilt of his predecessors in a broadly corresponding academic field. He does not deny the "dreadful events" and "the hate, fanaticism and sadism, which made Auschwitz possible". Lenz continues, "Your question about guilt is phrased in such an all-embracing manner that it can't be answered with a simple yes or no. Guilt for what? Guilt on account of what pronouncements, what actions, what silences, what omissions? After the fact that these dreadful events had taken place had been revealed, I believe that everyone was obliged to ask himself whether and how he had been an accomplice. Basically, everyone can only answer such a question of personal conscience for himself. A person standing on the outside to whom this whole period and the individuals involve aren't known through personal experience should be very careful how he judges it. I know that my father, like myself, felt a sense of complicity and suffered from it, even if he claimed otherwise. But, all the same, your question about guilt seems to me to be somewhat different from an attempt to understand this whole development from the historical point of view. To do this, I believe, we should start from what Fischer, Lenz, and von Verschuer knew about, and what they understood of these scientific, biological, and political questions, as well as from what they held to be desirable, given that they were children of their culture, their time, and their class.

It seems clear, to me at least, that in many cases, our present perceptions of malicious intentions are simply based on a faulty understanding of the reality of situations where intentions had, in fact, been basically good. I have never been able to recognize, in what these three men said or wrote, any path which might lead towards the hate, fanaticism, and sadism which made Auschwitz possible. As far as I can see, those responsible for Auschwitz never called on any of these three men to provide a justification of their brutality. Rather, they looked for models, or supposed models, in quite a different direction, where, in those years, the preaching of implacable antagonism, hate, and a fight to the death against opponents was the norm." "I am sure that you would have arrived at a fairer assessment of my father if you had known him personally and hadn't just looked through his published views for whatever can be used against him [...] Of course, I won't deny you the right to appear as a prosecutor and a preacher dedicated to a cause. Every man is subject to the moral judgments of others, especially when his views or actions involve the public. There must be prosecutors and advocates, but prosecutors are, by the very nature of their tasks, one-sided. You're performing a very important function in society, but you shouldn't set yourself up as a judge or a historian. When a prosecutor usurps the power of a judge, justice must suffer." Basically, Lenz defends his father in intellectual babble, declaring that his father was a child of that time, class and culture, but his intentions were honourable.

Dr. Helmut von Verschuer is the son of Professor Otmar von Verschuer. He studied at the University of Marburg and now works for the European Economic Community. Müller-Hill asked Verschuer about his father's reputed religiosity. Verschuer answers, "As soon as they arrived in Frankfurt in 1935, my parents started looking for a congregation which they could join. They rejected the local congregation of Dornbusch which was led by a minister of the German Christian Church." He joined the 'Confessional Church'. "After our move to Berlin-Dahlem in 1942, my father joined, Niemöller's congregation. Niemöller himself was in prison at the time. There, we often met Adam von Trott zu Solz." "What was your father's position on anti-Semitism?" I ask. "At home, there wasn't ever a trace of any such thing. We never spoke about Jews [...] I didn't know what Jews were, and I asked my parents. Later on, it became clear to me that the so-called Jewish question had something to do with my father's scientific field. But I don't remember my father making any anti-Semitic remarks in our house." "How about your father's party membership?" I ask. "I have a recollection that when we lived in Frankfurt, my father had to decide whether to be drawn into the Party, together with the other members of an organization to which he belonged, or to resign. Obviously, he didn't do the latter. "Did he ever tell you of his leading role in the student Freikorps in Marburg and of the workers they shot while they were 'trying to escape' from the custody of that corps?" "No, he didn't. "My father often said: "Render unto Caesar the things which are Caesar's and unto God the things which are God's." That was one of his precepts.

My father didn't show any understanding for [Adam von Trolls's participation in the 1944 plot to assassinate Hitler], steeped as he was in the

Prussian-Protestant tradition of loyalty to authority, and condemning, as he did, political assassination. "My father favoured a strict separation between 'pure' science and politics. He selected his co-workers on the basis of their professional qualifications, and not their political ideas. I ask about the expert report written by his father in Frankfurt in a race-dishonour trial. "Perhaps a co-worker wrote it," he says. I answer: "But not the letter to the Minister of Justice." "Perhaps not, I didn't know about this incident before. To my knowledge, my father helped some Jews with his expert reports. "Do you remember Mengele?" I ask. "Of course, above all, from our time in Frankfurt. I remember him as a friendly man. In the institute, he was called 'Papa Mengele' by the ladies on account of his kindliness. Like the other assistants, he sometimes used to come to tea in our house with his young family. My mother told me that when Mengele was asked during a meal in Berlin whether what he had to do was hard, he answered: "It's dreadful. I can't talk about it." I wonder myself whether he didn't deliberately keep my father in the dark about the context and background of Auschwitz, so that he could continue his scientific collaboration with him."

"The fact that your father destroyed his correspondence with Mengele indicates that he wasn't totally in the dark. Did he ever talk to you about that?" I ask. "No. During his time in Münster, I heard about the slanders spread by Nachtsheim and Gottschaldt. But my father thought it best not to respond. He maintained silence about everything which he thought to be slander. "Your father considered these attacks by Gottschaldt and Nachtsheim to be slanders," I say. "But these attacks by his former colleagues seem to me to have been based, in large part, on a correct interpretation of the facts. For example, Mengele sent the eyes of individuals whom he had killed in Auschwitz to the institute. Your father applied to the DFG for a grant for his collaboration with Mengele. When you speak of slander, I understand you to be quoting your father rather than expressing your own opinion based on the facts. But I agree that there is no doubt that your father was rather roughly attacked." "You're right in so far that I can't really form my own opinion about this matter, since these events weren't known to me at the time and weren't explained to me at the time and weren't explained to me later by my father." "Why didn't your father write any account of his life, any memoirs, after the war?" I ask. "I think that a public admission on his part of his culpable involvement in the events of the time would have been helpful, and would have relieved him from a great burden. But he couldn't bring himself to do it despite much urging on the part of Trott's relatives. In addition, he was convinced of his own scientific integrity. His talk to the Prussian Academy of Sciences in 1943,

‘The foundations of heredity as destiny and duty’. Appeared to be a relatively courageous one for the time.” According to Widukind Lenz, von Verschuer was a believer in God and in his viceroy, the Führer. He had a split personality, being “a member of the Confessional Church, but at the same time, he was bewitched by National Socialism.”

Miss Gertrud Fischer, the daughter of Professor Eugen Fischer has no professional training, and when her father worked in Berlin, she worked in the seminary of the Evangelical Charitable Society. When Müller-Hill asked her, “Did he ever have doubts about National Socialism?” “My father was a completely apolitical person. Early in life, he was a Catholic, but later he left the Church. He was no National Socialist. He was a nationalist and a conservative, but they all were at that time, that’s not a matter of politics. He joined the Party late, when pressure was brought to bear on him.” About 1938, she thought. “Was your father an anti-Semite?” I ask. “No, no.” she says. “He worried a lot about what happened to his Jewish colleagues and their wives.” “Did you discuss the persecution and extermination of the Jews with him, either during the war or afterwards? Did he ever question himself about his involvement?” “No,” she says, “we never spoke about that. I didn’t know anything about it during the war. Von Verschuer and he must have known. But we didn’t ever discuss it. It’s an entirely new thing that people talk about it now. In any case, why are you picking on him in particular? They were all guilty. He didn’t do anything special.” “When he retired, he went to live in a village. I lived there with my parents until 1950. He never complained. It was a very hard time for him. It’s difficult for you to understand. It was only in 1950 that the French left my grandparents’ home and we were able to move back here. Both my mother and he lived to be over ninety. My father was a kindly man. So sensitive. He was brave too. And unassuming. A piece of sausage, a roll, and a glass of wine, he wanted nothing more. It became lonely for him. Heidegger visited him now and then. His students all stuck by him. Abel also came to visit him; he was the only member of the SS among his students.” “What were the others really like?” “Bühler was a convinced National Socialist,” she says. I ask about von Verschuer. “My father had a special relationship with von Verschuer. He loved him like a son. Von Verschuer was his successor, of course. He was a member of the Confessional Church [...] Von Verschuer went to church every Sunday.” “Was von Verschuer an anti-Semite?” “No certainly not. He was just like my father. He never said “the Jews are bad,” he said “the Jews are different.” And she smiled at me. “He supported the segregation [Trennung] of the Jews. You know what it was like, when we came to Berlin in 1927. Cinema, theatre, literature, it was all in their hands.

He was for segregation. But he wasn't an anti-Semite. He was a very special father, you know."

Professor Edith Zerbin-Rüdin, the daughter of Professor Ernst Rüdin, is a psychiatrist, following in her father's footsteps investigating the inheritance of schizophrenia. She qualified in medicine in 1945 at the age of twenty-four. Müller-Hill asked her about sterilization. "My father was convinced of the importance of sterilization. There was an international eugenics movement at the time. He never took his duties in the appeal court which dealt with hereditary health and sterilization lightly. I raise objections concerning the propriety of the legal procedures for sterilization. "Yes," she says, "when my step-mother, who was a teacher, saw the questions to be answered on the forms, she also said: "Mere school-test questions which don't test intelligence. But the questions were altered later." "Did you father have any second thoughts about sterilization later on?" I ask. "He was always in favour of sterilizing those with hereditary defects; he was never in favour of sterilizing others, like psychopaths, for example." "He supported the legalization of such sterilization many times," I say. "That can't be true," she says. "In addition, he wasn't in favour of sterilizing homosexuals." "That I can corroborate," I say. In so far as Jews and Gypsies were concerned, he hoped that all that would come to an end, once the war was over. The only alternative to full collaboration which he could see was emigration. But he decided against that because, as he said to the Denazification Tribunal: "Emigration would have been desertion." That's the way he saw it." "And his vehement article in favour of the racial measures of National Socialism?" I ask. "Around the end of 1942, or the beginning of 1943, he wrote it as a neutral statement at first, then he rewrote it. It was like that in those days. What should he have done? He would have sold himself to the devil, in order to obtain money for his institute and his research." I ask: "What did he have to give to Heydrich, to get 30,000 Reichsmarks from him?" "I don't know anything about that." I tell her that a former co-worker of Rüdin, Theo Lang, had told the British Secret Service, while the war was still going on, that Rüdin was involved in a project on mass sterilization by X-rays. "That's not right. Lang is not a good witness. He was a member of the Party early on."

"Did your father know about euthanasia?" I ask. "My father protested to Dr. Linden that he was not asked and not informed. Dr. Linden replied that his attitude towards the question of euthanasia was known. I ask "Were your father's papers preserved?" "No. In the end my father was classified by the Denazification Tribunal as 'a fellow-traveller'. I find it difficult to believe that your father put up any firm opposition to euthanasia. I tell her about the draft of the law which was to regulate the killing of mental patients and I quote the proposed formulations for various parts of the law, including that by Professor Lenz suggesting killing "by medical means of which the patient remains unaware. (I forgot to mention her father's name on a memorandum advocating covert euthanasia). "But that just wasn't so," she says, "that was the terrible thing about it. Römer told my father that a review commission had come to his hospital in Ilmenau, and that the patients clung to the nurses as they were taken away. They knew very well what was going on." "Was your father an anti-Semite?" "No, not at all. My best girlfriend was half-Jewish. My father even tried to keep Kallmann.". "Was your father a National Socialist?" "No, certainly not. He only joined the party in 1937 under the pressure of the conditions prevailing at that time. He was denounced twice. "Did you speak about sterilization, euthanasia, and the final solution at home after the war?" I ask. "Only a little. There weren't many opportunities in any case, because of my father's frequent absences on account of internment and illness. He was a scientist, not a politician. Politics is a dirty game. Then just as now."

Gudrun, Himmler's daughter, was born in 1929, and he adored his only child by marriage to Margaret S. Boden, though he had two illegitimate children with his secretary. When Himmler lived in Berlin, he would telephone Gudrun almost daily in Munich and wrote letters weekly. Gudrun would accompany her father on some official duties, which included at least one concentration camp. The great divide between the Chief of SS and Gestapo responsible for murdering one and a half million children and his tender love for Gudrun is beyond human comprehension and possibly reflects the hard wired emotive difference between 'us' and 'them' or simply the loving bond between the daughter and an all-powerful father. After Himmler's death, Gudrun pursued her father's Nazi ideology, associating with SS officers and right-wing Germans, offering financial and legal help for Nazis to escape judicial procedures. She collects money for the neo-Nazi movement and by the age of eighty, she has been dubbed as the grandmother of the female neo-Nazis. Edda, the daughter of the 'Reichsmarschall' Herman Göring likewise defends her father, but she does not indulge in neo-Nazi activities.

Peter Sichrovsky interviewed children and grandchildren of leading Nazis and published their accounts under assumed names in the book 'Born Guilty'. Whilst a number felt guilty and considered themselves the sons of criminal fathers, others justified their fathers' actions. An example is presented here of the son of an SS doctor who volunteered to work in Dachau. The son followed in his father's footsteps, qualifying in medicine and here are his views and convictions related in the interview with Sichrovsky. "Perhaps one day we'll become the new elite. I'm certain that times will change and some aspects of the past will return [...] My friends and I – most of them are doctors – are ready. We have time. Unlike our fathers, we won't let any old idiot use us. As doctors we're indispensable to any political change. The nation, being a living entity, needs doctors. If need be they can also kill, not out of joy in killing but out of necessity. It's part of the job. Just as a doctor can save the life of a patient by removing an appendix he can save the body politic by excising big tumours. The extinction of life also forms the basis of the survival of others. This is where personal conviction comes in. My father serves as a model in this respect. I do things differently yet without being different."

The interviews of Gerald Posner in his book 'Hitler's Children' (1991) reveal how the children of prominent Nazis judge the sins of their fathers. Wolf Hess, is the only child of Rudolf Hess, who was a faithful deputy-Führer of the Nazi party and a close associate of Hitler. Hess was very proud of his son Wolf Rüdiger and Hitler was his godfather in a NSDAP 'naming ceremony'. Wolf beliefs in his father's total innocence and that the trial was a total sham of 'victors' justice'. He does not seem to deny the Holocaust, but claims that those Nazis responsible for the Holocaust crimes should have been tried by German courts. He feels bitter about his father's long imprisonment and does not admit any harm his father may have done from 1933 to 1941. He identifies entirely with his father's philosophy and considers him a victim, not a criminal. He denies German collective guilt, though at least by implications, he admits to some 'Nazi excesses'. The interview with Posner concludes by Wolf Hess saying, "In some years history will take a different perspective on these so-called crimes and my father will be seen in a proper and good way. It will be seen that the former Allies, the victors of World War II, are anything but the host of morality, justice, and humanity, as which they made themselves judges over Germany. It's changing already. You cannot hide the truth for ever."

However, there are other sons who condemn their fathers for their criminal activities and this is particularly well observed with Niklas Frank, the younger son of Hans Frank, a lawyer who was appointed by Hitler to become the governor-general of Poland (also known as the 'Butcher of Poland'). In the interview with Gerald Posner, Niklas Frank was most outspoken about his father also published in his book 'My Father, A reckoning'. Niklas says, "You cannot imagine how much I hate him. He was a pathetic arse-kisser, hare-brained and a numbskull". When Hans Frank, as Minister of Justice in Bavaria, was complicit in the arrest and murder of Röhm and the SA leaders, Niklas stated, "He knew the law and he walked all over it, all the more disgraceful. From the moment on he was co-opted, he had blood in his throat, on his hands, in his soul, and on his conscience. Niklas has no doubt that his love of prestige and power, utterly corrupted him: 'He sold his soul to become important'". In one of Frank's most vicious public pronouncements he stated, "When we began here, there were three and a half million of them; now, all that is left is little more than a few groups of Jewish labourers. All the others have, shall we say, emigrated. In another address he claimed that his consolation in case of military defeat would be 'that I will be able to say triumphantly that I have killed two million Polacks.'" Niklas tried to understand what drove his father to his crimes, by reading all that was written about his father and interviewing father's colleagues for his book. He said, "I still do not understand him. I have tried. He wasn't an ideologue. It was a career to him, and his ambition and weakness drove him. But still if he was alive there are a lot of questions I would ask him. A lot. I want the truth from him. I want him to tell me he is guilty. I know he wanted the big homes, the fine uniforms, all the luxury, but besides that I can't understand why he would do it. I hate him for it. I am furious at his weakness. When I used to meet his former colleagues and tell them I thought he was a criminal, they thought I was mentally deranged. They don't see it. To me it is so clear, only his motivation is hidden."

Niklas's brother Norman Frank, born in 1928, was eleven years older and was Frank's favourite child. He was very different to Niklas, being quiet, introspective, and physically less well built than Niklas. He deeply loved his father, still does at the age of sixty-two, and thinks of him every day, but differently from Niklas. "Norman is as perplexed as his younger brother. 'I do not understand my father at all. I have tried so much to understand him. I can't understand that he allowed himself to become so corrupted for junk. It is such a contradiction in a man I love. On the one hand I have the image of a good father and on the other is the man at the trial charged with crimes. And for me these two images belong together in my mind. When I visited him at Nuremberg, I had to accept this conflict, this contradiction. I saw that great intelligence can always come close to excess if it is mixed with ambition. Being highly educated does not shield you from horrible crimes".

Rolf Mengele is the only son of the SS Doctor Josef Mengele who carried out selections at the ramp in Auschwitz, Ravensbrück, and Bergen-Belsen for life or death, in addition to notorious lethal medical experiments on children and adults. He sent some 400,000 people to their deaths through his ramp selection – despite having been born into a prosperous Catholic family in Günzburg and highly educated first at the University of Munich with the doctorate in Medicine and then at the University of Frankfurt with the PhD in Heredity. Rolf himself studied law at the Universities of Freiburg, Hamburg, Munich, and Geneva. He hardly knew his father as a child, as he escaped to Argentina in the early 1950's. However, Rolf visited his father at the age of thirty-five, when he tried to find out about his father's role in Auschwitz. "I told my father I was interested in hearing about his time in Auschwitz. What was Auschwitz according to his version of events? What did he do there? Did he have a role in things he was charged with? The questions continued nightly. Mengele strayed from the essential points, justified his racist theories, filled his arguments with philosophical and pseudo-scientific verbiage. 'His arguments for why he thought some races were superior to others were quite unscientific. He waffled on and on. He was so sure he was right in all respects, I asked him why he had not turned himself in. My father replied, 'There are no judges, only avengers'. Mengele became angry as the exchanges continued. At one point, sensing Rolf's incredulity, he screamed: 'Don't tell me you, my only son, believes what they write about me?' 'I realized that this man, my father, was just too rigid. Despite all his knowledge and intellect, he just did not want to see the basis and rules for the simplest humanity in Auschwitz. He didn't understand that his presence alone had made him an accessory within the deepest meaning of inhumanity. In the end, it was impossible to discuss the concepts of evil or guilt because his father felt no guilt: 'I tried. These allegations, these facts left me speechless'. I was hoping he'd say, 'I tried to get a transfer to the front. I did this, I did that'. But it didn't even come to this preliminary agreement. Unfortunately, I realized that he would never express any remorse or feeling of guilt in my presence."

When his father died of a stroke at the age of sixty-seven, whilst swimming on the beach in Sao Paulo, Brazil, "Rolf's reaction to his father's death was one of enormous relief. 'I basically had a conflict that could never be resolved,' he said. 'On the one hand he was my father; on the other hand there were these charges, these horrific pictures of Auschwitz. I was very relieved that this solution came about. Rolf completely condemns him. He is the only family member to have publicly apologized for his father's crimes and to have admitted that he is 'ashamed' to be his son. Rolf does not share the 'pity' that some other children of prominent Nazis feel for their parents: 'I don't feel sorry for him. I feel he got the package he deserved. I don't pity him as my father, only that he wasted his life. I can't understand him. But Rolf will not bring himself to the position of Niklas

Frank who hates his father. I don't feel strongly enough about him to hate him [...] Rolf does not only have to cope for himself with his father's legacy. With three children, he must now pass the information to a new generation. 'It is hard,' he says. 'It's very hard for us. My eldest daughter [twelve years old] has already asked us. But they understand it when we explain we were also children. We were in their position, just one generation removed. We weren't involved. But instead we must tell them the truth. They must hear it from us instead of from friends or school. It is my obligation to them. In 1987 Rolf changed his surname for the sake of his children. They deserve to grow up without having to answer for what their grandfather did. He is gone, but he has left me here to answer the questions of what he did and why he did it. He is gone but I must bear the burden." Sichrovsky quotes a letter published in 'Der Spiegel' from Georg Kopp, a nineteen-year-old man living in Brunswick, in which he states: "As the child of fascist grandparents I feel guilty, guilty that even after forty years of post-Nazi rule National Socialist ideology is still so widespread."

These interviews are significant in so far that they indicate to some extent the unfettered domestic attitudes, despite cautious cover up by the sons or daughters through filial loyalty and love towards their father. The eleven interview responses can be divided into three groups (a) The largest group of six individuals, among whom Lenz, Fischer, Rüdin, Verschuer, Göring, and Norman Frank, all sons or daughters of highly educated university professors or influential fathers who were responsible for developing the ideological basis of 'racial hygiene' used by the Nazi regime to kill first Germans genetically and mentally defined categories of people. Later, this mutated into killing Jews, gypsies, and homosexuals. Norman Frank demonstrated the complexity of deep love for his father, yet being perplexed by his father's crimes – a dual reality that not surprisingly, he was unable to resolve. They all argued that their fathers were scientists (except Göring and Frank), not involved in politics, and some were devout Christians (Verschuer). They denied knowledge, culpability or guilt concerning the killing spree during the Nazi period. They claimed that none of their fathers were anti-Semites, they all helped Jews and at worst they advocated segregation of Jews from gentiles (Verschuer), in effect apartheid in Germany. In passing they admitted 'some terrible times' and the Holocaust that impacted on them only after the war, especially through films.

(b) The second group consists of Gudrun Himmler, Wolf Hess, and the anonymous Doctor whose father was an SS doctor in Dachau. These followed in their father's footsteps, supporting ex-Nazis (Gudrun Himmler) and justifying their fathers' activities. Wolf Hess's father was a politician, he denied any wrongdoing by his father and believed passionately that history will vindicate him. The Doctor even claimed that some of his medical friends are of the same mind and warned that the time will come when they will follow their fathers' ideology but carry out a thorough job! The critical question is whether Gudrun Himmler, Wolf Hess. and the son of the Dachau SS doctor are manifestations of epigenetic changes. These can be elicited by environmental agents that modify DNA by a chemical process, such as methylation, which may affect long-term memory. If these were to be passed onto the next generation, which has so far not been established, it would explain the different responses of the offspring of leading Nazis.

(c) The third group is represented by Niklas Frank and Rolf Mengele. Both condemn their fathers' activity; they feel responsible and tainted by being the sons of mass murderers and tried but failed to understand how their highly educated fathers could have fallen into the abyss of mass murder. Rolf Mengele studied law, he is a responsible son of a prominent Nazi, innocent as a child of his father's deeds, yet ashamed and apologizes for the dark legacy that affects him to a greater extent than other second generation Germans. This was well expressed above by Stolleiss "Sense of shared responsibility for the Nazi period and its crimes". Furthermore, Rolf Mengele raises the effect of the Nazi past on the third generation, namely his children. How does he explain to them that 'Grosspapa' (granddad) was a murderer? Does change of name 'Mengele' by deed poll to stop the shame and opprobrium of the third and subsequent generations? Rolf Mengele is anxious that his father's crimes should not affect his children, "This heritage must end with me." Indeed, Norman Frank decided not to have children because "after what my father did, I don't think the name Frank should go on." Other children of Nazi criminals expressed the view that the Holocaust must not be forgotten and that they have the obligation to prevent it from happening ever again. Niklas Frank openly declares hatred of his father and is most outspoken about the misdeeds of a highly educated man.

The three groups demonstrate polarisation of the post-war German society in their views of the National Socialist period. At one pole are those who feel responsible for their fathers' misdeeds, in the middle are the 'innocent bystanders' who deny culpability or guilt of their fathers, though admitting posthumously 'the terrible times'. At the other pole are those who fully justify their fathers' ideology and even threaten that they will complete their fathers' 'unfinished business'.

Muller-Hill argues that the 'apolitical scientists' maintained "separation of the 'good, pure' scientists and the 'wicked', 'political' scientists which had various consequences. Thus, the 'pure' scientists, who had been ensnared into crime, were threatened with the destruction of their scientific careers, if they were ever to tell the truth or attempt to understand what had really happened. So the dissemination of half-truths flourished. The 'pure' academics once again appreciated how advantageous it was to be an objective, apolitical, pure scientist. This applied equally whether, like Professors Hallervorden and von Verschuer, their own ends had been served by the large-scale murders, or whether, like Professors Fischer, Lenz, and Rüdin, they had done no more than act as advisors and expert witnesses to the machinery of murder. They had known nothing and could say nothing. And so they once again became a part of the scientific establishment. They made a cult out of their silence and of the 'incomprehensible mysteries' of National Socialism. Professor Fischer, for example, wrote in a draft letter to his old colleague Professor Muckermann. 'I confess that I am deeply shocked by what has been revealed. I believed, steadfastly and honestly, that I was serving the same ideals and that I was faithful to the same responsibilities as I always had been. And right up to the end I suspected nothing of the enormity of what happened. But this cannot be discussed here." However, "Professor von Verschuer wrote, to his old colleague, Professor de Rudder, now the Dean of the Faculty of Medicine in Frankfurt, where he hoped to return to take up his old chair: 'I thank you very much for the 'Persilschein' (Persil washing powder) which you sent me."

V. MEMORY – AMNESIA – SILENCE – GUILT – CHILDREN OF NAZIS

<table>
<tr><td>‘Nothing fixes a thing so intensely in the memory as the wish to forget it’

Michel de Montaigne, 1533-1592</td><td>‘A thousand years will pass and the guilt of Germany will not be erased’

Hans Frank, before he was hanged at Nüremberg, 1946</td></tr>
<tr><td colspan="2">‘In silence the sin of the Church is acknowledged as the sin that was part of what led to genocide.’

James Carroll, in ‘Constantine’s Sword’, 2001</td></tr>
<tr><td>‘Paralysed by memory and liberated by forgetting’.

Adapted from John Armstrong ‘Love, Life, Goethe’,2006</td><td>‘Memory not in vengeance but to prevent future inhumanity’

Paraphrased from W. Shawcross, Nüremberg Trial, 1946</td></tr>
</table>

Memory is a process of encoding, retaining, and retrieving information of past events. Recent studies suggest that infants as young as six months can recall information. At the other end of life span, memory declines with age and differs qualitatively, commonly

Affecting recall of names and past encounters or events. Short-term memory is a recall of events for a limited time and tends to be accurate. Long-term memory is the retention of past events, which can be recalled at a later time. It is more reflective, over a life-time and may be even passed on to the next generation. Individual memory is selective, dependent on one’s experience, whereas collective memory is a formal rendering of historical events.

A number of factors can influence retrieval of memory, of which odours are particularly potent agents. This may involve stressful events, such as exhaust fumes of a vehicle involved in arresting and transporting a person to prison, or pleasant smell of cooking or those of a sexual partner.

Emotional events are usually recalled with great clarity. Post-traumatic stress disorder may result in loss of memory and is associated with fear activating the amygdala in the brain. The extreme of memory loss is seen in Alzheimer disease. Amnesia is loss of memory due to brain damage and therefore a pathological condition. However, the term 'amnesia' is also used in everyday parlance to indicate purposeful loss of memory that is commonly encountered in criminal court cases. As with memory, amnesia may be individual or collective of which a recent example is that of the German Medical establishment.

The polluted German language of Goebbels and his comrades was in stark contrast to the palpable silence of the public, Churches, the literary establishment, and the universities. There was not an Emil Zola to stand up and be counted against the iniquities perpetrated to a religious minority of German citizens some of whose families lived in the land for centuries and succeeded to acculturate themselves to the German social environment. 'Stille Nacht', und nicht so 'Heilige Nacht' (silent night, and not so holy night) resonated among the 'Volk' when the Jews were disenfranchised, losing their livelihood, properties, liberties, and finally being transported to the East for the 'final solution'. The asymmetry between the 'big lie' that Goebbels was even proud of, as he and his cohort poisoned the language of Goethe and Schiller and the deafening silence of the 'innocent bystanders' who were blind to the disappearance of their neighbours, colleagues and friends and deaf to the screams of the innocent mothers, children, and babies. Civilization ceased to affect the spirit of humanity and barbarity prevailed.

After the war there was total denial by the professions, admitting unprofessional conduct but a 'few psychopath'. Attempts by three German physicians to explore the collapse of medical ethos by the profession resulted in them being considered as traitors, dishonouring the Medical Profession and named 'Nestbeschmutzers' (soiling their nest), and they were ostracized by their colleagues. All this happened despite the explicit prescient warning of no lesser authority than Professor Hufeland, physician to the King of Prussia, Goethe, and Schiller about 150 years ago. "The physician must not do anything else but maintain life. If that task is ever questioned, the physician becomes the most dangerous person of any nation".

The 'Kaiser Wilhelm Society', renamed the 'Max Planck Society' (MPS), carried out in 1999 an independent assessment of its war-time history. After fifty-seven years, in 2001 the president of the MPS Hubert Markl offered survivors of concentration camp experiments "the deepest regret, compassion, and shame at the fact that crimes of this sort committed, promoted, and not prevented within the ranks of German scientists. There is scientific evidence proving beyond the shadow of a doubt that directors and employees at Kaiser Wilhelm Institutes co-masterminded and sometimes even actively participated in the crimes of the Nazi regime. The Max Planck Society, as the Kaiser Wilhelm Society's heir, must face up to these historical facts and its moral responsibility." At the conclusion of the study in 2005, Markl re-stated his apology and asked survivors of the experiments on twins at the Auschwitz concentration camp for forgiveness for the suffering inflicted on the victims of these crimes in the name of science. Markl also apologized for the tardiness of the MPS in facing up to its historical responsibility.

It is noteworthy that Markl used the powerful words "the deepest regret, compassion and shame". The word shame does not commonly feature in the German quest to 'come to terms with the Nazi past'. It was Bernard Williams who pointed out that 'shame' cannot be really divided from 'guilt', nor can guilt be without shame. Indeed, shame may be the reason for the inability to admit guilt. The opposite of shame is honour, which played an important role in most nations, not least in Germany. The honour of Medicine, the Universities as well as the Wehrmacht were jealously guarded, yet they succumbed miserably to the myth of German culture 'Über Alles' (above all else), as sung in the national anthem. Guilt and shame can be countered by remorse and atonement in a variety of ways and Markl touched the sensitive area that may well lead to rehabilitation of otherwise great cultural past of Weimar classicism, Humboldtian liberal universities and the great contributions to Medical science by the likes of Virchow, Koch, and Ehrlich. Consistent denial or collective amnesia of medical atrocities lasted sixty-seven years, but at the 2012 meeting in Nuremberg, the German Medical Association ('Bundesärztekammer') adopted the following declaration: "We acknowledge the substantial responsibility of doctors for the medical crimes committed under the Nazi regime and regard these events as a warning for the present and the future. We express our deepest regret that despite their healing mission, doctors were guilty of violation of human rights. We ask for forgiveness from those alive and dead victims, as well as their descendants."

Whether the medical profession adopted the protective devise of 'collective amnesia' or that of being in denial is debatable. The most significant issue is the admission of responsibility for murder and experimental torture by the German healing profession and refute a conspiracy of silence pursued by perpetrators of the ultimate anti-Hippocratic oath –murder of children, men and women.

Learning and memory are related to the basic philosophical tenets discussed from the seventeenth century to the present day – empiricism and rationalism. The British view expressed by the empiricist John Locke was that the mind was a blank state, without any innate knowledge, that is filled subsequently by experience. Everything is learned and the more often we are exposed to an idea and the more effectively it is associated with other ideas, the more enduring it becomes in our mind. However, the German rationalist Immanuel Kant opposed this and argued that we are born with a template of knowledge. This *a priori* knowledge determines how sensory experience is preserved and interpreted. As is often the case both in philosophy and science when there are two opposing theories, both are right and complement each other. The anatomy of the neural circuit is consistent with Kantian *a priori* knowledge, whereas the strength of the neural connections is a function of experience and repetition consistent with Locke's notion. The persistence of such changes underlies memory.

Hitler, Himmler, and their mouth speak Goebbels hit instinctively on the 'Kant-Locke' formula of learning. They made use of the *a priori* Christian hostility towards the Jews, endorsing it repeatedly, haranguing the German 'Volksgemeinschaft' with the writing of 'Adversus Judaeos', selective excerpts from Martin Luther, and anti-Semitic writings in academia. The general public responded to de-humanization of their former colleagues, friends, and neighbours, preached effectively by the evil triad and their willing executioners. A great deal has been said about the 'primitive' unconscious mind, not least by Freud. Can we be held responsible for our actions that are made without conscious decision? This question has been dealt with by the psychologists Richard Gregory and Vilayanur Ramachandran. They argued that "our conscious mind may not have free will but it has free will not". Considerable progress has been made in mapping out the parts of the brain involved in memory. Short-term memory involves transient neural activation in the prefrontal cortex and the parietal lobe, whereas long-term memory is maintained by permanent neural connections involving the hippocampus (see next section).

VII. COGNITIVE AND EMOTIONAL INTERACTIONS IN THE BRAIN

> 'Descartes's concept of separating mind from matter, is merging into Spinoza's concept of single matter'
>
> *Author*

The brain constitutes the central nervous system, regulating the peripheral nerves in sensing the environment, temperature, pressure, pain, visual and auditory input, smell and taste. It initiates appropriate responses by passing messages to the periphery, such as muscular movement. The brain is the centre of reasoning, memory, judgment, emotion, appreciating art, social values and decision making process. It consists roughly of 100 billion neurons (a cell with long cytoplasmic extension) communicating in a network of neurons by synapses.

Archaeological evidence suggests that Homo sapiens existed in Africa around 300,000 years ago and moved to Europe some 50,000 years ago. Whilst the cranial capacity has not changed greatly over the past 300,000 years, as measured by the size of the skull, it is likely that the folding of the brain has increased its volume and with it the social and intellectual development of the brain. Recent advances in neuro-imaging by using 'functional magnetic resonance imaging' (fMRI) enables systematic studies linking distinct functional activities with defined regions of the brain. The complexity of interactions between neurons, traversing, connecting and transmitting impulses has yielded information with enormous significance to our perception and understanding of mental events. It appears that Descartes's most famous concept of separating mind from matter, 'I think therefore I am', is merging into Spinoza's concept of single matter.

The brain can be divided functionally into the cerebrum, limbic system, and cerebellum, which is connected by the brain stem to the spinal cord, serving all tissues. The cerebellum deals with coordination of movements and balance and will not be discussed further. The cerebrum accounts for about two-thirds of the brain mass (Fig.1, p.441) and is divided into the right and left lobes, connected by neurons, termed 'corpus callosum'. The outer layer of 'grey matter' constitutes the 'cerebral cortex', which is responsible largely for consciousness, reasoning, language, and motor skills. There are four major lobes. The Frontal lobe performs executive functions, organising responses to complex issues and coordinating memory with new data. The Temporal lobe controls memory, learning, hearing, emotion, and language, the latter is limited to the left side. The Parietal lobe receives and processes sensory information and localisation. The Occipital lobe is responsible for processing visual impulse and passes them on to other parts of the brain for further identification and storage.

A gross simplification of the relationship between defined sites in the brain and their functions is presented diagrammatically in Fig. The pre-frontal cortex (PFC) of the frontal lobe is involved in intelligence, reasoning, social behaviour, decision-making, language, memory, and control of impulses. Cognitive movement and social behaviour are also in the frontal cortex. Indeed, the PFC controls higher functions, executive control, goals and action, and has been called 'the organ of civilization'. It is considered to have developed later in evolution, and it matures more slowly than other areas and may take until adulthood. This is consistent with the immature adolescent social behaviour and self-control.

The cerebrum, and especially the PFC, is extensively connected with the older, more primitive 'limbic system', the description of which is based on that of Marco Catani and Michel Thiebaut de Schotten 'Atlas of Human Brain Connections' (2012). The limbic system is a group of functionally interconnected sub-cortical and cortical structures, linking emotion to cognitive functions, and includes behaviour, controlling special interactions, and memory. The cortical components of the limbic system include the 'hippocampus', which deals with memory, and spatial orientation, the 'insula', involved in empathy, distress, and hate and, 'cingulum', dealing with memory and pain. The subcortical limbic structures include the 'amygdala', an important neural structure responsible for emotion, fear, aggression, as well as empathy. 'Hypothalamus', interacts with the cerebrum, hormonal system, and monitors blood pressure, body temperature, pain, and fear. Parts of the 'thalamus' deals with pain, sorting and processing signals from the spinal cord. The 'accumbens' seems to be involved in reward and the 'putamen' in love and hate.

It is important to appreciate that whilst the major functions, such as emotion, pain, fear, memory, empathy, and reward are ascribed to certain parts of the limbic system, there is a great deal of interaction between them and the PFC. For instance, hate has been demonstrated by fMRI to be localized to the frontal gyrus, pre-motor cortex, putamen, and insula. It is noteworthy that whilst the neural pathways for hate are distinct from those of fear, anger, or aggression, they share the 'putamen' and 'insula' in passionate love. This finding underscores the all too frequent link between love and hate, with one readily mutating into the other.

Fig.1

Diagrammatic representation of functional correleates of the major parts of the brain. These regions are extensively inter-connected.

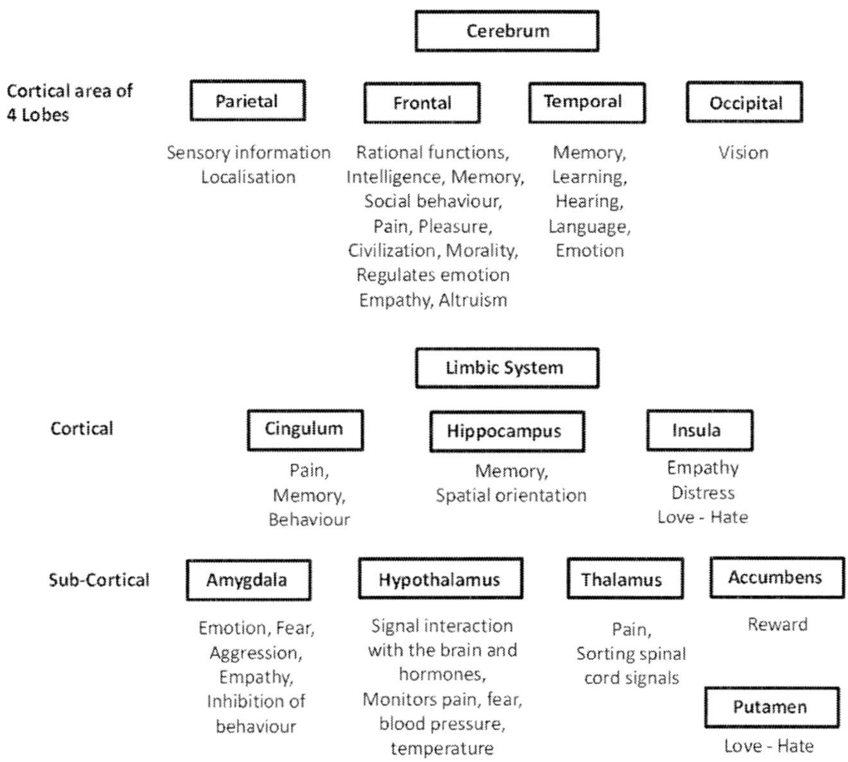

The different anatomical and functional areas of the brain interact by short and long distance neuronal extensions and this can be in one or both directions or applying Claude Bernard's concept of 'counter-current' mechanism to neuronal interactions. The most important link between the cognitive PFC and the non-cognitive emotional limbic system may well determine our social behaviour. The more ancient emotional response is likely to be tempered by censuring mechanism of the PFC. Altogether, wiring of neurons in the brain and their interconnections may determine our neural functions. Memory may depend on the connections made by the neurons between different parts of the brain.

A crucial function in neural interactions is served by neuro-chemicals produced by some of the sub-cortical structures. The most important are oxytocin (OXT), arginine vasopressin (AVP), corticotrophin releasing factor (CRF), noradrenaline (NA), serotonin and dopamine (DA). These are involved in stress, anxiety, fight and flight, sexual activity, aggression, reward, and punishment. The chemicals bind receptors expressed on the surface of neurons and function is determined both by the neurotransmitters and density of receptors. For instance, high receptor density for OXT and AVP correlates with long-term social bonding. OXT is released during social interactions and inhibits defensive behaviour, such as fight and flight. OXT and AVP levels are also associated with affectionate human relationships, trust, safety and impaired communication. This is consistent with the views expressed by Patricia Churchland that morality originates in the neurobiological changes linked with bonding. Indeed, individuals given intranasal OXT were significantly more cooperative within a group, but out-group hostility remained the same. OXT has also been explored as a therapeutic agent in borderline personality disorders with promising results.

Genetic polymorphism is another rapidly advancing area of research and has been demonstrated for OXT receptors. The allele of OXT is associated with changes in the size of most of the limbic structures and decreased amygdala activity. Impaired social behaviour was observed, such as empathy, long-term attachment, parenting and other manifestations. DA is also involved in social behaviour, learning, reward/punishment, and pair-bonding. The gene that codes for the enzyme MAOA (monoamine oxidase) seems to predispose to violence. Any predisposing genetic effect is influenced by the environment in early childhood, parental care, and physical or sexual abuse. Altogether, social behaviour is the end result of a multiplicity of factors, involving genes for OXT and their receptors, AVP, opiates, DA, serotonin and receptors, neural network, and the environment.

'Mirror neurons' are subset of neurons in the frontal, pre-motor, and parietal cortex, first reported in rhesus monkeys. They respond when a monkey sees another monkey place food into its mouth, as well as when the animal itself performs the same action. This discovery suggested that mirror neurons represent an intention or goal and may lead to understanding the neuro-biological basis of mental states. Indeed, on the basis of mirror neurons, a 'theory of mind' was postulated, whereby not only can one attribute to them an intention, but also fears, desires, feelings, and beliefs.

This was followed by the hypothesis that mirror neurons are responsible for mental states through a process of simulation. A great deal of speculation has attended this hypothesis and is well-argued by Churchland; one plausible suggestion is that simple actions are but a way to a complex end.

These experiments are difficult to reproduce in humans because of obvious ethical considerations. Nonetheless, the concept has been applied to empathy, in that a sad facial expression is simulated in the observer's brain, modulating activity in the limbic system, through the insula. This has been substantiated by fMRI demonstrating activation of the insula and the anterior cingula when the subjects are given a painful stimulus and are shown someone's painful facial expression. Furthermore, patients with damage to the insular cortex have a tendency not to feel empathy or emotions.

A remarkable insight of brain-imaging into what might be named as 'neuro-theology' suggests that the frontal lobes become active during meditation by Buddhist monks or during the prayers of Franciscan nuns. The temporal lobes are active during the perception of intense religious experience and during auditory hallucinations. Some believe this could be part of the brain activated when one 'hears the voice of God.' They may also be responsible for the emotional aspects of religious experience. The Bible deals with faith in terms of passionate concern and commitment. This view is consistent with the neurobiological division between the emotional limbic system and the rational pre-frontal cortex. However, whether faith is higher or lower than reason is not a point of contention, suffice to say that the two functions are different, though usually interactive. Polarisation towards the rational or emotional pole is evident throughout the spectrum of every religion. The appeal of faith to tradition is that human beings in the past have claimed to have met a Being who endowed their lives with moral worth and significance. They hear God speaking to them when, for instance, they read of how he had spoken to Isaiah, Jeremiah, or Micah.

It has been suggested that mimicry acts as 'social glue' derived from unconscious mimicry. Churchland argues that we like imitation in social situations (laugh when you laugh) because it tells us that "your frontal cortex is much like my frontal cortex and I can predict your behaviour – you are like me. Uncustomary behaviour, however, makes me anxious, because I cannot predict what you will do – whether you will be dangerous or nasty. Before accepting a stranger in society they will want assurance that he can acquire successful imitative behaviour, gets one 'past the gate' because it is a sign of social competence." In Kafka's 'The Trial', 'K' was waiting at the gate and he never gained entrance into the castle. 'Hume observed that we extend kindness more easily to those who are like us, who resemble us', he or she is 'one of us'; reminiscent of Goethe's 'elective affinity'. Furthermore, mimicking is discriminative, in that most people are likely to model themselves after successful rather than unsuccessful people. Social problems are solved when implicit standards emerge from shared values that most people adopt by observations and imitation. Neurological studies suggest that the 'social brain' is located in the PFC, especially the orbitofrontal and part of the cingulate cortices, connected to the amygdala and other areas of the subcortex.

The Neurobiology of violence has also made significant progress and its importance cannot be overstated. According to Baron Cohen, psychopaths have zero-degree empathy, they are exclusively preoccupied with themselves, they have a need to dominate, show complete detachment from other people's feelings, and are capable of mindless aggression and pleasure from someone's suffering. The limbic regions of the brain are often smaller in size and have lower level of activity in emotion and decision making process; the prefrontal cortex is also functioning poorly in psychopaths. A remarkable finding has been that the psychopath knows right from wrong, but cannot feel the difference between the two.

Adrian Rayne in his studies of the criminal mind published recently 'The Anatomy of violence', in which he suggested, as others did, that the amygdala functions as the centre of psychopathic behaviour. They lack conscience, remorse, and guilt, and the amygdala is less activated when they consider moral problems. Part of the pre-frontal cortex, linked with decision making and learning, is decreased in size. The anterior 'cingulate cortex' is also linked with regulating behaviour and impulsivity. The complexity of the interactions between these neural structures, the neurotransmitters, low serotonin and cortisol, with high testosterone levels have been well correlated with violence. Social structures are also of great significance and there is some hope that the knowledge gained from these studies will help to prevent and/or contain violence. Although Steven Pinker, in 'The Better Angels of Our Nature', has argued that whilst violence has dropped dramatically, there is still an enormous gap between the progress made in sciences and communication, compared with human behaviour and violence, and this warning should be heeded.

VII. EMPATHY, SOCIAL INTELLIGENCE, ALTRUISM

Fig.2:

Diagrammatical representation of the principal neurological interactions of Violence

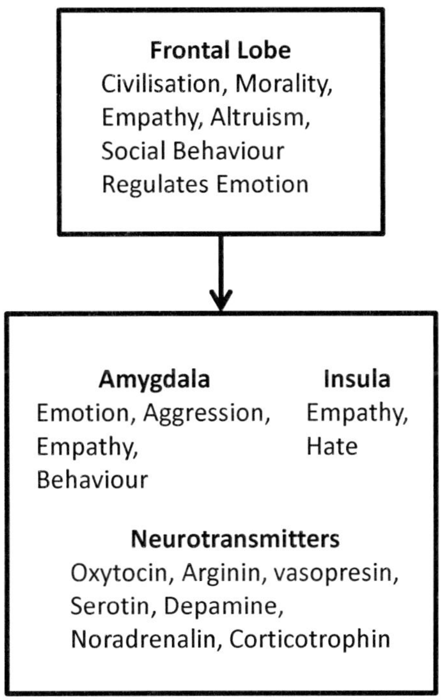

Recently, empathy has come to the forefront as a central factor in the process of evolution. Empathy is the key emotion that played an essential role in cognitive evolution of the human brain. It consists of the ability to think in the mind, anticipate the responses and interact with that of another individual; not dissimilar from the game of chess.

Simon Baron Cohen, in an examination of human cruelty in his book 'Zero Degrees of Empathy', he defined empathy as "our ability to identify what someone else is thinking or feeling, and to respond to their thoughts and feelings with an appropriate emotion." He developed an 'Empathy Quotient', based on two main components of empathy, recognition, and response. Baron Cohen defined seven levels along the empathy bell curve. At zero level, individuals can commit serious crime, assault, torture, rape, murder, without experiencing remorse or guilt, because they are incapable of appreciating other person's feelings. At level six, the empathy is in a constant state of hyper-arousal, being excessively concerned and supportive of another person. The limbic structures may be involved in the mechanism of the empathy circuit, and neuroscientists have placed the amygdala at the centre of the 'emotional brain'.

Daniel Goleman has written a ground-breaking account of 'Emotional Intelligence' in 1995. He focused then on the innate human capacity to manage one's emotion and self-awareness. More recently, Goleman extends this concept to inter-connections with other individuals, the 'inter-personal radar', which determines ones' social life, success or failure. He argues in his latest book entitled 'Social Intelligence' (2007), the capacity to enrich social aptitude that is getting on well with people and acting wisely in human relationship. Empathy and concern for ones' fellow human being, beyond the narrow self-interest are functions that have a neurological basis, which has lately undergone intensive studies, thanks to the emergence of fMRI.

According to Goleman, evolutionary psychologists argue that "Cooperation as well as competition drove the evolution of our larger brain size and of intelligence generally. And to recognise that intelligence can include noncognitive abilities." Paul Bloom, a developmental psychologist at the University of Yale, states that some aspects of morality, that is the sense of right and wrong is a product of biological evolution and is not learned, taught or acquired by religion. Rudimentary sense of fairness has been demonstrated in infants as young as three months by studying their eye movements in response to a variety of pictures. Co-operation, fairness, and reciprocity may have evolved because they were beneficial among a group of people. Bloom points out, the evolutionary price of help and co-operation in one group elicits prejudice towards strangers, the 'others'. Moral progress however, is acquired from parents, society, and the prevailing culture, based on the rudimentary sense of justice. He suggests that evolution provided the genetic imprint for empathy, fairness, and justice, but individual development is the result of reason, imagination, and compassion. The alternative view is that social intelligence is the application of general intelligence to social situations that is largely a cognitive aptitude. This view is countered by claiming that social intuition, empathy, and compassion, referred to by Goleman as 'non-verbal abilities', are at work. These may come to the fore in microseconds, before the cognitive brain is activated. Goleman suggests that human relationships are largely non-cognitive, such as empathy, coordination, feedback and the basic capability to adjust to the vicissitudes of life. Social intelligence might be the primordial talent of the human brain.

Neuroscientists seemed to be agreed that the 'social brain' involves interlocking circuits functioning for a task. Thus, stimulation of the temporal cortex communicates with the parietal and then the frontal cortex. In empathy, the most likely connector may reside in the insula, which ties the limbic area with the frontal cortex. However, after registering emotional information, the pre-frontal cortex – the executive centre – is responsible for the appropriate response. The neurologist Antonio Damasio has studied patients with impaired functions and suggested that decision making, especially in our social life is carried out by linking the pre-frontal parietal and cingulate areas, as well as the amygdala and the insula.

Altruism refers to a state in which an individual is moved by other's emotion or distress. Gazzaniga outlined the psychological basis of "The empathy altruism hypothesis, which seeks to explain the pro-social behaviour we engage in when we watch another human being in distress. We automatically and unconsciously simulate this distress in our minds, which in turn makes us feel bad. We became infected by other person's negative feelings, and in order to alleviate this state in ourselves, we are motivated to action. A number of studies support this – that manipulating feelings towards an individual increases helping behaviour. Looking at expressions of distress, for example, enhances helping behaviour". Indeed, Adam Smith wrote as early as 1759, "When we see a stroke aimed and just ready to fall upon the leg or arm of another person, we naturally shrink and draw back our leg or our own arm; and when it does fall, we feel it in some measure, and are hurt by it as well as the sufferer. This tendency to react to the distress of others appears to be innate: it has been demonstrated in new-born infants, who cry in response to the distress of other infants within the first days of life". This response can be interpreted in terms of mirror neurons, understanding the distress signals of others. Michael Burleigh's observation is pertinent here; "Businessmen, peasants, monks, nuns and priests did a great deal more rescuing than academic philosophers, of whom history has recorded not a single example of altruism in this era, although they do a lot of writing on these subjects." The shining exception was Professor Kurt Huber of the 'White Rose' student anti-Nazi movement. Solidarity, loyalty, help, and altruism was non-existent from Professor Klemperer's colleagues when he was dismissed from the Chair of Romantic Literature at the University of Romance languages at the Dresden Technical College.

Similarly, when Heidegger was appointed Rector of the University of Freiburg in 1933, he did not rescind or in any way offer to help Professor Husserl, his Jewish mentor who was dismissed from his post due to the Nazi racial laws. Heidegger demonstrated little empathy, no altruism, and crass disloyalty to his mentor that might be interpreted as a self-centred existence (or his own celebrated concept of 'Being and Time'). It would be, of course, of great interest to compare the Empathy Index in a well-defined socio-economic group between say Germany, England, and Switzerland, though the potential political repercussions might preclude such a study.

CHAPTER 12: SCIENTIFIC EVALUATION OF THE SIGNATURES OF GENOCIDE BY NETWORKING, MODELLING, ALGORITHM OR RETROSPECTIVE STUDIES

I. **Strategy to establish the template of genocide**
II. **Persistence of anti-Semitic violence from the 14th to 20th century**
III. **Retrospective historiography of anti-Jewish persecution from the 13th to the 1st century**
IV. **Epigenetic changes**

I. STRATEGY TO ESTABLISH THE TEMPLATE OF GENOCIDE

> 'The categorical imperative is to study the signatures of the template of genocide'
>
> *Author*

The interactions between race, religion, ethics, morality, history, art, literature, philosophy, economy, and politics are immensely complex and conventionally these are dealt with separately to gain in depth knowledge and understanding. They are more often than not written by academics to academics and integration between different disciplines is hard to establish. Reductionism is essential to gain detailed knowledge of a single issue, but to comprehend it fully in a wider context, needs to be followed by reconstruction that integrates other factors and disciplines into a comprehensive entity. This has been only lately appreciated in science with the emergence of a new discipline based on algorithms, networking and modelling, called 'Systems Biology'.

Whilst physics, chemistry, biology, and genetics lend themselves to an overall mathematical analysis or model building, is this approach also applicable to complex subjects in the humanities? The questions asked are common to both science and humanities. How does one component of a problem interact with other components and the environment? What regulates their function and what regulates the regulator? Are there critical pathways in a complex system and can the multiplicity of factors be reasonably weighted? Does a model offer a greater insight into the organization, interactions and regulation of the subject under investigation then conventional reasoning? As computers are capable of using a vast number of data repeatedly, unlike the human mind, can they unravel networks and models that lead to testable hypotheses? The system may also identify similar motifs, positive and negative feedback loops found within different networks which may aid in understanding the critical factors or pathways in the multifactorial complexity of the data. An example is the 'Brain Project', which offers insight into fundamental functions, such as learning and memory by computational models that integrate physical, biochemical, anatomical, genetic and environmental aspects associated with brain functions.

Historically, as early as (20BC – 50AD), Philo of Alexandria referred to the 'divine algorithms' and the creation of 'logos' (the natural law for men and matter). Thus, the intriguing suggestion has been made that God may be the very First Programmer. Perhaps he designed alternative universes, but ours showed structural and functional superiority, unless there are others better or different successful models that we do not know about. Among philosophers, Descartes was a reductionist in dividing mind and matter, though he then linked the two entities in his famous deduction "I think therefore I am". Spinoza came to the conclusion that mind and matter is one substance with different attributes. He argued that God is nature and all that we recognise is his creation. Indeed, Spinoza came nearest to 'Systems Biology' by applying the Euclidean system to derive his concepts; definition, axioms postulates, propositions, and corollaries. Isaac Newton, in his momentous discovery of gravity of the earth, may have used this as a 'module', which he then applied successfully to interstellar gravitational forces. The renowned physicist, Richard Feynman, stated that "What I cannot create I do not understand." This involves producing physical or biological models that function as predicted and demonstrate that we comprehend the principle of organisation of the natural system.

The complexity of multifactorial interactions in the field of literature has been studied by Franco Moretti at the Stanford Literary Laboratory by pursuing literary research of a digital and quantitative nature. Moretti points out that this harks back to the extraordinary vision of Goethe, discussing with Eckermann almost 200 years ago. "Nowadays national literature doesn't mean much: the age of world literature is beginning, and everybody should contribute to hasten its advent'. These sentiments were echoed some twenty years later by Marx and Engels, arguing that from the many national literatures, often narrow-minded, a world literature will emerge. Both Goethe and Marx had in mind World Literature ('Weltliteratur'). Moretti argues that of all the published literature one may read less than 1%, which consists of its canonical fraction, so the vast majority of novels are trashed which no one has read. He refers to this in the book called 'The Slaughterhouse of Literature' (2000). He quotes Max Weber that what matters "is not the actual interconnections of things but the conceptual interconnections of problems".

This may require a new critical method of study and Moretti has computerised thousands of nineteenth century novels which enabled analysis of what he calls 'big data'. He uses 'Network Theory', which through diagrams, demonstrates the connections between, say different characters or plots. He adopts a scientific approach in his book entitled 'Graphs, Maps and Trees' (2007), in which he argues that data collected enhance knowledge of literature per se, though ultimately it needs to be interpreted. This is data-driven research, very different from conventional 'Close Reading' of individual novels and he refers to this as 'Distant Reading', which he recently published (2013) as a book with that title. The new 'Brave World' of this approach marks a paradigm shift in our conceptual understanding of literature and though it yields new data, whether they tell us more than would conventional reading, is open to question. However, it started a novel strategy and might well be informative, provided the objective is clearly defined.

Moretti raises the issue that some people object to the literary value, as canonical masterpieces are compared with 'reams of derivative pulp'. Indeed, there is a trend away from interpretive criticism towards quantitative research methods, and those who have not heard of 'meta-data' are frightened by it. Any new development is embraced by some and violently opposed by others, yet the two approaches may be complimentary as they serve different objectives. 'Close Reading' develops a specific insight in characters, situations, unknown places and enriches one's perspective of people and the world. 'Distant Reading' deals with the general, not particular, knowledge and can be comparative on national or world scale. The latter using digitalised archives enables one to ask a different type of question than 'Close Reading'. Moretti is involved in 'data mining' the public products of the shared culture.

Whether this approach might be more informative in applying to the complex problem of genocide cannot be answered without actually pursuing a similar network analysis, with the aim of defining the principle interconnections, possibly their importance, and generating unexpected nuances, which 'Close Reading' may not have disclosed. The multifactorial analysis may not necessarily give the answer, but it is likely to increase our knowledge of a danger, which we know can engulf even the most sophisticated people. Some of the many interacting factors in the network are illustrated in Fig. 5 (p.449)

It is immensely important to unravel the interactions between the environment affecting the neural pathway, with the all-important communication between the older 'limbic system' dealing with emotion, empathy and aggression, and the pre-frontal cortex, the evolutionary more recently developed rational and regulatory centre. These interactions pave the way to empathy, tolerance, and altruism on the one hand, and hostile attitudes, aggression, and evil on the other. As Albert Einstein famously declared 'God does not play dice with the world.' Chaos results with loss of order and predictably, when there is a breakdown in some of the pathways, algorithms or homeostatic models in an individual or a whole nation, dire consequences may follow, with aggression, war or genocide. The objectives of Systems Biology applied to the humanities, perhaps to be named 'Systems Humanity', is to define the complexity of multifactorial interactions, recognise the pattern of danger signals and attempt to predict their effect on the welfare of the individual and society at large. It would require a multidisciplinary approach that would include applied statisticians to quantify each of the multiplicity of factors involved in the intricate network of human behaviour – the fine, fragile line between civilization and barbarity

(Fig. 5) Potential computational model of a network of interacting factors, which under a given set of circumstances may lead to genocide

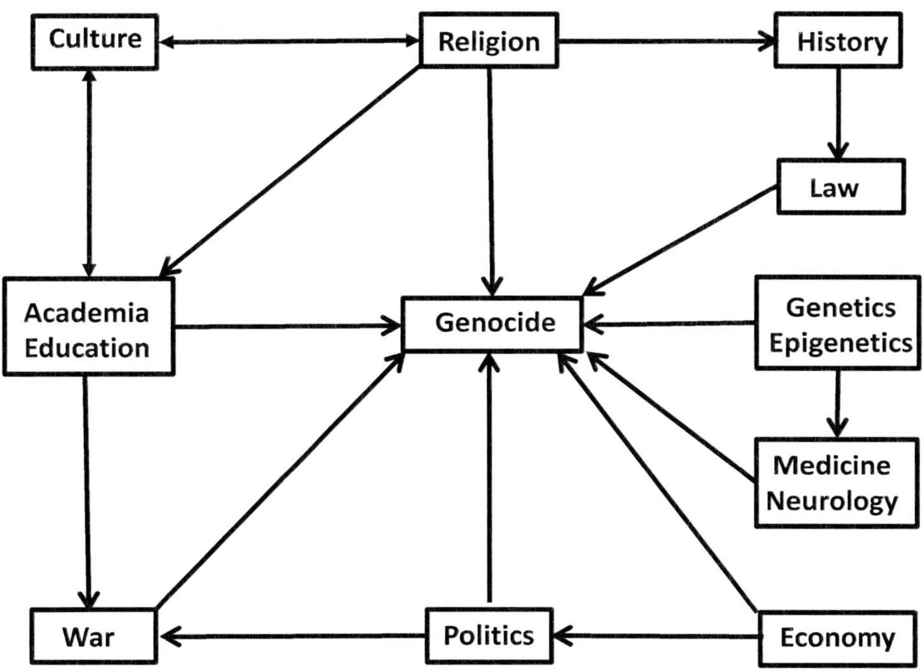

II. PERSISTENCE OF ANTI-SEMITIC VIOLENCE FROM THE 14TH TO THE 20TH CENTURY

The history of anti-Semitism has a long pedigree in religious strife and can be traced to Jews declaring their belief in one and only all powerful, omnipotent God who made the world and all living humans, animals, and plants. There is an extensive literature on the most persistent hatred of Jews and Judaism, which has entered the fabric of religion, literature, all the arts and cultural pursuits. This is not the place to even try to review the complex history of anti-Semitism.

In a remarkable investigation, Nico Voigtländer and Hans-Joachim Voth published in a paper entitled "Persecution perpetuated: the medieval origins of anti-Semitic violence in Nazi Germany" (2012). The rationale of the investigation was the emerging literature over the past decade that cultural attitudes are powerful determinants of behaviour and that they can persist over very long time. A sequel to this finding was to explore the influences responsible for transmission and long-term maintenance of 'memory' of that behaviour. They addressed specifically the historical roots of anti-Semitism and as this has an important bearing, both on the complex causes of the Holocaust and a novel statistical method of examination, it is presented in some detail.

Jews were blamed for the 'Black Death' which killed at least a third of Europe's population during 1348-50. They used plague-era pogroms as an indicator of medieval anti-Semitism and applied robust statistical analysis, which demonstrated that the same places in Germany, which had violent attacks on Jews during the plague in 1349, also showed anti-Semitism 500 years later. They write, "These inhabitants engaged in more anti-Semitic violence in the 1920s, were more likely to vote for the Nazi Party before 1930, wrote more letters to the country's most anti-Semitic newspaper 'Der Stürmer', organized more deportations of Jews, and engaged in more attacks on synagogues during the *Reichskristallnacht* in 1938." They also presented evidence that towns and cities that attacked their Jews in 1349 had more pogroms before the Black Death. They were also more likely to display anti-Semitic sculptures in public and attack Jews in the early nineteenth century.

Violent hatred of Jews persisted at the local level despite their virtual disappearance from Germany for centuries after 1550. They also found that medieval economic factors may have partly influenced early Jewish settlement and 'Black Death' pogroms, but this failed to explain 20th c. anti-Semitism. There was no evidence that Protestant compared with Catholic areas witnessed strongly different degrees of persistence. However, "the correlation between medieval pogroms and twentieth-century anti-Semitism underscores the importance of deeper historical antecedents of cultural attitudes at the local level. The findings add further weight to existing papers that demonstrate the historical origin of modern-day attitudes" (Example in Table 1). It is remarkable that they were also able to trace persistence of anti-Semitic attitudes at the local level as far back as the 11th century, thus spanning nine centuries, though the latter was not supported by statistical evidence.

Table 1 *Comparison of pogroms in Würzburg in 1147, 1298 and 1349, with no records of anti-Semitic violence in Aachen at the same periods*

	Würzburg	**Aachen**
Population in 1933	101,000	162,000
Jewish population recorded	1,100	1,242
Pogroms in 1349	Yes	No
Pogroms in the 1920s	Yes	No
NSDAP membership in 1928	6.3%	1%
Letters to the 'Stürmer'	23	10
Deported	44%	37%

"Most of the towns in our study were small, with a median population of no more than 9,000 inhabitants in 1933 and with at most a few thousand in the Middle Ages. Immigration and marriages across towns were relatively rare. These characteristics would have facilitated the persistence of beliefs at the local level. A large inflow of outsiders weakened the transmission of attitudes from one generation to the next". Numerous sites of mass killings in 1348-1350 were recorded especially in towns of the Rhineland, Franconia, and Hesse. In Thuringia, the Jews in Heiligenstadt were systematically killed and re-admitted only in 1469. They suggested that the overall pattern of persistence of anti-Semitism may reflect the effects of relatively low levels of migration of the population. However, they were not certain that vertical transmission from parents to children was crucial, though the decline in persistence of anti-Semitism in trading cities, such as the Hanseatic League, was more in line with models of parental influence on their children's attitudes.

They argue that symbolic practices and festivals may have helped to perpetuate hostile beliefs. Passion plays often portrayed Jews as engaged in deicide and anti-Semitic sculptures decorated churches and private houses. For instance, churches from Cologne to Brandenburg displayed a 'Judensau', the image of a female pig in intimate contact with Jews in suggestive sexual poses. Often festivals were commemorated by pogroms, such as in the Bavarian town of Deggendorf, attacks on the Jewish community in 1337 were celebrated every year until 1968. In Spain, until fairly recently, Spanish children played a game called 'Killing Jews' around Easter, despite that Jews were almost entirely absent since their expulsion in the inquisition in 1492.

Some of these findings are consistent with Goldhagen's arguments that a long-term history of anti-Semitism was responsible for the hatred of the perpetrators of the Holocaust. He also pointed out that anti-Semitism can be rife even without any knowledge, actions, or indeed presence of Jews, which is underpinned by the data of Voigtländer and Voth. These data argue strongly in favour of the long-term ingrained belief of anti-Semitism (the oldest hatred). Among a number of factors considered, two paradigms stand out. The constant issue present in 1349 and 1920 is the anti-Jewish teaching by the Church, and even documented attack on the Jewish community in a Bavarian town in 1337 being celebrated annually until 1968. By the same token, the Passion plays enacted yearly portrayed the Jews engaged in deicide. The Bishop of Nitra in Slovakia perpetuated the belief in 1942 that

Jews killed God to justify the deportation of Slovak Jews to concentration camps.

III. RETROSPECTIVE HISTORIOGRAPHY OF ANTI-JEWISH PERSECUTION FROM THE 13TH TO THE 1ST CENTURY

Following the rationale established by Voigtländer and Voth that cultural attitudes are powerful determinants of behaviour and that they persist over hundreds of years, a retrospective historiography of authenticated anti-Jewish activities, though without the statistical evidence is presented, harking back up to the beginnings of Christianity. A reverse chronological order is adopted, prior to the German Nazi genocide, presenting briefly the milestones which have had serious consequences on Jewish life and survival (see flow sheet, Fig.2).

'Stab in the back' alleged cause of surrender after the First World War and signing the Versailles Treaty in 1918-1919 was a 'Jewish conspiracy'. This rumour was spread among the demoralised, demobilised, and unemployed soldiers and the economically ruined population. A scapegoat for all the misery had to be found and the Jew served that purpose. Moreover, the armistice of unconditional surrender was signed by the politician Matthias Erzberger. Walter Rathenau was an exceptionally capable foreign minister serving in the Weimar Republic. Both were of Jewish origin and both were assassinated. The allegation was formally disproved, but the Volk was ever ready to blame the Jew for any misfortune. Among several learned individuals, such as the philosopher Johann Fichte, the lawyer Eugen Dϋhring, and the historian Heinrich von Treitschke stand out for their anti-Semitic polemics. Treitschke coined the oft-repeated phrase "Jews are our misfortune", not least as it had the authenticity of a highly regarded historian. Martin Luther (16th c.) first spoke highly of Jews, proclaiming that "Jews are the best blood on earth". However, when Jews refused to abandon their long-held belief, Luther turned against them and wrote the book "The Jews and their lies" (1541). He forbade rabbis to teach, confiscated rabbinical books, advocated burning down synagogues and Jews' homes, they should be driven out of the country and perceived them to be evil 'lords of the world'. Some 400 years later, Hitler and his acolytes used these words with great effect in his diatribe against the Jews. The Spanish inquisition under Ferdinand II and Isabella I in 1492-1501 ordered Jews to convert to Christianity. Some did convert to save their lives, many were killed and others expelled from Spain.

In the 13th C. Thomas Aquinas (1225-1274) was the greatest Dominican theologian. He argued against the notion that Jews rejected Jesus because of ignorance, but by deliberate defiance of the truth that Jesus was the Messiah, son of God. A failure of conversion after forced indoctrination of Jews by Christian teaching led Pope Gregory IX to investigate the Talmud, which was deemed blasphemous and a work of heresy. The order was made to eliminate the Talmud – arguably the first comprehensive attempt to destroy Jewish culture by burning some 12,000 books of the Talmud. It took place in Paris near the Notre- Dame and was a cultural vandalism 700 years before the Germans burned books in many German cities.

Innocent III convened the Lateran Council in 1215, which for the first time ordered that Jews should be segregated, that they should wear distinguishing dresses and wear yellow badges; they were banned from taking public office and were obliged to pay compulsory tax. Similar measures were perpetuated 800 years later by German Nazi legal authorities. Blood libels against Jews, accusing them of killing Christian boys and using their blood to prepare 'mazzah' (unleavened bread) for the Passover ritual. The first case was reported in 1144 in Norwich, England and later spread to most European countries, with concomitant reprisals and pogroms against Jews. Despite denials by the Emperor Frederick II and Pope Innocent IV, after thorough investigations, these accusations continued for the next eight centuries.

The Crusades were holy wars against the enemies of Christ. The 1st crusade in 1095 was preached by Urban II to liberate Jerusalem from Muslim Arabs. On route to the Holy Land, the mob discovered the 'Jewish Infidels' in cities such as Worms, Speyer, Trier Mainz, and Cologne, and they were let loose, robbing Jews of food, possessions and finally murder at large. The Bishops tried to prevent the violence, which was against Church policy, and Pope Callixtus issued a Papal Bull in defence of Jews. Nonetheless, Jews were subjected to forced baptism and ritual slaughter was perpetrated on entire families. The 2nd and 3rd crusades took place in the 12th century. The 11th century marks also the entry of St. Anselm (1033-1109), a great English theologian who applied reason in place of superstition and yet argued that God needs human blood sacrifice for redemption, to deliver from sin and damnation. Peter Abelard (1079-1142) was a brilliant Catholic theologian, who rejected the concept that God needs a human sacrifice in Jesus. However, he fell passionately in love with his beautiful pupil Heloise and predictably this violation of trust between pupil and teacher led to one of the greatest, all too human tragedies (see. Ch.5).

Abelard expressed the most memorable empathy and understanding of the Jewish predicament. "No nation has suffered so much for God as the Jews." He knew the true meaning of suffering.

The next 500 years, from the 10th to the 6th century, are noted for worsening of Christian-Jewish relationship and recourse to anti-Jewish legislation. However, the Visigoth (5th – 8th century) ruled the Iberian Peninsula, with friendly relationship between Christians and Jews. With the conversion of King Reccared in the late 6th century from Arianism to Catholicism, anti-Jewish legislation was enacted. Intermarriage was prohibited as was holding public office. Gregory the Great (540-604) protected Jews from physical violence and condemned desecration of synagogues and cemeteries. Nonetheless, later Jews were ordered to be baptised and all Jewish festivals and rituals were forbidden. Emperor Theodosius (408-450) marked the formal transition to Christianity as the religion of the Roman Empire. Although the Jewish religion was tolerated, intermarriage with Christians was forbidden, as was proselytising or holding public office.

St. Augustine, Bishop of Hippo (354-430) was a highly learned theologian, and well aware of the Jewish roots of Christianity. He opposed the arguments of his predecessors that Jews' continued existence cannot be justified. He introduced the concept that Jews scattered throughout the world serve as witnesses to the prophesy-based Christianity and this might have saved Jewish survival. Augustine was the disciple of St. Ambrose (339-397), Bishop of Milan, who declared that 'Jews are the Churches' last problem', reminiscent of words uttered about 1500 years later by Hitler and his cohort.

The anti-Jewish polemics, termed 'Adversus Judaeos' span over 2.5 centuries, (395-140). The major theologians were Chrysostom, Origen, Tertullian, Justin Martyr, and Marcion, all of whom use explicit anti-Jewish invectives, to the point of threatening Jewish existence, unless they undergo conversion. This brings us to the Gospel writers (75-100), who also present Jews in an adverse light and Matthew, most likely of Jewish parentage who made the most explicit and damaging statement to Pilate "His blood is on us and our children". This indictment had been perpetuated up to the present time, exonerating Pontius Pilate and the Romans to be responsible for both the jurisdiction and crucifixion of Jesus.

St. Paul's conversion, recognising Jesus as the Messiah (circa 33-36) was the very beginning of the missionary zeal, initially addressed to the Jews. Although some followed his sermons and converted, most Jews did not believe that Jesus was the Messiah. He wrote thirteen pastoral letters, and in the 'Acts' and the 'Romans', he stands by the Jewish teaching. When Jews largely rejected his views, Paul turned to preaching to the Gentiles, revised Judaism, and expressed overtly anti-Jewish views. In the letter to the 'Galatians', Paul claims that "the Jews killed both the Lord Jesus and the Prophets [...] but God's wrath has come upon them at last." Paul may well have been frustrated in his failure to convert Jewish people and his total conviction that Jesus was the Jewish Messiah may have driven him to initiate the anti-Jewish polemics.

As we have discussed above, location and anti-Semitism were significantly correlated using robust statistical data over a period of at least 600 years between 1369 and 1930. The written evidence of the language used from 20th down to the 1st century suggests a continuous chain of anti-Jewish polemics, demonising them and making Jews responsible for deicide. This was perpetuated by weekly sermons in churches, the annual festival over Easter, artistic representations in paintings, sculptures, literature, and poetry. Indeed, two millennia of systemic anti-Semitism had entered the fabric of homes, schools, educational establishments, civil and cultural institutions, and often underwritten by legal restrictions. Although, the Enlightenment has eased the plight of Jews, being freed from Ghetto existence and granted civil rights, the ingrained systemic prejudice remained dormant, intermittently breaking to the surface. The prime example are four true Christian theologians who risked their lives for the sake of humane and Christian values, despite ingrained, cultural anti-Jewish sentiments (see Ch.10).

Reverse Historiography of the major milestones of polemics, persecutions and mass murder against Jews over 2000 years, starting with the National Socialist period in the 20th Century down to St Paul in the 1st Century. The presistent chain of anti-Semitism suggests the paradigm of epigenetic changes in the memory DNA.

Century	**20**	**20**	**16**	**15**	**14**	**13**	**12**	**11**	**8**	**6**	**5**	**2-4**	**1**	**1**
	1920-1945	1894-1906	1483-1546	1492-1501	1349	1225-1274	1144	1095	779-840	540-604	354-430	395-140	75-100	36-67
Years	**National Socialism** 1933-1945	**Dreyfuss Affair**	**Martin Luther** 1517	**Spanish Inquisition Ferdinand II Isabella I**	**Black Death**	**Thomas Aquinas** (1225-1274) Gregory (1227) Innocent 1215	**Blood Libels** Poisoning Wells Crusades 2nd, 3rd	**Crusade 1st** Anselm Abelard	**Visigoth** 8th-5th C.	**Gregory The Great**	**Augustine** Theodosius Antioch 1st Ritual Murder 1st Pogrom Alexandria	**Adversus Judaeos** Chrysostom Ambrose Origen Tertullian J Martyr Marcion	**Gospels** Mark Matthew Luke John	**Paul**

600 Years

Location and anti-Semitism Correlated*

2000 Years

Language unchanged, reasoning revised

*Based on the statistical evidence of the local continuity of persecution of Jews over 600 years between Nazi Germany in 1930-1945 and the black death in 1349 (Voigtländer & Voth 2012).

V. EPIGENETIC CHANGES

Over the past few years, evidence has emerged that the genes residing in DNA can be modified by repeated exposure to environmental agents. The DNA sequence remains unchanged but chemical change, such as methylation or acetylation may alter the expression of DNA or histones (proteins that package the DNA). This may affect memory, as well as the long-standing controversy concerning nature versus nurture. Nature is inherited in DNA, which can be modified by nurture in the expression of DNA and may modulate the strength and speed of activation of the gene. Epigenetic changes in DNA affecting memory is a potential mechanism which would maintain a belief which is re-enacted during an individual's lifetime 'from the cradle to the grave' – and potentially beyond to the next generation.

Epigenetic change has been defined as "stably heritable phenotype resulting from changes in the chromosome without alterations in the DNA sequence." It is likely to influence the development of children, depending the way a child is brought up by its parents. The brain more than doubles in weight over the first two years of life and increases further up to adulthood. Hence, the importance of parental care on the child's social state of mind. Nurturing rodents over the first twelve hours after the birth has been shown by the neuroscientist Michael Meaney to determine the response of that pup's brain to stress associated with methylation of DNA. The more nurturing (licking and grooming her pups by the mother), the more confident and fearless the pup will become. This was associated with greater connections of brain cells, especially in the hippocampus, where learning and memory resides and the pre-frontal cortex dealing with cognition and emotion. Numerous studies in animals have shown that early life stress can leave persistent epigenetic marks in the genes, which alters their expression and can affect behavioural function through adulthood. Indeed, these findings in rodents seem to be very similar to those in the hippocampus of the human brain of persons abused during the formative stages of childhood. Long-term memory may be linked to a specific methyltransferase.

It would be surprising if the repetitive habit of prayer and Church service passed on in early childhood were not to have an epigenetic effect. However, the most remarkable finding discussed above is the correlation of persistence of anti-Semitic violence during the Black Death in the fourteenth century and Nazi atrocities in the twentieth century. Epigenetic changes might be a plausible interpretation of the statistical correlation of violent anti-Semitism over a span of six hundred years, but proof of this paradigm might be fraught with all sorts of difficulties. Apart from this important study, the paradigm has emerged that parents may pass not only the DNA to their offspring, but also functional expression of the DNA, which is modulated by parental care and empathy. Epigenetic modifications may last a lifetime, but whether altered genes might be passed on to the next generation has been demonstrated as yet only in rodents.

Epigenetics may serve as a bridge between nature and nurture or more precisely interactions between genes in the brain and the environment. Non-genetic environmental variables affecting gene expression are maternal care, nutrition, social stress, or hormonal factors. This creates an interface between the dynamic environment and fixed genome. The potential effect of epigenomes on the children of diehard SS parents has been discussed previously.

A potential biological basis of studying epigenetic persistence of anti-Semitism over 600 years in identified locations is now possible. Rapid developments in the methodology of studying epigenetic memory have recently raised the possibility of pursuing population studies and even eventual eradication of anti-social attitudes. Methylation of histones can activate or repress gene transcription through DNA methyl transferase. Indeed, long-term memory has been linked to a specific methyl transferase. DNA methylation and demethylation levels can be measured in white blood cells. Such epigenetic modifications have been studied as a function of age in many sites of the coding genes. One of the methods used for DNA methylation is chromatin immuno-precipitation. Although this is best done with blood, buccal epithelial smears or saliva can also be used.

CHAPTER 13: CONCLUDING THOUGHTS

I. **Christianity**
II. **Weimar Republic**
III. **War of the Swastika against Star of David**
IV. **Thuringia – Epicentre of Culture versus Barbarism**
V. **Universities of Jena and Heidelberg**
VI. **Complex Academic Structure of Genocide**
VII. **Acknowledgment of Guilt from four Academic Institutions**
VIII. **Psychological state of Nazi Leaders**
IX. **'Stunde Null' of Western Civilization**
X. **Anthology of 'The Deep Hurt'**

CONCLUDING THOUGHTS

<table>
<tr><td colspan="2">‘The Nϋremberg Trial struck a blow to the complaisant Christianity and Enlightened Humanity, which to this day failed adequately to explore, explain or deal with the radical evil to which they were a party’

Elsie Douglas, secretary to the Supreme Court of Justice in Nϋremberg, 1946</td></tr>
<tr><td>‘Doctors at the concentration camp ramps, selecting by Nazi diagnostic criteria for life or death were the ‘medical Einsatzgruppen’ of the Reich’

‘Killing Squad’, Author</td><td>‘The passivity of the bystander had effectively turned into collaboration’

James Carroll, 2002</td></tr>
<tr><td colspan="2">‘Nazi atrocities were ‘A crime without a name’

Winston Churchill, 1945</td></tr>
<tr><td colspan="2">‘Christianity in Germany bears a greater responsibility before God then the National Socialists, the SS and the Gestapo’

Protestant theologian pastor, Martin Niemöller, 1946</td></tr>
</table>

The burning question persisted over the past seven decades. How was it possible that a highly cultured nation in the centre of Western Christian civilization embraced the ultimate evil of mass murder of people who lived in their midst, spoke the same language, greatly appreciated and enhanced the same culture, but were different in religion? Those who value the moral and ethical principles of Western Civilization need to turn their attention to the critical issue of this paradox. It applies to theologians, philosophers, historians, scientists, medical doctors, and men or women with humanity, conscience, and empathy.

I. CHRISTIANITY

All roads of enquiry led to the original schism between Judaism and Jesus/Joshua's teaching, as presented by Paul/Saul, followed by the four Gospel writers. The critical issue of the historical Jesus in contrast to the believer's (posthumous) Jesus has recently come under scrutiny. The prophets chastising Jews for not adhering to God's commands, was interpreted by Paul, the Gospel writers, and early Christian Fathers that the Jewish people have forgone the Covenant and through Jesus the Covenant was passed on to the Christians – referred to by the Church as 'Supersession'. Christians thereby replaced the Jews as the 'Chosen people'. However, the Jews were chosen directly to be the bearers and exponents of the Covenant by God, whereas the Christians replaced Jews indirectly by dint of interpretation of the Prophets, undoing God's direct covenantal agreement or by 'deed poll'. As pointed out by many, only angels and not common flesh and blood people could satisfy all the tenets of the law. Indeed, in the past priests, just as rabbis, consistently chastise their congregation from the pulpit for committing sins in everyday life. Whilst any revised interpretation of Jesus is unlikely to change religious beliefs, it may help to appreciate the mutual misunderstandings, mistrust and polemics between Christianity and Judaism that have never been resolved.

For Christianity, the Messiah promised by the prophets to the Jews was Joshua who became Jesus (in Greek) and later Christ – the anointed son of God. The Jewish roots of Jesus have been amply demonstrated by many scholarly studies, of which Géza Vermes is the pre-eminent and authentic authority. Indeed, as Edward Kessler writes, "Christianity was one Jewish group amongst many, including the Sadducees, Zealots, Essenes and Pharisees. But only the Jewish followers of Jesus (the Christians) and the Jewish descendants of the Pharisees (the rabbis) survived the destruction of the Temple by the Romans in 70 CE." Judaism in ancient times up to the 20th century, was faced with many claims by charismatic rabbis and more so by their followers to be The Messiah. For the Jews the Messiah has not yet emerged and they pray daily for him to come. The historical evidence is clear at least on one crucial point that the promise of the 'Messianic Age' with 'Paradise on Earth' has not materialised.

Jews were involved in two unequal bloody wars with the Romans because of the strong belief in the one and only God, and they were not prepared to compromise with Roman deities. Christianity was in the process of evolving into a new religion and Helena's Cross with her son, Constantine's sword became a mighty force. Christianity assumed power throughout the Roman empire and the Jews lost all except their tenacious belief in the One God revealed to them on Mount Sinai, liberating them from Egyptian slavery and chosen to be 'the light unto the nations'. However, with Christianity gaining overall power, the Crusaders with the Popes' blessings, perpetrated repeatedly horrendous atrocities. Torture of individuals who deviated from the declared dogma of the Church, burning of heretics at the stake, inter-Christian denunciations and wars negated 'Messianic peace on earth'. The Spanish inquisition, the Reformation, Blood libels, pogroms, the Second World War culminating in the Holocaust are not consistent with the Messianic peace and harmony envisaged by 'His Coming'.

In Martin Luther's early period of the Reformation around 1537, he speaks highly of Jews, as a people having been chosen by God to transmit his message to the world. He says, "the Jews are the best blood on earth (Luther, l.c. xxv.409). Through them alone the Holy Ghost wished to give all books of Holy Scripture to the world [...] The Jews drink out of the original spring, the Greeks drink out of the stream flowing out of the stream, The Latins however, out of the puddle." Luther published an entire pamphlet in 1543, 'That Jesus was born a Jew' (i.b. xxix 45-74), and expected general conversion of Jews to Christianity. When his expectations were thwarted he became incensed for their refusal to convert. He pursued until his dying day crude, anti-Jewish polemics similar to those of the Christian Fathers, and published in 1541 a book entitled, 'On the Jews and their lies'. He advocated, 'confiscation of rabbinical texts, to forbid the rabbis to teach, burn down synagogues along with the Jews' homes. And all Jews should be driven out of the country for all time.' A new wave of anti-Jewish persecutions followed, only to be eased by the Napoleonic code of law, followed by the Enlightenment. Jews were largely freed from their Ghetto existence, and with liberating zeal and haste were more than able to overcome their formal educational and civic handicaps. They entered educational institutions, and excelled in the fields of science, law, medicine, the humanities, music, economy, and trade. They created new ideas that may have disturbed the harmony of the well-rehearsed ideas of the host countries. They moved rapidly up the social ladder to become leaders in many professional, educational, economic, as well as political fields. These developments were particularly evident in Germany and led to disharmony, competition, jealousy, and animosity between the emerging Jewish middle class and the establishment.

The heavy burden of 'deicide' of the very people who had been entrusted to declare the existence of the one and only God has taken two millennia (in 1965) to lift the accusation by Vatican II. Are we witnessing the Christian ecumenical movement extending to Judaism in a spirit of making amends for the past iniquities? Dare one raise the Jewish concept of repentance ('Teshuva'), the literal meaning being 'Return'? Acknowledging, regretting, and remembering the wrongs committed against their elder brethren and return to basic humane, moral and religious values? Is it so difficult for human nature to accept the rational – yet fiercely fought notion that there are diverse ways to God and salvation? Rabbi Lord Sacks argues cogently in his book 'Dignity of Difference': "We serve God, author of diversity by respecting diversity." This concept repudiates the notion held by religious authorities from the times of antiquity up to the present that diversity is damnable. One can identify at least ten fault lines in the Christian-Jewish rapture that had such a devastating effect on the original and elder partner of monotheism.

1. The first paradox of Jewish origin of Christianity has been demonizing Jews and their scriptures. Might this be interpreted as a testament to the insecurity of early Christianity expressed in persecution of Jews?
2. The second paradox is to blame Jews for Jesus's death and yet Jesus freely chose his death as a human blood sacrifice for redemption. The corollary of this is a further pernicious layer, possibly through St. Anselm's theology that Jews are blamed for the very deed that makes possible Christian salvation. Indeed, the Romans have been absolved from any responsibility, yet they were the real culprits, the prevailing power and brute force crucifying Jesus. However, Vatican II 'Nostra aetate' has absolved Jews of deicide.
3. The concept of Supersession of Christianity and a new covenant with the 'righteous chosen people of gentiles' is based on the interpretation of the Prophets' admonitions of Jews failing to abide by God's laws, is open to endless arguments. However, taking away by men what has been granted directly by God to the People of Israel has not been the most persuasive hermeneutic reasoning. This

has been partly admitted and revised by Vatican II. The Jews "remain most dear to God and have the glory and the covenant and the Law and the worship and the promise. For the gifts and the call of God are irrevocable."

4. Christianity is unfulfilled until Jews accept Jesus as the Messiah, for his primary mission was to convert his Jewish brethren to his teaching. The implication of this precept is that Jews are held to be responsible for the fulfilment of Christianity and blamed for any failure.
5. A closely related notion is that liberal Protestants wanted Jews to convert to Christianity in order to affect the Second Coming of Jesus and complete the eschatological process. Indeed, the Jews are responsible for the second coming of Jesus and if they do not convert they will be blamed for not fulfilling 'paradise on earth'. Hence, Jews hold the power for good or ill. The alternative, equally cogent, view but not argued, is that as long as Christianity persecutes Jews who have consistently, at great personal peril believed in the one and only God, the 'True Messiah' will not come.
6. The survival of Judaism is a constant negation of Christianity and reminder of the elder brethren with whom God chose to make the Covenant.
7. St. Augustine viewed the Jews and their Bible within the historical context. He fully acknowledged the Jewishness of Jesus and the apostles. He taught that Jews should be allowed to observe their laws and traditions. Augustine argued that God must have wanted them to be dispersed over the world, as witnesses to the prophecies of Christ and the Bible. Although conversion is their only way to salvation, this should be accomplished through persuasion not coercion. Thus, unlike teachings of many of the former Christian fathers, Augustine argued that Jewish survival is critical as witness to Christianity. Whilst Augustine's teaching may have enabled Jews to survive, they were largely denied freedom of expression, depriving them of livelihood, homes and isolating them in ghettos by the Christian rulers for over 1500 years. This purported to demonstrate God's rejection of Jews and superiority of Christianity, to which Jews are the living witnesses. It could be argued that this is a self-fulfilling prophecy, instigated and maintained by the Christian masters.

8. The possibility that the prophecy that Jews will be 'the Light unto the Nations', might have been accomplished through Jesus and Paul, spreading the God of Abraham, albeit in a modified, largely acceptable way to the 'Nations' may not have been adequately studied.
9. The burden to spread God's message was thrust onto the Jews and ever since, the Nations were engaged in killing the messenger; no exception to the cardinal rule, 'you do not kill the message by killing the messenger'.
10. Eradication of Jewish influence on Christianity has been attempted, such as omitting in the scriptures Jesus's Jewish parentage, or referring to him as a 'Galilean' has not worked. As convincingly argued by Susannah Heschel, to Aryanise Jesus so as to create a 'Judenrein' (free of Jews) Christianity was a figment of imagination by extricating the religion from its roots. Hitler believed that Christianity is an invention of the Jews, that if one removes Judaism from Christianity, there is little left of the religion; perhaps for a change, he was right.

II. WEIMAR REPUBLIC

The Weimar Republic, after the defeat of the First World War, was unpopular as it had to deal with insurmountable problems of economy, inflation, depression, unemployment, and unrealistic war compensation demanded by the Versailles Treaty. Recrimination about the shameful and dishonourable surrender, associated with the 'stab in the back' myth pointed the finger on the timeless culprit and scapegoat – the Jew. The clamour for the traditional strong leadership culminated in electing Hitler as the Chancellor of the 'Thousand Year Third Reich'. The National Socialist regime led by Hitler and his cohort embarked on war on three fronts. The first was the racial war against the Jews, the second Eastern front was ostensibly for liberating Germans in Eastern Europe, linked with territorial expansion under the banner of 'lebensraum' and undeclared enslavement of the Slav people. The third front was declared by the Anglo-French allies, when Hitler attacked Poland and belatedly they woke up to Hitler's aggressive design to rule over much of Europe ('Gross-Deutschland').

III. WAR OF THE 'SWASTIKA AGAINST STAR OF DAVID'

'The difficult decision had to be taken, to cause this 'Volk' to disappear from the earth' *Speech to the SS by Heinrich Himmler, 1943*
'Total solution to the Jewish question bluntly stated the 'Volkstod' (Death of a Nation)' *E. M. Zimmer Lederberg, meeting at the Frankfurt Institute, 1941*
'The war against the Jews – the Holocaust, was the ultimate premeditated crime' *Lucy Dawidowicz. 1975*

Considerable attention has been paid to the war against Jews, started in 1933 as a 'cold war', depriving German Jews of their nationality, freedom, livelihood, followed by Goebbels' dehumanisation of Jewish people, culminating in the 'hot war' with deportation to 'Extermination Camps' ('Vernichtungslagers'). The 'Racial War' can be defined as 'extermination of Jewish people, with Jewish ancestry up to the 4th generation, including the new-born and unborn foetuses. A census of Jewish people was carried out by Heydrich and his officials who identified about 11 million Jews world-wide to have been targeted for mass murder. This was a policy enacted by a central European government, imbued with Christian and Enlightenment ideals, and expounded by University educated individuals. 'Racial hygienists', in effect 'exterminators', many based at universities, argued that the evolutionary process, normally taking millennia, will be accelerated to a few years, by hanging, shooting, and gassing the 'inferior people', using impeccable German organisation and discipline. They aimed to generate the perfect individual with Nazi – Nordic – Brain – Body – Culture, characteristics defined by learned eugenic experts and executed by medical doctors.

This was a war by stealth, a war started by politicians, underwritten by racists with the connivance of academia, lawyers passing restrictive laws, releasing the elementary forces of the mob. Finally herding children, women, and men into cattle trucks, on route to the ultimate modern development, the German extermination camp. The final act of contempt for Civilization, Universities, the Enlightenment, and the Ten Commandments was perpetrated by the healers turned killers from the finest German universities. Even Heidegger, the man of 'Da Sein', lost his judgment, humanity, empathy, and ethics, the philosopher who owed a great deal of his intellectual development to Jewish philosophers and was emotionally nourished by some of his Jewish students.

The public was not party to the general plan of exterminating Jews and enslaving the Slav people, in order to produce 'lebensraum' for the superman. However, the war against the Jews was known to thousands of soldiers, especially those serving on the Eastern front, and some of their dependants at home or by anyone who wanted to know what happened to the dispossessed Jews transported to the 'East'. Nonetheless, the Church, academia, and altogether enlightened humanity, remained 'schtum'. They were not concerned, as poignantly expressed by Pastor Niemöller after the facts (see p.386). It is fairly easy with a modicum of prejudice to define an undesirable group of people as 'witches, heretics, Jews, communists, blacks, whites or simply 'others'' and dispose of them, as well documented by history. Humanity must not be smug that Germany of 1933-1945 was an aberration, which cannot and will not repeat itself; 'For whom the bell tolls, it rings for thee' (Hemingway). The Churches, Universities, and enlightened humanity carry a heavy burden of responsibility for the future, judging by the past. Human capacity for good, achieving spiritual and scientific heights, in equal measure with man's inhumanity to man, are hard-wired in his primordial psyche. The Nüremberg trial expressed in Elsie Douglas's words, the limits of the law to speak adequately on behalf of humanity's most traumatic history. "Altogether, it is fair to conclude that the trial struck a blow to the complaisant Christianity and Enlightened Humanity, which to this day failed adequately to explore, explain or deal with the radical evil to which they were a party, however indirectly, and cannot be exonerated."

IV. THURINGIA, THE EPICENTRE OF CULTURE VERSUS BARBARISM

> 'Goethe was not just a good and great man, but an entire culture'
>
> *Friedrich Nietzsche, 1880*

The rupture between Culture and Civilisation was singularly manifested in the state of Thuringia, the epicentre of Classical Weimar Culture of Goethe and Schiller. Goethe has been epitomized as 'the bedrock of German culture', especially during stressful times when the nation's morale was at a low ebb. Indeed, the president of the newly created Weimar Republic called upon Goethe when he addressed the German people and asked them to abandon imperialism and adopt Goethe's 'Spirit of Weimar'. Nietzsche described Goethe as not only a good and great man, but as an entire culture. A particularly apt description of Goethe by Schiller is that of an ideal, whole, well-rounded individual, who presented personalities in his books that may have influenced the educated Western European to be a human being – a 'Mensch'. A few miles east, Weimar was twinned with the University of Jena, a great seat of learning, among whom were counted the philosophers, Fichte, Hegel, and Marx, with Schiller occupying the chair of History and Goethe the Vice-Chancellor, playing an important role in the development of the university. To the west of Weimar, is Eisenach, where Johan Sebastian Bach was born and Martin Luther attended school and later was hiding from the Pope's agents in the local castle of Wartburg, where he completed the first translation of the New Testament into German. Despite Thuringia in the 19th century embodying Weimar classicism, one of the highest levels of culture, religion and learning, it was the first state early in the 20th century Germany to fall under National Socialist political influence and government. The barbarities perpetrated at the Buchenwald concentration camp, were almost within walking distance of Weimar.

V. UNIVERSITIES OF JENA AND HEIDELBERG

Once Thuringia became a Nazi-dominated State, under Frick and Sauckel, the University of Jena was the first to be transformed into a 'model Nazi university'. Hans Günther's appointment to the Chair in 'Social Anthropology' as early as 1931 heralded the new regime by an outspoken racist, anti-Semite and authority on 'Racial Science'; indeed, he was known as the 'Rassen Papst' (Race Pope). Between 1862 and 1909, the university had Professor Ernst Haeckel the foremost exponent of Darwin's theories in Germany. Günther and the Nazis used and adapted Haeckel's overall sound biological concepts to fit their ideology. The circle was squared in Jena when the avowed, fanatical Nazi, Dr. Karl Astel, a 'sport physician', responsible for thousands of forced sterilisations, was appointed in rapid succession to a professorship in the medical faculty, then the head of a newly established 'Institute of Human Genetic Research and Racial Politics', Rector of the University of Jena and more appropriately SS lieutenant colonel. The culturally and spiritually endowed Weimar-Jena-Eisenach was dishonoured, by Jena becoming a model Nazi university, discrediting Weimar Classicism and underwriting the barbarities perpetrated on their doorstep in Buchenwald. Thuringia reached a low point of humanity, creating the unsavoury triad between culture, civilization and barbarism.

In order to find out if other universities followed suit, the renowned university of Heidelberg was studied and compared with that of Jena. The University of Heidelberg, the oldest and arguably the most distinguished seat of learning in Germany, succumbed to Nazi influence without significant resistance from its academic establishment. Despite its impeccable liberal history, hailing as far back as 1673, when the Jewish philosopher Benedict de Spinoza was invited to the Chair of Philosophy, the University followed the downhill path of Jena. In 1933, Wilhelm Groh a legal scholar, was elected Rector of the University and dismissed a third of his staff for political and mostly racial reasons. About half of the remaining professors joined the Nazi 'Instructors League'. The liberal university principles laid down by Humboldt were converted to the 'Führer Principle'. From 1935 to 1945, the Rector of the university changed the 'Heidelberg Spirit' into the 'Heidelberg Myth'. The worst racial excesses were committed by the Nobel Prize physicist professor Philipp Lenard, the professor of philosophy, Paul Schmitthenner, and the surgeon Karl H. Bauer. Philipp Lenard introduced a new concept in science 'Aryan physics' and what he maliciously labelled 'Jewish physics', despite his acknowledged help he received from Hertz, Einstein, and Königsberger, all three being of Jewish origin. Carl Bauer found it equally easy to remove the racially targeted 'inferior people' by applying his surgical skills and excising the tumour. Yet, he was elected in 1945 as the first post-war Rector of the University. Thus, Heidelberg, arguably one of the greatest Universities in Europe, had for its first post-war Rector a surgeon, who protected former Nazis and even excluded those with anti-Nazi credentials.

Stephen Remy in his book, 'The Heidelberg Myth' (2002), comprehensively demolished the notion that Heidelberg was free of the racist virus. Whilst most professors remained silent, there were a number of honourable individuals with high moral, intellectual, and scholastic principles. Among these was Karl Jasper, professor of philosophy, Alfred Weber, professor of Sociology, and Gustav Radbruch, a legal scholar.

Robert Ericksen's studies of the culpability of the Churches and Universities, especially that of Göttingen, concluded by stating, "I argue that the killers who resemble those of us who are members of Western culture were given a license to kill by their churches and universities. By their endorsement of a regime that openly spoke of its brutal intentions towards Jews, a regime that increasingly tightened the screws of injustice and mistreatment".

Three pertinent case histories were discussed; Philipp Lenard, the Nobel Prize winning physicist, the infamous Joseph Goebbels, Minister of Propaganda and Martin Heidegger the eminent philosopher. They share in common an affinity to Jewish mentors, and ideas; two of them were also intimately involved with Jewish women. They were the products of highly regarded German universities, yet they emerged as dire racists, advocating the demise of the very people who supported them intellectually and some emotionally. This paradox of German-Jewish affinities turned to hatred still awaits an explanation. However, no lesser individuals than Johann Wolfgang Goethe, Thomas Mann, Bogumil Goltz, Herman Cohen, and Wolf Lepenies drew attention to the conundrum of German-Jewish affinities.

VI. COMPLEX ACADEMIC STRUCTURE OF GENOCIDE

> 'All the barbarities were in full swing, whilst Beethoven and Mozart played, Goethe and Schiller were read and recited, and 'Kultur' with its ennobling, spiritual élan thrived side by side of murder at large'.
>
> *Professor George Steiner's consistent post-Holocaust theme*

By the early 20th century, an institutional anti-Jewish prejudice prevailed, through teaching of the Churches and in most Christian homes. This was despite a wave of Jewish assimilation and acculturation, with some either joining the emerging Reform Synagogue or conversion to Christianity. Heinrich Heine was baptized in 1825 and declared that he has done so to obtain an "entry ticket to European civilization"; then he wrote, "I am now hated by both Christian and Jew". These sentiments were also pertinent to Gustav Mahler's conversion to Christianity before his appointment as conductor of the Viennese Opera. Historically, this heralded voluntary 'Cultural Conversion', to enable one to pursue one's artistic talent, as compared with 'forced Conversion' of survival. Millennia of persistent anti-Jewish teaching by Catholic and centuries by Protestant Christianity were the origins of the 'complex composite enabling academic structure of genocide'.

The second contributing factor was the academic, nationalist, racist, and anti-Semitic agenda against the outsider, the unprotected, despised Jew. He was the harbinger of all problems, all new ideas as disparate as capitalism and communism, in fact, any 'ism'. Comte Joseph A. de Gobineau, in his 'Essay on the Inequality of Human Races (1853-1855)', insisted that race explained everything in the past, present and future. In Germany, after the Reich had been established in 1870, political authority was aligned with those of racial identity. The call for Aryan superiority as well as the belief in 'Völkisch' nationalism gained momentum. This was especially evident in the writings of the prominent Prussian historian Heinrich von Treitschke in about 1880 that "Jews are Germany's misfortune. The Jew belonged to a rootless, inferior species of humanity". Presumably this is despite Abraham, Moses, Joshua/Jesus, Saul/Paul, some of the Apostles, Philo, Spinoza,

Freud, Marx, Mendelson, Mahler, Heine and Einstein; Nobel Prize winners out of all proportion to its number and excelling in every academic discipline. The same historian pronounced that "War was morally sublime".

Similarly, Eugen Dühring, lawyer and philosopher, argued in 1881 that the Jews, despite being an inferior race, were taking over Europe. They should be forced back into ghettos and their property confiscated. Houston Stewart Chamberlain published in 1910 'The Foundations of the Nineteenth Century', in which he presented the racial struggle, with Germany upholding the European Christian culture against the corrupting influence of the Jews. He also postulated that Christ was not Jewish. This fell on receptive ears of religious intolerance, identifying the Jew as a familiar culprit of hatred, a scapegoat of all misfortunes and calamities that offered a welcome relief. These views were propagated despite the 'Book of Genesis' that everyone was descended from Adam and Eve, leading to the doctrine of common humanity, though set aside during religious wars and persecutions.

A host of anthropologists, biologists and eugenicists locked into the fray, interpreting Charles Darwin's concepts expressed in 'Origin of Species' (1859) and Descent of Man (1871) to suit their ideology. Indeed, Darwin did not believe in distinct identities, though they may merge into each other, and it was not possible to find clear distinctive characters between them. Yet his argument that evolution was based on survival of the fittest was interpreted by some to mean that life was a struggle for existence among races, and that the stronger and more intelligent will survive by reason of natural selection over the weaker and less apt people, doomed to extinction. These ideas, led to the policy adopted by the Nazi followers to eliminate the 'weak races', defined by hatred and fictitious criteria by the 'supermen' constituting the 'Volk'. The state must intervene to advance human evolution. Selecting the Jewish people was based on being a rootless degenerate race, despite or more likely because of all the above mentioned key innovators of religion, philosophy, art, and science. Furthermore, Rudolf Virchow, one of the founding father of German anthropology (1871), carried out a survey of six million schoolchildren in Germany, according to the colour of their eyes, hair, and skin. He concluded that 'pure' and separate Aryan and Jewish races did not exist. This became more evident, when the proportion of Jews marrying non-Jews had risen from almost eight percent in the period 1901-1904 to about twenty-three percent by 1929. Later, in 1942, Ruth Benedict published 'Races and Racism', in which she dismissed the thought of race as 'a travesty of scientific knowledge', followed by Ashley Montagu's "Man's Most Dangerous Myth: The Fallacy of Race", both quoted by Cannadine.

Among the infamous university-educated individuals, Fritz Lenz (1887-1967) 'professor of eugenics for racial hygiene' – a misleading title approved by the University of Munich in 1923, deserves special mention. He argued that culture, evolution, and redemption are all dependent on race and claimed that these express all the criteria of Nazi ideology. He was aided and abated by a series of Eugenicists, mutating into 'Racial Hygienists', to mention only Eugene Fischer, Otmar von Verschuer, and Ernst Rüdin. 'Racial Hygiene', a euphemism for eliminating anyone the Nazis disapproved was described by Max Nordau: "Evolution acted as a cover for natural barbarism, allowing people to cover their instincts with the last word of science." Benno Müller-Hill Professor of Genetics at the University of Cologne concluded that the pure academic found it opportune to be an apolitical good scientist. "This applied equally whether, like professor Hallervorden and von Verschuer, their own ends had been served by the large-scale murders, or whether, like Professors Fischer, Lenz and Rüdin, they had done no more than act as advisors and expert witnesses to the machinery of murder. They had known nothing and could say nothing. And so they once again became a part of the scientific establishment. They made a cult out of their silence."

The basic ideology was to eliminate the Jewish inspired principle that it is forbidden – it is a sin – to kill another human being. Once this fundamental issue was out of the way, physicians started to prescribe 'Gnadetod' or euthanasia to children with incurable mental diseases. The weak adults should be denied medical care as this is counterproductive to natural evolution of survival of the fittest. The list for disposing of unfit people grew according to the ignorance of the aetiology of the disease to include tuberculosis, venereal diseases, crime, alcoholism, features of hereditary degeneration and schizophrenia. The novel medical diagnosis 'Unworthy of Life' was even queried by the medical staff at the specially designed killing centres. The celebrated paediatrician at the Jena Children Hospital, Professor Yusuf Ibrahim, sent a baby twelve months old called Sabine to the hospital Stadtroda with the diagnosis of 'Microcephaly' and the prognosis that normal development will not be achieved. He recommended euthanasia. At the centre, they queried the learned professor's conclusions, carried out further observations and found that the baby responded well to her environment and advised that she should be returned home and further observations should be made at the age of three.

Little Sabine's life was saved from the enthusiasm of the Professor for Euthanasia.

'Gnadetod' was then extended to adults and the method of killing perfected by applying modern science-driven methods. The 'Gnadetod' chain reaction activated anthropologists, anatomists, and biologists, all highly regarded university disciplines, to argue that certain categories of people are in the way of 'Kultur', indeed they were categorised as non-human or sub-human. Among these were Jews, Romanis, homosexuals, and Jehovah witnesses. By this stage, the chain reaction increased by several logs from thousands to millions and universities expanded their chairs through lavish financial support by the Nazi hierarchy. A more scientific terminology emerged for the new cadre of professors – 'racial hygiene'. Their scientific research led to the paradigm that the Slav people are to be next in line for purging humanity of undesirables or at least enslaving them to work for the German Volk. The concept of 'lebensraum' coupled with the 'bread basket' in the East may have endorsed these ideas. A start had been made by eliminating a fair proportion of Polish intelligentsia. If Germany had won the war, it is likely that the 'Gnadetod chain reaction' would have exploded, especially in East Europe and ensnared in one form or another the rest of the non-German 'inferior people'.

Among the philosophers, Martin Heidegger joined the Nazi party in 1933 endorsed the 'Führer principle' and declared, 'The Führer alone is the present and future Germany and its Law'. He was rewarded by becoming the first university Rector of Freiburg under the Nazis, but his communication skills, based on philosophical discourse were probably unsuitable and he soon resigned from the post. Richard Wolin suggested that Heidegger succumbed in 1933 to the delusion that the National Socialist Revolution represented the saving power of Western Humanity; a power capable of redeeming European culture from the dislocation of a rationalistic, modernizing and nihilistic bourgeois 'Zivilisation'. Heidegger's rare, though grossly insensitive, indeed contemptible thoughts about the holocaust does not reflect well on his humanity. This is even more pertinent in view of what he owed his Jewish mentor, Edmund Husserl, and the ideas of Emil Lask, another Jewish philosopher, as well as the close emotional relationship with Hannah Arendt, and supervising at least six out of his twelve Jewish doctoral students. A highly regarded philosopher but a flawed human being is perhaps not an unfair epitaph, despite endless arguments about his influence on Nazi ideology. Recent discovery of his

'Black Notebook' leaves little doubt of his racist anti-Semitic views, despite or perhaps because of his Jewish links.

The major third factor in the complex genocide structure was the judiciary. Whilst the Weimar constitution was not abrogated, the question arose whether the Third Reich is not really devoid of law, or that constitutional law ended in 1933. 'Protective custody' by the Gestapo, special death squads and concentration camps were not governed by conventional law but what may be called 'Führer's law'. There were also 'People's Courts' staffed by Nazi judges. The single exception was a flurry of restrictive laws against the Jews, within months of gaining power in 1933. The final extermination, which presumably came under the rubric of Führer's oral law, was largely interpreted by Himmler. The first law passed in 1933, the 'Law to restore the professional Civil Service', dismissed all individuals of Jewish descent and that included university staff. The 'Reich Citizenship Law' deprived German Jews of citizenship rights and redefined them as subjects of the state. Then followed the 'Law for the protection of German blood and honour', which outlawed marriage between Jews and non-Jews. Overall, about 250 decrees removed Jews from professions and economic life and made them outlaws in Germany.

The faithful guardians of German Law, reversed by the stroke of pen the citizenship that had been granted to German Jews between 1812 and 1869. Among these legal authorities featured Carl Schmitt, a scholar, converted to Nazi ideology, advocated Führer dictatorship and wrote on 'The Führer protects the law'. Of course he was an avowed anti-Semite. Otto Koellreutter was an early Nazi who wrote the new constitutional law. Theodor Maunz, professor of German constitutional law in Freiburg, was also an early member of the Nazi party. He was highly regarded by the judiciary, despite pronouncing that arrests by the Gestapo are acts outside the judicial realm, in effect giving free reign to an extra-judicial state, within the state; hence the Gestapo was given a free hand. These were not young opportunistic lawyers making their reputation on the wave of rising clamour for strong leadership and anti-Semitism. They were well established, reputable members of the legal fraternity, unlike Reinhard Höhn a young Nazi lawyer making his way in the profession, opposed the 'Roman-Jewish' thinking (in itself a novel contradictory concept). He characterised it as 'liberal, rational, abstract, individualistic, materialistic, alien to the people, nihilistic and corrupting'. The final stage of genocide was accomplished ostensibly by the Wannsee Conference, attended by a number of lawyers, doctors, and Adolf Eichmann under the chairmanship of Reinhard Heydrich. Indeed, Heydrich expressed surprise at the readiness of lawyers and doctors supporting mass murder of 11 million human beings. Eichmann spent his considerable administrative talent to collect and deliver European Jews to the Führer's designated destination, to accomplish Führer's dearest wish, the final solution that will bring purity, peace, and prosperity to the Volk. Eichmann's notoriety was spectacularly made public at the Jerusalem Trial, which did not demonstrate a monster but a banal man, yet capable of quoting Kant correctly. He disclaimed any responsibility for the fate of millions of Jews, he just obeyed orders.

> 'They were Scientific and medical methods, scientific and medical speeches that were used in carrying out these crimes in the name of science'
>
> *Professor Benno Müller-Hill, University of Cologne. 1988*

Doctors of medicine were the fourth and final nail in the coffin, selecting for life or death. They were the only professionals in direct face-to-face contact with the victims. This was the 'unkindest cut of all', for the exalted healing profession, educated and trained by some of the most famous Medical Schools in the world. They were personally involved in condemning millions of innocent human beings to death by injections, shooting or gassing. The blatant anti-Hippocratic act committed by highly cultured people, who for good measure proposed the most barbaric experiments, so as to gain some useful 'scientific information' from children and adults who are anyway going to die, is the ultimate unrestrained radical evil of those who 'do know what they are doing'. There are no words that can express the revulsion of the foul acts committed by some German and Austrian doctors of medicine.

The least the Medical Schools educating these contemptible members of the healing profession could have done, was to study the intake and end-product of some of their students, if there are any features in their selection or educational process that might account for the catastrophe. The institutions cannot be absolved from culpability and must bear some responsibility. The willing medical executioners of the Nazi regime have been noted previously and it remains appropriate here only to add the emerging 'Anti-Hippocratic Medicide Syndrome', the 'Mengele –

Clauberg – Eberl Syndrome' (p.417). Dr. Mengele and Dr. Eberl selected people for life and death at the ramp of the extermination camps, whilst Drs. Clauberg and Mengele for perpetrating lethal experiments, the former on women and the latter on children and adults. They were regrettable products of some great German and Austrian University Medical Schools.

The four enabling institutions – Christianity, Academia, Law, and Medicine created the infrastructure of genocide and all that was needed was a powerful trigger to set off the 'complex-composite act of genocide'. The prevailing conditions after the First World War, the shock of losing the war, the Versailles Treaty with its heavy reparations, global depression, unemployment, economic hardship, political dissatisfaction with the Weimar regime and distrust of the imposed untried democracy, were all contributing to the crisis. Hitler, and Goebbels, his devoted spokesman, empowered the 'Volk' with a communal hubris and arrogance over the 'others', who will become slaves unto the 'Volk' or eliminated – a winning formula – underwritten by the success of the 'Blitzkrieg', defeating the French and the British forces. The 'crooked cross and sword of Genocide' or the 'heavenly way to mercy killing' is depicted in the Figure.

VII. ACKNOWLEDGEMENT OF GUILT, REMORSE AND APOLOGY FROM THE FOUR INSTITUTIONS CREATING THE INFRASTRUCTURE OF GENOCIDE

'A little self-recrimination and a lot of self-justification'

Professor Michael Stolleis; the legal profession coming to terms with its past, 1992.

'Perhaps Nazis were good Christians who instinctively plucked the 'forbidden fruit of knowledge'. God will forgive them, that is his business'

Adapted from Heinrich Heine

The moral courage of the four anti-Nazi Protestant reform theologians demonstrated what true Christianity can and should mean. Alas, they were not supported by the bulk of the Church and paid a very heavy personal price. Karl Barth, a Swiss theologian, had to leave Germany, Dietrich Bonhoeffer was incarcerated in Buchenwald concentration camp and then murdered. Martin Niemöller and Heinrich Grüber were imprisoned in Sachsenhausen and Dachau but fortunately both survived.

Vatican II (Nostra aetate), declaration in 1965 on non-Christian religions, was described by Eugene J. Fisher in 'A dictionary of Jewish-Christian relations' "the most significant document concerning Jewish-Christian relations in Church history since Paul in Romans 9-11. It rejected anti-Judaic theological polemics and condemned anti-Semitism and replaced them with the foundations for a renewed vision of the continuing role of the Jewish people in God's plan of salvation for all humanity. Noting the New Testament records that some 'authorities of the Jews 'Pressed for the death of Christ', it stated that what happened 'cannot be blamed upon all the Jews then living, nor upon the Jews of today'. The Diaspora 'allowed Israel to carry to the whole world a witness – often heroic – of its fidelity to the one God'. Positively, the Council emphasised the Jewish origins of Christianity and that the Church draws spiritual 'sustenance' from the people of God of the 'Ancient Covenant'. The Jews 'still remain most dear to God' and 'have the glory and the covenant and the Law and the worship and the promise. For the gifts and the call of God are irrevocable'.

Vatican II was followed over thirty years later in 1998 by the pronouncement of the Holy See's Commission for Religious Relations with the Jews "We Remember: A Reflection on the Shoah". "The Shoah was the work of a thoroughly modern neopagan regime. Its anti-Semitism had its roots outside of Christianity". This statement denied responsibility of the Church for the Holocaust, and differed fundamentally from the declaration by the United States Catholic Conference in 2001 in the 'Catholic Teaching on the Shoah' implementing 'the Holy See's We Remember'. "Christian anti-Judaism did lay the groundwork for racial, genocidal anti-Semitism by stigmatizing not only Judaism but Jews themselves for opprobrium and contempt. So the Nazi theories tragically found fertile soil in which to plant the horror of an unprecedented attempt at genocide". This statement accepted culpability and was at variance with the above pronouncement in 1998.

At the World Council of Churches (1948), the Lutheran and Calvinist churches expressed remorse for their past commission of 'sin against God and man', of anti-Semitism. A small but increasing number of Christian theologians have re-examined their traditional views and teaching of Judaism, and some of these are discussed in the last chapter 'A Way Forward'.

Academia failed to express remorse with the exception of the Kaiser Wilhelm Society (now Max Planck Institute). In 2001, fifty-six years after the end of the war, and following a very thorough reassessment of its war-time activities, the president offered survivors of the concentration camp experiments "the deepest regret, compassion, and shame at the fact that crimes of this sort were committed, promoted, and not prevented within the ranks of German scientists." However, Heidegger displayed hubris, arrogance, and an appalling insensitivity of a philosopher of 'Da Sein' (Being and Time), demonstrating the division between conceptual ideas in philosophy and personal humanity and morality. After the war, Heidegger failed to express regret or contrition over his moral and ideological support during the Nazi years.

The Legal Profession, despite the Geneva Convention on war and the conduct towards civilians, failed to follow these guidelines. After the war, the profession, in the words of professor Michael Stolleis was concerned with 'Vergangenheitsbewältigung' (coming to terms with the past), characterised by "a little self-recrimination and a lot of self-justification."

This is a fair summary of the legal profession's attempt to exonerate themselves from their passive acceptance by some or active endorsement by others of 'Führer's law', as Hitler explained, 'The health of the German nation is more important than the letter of the law', or 'The Führer' protects the law'. The profession effectively abdicated its moral and legal responsibilities in favour of a lawless tyranny of dictatorship.

Stolleis notes with reference to military justice that more than 3000 judges passed about 50,000 death sentences. He quotes Messerschmidt and Wüllner's book, 'Military justice was part of the Nazi system'; "it supported that system right up to the last days of its downfall; its punishment was barbarically harsh, especially in comparison to that in other countries; and it has a still undetermined but very high number of innocent victims on its conscience. As described on p. the lawyers were immensely successful after the war in putting the past behind and rose to great heights in their profession. No member of the Association of Constitutional lawyers or professor was involved in active resistance, indeed silence, acceptance of 'legal justification' of murder was the rule. The legal profession has not acknowledged remorse and pursued 'business as usual', thriving in the new democratic and Federal Republic."

Sciences in the Third Reich were considered in a book entitled 'Science in the Third Reich' (2001), edited by Professor Margit Szöllösi-Janze, with chapters by historians on science, medicine, pharmacology, and contemporary history. There was virtually no opposition and no public expression of remorse or apology. In Sir Francis Simon's statement, "In my opinion German scientists as a group lost their honour in 1933 and did nothing to get it back. I admit that you cannot say that everybody should have risked his position or life, but such risks were no longer necessary after the war. The least you could expect after all that happened was that German scientists, as a group, would state publicly and clearly that they regretted what had happened. I did not notice anything of this kind." This statement sadly applies not only to science but all professional bodies in Germany, with the exception of a few just and honourable men. Albert Einstein was more pragmatic when he responded to Professor Max Born, a fellow Nobel Prize physicist, who also had to leave Germany after Hitler came to power. Born decided after the war to relinquish his professorial post in Edinburgh and return to Germany. In his correspondence with Einstein, a long-term friend of his, Born extolled the advantages of returning to Germany, arguing that post-war Germany is very different from the bad day's days under the Nazis. He tried to persuade Einstein to return to Germany, but he would not contemplate such a move. Indeed, Einstein consistently referred to Germany as "the land of mass-murderers."

The Medical Profession was in denial for sixty-seven years after the war, but in 2012, the German Federal Chamber of Physicians meeting appropriately in Nüremberg had fully admitted their guilt, remorse, and apology in the following declaration. "We acknowledge the substantial responsibility of doctors for the medical crimes committed under the Nazi regime and regard these events as a warning for the present and the future. In contrast to still widely accepted views, the initiative for the most serious human rights violations did not originate from the political authorities at the time, but rather from physicians themselves."

With this admission of guilt by the second generation of doctors, on behalf of the perpetrators responsible for murdering hundreds of thousands innocent children, women and men, and carrying out inhumane experimentation, a new chapter was opened in German Medicine. Whilst internationally, German medical scientists and practitioners have long ago normalised their high standing, it remains to be seen whether medical students learn the ethical and moral lessons of a profession that lost its way through hubris, prejudice, self-glorification and lack of critical intellectual, moral and social intelligence.

A pre-requisite for normalisation of relationships in any sphere of activity is to take responsibility for the past wrong and evil actions. Successive German governments have adhered to that moral imperative and this attitude needs to be adopted by the professional bodies and governments. The notable exception is Austria, whose people have enthusiastically embraced the ideology of National Socialism, racism and anti-Semitism, and played a disproportionately large role in the number of perpetrators of atrocities in concentration camps. Their 'defensive silence of denial' has worked well for them, by claiming that they were the first victims of the 'Anschluss', a ploy that is both amoral and false.

And finally, what about the 'innocent bystander', as stated by the historian Deborah Lipstadt in 'Aryan Nation', "Had the Nazi hierarchy encountered unambiguous and sustained realism by non-Jewish Germans at their anti-Semitic policies (as the Bishop of Galen had protested against euthanasia), there probably would have been no 'Final Solution'". James Carroll argued "that the passivity of the bystander had effectively turned into collaboration". After the war, in a memorable expression of the uncaring attitude of people, Martin Niemöller wrote "First they came for the Jews and I did not speak out because I was not a Jew; then they came for the Communists and I did not speak out because I was not a Communist; then they came for the unionists and I did not speak out because I was not a union man. Then they came for me – and there was no one left to speak out for me".

Racial Hygienists played a lethal game with evolutionary forces of nature. Alfred Ploetz coined the term 'Racial Hygiene', which advocated that Society should examine the moral and intellectual capacity of citizens to decide on marriage and the permitted number of children and may include prohibition of reproduction. Disabled children should be aborted, as this is counterproductive to natural evolution. Ploetz was not a racist, he was against anti-Semitism, ranked Jews along with Aryans, as two of the best cultured races. However, the Nazis appropriated Ploetz to their fold and subverted his concepts. They showered him with honours, until at an advanced age, Ploetz joined the Nazi party. However, Lenz, Fisher, Verschuer, and Rüdin, all respectable eugenicists, seemed to have succumbed to the prevailing hate, socio-economic advantages and the enthusiasm of a genocidal government to eradicate 'inferior races'. These were defined by fictitious criteria and considered themselves as the superior race. They were the creators of a novel, unique experiment, an opportunity not to be missed, by tampering with nature itself, and using science to accelerate evolutionary forces of survival of the fittest. They considered themselves the true followers of Darwinism and the unprecedented power they acquired appealed to their hubris and self-esteem. Racial hygienists were hailed as the seekers of future German 'Valhalla', and no body of academics has ever gained such high esteem in the eyes of the leadership and people. Although it all may have started as an innocent academic exercise, it ended in wholesale murder, unprecedented in the history of enlightened civilisation.

The common ground with all professions has been initially collective denial, silence, and fierce protection of territorial integrity, akin to that seen in animal behaviour, as well as accusation of soiling one's nest ('Nestbeschmutzer') of anyone stepping out of line and revealing the true facts. During denazification, the guilty testified in a 'loyalty network' for one another, pleaded upholding professional values and finding a morsel of anti-Nazi activity, which was magnified into active opposition to the regime. However, with time, marked in generations, once the righteous men with professional hubris and secret guilt passed away, the truth broke through either in trickles of painstaking investigations or in torrents of admissions. Broadly the chronological progress has been as follows:

1. The Roman Catholic Church has formally admitted remorse in Vatican II about twenty years after the end of the war. The World Council of the Lutheran and Calvinist Churches expressed remorse for their past anti-Semitism three years after the war.

2. The Universities, exemplified by Jena and Heidelberg, just carried on with their academic duties, arguing that they were unable to oppose the incursions from the regime. They were in denial, and silence prevailed, with the notable exceptions of the Kaiser Wilhelm Society (now Max Planck Institute), fifty-six years after the war, admitting guilt and shame in lieu of some of its scientists. Significantly, this is probably the first utterance of 'shame' by an important public institution.

3. The law profession extricated itself without any necessity to plead guilty and as self-appointed defence attorneys their professional training was brilliantly executed – yet guilty after the facts. Great legal and moral authorities, such as professor Michael Stolleis, paved the way to admitting culpability for the indefensible ethical surrender of individuals who betrayed the legal-ethical standards of Germany; they became the real 'Nestbeschmutzers' (soiling their nest) of German justice.

4. The Medical profession took fully sixty-seven years to acknowledge active participation in the Holocaust and to express remorse. The best one can say, "Never too late".

5. The military, especially the Wehrmacht, upheld their pristine innocence, claiming that all the atrocities were carried out by the SS, Gestapo, and the 'Einsatzgruppen' (special killing squads). The professed innocence may have prevailed early during the war, but after 1941, they joined in the fray, as was amply documented and they remained in denial.

6. The innocent bystanders of the Volk, who did not know, were not told and did not ask, went along with the regime's measures and in James Carroll's view 'they turned into collaborators'.

After an in-depth examination of pastors in the church and professors at the universities, Professor Robert P. Ericksen concludes that these "members of Western culture were given a license to kill by their churches and universities." He asks whether these people should be considered to be partly responsible for mass murder. Furthermore, Ericksen states, "The evidence suggests that both church and university gave Germans permission. Both institutions heaped praise on Adolf Hitler in 1933. Neither openly recanted this praise for Nazi ideas or seriously challenged Nazi policies. To enact a brutal policy by their endorsement of a regime that openly spoke of its brutal intentions towards Jews."

VIII. PSYCHOLOGICAL STATE OF NAZI LEADERS

A great deal has been written about the psychological state of Nazi leaders and personalities. Whilst Himmler had been labelled as a psychopath and Goering as a heroin addict, a common trait of Jewish self-hatred runs through a number of leading Nazis. The term 'self-hating Jew' had been applied largely to assimilated, enlightened, intellectual Jews who felt uncomfortable with the traditional Jewish life of their parents or altogether of their ancestry, on account of class, culture, education, and religious outlook. They express some of the rhetoric of anti-Semites. The classical example was Otto Weininger, a brilliant young Austrian Jewish writer. According to Amos Elon, the book of Weininger inspired the Viennese black joke that "anti-Semitism did not really get serious until it was taken up by Jews." Self-hatred by Gentiles on account of alleged or real Jewish ancestry can be coined by the term 'auto-aversion' and classified into three groups.

1. Alleged Jewish ancestry, which was most likely false, but the stigma and perceived 'odium' played relentlessly on their minds and may have led to murderous hatred. Hitler, Heydrich, and Wagner are prime examples of 'auto-aversion'.
2. Strong intellectual and/or emotional ties with Jews, elicited an association and a nagging feeling of debt, which they wished to deny or abrogate, as it may have hindered later ideological, academic, business or social norms. Examples of this type of 'auto-aversion' was seen in Goebbels, Lenard, and Heidegger.
3. Theological 'auto-aversion' might apply to the Christian religion, with its Jewish roots in Jesus (Joshua), Paul (Saul), probably Matthew and John and many of the Apostles. Christianity emerged from Judaism, the 'Old Testament' and supersession of the interpretation of the Prophets.

A fratricidal hatred developed towards the Jews, with persecutions, crusades, the inquisition, pogroms, and culminating in the Holocaust. The two-thousand-year history is consistent with an aversion of Christians to their Jewish origins, the people who are not willing to accept the historical status of Jesus. In addition to or alternatively, the wish to exorcise or kill the father of Christianity adds up in Freudian terms to a 'Theological

Oedipus complex'. Indeed, the two paradigms can be unified into the fratricidal aversion to the Jewish roots of Christianity, which had led to the miserable history of the two religions believing in one and the same God of Abraham. Altogether, the 'Syndrome that dares not speak its name' (SS-N), the co-existence of Culture and Barbarity combined with auto-aversion was manifested by the racists – Hitler and Heydrich, the chief polemicist – Goebbels, the Nobel laureate in science – Lenard, the renown philosopher – Heidegger and the celebrated composer – Wagner.

In the final analysis, the culprits were not the mob let loose at the prey. The men responsible were those with the primeval instinct of animal sacrifice practised by many tribes and religions. Men who focused on an ancient culprit, the Jew, who imposed on the world the heavy burden of One and Only God with the attendant Ten Commandments. The fratricidal war of the Abrahamic religions had created an absolute certainty of the one and only way to reach God. Two millennia of hostility, massacres, pogroms, culminating in the Jewish Genocide, failed to alter the 'stiff-necked' adherence of the 'Chosen People'. The men of letters had a culprit for all past, present and future calamities. From the 'black death' to 'blood libels', economic crises, political upheavals, wars, degrading culture, and creating communism and equally capitalism. Indeed, by this alleged account, the pernicious Jewish power will have attained mastery of the world. The enlightenment largely failed to remedy the overall view of the Jew. The freedom of expression embodied in the written or spoken word by Voltaire became the eleventh commandment.

Generally, everyone was courting favours with radical measures, so as to gain benefaction from Adolf Hitler the charismatic leader of the German Volk. The entire machinery of culture, education, and learning capitulated, with very few vocal exceptions, and the great majority of 'innocent bystanders'. The end-result, murder of six million Jews, death of millions of Germans and Allies. After the war, the suffering, destruction, and mayhem were placed at the feet of the Führer, absolving his willing accomplices and belittled the minds of some sixty million Germans, many of whom were directly or indirectly responsible for the genocide.

The racial ideology of the brave new Nazi world was to create a perfect, blood-defined, racially pure, fair, blond, blue-eyed Führer-led Volk, by eliminating the 'others'. Academic ideas by University-educated, enlightened, Christian individuals, were contrary to Darwin's 'Descent of Man', denial of Goethe's 'Wahlverwandtschaften', they violated Moses' 'Ten Commandments', and were in total contradiction to our knowledge of

DNA and heredity. The findings of the 'Human Genome Project' suggests that different 'races' share over 99.9% of their DNA and even the remaining 0.1% shows more variation within than between the so called racial groups. Thus, the evidence supports the biblical view of monogenic creation and denies the racist conjecture of polygenic origin.

IX. 'STUNDE NULL' (ZERO HOUR) OF WESTERN CIVILIZATION

The Nazi racial ideology created the authentic 'Stunde Null' of Western Civilization in generating a moral, legal, and medical vacuum. In biological terms, if one removes a microorganism from the community of organisms, the vacuum is filled by other adjacent organisms. Similarly, with animals or a power vacuum in a country, it will be overrun by its neighbour. The Holocaust created a total blackout, a vacuum of all the civilising values generated by Religion, Faith, and the Enlightenment in an advanced culture, which was unprecedented in the annals of history. After the horror was disclosed a stunned silence filled the vacuum of 'Stunde null' of civilization. Morality, law, and medicine were withdrawn from a selected population and the country entered an unchartered territory of lawlessness, criminality, and medicide. The Nüremberg trial had recognised the hopeless attempt to apply established jurisprudence to this unique crime and had to create a new category "crime against humanity" and coin the new term 'Genocide'.

Conceptually, the arguments based on inferior races, and Social Darwinism have proved to lack any scientific credence and if there were to be any substance to this concept, the way that German 'racial hygienists' embarked on correcting 'nature's failures' went against every civil, human, moral, and religious precept. The moral vacuum has been dealt with by regression to a primordial atavism, which may be buried deep in the human psyche, the limbic system of the brain. However, this begs the question, what repressive mechanism, which keeps the barbaric past at bay is released to allow it to break through and become dominant after a dormant period? Both the legal and medical professions fell into uncharted waters of criminality, members of these paragons of culture and upper echelon of education prevaricated, as each professional body failed to face responsibility for their murderous past. The chain reaction of perverse rationality, taken to irrational extremes, by educated and yet deluded individuals waits for an explanation by the new generations of German moral thinkers. A twelve-year-eclipse in German history of civilisation will not go away. It was tragically highlighted by the blood of the 'Weisse Rose Students'. "We will not be silent, we are your bad conscience" and expressed in the following anthology of 'Deep Hurt'.

X. ANTHOLOGY OF 'THE DEEP HURT'

You who live safe Consider if this is a man Who dies because of a yes or no. Meditate that this came about Repeat them to your children *Primo Levy, If This Is a Man*
Stood on a great plain in the falling snow, Ten thousand soldiers marched to and fro Looking for you and me, my dear, looking for you and me. *W H Auden, Refugee Blues*
An engine, an engine Chuffing me off like a Jew A Jew to Dachau, Auschwitz, Belsen I began to talk like a Jew I think I may well be a Jew *Sylvia Plath, Daddy*
And I myself am one massive, soundless scream Above the thousand thousand buried here I am each old man here shot dead I am every child here shot dead Nothing in me shall ever forget! *Yevgeny Yevtushenko, Babi Yar*

Black milk of day break we drink you at evening
We drink it at mid-day and morning we drink it at night
We drink and we drink
We shovel a grave in the air
there you won't lie too cramped

Paul Celan, Death Fugue

We, the rescued,
The noose wound for our neck still dangle
Before us in the blue air –
Hourglasses still fill with our dripping blood

Nelly Sacks, We the Rescued

Be embraced millions!
This kiss for the whole world!
Brothers, above the starry canopy
Must a loving father dwell

Friedrich Schiller, Ode to Joy,
Ludwig van Beethoven, 9th Symphony

CHAPTER 14: A WAY FORWARD

I. **Vatican II (Nostra aetate 1965) and pronouncements by other churches**
II. **Roman Catholic theological thoughts -Gregory Baum and James Carroll**
III. **Post-holocaust Jewish thoughts**
IV. **Academia and the professions**
V. **Post-war historians and professions**
VI. **The 'Jewish question' mutated into the 'German question'**
VII. **White Rose students**

A WAY FORWARD

'I have taken great care not to laugh at human actions, not to weep at them, not to hate them, but to understand them'.

Baruch Spinoza, Tractatus Politicus, 1676-1677

'The theological negation of Judaism and vilification of the Jewish people were translated into genocidal action of monstrous proportions'

Professor Gregory Baum, Roman Catholic, Theologian, 1979

'Christianity's oppression of Judaism is linked with Christianity's emergence from Jewish Origins'.

Author

'The same men who are held strictly in control by custom, respect, self-control, friendship and loyalty with one another, once they encounter the 'stranger' they turn to murder, arson, rape and torture, exhilarated and spiritually undisturbed'.

Paraphrased from Nietzsche's 'Basic Writings', 2011

'The overall ethical rules that apply to individual violence are erased from group violence and become an abstraction'.

Robert Toscano, 2009

'The Holocaust may be a manifestation of the predisposition to primeval aggressive instincts as expressed by Konrad Lorenz'.

Zygmunt Bauman, 1989

'Auschwitz reveals an illness operative not on the margins of our civilization but at the heart of it. The Holocaust challenges the Foundations of Western Society'.

Professor Aarne Siirala, Lutheran Theologian, 1976

<table>
<tr><td>‘The false ideology- Through an ocean of Blood to a kingdom of love’.

Author</td><td rowspan="2">‘The true ideology – we serve God, author of diversity, by respecting diversity’.

Rabbi Lord Jonathan Sacks, 2002</td></tr>
<tr><td>‘The Jewish Question mutated into the ‘German Question’

Author</td></tr>
</table>

I. VATICAN II (NOSTRA AETATE, 1965) AND PRONOUNCEMENTS BY OTHER CHURCHES

Vatican II may have proved to be a watershed in Christian-Jewish relationship after two millennia of anti-Jewish polemics in the Gospels, art, literature, and deprivation of civic rights. Gregory Baum outlined three major points. "In the first place, the Vatican II declaration asked Catholics to engage in dialogue and cooperation with Jews. To foster and recommend that mutual understanding and respect which is the fruit above all of biblical and theological studies, and of brotherly dialogues. By thus recognizing Judaism as a religion in its own right and an equal partner in dialogue, Vatican II abandoned, at least implicitly, the Church's missionary stance toward the Jews. Secondly, the Vatican declaration asked Catholic preachers and teachers to eliminate the various evil myths that have been projected upon the Jews in the Christian tradition, especially the myth that they are a rejected people, a people abandoned by God, condemned for their unbelief. Far from being repudiated, the Jews, according to the teaching of Vatican II, continue to be God's chosen people. Thirdly, the conciliar declaration gives expression to the common hope, shared by Christians and Jews, that God's ultimate victory will overcome the powers of evil and liberate the human family from all enemies of life. 'In company with the ancient prophets and the apostle Paul, the Church awaits that day, known to God alone, on which all peoples will address the Lord in a single voice and 'serve him with one accord' [Zeph 3:9; cf. Isa. 66:23; Ps. 65:4; Rom. 11:11-23].

" The Good Friday liturgy of the Catholics 'Let us pray also for the perfidious Jews' has been changed by John XXIII already in 1959, demonstrating that the prayers are not engraved in stone. According to Edward Kessler in 'The Jews, Christians, Muslims: The Way of Dialogue' (1988), by John Paul II, before his pilgrimage to Israel declared repentance of the Church of one of its major sins; Christian teaching against Jews over centuries and for the failure of the Church during the Holocaust. Regrettably, the Orthodox Churches have not followed the lead of the Roman Catholic Church.

The Protestant theologian Paul van Buren, in a comprehensive study of 'A Theology of the Jewish-Christian Reality' (1980-1987), argues that Gentiles attempted unsuccessfully to negate the eternal covenant between God and the Jewish people. He suggested that Christianity and Judaism should draw together, whilst retaining their distinctiveness. The Lutheran scholar Krister Stendahl, in his book 'Paul among Jews and Gentiles', posits the interpretation that Israel is the elect people of God and Christians are 'honorary citizens grafted on the rich tree of Jewish heritage'. Kessler quotes a most telling denunciation by the Anglican Communion, "Through catechism, teaching of school children, and Christian preaching, the Jewish people have been misrepresented and caricatured. In order to combat centuries of anti-Jewish teaching and practice, Christians must develop programmes of teaching, preaching, and common social action which eradicate prejudice and promote dialogue and sharing among biblical people."

Quite apart from the important pronouncement of Vatican II, the International Council of Christians and Jews agreed on a 'Ten Points' declaration in 1946 and updated in 2009. This reiterates the Jewishness of Jesus, the common bond between Christians and Jews in the commandments to love God and one's neighbour, as declared by Hillel and Jesus. Christians should avoid anti-Jewish polemics, choosing critical passages in the New Testament and blaming Jews for Christ's death. The Council, mostly a Protestant church, without Roman Catholic membership, admitted in a report in 1948 that Christian teaching was one of the causes of anti-Semitism. However, in a remarkably insensitive move, whilst acknowledging that six million Jews were murdered under the Nazis, and presumably sharing some responsibility by admitting that Christianity contributed to anti-Semitism, they resolved that even greater effort should be made to convert Jews. Presumably this is not to complete the demise of Judaism, perpetrated by the Nazis, but their salvation, only possible through Christ. This missionary zeal was pursued despite having done very little to save converted Jews from being deported to extermination camps. In 1979 they issued 'Guidelines on Dialogue with people of living faiths and ideologies.'

Furthermore, the Munich Cardinal Faulhaber compared allied bombing of German cities with Nazi crimes in concentration camps. The absurd analogy by the Cardinal has, however some merit, that he admitted German Nazi crimes. An equally bizarre argument was put forward by Bishop Wurm Warning "that the post-war German bureaucracy would be filled by individuals not up to the task and 'unsuited in terms of character' for the positions they would now hold". Thereby, the Bishop implied that Church members of a suitable character being excluded were former Nazis. Referring to denazification of the church, Ericksen writes, there was "No awareness of Christian guilt, no statement of repentance, and no acknowledgment of the suffering of Germany's victims [...] Pastors had written so many of the statements on behalf of the accused, that they were derisively known even at the time as Persilschein (that is, 'soap certificates' suitable for a whitewash)". A truly appalling case was that of Eduard Strauch in charge of the Sonderkommando 1b. He was tried and sentenced to death at Nüremberg. However, according to Ericksen, Heinrich Held, president of the Protestant Church in the Rhineland, pleaded for him; Strauch had, after all, studied theology. Almost identical case was that of Waldemar Klingelhöfer of 'Einsatzgruppe B, his pastor pleaded for him.

During the early years after 1945, the term Nazi and German were kept apart, in an attempt of separation ('trennung'), to shield the good Germans from crimes of the others, the Nazis, the emerging 'outsiders'. This is intriguing and reminiscent of the defensive ploy that some good Germans adopted when they claimed to have wanted only 'trennung' from the Jews and not their annihilation. Some forty years after the end of the war, with the second and third generations of Germans, the influence of Nazis and their students, sons and daughters became less pervasive. Awkward questions have been raised about their history, with critical appraisal by young German scholars. The awkward polysyllabic word entered the vocabulary 'Vergangenheitsbewältigung' (coming to terms with the past).

Nonetheless, many Christian theologians pursued critical analysis of the Holocaust tragedy. The Lutheran scholars, Alice and Roy Eckardt, linked the tragedy of the Holocaust with the re-birth of the State of Israel. They termed the Holocaust a 'uniquely unique' event because the Nazis were resolved to exterminate the entire European Jewish population. Alice Eckardt proposed that Christian Liturgy should admit Christian failure to respond to the suffering of the Jewish people, culpability in the tragedy and to resolve that 'never again' should a Christian people tolerate such iniquities. Kessler quotes the German Catholic theologian Johann Baptist Metz questioning in 1984, how Christians may speak of 'God after Auschwitz'. His response was based on the scriptural principle 'authority of those who suffer' and called for revision of Christian theology. Metz wrote, "There is no truth for me, which I could defend with my back turned toward Auschwitz. There is no sense for me, which I could save with my back turned toward Auschwitz. And for me there is no God to whom I could pray with my back turned toward Auschwitz."

Furthermore, Kessler points out that a combination of the changes wrought by the Holocaust, the establishment of the State of Israel, the significant pronouncements made by Vatican II, and the ecumenical movement, have all made an impact on re-examination of the relations between Christians and Jews. He argues that "Christianity shifted from what was, for the most part, an inherent need to condemn Judaism to one of condemnation of Christian anti-Judaism". Furthermore, that there has been "a demonstrable shift from a Christian monologue about Jews to an instructive dialogue with Jews." However, Kessler rightly cautions whether the message, actions and violence against Jews over two millennia will ameliorate the long-standing hatred and especially whether the revised teaching of the Roman Catholic Church will reach the grass roots of Christianity. Similar doubts have been voiced by James Carroll.

The Roman Catholic theologian Gregory Baum is well aware of the difficulties in integrating the revised teaching in the catechism and religious education, because they contradict the central tenets of the Christian Gospel. Indeed, the success of the newly revised teaching of Christianity had next to no effect. "Under the impact of the holocaust that destroyed six million Jews, some Christian theologians have been ready to submit Christianity to a radical ideological critique. They have been willing to face the possibility that anti-Jewish trends in Christianity are not simply peripheral and accidental, but woven into the core of the message. As long as the Christian Church regards itself as the successor of Israel, as the new people of God substituted in the place of the old, and as long as the Church proclaims Jesus as the one mediator without whom there is no salvation, no theological space is left for other religions, and in particular, no theological validity is left for Jewish religion. In his 'Voice of Illness' Aarne Siirala tells us that his visit to the death camps in eastern Europe after the war overwhelmed him with shock and revealed to him that something was gravely sick at the very heart of our spiritual tradition. The holocaust may not be reduced to a monstrous criminal act to be deplored and then forgotten. Auschwitz has a message that must be heard: it reveals an illness operative not on the margin of our civilization but at the heart of it, in the very best we have inherited. The holocaust challenges the foundations of Western Society. Aarne Siirala has understood his theological quest as an effort to diagnose and confront this illness alive in the Christian tradition."

II. THEOLOGICAL THOUGHTS BY ROSEMARY REUTHER, GREGORY BAUM, AND JAMES CARROLL

Rosemary R. Reuther (1936) was born to a Roman Catholic mother and Episcopal father. She studied Philosophy and Ancient History, followed by PhD in Classics and Theology. She taught theology at universities and colleges and has authored many books on the Bible, Christianity, and feminist theology in North America. In her seminal book, 'Faith and Fratricide – The Theological Roots of Anti-Semitism' (1974), Reuther proposed a new relationship between Christianity and Judaism. "Christians learn who they are by learning the story of the Jews from Abraham to the time of Jesus and, through Jesus, carrying down a history created by the Christian Church and society. The history of the Jews disappears at the time of Jesus. This testifies to the Christian claim that it is the true Israel which alone carries on the biblical legacy. The Christian way of learning history negates ongoing Jewish existence. If we learned not only New Testament, but rabbinic midrash; if we viewed the period of the Second Temple, not merely through the eyes of early Christianity, but through the eyes of the disciples of Rabbi Yohanan ben Zakkai; if we read Talmud side by side with the Church Fathers; if we read the Jewish experience of Christendom side by side with the Christian self-interpretation, this Christian view of history would fall into jeopardy. For this reason, Jewish history 'after Christ' is not merely unknown, but repressed. Its repression is essential for the maintenance of Christian identity. Because the anti-Judaic myth and its social workings in Christendom is almost never taught in Church history or 'Western civilization,' the dubiousness of Christendom and the roots of anti-Semitism remain buried. The very suppression of Jewish history and experience from Christian consciousness is tacitly genocidal. What it says, in effect, is that the Jews have no further right to exist after Jesus. We repress the memory of their continued existence and our dealings with them so that it appears that 'after Christ' Jews disappear, and only Christians remain as the heirs of Jewish history and the people with a future."

Reuther expressed these robust arguments and proposed an end to the 'Christian anti-Judaic myth', allowing the 'return of the repressed' and a new way of formulating Christian identity 'that allows space for the Jewish brother to live – live not on our terms, but on his.' These are powerful sentiments followed up by concrete proposals, suggesting a template of remedial action, delivered to a 'Committee of the American Association of Theological Schools.'

Reuther concludes with further arguments concerning Christian theology, "Since the Christian anti-Judaic myth has been not only a means of hating Jews, but a means establishing Christian identity as the 'true Israel', this Jewish consciousness means also a rethinking of Christian identity in such a way as to accept Judaism as still the 'true Israel.' God, who creates the many peoples, also can allow for many ways to the Father, which only become one at that end of history which is truly 'final.' The fratricidal side of Christian faith can be overcome only through genuine encounter with Jewish identity. Only then might a 'Judaeo-Christian tradition,' which has heretofore existed only as a Christian imperialist myth, which usurps rather than converses with the Jewish tradition, begin to happen for the first time."

Gregory Baum strongly endorsed Reuther's forthright analysis and recommendations for revision of Christian theology towards Judaism came from Baum (1923). He is a highly regarded Roman Catholic theologian, who studied first mathematics and physics in Canada and later for his doctorate in Theology at the University of Fribourg. Baum was a theological adviser during Vatican II, he participated in writing the Vatican conciliar documents on 'Religious Liberty, Ecumenism, and on Church's Relation to Non-Christian Religions'. He published many books, joined the priesthood, which he then left in 1976. Among many theological appointments, he became Professor of Theological Ethics at McGill University in Canada.

In a perceptive and long Introduction to Reuther's book, Baum writes of the reasons why he denied his previous position as a Christian theologian when he defended the New Testament from the accusation of prejudice and falsification. This was in response to the book entitled, 'The Jews and the Gospel', written by the French historian Jules Isaac in 1948, himself a Jew who is believed to have also inspired Pope John XXIII to prepare the 'Declaration on the Church's Attitude to Non-Christians' for the Second Vatican Council. Baum wrote, "I had to admit in the course of my study that biblical passages reflected the conflict between Church and Synagogue in the first century. While I was bound to acknowledge that already the New Testament proclaimed the Christian message with a polemical edge against the religion of Israel, I refused to draw the consequences from this. I was still convinced that the anti-Jewish trends in Christianity were peripheral and accidental, not grounded in the New Testament itself but due to later developments, and that it would consequently be fairly easy to purify the preaching of the Church from anti-Jewish bias. Since then, especially under the influence of Rosemary Ruether's writings, I have had to change my mind."

Baum concedes a critical point that whilst the crimes committed by Hitler and his regime cannot be blamed directly on the Church, it helped and enabled him through the contempt among Christians for Jews and all things Jewish, being a symbol of unredeemed humanity, a carnal and perverse people, to pursue his extermination 'final solution'. In all honesty, Baum poses the frightening question: "Is such a radical reinterpretation of the Gospel possible? Is it possible to purify the Christian message of its anti-Jewish ideology without invalidating the Christian claims altogether?" He struggles with the conundrum of traditional scripture he believes in, and the 'Tremendum' of the Holocaust, right now for all to see – for those who have eyes with vision of reality.

The following thoughts are some of the most powerful expressions by any theologian, imbued with honesty and self-deprecation, echoing a deep and disturbing truth by a devout Christian theologian. "What if a message is revealed there, in the light of which we must examine the entire Christian religion? The holocaust teaches the Church that any monopolistic claim to divine truth or any form of ecclesiastical self-evaluation will eventually translate itself – because Christianity has achieved cultural dominance, even if its membership should diminish – into social attitudes and political action and hence generate grave injustices that eventually accumulate to become major crimes. Christian love – the subjective factor – is unable to stop the harmful effects of the symbols of power and domination – the objective factor – woven into Christian preaching and teaching. This, I hold, is the message of Auschwitz addressed to the Church. Why? Because here the theological negation of Judaism and the vilification of the Jewish people that were part of the Christian tradition were translated into genocidal action of monstrous proportions, not indeed by Christians themselves, but by a political party that used for its own purposes a heritage built up by Christianity and counted on a good deal of Christian cooperation."

Baum admits that Reuther's 'Faith and Fratricide' is a brilliant but at the same time disturbing book, as the Christian critical eye of the repressed side of Christianity, which remains unacknowledged and hidden in the Churches doctrine and collective unconscious. He argues that Christians, indeed some historians, have dismissed Judaism as an extinct religion, overlooking living Jewish religious practice that has survived and the disproportionally large cultural and scientific contribution they have made to the welfare of the nations. The survival of their resilient, ancient religion is epitomised in a graffiti scribbled on the Triumphal Arch of Titus in Rome 'Am Israel Chai' (Israel is alive).

James Carroll called for 'Vatican III' with an agenda for a new reformation, not surprisingly in line with Reuther's and Baum's view. He suggests dealing firstly with the anti-Judaism text in the New Testament, with emphasis on love instead of hate. He proposes the following items to be considered in a chronological order: "power (Constantine, Ambrose, Augustine), Christology (Crusades, Anselm, Abelard), Church intolerance (Inquisition, Nicolaus of Cusa, the ghetto, democracy (Enlightenment, Spinoza, modernism), and only then of repentance (Holocaust, Silence, Edith Stein)." As this book has demonstrated, the Church's attitude toward Jews is at the dead centre of each of these problems, and a fundamental revision of that attitude is the key to the solution of each problem. It seems clear that authentic Church reform, defined as shaping something according to its own essential being, is tied to the Jews, if only because the perversion of that essential being, the perversion, that is, of the message of love preached and lived by Jesus – has so clearly been tied to the Jews from the beginning."

Carroll argues that "repentance presumes change – at every level of the Church's life, because it is at every level that the poison of anti-Semitism has had its effect. 'Teshuva' is the word Jews use to describe the process by which repentance and forgiveness take place". This would require changes in education, mission, relations, and doctrine, and Carroll calls for "those changes as a Catholic, but in fact I am following. Jewish theology which, in its reflections on the reality of God since the 'Tremendum' of the Holocaust, has led the way for all serious theological reflection." He points out that whilst Catholic history has not caused the Shoah, there was "a necessary, unbroken thread in the rise of genocidal anti-Semitism as well as the source of the Church's failure to openly oppose it. In silence the sin of the Church is acknowledged as the sin that was part of what led to genocide. There is no more talk that exempts 'the Church as such' from this judgment."

With the demonstrably sad history of the last two millennia, is it inconceivable that God's testing ground of Christian morality, tolerance and 'love your neighbour' principle is enshrined in the treatment of Jews in Christian countries. This may well be the only constant point of reference of judgment of morality of Christianity since its birth, as God has not revoked his covenant with the Jewish people, as has now been endorsed by the Vatican, despite the doctrine of supersession that seems to lack direct divine sanction. When the Jewish people waited for Moses forty days in the desert to return from his parley with God, they failed the test and reverted to idolatry of 'the golden calf'. By the same token, when Christianity assumed worldly power through Constantine's conversion, God's critical test may have been the basic teaching of Jesus in relation to God's chosen people. The longest hatred has been the longest trial of the Christian religion that has lofty principles, but denied breathing space to those whose ideals they adopted. Is it not evident that both the message and messengers were Jews and is it inconceivable that this was God's way of passing on his teaching – albeit modified to suit the other nations? God is a long-term strategist, governed by a unique algorithm. He has embedded in the Jewish and Christian psyche the concept of hope of the coming of Messianic age of paradise on earth. The establishment of the State of Israel has been a milestone in Jewish/Christian history, though thwarted by the surrounding countries, the Muslim world and anti-Semitism. The 'tragic historical mistake' can be and must be corrected', without further recrimination and justification. All it needs to prevent the apocalypse of both Abrahamic Religions, divided by a Common God, is a modicum of divine inspiration and human accommodation.'

Among the welter of possibilities that does not seem to have been formally raised is the simple, all too naïve question whether God is not punishing the world for the sin of persecuting Jews. The people He chose for the covenant and designated to be 'the light unto the nations'. For a non-theologian, this blatantly obvious question must have been raised by some Christian theologian and dismissed out of hand.

Up to the time of the Holocaust, both Christianity and Judaism seemed to have largely forgotten or found it disturbing to accept that Jesus was a Jew, though a robust reminder was made by Martin Luther in 1523 'That Jesus Christ was Born a Jew'. A number of rabbis and Jewish scholars also reminded Jews that Jesus was a learned practising Jew – a rabbi who kept most of the precepts of Judaism. This has been noted according to Kessler by Rabbi S. R. Hirsch (1808-1888), A. I. Cook (1865-1935) Chief Rabbi of Palestine, and reform rabbis A. Geiger (1810-1874), S. Wise (1874-1949), and L. Baeck (1823-1956). Among the Jewish scholars were M. Buber (1878-1965), H. Cohen (1842-1918), and F. Rosenzweig (1886-1929). More recently, the book by S. Boteach, 'Kosher Jesus', has underlined the traditional Jewishness of Jesus. However, the classical work on the historical Jesus was written by the biblical scholar Géza Vermes (1924-2013) in a series of eleven books, beginning in 1973 with 'Jesus the Jew' and completed in 2012 with 'Christian Beginnings'. A denial of Jesus's Jewish origin was attempted by professor Walter Grundmann of 'The Institute for the study and eradication of Jewish influence on German Church life' (1932-1942), and critically analysed in the scholarly book 'The Aryan Jesus' by Susannah Heschel (2008).

A history of almost two millennia of validating Christianity, keeping the Jews wretched, was by adopting an extreme view of St. Augustine's argument. Hitler, his racist mentors, and fellow-travellers perceived the weakness of this concept and that of Luther's teachings and ordained mass murder. The long line of 'tragic historical mistakes' must be redeemed from being revisited. The lesson not yet learned is that religion, the enlightenment, science, or culture are no safeguards from future calamity, indeed they may be collateral enabling factors in the human capacity for hatred, intolerance and persecution. The next time it may involve not only the historical scapegoat, Abraham's son Isaac, but others selected at the whim of people with an urge of hatred, reaching the depth of the killer instinct. Humanitarian reasoning, as well as biblical precepts are in agreement that Christianity and Judaism need to arrive at a common understanding in order to shape the ultimate destiny.

With the appalling history of the last two millennia, is it inconceivable that God's testing ground of Christian morality, tolerance and 'love your neighbour' principle is enshrined in the treatment of Jews in Christian countries. This may well be the only constant point of reference of judgment of morality of Christianity since its birth, as God has not revoked his covenant with the Jewish people. Indeed, this has now been endorsed by the Vatican, despite the doctrine of supersession that seems to lack direct divine sanction. When the Jewish people waited for Moses forty days in the desert to return from his parley with God, they failed the test and reverted to idolatry of 'the golden calf'. By the same token, when Christianity assumed worldly power through Constantine's conversion, God's critical test may have been the basic teaching of Jesus in relation to God's chosen people.

The longest hatred has been the longest trial of a religion that has lofty principles, but denied breathing space to those whose ideals they have largely adopted. Is it not evident that both the message and messengers were Jews and is it inconceivable that this was God's way of passing on his teaching – albeit modified to suit the other nations? God is a long-term strategist, governed by a unique algorithm. He has embedded in the Jewish and Christian psyche the concept of hope of the coming of Messianic age of paradise on earth. The establishment of the State of Israel has been a milestone in Jewish/Christian history, though thwarted by the surrounding countries, the Muslim world and anti-Semitism. The 'tragic historical mistake' can be and must be corrected, 'without further recrimination and justification. All it needs to prevent the apocalypse of the two Abrahamic Religions, divided by a Common God, is a modicum of divine inspiration and human accommodation.'

III. POST-HOLOCAUST JEWISH THOUGHTS

Religion had played a central role ever since the split of Christianity from Judaism. The 'Jewish Diaspora' has been interpreted according to one's religious persuasion. To Christians, it signifies God's wrath and punishment of his 'Chosen People' for the sins of rejecting Christ, their Messiah. The Jewish Diaspora started with the destruction of the First Temple in Jerusalem by the Persians in the 6th C. BCE, and some 600 years later in 90 CE the Second Temple by the Romans. They were instructed to wait for the true Messiah who will gather the children of Israel and return them to Jerusalem. Isaiah stated that the destiny of the Jews is to be the 'Light unto the Nations'. This task has not been received with grace but 'perpetual bondage' in the disguise of anti-Semitism – the longest hatred. Is it beyond the wit of humanity to halt the 'original theological sin'? The 'Hillel-Jesus' principle of love, so ardently taught by Jesus, has failed to make an impact in the singular hatred of Jews, who persisted in the steadfast belief of the one and only God shared by Christians, but not requiring an intermediate deity or son of God by the Jews.

After six million Jews were murdered within the heart of European culture, students in Jewish seminaries still recite, debate, and argue about the minutiae of dietary laws, the Sabbath, Festivals, and prayers. The six million murdered, after suffering torment of the mind and physical atrocities are largely accepted by a conspiracy of silence. The incomprehensible horror of the dead mutates into statistics, when individual suffering, dying, without funerals, without prayer, without resting place, without knowing how, why wherefore, – the off-chance of being still alive somewhere – eludes conventional wisdom and emotional expression. There are no sages to help, because there were no supernatural manifestations, just murder at large. Any attempt to explain the premeditated wilful murder of one and a half million children sacrificed on the altar of the belief in 'One and Only God' defies human ingenuity. The cowardly silence is only marginally less objectionable than the blasphemous indictment of 'having sinned'. Perhaps the only sin perpetuated over the two thousand year history of harassment – suffering – isolation – murder, is not devoting the outstanding Jewish gift of intelligence and inventiveness to study the causes, manifestations and prevention of the longest hatred of humanity. To wait for the Messiah is to abdicate one's responsibility towards the future generations. If and when the Messiah comes, this will be a bonus to the 'modus vivendi' and a promise to solve all problems on this earth.

Post-Holocaust Jewish relations with Christianity was declared in the statement 'Dabru Emet' (Speak Truth), in an attempt towards Jewish reassessment of Christianity. Kessler points out that 'Dabru Emet' is a "positive affirmation of Christianity", and summarises it as follows: "Jews and Christians worship the same God and they seek authority from the same book (the Bible). Christians can respect the claim of the Jewish people upon the Land of Israel. Jews and Christians accept the moral principles of Torah. Nazism was not a Christian phenomenon. The humanly irreconcilable differences between Jews and Christians will not be settled until God redeems the world. A new relationship between Jews and Christians will not weaken Jewish practice, and Jews and Christians must work together for justice and peace." However, it caused some controversy within the Jewish community, questioning that "Jews and Christians worship the same God, and that Nazism was not a Christian phenomenon. A welcome note in the interfaith relationship has been the common ancestry claimed by all three 'Abrahamic Faiths', with corresponding Institutes having been established in Cambridge (England) and New York. Recall of Abraham might facilitate a working relationship in the division between Judaism, Christianity and Islam".

The most cogent Jewish view of the way forward was argued in a rational, philosophical and pragmatic way by Rabbi Jonathan Sacks in his book 'The Dignity of Difference' (2002). "In the course of history, God has spoken to mankind in many languages: through Judaism to Jews, Christianity to Christians, Islam to Muslims. How could a sacred text convey such an idea? It would declare that God is God of all humanity, but no single faith is or should be the faith of all humanity. Only such a narrative would lead us to see the presence of God in people of other faiths. Only such a worldview could reconcile the particularity of cultures with the universality of the human condition. This means that religious truth is not universal. God no more wants all faiths and cultures to be the same than a loving parent wants his or her children to be the same. That is the conceptual link between love, creation and difference. We serve God, author of diversity, by respecting diversity. The critical test of any order is: does it make space for otherness? Does it acknowledge the dignity of difference? We will need to understand that just as the natural environment depends on biodiversity, so the human environment depends on cultural diversity, because no one creed has a monopoly on spiritual truth; no one civilization encompasses all the spiritual, ethical and artistic expressions of mankind." These wise, powerful, and challenging sentiments might be the guiding spirit – a template for religious leaders, instead of practitioners of the false ideology 'through an ocean of blood to the kingdom of love'.

It is remarkable that in an essay Michael Ignatieff, as visiting professor of human rights at the Kennedy School of Government at Harvard University, expressed rather similar thoughts. "Our whole heritage is a product of the contributions of all peoples. We can best understand this when we realize how impoverished our culture would be if the so-called inferior peoples doomed by Germany, such as the Jews, had not been permitted to create the Bible, or to give birth to an Einstein, a Spinoza; if the Poles had not had the opportunity to give to the world a Copernicus, a Chopin, a Curie; the Czechs, a Huss, a Dvorak; the Greeks, a Plato and a Socrates; the Russians, a Tolstoy and a Shostakovich. A sense of otherness, of distinctness, is the very basis of the consciousness of our individuality, and this consciousness, based in difference, is to attack the shared element that makes us what we are as a species. This reality of difference, both fated and created, is our common inheritance, the shared integument that we must fight to defend whenever any of us is attacked for manifesting it." These powerful and wise arguments have not been at the forefront of either Jewish or Christian religion. Indeed, diversity was considered to be dangerous, usually condemned, even as heretical, from the very beginnings of both Judaism and Christianity.

To attain the lofty ideals, Christian religious leaders and theologians will have to look deep into their hearts and consider the pain, atrocities, torture and ultimately murder perpetrated against innocent children, women and men in the name of the one and only God shared and recognised by all. Christians will need to reinterpret supersession of Israel, reorient Matthew's deicide to the real culprit the Romans, neutralize the racial and religious anti-Jewish polemics in the scriptures. Jews will need to interpret Isaiah's "Israel will be the light unto the nations" pragmatically. The dominant Christianity has followed many of the tenets of Mosaic laws, albeit in a revised, restructured trinity that suited 'other nations' – the gentiles. In the long run, Christianity was created by two Jewish rabbis – Jesus (Joshua) and Paul (Saul) and further re-interpreted by the four Gospel writers, some of whom were Jews. A crucial question needs to be studied by theologians whether Jesus and Paul have not fulfilled the promise that 'Jews will be the light unto the nations'. Whilst the Romans killed the messenger – Jesus – they failed to kill the message of the one and only God. Indeed Christianity has adapted Judaism, monotheism, the belief in God of Abraham, and well over a billion people profess Christianity, all of which is the challenging evidence. A critical convergence of fundamental beliefs emerged between Rabbi Hillel the most celebrated Jewish scholar (around the latter half of the first century BCE and the early part of the first century CE) and Jesus. Hillel expressed the Torah in the golden rule "that which is hateful to you do not do unto others", whereas Jesus paraphrased the dictum in his famous statement "Do unto others as you would do unto yourself". Since Hillel followed up his golden rule by adding that "all the rest of the Torah's laws are specifications of this principle" one might argue that Jesus has passed the Torah to the 'Nations' and Isaiah's prophecy has been fulfilled. Or is this too naïve a non-theological reasoned conclusion?

To reconstitute the theological-hard wired prejudice of two millennia, knowing the total commitment to the one and only way, taught by priests and parents, the loyalty these ties evoke is a serious obstacle that must not be underestimated. Formal declarations are helpful but they do not reach the grass roots of the people. It requires the inspiration of Hobbs's philosophy – the practical, emotional link with the rational approach, in persuading the religious leadership, its theologians and ultimately the people. In the emerging modern, neurological terminology, the reasoning of the evolution-dependent pre-frontal cortex will need to coordinate its act with the emotional, older limbic system and this challenges humanity with a critical commitment to the true Judeo – Christian morality.

IV. ACADEMIA AND PROFESSIONS

> ‘The pursuit of culture, a characteristic feature of German people has not been a moderating force but was co-existent with mass murder.
>
> *Author*

The Universities and Academia have largely failed to admit culpability for their support of or accommodation with an evil ideology. With a few exceptions, they failed to oppose during the early period the student-lead racism, shouting down lecturers given by opponents of Nazism or Jewish teachers. They acquiesced to sacking these members of staff and as recorded by Victor Klemperer in his diaries, faculty colleagues gradually cut all associations with them, thus isolating them not only from the university but also social contact. Later when most of the senior appointments were heavily biased in favour of members of the National Socialist party and the ‘Führer Principle’ took over freedom of expression, any of the professors not actively supporting the Nazi diktats, got on with their subject, closing their eyes and shutting their ears to all the iniquities and to the Humboldtian principles of yesterday.

The inhumanity of the experiments carried out during the Third Reich on concentration camp inmates are universally abhorred. The prevailing view by German scientists was that this was caused by a few psychopaths – ‘a few rotten apples’. The universities and research institutions have largely acquiesced to this view for half a century. However, in 1999 the Max Planck Society (MPS), previously known as Kaiser Wilhelm Society, which administers eighty research institutes in Germany, was moved by historians to reassess their war-time history. A six-year programme was launched in 1999 by Hubert Markl, then president of the MPS, and first reported in 2001 in which ‘Max Planck offers a historic apology’. The pronouncement was made at a symposium on human experimentation sponsored by the Max Planck presidential commission that was investigating the KWG’s activities from 1933 to 1945. Max Planck Society president Hubert Markl offered survivors of concentration camp experiments “the deepest regret, compassion, and shame at the fact that crimes of this sort were committed, promoted, and not prevented within the ranks of German scientists." Markl stated that "there is scientific evidence proving beyond the shadow of a doubt that directors and employees at Kaiser Wilhelm Institutes co-masterminded and sometimes even actively participated in the crimes of the Nazi regime. The Max Planck Society, as the Kaiser Wilhelm Society's 'heir', must face up to these historical facts and its moral responsibility."

The final report of the programme conducted by independent science historians who systematically analysed the role of the MPS concluded that many scientists far from being subjected by force, voluntarily oriented their work to fit the regime's policies – as a way of funding their research. Indeed, most researchers have regarded the regime not as a threat, but as an opportunity for their research ambitions. The work has shed light on the behaviour of scientists and it serves as a timely reminder of the need for strict ethical limits to be defined, and adhered to. The work of the program has been documented in a series of German-language books running to 11 volumes, one of which has already been published in English [Politics and Science in Wartime. Comparative International Perspectives of the Kaiser Wilhelm Institutes, Ed. Carola Sachse and Mark Walker (2005)]. Hubert Markl asked survivors of the experiments on twins at the Auschwitz concentration camp for forgiveness for the suffering inflicted on the victims of these crimes in the name of science. Markl also apologized for the tardiness of the MPS in facing up to its historical responsibility. Furthermore, he joined with the 'Deutsche Forschungsgemeinschaft' to unveil a memorial in reminder of the state-sponsored program of murder by euthanasia and the abuse of victims for research purposes. He stated at the final conference that "Those who are fixated only on the past will move blindly into the future, as will those who are concerned only with the present."

Denazification of Germany after the war did not work, as remarkably no one was a Nazi and they all helped the Jews. Erickson succinctly concluded that "Denazification records are absolutely filled with fabrications told by every sort of person, from university professors, who were among the most creative, to pastors, who were among the most enthusiastic. Denazification made an important contribution toward achieving its desired goal: a post-war Germany committed to democracy and without any significant Nazi resurgence. Every post-war German who lied about the past, who denied ever having been a Nazi, helped establish in the public mind the toxic reality of the Nazi ideology and the Nazi regime. These denials also made it difficult, if not impossible, for individuals to revert to praise or promotion of the Nazi ideology by 1950."

The Enlightenment's declaration of 'Freedom of speech' has become axiomatic in Western universities and liberal societies. It has become untouchable and canonical irrespective of some of its consequences. The conundrum that university chancellors had to deal with up to the present time is to differentiate between speech that incites violence, which is forbidden and that which incites tension and hatred against a religion or minority people, which seems to be permitted. Quite apart from the difficulties of differentiating between these, it cannot have escaped the attention of people in charge of educational institutions that inflaming tension leads to a point when violence breaks out. This has been amply demonstrated in German schools, universities, and the church in exposing the formative, receptive minds of young people to anti-Semitic diatribe, which has led to the Jew being the bearer and perpetrator of all the evil in the world. Hence, eliminatory anti-Semitism was the right treatment of the 'Jewish problem'. By the same token, the notorious anti-Semitic falsehood of 'The Protocols of the Elders of Zion' would not be banned, under the rubric of 'freedom of speech and expression', despite its effect of poisoning the minds of people over many generations. The book is currently advertised all over the Muslim world, as well as sold in the Red-Square near the Kremlin in Moscow. Most people will accept any plausible conspiracy theory, especially if they are conditioned to it and not bother to analyse the claim.

The total denial of what Daniel Goleman calls 'Social Intelligence', with all the emotional baggage that one accumulates throughout life, ignores the fundamental tenet how people make a judgment. Preserving free speech appears to be more fundamental and takes priority over the abuses of people for their religion, 'ism', or sexual preference, which leads to hatred, persecution, and even extermination. There is something wrong in defending the right of speech and writing that leads to denial of freedom of other groups of people. 'My freedom should not restrict your freedom', an obvious right of the individual, which can be denied by the canonical 'freedom of speech', and has been accepted in drawing up laws in democratic countries.

All the wisdom of academia has been unable to this day to draw a red line between freedom of speech and freedom of hate. The reluctance of university Chancellors to challenge and revise this principle is understandable but wrong, if one considers the havoc wrought by the rubble of Nazi students and teachers, silencing anyone not supporting their ideology or expelling unilaterally undesirable religious or racial individuals. The excuse that this does not prevail in democratic countries is counter to the evidence on university campuses, with religiously, racially, or ideologically motivated student bodies adopting fascist methods and threatening others who dare to oppose them.

V. POST-WAR HISTORIANS AND PROFESSIONS

Both German and non-German historians have objectively analysed and presented the Weimar Republic, and the critical period before Hitler gained power through a democratically elected process. The role of humanities in the Third Reich was subjected to serious studies, and the detailed repost by Nicolas Berg on West German historians and their relationship to the Holocaust in 2003 concluded that German scholars in history and other humanities supported the Nazi ideology and regime, often with enthusiasm. However, revisionist historians have predictably appeared on the horizon in an attempt to remove the horrendous crimes, and the evil events from German conscience, and to regain their ideal of the 'Kulturnation' (nation of culture). Re-writing an acceptable history for posterity was initiated in about 1986 by *bona fide* historians, especially Ernst Nolte, Michael Stürmer, and Jürgen Habermas. They placed the onus of responsibility squarely on Hitler alone, or the British for the policy of appeasement, or the Versailles treaty or equating the Holocaust with the expulsion of Germans from Eastern Europe, which even Martin Heidegger, the architect of 'Being and Time' had supported.

The relativisation of history, especially by Nolte, was to equate the Nazi mass murder with the Soviet Gulag. So two wrongs somehow make them commonplace and as such more acceptable, or really, the Nazis just followed the Russians, whom otherwise they considered to be inferior human beings. Hans Mommsen has been critical of this development, termed 'Historikerstreit' ('Historians' controversy' or 'unresolved past'), a controversy over the singularity of the Holocaust. He stated, "To accept with resignation the acts of screaming injustice and to psychologically repress their social prerequisites by calling attention to similar events elsewhere and putting the blame on the Bolshevist world threat recalls the thought patterns that made it possible to implement genocide." The thrust of the argument was to displace the historical guilt, not by solid argument, but by tentative questions, and comparisons, to insinuate the desired answer and to trivialize the unique aspect of the 'Final Solution'.

These are dark clouds on the horizon in an otherwise enlightened Germany. Hopefully, the present generation that lost its high moral and cultural standing, through no fault of their own, will not take the easy option to whitewash their stained history. Chancellor Kohl thought in 1985 that the time had come to bury the past, when he conducted President Reagan to the graves of German soldiers, including the Waffen-SS. His and his advisers' naivety failed to appreciate that the immensity of anti-Christian, anti-Enlightenment, and anti-human acts by a people endowed by Goethe, Beethoven, Kant, and the entire culture of a gifted people is a unique evil which can be only mitigated by evidence of right actions in the future. The 'White Rose' students saw it clearly. "We will be your bad conscience. We will not leave you in peace", what some historians do not wish to accept. Does the historian's debate matter? Yes, it does. Historians propagate the notion that they are protectors of collective memory, protecting it from legends and manipulations. A fair example of this is the historian David Irving versus Deborah Lipstadt, defended by Richard Evans, though it needed a court case to declare Irving guilty by manipulating, anti-Semitic and falsified history.

The Legal profession carried on after the war, as if they were free of any guilt in sustaining an evil regime and enthusiastically writing and enacting the laws, depriving hundreds of thousands of German Jews of citizenship, livelihood, freedom, and education. They failed miserably to protect the Law, and declared 'Führer's Law' the guiding light of the Third Reich – tantamount to a lawless country. Professor Michael Stolleis, a second generation eminent German lawyer, broke the conspiracy of silence lead by lawyers and judges from the Nazi period. Stolleis, the 'Director of the Max Planck Institute for European Legal History', represents the new post-war generation of lawyers, with high ethical standards, who has confronted the dismal past of his profession. He has bravely attempted to rectify the lack of any disclaimer or apology by the legal body.

Unfortunately, the medical profession was the major culprit – the mass murderers, in face-to-face encounter with their victims. The exquisite humane history of medicine has been soiled by the most educated, Christian, and Enlightened individuals, a reality that was admitted by the German medical profession in 2012, after sixty-seven years of denial. There were a number of exceptions among the doctors, who behaved in an ethically correct, Hippocratic way and they must be recognised and excluded from the stigma of the rest of the profession. The shining light were the 'White Rose' medical and other students who in their educational infancy recognised right from wrong and deserve a place of pride in the moral pantheon of German universities. A number of international conventions have defined the basic Hippocratic principle – 'Do No Harm' and Germany has been supporting these. The Medical Schools must bear the responsibility of ethical education, with historical narrative of selection for life and death in concentration camps and the horrendous experiments perpetrated by German doctors of medicine on innocent victims.

VI. THE 'JEWISH QUESTION' MUTATED INTO THE 'GERMAN QUESTION'

<table>
<tr>
<td>'The critical test of any order: does it make space for otherness? Does it acknowledge the dignity of difference?'

Rabbi Lord Jonathan Sacks, 2002</td>
<td>'Right actions in the future are the best apologies for bad actions in the past'.

Tryon Edwards, Theologian, 1908</td>
</tr>
<tr>
<td colspan="2">'The Nüremberg trial struck a blow to the complaisant Christianity and Enlightened humanity, which to this day failed adequately to explore, explain or deal with the radical evil which they were a party, however indirectly, and cannot be exonerated'.

Professor Lawrence Douglas in 'The Memory of Judgement, 2001</td>
</tr>
<tr>
<td>'While I do not have a sense of personal guilt, I do feel a sense of shared responsibility for that period and its crimes'.

Professor Michael Stolleis, 2002</td>
<td>'All the persecutions and atrocities are revolting to all of us. I assure you it just isn't German'.

Baldur von Ribbentrop; Nüremberg Trial, 1946</td>
</tr>
</table>

The entire edifice of genocide was based on millennia-long, anti-Jewish teaching by the Christian Churches. The academic anti-Semitic polemics were propagated largely by university-trained individuals, unhindered by 'freedom of expression, and practised by most universities. The lawyers were only too willing to enact the anti-Jewish laws that were for them a pen and paper exercise in the comfort of their offices, having no compassion or ethical constraint with their deadly deeds. However, the most shocking revelation was that of 'healers turned killers'. The final common pathway was to have led to the 'Judenrein' (Clear of Jews) Europe, with the principal components shown below. Even a museum of an extinct people was planned.

The 'Moral Enormity' of the crime made possible by highly educated individuals, imbued by the Enlightenment in the midst of the Christian

Western civilisation, has a wider meaning to those who value humanity and ask fundamental questions about Religion, the Enlightenment, Morality, Modernity, Ethos at Universities and centres of Education of Humanities, Science, and Art. These are critical issues that need to be explored in depth, so as to prevent a further catastrophe, which in our ignorance might be in the making and we fail to recognise it.

The awesome question has to be answered on behalf of the six million murdered individuals who cannot speak for themselves. The answer will require a great deal of thought, wisdom, and good judgment by the four institutions as they are the real culprits, which underpinned Hitler's racist ideology releasing the all too willing natural forces of hatred of the 'Other'. It needed a fellow suffering being the Catholic theologian Peter Abelard to appreciate and express as early as 1130 some of the most poignant and wise words about the suffering Jew. "To mistreat the Jews is considered a deed pleasing God [...] The life of the Jews is in the hands of their worst enemies [...] Christian rulers who actually wish for their death so that they can confiscate their possessions. Heaven is their only refuge."

The initial reaction of disbelief and disgust after the full disclosure of the ultimate barbarity that cultured, God-fearing, enlightened people were capable of perpetrating, was a period of silence. The churches made public statements, as discussed above, a few theologians endowed with humanity and empathy deplored the church's teaching and hostility to Judaism and Jews, which may have led to the Holocaust. There is little concrete evidence that these sentiments had a great impact, as anti-Semitism has again been spreading in Europe. The hate virus has mutated under the guise of anti-Israeli, linked with anti-Jewish attitude, and the churches have demonstrated little evidence of countering this trend. The wise thoughts expressed by Baum, Reuther, and Carroll among others have not been heeded.

Academia, with a few individual exceptions, has not covered itself with glory. Indeed, the Universities maintained that they were the victims of Nazi dictatorship. Little responsibility or regret was expressed towards the inhumane attitude meted out to their Jewish or political colleagues, mentors and teachers, as chronicled by Victor Klemperer. Denazification was perfunctory, professors and lecturers with active Nazi involvement were re-installed, and their pensions were honoured. This did not apply to those members of staff who were dismissed. Universities will have to seriously devote a great deal of effort, time and studies to define their function and responsibilities towards humanity. Back to Goethe, back to Humboldt, and back to Virchow are the obvious routes, within a modern idiom.

Can the future generations of Germans stand up to the challenge? Paradoxically, leading politicians are steadfast about their responsibilities towards the victims, although not directly involved in the massacre of the innocents. The prime example among the Chancellors of Germany is Angela Merkel (née Kasner), born in 1954 in Hamburg under the German Democratic Republic (East Germany). Is it fortuitous, that like Margaret Thatcher she studied Chemistry at the University of Leipzig and was awarded the doctorate of the Academy of Sciences in Berlin? Merkel has demonstrated her commitment in support of Israel before and during the time she assumed the Chancellorship and visited Israel four times. In 2014, she was awarded Israel's highest civilian award by President Shimon Peres for her "unwavering commitment to Israel's security and the fight against anti-Semitism and racism". The Universities by and large denied any culpability for the Nazi period and went on 'business as usual'. So did the legal profession. The medical profession after sixty-seven years of denial, made an apology and acknowledged responsibility for the medical crimes committed under the Nazi regime and admitted that doctors were guilty of violation of human rights.

However, some of the post-war historians, forty years after the end of the war, started the revisionist process, arguably with an eye to posterity, and to redeem the evil deeds from the German 'Kulturnation'. Historians, such as Ernst Nolte, Michael Stürmer, and Jürgen Habermas engaged in the 'Historikerstreit' (controversy over the unique nature of Nazi atrocities), attempting to minimise Hitler's crimes by equating Nazi mass murder with those of Soviets, who killed even more people in the Gulag. This ostensibly spreads the evil to others and thereby removes the odium of uniqueness. Another ploy is to equate the murder of six million people in the Holocaust with the post-war expulsion of Germans from Eastern Europe who were at the vanguard of supporting Nazi takeover of places such as the Sudetenland in Czechoslovakia. This really defies reason and common judgment and does not bode well for the future. The 'Irving virus' of false history has not lost its virulence. Fortunately, however, there are honest historians, such as Hans Mommsen, who is critical of those who try to whitewash the past and one can only hope that the truth will prevail.

Schools and Universities have a responsibility to teach without equivocation the depth of depravity attained by the evil ideology preached by evil-minded men and women. It is easy to teach glories of the past, but difficult to present the ugly face of the nation's past. How does one deal with the 'Other', when religion, art, literature and often parental home are all biased against it? The emotional response is complex, but an innate lack of empathy, suspicion of the stranger, distrust, and jealousy come into play. Competition for jobs at any level of labour, business, profession or university are issues of concern, both in material and intellectual spheres. If egged on by disgruntled people, who see a person 'not one of us' doing well, can lead to hostility, hatred and verbal or physical abuse. Politicians will generally go to any lengths to curry favour and gain support. Among the many basic emotive factors are 'Schadenfreude' (pleasure at someone's expense), atavism – returning to one's primeval roots and resort to physical violence.

An idiosyncratic view has been voiced by Thomas Mann in his speech before the 'Library of Congress' in Washington that Goethe wished for a German Diaspora. "Like the Jews the Germans must be transplanted and scattered over the world, in order to develop the good that lies in them, and to the benefit of the nations. That the Germans let themselves be suppressed everywhere, like the Jews, but that they were, again like the Jews indestructible. The Germans kept close together only when they had no fatherland. Like the Jews, they would not perish, because they were individuals". These thoughts of Goethe in 1807-1808 are even more evocative and significant by Goethe's actual statement, "I have often felt a bitter pang at the thought of the German people, as estimable as individuals and so wretched on the whole". The prescience of Goethe over a century before the Germans inflicted the ultimate catastrophe upon the Jewish people suggests almost a prophetic vision of the poet, writer, and a man of wisdom and judgment. Carl Jaspers's 'Schuldfrage' (assuming responsibility) was the most important declaration by a German to assume responsibility for the crimes of the National Socialist era. He demanded a change of Germans to a stateless nation with the 'pariah' status comparable to that of the Jews and assume the burden of moral responsibility and 'political diaspora', thus echoing Goethe's thoughts. These were expressions of deep anguish by a philosopher, who unlike his friend Heidegger, was stricken by the national disaster and recognized the ultimate evil perpetrated by his German compatriots that led to the collapse of a proud culture devoid of civilization.

Whereas the book attempted to deal with the 'Jewish Question' as envisaged by the perpetrators of the Genocide, at the end of the narrative it mutated into the 'German Question' – "how was it possible". At the moment of truth, at the Nüremberg Trial, Hans Frank finally grasped the enormity of the catastrophe, of which he was a major party and declared, "A thousand years will pass and the guilt of Germany will not be erased". A naïve and hollow plea was uttered by the ever engaging simple diplomat, Baldur von Ribbentrop facing his nemesis. "All the persecutions and atrocities are revolting to all of us. I assure you it just isn't German". This is the nub of the 'German Question', as Ribbentrop was right, though not by his personal assurance, that this is not German, but by the standards of Goethe, Schiller, Humboldt, and Virchow. He was wrong, however by the standards of Hitler, Himmler, and Goebbels, who presumed to be 'echt Deutsch' (Real Germans), whilst Hitler himself was a dubiously naturalised German of Austrian origin.

How is one to explain the transition from centuries of Christianity, imbued with the ideals of liberty, contributing to the world the best in literature, art, and science, excelling in music and yet returning to an orgy of primeval barbarism? Has the deeply buried evolutionary process of their psyche or limbic part of the brain, resurfaced in the guise of scientifically ordained atavism? The 'German Question' raises the meaning of Christianity, humanity, the practice of justice, and Hippocratic medicine in Germany. This deals with civilised behaviour, the natural laws of God, humanity, and the Enlightenment. They were the principal victims of Nazi terror, primarily aimed at the Jewish scapegoat. However, they were also atrocities against civilisation, unless one adopts the view that Nazi atrocities were an act of civilization, which does not have or has lost the moral force. It has been argued that Nazi atrocities and the extermination of the Jews are so completely incompatible with the morality of Christian teaching and the Enlightenment that they threaten humanity as a whole. 'The German Question' is to explore and comprehend the Holocaust through the ethical principles of Religion – Academia – Law and – Medicine, the true culprits enabling Hitler and his 'Willing Executioners' to commit the 'Second Fall of Man'.

The lesson we might have, should have, learnt that the sad realisation from the German-Nazi history is that religion, reason, and morality can be set aside under a set of conditions, and have to be further studied. The 'German problem' may well be considered a 'Universal problem' as the 'Other' can be readily identified and all moral scruples abandoned in defence of 'Us'. The attraction of nationalists declaring to be a master race is a simple, effective formula that Goebbels well understood to work miracles. Rationalising injustice, moralising immorality, murder in defence of ‘Us’, all with or without culture, has become ‘the art of the possible’. Our awareness of evil must be heightened, and the Church and educational institutions have a task, which so far they have not addressed adequately, if at all.

As long as a rational or religious interpretation is not forthcoming, study of institutional genocide, linked with enlightenment ideology and religious doctrine, is a categorical imperative for humanity. Twelve years of the ‘Nazi Thousand Year Reich’ may have resulted in the ‘Thousand Year Genocide Memory’, underwritten by the ‘Trinity of Evil’, Hitler – Himmler – Goebbels. The ‘Jewish Question’ of the Third Reich has mutated into the ‘German Question’ post-Third Reich. ‘How was it possible for a highly cultured nation to transform into a barbaric nation of the ‘Volk’? The answer to this burning question has not been forthcoming and is equally pertinent to-day – long after the ‘Tremendum’ – when the unimaginable, incomprehensible, inhumane, turned to stark reality, after 2000 years of Christianity and 200 years of Enlightenment.

VII. WHITE ROSE STUDENTS

In the midst of the morass of evil, a shining light of Humboldtian ideals and Goethe's spirit – the true Enlightenment – emerged an alternative Germany of Civilization in step with culture. Whilst German university students in the 1930s were the vanguard of nationalist, anti-liberal, anti-Semitic ideology, actively hounding out scholars for political or religious reasons, a small group of medical and philosophy students at the University of Munich formed an anti-Nazi resistance group between June 1942 and February 1943. This consisted of a core of six students, all about twenty years old, calling themselves the 'White Rose' (Weisse Rose) that included Hans, Sophie and Inge Scholl, Alexander Schmorell, Willi Graf, and Christoph Scholl, with the professor of philosophy Kurt Huber. They had been horrified by witnessing shooting of naked Jews in a pit by German soldiers on the Eastern front. At great danger to their personal safety, they wrote and distributed anti-Nazi leaflets, advising Germans to resist the Nazi oppression and tyranny. They rejected fascism and believed in a federated Europe, based on principles of tolerance and justice. Inevitably, in February 1943, the Gestapo apprehended first Hans and Sophie Scholl, and then Christoph Scholl. They were brought before the People's Court in Berlin, presided by Judge Roland Freisler, and after a few hours they were convicted of treason and sentenced to death, which was carried out within hours of the verdict by the guillotine. Hans cried out, "Long Live Freedom". Later that year, Alexander Schmorell, Willi Graf, and Kurt Huber were tried and executed; many other students implicated with the "White Rose" received prison sentences.

Fig. 1 *The anti-Nazi leaflets embedded in the pavement at the entrance to the Ludwig Maximillian University of Munich in the 'Geschwister Scholl Platz' (the author reading them).*

The 'White Rose' was the sole University-inspired resistance, indeed the only true opposition to the atrocities perpetrated by the barbaric Nazi regime, in contrast to the later attempt on Hitler's life when it became clear to the German military that the war was lost. As a postscript, Roland Freisler was the most notorious judge dispensing Nazi 'blood justice' and he was justly rewarded, when he was killed by a direct hit during an air raid. The anti-Nazi leaflets embedded in the pavement at the entrance to the Ludwig Maximillian University of Munich in the 'Geschwister Scholl Platz' (The Scholl Square) is the most heroic monument of the other Germany (Fig. 1). One of these leaflets states: "Why do German people behave so apathetically in the face of all these abominable crimes, crimes so unworthy of the human race? The German people slumber on in their dull, stupid sleep and encourage these fascist criminals. [The German] must show not only sympathy; no, much more: a sense of complicity in guilt [...]. For through his apathetic behaviour he gives these evil men the opportunity to act as they do. He himself is to blame for the fact that it came about at all! Each man wants to be exonerated but he cannot be exonerated; he is guilty, guilty, guilty! Now that we have recognized [the Nazis] for what they are, it must be the sole and first duty, the holiest duty of every German to destroy these beasts."

Germans at large, and especially the student body, owe a debt of gratitude to the martyrdom of the 'White Rose' students and Professor Huber who attempted to salvage the other Germany, the one that cares for the spirit of humanity, where empathy, love, and altruism are enacted and where civilisation, culture, and morality are the guiding principles.

German people are fortunate to be able to redeem their great past by falling back on their giants of culture and create the renaissance of Goethe, Schiller, Kant, Beethoven and Humboldt, to mention just a few. The religious authorities, universities, historians and the legal profession have immense talent to face the future by dealing effectively with the past. However, the medical profession had the foreboding by no lesser man than Christoph W. Hufeland, Professor of Medicine, University of Jena, Physician Royal to the King of Prussia, as well as medical adviser to Goethe and Schiller,

Hufeland's astonishing statement published about 135 years ago strongly advised "The physician should and must not do anything but maintain life, irrespective whether it is happy or miserable, worth living or not, is not for the physician to decide. If that issue were ever to be considered, then the consequences are unpredictable and the physician becomes the most dangerous person in the land. Should this line be crossed and the physician decides on the life of his patient, then all it takes is stepwise progression to extend the decision on the worthlessness and uselessness of human life to apply to the lives of others." The German Hippocrates could not be more prescient and explicit of the future catastrophe and his pronouncement should be inscribed not only in the mind of every physician but also lawyers, academics and theologians concerned with the welfare and safety of humanity.

BIBLIOGRAPHY

Adorno, Theodor W., and Benjamin W., The Complete Correspondence 1928-1940, Edited by Henri Lonitz, transl. by Nicholas, Walker, (Polity Press 2003)

Amery, Jean, transl. by Sidney Rosenfeld and Stella P. Rosenfeld, At the Mind's Limits (Granta Books Ltd. 1977)

Annas, George J, and Michael A. Grodin, The Nazi Doctors and The Nüremberg Code, Human Rights in Human Experimentation (Oxford University Press, 1992)

Arendt, Hannah, Eichmann in Jerusalem, A Report on The Banality of Evil (Penguin Books, 1963)

Armstrong, John, In Search of Civilization, Remaking A Tarnished Idea (Allen Lane, 2009)

Love, Life, Goethe, How to Be Happy in An Imperfect World (Penguin Books, 2007)

Astor, Gerald, The Last Nazi, The Life and Times of Dr. Joseph Mengele (SPHERE Books Ltd., 1986)

Ball, Philip, Serving the Reich, The Struggle for The Soul of Physics Under Hitler (The Bodley Head, London, 2013)

Critical Mass, How One Thing Leads to Another (Arrow Books, 2005)

Bankier, David, The Germans And the Final Solution, Public Opinion Under Nazis (Blackwell, 1992)

Baron-Cohen, Simon, Zero Degree of Empathy, A New Theory of Human Cruelty, (Allen Lane, 2011)

Bauer, Yehuda, Rethinking the Holocaust (Yale University Press: New Haven and London, 2002)

Bauman, Zygmunt, Modernity and The Holocaust (Polity Press, 2000)

Bell, Matthew, The Essential Goethe (Princeton University Press: Princeton & Oxford, 2016)

Berkovits, Eliezer, Faith After the Holocaust (Ktav Publishing House, Inc. New York, 1973)

Berlin, Adele and Marc Zvi Brettler, The Jewish Study Bible, Tanakh transl. (Oxford University Press, 1999)

Berlin, Isaiah, The Proper Study of Mankind, Edited by Henry Hardy & Roger Hausheer (Chatto & Windus London, 1997)

Freedom and Its Betrayal, Six Enemies of Human Liberty (Pimlico, 2003)

Bernstein, Michael A., Five Portraits, Modernity and The Imagination in Twentieth Century German Writing (Northwestern University Press, Evanston, Illinois, 2000)

Bettelheim, Bruno, Recollections and Reflections (Thames and Hudson, 1990)

Bialas, Wolfgang and Anson Rabinbach (eds.), Nazi Germany and the Humanities How German Academics Embraced Nazism (Oneworld Publications, 2014)

Bigsby, Christopher, Remembering the Holocaust the Chain of Memory (Cambridge University Press, 2006)

Blanning, T. C. W., The Culture of Power and The Power of Culture, Old Regime Europe, 1660-1789 (Oxford University Press,2002)

Boos, Sonja, Speaking of The Unspeakable in Postwar Germany, Towards A Public Discourse on The Holocaust (Cornell University Press,2014)

Born, Max, and Einstein, Albert, The Born Einstein Letters, Correspondence From 1916 to 1955, transl. by Irene Born (Macmillan Press,1971)

Braudel, Ferdinand, A History of Civilizations, transl. by Richard Mayne (Penguin Books 1997)

Bridgman Jon, The End of the Holocaust the Liberation of The Camps (B.T. Batsford Ltd. London, 1990)

British Medical Association, Medicine Betrayed (Zed Books, 1992)

Brooks, David, The Social Animal (Published by Short Books, 2011)

Brooks, Martin, Extreme Measures, The Dark Visions and Bright Ideas of Francis Galton (Bloomsbury Publishing, 2004)

Buber, Martin, I And Thou, transl. By Walter Kaufmann (T.& T. Clark, Ediburgh,1970)

Buch, Esteban, Beethoven's Ninth, A Political History (The University of Chicago Press, 2003)

Burleigh, Michael, Sacred Causes (Harper Press, 2006)

The Third Reich a New History (Macmillan, 2000)

Moral Combat, A History of World War II (Harper Press 2010)

And Wolfgang Wippermann, The Racial State Germany 1933-1945 (Cambridge University Press, 1991)

Canetti, Elias, The Human Province, transl. by Joachim Neugroschel (Andre Deutsch, 1985)

Carey, John, What Good Are The Arts? (Faber and Faber,2005)

Carroll, James, Constantine's Sword, The Church and The Jews (A Mariner Book, Houghton Mifflin Company,2002)

Churchland, Patricia S., Braintrust, What Neuroscience Tells Us About Morality (Princeton University Press, 2011)

Cohen, Josh, Interrupting Auschwitz, Art, Religion, Philosophy (Continuum, 2003)

Connot, Robert E., Justice at Nuremberg (Carroll & Graf Publishers, Inc. New York, 1983)

Cornwell, John, Hitler's Pope, The Secret History of Pius XII (Viking 1999)

Hitler's Scientists, Science, War and The Devil's Pact (Viking, 2003)

Craig, Gordon A., The Germans (Penguin Books, 1984)

Dahrendorf, Ralf, The Unresolved Past, A Debate in German History, Ed by Gina Thomas (Weidenfeld and Nicolson, London, 1990)

Davies, Norman, Europe A History (Oxford University Press, 1996)

Dawidowicz, Lucy, The War Against the Jews 1933-1945 (Penguin Books, 1975)

De Gaulle Anthonioz, Genevieve, God Remained Outside, An Echo of Ravensbrück (Souvenir Press, 1998)

Dennis, David B., Inhumanities, Nazi Interpretation of Western Culture (Cambridge University Press, 2012)

Douglas, Lawrence, The Memory Of Judgment, Making Law And History In The Trials Of The Holocaust (Yale University Press, 2001)

Eagleton, Terry, On Evil (Yale University Press, 2010)

Eerdmans Dictionary of Early Judaism, Ed by John J. Collins and Daniel C. Harlow (W. B. Eerdmans Publishing Co., 2010)

Elias, Norbert, The Germans Edited by Michael Schröter, transl. by Eric Dunning & Stephen Mennell (Polity Press 1996)

Elon, Amos, The Pitty Of It All, A Portrait Of Jews In Germany, 1743-1933 (Penguin Books,2004)

Ericksen, Robert P., Complicity In The Holocaust, Churches, Universities In Nazi Germany (Cambridge University Press, 2012)

Evans, Richard, J., The Third Reich In Power 1933-1939 (Penguin Books,2005)

The Third Reich At War (Penguin Books, 2008)

In Defence Of History (Granta Books, London,1997)

Felstiner, John, Paul Celan : Poet, Survivor, Jew (Yale University Press,1995)

Ferguson, Niall, The War Of The World, History's Age Of Hatred (Allen Lane, 2006)

The West And The Rest (Allen Lane, 2011)

Fest, Joachim, Not Me, Memoirs Of A German Childhood, transl. by Martin Chalmers (Atlantic Books, London, 2012)

Fishburn, Matthew, Burning Books (Palgrave Macmillan,2008)

Freudmann, Lillian C., Antisemitism In The New Testament (University Press of America, Lanham, New York, London,1994)

Friedlander, Saul, Edited , Probing The Limits Of Representation, Nazism and The Final Solution (Harvard University Press,1992)

Fulbrook, Mary, Dissonant Lives, Generations and Violence Through The German Dictatorship (Oxford University Press, 2011)

Gay, Peter, The Cultivation Of Hatred, The Bourgeois Experience Victoria To Freud (Harper Collins Publishers, 1993)

Gazzaniga, Michael, S., The Ethical Brain (Dana Press, New York, Washington,D.C.

Gilbert, Martin, The Holocaust, The Jewish Tragedy (Collins, London,1986)

Gilmour, Ian, Hitler, The Germans, and the Final Solution (Yale University , 2008)

The Nazi Dictatorship. Problems and Perspectives of Interpretation, (Hodder Arnold Publication, 2000)

Glover, Jonathan, Humanity, A Moral History Of The Twentieth Century, 2001)

Goldhagen, Daniel, J., Hitler's Willing Executioners, Ordinary Germans And The Holocaust (Little Brown and Company, 1996)

A Moral Reckoning, The Role Of The Catholic Church In The Holocaust And Its Unfulfilled Duty Of Repair (ABACUS, 2002)

Goethe, Johann, Wolfgang, The Sufferings Of Young Werther, transl. by Stanley Corngold (W. W. Norton & Company, 2012)

Elective Affinities, transl. by David Constantine (Oxford University Press, 1994)

Goleman, Daniel, Social Intelligence (Arrow Books,2007)

Emotional Intelligence, Why It Can Matter More Than IQ (Bloomsbury Publishing, 1996)

Goodrick-Clarke, Nicholas, The Occult Roots Of Nazism, Secret Aryan Cults And Their Influence On Nazi Ideology (I.B. Tauris & Co. Ltd Publishers, 1992)

Gordon, Peter E. and McCormick, John P., Editors, Weimar Thought, A Contested Legacy (Princeton University Press, 2013)

Harper Collins Study Bible, Ed. By Wayne A. Meeks et al (Harper Collins Publishers, 1993)

Hasting, Max, Victory in Europe: D-Day to V-E Day ((Little Brown & C, 1992)
Hawking, Stephen and Mlodinow, Leonard, The Grand Design (Bantam Press, 2010
Helm, Sarah, Ravensbrück, Life And Death In Hitler's Concentration Camp For Women (Nan A. Talese , Doubleday, 2014)
If This Is A Woman, Inside Ravensbrück (Abacus, 2016)
Hemmendinger, Judith & Robert Krell, The Children of Buchenwald, Child Survivors Of The Holocaust (Gefen Publishing House, Jerusalem,2000)
Hertz, J.H., The Pentateuch And Haftorahs, Hebrew Text, English Translation And Commentary (Soncino Press, London, 1952)
Heschel, Susannah, The Aryan Jesus, Christian Theologians And The Bible in Nazi Germany (Princeton University Press, 2008)
Hobsbawm, Eric, The Age Of Extremes, 1914-1991 (ABACUS Book,2004)
Hoedeman, Paul, Hitler Or Hippocrates (The Book Guild Ltd. Sussex, England, 1991)
Hoess, Rudolf, Commandant Of Auschwitz, The Autobiography, transl. by Constantine FitzGibbon (Phoenix Press,2000)
Huntington, Samuel P., The Clash Of Civilizations And The Remaking Of World Order (The Free Press, 2002)
Jacobs, Louis, The Jewish Religion, A Companion (Oxford University Press, 1995)
Kandel, Eric R., In Search Of Memory, The Emergence Of New Science Of Mind (W. W. Norton & Company, 2006)
Kater, Michael H., Doctors Under Hitler (The University Of North Carolina Press, 1989)
Katz, Steven T., Shlomo Biderman, Gershon Greenberg, Wrestling With God, Jewish Theological Responses During And After The Holocaust (Oxford University Press, 2007)
Kekes, John, The Roots Of Evil (Cornell University Press, 2005)
Kershaw, Ian, The Hitler Myth, Image Of Reality In The Third Reich (Oxford University Press, 1987)
Kertesz, Imre, Fatelessness, transl. by Tim Wilkinson (Vintage Books, New York, 2004)
Kessler, Edward, An Introduction To Jewish-Christian Relations (Cambridge University Press, 2010)
And Neil Wenborn, A Dictionary Of Jewish-Christian Relations (Cambridge University Press, 2005)

Kirk, Tim, Cassell's Dictionary Of Modern German History, Ed. By Chris Cook (Cassell,2002)

Klee, Ernst, Willi Dressen and Volker Riess, transl. by Deborah Burnstone, Those Were The Days (Hamish Hamilton, London,1988)

Klemperer, Victor, I Shall Bear Witness, The Diaries Of Victor Klemperer 1933-1941, transl. by Martin Chalmers (Weidenfeld & Nicolson,1998)

Kramer, Alan, Dynamics Of Destruction, Culture And Mass Killing In The First World War (Oxford University Press, 2007)

Krebs, Christopher B., A Most Dangerous Book, Tacitus's Germania From The Roman Empire To The Third Reich (W.W. Norton & Company, 2011)

Küng, Hans, The Beginning Of All Things, Science And Religion, transl. by John Bowden (William B. Eerdmans Publishing Company, 2007)

Langer, Lawrence, L., The Holocaust And The Literary Imagination (Yale University Press, 1975)

Lau, Israel Meir, Out Of The Depths, The Story Of A Child Of Buchenwald Who Returned Home At Last, A Memoir (STERLING Publishing, New York, 2011)

Lepenies, Wolf, The Seduction Of Culture (Princeton University Press, 2006)

Levi, Primo, If This Is A Man And The Truce, transl. by Stuart Woolf (ABACUS,1958)

The Periodic Table, transl. by Raymond Rosenthal (Michael Joseph London, 1985)

The Drowned and The Saved, transl. by Raymond Rosenthal (ABACUS 1988)

Lifton, Robert J., The Nazi Doctors, Medical Killing And The Psychology Of Genocide (Macmillan, London, 1986)

Lilla, Mark, The Stillborn God, Religion, Politics, And The Modern West (Alfred, A. Knopf, New York, 2007)

Longerich, Peter, transl. by Jeremy Noakes and Lesley Sharpe, Heinrich Himmler (Oxford University Press, 2012)

Goebbels transl. by Alan Bance, Jeremy Noakes and Lesley Sharpe (VINTAGE, London 2015)

Holocaust, The Nazi Persecution And Murder Of The Jews (Oxford University Press, 2010)

Mack, Michael, Spinoza And The Specters Of Modernity ,The Hidden Enlightenment Of Diversity From Spinoza To Freud (Continuum, London, New York, 2010)

Mann, Thomas, Lotte In Weimar, transl. by H.T. Lowe-Porter (Penguin Books, 1982)

Martin, Nicholas, Schiller: National Poet- Poet Of Nations, A Birmingham Symposium (Rodopi, Amsterdam, New York,2006)

Mayer, Arno J., Why Did The Heavens Not Darken, The Final Solution In History (VERSO, London, New York, 1988)

McElligott, Anthony, editor, The Short History Of Germany, Weimar Germany (Oxford University Press, 2009)

Mazower, Mark, Dark Continent, Europe's Twentieth Century (Penguin Books, 1998)

McNeill, William H., History Of Western Civilisation, A Handbook (The University of Chicago Press, 1986)

Medawar, Jean and David Pyke, Hitler's Gift, Scientists Who Fled Nazi Germany (Richard Cohen Books, London, 2000)

Mitscherlich, Aexander and Fred Mielke, Medizin Ohne Menschlichkeit, Dokumente Des Nürnberger Ārzteprozesses (Fischer Taschenbuch Verlag, 1960)

Müller-Hill, Bennno, transl. by George, R., Fraser, Murderous Science, Elimination By Scientific Selection Of Jews, Gypsies, And Others, Germany 1933-1945 (Oxford University Press, 1988)

Mulisch, Harry, Siegfried, transl. by Paul Vincent (Viking, 2003)

Murray, CharleA., Human Accomplishments, The Pursuit Of Excellence In The Arts And Sciences, 800B.C. to 1950 (Perrenial, Harper Collins Publishers, 2004)

Nadler, Steven, Spinoza, A Life (Cambridge University Press, 1999)

Overy, Richard, Interrogations: Inside the Minds of the Nazi Elite (Peguin books, 2002)

Padfield, Peter, Himmler Reichsführer-SS (Macmillan, London 1990)

Perutz, Max, I wish I'd Made You Angry Earlier, Essays On Science And Scientists (Oxford University Press, 2002)

Pinker, Steven, The Blank Slate, Modern Denial Of Human Nature (Penguin Books, 2002)

Posner, Gerald, Hitler's Children, Inside The Families Of The Third Reich (Heinemann, 1991)

Power, Samantha, A Problem From Hell, America And The Age Of Genocide, London, 2002)

Proctor, Robert N., Racial Hygiene, Medicine Under Nazis (Harvard University Press, 1988)

Rabinbach, Anson, In The Shadow Of Catastrophe, German Intellectuals Between Apocalypse And Enlightenment (University of California Press,2000)

Reed, T. J., Light In Germany (The University of Chicago Press, 2015)
Remy, Steven P., The Hydelberg Myth, The Nazification And Denazification Of A German University (Harvard University Press, 2003)
Richards, Robert J., The Tragic Sense Of Life, Ernst Haeckel and The Struggle Over Evolutionary Thought (The University of Chicago Press, 2008)
Robertson, Ritchie, Heine (Peter Halban Publishers, Ltd, 1988)
Rose, Paul Lawrence, Revolutionary Antisemitism In Germany From Kant To Wagner (Princeton University Press, 1900)
Ross, Alex, The Rest Is Noise, Listening To The Twentieth Century (Fourth Estate, London, 2007)
Rummel, R. J., Democide, Nazi Genocide And Mass Murder (Transaction Publishers, 1992)
Sacks, Jonathan, The Dignity Of Difference, How To Avoid The Clash Of Civilization (Continuum, London, New York, 2002)
Not In God's Name, Confronting Religious Violence (Hodder & Stoughton,2015)
The Persistence Of Faith, The Reith Lectures 1990, Religion, Morality & Society In A Secular Age (Weidenfeld and Nicolson, 1991)
Schama, Simon, The Story Of The Jews, Finding The Words, !000 BCE – 1492 CE (Bodley Head, London, 2013)
Scruton,Rogers, Culture Counts, Faith And Feeling In A World Besieged (Brief Encounters, 2007)
Sherratt, Yvonne, Hitler's Philosophers (Yale University Press, 2013)
Shirer, William L., The Rise And Fall Of The Third Reich (Pan Books, 1960)
Sichrovsky,Peter, Born Guilty, Children Of Nazi Families, transl. by Jean Steinberg (I.B. Tauris & Co Ltd., Publishers, 1988)
Snyder, Louis L., Hitler's German Enemies, Portraits Of Heroes Who Fought The Nazis (Berkley Books New York, 1992)
Spivey, Nigel, Enduring Creation, Art, Pain And Fortitude (Thames and Hudson, 2001)
Spotts, Frederic, Hitler And The Power Of Aesthetics (Pimlico,2003)
Steigmann-Gall, Richard, The Holy Reich, Nazi Conception Of Christianity, 1919-1945 (Cambridge University Press, 2003)
Steiner, George, Language And Silence, Essays 1958-1966(Penguin Books,1967)
Bluebeard's Castle, Some Notes Towards The Redefinition Of Culture (Faber and Faber, 1971)

Extraterritorial, Papers On Literature And The Language Revolution (Penguin Books, 1971)

Grammars Of Creation (Faber and Faber, 2001)

My Unwritten Books (Weidenfeld & Nicolson London, 2008)

The Poetry Of Thought, From Hellenism To Celan (A New Directions Book, 2012)

Stewart, Matthew, The Courtier And The Heretic, Leibniz, Spinoza, And The Fate Of God In The Modern World (Yale University Press, 2005)

Szöllösi-Janze, Margit, Editor, Science In The Third Reich (BERG, Oxford, New York, 2001)

Taylor, A.J.P., The Course Of German History (Routledge, 1988)

Todorov, Tzvetan, transl. by Gila Walker, In Defence of the Enlightenment (Atlantic Books, London, 2006)

Vermes, Geza, Christian Beginnings. From Nazareth to Nicaea (AD 30-325), (Allen Lane 2012)

Voigtländer, Nico, and Hans-Joachim Voth, "Persecution Perpetuated: The Medieval Origins of Anti-Semitic Violence in Nazi Germany 2012. The Quarterly Journal of Economics, Oxford University Press, 2012, vol. 127(3), pages 1339-1392

Ward, Keith. God, A Guide For The Perplexed (One world, Oxford,2003)

Watson, Peter, The German Genius, Europe's Third Renaissance, The Second Scientific Revolution, and The Twentieth Century (Simon & Schuster, 2010)

Weindling, Paul J., Nazi Medicine And The Nüremberg Trials, From Medical War Crimes To Informed Consent (Palgrave Macmillan, 2004)

Health, Race And German Politics Between National Unification And Nazism, 1870-1945 (Cambridge University Press, 1989)

Weikart, Richard, From Darwin To Hitler, Evolutionary Ethics, Eugenics And Racism In Germany (Palgrave Macmillan, 2004)

Wiesel, Elie, All Rivers Run To The Sea, Memoirs (Schocken Books, New York, 1995)

Wasserstein, Bernard, Barbarism and Civilization, A History Of Europe In Our Time (Oxford University Press, 2007)

Winder, Simon, Germania, A Persona History Of Germans Ancient And Modern (Picador,2010)

Wistrich, Robert S., Who'S Who In Nazi Germany (Routledge,2002)

Anti-Semitism, The Longest Hatred (Thames Methuen, 1991)

Wright, Robert, The Evolution Of God, The Origins Of Our Beliefs (ABACUS, 2009)

Zagorin, Prez, How The Idea Of Religious Toleration Came To The West

(Princeton University Ppress,2003)
Zeldin, Theodore, An Intimate History Of Humanity (Sinclair-Stevenson, 1994)

Index